World Social Protection Report 2014/15

Building economic recovery, inclusive development and social justice

World Social Protection Report 2014/15

Building economic recovery, inclusive development and social justice

INTERNATIONAL LABOUR OFFICE • GENEVA
ACADEMIC FOUNDATION • NEW DELHI

First published in 2015 by

International Labour Office,
CH-1211 Geneva 22, Switzerland
www.ilo.org

in association with

Academic Foundation
(co-publication partners for South Asia)
4772/23 Bharat Ram Road, (23 Ansari Road), Darya Ganj,
New Delhi - 110002, India.
www.academicfoundation.org

First published 2014

World Social Protection Report 2014/15: Building economic recovery, inclusive development and social justice
International Labour Office – Geneva: ILO, 2014

ISBN 978-92-2-128660-8 (print)
ISBN 978-92-2-128661-5 (web pdf)
ISBN 978-92-2-128662-2 (e-pub)
ISBN 978-92-2-128663-9 (Kindle)

International Labour Office

social security / scope of coverage / gaps in coverage / social security policy / ageing population / pension scheme / health insurance / role of ILO / developed countries / developing countries

02.03.1

ILO Cataloguing in Publication Data

ISBN 978-93-327-0175-5 (Academic Foundation / for South Asia)

Printed and bound in India.

Preface

Since its creation in 1919, the ILO has been supporting countries to develop and implement social security systems for all. There has been tremendous progress since then. At the outset, some 40 countries were starting to build such schemes; today, all countries in the world have a social security system.

What is more, social protection coverage and benefits continue to expand, as reflected in the groundbreaking ILO Recommendation concerning National Floors of Social Protection (No. 202), adopted in 2012. The Recommendation bears witness to the joint commitment of governments, employers and workers to building nationally defined social protection floors which guarantee at least a basic level of social security to all, encompassing access to health care and income security throughout people's lives and ensuring their dignity and rights. While social protection floors are essential, the Recommendation does not stop there: it also sets out detailed guidance on building comprehensive social protection systems.

Two years after the adoption of the Recommendation, this *World Social Protection Report* offers a comprehensive body of evidence both on the impressive progress made over the last few years and on the remaining gaps that need to be filled. Based on a life-cycle approach, the report provides an overview of the current organization of social protection systems, coverage, benefits and expenditures. With its global scope and valuable statistical annexes, it is an essential reference for anyone interested in social protection.

In recent years, the ILO has provided technical assistance on social protection to no fewer than 136 countries. And we are proud to continue our support all over the world, as more and more evidence shows that social protection systems play a key role in the functioning of modern societies and are an essential ingredient of integrated strategies for economic and social development. Furthermore, experience since 2008 shows that countries with adequate social protection systems were able to respond more quickly and effectively to the global crisis.

Yet some 73 per cent of the world's population continues to live without adequate social protection coverage. In other words, for the large majority of people the fundamental human right to social security is only partially realized or not at all. In 2014, it is clear that the global community needs to make greater efforts in realizing this right. With this in view, it is opportune to recall the many countries that historically have built sound economies at the same time as decent societies with social protection.

Still grappling with the economic repercussions of the global financial crisis, the world is faced with a deep social crisis which is also a crisis of social justice. Fiscal consolidation and adjustment measures threaten household living standards in a significant number of countries. Despite progress made in reducing levels of extreme poverty in some parts of the world, high levels of poverty and vulnerability persist; what is more, poverty is actually increasing in many high-income countries. In addition, high and still rising levels of inequality in both advanced and developing economies are widely acknowledged as cause for great concern.

Social protection measures are essential elements of a policy response that can address those challenges. They not only support the realization of the universal human right to social security, but are both a social and an economic necessity. Well-designed social protection systems support incomes and domestic consumption, build human capital and increase productivity. The bold efforts in extending social protection in many developing countries, from Brazil to China, from Ecuador to Mozambique, have underlined its key role in reducing poverty and vulnerability, redressing inequality and boosting inclusive growth.

This is an issue that the international community should embrace as a priority in the post-2015 development agenda. Social protection can ensure that all people have the security of knowing that if they lose their job or fall ill, and also when they grow old, they will not face the risk of poverty and insecurity. Our modern society can afford to provide universal social protection everywhere.

I hope that this report will be a useful tool for practitioners, and provide the basis for better informed policy-making.

Geneva, June 2014

GUY RYDER
Director-General
International Labour Office

Acknowledgements

This report was drafted by a team supervised by the Director of the ILO Social Protection Department, Isabel Ortiz, consisting of Krzysztof Hagemejer, formerly Chief of the Social Policy, Governance and Standards Branch; Anne Drouin, Chief of the Public Finance, Actuarial and Statistics Services Branch; Florence Bonnet, Social Security Statistics Coordinator; Christina Behrendt, Senior Social Protection Policy Specialist; Emmanuelle St-Pierre Guilbault, Legal Specialist; Xenia Scheil-Adlung, Coordinator Social Health Protection; and John Woodall, formerly Coordinator Pension Policy.

Substantial inputs to the report were received from Matthew Cummins, Social and Economic Policy Specialist at the United Nations Children's Fund (UNICEF), and several colleagues in the ILO Social Protection Department, including Fabio Durán Valverde, Senior Specialist Social Security; Aidi Hu, Coordinator Country Operations, Asia; Cristina Lloret, Junior Social Security Actuary; Helmut Schwarzer, Senior Social Security Specialist for the Americas and the Caribbean; Maya Stern-Plaza, Junior Legal Officer; Victoire Umuhire, Junior Legal Officer; Veronika Wodsak, Technical Officer Social Security; Hiroshi Yamabana, Social Security Actuary; and Katharina Diekmann, Zita Herman, Vinu Parakkal Menon and Nicholas Teasdale-Boivin.

The report benefited from comments from colleagues in other ILO technical departments and field offices, including Manuela Tomei, Director of the Conditions of Work and Equality Department; Michelle Leighton, Chief of the Labour Migration Branch; Philippe Marcadent, Chief of the Inclusive Labour Markets, Labour Relations and Working Conditions Branch; Shauna Olney, Chief of the Gender, Equality and Diversity Branch; Alice Ouedraogo, Chief of the HIV/AIDS and the World of Work Branch; Laura Addati, Maternity Protection and Work–Family Specialist; Janine Berg, Senior Development Economist; Fabio Bertranou, Senior Labour Market and Social Protection Specialist, ILO Buenos Aires; Theopiste Butare, Senior Social Security Technical Specialist, ILO Yaoundé; Pablo Casalí, Senior Social Security Specialist, ILO Lima; Luis Casanova, National Officer, ILO Buenos Aires; Raphael Crowe, Senior Gender Specialist; Adrienne Cruz, Senior Gender Specialist; Loveleen De, Social Security Consultant, ILO Bangkok; Juan De Laiglesia, Economist and Labour

Market Specialist; Maria Gallotti, Specialist in Migration Policies; Youcef Ghellab, Head Social Dialogue and Tripartism Unit; Frank Hoffer, Senior Research Officer, ILO Bureau for Workers' Activities; Lee-Nah Hsu, Technical Specialist on HIV/AIDS; Kroum Markov, Legal Specialist; Barbara Murray, Senior Disability Specialist; Susan Maybud, Senior Gender Specialist; Seil Oh, Social Security Officer, ILO Bangkok; Céline Peyron Bista, Chief Technical Adviser, ILO Bangkok; Markus Ruck, Senior Social Security Specialist, ILO New Delhi; Catherine Saget, Senior Economist; Francis Sanzouango, Employer Relations Specialist, Bureau for Employers' Activities; Sinta Satriana, Social Security Consultant, ILO Bangkok; Valérie Schmitt, Senior Social Security Specialist, ILO Bangkok; Stefan Trömel, Senior Disability Specialist; Catherine Vaillancourt-Laflamme, Chief Technical Adviser, ILO Manila. Comments and guidance from the ILO's Deputy Director-General for Policy, Sandra Polaski, are especially appreciated.

The ILO is also grateful for the helpful comments received from other United Nations organizations, including from Diana Barrowclough, Senior Economic Affairs Officer at the United Nations Conference on Trade and Development (UNCTAD); Michael Clark, Special Adviser on International Governance at the Food and Agriculture Organization (FAO); Sarah Cook, Director of the United Nations Research Institute for Social Development (UNRISD); Christian Courtis, Human Rights Officer at the Office of the UN High Commissioner for Human Rights (OHCHR); Frédéric Dévé, Governance Adviser, FAO; David Evans, Director of the Department of Health Systems Financing, World Health Organization (WHO); Lynn Gentile, Human Rights Officer, OHCHR; Catalina Gomez, Social Protection Consultant, UNICEF; Katja Hujo, Research Coordinator, UNRISD; Alex Izurieta, Senior Economic Affairs Officer, UNCTAD; Gabriele Köhler, formerly South Asia Regional Adviser on Social Policy, UNICEF; Hans-Horst Konkolewsky, Secretary-General, International Social Security Association; Joseph Kutzin, Coordinator, Health Financing Policy, WHO; Daniel Lopez Acuña, Adviser to the Director General, WHO; Sheila Murthi, Social Protection Consultant, UNICEF; Krista Orama, Focal Point for the Rights of Persons with Disabilities, OHCHR; Shahra Razavi, Chief Research and Data Section, UNWOMEN; Stefania Tripodi, Human Rights Officer, OHCHR; Jenn Yablonski, Social Protection Specialist, UNICEF; Ilcheong Yi, Research Coordinator, UNRISD; Michael Cichon, former Director of the ILO Social Security Department and now President of the International Council on Social Welfare; and for the comments of three anonymous peer reviewers.

Thanks are also due to those who facilitated the editing, production, publication and dissemination of this report in their different roles, including Charlotte Beauchamp, Raphaël Crettaz, Laetitia Dard, Chris Edgar, José Antonio Garcia, Victoria Giroud-Castiella, Jean-Luc Martinage, Michel Masurel, Martin Murphy, Marcia Poole, Karuna Pal, Ksenija Radojevic Bovet, Damien Riunaud, Dalibor Rodinis, Hans von Rohland, Gillian Somerscales and Hans Christian Weidmann.

Contents

ANNEXES

List of figures

List of tables

List of boxes

List of abbreviations

AAAQ	availability, accessibility, acceptability and quality (criteria)
ADB	Asian Development Bank
CCT	conditional cash transfer
CIS	Commonwealth of Independent States
CRPD	UN Convention on the Rights of Persons with Disabilities
DfID	Department for International Development (United Kingdom)
ECLAC	United Nations Economic Commission for Latin America and the Caribbean
EU	European Union
EU-SILC	European Union Statistics on Income and Living Conditions
FAO	Food and Agriculture Organization of the United Nations
GDP	gross domestic product
HIC	high-income country
ICESCR	International Covenant on Economic, Social and Cultural Rights, 1966
IFF	illicit financial flows
IILS	International Institute for Labour Studies
ILO	International Labour Office/Organization
IMF	International Monetary Fund
ISSA	International Social Security Association
LEAP	Livelihood Empowerment Against Poverty programme (Ghana)
MDG	Millennium Development Goal
MGNREGS	Mahatma Gandhi National Rural Employment Guarantee Scheme (India)
NDC	notional defined contribution
NGO	non-governmental organization
NHIS	National Health Insurance Scheme (Ghana)
OECD	Organisation for Economic Co-operation and Development
OHCHR	Office of the United Nations High Commissioner for Human Rights

OOP	out-of-pocket payments
PAYG	pay-as-you-go
PEP	public employment programme
PPP	purchasing power parity
SSA	Social Security Administration of the United States
SWF	sovereign wealth fund
UDHR	Universal Declaration of Human Rights, 1948
UN	United Nations
UNCTAD	United Nations Conference on Trade and Development
UNDP	United Nations Development Programme
UNESCO	United Nations Educational, Scientific and Cultural Organization
UNICEF	United Nations Children's Fund
UNRISD	United Nations Research Institute for Social Development
VAT	value added tax
WHO	World Health Organization

Executive summary

Social protection policies play a critical role in realizing the human right to social security for all, reducing poverty and inequality, and supporting inclusive growth – by boosting human capital and productivity, supporting domestic demand and facilitating structural transformation of national economies. This ILO flagship report: (i) provides a global overview of the organization of social protection systems, their coverage and benefits, as well as public expenditures on social security; (ii) following a life-cycle approach, presents social protection for children, for women and men of working age, and for older persons; (iii) analyses trends and recent policies, e.g. negative impacts of fiscal consolidation and adjustment measures; and (iv) calls for the expansion of social protection in pursuit of crisis recovery, inclusive development and social justice.

While the need for social protection is widely recognized, the fundamental human right to social security remains unfulfilled for the large majority of the world's population. Only 27 per cent of the global population enjoy access to comprehensive social security systems, whereas 73 per cent are covered partially or not at all.

The lack of access to social protection constitutes a major obstacle to economic and social development. Inadequate or absent social protection coverage is associated with high and persistent levels of poverty and economic insecurity, growing levels of inequality, insufficient investments in human capital and human capabilities, and weak aggregate demand in a time of recession and slow growth.

The strong positive impacts of social protection have brought social protection to the forefront of the development agenda. Social protection is a key element of national strategies to promote human development, political stability and inclusive growth. The ILO Social Protection Floors Recommendation, 2012 (No. 202), reflects a consensus on the extension of social security reached among governments and employers' and workers' organizations from 185 countries at all levels of development. Further, the roll-out of social protection floors is endorsed by the G20 and the United Nations.

However, while there has been a global trend towards the extension of social protection, particularly in middle-income countries, the effectiveness of social security systems in a number of countries is at risk as a result of fiscal consolidation and adjustment measures. These trends are presented in the different chapters of the report, following a life-cycle approach.

Social protection for children and families: A right unfulfilled

Social protection policies are an essential element of realizing children's rights, ensuring their well-being, breaking the vicious cycle of poverty and vulnerability, and helping all children realize their full potential. Despite a large expansion of schemes, existing social protection policies do not sufficiently address the income security needs of children and families, particularly in low- and middle-income countries with large child populations. About 18,000 children die every day, mainly from preventable causes: many of these deaths could be averted through adequate social protection.

Social protection also has a key role in preventing child labour by reducing economic vulnerability of families, enabling children to go to school and protecting them from exploitation.

More efforts are needed to step up measures to ensure income security for children and families. Many children do not receive the essential cash transfers that could make a real difference, in terms of nutrition, health, education and care services, to their chances of realizing their full potential. Specific child and family benefit programmes rooted in legislation exist in 108 countries, yet often cover only small groups of the population. In 75 countries, no such programmes are available at all.

On average, governments allocate 0.4 per cent of GDP to child and family benefits, ranging from 2.2 per cent in Western Europe to 0.2 per cent in Africa, and in Asia and the Pacific. Underinvestment in children jeopardizes their rights and their future, as well as the economic and social development prospects of the countries in which they live.

Fiscal consolidation and adjustment measures in higher-income economies threaten progress on income security for children and their families. Child poverty increased in 19 of the 28 countries of the European Union between 2007 and 2012.

Social protection in working age: The quest for income security

Social protection plays a key role for women and men of working age by stabilizing their incomes in the event of unemployment, employment injury, disability, sickness and maternity, and by ensuring that they have at least a basic level of income security. While the labour market serves as the primary source of income security during working life, social protection plays a major role in smoothing incomes and aggregate demand, thereby facilitating structural change within economies.

Worldwide, 2.3 per cent of GDP is allocated to social protection expenditure for women and men in ensuring income security during working age; regionally, levels vary widely, ranging from 0.5 per cent in Africa to 5.9 per cent in Western Europe.

Unemployment protection

Where they exist, unemployment benefit schemes play a key role in providing income security to workers and their families in the event of temporary unemployment, contributing thereby to preventing poverty; supporting structural change in the economy; providing safeguards against informalization; and, in the event of a crisis, stabilizing aggregate demand, helping the economy to recover more quickly.

However, only 28 per cent of the labour force worldwide is potentially eligible for benefits (contributory or non-contributory) under existing legislation should they become unemployed. Within this overall figure, regional differences are considerable: 80 per cent of the labour force is so covered in Europe, 38 per cent in Latin America, 21 per cent in the Middle East, 17 per cent in the Asia and Pacific region, and 8 per cent in Africa. Only 12 per cent of unemployed workers worldwide actually receive unemployment benefits, and again regional differences are large, with effective coverage ranging from 64 per cent of unemployed workers in Western Europe to just over 7 per cent in the Asia and Pacific region, 5 per cent in Latin America and the Caribbean, and less than 3 per cent in the Middle East and Africa.

A number of emerging economies have introduced unemployment benefit schemes, such as Bahrain or Viet Nam, as a means to ensure income security for unemployed workers and facilitate their search for jobs matching their skills in the formal economy. India's employment guarantee scheme (Mahatma Gandhi National Employment Guarantee Scheme) also provides a form of unemployment protection by guaranteeing 100 days of public employment to poor rural households.

Employment injury protection

In 2013, shaken by the Rana Plaza tragedy in Bangladesh, the world became aware that social protection in case of employment injury is essential to protect workers and their families from the financial consequences of accidents at work and to facilitate their rehabilitation. At present, however, only 33.9 per cent of the global labour force is covered by law for employment injury through mandatory social insurance. Even if voluntary social insurance coverage and employer liability provisions are included, only 39.4 per cent of the labour force is covered by law. In practice, actual access to employment injury protection is even lower, largely owing to incomplete enforcement of the legislation in many countries.

The low coverage of employment injury compensation in many low- and middle-income countries points to an urgent need to enhance working conditions in respect of occupational safety and health, as well as improving employment injury coverage for all workers, including those in the informal economy. As more countries move from employer liability as the basis for employment injury protection to a mechanism based on social insurance, levels of protection for workers are likely to improve – but only if new laws are effectively enforced.

Disability benefits

Social protection plays a key role in meeting the specific needs of persons with disabilities with regard to income security, access to health care and social inclusion. Effective measures to support persons with disabilities in finding and retaining quality employment are a key element of non-discriminatory and inclusive policies that help to realize their rights and aspirations as productive members of society.

Complementing contributory schemes, non-contributory disability benefits play a key role in protecting those persons with disabilities who have not (yet) earned entitlements to contributory schemes. Only 87 countries offer such non-contributory benefits anchored in national legislation, which would provide at least a minimum level of income security for those disabled from birth or before working age, and those who for any reason have not had the opportunity to contribute to social insurance for long enough to be eligible for benefits.

Maternity protection

Effective maternity protection ensures income security for pregnant women and mothers of newborn children and their families, and also effective access to quality maternal health care. It also promotes equality in employment and occupation.

Worldwide, less than 40 per cent of women in employment are covered by law under mandatory maternity cash benefit schemes; 57 per cent if voluntary coverage (mainly for women in self-employment) is included. Due to the ineffective enforcement and implementation of the law in some regions (Asia and the Pacific, Latin America and Africa in particular), effective coverage is even lower: only 28 per cent of women in employment worldwide are protected through maternity cash benefits which provide some income security in during the final stages of pregnancy and after childbirth; the absence of income security forces many women to return to work prematurely.

An increasing number of countries are using non-contributory maternity cash benefits as a means to improve income security and access to maternal and child health care for pregnant women and new mothers, particularly for women living in poverty. However, significant gaps remain.

Ensuring effective access to quality maternal health care is of particular importance, especially in countries where the informal economy accounts for a large proportion of employment.

Old-age pensions: A state responsibility

The right to income security in old age, as grounded in human rights instruments and international labour standards, includes the right to an adequate pension. However, nearly half (48 per cent) of all people over pensionable age do not receive a pension. For many of those who do receive a pension, pension levels are not adequate. As a result, the majority of the world's older women and men have no income security, have no right to retire and have to continue working as long as they can – often badly paid and in precarious conditions. Under existing laws and regulations, only 42 per cent of people of working age today can expect to receive social security pensions in the future, and effective coverage is expected to be even lower. This gap will have to be filled also by an expansion of non-contributory provisions.

In recent years, many middle- and low-income countries have made efforts to expand the coverage of contributory pension schemes and to establish non-contributory pensions so as to guarantee at least basic income security in old age to all.

At the same time, countries undertaking fiscal consolidation are reforming their pension systems to make cost savings, by such means as raising the retirement age, reducing benefits and increasing contribution rates. These adjustments are reducing state responsibility for guaranteeing income security in old age and shifting large parts of the economic risks associated with pension provision on to individuals, thereby undermining the adequacy of pension systems and reducing their ability to prevent poverty in old age. Future pensioners will receive lower pensions in at least 14 countries of Europe.

It is important to note that a number of countries are reversing the earlier privatizations of pension systems, implemented in the 1980s and 1990s. Argentina, the Plurinational State of Bolivia, Chile, Hungary, Kazakhstan and Poland either have renationalized or are renationalizing their pension systems to improve old-age income security.

Towards universal coverage in health

The urgency of striving for universal coverage in health is illustrated by the fact more than 90 per cent of the population living in low-income countries remains without any right to coverage in health. Globally, 39 per cent of the population is lacking such coverage. As a result, about 40 per cent of all global health expenditure is shouldered directly by the sick. However, even people who are legally covered experience limited health benefits, high out-of-pocket payments and a lack of the health workers needed to deliver services. In such circumstances, despite coverage, health care is frequently neither available nor affordable, and the cost of accessing needed services can lead to poverty.

The ILO estimates that there is a global shortfall of 10.3 million health workers required to ensure that all in need receive quality health services. This gap, and the often close-to-poverty wages of health workers, are blocking progress towards universal health coverage.

Globally, 88 countries in several regions of the world have proved that it is possible to close the gaps in health coverage. Many of them began the process of reform at lower levels of national income and invested in times of economic crisis. Further, they have shown that countries can achieve high coverage rates and even universal coverage using either tax- or contribution-funded systems and schemes or a mix of both. However, countries undergoing fiscal consolidation have often initiated health reforms to make cost savings, through such means as rationalizing the costs of public health facilities, introducing patient co-payments and cutting wage bills for medical staff. These adjustment measures have sharpened inequities in access to health care and increased exclusion by shifting the burden from the public purse to private households.

Investing in health protection, including paid sick leave, yields returns. However, public expenditure on health is at present too low to be sufficiently effective: the potential economic returns from increased productivity and employment cannot be realized while gaps in coverage persist. Closing these gaps would lead to the highest rates of return in the world's poorest countries.

Greater joint efforts are necessary to work towards universal health coverage, and towards the associated goal of establishing social protection floors, as recently called for by the UN General Assembly.

Expanding social protection: Key to crisis recovery and inclusive development

The global financial and economic crisis has forcefully underlined the importance of social security as a human right, and as an economic and social necessity, as set out in the ILO Social Protection Floors Recommendation, 2012 (No. 202).

In the first phase of the crisis (2008–09), social protection played a strong role in the expansionary response. At least 48 high- and middle-income countries announced fiscal stimulus packages totalling US$2.4 trillion, of which approximately a quarter was invested in counter-cyclical social protection measures.

In the second phase of the crisis (2010 onwards), governments embarked on fiscal consolidation and premature contraction of expenditure, despite an urgent need of public support among vulnerable populations. In 2014, the scope of public expenditure adjustment is expected to intensify significantly: according to IMF projections, 122 countries – of which 82 are developing countries – will be contracting expenditures in terms of GDP. Further, a fifth of countries are undergoing excessive fiscal contraction, defined as cutting public expenditures below pre-crisis levels.

Contrary to public perception, fiscal consolidation measures are not limited to Europe; many developing countries have adopted adjustment measures, including the elimination or reduction of food and fuel subsidies; cuts or caps on wages, including for health and social care workers; rationalizing and more narrowly targeting social protection benefits; and reforms of pension and health-care systems. Many governments are also considering revenue-side measures, for example increasing consumption taxes such as VAT on basic products that are consumed by poor households.

In developing countries, some of the proceeds of these adjustments, e.g. from the elimination of subsidies, have been used to design narrowly targeted safety nets, as a compensatory mechanism to the poorest. However, given the large number of vulnerable low-income households in developing countries, more efforts are necessary to increase the fiscal space to meet the social protection needs of populations.

Of particular significance are the divergent trends in richer and poorer countries: while many high-income countries are contracting their social security systems, many developing countries are expanding them.

High-income countries have reduced a range of social protection benefits and limited access to quality public services. Together with persistent unemployment, lower wages and higher taxes, these measures have contributed to increases in poverty or social exclusion now affecting 123 million people in the European Union, 24 per cent of its population, many of them children, women, older persons and persons with disabilities. Several European courts have found cuts unconstitutional. The cost of adjustment has been passed on to populations, who have been coping with fewer jobs and lower income for more than five years. Depressed household income levels are leading to lower domestic consumption and lower demand, slowing down recovery. The achievements of the European social model, which dramatically reduced poverty and promoted prosperity in the period following the Second World War, have been eroded by short-term adjustment reforms.

Many middle-income countries are boldly expanding their social protection systems, thereby contributing to their domestic demand-led growth strategies: this presents a powerful developmental lesson. China, for instance, has achieved nearly universal coverage of pensions and increased wages; Brazil accelerated the expansion of social protection coverage and minimum wages since 2009. Continued commitment is necessary to address persistent inequalities.

Some lower-income countries have extended social protection mainly through temporary safety nets with very low benefit levels. However, in many of these countries debates are under way on building social protection floors as part of comprehensive social protection systems.

The case for social protection is compelling in our times. Social protection realizes the human right to social security and is a key element of sound economic policy. Social protection powerfully contributes to reducing poverty, exclusion and inequality – while enhancing political stability and social cohesion. It also contributes to economic growth by supporting household income and thus domestic consumption; this is particularly important during this time of slow recovery and low global demand. Further, social protection enhances human capital and productivity, so it has become a critical policy for transformative national development. Social protection, specifically social protection floors, are essential for recovery, inclusive development and social justice, and must be part of the post-2015 development agenda.

Introduction

1

KEY MESSAGES

- While the need for social protection is widely recognized, the fundamental human right to social security remains unfulfilled for the large majority of the world's population. Only 27 per cent of the global population enjoy access to comprehensive social security systems, whereas 73 per cent are covered partially or not at all.
- The lack of access to social protection constitutes a major obstacle to economic and social development. Inadequate or absent social protection coverage is associated with high and persistent levels of poverty and economic insecurity in some parts of the world, high and growing levels of inequality, insufficient investments in human capital and human capabilities, and weak automatic stabilizers of aggregate demand in the event of economic shocks.
- Social protection policies contribute to fostering both economic and social development in the short and the long term, by ensuring that people enjoy income security, have effective access to health care and other social services, and are empowered to take advantage of economic opportunities. Such policies play a key role in boosting domestic demand, supporting structural transformation of national economies, promoting decent work, and fostering inclusive and sustainable growth.
- National social protection floors and broader social security systems provide an enabling framework within which to reduce and prevent poverty, as well as to redress inequalities. They are key elements of national policies to promote human development, political stability and inclusive growth.
- The ILO Social Protection Floors Recommendation, 2012 (No. 202), provides practical guidance for setting national social protection floors and building comprehensive social security systems. It reflects a consensus on the extension of social security reached among governments and employers' and workers' organizations from 185 countries at all levels of development.
- While there has been a global trend towards the extension of social protection, particularly in middle-income countries, the effectiveness of social security systems in a number of high-income countries is at risk as a result of fiscal consolidation measures. These trends are presented in the different chapters of the report, following a life-cycle approach.

1.1 A right unfulfilled

While the need for social protection is widely recognized, the fundamental human right to social security remains unfulfilled for the large majority of the world's population.[1] Despite the impressive extension of social protection coverage over the past century, especially over the past decade, only a minority of the world's population is effectively protected. According to ILO estimates, in 2012 only 27 per cent of the working-age population and their families across the globe had access to comprehensive social security systems. In other words, almost three-quarters, or 73 per cent, of the world's population, about 5.2 billion people, do not enjoy access to comprehensive social protection. Many of those not sufficiently protected live in poverty, which is the case for half the population of middle- and low-income countries (World Bank, 2014).[2] Many of them, about 800 million people, are working poor (ILO, 2014a), and many work in the informal economy.[3]

The lack of access to social protection constitutes a major obstacle to economic and social development (ILO, 2010a; ILO, 2011a; ILO, 2012a; UN, 2008; UN, 2012b). In fact, the widespread lack of social protection coverage is associated with high and persistent levels of poverty and economic insecurity in some parts of the world (e.g. World Bank, 2014), high and growing levels of inequality (UNDP, 2014; UN, 2013d; UNRISD, 2010), insufficient investments in human capital and human capabilities, and weak automatic stabilizers of aggregate demand in the event of economic shocks (e.g. ADB, 2014).

Social protection policies contribute to fostering both economic and social development in the short and the long term, by ensuring that people enjoy income security, have effective access to health care and other social services, and are empowered to take advantage of economic opportunities. They play a key role in boosting domestic demand, supporting structural transformation of national economies, promoting decent work, and fostering inclusive and sustainable growth (e.g. G20, 2011; G20, 2012; ILO, 2012a; OECD, 2009a; World Bank, 2012). Social protection policies also accelerate progress towards the Millennium Development Goals (UN, 2010a; UNICEF, 2010). Sustainable and equitable growth cannot be achieved in the absence of strong social protection policies which guarantee at least a basic level of social protection to all in need and progressively extend the scope and level of social security coverage.[4] Such basic levels of social security should be guaranteed as part of national social protection floors, which constitute the fundamental elements of national social security systems.

Many countries have significantly extended their social security coverage during recent years and have stepped up their efforts to ensure that all in need benefit from at least basic protection, while continuing to develop their social security systems. In Brazil, Cabo Verde, China, Ghana, India, Mexico, Mozambique, South Africa and Thailand, for example, the gradual extension of social security coverage has had a significant impact on the well-being of the population, and has contributed, in conjunction with economic, labour market and employment policies, to fostering economic and social development and inclusive growth.

On the other hand, in the aftermath of the global financial and economic crisis a number of governments have reduced public spending in areas including social security systems, resulting in limits on the coverage or level of benefits. Fiscal consolidation[5] measures have slowed progress towards the realization of the

---

[1] There are varying definitions of the terms "social protection" and "social security". In many contexts, as in this report, the two terms are used interchangeably. The ILO usually uses the term "social security", with reference to the human right to social security set out in the Universal Declaration on Human Rights, 1948 (Art. 22), the International Covenant on Economic, Social and Cultural Rights, 1966 (Art. 9) and other UN human rights instruments. This term encompasses a broad variety of policy instruments, including social insurance, social assistance, universal benefits and other forms of cash transfers, as well as measures to ensure effective access to health care and other benefits in kind aiming at securing social protection. For more detail, see the glossary at the end of this report (Annex I), as well as ILO, 2010a, pp. 13–17.

[2] These World Bank estimates are based on a poverty line of US$2.50 PPP for 2010.

[3] The informal economy is understood as the set of all economic activities by workers and economic units that are – in law or in practice – not covered or insufficiently covered by formal arrangements. Workers in the informal economy are usually covered insufficiently or not at all by social protection; indeed, the lack of social protection coverage is sometimes used as a criterion by which to identify informal employment. At the same time, extending social protection coverage to workers in the informal economy helps to address some of the risks that trap workers in informality (such as the lack of health coverage) and support transitions to formalization (ILO, 2013g; ILO, 2013h).

[4] This recognition reflects an important policy paradigm shift in international development (Cichon and Hagemejer, 2007; Cichon, 2013). This can be seen in policy documents and academic studies, but also in the wide range of recent policy reforms in a growing number of developing countries.

[5] In this report, fiscal consolidation refers to the wide array of adjustment measures adopted to reduce government deficits and debt accumulation. Fiscal consolidation policies are often referred to as austerity policies.

Figure 1.1 Towards comprehensive social security systems: Number of areas covered in social protection programmes anchored in national legislation, 1900–2012

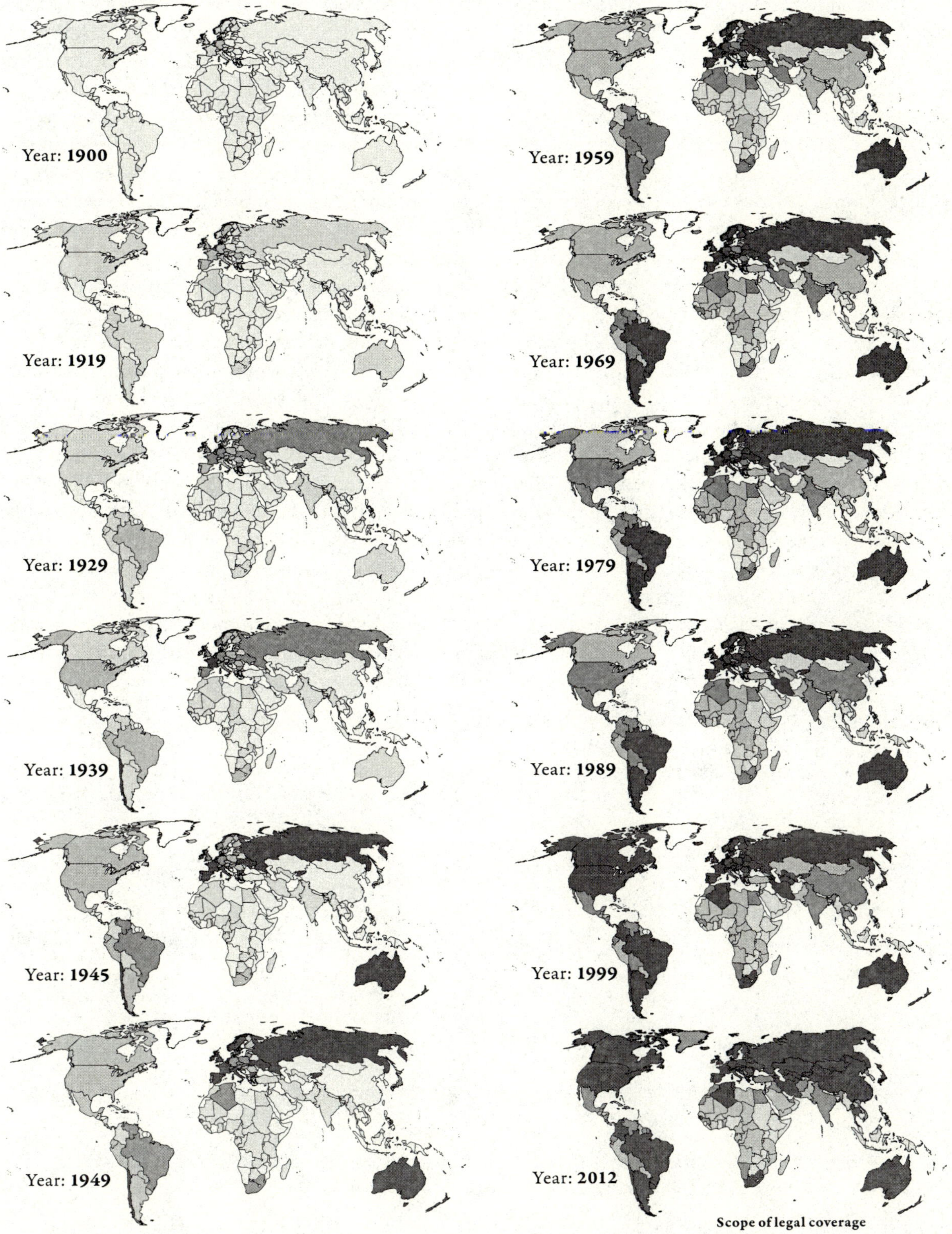

Scope of legal coverage

- None
- Very limited scope (1–4 policy areas)
- Limited scope (5–6 policy areas)
- Semi-comprehensive scope (7 policy areas)
- Comprehensive scope (all policy areas)

Note: The following areas are taken into consideration: sickness benefits, unemployment benefits, old-age benefits, employment injury benefits, family/child benefits, maternity benefits, invalidity/disability benefits and survivors' benefits. Date of adoption of first law taken as a basis for the construction of the maps.

Sources: Based on SSA and ISSA, 2012; SSA and ISSA, 2013a; SSA and ISSA, 2013b; SSA and ISSA, 2014.

Link: http://www.social-protection.org/gimi/gess/RessourceDownload.action?ressource.ressourceId=36923 human right to social security and other human rights (OHCHR, 2013) in many countries, as well as weakening the contribution that social security systems can make to socio-economic recovery.

1.2 Building social protection systems: A historical overview, 1900–2012

Since the beginning of the twentieth century, significant progress has been made in extending social security coverage and building comprehensive social security systems. From early steps taken in a number of pioneer countries, the scope of legal coverage,[6] as measured by the number of areas covered by social protection programmes anchored in national legislation, was extended at an impressive pace to more countries and more areas (see figure 1.1).[7] By 2012, the majority of countries had social security schemes established by law covering all or most areas, albeit in many cases only for a minority of their populations. This was the case in most European countries, large parts of the Americas, and increasingly also in Asia and the Pacific and in North Africa. Significant progress has also been made in the Middle East and sub-Saharan Africa.

Countries tend to extend their national social security systems in a sequence of steps, depending on their national circumstances and priorities. In many cases, when building social security systems, countries first addressed the area of employment injury, then introduced old-age pensions, disability and survivors' benefits, followed by sickness, health and maternity coverage. Benefits for children and families, and unemployment benefits, typically came last (see figure 1.2).

However, the extension of legal coverage does not in itself ensure either the effective coverage of the population or improvements in the quality and level of benefits. In fact, the extension of effective coverage has significantly lagged behind that of legal coverage, due to problems in implementation and enforcement, a lack of policy coordination and weak institutional capacities for the effective delivery of benefits and services. It is therefore essential to monitor legal and effective coverage in parallel, as will be done throughout this report, as far as the available data allow.

In many countries, a number of programmes have emerged in recent years that provide some degree of protection but lack a legal foundation. These cannot be considered as offering the same quantity and extent of protection as programmes grounded in law, as they do not establish legal entitlements or enforceable rights. Still, they play an important role in improving the situation of those benefiting from them. Many governments recognize the importance of anchoring social

Figure 1.2 Development of social protection programmes anchored in national legislation by area (branch), pre-1900 to post-2005 (percentage of countries)

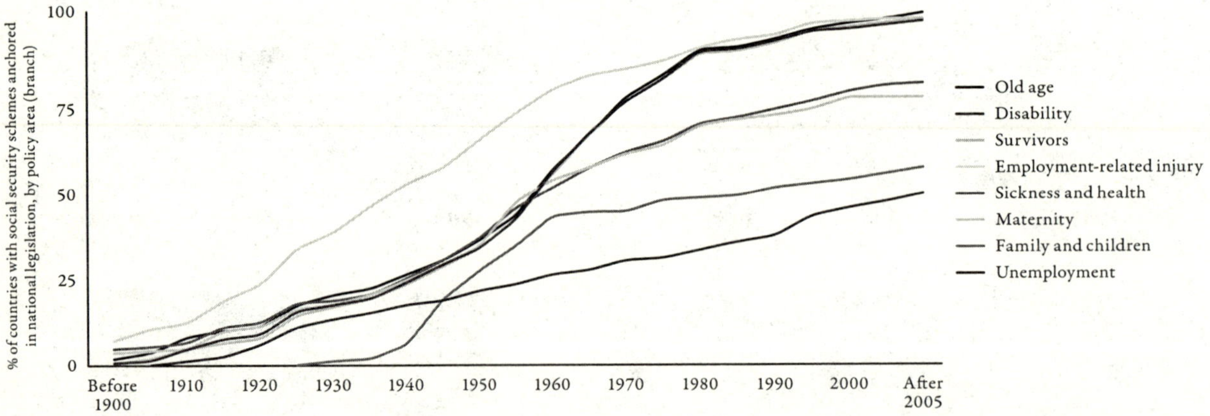

Sources: Based on SSA and ISSA, 2012; SSA and ISSA, 2013a; SSA and ISSA, 2013b; SSA and ISSA, 2014; ILO NATLEX database.
Link: http://www.social-protection.org/gimi/gess/RessourceDownload.action?ressource.ressourceId=36924

[6] For more detail on the concepts of legal and effective coverage and their measurement, see Annex II of this report.

[7] The following areas are taken into consideration: sickness benefits, unemployment benefits, old-age benefits, employment injury benefits, family/child benefits, maternity benefits, invalidity/disability benefits and survivors' benefits, as defined in the Social Security (Minimum Standards) Convention, 1952 (No. 102), as listed in the note to figure 1.1. Health is not included in figure 1.1 for methodological reasons, but is discussed in detail in Chapter 5.

security programmes in a sound framework of national legislation, thereby clarifying individuals' rights and obligations, enhancing the predictability and adequacy of benefits, strengthening institutional capacities promoting transparency and accountability, providing safeguards against corruption and establishing a more stable and regular funding base.

1.3 Fiscal consolidation: Setbacks 2010–15

The report also focuses on the setbacks resulting from fiscal adjustment processes initiated from 2010 onwards. In 2014, 122 countries are limiting their public expenditures in terms of GDP, at a time when populations are most in need. Fiscal consolidation measures have contributed to increases in poverty and social exclusion in several high-income countries, adding to the effects of persistent unemployment, lower wages and higher taxes. The resulting depressed household income levels are jeopardizing domestic consumption and demand, and slowing down recovery.

Contrary to public perception, fiscal consolidation policies have been applied not only in European countries, but also in some middle- and low-income countries, which are currently grappling with dwindling economic growth rates (IMF, 2013a). The combination of food and fuel price increases, followed by the global economic slowdown, jobless recovery and now cutbacks in public expenditure, have taken a toll on families in developing countries. The crucial importance of governments' commitment to continuing investments in social protection, in order to ensure inclusive growth and limit the harmful effects of persistent poverty and growing inequality, is highlighted in the different chapters of the report.

1.4 The way forward: Building national social protection floors and social security systems

With the adoption of the ILO's Social Protection Floors Recommendation, 2012 (No. 202), the world has taken a significant step forward in the realization of the human right to social security.[8] This Recommendation is the first international legal instrument that explicitly recognizes the triple role of social security as a universal human right and an economic and social necessity. It recognizes the importance of national social protection floors, which provide basic social security guarantees to all with the aim of ensuring effective access to at least essential health care and a basic level of income security as a matter of priority, as the indispensable foundation for more comprehensive national social security systems (ILO, 2012a). The ILO's two-dimensional extension strategy provides clear guidance on the future development of social security in the ILO's 185 member States towards the achievement of universal protection of the population by ensuring at least basic levels of income security and access to essential health care (national social protection floors: horizontal dimension) and progressively ensuring wider scope and higher levels of protection, guided by ILO social security standards (vertical dimension).[9]

The importance of building national social protection floors has also been recognized by the United Nations and the wider international development community. Following the call for the establishment of social protection floors by the UN Chief Executives Board in 2009 (UN, 2009a; Social Protection Floor Advisory Group, 2011), the role of social protection in general, and social protection floors in particular, for economic and social development has been acknowledged in a number of international, regional and multinational forums, including the United Nations (e.g. UN, 2010b; UN, 2012a) and the G20 (G20, 2009; G20, 2011; G20, 2012).

The emerging global consensus on social protection floors has been accompanied by a stronger emphasis on coherent and effective social protection systems in the strategic frameworks of other major international and multilateral organizations (FAO, 2012; OECD, 2009a; UNICEF, 2012; WHO, 2010; World Bank, 2012; European Commission, 2011a; European Commission, 2012a). Along with the ILO, they emphasize the need for a systemic approach to social protection, aiming at building inclusive and sustainable social protection systems that are closely coordinated with other social and economic policies. Together with other

[8] Recommendation No. 202 was adopted almost unanimously (one abstention) by governments and employers' and workers' representatives of the ILO's member States at the 101st Session of the International Labour Conference. The core elements of this Recommendation, and wider perspectives, were reflected in the Resolution and conclusions concerning the recurrent discussion on social protection (social security), adopted at the previous session of the International Labour Conference in 2011. Both documents are included in ILO, 2012a.

[9] This strategy was adopted by the International Labour Conference in 2011 (ILO, 2012a).

Box 1.1 The ILO's normative framework for the extension of social security

Since its establishment in 1919, the ILO has played a major role developing an internationally defined normative framework guiding the establishment, development and maintenance of social security systems across the world, and has become the world's leading point of reference for efforts to this end. Elaborated and adopted by the Organization's tripartite constituents, governments, employers' and workers' representatives of all ILO member States, and stemming from the Organization's mandate, the Conventions and Recommendations that compose this framework are unique: they establish standards that States set for themselves, building on good practices and innovative ways of providing enhanced and extended social protection in countries from all regions of the world. At the same time, they are built on the notion that there is no single perfect model for social security; on the contrary, it is for each society to develop the best means of guaranteeing the protection required. Accordingly, they offer a range of options and flexible routes for their application, which can be achieved through a combination of contributory and non-contributory benefits, general and occupational schemes, compulsory and voluntary insurance, and different methods for the administration of benefits, all directed at ensuring an overall level of protection which best responds to each country's needs.

Complementing and giving specific form to the provisions regarding the right to social security in international human rights instruments, the ILO's normative social security framework consists of eight up-to-date Conventions and Recommendations. The most prominent instruments are the Social Security (Minimum Standards) Convention, 1952 (No. 102), and the Social Protection Floors Recommendation, 2012 (No. 202).[1]

The long-standing Convention No. 102 regroups the nine classical social security contingencies (medical care, sickness, unemployment, old age, employment injury, family responsibilities, maternity, invalidity, survivorship) into a single comprehensive and legally binding instrument.

The recent Recommendation No. 202 provides guidance on closing social security gaps and achieving universal coverage through the establishment and maintenance of comprehensive social security systems. It calls upon States to achieve universal coverage with at least minimum levels of protection through the implementation of social protection floors as a matter of priority; and to progressively ensure higher levels of protection. National social protection floors should comprise basic social security guarantees that ensure effective access to essential health care and basic income security at a level that allows people to live in dignity throughout the life cycle These should include at least:

- access to essential health care, including maternity care;
- basic income security for children;
- basic income security for persons of working age who are unable to earn sufficient income, in particular in cases of sickness, unemployment, maternity and disability;
- basic income security for older persons.

Complementing existing standards, Recommendation No. 202 sets forth an integrated and coherent approach to social protection across the life cycle, underscores the principle of universality of protection through nationally defined social protection floors, and embodies a commitment to their progressive realization in terms of benefits and people covered. It thereby aims at ensuring that all members of society enjoy at least a basic level of social security throughout their lives, ensuring their health and dignity. Poverty, vulnerability and social exclusion are established as priority areas of attention, with the clear objective of reducing poverty as soon as possible. The Recommendation calls for systems that are country-led, are aligned to national circumstances, are reviewed in the light of population needs, and include the participation of all stakeholders. In an innovative way, it contains guidance on monitoring to help countries assess their progress in moving towards enhanced protection and improve the performance of national social security systems.

[1] Convention No. 102 has been ratified to date by 50 countries, most recently by Brazil (2009), Bulgaria (2008), Honduras (2012), Jordan (2014), Romania (2009) and Uruguay (2010), and provides guidance for all 185 ILO member States. ILO Recommendations are not open for ratification.

international standards, the ILO's normative framework on social security (see box 1.1) guides the development and continuous evolution of national social security systems to provide populations with meaningful social protection.

1.5 Objective and structure of the report

Two years after the adoption of Recommendation No. 202, this report takes stock of the state of social security coverage around the world, particularly with regard to the building of national social protection floors and comprehensive social security systems. This report is the second in a series of reports[10] that provide an assessment of social security coverage around the world, highlight progress made in enhancing protection, identify remaining coverage gaps, and discuss major challenges for further progress in realizing the right to social security for all.

Reflecting the approach set out in Recommendation No. 202, this report is structured in a sequence of chapters following the life cycle, so that relevant clusters of contributory or non-contributory social security schemes and programmes are addressed together.[11] Chapters 2–4 focus on social protection benefits that enhance income security throughout the life cycle, gathered into three major clusters: Chapter 2 focuses on social protection benefits for children and families, including child and family benefits; Chapter 3 addresses various elements of income security for people of working age, addressing specifically benefits in case of unemployment (section 3.2), employment injury (section 3.3), disability (section 3.4) and maternity (section 3.5). Chapter 4 addresses income security in old age, with a particular focus on old-age pensions.[12] Chapter 5 is devoted to achieving universal coverage in health throughout the life cycle, including medical care and sickness benefits. Chapter 6 is devoted to issues of social security financing and expenditure, and reflects specifically on the divergent trends of expansion and contraction, and their implications for future policy-making in social security and the post-2015 development agenda. Throughout the report, reference is repeatedly made to the rights underpinning social security systems, which remain as valid and as important as ever.

Annex I includes a short glossary of key terms used in this report, and Annex II summarizes the concepts and measurement of social security coverage applied. Annex III includes summary tables regarding some of the main minimum requirements set out in ILO social security standards. Annex IV includes the statistical tables.

1.6 Building the knowledge base on social protection statistics

Conceived as a tool to facilitate monitoring of the state of social protection in the world, the *World Social Protection Report* offers in its successive editions an extensive statistical resource in relation to social protection, including a set of detailed tables in the Statistical Annex (Annex IV) of this report, and more on a dedicated website.[13] This database draws to a large extent on the ILO Social Security Inquiry database, which provides in-depth country-level statistics on various dimensions of social security systems, including key indicators.[14]

Having published such data since the 1950s in various forms, the ILO maintains its databases in collaboration, as far as possible on a consistent basis, with a number of other international and regional actors, notably the Asian Development Bank (ADB), the Statistical Office of the European Commission (Eurostat), the Economic Commission for Latin America and the Caribbean (ECLAC) and other regional commissions of the United Nations, the International Social Security Association (ISSA), the Organisation for Economic

[10] The first report in the series was published as the *World Social Security Report* in 2010 (ILO, 2010a). This report is published as the *World Social Protection Report* in order to reflect the greater interest in social protection issues in many parts of the world, and at the international level.

[11] In doing so, both the horizontal and vertical dimensions of the extension of social security (ILO, 2012a) are addressed in an integrated way in each chapter.

[12] General social assistance is not treated under a separate heading but is referred to throughout the report.

[13] The Statistical Annex (Annex IV) of this report includes two sets of tables. Tables AIV.A1–AIV.A12 provide key demographic, economic and social indicators and are available online; tables AIV.B1–AIV.B13, which are more specifically concerned with social protection, are included also in the printed version. All material is available at http://www.social-protection.org/gimi/gess/ShowTheme.do?tid=3985.

[14] The ILO Social Security Inquiry database is available at: http://www.ilo.org/dyn/ilossi/ssimain.home?p_lang=en.

Co-operation and Development (OECD), the World Bank and the World Health Organization (WHO). The ILO Social Security Inquiry database is linked to various other databases on social protection, including the Eurostat European System of Integrated Social Protection Statistics database (ESPROSS), the OECD Social Expenditure database (SOCX), the World Bank pensions and ASPIRE databases, the ISSA's Social Security Observatory, the ADB Social Protection Index database (SPI), the WHO's Global Health Observatory and National Health Accounts, and ECLAC's databases.[15] The ILO Social Security Inquiry database also draws on national official reports and other sources, which usually are largely based on administrative data; and on survey data from a range of sources including national household income and expenditure surveys, labour force surveys, and demographic and health surveys, to the extent that these include variables on social protection. This report is also intended as a contribution to the joint efforts at national and international level[16] to ensure the availability of high-quality social security statistics, not least to support ILO member States in monitoring and reviewing their social protection floors and social security systems, and to ensure their effectiveness and efficiency in meeting the social protection needs of their populations.

[15] A list of databases used for the production of this report is provided at the end of the bibliography.

[16] Efforts are under way in the framework of the Social Protection Inter-Agency Coordination Board (SPIAC-B) to strengthen collaboration between international agencies in the field of social protection statistics and to develop integrated guidance material for national actors (ILO et al., 2013; Bonnet and Tessier, 2013). This work aims at carrying further the international community's earlier efforts to agree on a set of core indicators in the field of social security statistics, as set out in the "Resolution concerning the development of social security statistics", adopted by the International Conference of Labour Statisticians in 1957, which continues to provide relevant guidance for the further development of social security statistics at the national level.

Social protection for children and families

2

KEY MESSAGES

- Social protection policies are an essential element of realizing children's rights, ensuring their well-being, breaking the vicious cycle of poverty and vulnerability, and helping all children realize their full potential.
- Despite a large expansion of schemes, existing social protection policies do not sufficiently address the income security needs of children and families, particularly in low- and middle-income countries with large child populations. About 18,000 children die every day, mainly from preventable causes. Many of these deaths could be prevented through adequate social protection.
- More efforts are needed to step up measures to ensure income security for children and families, including child and family benefits. Specific child and family benefit programmes rooted in legislation exist in 108 countries, yet often cover only small groups of the population. In 75 countries, no such programmes are available at all.
- On average, governments allocate 0.4 per cent of GDP to child and family benefits, ranging from 2.2 per cent in Western Europe to 0.2 per cent in Africa, and in Asia and the Pacific. Underinvestment in children jeopardizes their rights and their future, as well as the economic and social development prospects of the countries in which they live.
- Fiscal consolidation and adjustment measures in higher-income economies threaten progress on income security for children and their families. Child poverty increased in 19 of the 28 countries of the European Union between 2007 and 2012.
- Social protection is a human right, further supported by the UN Convention on the Rights of the Child, 1989, and yet many children do not receive the essential cash transfers that could make a real difference, in terms of nutrition, health, education and care services, to their chances of realizing their full potential. Social protection also has a key – yet often neglected – role in preventing child labour.

2.1 The role of social protection in ensuring children's well-being

Social protection is essential in preventing and reducing poverty for children and families, in addressing inequalities and in realizing children's rights.

Despite recent progress in many parts of the world, too many children live in poverty and are deprived of their most elementary rights (UNICEF, 2012; UNICEF, 2014). In, fact, in most parts of the world, children and families with children are at greater risk of poverty than other groups of the population, with respect to both monetary and other forms of poverty.

The consequences of poverty are very significant for children. Children experience poverty differently from adults; they have specific and different needs. While an adult may fall into poverty temporarily, a child who falls into poverty may be poor for a lifetime – rarely does a child get a second chance at an education or a healthy start in life. Even short periods of food deprivation can be detrimental to children's long-term development. If children do not receive adequate nutrition, they lag behind their peers in size and intellectual capacity, are more vulnerable to life-threatening diseases, perform less well in school, and ultimately are less likely to be productive adults. Child poverty threatens not only the individual child, but is likely to be passed on to future generations, entrenching and even exacerbating inequality in society (see, e.g. UNICEF, 2012; UNICEF, 2014; Minujin and Nandy, 2012; Ortiz, Moreira Daniels and Engilbertsdóttir, 2012). Many of the 18,000 children under the age of five who die every day, mainly from preventable causes, could be saved through adequate social protection (UNICEF, 2014). Where children are deprived of a decent standard of living, access to quality health care (see Chapter 5), education and care, and where they suffer from social exclusion, their future is compromised. Where children are forced to engage in child labour, such exploitation takes a heavy toll on their physical and cognitive development, and on their future life chances (ILO, 2013a). Child poverty affects not only the well-being and aspirations of individual children, but also the wider communities, societies and economies in which they live.

Child and family benefits, in cash and in kind, play a particularly important role in realizing children's rights and addressing their needs, particularly for the most vulnerable members of society (see, e.g. UNICEF, 2012; Sanfilippo, de Neubourg and Martorano, 2012; UNESCO, 2014). Evidence from many parts of the world demonstrates that social protection benefits have led to a marked improvement in the nutritional status of children (see ILO, 2010a; UNICEF, 2012; Save the Children, 2012a). Cash transfer programmes have also contributed to a significant increase in the utilization of pre- and post-natal health visits and in a reduction in the proportion of home-based births, thus enhancing maternal and child health. More generally, such programmes have been shown to increase the utilization of health services, again contributing to improvements in children's health (e.g. Attanasio et al., 2005). Cash transfers for children and families, both conditional and non-conditional, have also contributed to significant increases in children's enrolment and attendance at school in different parts of the world, as well as, although with less conclusive evidence, improvements in education outcomes (e.g. additional years of schooling, impact on wages) (Fiszbein and Schady, 2009; Baird et al., 2013; UNICEF, 2012; ILO, 2010b; ILO, 2013a). Through these various channels, social protection benefits contribute to enhancing children's current and future well-being, and their ability to seize economic and social opportunities in later life. Child and family benefits, together with other forms of benefits and services, are also an important means of responding to the special needs of children with disabilities (UNICEF, 2013), orphans and vulnerable children, children affected by violence and abuse, and other disadvantaged children (Save the Children, 2012b; Barrientos et al., 2013).

This chapter focuses in particular on the income security of children and families, which constitutes a key dimension of their well-being. Strengthening income security is therefore a key element of policies that aim at reducing and preventing child poverty, at breaking the intergenerational transmission of poverty, and at facilitating children's access to nutrition, care, education and health care. The ILO's Social Protection Floors Recommendation, 2012 (No. 202), explicitly recognizes income security for children as one of the basic social security guarantees constituting a national social protection floor, based on an integrated approach that addresses the multiple dimensions of child well-being. This basic social security guarantee provides an effective framework for national policies (see box 2.1). The notion of income security is not limited to a sufficient level of cash income, but encompasses income in kind, such as nutrition and access to services – indeed, the broad range of resources that is necessary to secure a decent standard of living and life in dignity for all children. Social services (e.g. care, education, health care) are essential in ensuring income security, as these

Box 2.1 International standards for child and family benefits

The UN legal framework on human rights contains a number of provisions spelling out various rights of children that form part of their right to social protection. These comprise the right to social security, taking into consideration the resources and the circumstances of the child and persons having responsibility for their maintenance;[1] the right to a standard of living adequate for their health and their well-being; and the right to special care and assistance.[2] The ICESCR further requires States to give the widest possible protection and assistance to the family, particularly for the care and education of dependent children.[3]

ILO social security standards complement this framework and provide guidance to countries on how to give effect to the various rights that form part of the right of children to social protection. The ILO Social Security (Minimum Standards) Convention, 1952 (No. 102), Part VII, sets minimum standards for the provision of family (or child) benefits in the form of either a periodic cash benefit or benefits in kind (food, clothing, housing, holidays or domestic help) or a combination of both, allocated for the maintenance of children. The fundamental objective of family benefits should thus be to ensure the welfare of children and the economic stability of their families.

As specified by the ILO's Committee of Experts on the Application of Conventions and Recommendations, these standards require that family benefits be granted in respect of each child in the family and to all children, for so long as the child is receiving education or vocational training on a full-time basis and is not in receipt of an adequate income determined by national legislation. They should be set at a level which relates directly to the actual cost of providing for a child and should represent a substantial contribution to this cost. Family allowances at the minimum rate should be granted regardless of means. Benefits above the minimum rate may be subject to a means test. Furthermore, all benefits should be adjusted in order to take into account changes in the cost of providing for children or in the general cost of living (ILO, 2011c, paras 184–86).

ILO Recommendation No. 202 further refines and extends the normative framework, aiming at universal protection. Income security for children is one of the basic social security guarantees constituting a national social protection floor, and should ensure "access to nutrition, education, care and any other necessary goods and services" (para. 5(b)). Although the guarantee should be nationally defined, the Recommendation provides clear guidance on its appropriate level: the minimum level of income security should allow for life in dignity and should be sufficient to provide for effective access to a set of necessary goods and services, such as may be set out through national poverty lines and other comparable thresholds (para. 8(b)). Providing for universality of protection, the Recommendation sets out that the basic social security guarantee should apply to at least all residents, and all children, as defined in national laws and regulations and subject to existing international obligations (para. 6), that is, to the respective provisions of the CRC, the ICESCR and other relevant instruments. Representing an approach strongly focused on outcomes, Recommendation No. 202 allows for a broad range of policy instruments to achieve income security for children, including child and family benefits (the focus of this chapter).

[1] Universal Declaration of Human Rights, 1948 (UDHR), Art. 22; International Covenant on Economic, Social and Cultural Rights, 1966 (ICESCR), Art. 9; UN Convention on the Rights of the Child (CRC), Art. 26. [2] UDHR, Art. 25(1) and (2). [3] ICESCR, Art. 10(1).

reduce families' spending needs and can facilitate parents' availability to engage in paid employment knowing that their children are well cared for (e.g. UNICEF and ILO, 2013). Measures to facilitate access to health, education and care services, combined with measures to improve the availability and quality of those services, are necessary to ensure that children may realize their full potential.

Obviously, income security for children is impossible to achieve in isolation from the family and household context. Income security for children therefore mirrors the income security of their parents, grandparents and/or other carers. As a result, the range of policies and policy instruments available to achieve this goal is very broad, and reaches well beyond child and family benefits in a narrow sense: it also includes other social protection programmes as part of the national social security system, as well as broader policies that address decent and productive employment, wages and incomes, access to health care, education and other social services, as well as gender equality and care arrangements.[1]

The broad range of policies that are necessary to achieve income security for children is reflected in the

[1] In this respect, the Joint Statement on Advancing Child-sensitive Social Protection (DfID et al., 2009) provides important guidelines for the design, implementation and monitoring of social security schemes and programmes (see box 2.2).

Box 2.2 Child-sensitive social protection

The Joint Statement on Advancing Child-sensitive Social Protection sets out that the design, implementation and evaluation of child-sensitive social protection programmes should aim to:

- avoid adverse impacts on children, and reduce or mitigate social and economic risks that directly affect children's lives;
- intervene as early as possible where children are at risk, in order to prevent irreversible impairment or harm;
- consider the age and gender-specific risks and vulnerabilities of children throughout the life cycle;
- mitigate the effects of shocks, exclusion and poverty on families, recognizing that families raising children need support to ensure equal opportunity;
- make special provision to reach children who are particularly vulnerable and excluded, including children without parental care, and those who are marginalized within their families or communities due to their gender, disability, ethnicity, HIV and AIDS, or other factors;
- consider the mechanisms and intra-household dynamics that may affect how children are reached, paying particular attention to the balance of power between men and women within the household and broader community;
- include the voices and opinions of children, their care-givers and youth in the understanding and design of social protection systems and programmes.

The joint statement (DfID et al., 2009) was issued by the DfID, HelpAge International, Hope & Homes for Children, Institute of Development Studies, ILO, Overseas Development Institute, Save the Children UK, UNDP, UNICEF and the World Bank.

Joint Statement on Advancing Child-sensitive Social Protection issued in 2009 by a coalition of agencies, bilateral donor agencies and international NGOs (see box 2.2). This statement sets out important guidelines for the design, implementation and monitoring of social security schemes and programmes in order to ensure that the needs of children are addressed in a broad range of policies, including in national social protection systems and particularly national social protection floors.

The need for a broad social protection approach to realizing children's rights is also reflected in the recent *World Report on Child Labour* (ILO, 2013a; see box 2.3), which has highlighted the need to take a comprehensive and systemic view, considering the full range of social protection instruments, including those which ensure income security for working-age adults (e.g. unemployment protection, maternity benefits, disability benefits) and older persons (e.g. old-age pensions). Social health protection occupies a key role in protecting households from health-related poverty risks which are closely associated with the incidence of child labour. Child-sensitive measures aimed at reducing and preventing child labour should therefore form part of an approach that sets out not only to strengthen national social security systems but also to ensure effective coordination with other related policy areas, including employment, wages and broader social policies.

2.2 Expenditure on social protection for children and families

Public expenditure on social protection benefits aimed specifically at meeting the needs of children amounts to 0.4 per cent of total GDP worldwide, or 7.4 per cent of total social protection expenditure (excluding health expenditure) (see figures 2.1 and 2.2). These figures include child benefits and benefits targeting families with children, such as cash transfer programmes for children and families,[2] whether provided in cash or in kind, but exclude provisions for health and education,[3] two important related policy areas.

There is wide variation across regions. Whereas countries in Western Europe spend on average 2.2 per cent of their GDP on child and family benefits, representing about one-tenth of their public social protection expenditure (excluding health expenditure), in all

[2] General social assistance and other benefits which may indirectly benefit children (e.g. maternity benefits) are not included.

[3] The figures do, however, take into account some provisions designed to facilitate children's participation in education, such as textbooks, uniforms and school meals, where these are provided as part of social protection programmes.

Box 2.3 Social security systems and the prevention of child labour

Social protection is highly relevant to the prevention and reduction of child labour. Economic vulnerabilities associated with poverty and shocks are important drivers of child labour. Social protection instruments can play an important role in reducing child labour by mitigating these vulnerabilities and enhancing poor families' resilience. These links are explored in detail in the *World Report on Child Labour* (ILO, 2013a).

The links between social protection and child labour have received more attention with the emergence of conditional cash transfer programmes that explicitly link the receipt of cash benefits to school attendance or similar conditions. Many programmes have been found to have a significant effect in promoting school enrolment and attendance, yet it is not fully clear whether these effects result directly from the behavioural conditions, or indirectly through the income effect and a stronger emphasis on supply-side factors, that is, in ensuring that schools are actually available and accessible for poor children (ILO, 2013a; Barrientos et al., 2013). From the few evaluations that have systematically assessed the impact on children's work, it can be deduced that, while cash benefits tend to have a strong impact on school attendance, they may not reduce child labour to the same extent: many children combine school and work. Reductions in child labour are more evident where cash benefits are integrated with additional programme elements, such as after-school programmes, as in Brazil.[1]

Economic vulnerability is not the only cause of child labour, and social protection is not by itself a complete answer to it. Nonetheless, social protection is a critical pillar of a broader policy response to child labour. Efforts against child labour are unlikely to be successful in the absence of a social protection floor to safeguard vulnerable households and to enable them to seize opportunities and to break the intergenerational transmission of poverty.

Although other elements of social security systems have not been systematically assessed with regard to their impact on child labour, it can be assumed that they also have a positive effect in so far as they reduce the vulnerability of poor households and address poverty risks that may otherwise promote child labour. This is, for example, the case for social health protection, reflecting the fact that ill health constitutes a major poverty risk for vulnerable households. Measures to reduce the income insecurity of adults, including unemployment protection, employment guarantee schemes, disability benefits, maternity benefits and social pensions, also contribute to mitigating vulnerability for poor households, and can contribute to preventing and reducing child labour.

Within any broader social security system, building a national social protection floor is particularly relevant to addressing vulnerabilities associated with child labour. Social protection floors provide a set of basic social security guarantees, including a basic level of income security throughout the life cycle and access to essential health care. These basic guarantees, in turn, are essential in addressing the multifaceted economic and social vulnerabilities which promote and sustain child labour. Where children and their families enjoy basic income security and access to essential health care, and where the necessary education and other services are in place, child labour can be effectively prevented. Indeed, evidence presented in this report suggests that an approach linking cash and in-kind benefits with access to education and health services can be particularly effective in addressing child labour.

[1] Such elements were successfully implemented in the Brazilian PETI programme, which was integrated into the Bolsa Família programme in 2006.

Source: Based on ILO, 2013a.

other regions, less than 1 per cent of GDP is allocated to child and family benefits, even though in most of them children form a significantly higher proportion of the total population than in Europe. Despite the recent extension of cash transfer programmes, public expenditure on child benefits in Latin America and the Caribbean reaches only 0.7 per cent of GDP, or 6.5 per cent of public social protection expenditure (excluding health expenditure), a level similar to that prevailing in North America, the Middle East, and Central and Eastern Europe. In Asia and the Pacific, and in Africa, on average 0.2 per cent of GDP is allocated to child and family benefits. In the case of Africa, in particular, the low proportion of public expenditure on child and family benefits is particularly striking, considering the high proportion of children in the total population (children under 15 make up 42 per cent of Africa's population).

It is clear that the level of resources allocated is not sufficient to respond adequately to the income security needs of children and families, even when taking into account that these needs are also addressed through other means, including public health, education and care services. Underinvestment in the social protection needs of children is particularly critical in low-income countries, which on average allocate less than 0.1 per cent of their GDP to child and family benefits. This points to a significant underinvestment in children,

Figure 2.1 Public expenditure on child benefits by region, and proportion of children aged 0–14 in total population, 2010/11 (percentage of GDP)

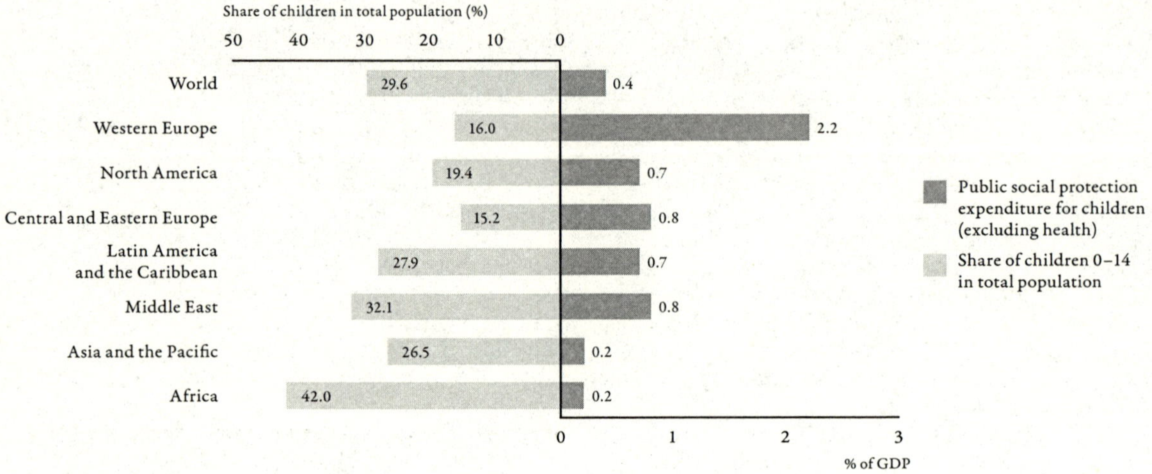

Sources: ILO Social Protection Department database. For detailed sources, see Annex IV, table B.13.
Link: http://www.social-protection.org/gimi/gess/RessourceDownload.action?ressource.ressourceId=42077.

which is likely to have negative effects on the future productivity of these countries' workforce, and their future economic and social development prospects.

The overall level of resources allocated to children and families depends, among other factors, on the composition of the set of benefits and services available. These reach beyond social protection in a narrow sense, and are only partly included in measures of social protection expenditure. While in some countries cash benefits play a major role in the overall package of benefits and services available to families, in others the provision of benefits in kind (e.g. school meals and other nutrition interventions, affordable housing) or the provision of services (e.g. childcare) plays a more dominant role, and obviously also affects the income security of families with children. The provision of quality public education, childcare and health services (see Chapter 5) also has implications for ensuring income security for families with children by reducing their need to allocate scarce resources to school fees and the costs of health and other care; yet these services also suffer from considerable underinvestment in some parts of the world. The availability of childcare services, along with the presence of public policies and measures adopted by employers to facilitate sharing work and family responsibilities for parents with children, will also affect the income security of children.

2.3 Extent of legal coverage: Child and family benefit programmes anchored in national legislation

Taking account of the wide range of social protection benefits and services needed to ensure children's well-being and the realization of their rights, this chapter focuses in particular on child and family benefits aiming at enhancing income security, and considers them in relation to the social security benefits discussed in other chapters of this report.[4]

Child and family benefits include various types of social protection benefits or combinations thereof (see figure 2.3). Some countries provide universal child benefits that cover all children, independently of the employment or income status of their parents, and are usually financed out of general taxation. Benefits are usually flat, but benefit rates may be differentiated by the age of the child or by taking into account

[4] In this respect, it is also useful to consider the labour market and employment implications of child and family benefits. These can also influence labour markets and wage-setting, and in terms of policy-making this may be seen as an important function in its own right. If the costs of bringing up children are at least partially met through collectively financed benefits (from general taxation or social insurance contributions), the differential needs of workers with children, as compared to workers without children, will not have to be met (exclusively) through wages. This may be seen as providing a more "level playing field" between workers with and without family obligations, and thus minimizing one possible source of distortion in the general wage structure. This outcome is seen in many high-income countries, where child benefits are available on an equal basis for all children, usually without means testing.

Figure 2.2 Public social protection expenditure on child and family benefits (excluding health), 2010/11 (percentage of GDP)

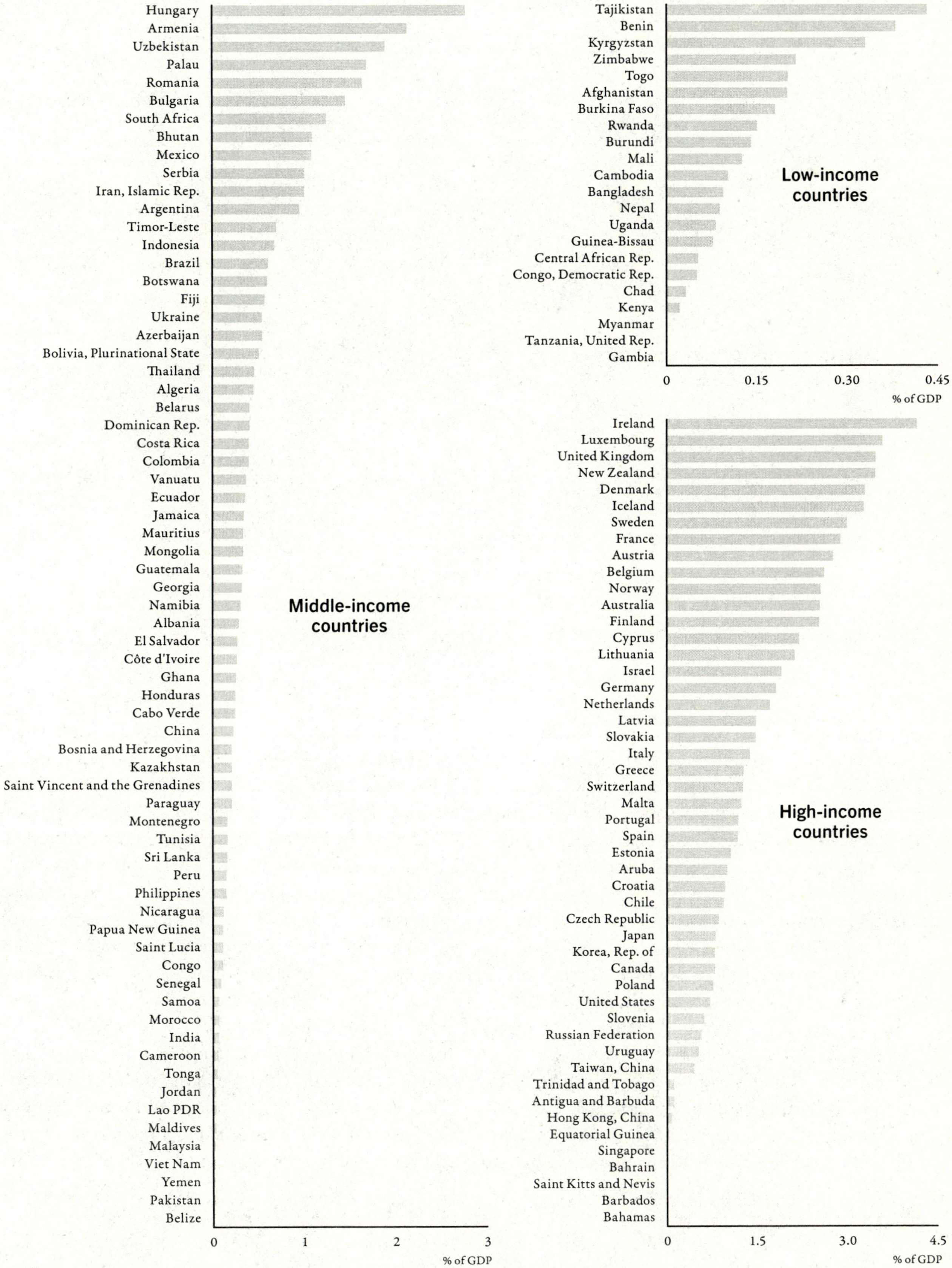

Sources: ILO Social Protection Department database. For detailed sources, see Annex IV, table B.13.

Link: http://www.social-protection.org/gimi/gess/RessourceDownload.action?ressource.ressourceId=44437.

Figure 2.3 Overview of child and family cash benefit programmes anchored in national legislation, by type of scheme and groups covered, 2012/13

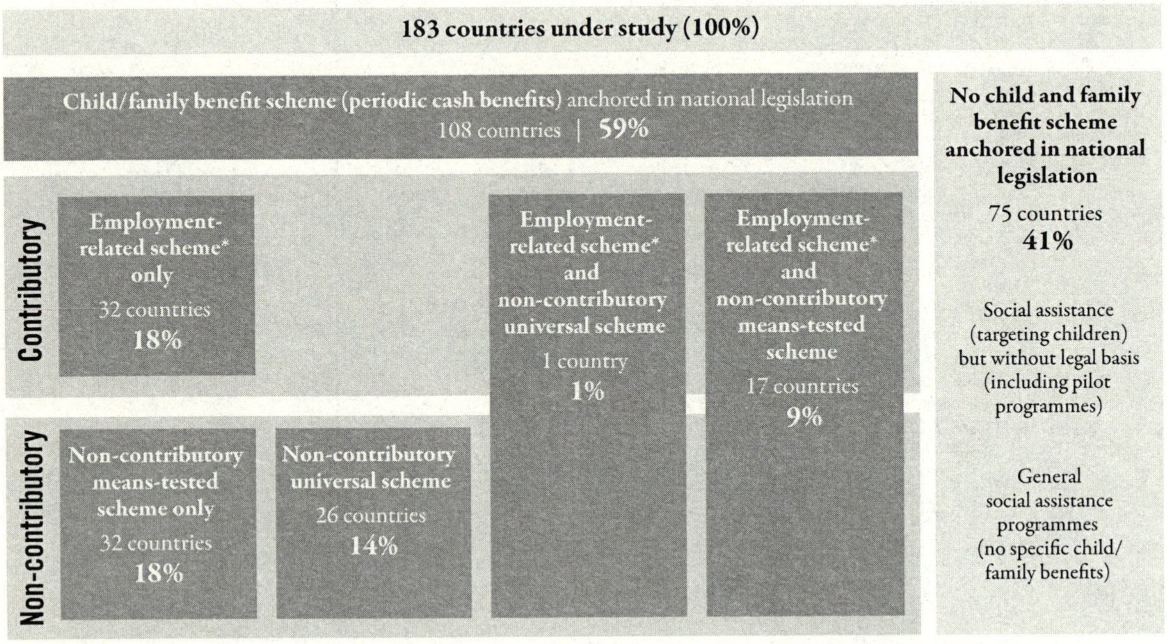

* Employment-related schemes include those financed through contributions from employers and workers, as well as those financed exclusively by employers.

Sources: Based on SSA and ISSA, 2012; SSA and ISSA, 2013a; SSA and ISSA, 2013b; SSA and ISSA, 2014; European Commission, Mutual Information System on Social Protection (MISSOC); Council of Europe, Mutual Information System on Social Protection of the Council of Europe (MISSCEO).

Link: http://www.social-protection.org/gimi/gess/RessourceDownload.action?ressource.ressourceId=42497.

the total number of children in the family. In some countries, benefits are fully or partially organized through the tax system, by providing tax rebates or a negative income tax to families with children.[5] Employment-related child or family benefits, usually financed through contributions and organized through social insurance schemes, cover mostly employees in the formal economy. Means-tested child and family benefits (specific social assistance benefits for children and families) are usually targeted towards poor families and children. They include a wide range of cash transfer programmes for children and families introduced in recent years, including conditional and non-conditional benefits.[6] These programmes have had a major impact on extending coverage and providing at least a minimum level of income security to children and families. Figure 2.3 summarizes the different types of programmes, and combinations thereof, through which cash benefits for children and families are provided. It focuses on programmes anchored in national legislation, as these are usually more stable in terms of funding and institutional frameworks, guarantee coverage as a matter of right, and provide legal entitlements to eligible individuals and households. In addition to these programmes, in some countries other programmes exist which are not yet anchored in national legislation, including pilot or temporary programmes, often limited to certain regions or districts.

In 108 countries out of the 183 for which sufficient data are available, periodic child or family benefits in cash are provided to eligible families and/or children. Many of the remaining 75 countries do, however, have more general social assistance programmes, which may provide benefits contributing to income security for

[5] In fact, the tax system plays a strong – and often neglected – role in redistributive policies for children and families (e.g. Adema, Fron and Ladaique, 2014).

[6] Some of these programmes include benefits for categories of the population other than children, and would therefore, strictly speaking, be classified as general social assistance programmes rather than child and family benefits. Indeed, some tend to be perceived as focusing exclusively on children and families, although in fact they have a broader remit.

Figure 2.4 Child/family allowances: Distribution of programmes anchored in legislation, by type of programme, 2011–13

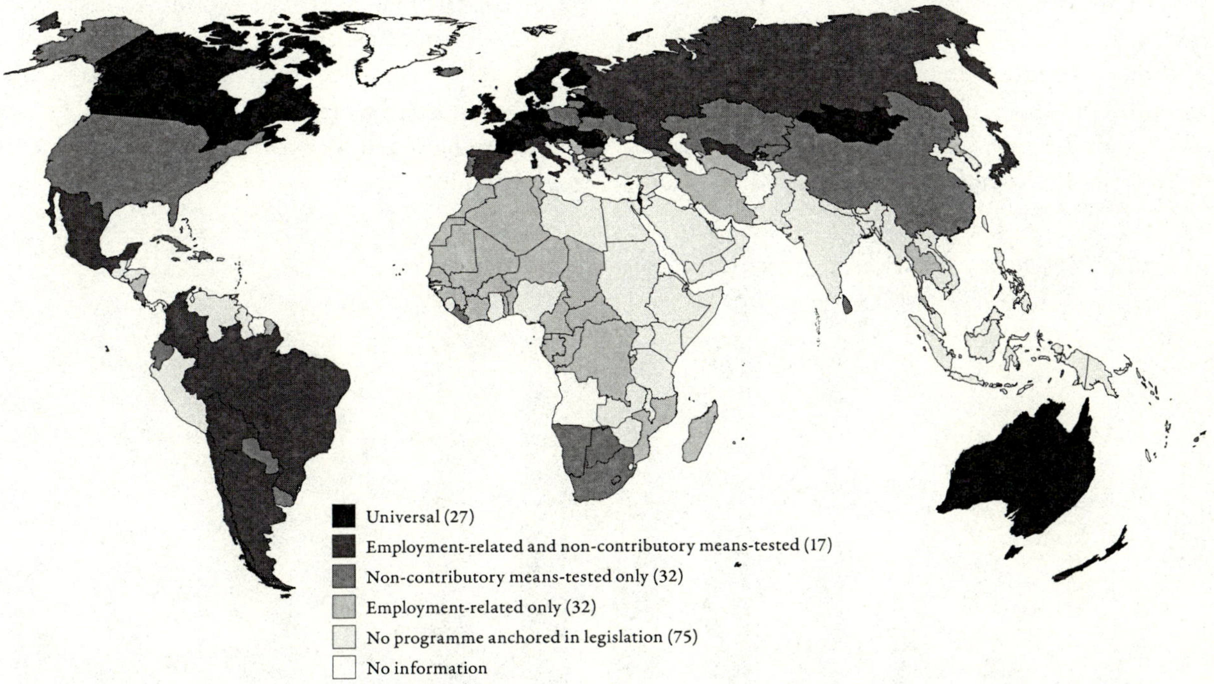

Note: Figures in brackets refer to the number of countries in each category.

Sources: SSA and ISSA, 2012; SSA and ISSA, 2013a; SSA and ISSA, 2013b; SSA and ISSA, 2014; European Commission, Mutual Information System on Social Protection (MISSOC); Council of Europe, Mutual Information System on Social Protection of the Council of Europe (MISSCEO).

Link: http://www.social-protection.org/gimi/gess/RessourceDownload.action?ressource.ressourceId=43301.

children and families, in the absence of specific child or family benefits. In addition to these cash benefits, many countries provide benefits in kind of various types, including access to free or subsidized goods (e.g. school meals).

Figure 2.4 illustrates the global distribution of child or family benefit programmes anchored in legislation. Some countries, particularly in Western Europe, provide such benefits to all children on a universal basis, financed out of general taxation, sometimes supplemented by specific social assistance benefits. Other countries, particularly in Africa and Latin America, have traditionally provided family allowances as part of their social insurance system or rely on a system of employer liability, requiring employers to pay family benefits to their workers. Where the provision of child benefits is directly or indirectly linked to an employment relationship, coverage rates tend to be lower than for universal provision, especially in countries with a large informal economy. In some of these countries, however, means-tested benefits complement employment-related family benefits and provide an important support for workers in the informal economy. In another group of countries, means-tested benefits constitute the dominant form of provision, either focusing on a relatively small group of vulnerable children and families, or providing a much wider coverage.[7]

While many countries in Latin America and the Caribbean combine employment-related benefits with non-contributory benefits anchored in legislation, thereby covering a substantial proportion of children and families, this is not the case in large parts of Africa and of Asia and the Pacific. Here, non-contributory programmes are not yet well enough developed to cover substantial numbers of children and families; many programmes still remain at a "pilot" stage with limited geographical coverage. More efforts are needed to anchor programmes in legislation in order to establish a clear definition of eligibility criteria and benefits, and a more stable basis for the implementation of these

[7] While most of these countries target child and family benefits to the poor in the form of specific social assistance benefits for families with children, there is a small group of countries which use a relatively light income or asset test to exclude affluent population groups from the provision of child benefits but maintain provision for the broad majority of the population (e.g. Cyprus, following a recent reform).

programmes, especially with regard to financial sustainability and institutional capacities.

An important aspect of the observed trends around the world is the extent to which countries are able to make provision for all residents, or at least those in need. Figure 2.5 shows that the achievement of this objective is linked to different priorities and traditions, and to some extent also to economic capacities available in the different parts of the world. While universal provision of child benefits is prevalent particularly in Europe and North America, in other parts of the world coverage tends to be more limited, usually to children of those employed in the formal economy and/or those in poor families.

Figure 2.5 Child/family allowances: Existence of programme anchored in legislation and main group(s) covered, by region, 2011–13 (percentage of countries)

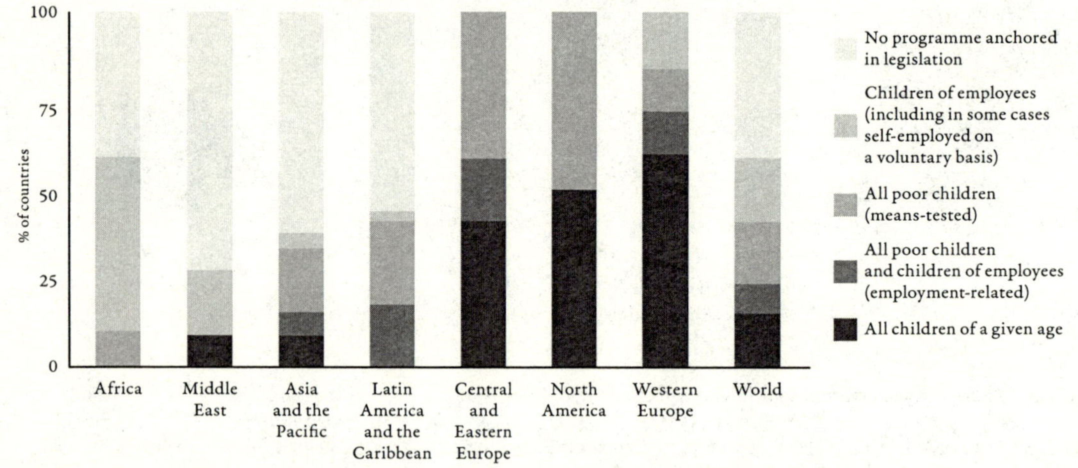

Source: ILO Social Protection Department, based on SSA and ISSA, 2012; SSA and ISSA, 2013a; SSA and ISSA, 2013b; SSA and ISSA, 2014.
Link: http://www.social-protection.org/gimi/gess/RessourceDownload.action?ressource.ressourceId=37002.

Figure 2.6 Child/family allowances: Main sources of financing, 2011–13

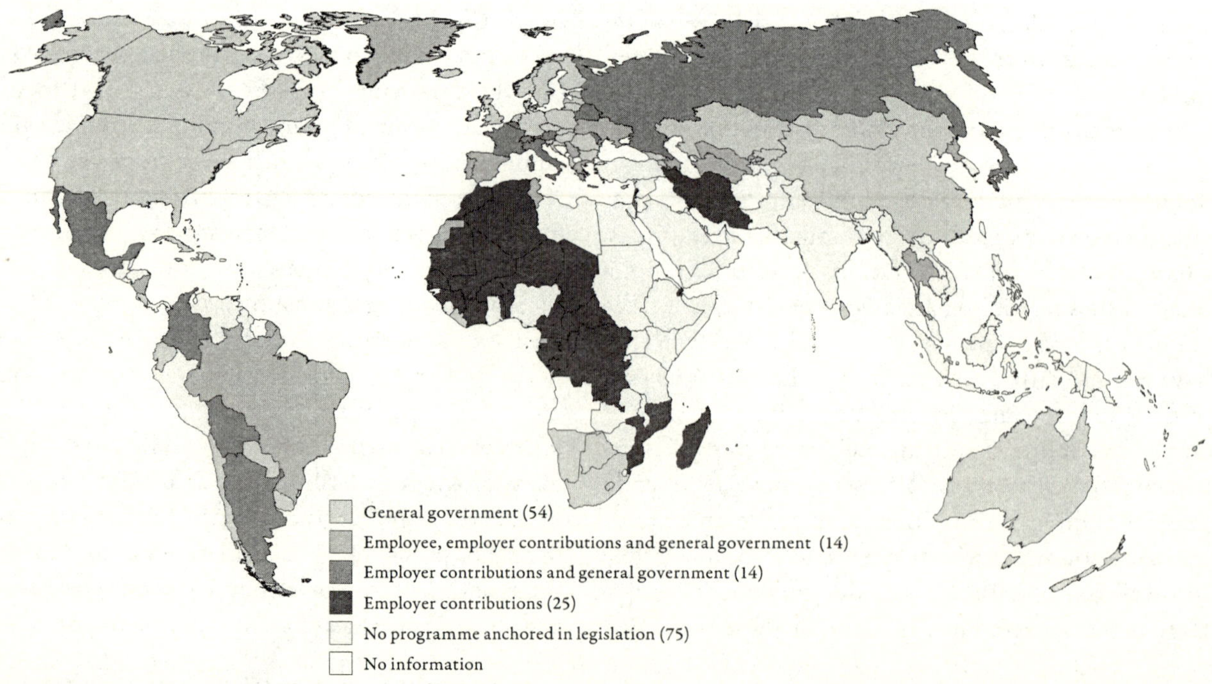

Note: Figures in brackets refer to the number of countries in each category.
Source: ILO Social Protection Department database, based on SSA and ISSA, 2012; SSA and ISSA, 2013a; SSA and ISSA, 2013b; SSA and ISSA, 2014.
Link: http://www.social-protection.org/gimi/gess/RessourceDownload.action?ressource.ressourceId=37004.

As with other areas of social security, the level of legal coverage of cash child and family benefits is correlated with the mode of provision and financing (see figure 2.6). Where child benefits are financed mainly through employers, particularly in countries where informality of employment prevails, coverage levels tend to be rather low. High levels of coverage usually require that the government take responsibility for financing the benefits by complementing coverage through existing contributory programmes for those groups of the population not or not sufficiently covered, whether through the provision of non-contributory benefits (as e.g. in Argentina or France) or through a large-scale non-contributory universal programme (as e.g. in Canada, Germany or Mongolia), in either case financed from either general taxation or other government revenue.

2.4 Closing coverage gaps and strengthening income security for children and families

Closing gaps in the coverage of child and family benefits is essential for ensuring income security for children and families. While universal or near-universal coverage is a reality in many OECD countries, and in many low- and middle-income countries the introduction of new child and family benefit programmes and the reform of existing ones have improved coverage to some extent, large gaps nevertheless remain.

The most prominent new development is the emergence of non-contributory cash transfer programmes in many low- and middle-income countries.[8] These programmes provide regular cash benefits to all families, or to poor families in particular, and have been found to have a strong impact on various dimensions of human development, whether they are explicitly linked to health- and education-related conditions (conditional cash transfer programmes) or not (unconditional cash transfer programmes). Conditional cash transfer programmes make the payment of cash benefits conditional upon compliance with specific "behavioural" conditions. Typically, the programmes require that families ensure their children's enrolment and attendance at school, and participate in specified health programmes, for example making regular visits to a clinic, or presenting children for vaccinations – stipulations that make demands on the availability, accessibility and quality of such services. If beneficiaries do not meet the specified conditions, sanctions may be applied, typically through the suspension or termination of benefits. Given that the beneficiaries are likely to be poor or very poor, the very potential for sanctions may itself be controversial, and the human rights implications of behavioural conditions in cash transfer programmes have been subject of intense debate (see e.g. ILO, 2011a, pp. 118–120; de Brauw and Hoddinott, 2008; Dornan and Porter, 2013).[9]

The considerable variety of cash transfer programmes that have emerged in recent years is only insufficiently described by the usual dichotomy of conditional and non-conditional programmes. Following the establishment of the Progresa/Oportunidades programme in Mexico, the first wave of conditional cash transfer programmes was concentrated in Latin America (Fiszbein and Schady, 2009; Barrientos, 2013), where conditional cash transfer programmes are now firmly established as an integral element of many national social security systems (see figure 2.7). By now, the largest programme in absolute terms is Bolsa Família in Brazil, which reaches around 11.3 million families comprising 46 million people, corresponding to about a quarter of Brazil's population – at an annual cost of US$3.9 billion (0.4 per cent of GDP). Similar programmes were implemented in 16 other Latin American and Caribbean countries, covering around 70 million people or 12 per cent of the population in the region (figure 2.7). Some programmes have developed distinctive features, such as the individualized support and transformational nature of the Chilean Chile Solidario programme (replaced by the Ingreso Ético Familiar programme in 2012; see UNICEF, 2012). Several cash transfer programmes for children and families also exist in Africa (e.g. in Ghana, Kenya, Malawi and South Africa) and in Asia (e.g. in Indonesia, the Philippines and Pakistan).

Some programmes combine conditional and non-conditional elements, such as the universal child allowance in Argentina (see box 2.4 below). In other countries, many of them in Africa, behavioural conditions are nominally part of the design of cash transfer programmes, yet are not fully implemented and monitored in practice. Some of these programmes have been introduced with "soft" conditions, under which the extent to which sanctions (usually the suspension or

[8] Because of their strong focus on children, cash transfer programmes are often considered as child or family benefit programmes, although it may also be argued that they share many features with generalized social assistance schemes.

[9] Moreover, as the responsibility for meeting these conditions mostly falls on mothers, these programmes have further-reaching implications for women's social and economic rights (e.g. Molyneux, 2007).

Figure 2.7 Level of expenditure and proportion of population reached by non-contributory conditional cash transfer programmes in selected Latin American countries, latest available year (percentages)

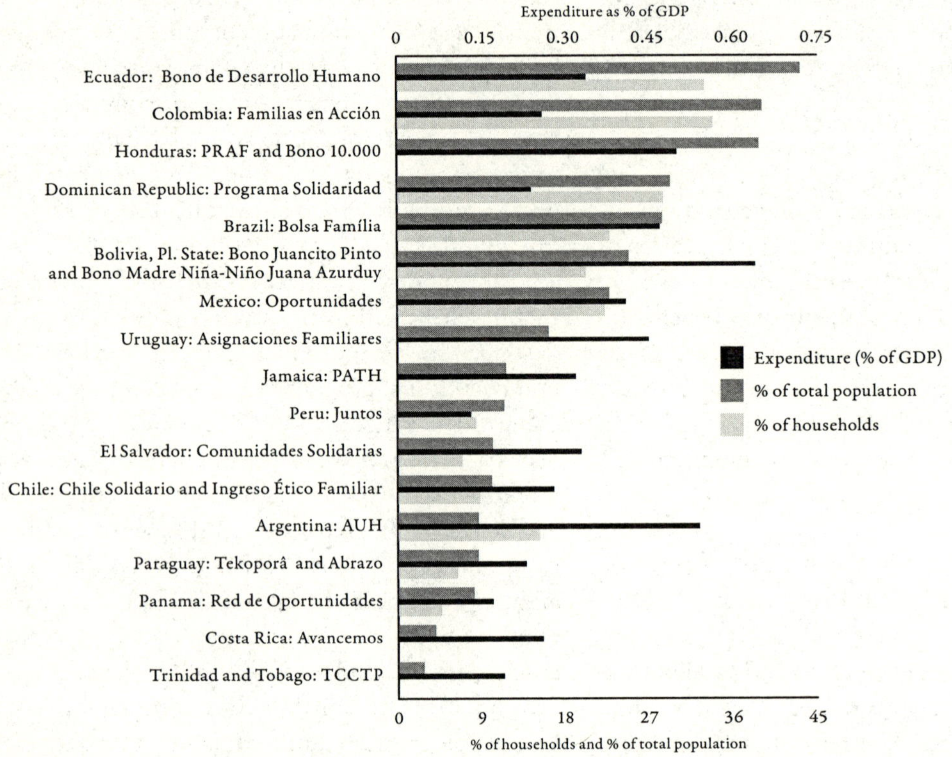

Sources: ECLAC, Conditional Cash Transfer Programmes database: Non-contributory social protection programmes in Latin America and the Caribbean database, http://dds.cepal.org/bdptc/en/ [accessed Jan. 2014].

Link: http://www.social-protection.org/gimi/gess/RessourceDownload.action?ressource.ressourceId=39338.

termination of benefits) are applied in cases of non-compliance takes into account the influence of factors beyond the beneficiaries' control, especially in respect of the poorest and most vulnerable. In some cases, conditions are applied, if at all, with considerable discretion, particularly in contexts where there is a significant lack of infrastructure and qualified staff. Where institutional capacities are limited, a strict adherence to behavioural conditions would be neither feasible nor equitable, given the often insufficient supply of education and health services, in terms of both quantity and quality, especially in remote areas.

The extension of cash transfer programmes for children and families has continued during recent years, and in some countries has even accelerated, whether in order to cushion the impact of the global crisis on children and families or with a more general objective of reducing poverty. In Haiti, a new conditional cash transfer scheme (Ti Manman Cheri) was introduced in 2012, with an initial annual budget estimated at US$13 million. In Honduras, the Bono 10,000 conditional cash transfer programme now provides cash benefits to poor families with children under 18 or pregnant women on condition that they commit to obligations with regard to school attendance and health care. In Mexico, the nutrition support programme Programa de Apoyo Alimentario (PAL) was expanded within the framework of the Oportunidades programme in 2010. Brazil extended coverage of the Bolsa Família programme by including more beneficiary categories, implementing an "active search" strategy to register extremely poor families not yet covered and increasing the amount of benefit paid. The budget has increased from 11.9 billion real (BRL) in 2009 to BRL23 billion in 2013, constituting approximately 0.5 per cent of GDP (Hermeto and Caetano, forthcoming). Thailand extended its education policy from 12 years of free basic education to 15 years in 2009 as part of its first stimulus package, allocating 18 billion baht to this programme in the first year with a view to drawing all children, including stateless and ethnic minority children, and children of migrants, into education from pre-school through high school and vocational education. Germany increased the level of child benefits in 2009 and 2010. Japan established a new universal allowance for children "of junior high school age" in 2010, and in 2012 made further changes to the law to allow for higher benefit levels,

Box 2.4 The universal child allowance in Argentina

Argentina closed a gap in the coverage of child benefits through the introduction of the universal child allowance (Asignación universal por hijo) for up to five children per family in 2009. This benefit complements the existing contributory family benefits for formal sector workers in the low and middle wage brackets and income tax rebates for workers in the highest income group. The scheme covers children of Argentinian nationality or children who have been resident in the country for at least three years whose parents fall into one of the following categories and do not already receive any other type of social assistance payments: those subject to the *social monotributo* (simplified social security regime for workers with very low incomes); the unemployed; those working in the informal economy; and domestic workers earning less than the adjustable minimum living wage. In addition to the 4.3 million children already covered through the other schemes (contributory family allowance and income tax rebate), the scheme now provides benefits to 3.3 million more children, representing 29 per cent of all children under the age of 18.

Families receive 460 pesos (ARS), equivalent to about US$69, for each child under 18, or ARS1,500 (about US$224) for a child with an assessed disability (without age limit). Of the total benefit, 80 per cent is paid monthly to benefit recipients through the social insurance institution. The remaining 20 per cent is deposited in a savings account in the name of the beneficiary with the National Bank. This sum can be recovered (on behalf of children in their care up to the age of six) when the beneficiary provides evidence of the children having undergone medical check-ups and necessary vaccinations or (for children aged 5–18) being enrolled in public education.

The cost of the scheme is estimated at approximately 0.5 per cent of GDP, financed out of earnings-related contributions and taxes and the annual interest on the Sustainability Guarantee Fund of the state pension system, created in 2007.

It is estimated that the scheme reaches 70 per cent of children living in poverty (between 80 and 90 per cent of very poor children) and that it reduces the proportion of poor and very poor children by 18 per cent and 65 per cent, respectively. Some 40 per cent of those who receive this benefit are not poor, most of them belonging to households with total incomes only slightly above the value of the poverty line. The Gini index shows a drop of approximately one percentage point as a result of the scheme. The combined impact of the contributory and non-contributory schemes is to reduce inequality by approximately 5 per cent. The total income of the poorest 10 per cent is increased by approximately 30 per cent as a result of the benefit.

Sources: Bertranou and Maurizio, 2012a; Bertranou and Maurizio, 2012b; national sources.

depending on age and number of children in a household, while also reintroducing an income ceiling above which a household was not eligible for the allowance.

While universal or quasi-universal coverage of all children is achieved predominantly in high-income countries, some middle-income countries have made great strides towards universal coverage: for example, in Argentina (see box 2.4), the universal child allowance introduced in 2009 extended coverage to families of unemployed people and those in the informal economy who were previously uncovered (Bertranou and Maurizio, 2012a). Mongolia also reintroduced its child allowance with virtually universal coverage, covering close to 900,000 children (99.6 per cent of all children) in 2012; the programme is funded from a mineral resource tax accumulated in the country's Human Development Fund.

Some initiatives represent notable progress towards more nearly universal coverage anchored in national legislation. The South African Child Support Grant, for example (see box 2.5), although means tested, covers more than half of all children under the age of 18, and has had significant impacts on children's nutrition, physical development and education (e.g. Patel et al., 2012; Patel, Hochfeld and Moodley, 2013; DSD, SASSA and UNICEF South Africa, 2012; Eyal and Woolard, 2013). In Colombia, a law was passed in 2011 that rendered access to the Más Familias en Acción programme a right, and raised benefit levels; as a result, the number of beneficiaries increased from 2.1 million to 2.6 million (Alviar García, 2013).

In many low- and middle-income countries, only a small minority of children and families receive child benefits. Where specific child or family benefit programmes do exist, they tend to be largely focused on workers in the formal economy and/or selected categories of disadvantaged children, such as orphans and vulnerable children. For example, the Kesejahteraan Sosial Anak programme (PKSA) in Indonesia provides conditional cash benefits for several categories of vulnerable children, including abandoned children, street children, young offenders and children with disabilities.[10] Many general social assistance programmes also

[10] Due to challenges in identifying eligible children, many vulnerable children remain outside the reach of this programme (ILO, 2012c).

Box 2.5 The Child Support Grant in South Africa

The Child Support Grant (CSG) in South Africa plays an important role in providing income security to poor children. Although the grant is means tested, the scheme reached 10.8 million children in 2012, that is, more than half of all children under the age of 18.[1] Coverage has been significantly extended by gradually increasing the maximum age threshold from seven years before 2003 to 18 years in 2008, and by adjusting the income threshold to inflation.

A monthly benefit of 300 rand (ZAR), equivalent to about US$28, per child is provided to caregivers who are South African nationals or permanent residents, and whose annual earnings are below ZAR34,800 for a single adult and ZAR69,600 for a couple. Applicants need to provide proof of income or of their status as unemployed, as appropriate. However, in order to facilitate access to the benefit for eligible families, particularly the poorest, the Government made efforts to disseminate information about eligibility criteria, simplify the procedure and reduce the number of documents applicants needed.

By and large, the grant is considered to have been successful in targeting poor households and to have had a marked impact on children's lives. In addition to poverty alleviation, studies also demonstrated positive effects on early childhood development, school attendance and educational attainments, including narrowing the schooling gap between children whose mothers have less education and those with more, improvements in overall health status, and reductions in risky behaviours by adolescents. Early enrolment in the programme was found to produce stronger impacts. Beyond the children themselves, the grant also facilitated access to the labour market for unemployed caregivers, especially for women.

[1] Conclusive interpretation of the available coverage data presents some difficulties.

Sources: Patel et al., 2012; Mokomane, 2012; Hagen-Zanker and Morgan, 2011.

Box 2.6 Providing benefits for orphans and vulnerable children: The Livelihood Empowerment Against Poverty (LEAP) programme in Ghana

The Livelihood Empowerment Against Poverty programme (LEAP) is a conditional cash transfer programme, currently implemented in about half of Ghana's districts, which targets extremely poor households that include one or more orphans and vulnerable children, people over the age of 65 or people with a severe disability. Orphans and vulnerable children are defined as children under 18 years of age who have lost one or both parents, who are chronically ill or living in a household headed by a child or a chronically ill person, or whose parents' whereabouts are unknown.

Of the 246,115 beneficiaries, 48.2 per cent are children up to 17 years of age. Depending on the number of eligible individuals in the household, the monthly benefit amounts to 24–45 cedi (about US$9–17), paid every two months. A recent UNICEF study (Cooke et al., 2014) showed that scaling up the LEAP programme to 500,000 beneficiaries could alleviate the impact on the poorest groups in the population of the removal of the fuel subsidy; even so, further measures will be necessary to have a broader impact on the reduction and prevention of poverty.

Beneficiary households with children under the age of 15 commit themselves to certain co-responsibilities when they sign up for LEAP. These include school attendance (with a maximum absenteeism of 20 per cent) and vaccinations and health check-ups for children under the age of five. Households in communities that are not covered by education or health facilities or where the capacity of existing facilities is insufficient are exempted from these conditions. Monitoring of compliance should take place every three months, and households not complying should receive warnings, house visits and, in the case of repeated non-compliance, penalties; but for the time being these are soft conditions, as no reliable mechanism to monitor compliance is currently in place.

In order to ensure they have access to health care, LEAP beneficiaries are automatically registered in the National Health Insurance Scheme (NHIS). As a result, beneficiaries are more likely to be covered under the NHIS than non-recipient households, although those also benefit from contribution exemptions for children, pregnant women, older people and the very poor (Handa et al., 2013).

Source: Based on national sources.

benefit children living in vulnerable households, such as the Programa Subsidio de Alimentos cash transfer programme in Mozambique, whose total budget allocation more than doubled from 0.16 to 0.35 per cent of GDP between 2008 and 2013 (Cunha et al., 2013). Many of the newer programmes in African countries, though they may be of significant size, operate as pilot programmes covering only certain districts, such as the LEAP programme in Ghana (see box 2.6) and similar schemes in Kenya and Malawi (García and Moore, 2012; Monchuk, 2014).

Recent developments have also demonstrated that cash transfers alone cannot offer income security for all children and families. More attention is needed to the formulation and application of integrated approaches that ensure effective coordination between different policy areas addressing children's needs, including health, education, care and child protection. In addition, connection with employment policies is of critical importance. A particular policy concern is establishing the optimal mix in provision of allowances in cash, on the one hand, and the availability and accessibility of quality childcare services and early childhood education, on the other – the latter playing a key role in protecting children from poverty by allowing their parents to work knowing that their children are well cared for (e.g. OECD, 2011a; UNICEF and ILO, 2013; ILO and UNDP, 2009; UNESCO, 2014). Such measures can have a significant impact on the income security of families with children, in particular for single-parent families.

Rich evidence of the impact of social protection policies, combined with other social policies, on the income security of children can be found in many European and some other OECD countries. The OECD has developed a sophisticated monitoring system, using a set of indicators and focused research studies, to analyse the availability of child and family benefits and other family-oriented policies and their outcomes (OECD, 2009c; OECD, 2011a; OECD, 2014b). Such a monitoring system can also facilitate national monitoring of the implementation of ILO Recommendation No. 202. Strengthening such national monitoring capacities should be a priority in many low- and middle-income countries.

2.5 How fiscal consolidation and adjustment measures threaten income security for children and families

While many countries have in recent years taken decisive steps to extend coverage of child and family protection measures and increase benefit levels, others have cut back provision in this area as part of fiscal consolidation measures implemented in the wake of the global crisis (see box 2.7). Some countries (e.g. Denmark, Ireland, Israel) have reduced the level of child benefits for all children, or for children in larger families; others (e.g. Denmark, Latvia) have introduced an effective ceiling on the total amount of child benefits or lowered the maximum age up to which children are eligible for child benefits (e.g. Ireland, Latvia). Some countries

Box 2.7 The effects of fiscal consolidation and adjustment measures on child and family benefits

Several countries, in particular in the developed world, have in recent years adopted contraction measures that have affected child and family benefits, a few in the early stages of the crisis (e.g. Ireland, Estonia) and more since 2010. Examples of such measures include the following:

- In Denmark, child benefits were successively reduced by 5 per cent each year in 2011, 2012 and 2013, and a ceiling on total child benefits was set at 35,000 kroner per year.
- In Ireland's 2013 budget, the child benefit payment level was reduced for the third time since 2010, in addition to other measures. Overall, a family with two children will have lost €864 in annual support since 2010. Back-to-school allowances were also cut in the 2012 and 2013 budgets.
- Israel announced the reduction of child allowances for children born after 1 June 2003 to a flat amount of 140 shekels (ILS), about US$39, for each child, replacing the earlier system of benefit rates increasing with the number of children. The cuts in child allowances are expected to save the Government ILS2.9 billion in 2014.
- In Latvia, family benefits were reduced to a flat amount per child, replacing the higher benefit rates for subsequent children in a household, thereby effectively reducing the total amount of child benefits for larger families. In addition, the maximum eligible age was reduced from 20 to 19 years for children in education.
- In Mongolia, the Child Money Programme was terminated at the end of 2009. However, in 2012 it was reintroduced as a universal programme.
- The United Kingdom's 2012 budget introduced a progressive income tax charge on child benefit in order to offset the value of the benefit for people earning over £60,000. Individuals earning between £50,000 and £60,000 will be charged with a portion of the amount of the benefit. The charge applies to the higher-earning partner in households receiving child benefit. Changes to the rules on child benefit are expected to reduce the entitlement of about 1.2 million families.

Sources: Jackson et al., 2011; Gauthier, 2010; national sources.

effectively excluded more affluent families by introducing an asset test (e.g. Cyprus) or a tax for those earning above a certain threshold which claws back the child benefit (United Kingdom), thus restricting the universal scope of such benefits.

Unless other compensatory measures are taken, these developments are likely to threaten the income security of families with children, particularly that of larger families, many of which are already at higher risk of poverty than others. There is a risk that in some countries such measures may jeopardize the progress achieved in reducing child poverty in recent years.

Indeed, child poverty has increased in 19 of the 28 Member States of the European Union between 2007 and 2012; by the latter year, more than one-quarter of children in Bulgaria, Greece, Italy, Romania and Spain were living at risk of poverty.[11] This increase in child poverty has given rise to concern about negative long-term effects with regard to the future employment prospects of today's children, and about the future productivity and competitiveness of European economies (European Commission, 2014a).

The increasing pressure on public budgets in many emerging economies may slow down further progress with respect to the income security of children and families, or even reverse the improvements already achieved. It is therefore essential to ensure that fiscal consolidation measures do not compromise the successes achieved to date in many countries through a broad and integrated range of social protection policies for children.

[11] Based on Eurostat database (at-risk-of-poverty line of 60 per cent of median equivalent income; children under 18 years).

Social protection for women and men of working age

3

3.1 Introduction: The quest for income security

Social protection for women and men of working age[1] includes a range of aspects. This chapter will focus in particular on income security, which is an essential component of the well-being of individuals and families. An overall majority of people of working age are economically active, and generally gain their livelihoods through income-generating activity, whether in formal or informal employment, and whether such activity can be categorized as decent work[2] or not. The social security needs of people of working age generally fall into three broad categories: first, the need to replace income lost temporarily or permanently as a result of

KEY MESSAGES

- Social protection supports women and men of working age by stabilizing their incomes in the event of unemployment, employment injury, disability, sickness and maternity, and by ensuring that they have at least a basic level of income security.
- While the labour market serves as the primary source of income security during working life, social security plays a major role in smoothing incomes and aggregate demand, thereby facilitating structural change within economies.
- Worldwide, 2.3 per cent of GDP is allocated to public social protection expenditure ensuring income security during working age; regionally, levels vary widely, ranging from 0.5 per cent in Africa to 5.9 per cent in Western Europe.
- Better social protection, including support in coping with the financial consequences of life events and improved access to health care, will help workers to find and sustain decent and productive employment.
- Policy coherence between social protection policies on the one hand, and employment, labour market and wage policies on the other, is essential in order to ensure that social security systems are efficient, effective and sustainable.

---

1 Working age is broadly defined here as the age range during which most people are, or seek to be, economically active, reflecting the life-cycle approach of the Social Protection Floors Recommendation, 2012 (No. 202), and being aware that in many contexts women and men continue to be economically active, out of choice or necessity, until well into old age (see Chapter 4). The upper and lower boundaries of "working age" are highly dependent on national contexts, as defined by national legislation and practice, and often depend on the length of time that people spend in education and statutory pensionable ages. For the purpose of the comparability of statistical indicators, this report follows established international practice in using an age range of 15–64 years, but this is not to imply that all individuals within this age range can or should conform to a specific notion of "work" or "activity".

2 Decent work has been defined by the ILO and endorsed by the international community as productive work for women and men in conditions of freedom, equity, security and human dignity. Decent work involves opportunities for work that is productive and delivers a fair income; provides security in the workplace and social protection for workers and their families; offers better prospects for personal development and encourages social integration; gives people the freedom to express their concerns, to organize and to participate in decisions that affect their lives; and guarantees equal opportunities and equal treatment for all.

unemployment, employment injury, disability, sickness or maternity; second, the need for income support or other social protection measures where income is insufficient to avoid poverty and/or social exclusion; and third, the need for support to restore earning capacity after any of the contingencies listed above and to facilitate participation in employment.

According to the Social Protection Floors Recommendation, 2012 (No. 202), the objective of national social protection floors is to guarantee, at a minimum, "basic income security, at least at a nationally defined minimum level, for persons in active age who are unable to earn sufficient income, in particular in cases of sickness, unemployment, maternity and disability". Other ILO social security standards provide more detailed guidance for specific policy areas. The following sections of this chapter will focus on four policy areas most relevant to people of working age, namely, unemployment protection (section 3.2), employment injury protection (section 3.3), disability benefits (section 3.4) and maternity protection (section 3.5). Access to health and sickness benefits, which also have important implications for income security during working age, is discussed in Chapter 5.

Most people seek income security during working life in the first instance through participation in the labour market. Income security is strongly dependent on the level, distribution and stability of earnings and other income from work, and is therefore significantly influenced by policy choices and the adoption and enforcement of legislation in a number of areas. Policy areas particularly relevant to income security include employment, employment protection, wages (including minimum wages) and collective bargaining, and active labour market policies, as well as policies to support workers with family and care responsibilities and to promote gender equality in employment. Recent labour market and employment trends have increased the pressure on social security systems to ensure income security for persons of working age. These trends include in particular higher risks of unemployment, underemployment and informality (e.g. ILO, 2014a; ILO, 2014b); increasing prevalence of precarious forms of work; and declining wage shares, dwindling real wages and inadequate wages (e.g. ILO, 2013b; ILO, 2014c), leading to persistently high proportions of working poor (ILO, 2014a).

In the light of these observations, it is very clear that income security cannot be achieved by social security alone. Social protection policies need to be coordinated with well-designed policies to address these challenges in the fields of employment, labour market and wage policies, with a view to alleviating excessive burdens on national social security systems and allowing them to work more efficiently and more effectively.

Most employment-related, contributory social security programmes cover those people (and their dependants) who have been economically active in the past, but have lost their income from work either permanently or temporarily owing to loss of their current job (unemployment benefits), sickness, longer-term disability or death resulting from a work-related accident or disease (employment injury benefits), circumstances not directly related to work (general sickness, disability and survivors' benefits) or pregnancy, childbirth and family responsibilities (maternity, paternity or parental benefits, child or family benefits).

However, these types of programme often do not cover the situations and needs of people (and their dependants) who are economically active but not in formal employment, whose income from employment is too low to prevent them and their families from falling into poverty, or who simply have no income at all, having been unemployed or underemployed for too long to qualify for benefits, with no prospect of such a situation coming to an end, even in the long term. These three groups – those in the informal economy, the working poor in formal employment and the long-term unemployed – usually fall outside the coverage of contributory social security programmes.

People in these groups may be covered by non-contributory programmes providing benefits in cash and in kind, such as social assistance or universal schemes. In countries where a large majority of the labour force is covered by contributory social insurance programmes, non-contributory programmes are most frequently addressed to those who are not covered by social insurance, namely, the long-term unemployed and the working poor. In economies where informality and large-scale poverty prevails, for many decades social assistance programmes, if they existed at all, were typically small and fragmented. However, in many such countries the last two decades have seen the development of large-scale non-contributory programmes targeted mainly at poor households. These sometimes link entitlements to benefits to beneficiaries' participation in public service programmes such as health care or education (usually referred to as conditional cash transfers or CCTs), or to participation in public employment programmes (often referred to as cash-for-work programmes), vocational training or entrepreneurship support programmes.

While this chapter will focus mainly on cash benefits, it is important to note that benefits in kind, in

Figure 3.1 Non-health public social protection expenditure for people of working age, and share of people of working age (15–64) in the total population, 2010/11

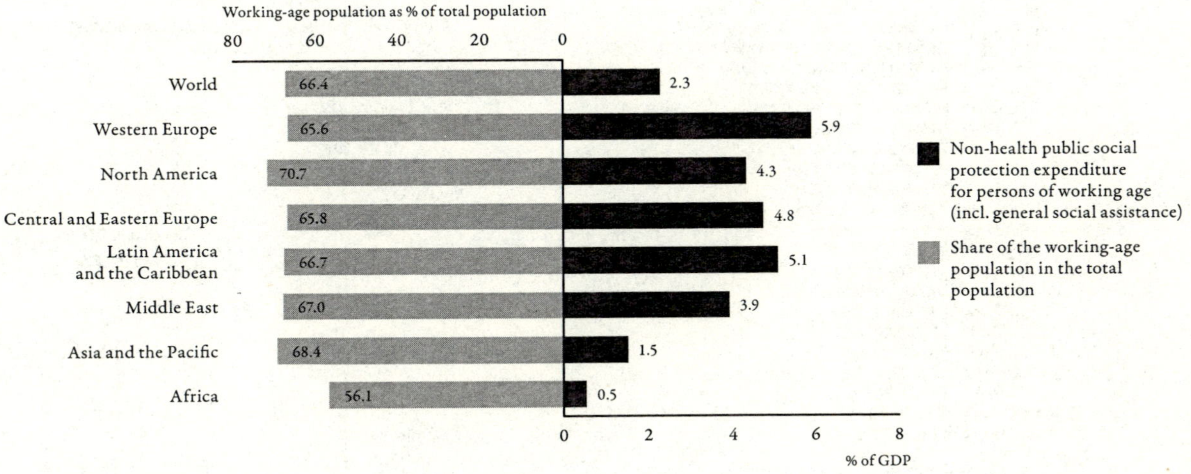

Source: ILO Social Security Inquiry database, see Annex IV, table B.13.
Link: http://www.social-protection.org/gimi/gess/RessourceDownload.action?ressource.ressourceId=42397.

particular health care and other social services, play an important role in ensuring income security for people of working age. The role of health-care provision (see Chapter 5 for more detail) is particularly important in this respect: people who enjoy effective access to quality public health services or are financially protected through affordable (social) health insurance will have higher income security than those at risk of having to pay high out-of-pocket costs for health care in times of need. The provision of other social services and related benefits in kind that have a monetary value, including education and care services, can also significantly reduce people's income needs. The provision of services such as employment services, skills development programmes, childcare facilities and long-term care services may also have an impact on people's ability to engage in paid employment, with important implications for income security, particularly for women (e.g. Martínez Franzoni and Sanchéz-Ancochea, 2014).

Worldwide, about one-third of total non-health public social protection expenditure, amounting to 2.3 per cent of GDP, is spent on benefits for people of working age (see figures 3.1 and 3.2).[3] These include unemployment benefits, employment injury benefits, disability benefits, maternity benefits and general social assistance. Within this overall figure, regional variations are significant, ranging from less than 0.5 per cent in Africa and 1.5 per cent in Asia and the Pacific to 5.9 per cent in Western European countries. While non-health public social protection expenditure for people of working age accounts for close to one-third of overall non-health social protection expenditure in Western Europe, it accounts for roughly half of this category of expenditure in Latin America and in the Middle East. In Africa, such expenditure accounts for about one-quarter of non-health social protection expenditure, a lower proportion which can partly be explained by a lower share of working-age population in total population and a relatively high proportion of expenditure on pensions in total public non-health social protection expenditure.

The remainder of this chapter is divided into four sections, dealing respectively with the areas of social security that are most relevant to people of working age, namely:

- unemployment benefits;
- employment injury benefits;
- disability benefits;
- maternity protection.

Many countries have already put in place or are designing new schemes that are broader in scope and less closely focused on the occurrence of specific contingencies. In many cases, national social security systems combine contributory schemes with non-contributory schemes in order to extend social protection to those with no or weak contributory capacities. Together, these schemes contribute to building national social protection floors and national social security systems.

---

[3] This also includes expenditure on general social assistance programmes, which accounts for 0.8 per cent of GDP worldwide (2.7 per cent in Latin America).

Figure 3.2 Non-health public social protection expenditure for people of working age, by national income (percentage of GDP), 2010/11

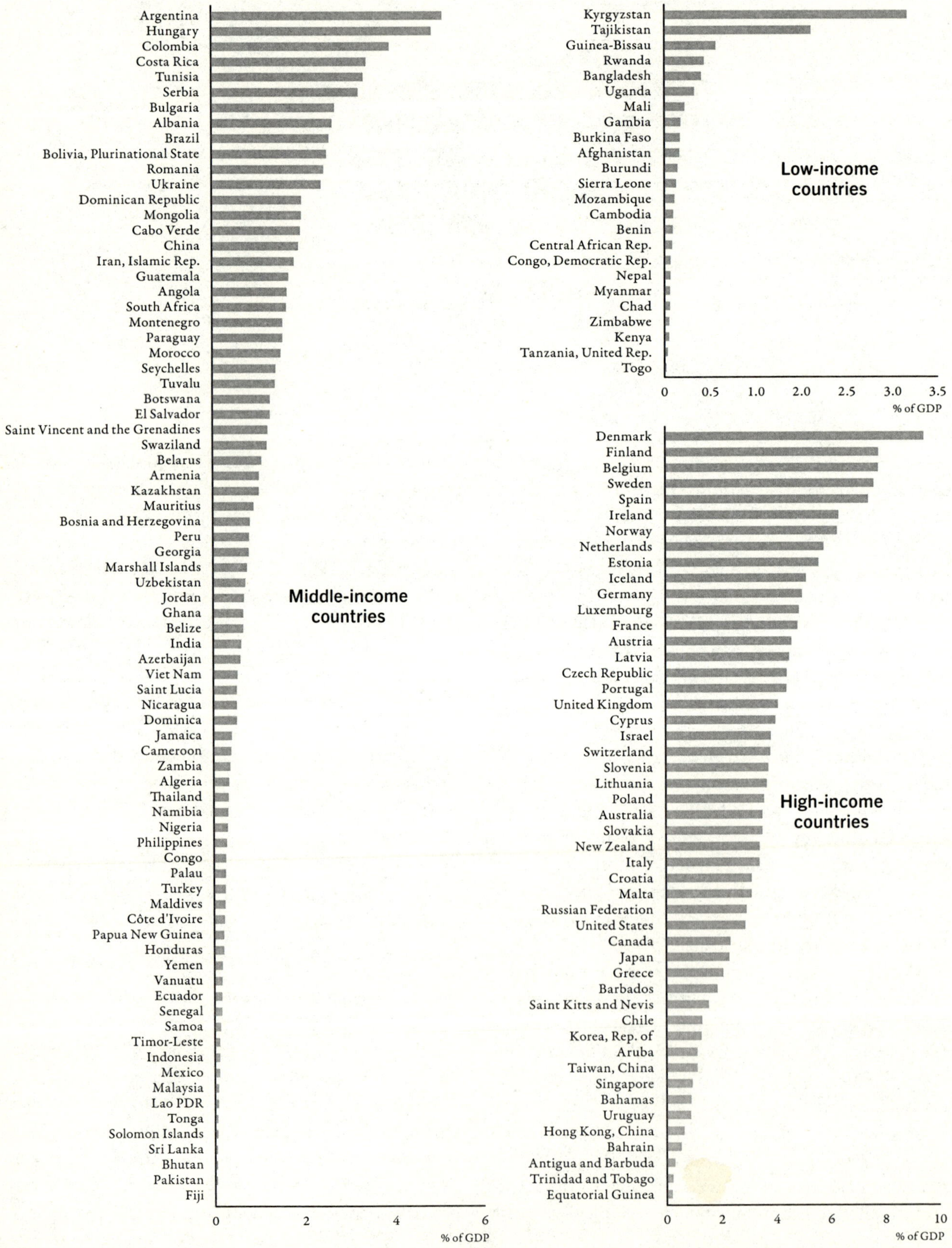

Source: See Annex IV, table B.13.

Link: http://www.social-protection.org/gimi/gess/RessourceDownload.action?ressource.ressourceId=44418.

3.2 Unemployment protection

KEY MESSAGES

- Where they exist, unemployment benefit schemes play a key role in providing income security to workers and their families in the event of temporary unemployment, thereby contributing to preventing poverty; supporting structural change in the economy; providing safeguards against informalization; and, in the event of a crisis, stabilizing aggregate demand, helping the economy to recover more quickly.
- Only 28 per cent of the global labour force is potentially eligible for benefits (contributory or non-contributory) under existing legislation in case of unemployment. Within this overall figure, regional differences are considerable: 80 per cent of the labour force is so covered in Europe, 38 per cent in Latin America, 21 per cent in the Middle East, 17 per cent in the Asia and Pacific region, and 8 per cent in Africa.
- Only 12 per cent of unemployed workers worldwide actually receive unemployment benefits, and again regional differences are large, with effective coverage ranging from 64 per cent of unemployed workers in Western Europe to just over 7 per cent in the Asia and Pacific region, 5 per cent in Latin America and the Caribbean and less than 3 per cent in the Middle East and Africa.
- A growing number of countries are extending the scope of protection offered under unemployment benefit schemes by including employment promotion measures such as skills development and employment services as part of the package, in combination with unemployment cash benefits.
- Linking employment and social protection policies, by combining cash transfers with public employment programmes (employment guarantee schemes), vocational training and/or support for entrepreneurship, offers new possibilities for providing income security to unemployed and underemployed workers in countries with high levels of informality.

3.2.1 Protecting incomes, cushioning demand shocks and facilitating structural change in the economy

Unemployment protection schemes provide income support over a determined period of time to unemployed people who are capable of working. Their objective is to provide at least partial income replacement for the loss of earnings resulting from temporary unemployment, enabling the beneficiary to maintain a certain standard of living during the transition period until he or she obtains suitable employment (see ILO, 2010a, pp. 57–58) and, increasingly, also to provide support in finding employment through a range of promotional measures and services. Under most schemes, cash benefits are available only in cases of involuntary unemployment,[4] and are restricted in duration (see box 3.1); under many schemes, they are combined with services such as support, counselling and advice in looking for employment, and facilities for enhancing, updating and developing skills.

In "normal" times, such schemes aim to meet the needs of individuals whose job losses reflect basic levels of turnover in the labour market, and thus to play a key role in supporting job mobility and facilitating structural change in the economy. In addition to guaranteeing income security for unemployed workers, unemployment protection schemes can also help protect them from slipping into informality, and support their search for new jobs in which they can apply existing or new skills in a productive way.

The repercussions for employment of the global crisis of 2008–09 have highlighted the wider role of unemployment benefits in helping both people and economies to adjust to shocks and to structural changes in the economy. Indeed, following sharp increases in unemployment rates in many parts of the world in the wake of the global crisis (ILO, 2013c), unemployment protection schemes have proved more important than ever both in providing income security to individuals and households and, by stabilizing aggregate demand, in fostering rapid recovery from the crisis.

Whether temporary unemployment is the result of covariant shocks, as in the event of the global crisis, or of the constant structural change undergone by economies and labour markets, unemployment benefits represent an effective tool to guarantee income security to

[4] Involuntary unemployment excludes cases where an employee leaves a job of her or his own volition, without just cause (e.g. harassment, resignation under threat), or where the employee has deliberately contributed to her or his own dismissal.

Box 3.1 International standards on unemployment protection

Giving effect to the right to social security enshrined in various international human rights instruments requires that effective social protection be guaranteed in the event of unemployment. Unemployment is recognized in the Universal Declaration of Human Rights, 1948 (UDHR) as one of the contingencies to be covered by national social security systems (Art. 25(1)). The right to access and maintain benefits, in cash or in kind, without discrimination, to secure protection from, among other things, unemployment, is considered as forming part of the right to social security as laid down in the International Covenant on Economic, Social and Cultural Rights, 1966 (Art. 9) (see also UN, 2008, paras 2 and 16).

ILO Conventions and Recommendations take a broad approach to unemployment protection by setting standards for the provision of cash benefits and services during periods of unemployment involving a suspension of earnings, thereby giving practical guidance for the implementation of the right to social security. Their objective is twofold: to ensure that individuals enjoy income security despite the loss of earnings suffered as a result of unemployment, and to support beneficiaries in finding productive and freely chosen employment.

The Social Security (Minimum Standards) Convention, 1952 (No. 102), requires the provision of cash benefits to unemployed persons capable of and available for work but unable to obtain suitable employment. It sets qualitative and quantitative benchmarks that must be met, at a minimum, (1) to ensure the coverage of a substantial amount of the population, (2) to ensure that the level of cash benefits represents at least a certain percentage of beneficiaries' former earnings and are thus deemed sufficient to serve as income replacement, or that they are sufficient to allow beneficiaries and their families to enjoy decent standards of living and health (see Annex III), and (3) to ensure that cash benefits are provided for a period of time that is long enough for them to serve their purpose.

The Employment Promotion and Protection against Unemployment Convention, 1988 (No. 168), increases the level and scope of protection that should be provided to the unemployed. In addition to full unemployment, it covers partial unemployment (i.e. temporary reduction in the number of working hours) and temporary suspension of work, as well as part-time work for those who are seeking full-time work. It also requires the provision of social benefits to certain categories of persons who have never been, or have ceased to be, recognized as unemployed or covered by unemployment protection schemes (e.g. new entrants to the labour market, those previously self-employed, etc.). Convention No. 168 further expands the scope of support that should be provided to the unemployed by calling upon the combination of cash benefits with measures that promote job opportunities and employment assistance (e.g. employment services, vocational training and guidance), prioritizing support to disadvantaged persons. Its accompanying Recommendation, No. 176, provides guidance on how to assess the suitability of employment for those seeking it, taking into account the age of unemployed persons, their length of service in their former occupation, their acquired experience, the length of their unemployment and the state of the labour market.

The Social Protection Floors Recommendation, 2012 (No. 202), guides countries in defining and guaranteeing basic income security, at least at a nationally defined minimum level, to all persons of working age who are unable to earn sufficient income, for reasons including unemployment, as part of a national social protection floor. Such guarantee should be provided at least to all residents, and may be furnished through a variety of means including universal schemes, social insurance, social assistance, negative income tax, and/or public employment and employment support programmes. In a spirit similar to that of Convention No. 168, it recommends that the design and implementation of social protection floor guarantees combine preventive, promotional and active measures; that they promote productive economic activity and formal employment through labour market policies and policies that promote education, vocational training, productive skills and employability; and that they are well coordinated with other policies that enhance formal employment, income generation, education, literacy, vocational training, skills and employability, that reduce precariousness, and that promote secure work, entrepreneurship and sustainable enterprises within a decent work framework.

individuals, smooth economic changes and stabilize aggregate consumption.

Most unemployment benefit programmes are designed to cover workers in formal employment who lose their jobs and find themselves temporarily unable to obtain suitable new employment. Most such programmes do not protect unemployed people who have had no formal employment in the recent past, the long-term unemployed, the underemployed or the working poor.

In countries with high levels of informality, wider non-contributory social assistance programmes combining employment and social protection policies have been developed to provide some income security for unemployed and underemployed workers. These include employment guarantee schemes and other public employment programmes, as well as programmes that combine cash transfers with support for skills development and creation of employment and entrepreneurship opportunities.

3.2.2 Types of unemployment protection schemes

Countries use different contributory or non-contributory mechanisms of unemployment protection, or combinations thereof (figure 3.3). The main types may be summarized as follows.

Contributory unemployment benefit schemes. These most commonly take the form of social insurance *(unemployment insurance)*, financed by contributions paid by employers, or shared between employers and employees, and usually cover workers in formal employment, on whose behalf regular contributions can be collected.[5] Unemployment insurance schemes have strong merits in terms of solidarity-based risk-sharing, their capacity to provide benefits in the form of periodical payments, and their potential to act across national economies as automatic stabilizers.

Non-contributory unemployment benefit schemes. These are often referred to as *unemployment assistance*, are usually funded at least partially through general taxation, and tend to provide a lower level of benefits than insurance schemes to unemployed workers who either do not qualify for contributory benefits (e.g. because of a short contribution period) or have exhausted their entitlement to unemployment insurance benefit.

Social security systems providing both contributory and non-contributory unemployment benefits are closely aligned with the fundamental framework of ILO standards, which stipulates that risk should be shared on a collective basis and contribution payments organized accordingly. These benefits are also in nearly all cases combined with measures to facilitate a rapid return to employment and/or upgrading of skills, thereby embodying the combination of income replacement and employment promotion that lies at the core of Convention No. 168 and Recommendations Nos 176 and 202 (see box 3.1).

Unemployment savings schemes (sometimes misleadingly called *unemployment insurance savings accounts*

Figure 3.3 Overview of unemployment protection schemes anchored in national legislation, by type of scheme and benefit, 2012/13

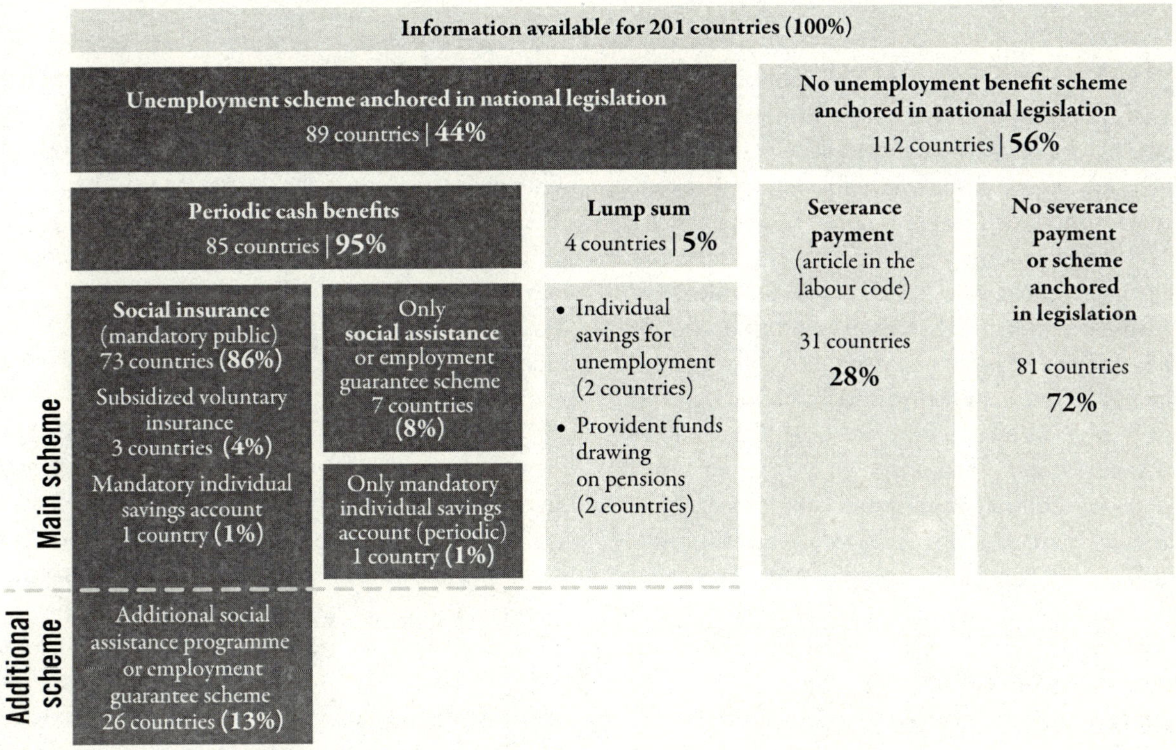

Sources: SSA and ISSA, 2012; SSA and ISSA, 2013a; SSA and ISSA, 2013b; SSA and ISSA, 2014; Employment protection legislation database (EPLex), accessed 18 November 2013.

Link: http://www.social-protection.org/gimi/gess/RessourceDownload.action?ressource.ressourceId=42257.

[5] While in most countries unemployment insurance is mandatory, voluntary unemployment protection schemes exist in several Scandinavian countries, where unemployment protection has traditionally been provided by trade unions and is supplemented by non-contributory schemes.

Figure 3.4 Distribution of unemployment protection schemes worldwide by type of scheme, 2012/13

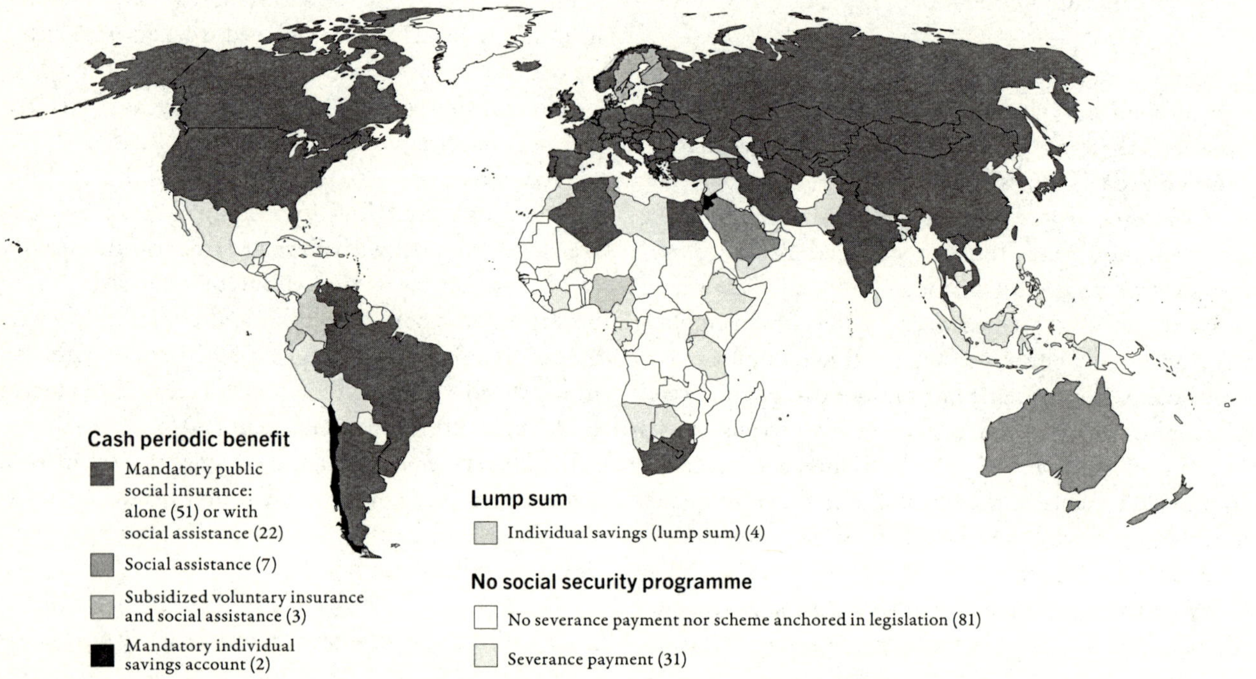

Note: Figures in brackets refer to the number of countries in each group. Information on the type of programme by country is available in Annex IV, table B.3.
Sources: SSA and ISSA, 2012; SSA and ISSA, 2013a; SSA and ISSA, 2013b; SSA and ISSA, 2014; ILO Employment Protection Legislation Database (EPLex).
Link: http://www.social-protection.org/gimi/gess/RessourceDownload.action?ressource.ressourceId=37034.

or UISA) require workers to accumulate savings in individual accounts, which provide for a stream of income in case of unemployment. Schemes of this type lack the key design element of risk-pooling; as a result, when an individual's savings run out, so does her or his income protection – and this may happen quickly. In addition, those workers who will be able to save most in their individual accounts tend to be the ones least prone to the risk of unemployment, while those at highest risk tend to have difficulties in building up sufficiently high savings to generate a significant income. So it cannot be said that such schemes either provide the same level of individual protection offered by social insurance schemes or are capable of acting as automatic stabilizers of aggregate demand in the same way. In addition, where such schemes allow borrowing from pension accounts, the result may be seriously reduced income security in old age.

Employment guarantee schemes. These provide a legal entitlement to employment in public works and cash transfers to poor workers in rural settings, and constitute one of the policy options that can be used to enhance income security for the working poor and employability. The largest and most closely studied scheme of this type is the Mahatma Gandhi National Rural Employment Guarantee Scheme (MGNREGS) in India (see box 3.3). Ethiopia, too, has implemented a large-scale programme which, although not providing a legally guaranteed income, combines public works with food and cash benefits: the Productive Safety Nets Programme (PSNP).

Severance pay. In many countries, this is the only form of income protection available to workers dismissed from certain forms of formal employment. This type of compensation, however, should be seen as representing a form of deferred pay or enforced savings by workers, rather than a form of social risk-sharing. It offers little help to the unemployed in terms of helping them back to work, or to employers who may need to make structural changes to their businesses, and may indeed have negative effects.[6] For this reason, unemployment benefits – generally in the form of

[6] In imposing an obligation to pay laid-off workers a lump sum proportionate to their prior job tenure, severance pay may pose a high burden on employers, especially those in economic difficulties, and is therefore prone to evasion and poor enforcement. Many employers that go bankrupt face difficulties in finding the severance payments due to their dismissed workers. Thus, severance pay cannot be considered as a substitute for periodic unemployment benefits (see ILO, 2010a; Holzmann et al., 2011; Sarra, 2008).

periodic payments – are considered more supportive of structural transformation in the economy than severance pay.

Not all of these different mechanisms of unemployment protection provide a clearly defined legal entitlement to a periodic unemployment benefit, setting out eligibility conditions, the nature and level of the benefit, the duration of payment, and obligations with regard to jobseeking and the acceptance of a suitable job.

At present, the majority (112 countries; 56 per cent) of the 201 countries reviewed in this report have no unemployment benefit scheme anchored in national legislation. However, 31 of these countries provide severance payment for workers covered by the labour code, which provides a limited level of protection to some workers.

Of the 89 countries (44 per cent) that have legislative provision for some sort of social security benefits in case of unemployment, more than 95 per cent (85 countries) provide *periodic cash benefits* to unemployed persons meeting the prescribed qualifying conditions. Public social insurance is by far the most common mechanism used to provide such regular income replacement. Social insurance, subsidized voluntary insurance or mandatory private insurance are complemented in one-third of these 89 countries by social assistance when rights to insurance payments have been exhausted or are not met. A few countries, including Australia, New Zealand and the Seychelles, provide only non-contributory benefits.

Contributory or non-contributory unemployment benefit schemes are predominantly to be found in advanced economies, but schemes providing for some form of unemployment benefits have also been introduced in middle-income countries (see figure 3.4).

3.2.3 Legal coverage for unemployment benefits

Figure 3.5 sets out the overall picture as to the proportion of the labour force protected by unemployment protection schemes according to national legislation (legal coverage ratio).

At the global level, only 28.1 per cent of the labour force is potentially eligible for unemployment benefit under existing national legislation, providing the fact that the laws are properly implemented and enforced. This proportion is based on a broad definition including mandatory unemployment insurance,

Figure 3.5 Distribution of unemployment protection schemes worldwide by extent of legal coverage of the labour force, latest available year

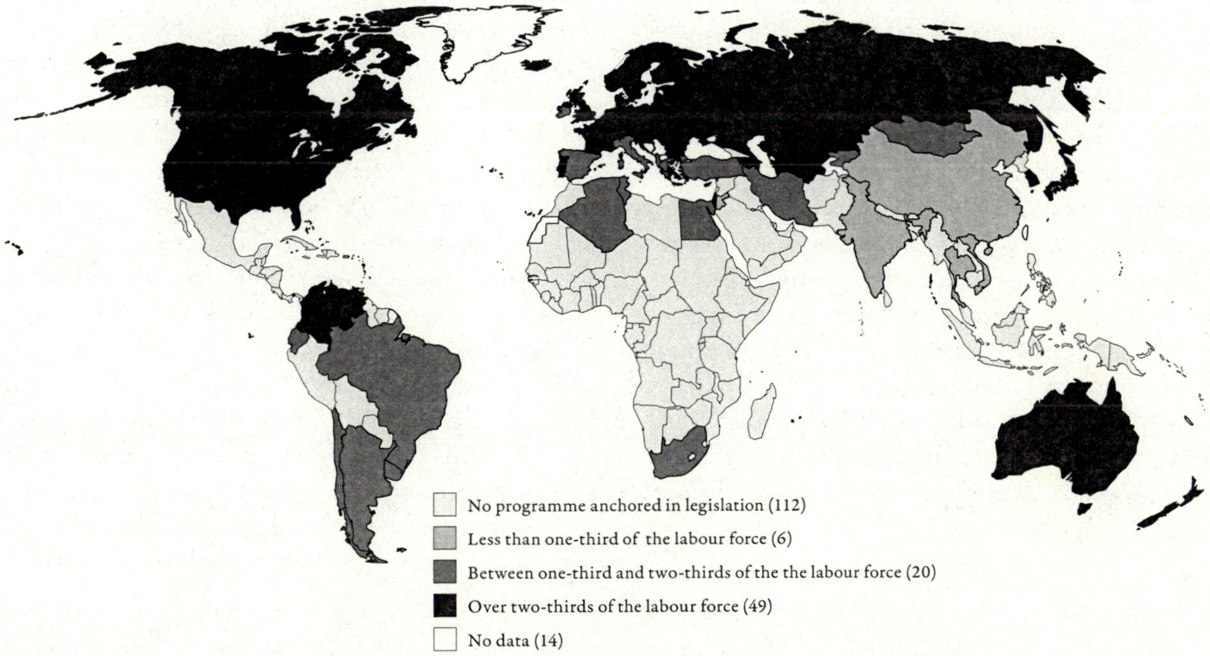

Note: Figures in brackets refer to the number of countries in each group. Data from 2009–13; for most countries, 2012/13.

Sources: Based on SSA and ISSA, 2012; SSA and ISSA, 2013a; SSA and ISSA, 2013b; SSA and ISSA, 2014; ILO LABORSTA database, and national legislative texts and statistical sources.

Link: http://www.social-protection.org/gimi/gess/RessourceDownload.action?ressource.ressourceId=37039.

Figure 3.6 Unemployment protection schemes: Extent of legal coverage, regional estimates, latest available year (percentage of labour force)

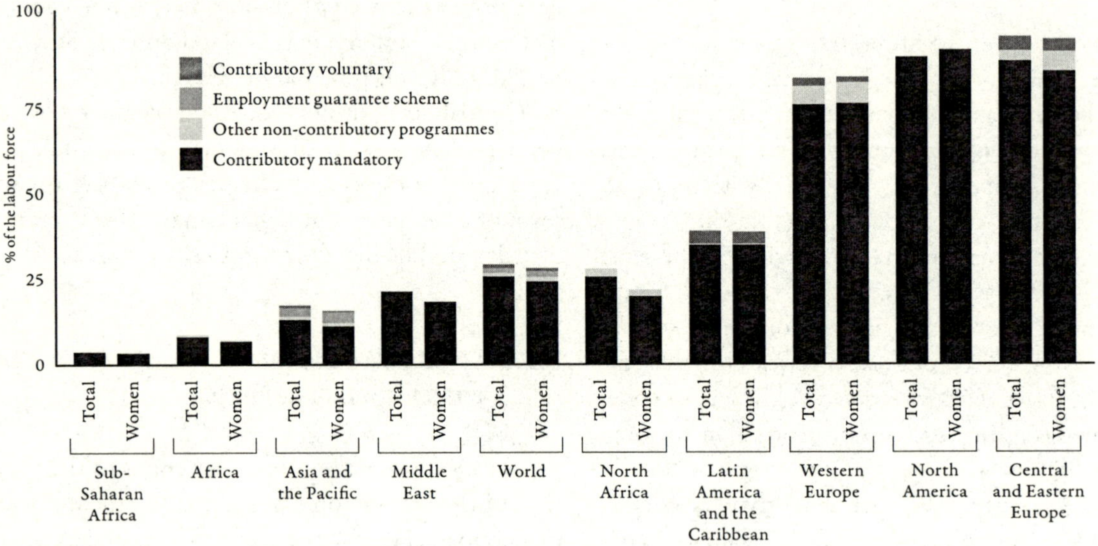

Note: Regional estimates are weighted by the labour force.

Sources: ILO Social Protection Department, based on SSA and ISSA, 2012; SSA and ISSA, 2013a; SSA and ISSA, 2013b; SSA and ISSA, 2014; national legislative texts; ILO LABORSTA, completed with national statistical data for the quantification of the groups legally covered.

Link: http://www.social-protection.org/gimi/gess/RessourceDownload.action?ressource.ressourceId=37040.

unemployment assistance and employment guarantees, as well as a very few voluntary schemes (see figures 3.3 and 3.4). The variation between regions is considerable (see figures 3.5 and 3.6): while 80–90 per cent of the labour force in North America and Europe is covered by law by an unemployment benefit scheme, only 37.6 per cent of the labour force in Latin America is so protected, along with 20.6 per cent of the labour force in the Middle East, 16.6 per cent in the Asia and Pacific region,[7] and just 8.4 per cent of the labour force in Africa. Where coverage is low, this is usually because unemployment benefit schemes do not exist and, where they do exist, usually cover only those working in the formal economy. There are marked gender differences in unemployment protection coverage in some regions, especially the Middle East, where only 17.7 per cent of the female labour force is protected by law, compared to 20.6 per cent of the total labour force, and in North Africa, where 20.9 per cent of the female labour force is protected, compared to 27 per cent of the overall labour force.

3.2.4 Effective coverage by unemployment benefits

Unemployment benefits play a key role in ensuring income security for unemployed workers and in facilitating their transition to new jobs, particularly if properly linked to employment services. However, the proportion of jobseekers receiving unemployment benefits varies widely across and within regions. The extent and level of effective coverage of unemployment benefit schemes can be measured by relating the number of actual recipients of such benefits to the number of unemployed workers at a given point in time.

What is observed, not surprisingly, is that *effective* coverage by unemployment benefits is lower than legal coverage,[8] and that this varies widely across regions and countries (see figures 3.7 and 3.8). While 63.8 per cent of the unemployed in Western Europe (in some countries, more than 90 per cent) receive unemployment benefits, including non-contributory benefits, only 21.6 per cent of unemployed workers in Central and Eastern Europe and 28 per cent of the unemployed in

[7] This includes an estimate of legal coverage for India's employment guarantee scheme, which is based on an estimate of the proportion of working or unemployed adults in the total rural labour force.

[8] It should be noted that indicators for legal and effective coverage are not strictly comparable, as they refer to two different dimensions of coverage and different reference populations (denominators). The legal coverage indicator refers to people eligible under legislation for unemployment benefits as a proportion of the total labour force. The effective coverage indicator refers to the proportion of those receiving unemployment benefits as a proportion of those currently unemployed.

Figure 3.7 Effective coverage of unemployment benefits: Unemployed who actually receive cash benefits, regional estimates, 2007, 2009 and 2012/13 (percentages)

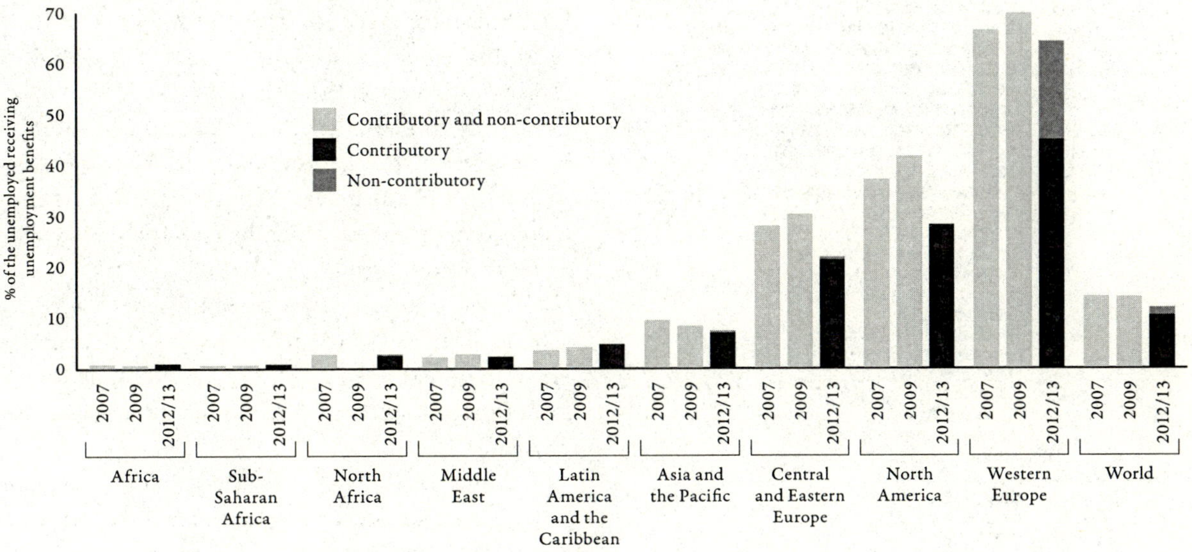

Notes: Numbers of unemployed receiving unemployment benefits collected from national social security unemployment schemes. Global average weighted by the labour force. For detailed information by country see Annex IV, table B.3.

Sources: Based on ILO Social Security Inquiry database, ILO LABORSTA and national sources.

Link: http://www.social-protection.org/gimi/gess/RessourceDownload.action?ressource.ressourceId=37042.

Figure 3.8 Effective coverage of unemployment benefits: Unemployed who actually receive cash benefits, latest available year (percentages)

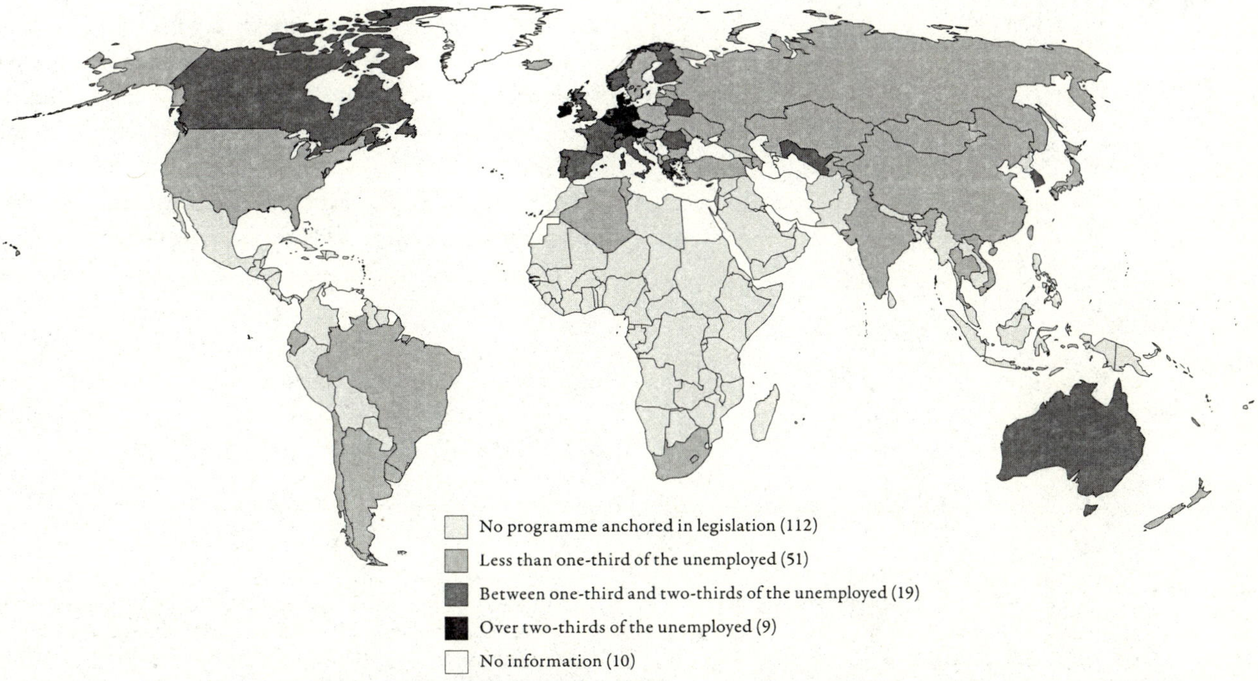

Notes: Data from 2009–13; for most countries, 2012/13. Unemployed beneficiaries of general social assistance schemes are not included due to unavailability of data. Their inclusion would increase coverage rates, but only in countries where such schemes exist on a large scale (high-income and some middle-income countries). Employment guarantee schemes are not included. For detailed information by country, sex and type of scheme, see Annex IV, table B.3. Figures in brackets refer to the number of countries in each category.

Sources: Based on ILO Social Security Inquiry database, ILO LABORSTA and national sources.

Link: http://www.social-protection.org/gimi/gess/RessourceDownload.action?ressource.ressourceId=37041.

Figure 3.9 Effective coverage of unemployment benefits: Unemployed who actually receive cash benefits, latest available year (percentages)

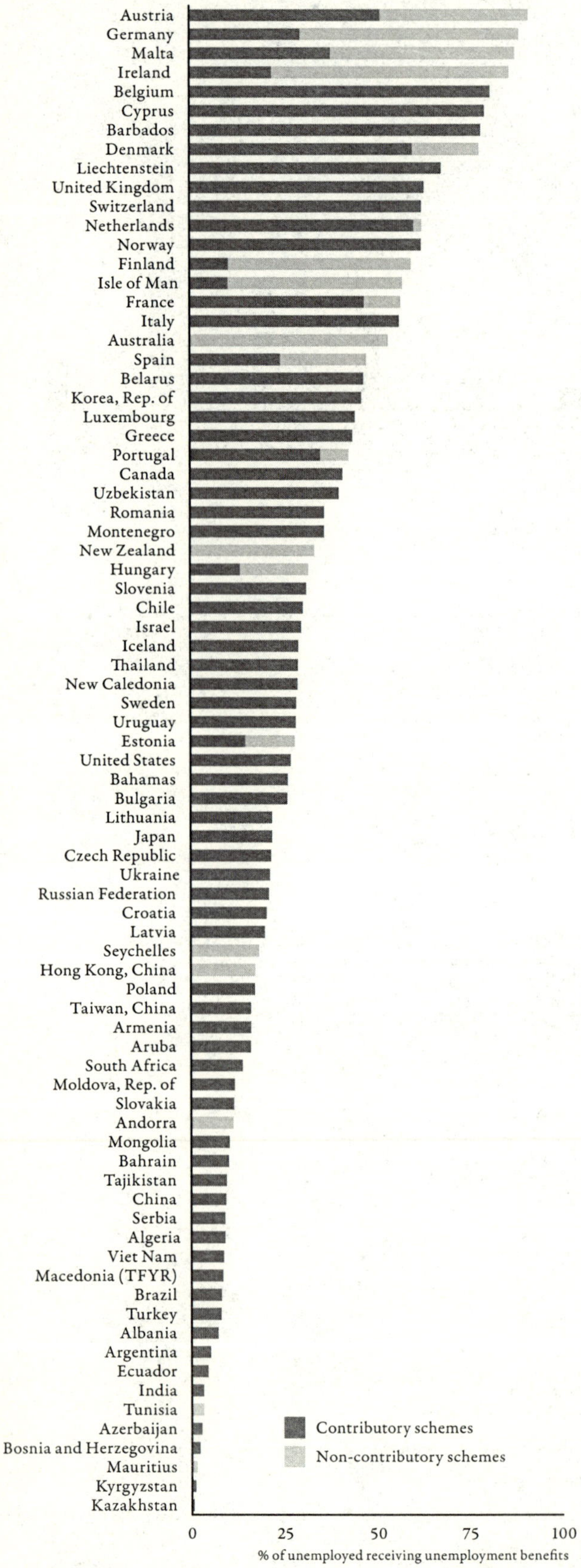

Note: See figure 3.8.

Source: Based on ILO Social Security Inquiry database (see Annex IV, table B.3).

Link: http://www.social-protection.org/gimi/gess/RessourceDownload.action?ressource.ressourceId=44417.

North America do so. Only a small minority of unemployed workers in many developing countries can expect to receive any kind of cash unemployment protection benefits: 7.2 per cent of unemployed workers in Asia and the Pacific, 4.6 per cent in Latin America and the Caribbean, and less than 3 per cent in the Middle East, North Africa and sub-Saharan Africa. Across the world, only 11.7 per cent of the unemployed receive unemployment benefits, while the remaining 88.3 per cent are left without income support.

While the lack of an unemployment protection scheme is certainly the major reason for the low coverage in global terms, other factors include long contribution periods,[9] and a short maximum duration of payment.[10]

In most regions – with the notable exception of Latin America – effective coverage rates have fallen since 2007 (see figure 3.7). This decrease may be due to changes in the structure of the unemployed population (for example, more first-time jobseekers or long-term unemployed) or changes in entitlement rules in unemployment benefit schemes. In Europe and North America, factors contributing to the steep rise in coverage rates between 2007 and 2009 are likely to have included more generous rules with regard to eligibility for unemployment benefits and a higher proportion of new beneficiaries. The subsequent dramatic fall in effective coverage ratios in these regions by 2012 may be attributed to a higher share of long-term unemployment and a consequently higher share of unemployed having exhausted their entitlement to unemployment benefit.

Figures 3.7–3.9 indicate that in many countries with unemployment benefit schemes in place, only a relatively small proportion of the unemployed actually receive periodic unemployment cash benefits.[11] Coverage ratios of more than two-thirds of the unemployed are reached in only nine out of the 89 countries that have schemes of some type in place. Several factors may contribute to low effective coverage rates. A high proportion of

---

[9] Conventions Nos 102 and 168 both require that the qualifying period be no longer than necessary to preclude abuse. Countries usually require either six or 12 months of contributions to qualify. Mongolia has the highest requirement, at 24 months of contributions, the last nine of which must be continuous, thereby excluding those with seasonal or temporary work contracts (Carter, Bédard and Peyron Bista, 2013).

[10] While the duration of protection varies widely, on average the maximum duration for benefit is 45 weeks (55 weeks in advanced economies; 17 weeks in Latin American countries).

[11] Some of those not covered by unemployment benefit schemes may, however, receive other benefits, such as general social assistance benefits.

Figure 3.10 Proportion of unemployed receiving unemployment benefits and relative poverty rates for the unemployed, selected European countries, 2012

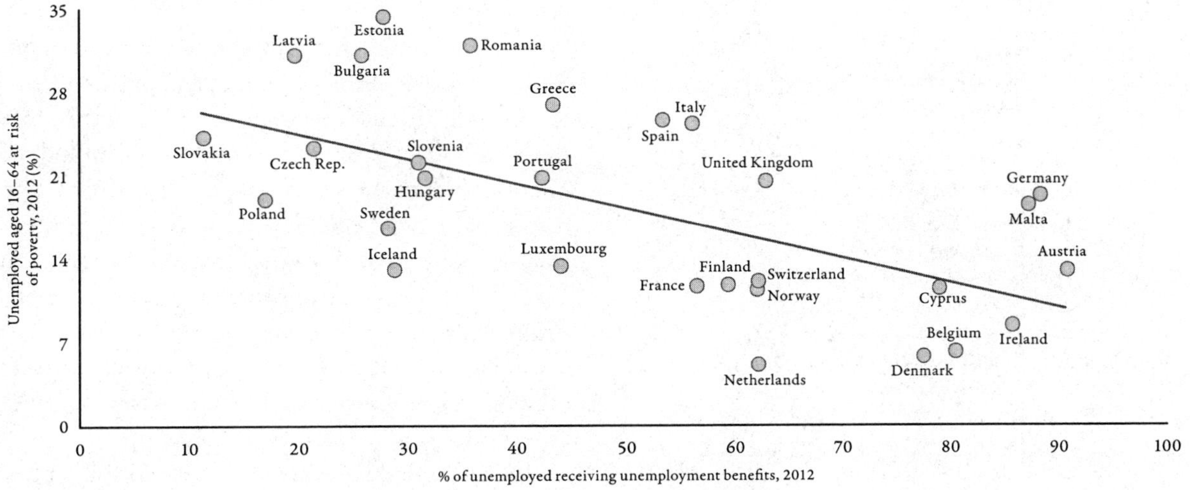

Note: Calculations based on a poverty line of 40 per cent of equivalized median household income, which is lower than the threshold used by the European Union for identifying those who are at risk of being poor (60 per cent of median income).

Source: Eurostat Income and Living Conditions Database; various sources (see Annex IV, table B.3).

Link: http://www.social-protection.org/gimi/gess/RessourceDownload.action?ressource.ressourceId=42961.

unemployed workers may belong to categories often excluded from legal coverage, such as domestic workers or part-time workers. A high share of long-term unemployed who have exhausted their benefit entitlement can also lower the coverage ratio. Other groups may be excluded from effective coverage because they do not meet the entitlement conditions, such as unemployed people (often young people or other workers with short and/or interrupted employment careers) who have not accumulated a sufficient contribution or employment record to be eligible for contributory unemployment benefits, or, in the case of means-tested benefits, whose own means are above the threshold set for eligibility for benefits.

High coverage rates of unemployment benefits are associated with higher income security for beneficiaries, provided that benefit levels are adequate. Unemployment benefits play a major role in preventing poverty for the unemployed, as shown by figure 3.10 for the Member States of the European Union. In countries where effective coverage rates of unemployment benefits are lower, the unemployed are more likely to live in poverty.

Evidence from the European Union also demonstrates that unemployed workers receiving unemployment benefits are more likely to return to work than those who do not receive any benefits (European Commission, 2014b, p. 163). Unemployment protection thus plays a key role in facilitating transitions back into employment and preventing poverty.

3.2.5 Unemployment protection for young people

Unemployment protection for young people constitutes a particular challenge, exacerbated by the high, and often growing, unemployment rates of young people in many countries (ILO, 2013d). The fact that very large numbers of young people around the world are unable to gain access to labour markets constitutes an important problem in itself (ILO, 2012b). Many aspects of this problem, moreover, bring into sharp focus specific issues in relation to the objectives, design and implementation of unemployment protection schemes more generally.

Only a small number of countries (20 out of the 201 reviewed for this report) provide unemployment benefits for first-time jobseekers, a category of the active population by definition excluded from the protection conferred by unemployment protection schemes based on contributory coverage. In some countries, first-time jobseekers may be eligible for some form of unemployment assistance; in others, they may have access to non-contributory benefits provided through, for example, a general social assistance programme. In most countries, however, first-time jobseekers do not fall within the remit of any social security schemes.

Even in systems where young unemployed women and men who have already acquired some work experience may be eligible for some contributory unemployment insurance benefits, they remain less likely to be eligible for such benefits than older adults, for

Figure 3.11 Unemployed receiving unemployment cash benefits, all ages and youth, 2012/13 (percentages)

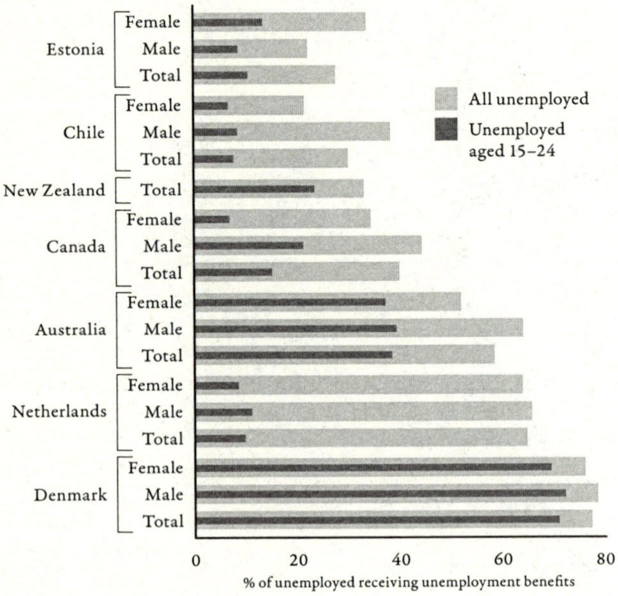

Source: ILO calculations, based on national sources.

Link: http://www.social-protection.org/gimi/gess/RessourceDownload.action?ressource.ressourceId=42960.

two reasons. First, minimum contribution periods in contributory unemployment insurance programmes effectively exclude young adults who are made redundant before meeting these minimum contribution periods. Second, young people are more likely to work in conditions which are not covered by unemployment insurance, including employment on temporary and part-time contracts, or in other forms of precarious or informal employment (see figure 3.11).

Many countries have strengthened their efforts to combine income support benefits with assistance in finding new employment, training, retraining and other measures aimed at increasing employability. These include specific programmes addressing youth unemployment, including increasing the quality of apprenticeship systems and other school-to-work transition programmes, providing career guidance and introducing measures to support the acquisition of work experience.

3.2.6 Expanding unemployment protection in emerging economies

One of the most remarkable policy developments in recent years is the strengthening of unemployment protection policies in emerging economies, in response to the need both to provide income security for individual unemployed workers and protect them from slipping into the informal economy, and to safeguard the nation's human capital (see e.g. Berg and Salerno, 2008). Several distinct forms of protection have emerged, including various types of unemployment insurance and assistance, and employment guarantee schemes. These different forms respond to different needs and contexts, and provide different levels of protection.

In some middle-income countries with high level of informal employment and weak employment services, unemployment savings schemes (see section 3.2.2 above) have been promoted, following the example of Chile.[12] It has been argued that in such contexts individual accounts are less prone to moral hazard than collectively financed unemployment insurance schemes.[13] The Chilean scheme partially addresses the inability of many workers to build up sufficiently high savings – one of the major shortcomings of this type of programme – through a tax-subsidized solidarity component, which effectively makes it a hybrid scheme. Some similar programmes, however (for example in Jordan), lack this component, instead allowing account-holders to tap into their pension entitlements, which effectively perpetuates income insecurity into old age. Experience from Chile shows that coverage remains low and is of greatest benefit to those at lowest risk of becoming unemployed while not sufficiently protecting those at greatest need; moreover, replacement rates tend to be insufficient to provide even a minimum level of income security (OECD, 2010a). These difficulties raise fundamental questions as to the viability of such programmes, unless supported by a large tax-funded solidarity component.[14]

A growing number of emerging economies have chosen instead in recent years to introduce or significantly expand contributory or non-contributory unemployment benefit schemes. These include Bahrain,[15]

[12] Chile's Seguro de Cesantía scheme was introduced in 2002 (see Sehnbruch, 2006; Chile Superintendencia de Pensiones, 2010).

[13] Proponents of unemployment savings accounts (e.g. Vodopivec, 2009; Robalino, Vodopivec and Bodor, 2010) argue that the fact that they require the unemployed to draw on their own savings, rather than offering access to a collectively financed unemployment fund, limits moral hazard in contexts where government authorities do not have the capacity to prevent abuse.

[14] Such a solidarity component would introduce through the back door the very risk of moral hazard that these schemes are supposed to minimize, thereby severely detracting from their purported advantages.

[15] Bahrain introduced a contributory unemployment benefit scheme in 2006, providing earnings-related benefits to the insured and flat-rate benefits to first-time jobseekers and those lacking a sufficient contribution record.

Box 3.2 Public employment programmes and their contribution to social protection

Public employment programmes (PEPs), a term used to describe any programme involving direct employment creation by government, are often used as one component of national social protection strategies. Among a broad variety of PEPs, two specific forms stand out:

- Public works programmes (PWPs), which may offer cash payments or food for work. This more common and traditional form is often adopted as a temporary response to specific shocks and crises, but may also have a longer-term horizon.
- Employment guarantee schemes (EGSs) refer to long-term rights-based programmes in which some level of entitlement to work is provided.

While PEPs can contribute to several development objectives, they are not able to serve all objectives to the same extent at the same time. In practice, the policy design and implementation requires the prioritization of one function over others, along the following lines:

- Employment function: emphasis on job creation in programmes that focus on the State as the employer of last resort.
- Social protection function: emphasis on income security and transfers in cash or in kind.
- Labour-based investment function: emphasis on the quality and nature of infrastructure constructed or services provided.

Where the main priority is not clearly defined, the monitoring and evaluation of a programme against its objectives will be hampered. It is therefore necessary to clearly define, separate and articulate the objectives of a programme, and to link it effectively to other employment and social protection policies.

Employment guarantee schemes can contribute to building national social protection floors in several respects. They can enhance income security for people of working age with no or insufficient earnings, by providing income that is regular and predictable and is provided as an entitlement. They can also be used to construct or improve infrastructure that enhances the supply of health, education and other public services. However, these schemes do not address all needs, given that the central element of employment excludes those who are not able to work, for whatever reason. Some PEPs (e.g. in Ethiopia and India) therefore combine employment guarantee schemes with cash transfers for those who are permanently or temporarily unable to work, or for whom work is not available.

Source: Based on Lieuw-Kie-Song et al., 2011.

Mauritius,[16] Saudi Arabia[17] and Viet Nam.[18] While these had been planned before the global crisis, their timely implementation was very helpful in coping with its repercussions. In each of these countries, the disbursement of unemployment benefits is closely linked to the provision of employment services that support jobseekers in finding a new job or acquiring new skills.

Other emerging economies have expanded coverage of their unemployment insurance schemes to cover workers at the margins of the formal economy. The Brazilian unemployment insurance scheme now covers not only waged workers, including domestic workers, but also small-scale fishermen, workers rescued from forced labour and workers in the Bolsa Qualificação (training scholarship) programme. In South Africa, domestic workers were brought under the umbrella of unemployment insurance in 2003.

Employment guarantee schemes and other forms of public employment programmes (see box 3.2) have emerged as a further policy option to provide temporary employment and a certain level of income security to rural populations during lean seasons when many rural workers are unemployed or underemployed. India's MGNREGS, introduced in 2005, provides a legally guaranteed right to a maximum of 100 days of employment a year to rural households (see box 3.3). Many other countries have been using public employment programmes to provide poor people with some level of income security at least for a limited period of time, although this is usually not based on a legal entitlement.

---

16 Mauritius complemented its unemployment assistance scheme with a social insurance scheme in 2009.

17 Saudi Arabia's Hafiz programme, implemented in December 2011, provides financial assistance of up to 2,000 riyal (SAR) a month to jobseekers and offers a broad range of placement and upskilling services.

18 Viet Nam introduced an employment insurance scheme in 2009, following the adoption of the Law on Social Insurance in 2006. The scheme is now being converted into an Employment Insurance scheme, expanding the scope of employment promotion measures provided in combination with cash benefits.

Box 3.3 India's Mahatma Gandhi National Rural Employment Guarantee Scheme (MGNREGS)

The MGNREGS was established under the corresponding Act (the National Rural Employment Guarantee Act: NREGA), adopted in 2005. Reflecting the constitutional right to work, the scheme confers legal rights on beneficiaries, which distinguishes it from programmes that are not anchored in national legislation and are therefore prone to discretionary changes. There are, however, some concerns that poor, often illiterate, households cannot realize their rights in practice.

Under the MGNREGS, a rural household is entitled to demand up to 100 days of employment per year, which is made available on agreed public works sites. A share of places in this programme is reserved for women. The programme undertakes projects facilitating land and water resource management, together with infrastructure development projects such as road construction. The programme is designed to be self-targeting, with wages equal to the prevailing, officially declared, minimum wage for agricultural labourers in the area. If work is not provided within the stipulated time, the applicant is entitled to receive an unemployment allowance.

The allocation for the programme from the national budget for the financial year 2012/13 was equivalent to 0.3 per cent of GDP. The programme is acknowledged as one of the largest rights-based integrated employment and social protection initiatives in the world, reaching close to 50 million rural households – approximately 30 per cent of rural households – in 2012.

Sources: Based on ILO, 2010b, pp. 89–90; ILO, 2011a, p. 68; Ahluwalia, forthcoming; Ehmke, forthcoming.

While the possibility of using public employment programmes to pursue simultaneously a multiplicity of objectives (investment, employment and social protection) renders them an attractive tool, the concomitant lack of a clearly defined primary objective can limit their effectiveness in fulfilling social protection objectives (e.g. ILO, 2014b; Lieuw-Kie-Song et al., 2011; McCord, 2012; Subbarao et al., 2013). Nevertheless, several countries (including Ethiopia and South Africa) have taken deliberate steps to emphasize social protection objectives in their public employment programmes (McCord, 2012). Public employment programmes will only help to alleviate poverty in the long term if they are designed to provide decent work, including an adequate level of wages, an integral skills development component and full respect for the occupational safety and health of workers, while also ensuring beneficiaries are covered by existing social security schemes and provided with access to health care.

3.2.7 Unemployment benefits as a key element of crisis response and fiscal consolidation measures

During the recent global crisis, many countries benefited from the capacity of unemployment benefit schemes to stabilize aggregate demand, and thus foster quick recovery (ILO 2011a; IILS, 2011c), in line with the Global Jobs Pact (ILO, 2009a; ECOSOC, 2009). Countries that had unemployment benefit schemes in place before the crisis were able to scale them up quickly to enhance their power as automatic stabilizers. Where partial unemployment benefits were available to compensate for crisis-induced reductions in working hours, they helped workers to keep their jobs, and employers to retain their workforces, during troughs in demand, and supported a rapid response to the first signs of recovery (ILO, 2011a; IILS, 2011c). A number of countries implemented these and other expansionary measures at a relatively early stage of the financial crisis. As the crisis continued and pressures on public budgets increased, some of these expansionary measures gave way to fiscal consolidation measures.[19]

Expansionary measures: Using unemployment benefits to ensure income security for the unemployed and to preserve jobs for the employed

Extension of coverage and increase in the level and duration of benefit. Several countries facilitated or extended access to existing or new unemployment benefits in response to the global crisis (ILO and World Bank, 2012; Bonnet, Saget and Weber, 2012). Some countries, such as Australia, reduced the waiting period for unemployment benefits; others, such as Latvia, reduced the length of the period of contributions required to be eligible for benefits. Most countries extended coverage to workers previously excluded, such as non-regular

[19] In this report, "fiscal consolidation" refers to the wide array of adjustment measures adopted to reduce government deficits and debt accumulation. Fiscal consolidation policies are often referred to as "austerity" policies.

Box 3.4 Keeping people in employment through part-time unemployment benefits: The example of Germany

Germany's part-time unemployment benefit (*Kurzarbeitergeld* or short-time work compensation), was one of the country's main policy instruments during the global financial and economic crisis. This benefit allowed companies faced with a drop in demand to retain workers on shorter working hours while guaranteeing them at least a degree of income security. Partial compensation for their loss in direct earnings was made through a cash benefit paid for a maximum period of six months. At the peak of the crisis, in May 2009, these benefits were being paid to around 1.5 million workers (5.4 per cent of the workforce).

As a result, the sudden downturn of the economy led to only a moderate increase in the number of unemployed and the number of recipients of unemployment insurance benefits, the employment impact of the downturn being largely cushioned by the remarkable expansion of partial unemployment benefits.

This policy is considered to be one of the factors explaining the relatively quick recovery of the German economy, because it ensured that employers were in a position to retain their workers throughout the crisis, thus avoiding firing and rehiring costs, and were able to respond quickly as the markets picked up again. The average reduction in working time was 30.5 per cent, the equivalent of about 432,000 full-time jobs. A loss of jobs of this magnitude would have resulted in an increase in the unemployment rate of about 1 percentage point.

Sources: Based on ILO, 2011a, box 3.10; see also ILO, 2010c; IILS, 2011a.

workers in Germany and Japan, the self-employed in Austria, and young people in Argentina (Bonnet, Saget and Weber, 2012). Other countries extended the duration of coverage to ensure inclusion of those who would otherwise be deemed to have exhausted their rights (these included Argentina, Brazil,[20] Japan,[21] Latvia,[22] Spain[23] and, in the case of older workers, Uruguay[24]), or provided emergency benefits to this group (for example, the United States[25]). Another strategy followed by some countries (for example, India and South Africa)was to use public employment programmes as a means to ensure a predictable income stream for unemployed and underemployed workers. Finally, some countries (for example, France and the United Kingdom) increased the level of benefits or provided one-off benefit payments to some categories of unemployed workers.

Keeping people in employment. Several countries (including Canada,[26] France, Germany (see box 3.4), the Netherlands and Poland) used partial unemployment benefits to allow employers to retain workers during the trough in demand. Various social dialogue instruments, especially tripartite cooperation and collective bargaining, were used to shape these policies. Partial unemployment benefits helped not only to contain the rise in unemployment and the number of recipients of (full) unemployment benefits, but also to keep experienced workers in place so that their employers could take prompt advantage of the eventual upturn (see Bonnet, Saget and Weber, 2012; ILO, 2010a (pp. 106–111); ILO, 2011a; Arpaia et al., 2010). Such measures are widely considered to have been successful in fostering quick economic recovery and preventing the "dequalification" and discouragement of workers. Other countries (for example, China) introduced or extended programmes that aimed at upgrading the skills of employed workers and workers in vulnerable situations (Aleksynska et al., 2013).

[20] In 2009, a temporary increase was implemented in the maximum duration of unemployment benefits for sectors hit particularly badly by the recession. This extension reached around 103,000 people, or 20 per cent of those receiving unemployment benefits. Also, those lacking formal income-earning opportunities have been targeted through extended access to the Bolsa Família programme. The stabilization of aggregate consumption through this measure, together with other social security programmes and the minimum wage policy, is observed to have contributed substantially to accelerating recovery in Brazil (IILS, 2011b.)

[21] At the end of 2008, Japan adopted a 60-day extension of the period during which unemployment benefits were payable to those who faced difficulty in finding re-employment (taking into consideration place of residence and age).

[22] The duration of unemployment benefit payment in Latvia was temporarily increased (from 1 July 2009 to 31 December 2011) to nine months across the board.

[23] This provision, introduced in Spain at the end of 2009 and extended in 2010, was complemented by measures to promote employability of the long-term unemployed involving their active participation.

[24] Introduced in 2009: see Amarante, Arim and Dean, 2013.

[25] The extension of Emergency Unemployment Compensation (EUC) in the United States began in June 2008 and expired on 1 January 2014.

[26] Canada's Work Sharing programme aimed at avoiding lay-offs by offering benefits from employment insurance to qualifying workers willing to work reduced hours while their employer recovers from adverse economic conditions.

Contraction measures: Tightening entitlement conditions for jobseekers' access to benefits

While many countries took bold measures to expand unemployment benefit coverage in order to mitigate the effect of the crisis, others adopted fiscal consolidation measures even in the early stages of the global crisis. These included the tightening of entitlement conditions for unemployment benefits (for example, in Ireland, Ukraine and the United Kingdom), increases in the number of contribution payments required to qualify for the receipt of unemployment benefits (in Ireland and Switzerland), the introduction of a higher earnings threshold for eligibility (in Ireland), reductions in the maximum period for which benefits could be paid (in the Czech Republic, Portugal, Serbia and Switzerland), and reductions in the level of benefits (in Romania and Serbia) (see Bonnet, Saget and Weber, 2012). While such measures may have helped to contain the rising cost of unemployment benefits, they may have led conversely to an increase in expenditure on social assistance benefits. Reductions in the maximum duration of entitlements (as in the Czech Republic and Ireland) or in the level of benefits (in Hungary and Latvia) had a strong impact on both current recipients of unemployment benefits and the newly unemployed.

Inevitably, the rise in unemployment rates led to a steep increase in the number of recipients of unemployment benefits, which rose on average by some 50 per cent between January 2008 and early 2009. In several countries, including Australia, New Zealand and the United States, the number of beneficiaries had roughly doubled by 2009 compared to pre-crisis levels. Since then, the number of beneficiaries has decreased, yet in most countries it still remains well above the levels of 2008. Considering the dim prospects for a global employment recovery (IMF, 2013a; ILO, 2014a), this situation is likely to continue. The expansion of unemployment benefits in some countries, together with the rising numbers of beneficiaries, have led inevitably to an increase in expenditure on such schemes. In some countries the existing reserves in unemployment insurance funds have been exhausted, necessitating budget allocations for tax-financed benefits.

As a consequence, from 2010–11 more countries started implementing fiscal consolidation measures with the objective of redressing the financial situation of both unemployment insurance funds and public budgets. This included some countries (such as Slovenia and Spain) which had taken bold measures to expand unemployment benefits at the onset of the crisis, but now felt the need to withdraw some of these expansionary measures and curtail unemployment benefits (see box 3.5).

Several countries implemented measures which changed the rights and obligations of jobseekers with regard to accessing benefits. For example, Canada, Spain, the United Kingdom and the United States all strengthened the requirements of unemployment benefit recipients in respect of searching for work.

Box 3.5 From expansion to fiscal consolidation: The examples of Slovenia and Spain

In several countries, an initial expansion of unemployment benefits in response to the global crisis was later reversed with the objective of consolidating public finances.

In January 2011, the Slovenian government introduced the new Labour Market Regulation Act (LMRA) as a response to the economic crisis, aiming thereby "to increase the security of jobseekers, especially the security of unemployed persons and persons whose employment is at risk, through the government's quicker response in the labour market". However, measures adopted in 2013 as part of a Bill on Emergency Measures, temporarily reduced the levels of unemployment cash benefits and maternity benefits for budgetary reasons. Unemployment cash benefits were reduced by 3 per cent to a monthly level no lower than €350 but no higher than €890 (the previous ceiling was €1,050). In addition, instead of unemployment benefits the long-term unemployed would receive wages and reimbursement of employment-related costs in exchange for their participation in public employment programmes.

In the early phase of the crisis, the Spanish government decided to extend unemployment protection temporarily to those who had exhausted their eligibility to benefits and subsidies and were in need, due to lack of other income, with an allowance of €420 per month for a maximum period of six months in combination with measures to promote employability. More recently, various measures have been taken with a view to reducing expenditure, including lowering the level of contributory unemployment benefits after six months, increasing the minimum age of qualification for non-contributory unemployment benefits for the older unemployed, and introducing new requirements for the long-term unemployed and persons with disabilities with regard to the acceptance of offers of employment or training.

Sources: Based on information from Labour Law Network, European Employment Observatory and national sources.

Measures to this end included a broader definition of suitable employment and stricter obligations for job-seekers with regard to their efforts in actively looking for a new job (e.g. in Canada[27]), compulsory participation in training and other active labour market programmes for certain categories of the unemployed (e.g. in Brazil,[28] Saudi Arabia,[29] Spain, the United Kingdom, the United States and Uruguay[30]) and stricter sanctions for recipients who refuse an offer of suitable employment (e.g. Ireland[31] and New Zealand[32]), as well as measures to enhance the effectiveness of employment services in getting people into employment and shortening the duration of unemployment claims (e.g. the United States[33]).

The role of unemployment benefits during the global crisis has highlighted two major policy lessons. First, it has underscored the importance of having well-designed unemployment benefit schemes in place which not only support the structural transformation of the economy in "normal" times, but can also be quickly scaled up in the event of major economic shocks in order to realize their full potential as automatic stabilizers of aggregate demand. Second, unemployment benefit schemes can achieve their potential only if they are financed appropriately from contributions and general taxation. Where financing is insufficient, ill-timed and ill-designed curtailments of benefits may have pro-cyclical effects, which may thwart economic recovery and lead to substantial increases in poverty and vulnerability.

3.2.8 Renewed emphasis on (re-)integrating unemployed workers into the labour market

Some of the measures recently implemented aimed at (re-)integrating unemployed workers into the labour market, accelerating a trend that started well before the global crisis (e.g. Lødemel and Trickey, 2001; Eichhorst, Kaufmann and Konle-Seidl, 2008). Some have been adopted as part of the crisis response, while others are not directly related to it. Aiming at better linking "active" and "passive" labour market policies, some measures focus on encouraging unemployed workers to participate in training, job matching and subsidized employment programmes, while others are more coercive in character.

Many of the recent reforms have been aimed at promoting and facilitating (re-)entry into employment for various specific groups, including the long-term unemployed, youth, single parents and persons with disabilities. Since 2010, most measures adopted in developed countries in particular have aimed at reducing unemployment by providing better support to the unemployed to enter or re-enter employment and by stimulating job creation. This is the case, for example, of measures introduced in pursuit of the objectives of the European Commission's "Social Investment Package" (SIP) (European Commission, 2013a). In recent years, too, wage and job subsidies and credit provision have been initiated to encourage job creation in many countries, e.g. Argentina, Brazil, Canada, France, Russian Federation, Saudi Arabia, South Africa and the United States.

---

[27] Changes introduced in the Canadian legal framework governing the employment insurance scheme included a clarification of the definition of "suitable employment" and of what constitutes a "reasonable job search" by those claiming unemployment benefits. The new definition of suitable employment widened the range of jobs that some beneficiaries (those with frequent unemployment spells) are required to accept, including jobs unrelated to previous fields of work, jobs paying 70 per cent of their former earnings and jobs entailing long commutes.

[28] In Brazil, additional vocational training opportunities were created for beneficiaries of income transfer programmes, including those receiving unemployment benefits and transfers under the Bolsa Família programme.

[29] In Saudi Arabia, a series of measures targeted the recipients of Hafiz: these included referral of hard-to-place beneficiaries to job placement centres, compulsory training, establishment of partnerships with private sector enterprises to provide training and employment opportunities for beneficiaries, and strengthened employment services (ILO and World Bank, 2012).

[30] In Uruguay, increases in the amounts of benefit and the extension of duration of payment from six to eight months were accompanied by a new obligation to take training courses.

[31] In Ireland, the conditionality of benefits was changed in the extended social welfare legislation that took effect from January 2011, stipulating disqualification for receipt of certain benefits (or reductions in payments) when a person refuses an offer of suitable employment or refuses to participate in an appropriate course of training or other support programme. Prior to this, the legislation required only that a recipient be seeking a job and be available for work, a provision that was applied in a somewhat benign manner (European Commission, 2012b).

[32] From July 2013, unemployed people in New Zealand have to comply with new conditions for the payment of benefits. If a suitable job is turned down without good reason, benefits may be reduced by half for unemployed with dependent children and for others stopped for 13 weeks. Other conditions include accepting (and passing) drug tests when applying for a job in certain sectors such as truck driving, construction and forestry; giving advance notice if leaving the country; and, for unemployed with children, meeting conditions with regard to children's school attendance and parents' childcare obligations.

[33] A reform of the Re-employment Services (RES) and Re-employment and Eligibility Assessments (REA) programmes aimed at ensuring more rapid re-employment, shorter claim durations and fewer erroneous payments of unemployment compensation.

Box 3.6 Measures facilitating return to work for parents with young children

Several countries have taken measures to help parents (particularly mothers) with young children return to work.

In Australia, a set of policy measures aimed at facilitating the (re-)entry into the labour market of single parents include more generous earnings disregards under various income support benefits, career counselling and enhanced childcare provision.

In Japan, a programme which supports women looking for work while raising their children, for instance through offering childcare services and information services, was re-invigorated. In 2011, 69,000 women used the programme and successfully found jobs.

In Pakistan, in 2009, the Benazir Income Support Programme (BISP) was introduced. The programme supports women in poor households with a combined package of cash benefits (1,000 Pakistan rupees (PKR) per month: approximately US$12) and in-kind social services. In addition to extending health insurance coverage to its beneficiaries (Waseela-e-Sehat), the programme provides vocational training opportunities (Waseela-e-Rozgar) to every beneficiary and access to interest-free financial support (Waseela-e-Haq) for certain women receiving the monthly benefit. The BISP is now being implemented across the whole country, with special attention to remote areas.

In the Russian Federation, access to training programmes designed for jobseekers was extended to women on leave to care for a child under the age of three. In 2011, 26,200 women on leave benefited from these programmes, of whom 15,700 found jobs. Additional measures included the introduction of flexible forms of work, self-employment programmes for women, and pre-school education for children aged three to seven.

Sources: Preparatory work for ILO and OECD, 2013; Aleksynska et al., 2013; national sources.

Many of these measures focus on linking the disbursement of cash benefits to active labour market policies, such as programmes for the provision of training, skills development, better job-matching, or career guidance and mentorship. These include efforts to provide jobseekers and recipients of unemployment benefits with better access to training, retraining, certification and job-matching (e.g. in the Russian Federation[34] and Saudi Arabia), personalized support (e.g. in the United Kingdom[35]), training and subsidized employment opportunities (e.g. Saudi Arabia[36]), and support in complying with job-search and activity requirements (Spain), as well as specific measures to support young people (e.g. in Argentina), older workers (e.g. in Canada[37]) and other specific groups (e.g. in the United States[38]). In some countries (including Japan, Pakistan, and the Russian Federation), measures to facilitate the employment of parents, particularly women, with young children have been introduced (see box 3.6).

Such policies have often been linked to broader efforts to provide an integrated package of "active" and "passive" labour market policies, or, more broadly, to offer integrated employment and social protection services (e.g. in Argentina,[39] Brazil and Germany[40]).

---

[34] A programme was initiated in the Russian Federation in 2010 to provide jobseekers with professional training, retraining, advanced training and certification.

[35] The United Kingdom's Work Programme offers personalized support to jobseekers through public, private or voluntary sector providers, who are paid on the basis of employment and job retention results.

[36] In Saudi Arabia, vocational training opportunities, specialized training and on-the-job training are provided through partnerships with private employers.

[37] Canada's Targeted Initiative for Older Workers helps unemployed older workers from small and vulnerable communities to upgrade their skills in order to go back to work.

[38] The Veterans Retraining Assistance Program (VRAP) supports military veterans in getting back to work by supplying up to 12 months of training programmes.

[39] The Argentinian Ministry of Employment and Labour implements several income transfers and support programmes to address the risks and consequences associated with unemployment and underemployment. The overall set of policies provides responses targeted at the specific needs of different groups. The contributory unemployment insurance programme (Seguro de Desempleo) provides some income compensation for formal employees who lose their jobs. As a complement, for formal employment, the programme for productive recovery (Programa de Recuperación Productiva) supports enterprises finding it difficult to retain jobs. In addition, for those not covered by the unemployment insurance programme and those who have exhausted their entitlement to benefits, the training and employment insurance scheme (Seguro de Capacitación y Empleo) provides vocational training and counselling through municipal employment offices. Also, the Interzafra programme facilitates transition between temporary or seasonal contracts by supporting workers with a cash allowance. Finally, the programme for more and better work for young people (Programa Jóvenes Más y Mejor Trabajo) aims at promoting social and labour market inclusion for young people through cash transfers, job counselling and educational support.

[40] The so-called "Hartz reforms" in Germany, particularly the unifying of unemployment assistance with social assistance in 2005 for those beneficiaries who are deemed employable, aimed at providing an integrated set of benefits and services for jobseekers and enhancing employability for recipients of social assistance (see, e.g., Alber and Heisig, 2011; Clasen and Goerne, 2011).

These integrated packages are aimed not only at recipients of unemployment benefits, but also at bringing recipients of other types of social assistance benefits under a common umbrella of activation policies (Clasen and Clegg, 2011). For example, Germany and France have implemented measures to combine unemployment benefits with social assistance for employable beneficiaries, and to merge their administration with employment services into "one-stop shops", with a stronger emphasis on decentralized services based on individualized "inclusion contracts".[41] Such policies are particularly relevant in the context of high levels of long-term unemployment, taking into account that discouraged workers may cease to be registered with employment services.

While such measures are intended to provide an integrated package of support to individuals, combining cash benefits with employment services, skills development and psycho-social support where necessary, some concerns have been expressed that individualized inclusion contracts may weaken social rights, if they lead to legal frameworks not being applied in a homogeneous manner (Künzel, 2011).

Also, while participation in training, retraining and other similar measures is intended to facilitate a quicker return to employment, an expectation or requirement to participate can also mean stricter control in the provision of benefits and additional obligations for jobseekers with regard to their entitlements to benefits. These measures may lead to the exclusion of, or discrimination against, certain groups of beneficiaries and the restriction of effective access to benefits. Careful design and implementation of activation measures is therefore necessary to ensure that these do not lead to unintended effects.

3.2.9 Challenges

As highlighted in this section, unemployment protection plays a multiple role in guaranteeing income security for unemployed workers while also supporting the structural transformation of national economies and mitigating demand shocks. One of the lessons learned from the global crisis is the importance of having effective unemployment benefit systems in place prior to a crisis in order to ensure that these are fully functional as automatic stabilizers of aggregate demand in the event of an economic downturn. However, a large number of countries lack effective unemployment benefit schemes and many others have schemes that provide only limited coverage. Consequently, the potential of such schemes to address employment shocks, as well as to support economic change, remains largely unfulfilled. In view of this, it is all the more encouraging that unemployment protection schemes have been recently introduced in several emerging economies, and that other countries are considering similar reforms. At the same time, increased efforts are needed to introduce measures, where possible, to enhance the effectiveness of existing schemes and to strengthen their links with programmes that support entry or re-entry into employment, skills upgrading and other active labour market policies.

In order to improve protection in countries with a high proportion of informal employment, which is usually accompanied by large-scale structural underemployment, it may be necessary to combine a variety of measures. These may include unemployment insurance alongside employment guarantee schemes and social assistance or other cash transfer programmes, depending on national context, which together can form an effective social protection floor for unemployed workers and their families, in accordance with Recommendation No. 202.

Unemployment benefits have not functioned alone in protecting incomes, promoting employment and enabling a quick recovery during the global crisis. Measures taken to strengthen other social security benefits, such as pensions, sickness benefits, social assistance benefits and access to health care, also play an important role in softening the impact of the crisis on private households and economies alike.

Coordination of unemployment protection with other social security policy areas is thus essential, as is coordination with employment and employment-related services. In order to be fully effective in supporting economic change and responses to shocks, unemployment benefits need to be complemented by training, retraining and other active labour market policies. These opportunities should be available to recipients of unemployment benefits as well as to non-recipients, and to all workers, whether in formal employment or operating in the informal economy. Effective coordination with such employment policies will enable unemployment benefits to fulfil their role in the most efficient way.

[41] In Germany, since the reforms of 2005 (see note 40), the administration of these cash benefits is combined with employment services in job centres. Social assistance is now limited to those who are not employable, and is administered separately. In France, an active inclusion policy is followed through the Revenu de Solidarité Active (2009), whose administration and linkage with employment services is highly decentralized.

3.3 Employment injury protection

KEY MESSAGES

- Worldwide, only 33.9 per cent of the labour force is covered by law for employment injury through mandatory social insurance. If voluntary social insurance coverage and employer liability provisions are included, 39.4 per cent of the labour force is covered by law.
- In practice, actual access to employment injury protection is even lower, largely owing to incomplete enforcement of the legislation in many countries.
- The low coverage of employment injury compensation in many low- and middle-income countries points to an urgent need to enhance working conditions in respect of occupational safety and health, as well as improving employment injury coverage for all workers, including those in the informal economy.
- As more countries move from employer liability as the basis for employment injury protection to a mechanism based on social insurance, levels of protection for workers are likely to improve – but only if new laws are effectively enforced.

3.3.1 Protecting workers affected by employment injury

Employment injury benefit schemes, providing benefits in cash and in kind in cases of work-related accidents and occupational disease, constitute in many countries the oldest branch of social security. These schemes were established to address one of the key challenges in modern workplaces. As a corollary of their responsibility to ensure working conditions which secure the occupational safety and health of their workers, employers are responsible for ensuring fair, equitable and effective compensation of workers (and, in the event of death, of their survivors) for the loss of income suffered as a consequence of an accident or occupational disease and for their access to the necessary health care (covering medical and allied care services and goods, including rehabilitation). Where such mechanisms are not in place, the only hope of redress for a person injured at work, or for her or his survivors, lies in action against the employer in the ordinary courts. Lawsuits of this type are generally lengthy, expensive and stressful for victims, and thus are rarely efficient in providing effective compensation to injured workers and the family or other dependants of deceased workers.

Non-adversarial schemes were thus introduced in a number of countries at an early stage, with a view to ensuring the timely provision of benefits to injured workers and their dependants, the establishment of predictable and sustainable financing mechanisms, and the efficient administration of funds. The first generation of such schemes consisted in "workmen's compensation schemes", under which the compensation of a worker or his/her surviving family dependants is a legal liability placed upon the employer. Underpinning this approach is the principle that employers must provide their workers with a safe and healthy working environment, and that failure to do so renders them liable for the consequent losses suffered by workers or their family members. Given that the financial burden of meeting this obligation rests solely on employers, these schemes often require them to take out private insurance. Experience has shown, however, that even where such an obligation exists in law, the outcomes of these schemes are often sub-optimal. The need to process an insurance claim, involving the need to obtain relevant information and undergo rigorous medical assessments, can cause serious delays in obtaining treatment and benefits. In addition, an employer may be reluctant to make a claim for fear of other legal implications. In recognition of these drawbacks, many countries have replaced employer liability provisions with social insurance, which in effect extends the no-fault principle to share the costs of employment injury across society (or at least that part represented in the formal labour market) as a whole.

This shift in approach to employment injury protection has been reflected in the standards adopted by the ILO from its early days (see box 3.7).

The effectiveness of programmes in addressing the specific contingency of employment injury relies on a specific set of principles:

1. "no fault": a worker who is injured, or his/her survivor(s) in case of death, should qualify for benefits without any necessity to prove "fault" on behalf of the employer;
2. collective sharing of liability; and
3. neutral governance at some specified level of administration of the scheme, meaning that the right to benefit can be established outside the contractual relationship between a worker and her or his employer.

Box 3.7 International standards relevant for employment injury protection

The right to protection against employment injury is enshrined in the Universal Declaration of Human Rights (UDHR), 1948, and the International Covenant on Economic, Social and Cultural Rights (ICESCR), 1966. The realization of this right requires the application of safe and healthy working conditions, the prevention, treatment and control of occupational diseases, and the provision of adequate benefits, in cash or in kind, that ensure access to adequate health care and income security to victims of employment injury and their dependent family members.[1]

Protection from employment injury has been the object of a number of Conventions and Recommendations adopted by the ILO from its early days. According to Convention No. 102 (Part VI), any condition that impacts negatively on health and which is due to a work accident or an occupational disease, and the incapacity to work and earn that results from it, whether temporary or permanent, total or partial, must be covered. The protection also includes, where a worker dies as a consequence of an employment injury or occupational disease, the loss of support suffered by her or his dependants. Accordingly, the provision must include medical and allied care, with a view to maintaining, restoring or improving the health of the injured person and her or his ability to work and attend to personal needs. A cash benefit must also be paid to the injured person or his/her dependants, as the case may be, at a guaranteed level and on a periodic basis, serving an income replacement or support function. Where the disability is slight, the benefit can, under certain conditions, be paid as a lump sum.

The Employment Injury Benefits Convention, 1964 (No. 121), and its accompanying Recommendation, No. 121, set higher standards, mainly in terms of population coverage and level of benefits to be provided (see Annex III). Convention No. 121 also recognizes the importance of an integrated approach for improving working conditions, limiting the impact of employment injuries and facilitating the reintegration of persons with disabilities in the labour market and in society; for such purposes this Convention requires the State to take measures to prevent employment injuries, provide rehabilitation services and ensure that displaced workers find suitable re-employment.

The approach taken by Recommendation No. 202 is different, reflecting its focus on preventing or alleviating poverty, vulnerability and social exclusion through income security guarantees, rather than on specific life risks; as such, it recognizes sickness and disability, in whatever cause or degree, as a potential source of financial insecurity which should be addressed, in so far as it prevents people of working age from earning sufficient income. In the same way, Recommendation No. 202 calls for guaranteed access to at least essential health care for all in need, over the life cycle, irrespective of the origin of the disability or ill health for which such care is required. Basic income security and access to essential health care can be ensured through a variety of approaches, combining contributory and non-contributory schemes and different types of benefits, such as disability and employment injury benefits, as well as other social benefits, in cash or in kind. Particularly relevant to employment injury protection is the Recommendation's further call for the combination of preventative, promotional and active measures with benefits and social services, and the coordination of social protection policies with policies that promote, among other things, secure work within a decent work framework.

[1] UDHR, Article 25(1), ICESCR, Art. 7 (b), 12 (b) and (c). See also ICESCR, General Comment No. 19, "The right to social security" (Art. 9), paras 2 and 16(e).

Within this framework, the aim of employment injury provisions in most countries is to meet the needs of workers who are incapacitated by injury at work or occupational disease, or of their dependent family members, by way of:

- appropriate and relevant medical and allied care,
- income replacement, by way of periodic cash benefits, in case of disablement, which may be assessed as
  - temporary or permanent,
  - partial or total, and
- contingent benefits (periodic cash payments and funeral grants) payable to survivors (widow/er, children or other dependent relatives, as the case may be) in case of death.

Many national employment injury schemes have a set of wider aims, such as the re-employment of injured or sick workers, and the promotion and maintenance of decent levels of safety and health in the workplace. These objectives can only be achieved effectively if there is a high level of policy integration, not only between the various branches of social security schemes, but also between those and policies relating to labour markets, labour inspection and occupational safety and health (OSH).

The provision of adequate compensation in case of permanent partial disability represents one of the greatest challenges in the employment injury branch of social protection. An approach which focuses on the loss of *bodily function* tends to compensate essentially for the physiological loss and may result in either over- or under-compensation from the economic point of view, even if the degree of disability is not assessed exclusively on the basis of medical factors. An approach based on *earning capacity* attempts to relate the level of benefit to the economic loss arising from the injury; this imposes demanding administrative requirements for the management of claims, and needs to be complemented by well-developed rehabilitation services in order to develop the residual capacities of injured workers. This in turn requires the full engagement of employers in the rehabilitation programme if it is to succeed. To achieve it, a rating system considering the past performance of employers in respect of occupational injury and disease can be used as an incentive to encourage employers' participation in facilitating the return to work of injured workers, but this is possible only in medium and large firms.

When it comes to implementation, another important criterion for measuring the effectiveness of employment injury schemes is the ability of the system to ensure that injured workers have access to the health-care facilities, goods and services they need, and that cash benefits reach injured workers or their survivors without delay. The timely delivery of benefits requires the setting-up of effective reporting systems and accompanying measures to assist victims and their survivors in accessing employment injury insurance through simple and efficient claims procedures. Online reporting systems of occupational accidents and diseases are among the tools that can be used to facilitate access.

3.3.2 Types of employment injury protection schemes

The majority of countries have adopted a social insurance approach to employment injury, though some countries have retained some elements of the employer liability approach. This may facilitate the coverage of workers who are not compulsorily included in such schemes, but who may wish to participate on a voluntary basis. In a very few countries, most notably the Netherlands, employment injury coverage has been fully integrated with schemes providing coverage for non-work-related disabilities.

Figure 3.12 Employment injury protection: Distribution by type of programme, 2012/13

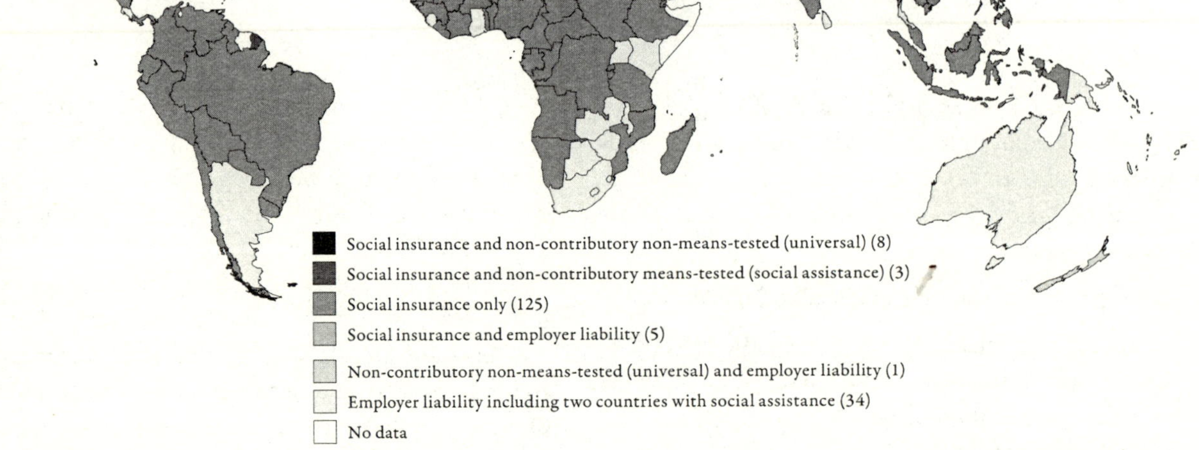

Notes: Figures in brackets refer to the number of countries in each category. In the Netherlands, there is no specific employment injury programme. The provisions of the 1966 and 1968 legislation pertaining to sickness and maternity benefits and disability pensions programmes (social insurance type) apply to all incapacities, whether work-related or not. These schemes are classified here as social insurance. In the eight countries that combine a universal type of scheme with social insurance, "universal" applies to medical care. For individual country information, see Annex IV, table B.4.

Sources: ILO calculations based on SSA and ISSA, 2012; SSA and ISSA, 2013a; SSA and ISSA, 2013b; SSA and ISSA, 2014.

Link: http://www.social-protection.org/gimi/gess/RessourceDownload.action?ressource.ressourceId=43177.

Figure 3.12 illustrates the patterns of coverage worldwide. It can be seen that the emphasis on social insurance, as opposed to first-generation schemes operating under employer's liability, is strongest in Europe, Central Asia and the Middle East, and lower in the Americas, Africa, and Asia and the Pacific. In the latter regions, employer liability provisions are still in place in a number of countries.

3.3.3 Extent of legal coverage

Legal coverage for employment injury protects mostly those in formal employment, whereas workers in informal employment are rarely covered. Figure 3.13 summarizes worldwide coverage and regional variations. At the global level, only 33.4 per cent of the total labour force, and only 31.7 per cent of the female labour force, is mandatorily covered by law through social insurance. When voluntary social insurance coverage and employer liability provisions are included, 39.6 per cent of the labour force is covered by law (36.7 per cent of the female labour force); effective coverage rates, however, may be significantly lower (see below). Not surprisingly, legal coverage rates reflect the general pattern of social protection coverage, with high levels in Europe (both Western and Eastern) and North America, more moderate but still substantial levels in Latin America, and much lower levels in sub-Saharan Africa and most of Asia.

Gender differences in legal coverage for employment injury are particularly high in the Middle East and Africa, where the coverage rates for women are respectively 18 and 13 percentage points lower than the overall coverage rates. In Latin American countries, the major gender difference is in access to social insurance, which reflects to a large degree the over-representation of women in various types of occupation that are usually excluded from legal coverage, ranging from unpaid family work to self-employment.

3.3.4 Extent of effective coverage

Legal coverage does not necessarily translate into effective coverage, for a variety of reasons; indeed, as figure 3.14 shows, the two diverge widely in many countries. In most countries for which data are available, the number of contributors (in most cases employers contribute on behalf of their employees) lags behind the number of those covered by law. The figure highlights in particular a small group of countries which, on a theoretical basis, reach high levels of coverage, but on the basis of voluntary participation (a principle adopted in particular to promote scheme access for self-employed workers). This is most striking in the cases of Indonesia and the United Republic of Tanzania, where legal coverage ratios, including voluntary coverage, stand at well above 70 per cent of the labour force, but where less than

Figure 3.13 Employment injury protection: Regional estimates of legal coverage (total and women), latest available year (percentage of labour force)

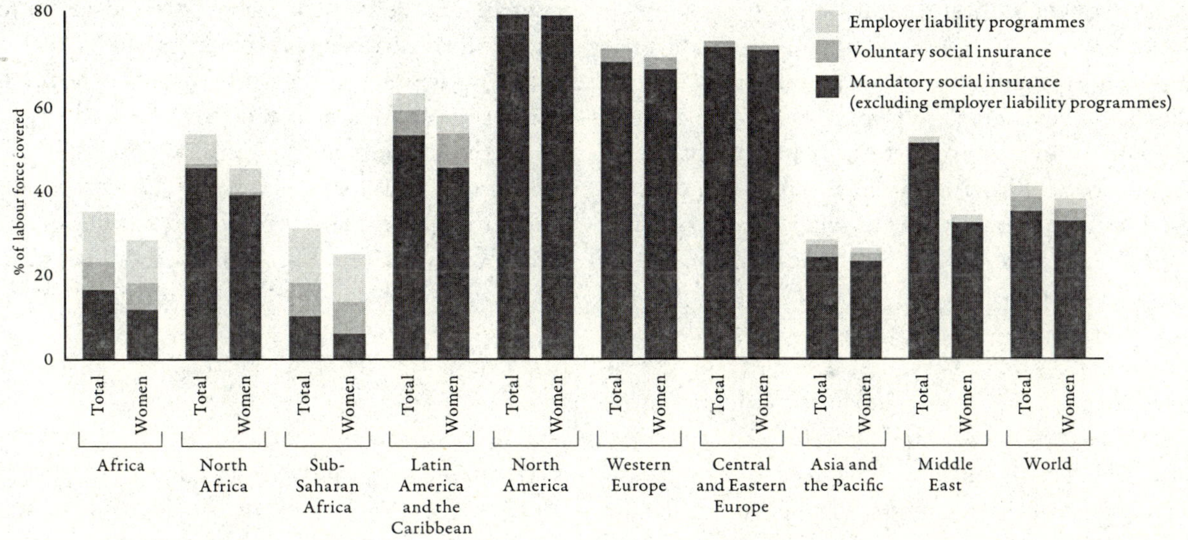

Notes: Regional and global estimates weighted by the labour force 2012 (ILO KILM, 8th ed.). For individual country information, see Annex IV, table B.4.

Sources: ILO Social Protection Department, based on SSA and ISSA, 2012; SSA and ISSA, 2013a; SSA and ISSA, 2013b; SSA and ISSA, 2014; ILO, LABORSTA (2014 data); ILO KILM (8th ed.); national legislative texts; national statistical data for estimates of legal coverage.

Link: http://www.social-protection.org/gimi/gess/RessourceDownload.action?ressource.ressourceId=37025.

Figure 3.14 Employment injury protection: Legal and effective coverage, latest available year (percentage of labour force)

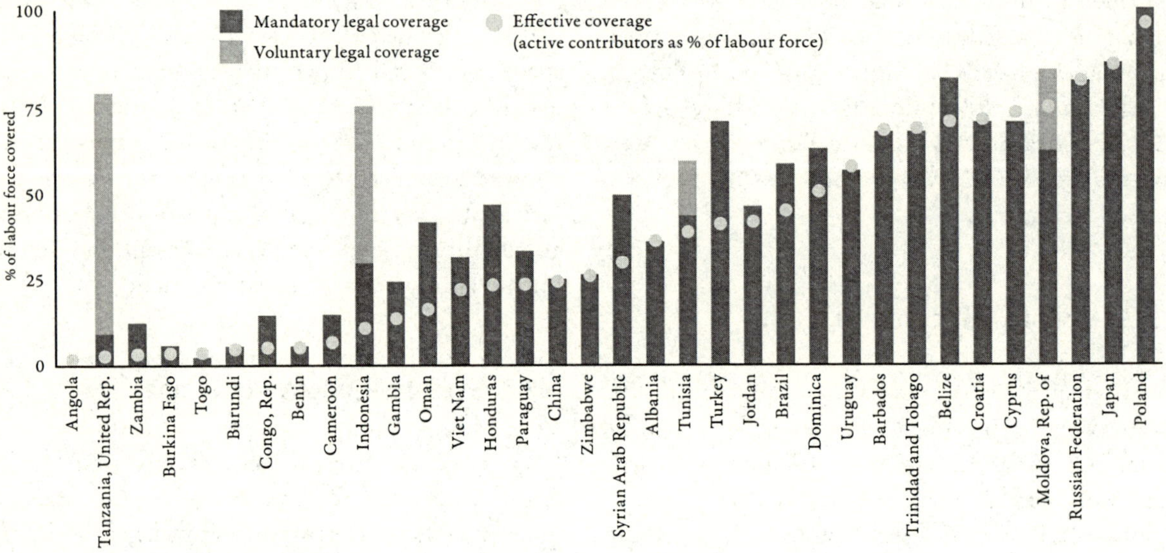

Source: For legal coverage, see figure 3.13. For effective coverage: ILO Social Security Inquiry database.
Link: http://www.social-protection.org/gimi/gess/RessourceDownload.action?ressource.ressourceId=37029.

10 per cent of the labour force is effectively covered in practice. It is in fact not uncommon for voluntary coverage to be taken up by a fraction of those eligible under the law. Possible reasons for this low take-up include low contributory capacities in the population covered, a lack of understanding of the importance of coverage, a mismatch between benefits offered and needs experienced, or overly complex procedures that deter participation.

3.3.5 Adequacy of benefits to cover workers' needs

Employment injury benefits for permanent disability are usually provided in the form of pensions. Schemes vary widely in the proportion of pre-disablement income provided (the replacement rate), as shown in figure 3.15. The same applies to temporary incapacity, as shown in figure 3.16, with further variation in the duration of the benefit.

The provision of suitable employment opportunities for workers disabled as the result of an employment injury is important.[42] China provides an interesting example. For certain degrees of disability, the employer must provide suitable employment or pay a pension equal to 60 per cent or more of the monthly net income of the injured worker.

3.3.6 Recent developments

From a global perspective, it is striking that while employment injury systems of some kind have been put in place in most countries, many low-income countries continue to rely on the principle of employer's liability rather than social insurance. It is, moreover, questionable whether countries with weak systems of enforcement and supervision have the capacity to monitor and ensure compliance with the law. In addition, workers' needs for effective protection in the event of employment injury are inadequately addressed in contexts where informality of employment prevails.

In this context, it is germane to note the implications of the accident which occurred at Rana Plaza in Dhaka, Bangladesh, in April 2013. Over 1,000 workers in industrial units located in the building lost their lives when it collapsed, and some 2,500 were injured (for more details, see box 3.8). It has been all too clear in the aftermath of this event that – among a host of interlinked issues of concern in respect of occupational health and safety, social protection and labour market conditions – the toll of human suffering is being compounded as a result of the lack of an effective scheme of employment injury protection. Recently, many countries have been developing and implementing national occupational safety and health programmes in line with

[42] This observation has similar aspects to the discussion of employment opportunities for older workers at the International Labour Conference in 2013 (ILO, 2013i).

Figure 3.15 Employment injury protection: Replacement rates for permanent disability

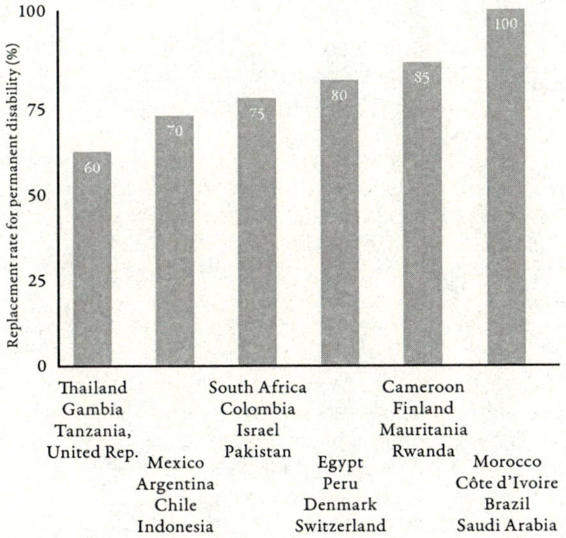

Sources: ILO calculations based on SSA and ISSA, 2012; SSA and ISSA, 2013a; SSA and ISSA, 2013b; SSA and ISSA, 2014.

Link: http://www.social-protection.org/gimi/gess/RessourceDownload.action?ressource.ressourceId=37031.

Figure 3.16 Employment injury protection: Replacement rates for temporary disability

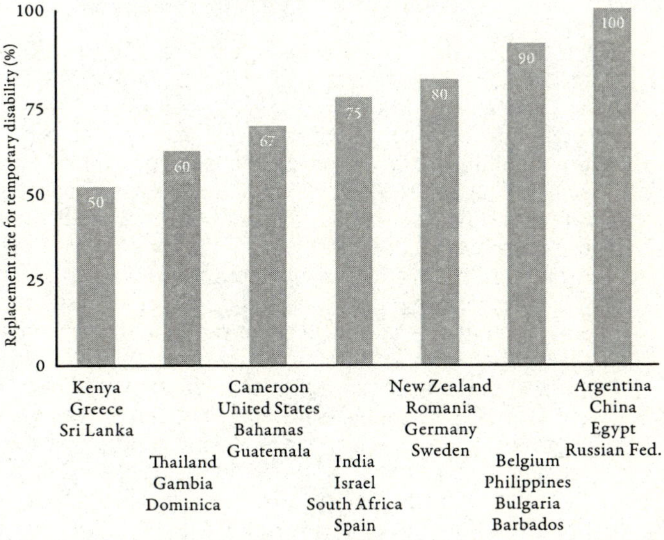

Sources: ILO calculations based on SSA and ISSA, 2012; SSA and ISSA, 2013a; SSA and ISSA, 2013b; SSA and ISSA, 2014.

Link: http://www.social-protection.org/gimi/gess/RessourceDownload.action?ressource.ressourceId=37030.

the ILO's Promotional Framework for Occupational Safety and Health Convention, 2006 (No. 187). These programmes can include employment injury insurance, strengthened reporting systems for occupational accidents and diseases, and mechanisms for timely compensation, and preventive measures.

The transition from employer's liability provisions to social insurance-based employment injury schemes, and the establishment of such schemes in countries which previously had no protection mechanism, constitutes a significant improvement in the social security of workers. In Cambodia, the employment injury scheme introduced in 2009 as the first branch of the social insurance scheme covered 1,800 enterprises and more than 500,000 workers (representing close to 20 per cent of employees, most of them women) by the end of 2010 (GIZ, ILO and P4H, 2012).

Another trend in recent years has been a stronger focus on enabling a faster return to work for beneficiaries. In a number of countries reforms were introduced to strengthen provisions for rehabilitation, among other measures (ISSA, 2012; OECD, 2010b; OECD, 2012a). While in some countries such measures were adopted with the objective of promoting rapid re-integration into working life, often requiring substantial additional upfront investments, in others such measures were taken with a clear cost-saving motive, often with ambivalent effects on the situation of beneficiaries.

3.3.7 Challenges

Employment injury coverage interacts with coverage in other areas of social security, such as health care. Nevertheless, the health-care needs of victims of occupational injury or disease may go beyond or differ from those of the majority of the people protected under general health-care schemes: for instance, the treatment of certain occupational diseases may require specific types of specialist care. It is therefore important to ensure that possible gaps are addressed. In this light, it is a matter of concern that, even within Europe, there are a number of countries where fiscal consolidation measures have entailed severe cutbacks in health care (see Chapter 5).

The financial needs addressed by employment injury schemes are similar to those of persons with disabilities incurred outside work. Contributory disability schemes which cover loss of earning capacity due to non-work-related disablements usually require the completion of a qualifying period before the person covered becomes entitled to a benefit. This requirement serves as a safeguard against abuse, and allows the proper financing of schemes to ensure the due payment of disability benefits on a long-term basis. By contrast, the qualifying conditions of employment injury benefit schemes should be designed in such a way that workers are protected against the consequences of employment

Box 3.8 The Rana Plaza disaster and its implications for social security in cases of employment injury

On 24 April 2013, the Rana Plaza building in Dhaka, Bangladesh, which housed five garment factories, collapsed, killing at least 1,132 people and injuring more than 2,500. Only five months earlier, at least 112 workers had lost their lives in another tragic accident, trapped inside the burning Tazreen Fashions factory on the outskirts of Dhaka. These disasters, among the worst industrial accidents on record, awoke the world to the poor labour conditions faced by workers in the ready-made garment sector in Bangladesh. For some of the lowest wages of the world, millions of people, most of them girls and women, are exposed every day to an unsafe work environment with a high incidence of work-related accidents and deaths, as well as occupational diseases. Most of the factories do not meet standards required by building and construction legislation. As a result, deaths from fire incidents and building collapses are frequent. In the absence of a well-functioning labour inspection system and of appropriate enforcement mechanisms, decent work and life in dignity are still far from reality for the vast majority of workers in the garment industry and their families.

Given the hazardous working conditions and the high risk of exposure to employment injury in this sector, the provision of adequate benefits is of critical importance to compensate injured workers for the loss of earnings they are likely to suffer, and to ensure that they have access to the medical and associated care required by their condition. Access to some form of financial compensation or support for dependent family members who lose their breadwinner can also make the difference between life in dire poverty, where children and older people are forced to work to survive, and life at or just above subsistence level. At present, the only form of financial protection available to workers and their dependants is set out in the labour code, which requires employers, when liable, to provide specified payments to injured workers or survivors.

A recent amendment to the labour code requires employers to insure themselves against liability, but no such obligation was in force at the time Tazreen caught fire, or when Rana Plaza collapsed. The amounts of compensation envisaged are also very low and take the form of lump sums, offering inadequate protection to beneficiaries against ill health and poverty in the medium and long term. The system is also plagued with major practical application issues (e.g. evasion, lack of proper enforcement, absence of effective recourse), with the result that legal entitlements very rarely materialize.

Despite the magnitude of the losses suffered by victims of the Tazreen and Rana Plaza accidents and their survivors, no compensation was paid in application of the labour code provisions on employer liability. A small number of global buyers and local players made some payments to victims in the months following the disasters, albeit on a voluntary basis. To redress the situation more substantively and ensure that injured workers and dependants of the deceased were effectively compensated, both financially and in respect of medical and other relevant care, global and local stakeholders got together and agreed to an unprecedented coordinated framework. With the ILO acting as a neutral chair, an "Arrangement" was adopted, providing a single approach to compensation consistent with ILO standards, and more specifically with the Employment Injury Benefits Convention, 1964 (No. 121).[1]

The Tazreen fire and the Rana Plaza accident prompted local authorities and other stakeholders to take major steps to strengthen occupational safety and health, labour inspection services, and skills training and rehabilitation services in the long term, with the support, notably, of the ILO and of global buyers. No concrete action has been taken, however, to develop a sound and effective framework for the provision of employment injury benefits, in line with ILO standards and Convention No. 121, that would apply beyond these specific incidents. There is, nevertheless, hope for the future, as such a measure is included in the National Tripartite Action Plan on Fire Safety for the Ready-Made Garment Sector adopted in May 2013.

[1] For more information on the Rana Plaza Arrangement, see the dedicated website at: http://www.ranaplaza-arrangement.org/ [accessed 24 Apr. 2014].

injury from their first day at work, and do not bear the health and financial risks of an unsafe or unhealthy work environment.

Employment injury benefits in case of permanent disability are long-term periodic payments, similar to other pensions, hence the need for an integrated approach within national systems. Integration prevents the duplication of benefits and enables the standardization of adjustment mechanisms to ensure that the purchasing power of benefits is maintained.

The global trend towards coverage under social insurance is encouraging. Such a framework helps to promote the rights- and solidarity-based perspective which is essential to the long-term health of social protection systems.

Complex issues may arise in the treatment of occupational diseases with long latency periods. While determining the time of occurrence of a work accident may not be problematic, determining the onset of an occupational disease may be more difficult. Many workers are currently exposed to working conditions that may or may not lead to the development of an occupational disease over a long period of time. Such problems can be even more difficult to manage in the circumstances of developing countries where relevant regulations, relating for example to protective clothing and other safeguarding measures, may be poorly enforced.

In those countries which have put in place employment injury insurance and workers' compensation schemes to address these needs, it is important that the schemes be administered on a fair and consistent basis. Medical examinations, diagnostics and assessments must be rigorous, and based on a national list of occupational diseases. Such lists, however, may not always be seen as sympathetic to claimants, and tend to reflect a particular set of national or local conditions and perceptions.[43]

Providing protection in cases of employment injury is an area of social security in which effective administration, and equitable treatment of claimants, plays a particularly crucial role. The role of administrators may be very wide, and closely interrelated with that of labour inspectors responsible for checking workplace safety as well as the whole range of measures to help prevent accidents at work, occupational injury and work-related diseases. An integrated framework comprising comprehensive occupational safety and health measures, strong inspection services and enforcement measures, as well as adequate cash and health-care benefits in the event of employment injury, accompanied by appropriate rehabilitation services, remains the best way to ensure that workers and their family dependants are effectively protected against the risks of employment injury.

3.4 Disability benefits[44]

KEY MESSAGES

- Effective measures to support persons with disabilities in finding and retaining quality employment are a key element of non-discriminatory and inclusive policies that help to realize their rights and aspirations as productive members of society.
- Complementing contributory schemes, non-contributory disability benefits play a key role in protecting those persons with disabilities who have not (yet) earned entitlements to contributory schemes, in particular those disabled from birth or before working age, and those who for any reason have not had the opportunity to contribute to social insurance for long enough to be eligible for benefits.
- Activation policies can play an important role in supporting persons with disabilities in finding suitable employment. They should be designed in such a way that they protect the rights of those who, for various reasons, are not able to find suitable employment, and for whom the introduction of such policies may result in a reduction of income security and potentially higher risk of poverty.
- Policy reforms should therefore pay special attention to finding the right balance between supporting engagement in employment and providing an adequate level of income security for persons with disabilities.

3.4.1 Protecting and enabling persons with disabilities

According to global estimates, persons with disabilities constitute some 15 per cent of the world's population; many of them live in developing countries. Around 785 million persons with disabilities are of working age (15 years or over) (WHO and World Bank, 2011). Many of them are engaged in the labour market, and many of them face greater disadvantage than others in accessing decent work that matches their skills and qualifications. Compared to others, persons with disabilities are less likely to be in full-time employment, more likely to find themselves in the informal economy and among the ranks of the working poor, and more likely to be unemployed and economically inactive (OHCHR, 2012; UN, 2013a; ILO, 2013d). Some persons with disabilities may also find it difficult to obtain

---

[43] As a result, statistics on employment injury benefits may reflect a considerably lower degree of cross-national comparability than is the case for other areas covered in this report.

[44] This section focuses on disability which arises outside employment and that is not the result of an employment injury. For an overview of the state of the world's social security coverage of disability resulting from employment injury, see section 3.3 above.

Box 3.9 Disability benefits for income protection: Relevant international standards

The international human rights legal framework contains many explicit references to the right to social protection of persons with disabilities. The Universal Declaration of Human Rights, 1948, and the International Covenant on Economic, Social and Cultural Rights, 1966, contain a general recognition of this right, while the UN Convention on the Rights of Persons with Disabilities (CRPD) goes into more detail.[1] Together, they recognize the right of persons with disabilities to an adequate standard of living for themselves and their families, including adequate food, clothing and housing, to the continuous improvement of living conditions, to social security and to the highest attainable standard of health. More specifically, according to the CRPD, States must safeguard and promote the realization of their right to social protection without discrimination on the basis of disability, providing equal access to appropriate and affordable services and devices and other assistance with disability-related needs; social protection and poverty reduction programmes; assistance with disability-related expenses; public housing programmes; and retirement benefits and programmes. The Convention also lays down the right of persons with disabilities to the enjoyment of the highest attainable standard of health without discrimination on the basis of disability. To this end, States must take all appropriate measures to ensure access for persons with disabilities to health services that are gender-sensitive, including health-related rehabilitation.

In a complementary way, successive standards adopted by the ILO set both basic minimum and higher standards of income protection which should be guaranteed to persons with disabilities in replacement of the income they were earning before disablement, or would have been earning from employment had they been able to work. More specifically, Convention No. 102 (Part IX – Invalidity Benefit) deals with the contingency of total disablement (not due to an employment injury) which results in a person's inability to engage in any gainful activity and which is likely to be permanent. In these circumstances, protection is to be provided through periodic cash benefits, subject to certain conditions. The Invalidity, Old-Age and Survivors' Benefits Convention, 1967 (No. 128), in its Part II, deals with the same subject matter but sets higher standards for disability benefits schemes. Its accompanying Recommendation, No. 131,[2] broadens the definition of the contingencies that should be covered under national schemes by including partial disability, which should give rise to a reduced benefit, and by introducing the incapacity to engage in an activity involving substantial gain among the criteria for disability assessments. Convention No. 128 also requires the provision of rehabilitation services designed to enable persons with disabilities to either resume their employment or perform another activity suited to their aptitudes.

Although medical care, including medical rehabilitation, is dealt with in separate provisions in Convention No. 102 (Part II) and the Medical Care and Sickness Benefits, Convention, 1969 (No. 130) – discussed at greater length in Chapter 5 – a comprehensive, coherent and integrated approach to disability benefits, such as the one set forth in the ILO's normative framework, requires that equal attention be given to the income support and medical needs of persons with disabilities. Hence, the standards set as regards the provision of medical care, including medical rehabilitation,[3] are highly relevant; such care should be "afforded with a view to maintaining, restoring or improving [their] health … and [their] ability to work and to attend to [their] personal needs".[4] Convention No. 102 further requires the institution or government department administering medical care to cooperate with the general vocational rehabilitation services "with a view to the re-establishment of handicapped persons in suitable work" (Art. 35).

Recommendation No. 202 also puts forward an integrated and comprehensive approach to social protection and disability benefits, according to which persons with disabilities should enjoy the same guarantees of basic income security and access to essential health care as other members of society through national social protection floors. These guarantees can be provided through a variety of schemes (contributory and non-contributory) and benefits (in cash or kind), as is most effective and efficient in meeting the needs and circumstances of persons with disabilities to allow them to live in dignity. Some of the principles set out in the Recommendation are of particular relevance for persons with disabilities, including the principles of non-discrimination, gender equality and responsiveness to special needs, as well as respect for the rights and dignity of people covered by the social security guarantees.

[1] UDHR, Art. 25(1), ICESCR, Art. 9, 11, 12, CRPD, Art. 25, 28. [2] Invalidity, Old-Age and Survivor's Benefits Recommendation, 1967 (No. 131). [3] Convention No. 130, Art. 13(f). [4] Conventions Nos 102, Art. 34(4), and 130, Art. 9.

or hold down employment due to their impairments or a non-supportive environment, or may be able to work only to a limited extent because of their impairments, and therefore have specific social protection needs.

Social protection systems play a key role in meeting the specific needs of persons with disabilities with regard to income security, social health protection and social inclusion. Elements of social security systems that explicitly address disability-related needs include schemes or programmes that provide income support to persons with disabilities and their families (such as contributory or non-contributory disability pensions, other disability-related benefits and general social assistance), social health protection and other mechanisms to ensure universal health coverage.[45] Schemes and programmes that support the (re-)integration of persons with disabilities into the labour market and facilitate their participation in employment also play a key role. In this respect, financial support to cover the disability-related costs associated with having a job can help persons with disabilities to avoid falling into poverty traps and facilitate their participation in productive employment (OHCHR, 2012; UN, 2013a).

Almost all countries offer at least a basic level of protection for persons with disabilities, but do so within a variety of frameworks. In general, schemes tend to distinguish between permanent and temporary disability, and between different types and degrees of disability, in recognition of the fact that people with different kinds and duration of disability can have very different needs.[46] This is so not only in terms of benefits to provide for income and livelihoods, and of appropriate health care, but also in terms of rehabilitation, retraining and re-employment services. In respect of all of these factors, and also in the very definitions adopted, schemes designed in individual countries vary widely.

Employment injury benefits (see section 3.3 above) are highly relevant for persons with employment-related disabilities who benefit from coverage (mainly workers in the formal economy). For those who are not covered by such provisions, or where these do not exist, income security is largely dependent on general disability benefits. In line with international standards (see box 3.9), such benefits should meet a number of criteria in order to produce the desired outcomes: schemes should be designed to meet specific disability-related needs; they should not prevent access to other social security benefits, unless serving the same function; benefits should be provided on a non-discriminatory basis; and benefits should not act as a disincentive to seeking employment.

3.4.2 Types of disability benefit schemes

Disability benefits may take various forms, depending on the type and objectives of the scheme(s) in place in a given country. In many countries, disability cash benefits are accompanied by benefits in kind, such as free and adapted public transport, access to other public services free of charge, free or subsidized ergonomic equipment, etc. While these benefits in kind have a monetary value and therefore contribute to guaranteeing income security, this section of the chapter focuses on cash benefits, which account for the majority of disability benefits. Almost all countries have a scheme anchored in law that provides cash benefits to persons with disabilities (see figure 3.17). In a majority of countries (155) this is done at least partly through social insurance schemes. These mainly cover employees in the formal economy, and generally provide earnings-related disability benefits that serve as income replacement in case of full or partial disability. In 27 countries (20 of which also have social insurance schemes), disability benefits are provided through a non-contributory universal scheme to all persons with assessed disabilities without regard to their income status. In 54 countries, social insurance is combined with means-tested benefits. In a further six countries, disability benefits are limited to means-tested benefits only. In 11 countries, the law provides for lump sums to be paid; four countries have no such scheme anchored in national legislation.

As figure 3.17 shows, in a significant number of countries (81) the only form of income protection available to persons with disabilities consists of benefits paid through employment-related social insurance. Although in some countries disability-related needs may be covered through general social assistance benefits, the lack of specific non-contributory disability benefits raises concerns about the lack of protection of children with disabilities (UNICEF, 2013), and of adults with disabilities who have never been able to work (whether because their disability existed at birth, or they became disabled before working age, or they had no access to education and, consequently, no access to employment) and so have never been able to contribute to social insurance. Without access either to employment with social security coverage, or to non-contributory benefits, persons with disabilities and their families are more at risk of poverty.

Some important regional differences can be observed regarding the scope of coverage (see figure 3.18). A first group of countries ensure the provision of disability cash benefits to eligible persons through social insurance mechanisms. These may be combined with non-contributory universal (or categorical) benefits, as in several countries in northern Europe (Finland, Denmark, Iceland), Eastern Europe and the CIS (Armenia, Azerbaijan, Russian Federation, Hungary), together

[45] For discussion of universal health coverage, see Chapter 5 below.

[46] It is also necessary to recognize that disability is a result of the interaction between a person with impairments and barriers in society, in line with the UN Convention on the Rights of Persons with Disabilities.

Figure 3.17 Overview of cash disability benefit programmes anchored in national legislation, by type of programme and benefit, 2012/13

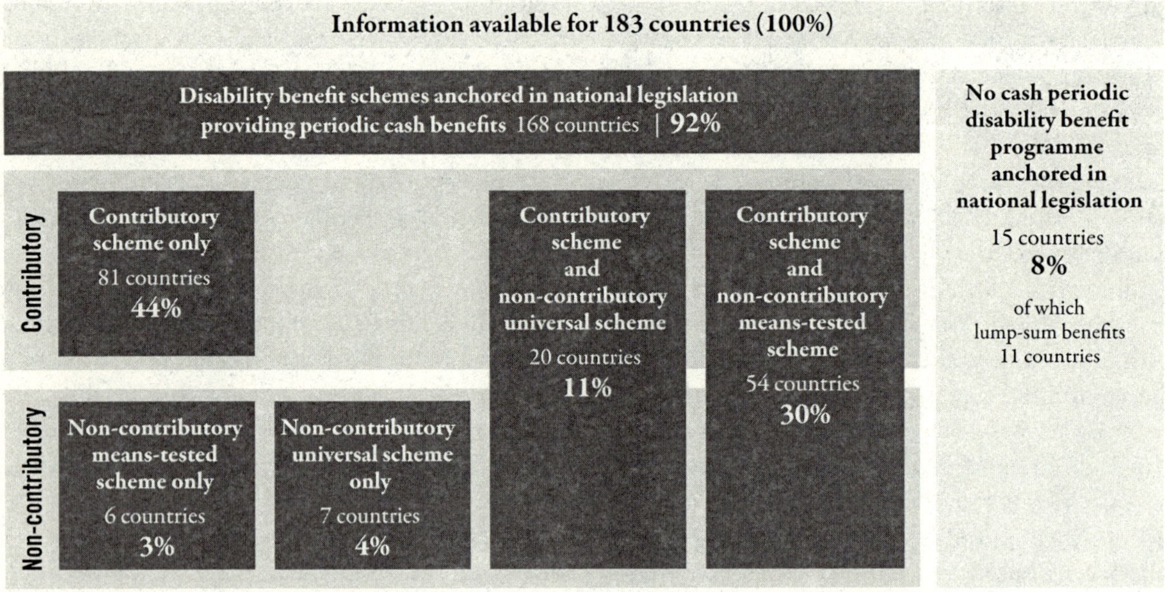

Sources: SSA and ISSA, 2012; SSA and ISSA, 2013a; SSA and ISSA, 2013b; SSA and ISSA, 2014; European Commission, Mutual Information System on Social Protection (MISSOC), accessed Dec. 2013; Council of Europe, Mutual Information System on Social Protection of the Council of Europe (MISSCEO), accessed Dec. 2013); OHCHR, 2012.

Link: http://www.social-protection.org/gimi/gess/RessourceDownload.action?ressource.ressourceId=42448.

Figure 3.18 Income support for persons with disabilities: Existence and type of programmes, 2012/13

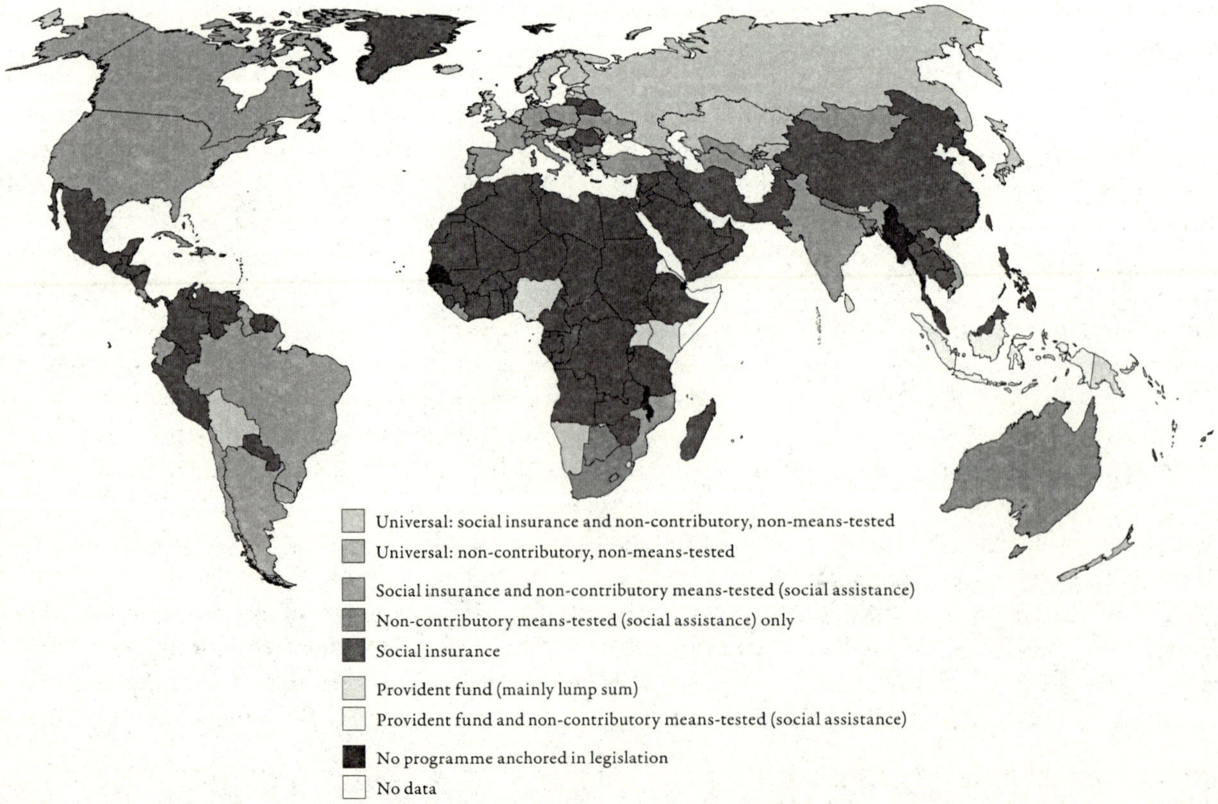

Sources: See figure 3.17.

Link: http://www.social-protection.org/gimi/gess/RessourceDownload.action?ressource.ressourceId=42317.

with a few from other regions (notably the Plurinational State of Bolivia, Namibia and Mauritius); some other countries (Brunei, Hong Kong (China), New Zealand, Timor-Leste) rely simply on non-contributory provision.

In 54 countries, mainly in Western Europe and Latin America, social insurance is complemented by poverty-targeted schemes, either specific to persons with disabilities or within more widely integrated social assistance programmes (as for instance Bono de Desarrollo Humano in Ecuador). A third group of countries, including Australia, South Africa and Nepal, have schemes which simply target poor persons with disabilities. A fourth group of 81 countries, mainly in Africa, the Middle East as well as Asia and the Pacific, provide social insurance benefits but exclude from that protection people outside formal employment. In these countries, it can be assumed that more limited coverage is likely to be achieved in the absence of a specific disability scheme to respond to the needs of persons with disabilities who are not in formal employment. In many of these cases, such people can gain access to benefits only through general social assistance programmes which cater partially for their specific needs. In addition, the extent to which national schemes provide for persons with disabilities may be curtailed by "capped" budgetary allocations: this has been the case for the scheme in Nepal, which has notionally wide outreach, and seems likely to happen as a result of recent reforms taken in the light of moves towards fiscal consolidation even in the better-off European countries, including the United Kingdom. Similarly, Indonesia's Jaminan Sosial Penyandang Cacat programme, while in principle providing cash transfers to people with severe disabilities in the poorest 40 per cent of the population, is subject to a limitation on funds resulting in very low coverage, estimated at 1.8 per cent of the target group (ILO, 2012e). On the other hand, the integrated Bono de Desarrollo Humano programme in Ecuador offers an encouraging illustration of extension of coverage to a significant proportion of persons with disabilities, who made up 1.7 per cent of beneficiaries in 2012, as compared with just 0.1 per cent before 2007 (Cecchini and Madariaga, 2011).

3.4.3 Effective coverage for disability benefits

From the above review of the types of programmes in existence, it is possible to draw some inferences about levels of coverage, although the extent of available data does not allow for a fully detailed statistical assessment on the global scale. In order to calculate effective coverage ratios, it would be necessary to relate the number of beneficiaries of disability benefits to the number of persons with disabilities affecting their earning capacity in each country.

In countries of the European Union, on average 27.9 per cent of persons with disabilities receive a disability benefit (see figure 3.19).[47] This coverage ratio

Figure 3.19 Europe: Persons with disabilities in working age and recipients of disability benefits, 2010

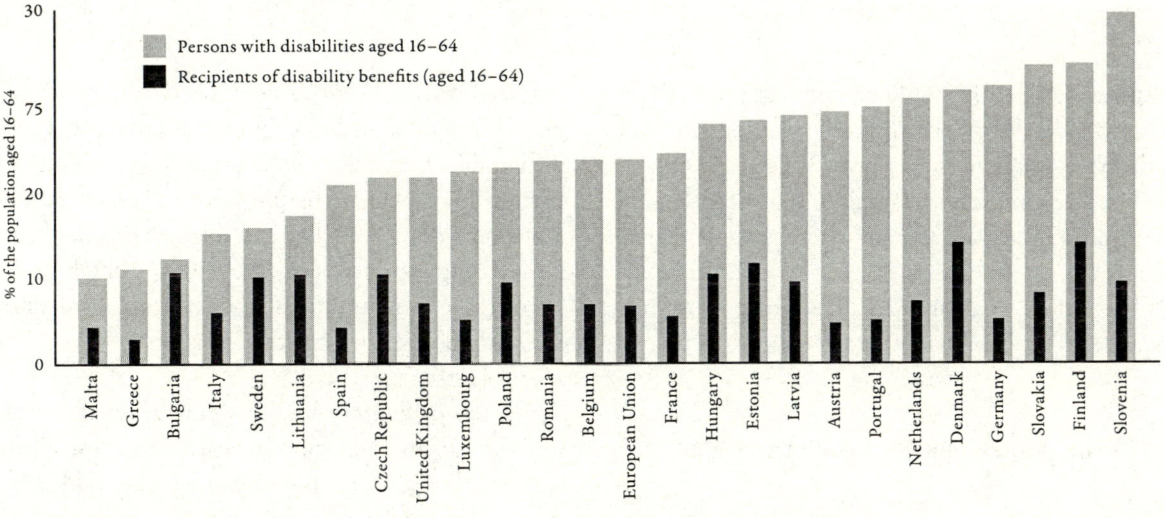

Source: Grammenos, 2013, based on EU-SILC data.

Link: http://www.social-protection.org/gimi/gess/RessourceDownload.action?ressource.ressourceId=42997.

[47] Unweighted average.

Box 3.10 Income security for persons with disabilities: Illustrations from Europe

Income security for persons with disabilities is a critical issue, in view of functional limitations and difficulties in accessing quality employment. At the EU level, the employment rate of persons with disabilities is much lower (45.5 per cent in 2010) than that of those without disabilities (71.7 per cent), and for those with severe disabilities it is lower still (26.2 per cent).

Disability benefits and other social security benefits can partially correct for some labour market inequalities, but only to a certain extent. In 2010, 19.1 per cent (19.9 per cent in 2009) of persons with disabilities compared with 14.7 per cent (14.3 per cent in 2009) of persons without disabilities lived in households classified as being at risk of poverty. The differential varies sharply between countries: it is relatively low in Hungary, Lithuania, Slovakia and the Netherlands but significantly greater in, for example, the United Kingdom, Slovenia and Portugal.

Figure 3.20 Europe: Rates of poverty risk among those of working age (16–64) by disability status, 2010 (percentages)

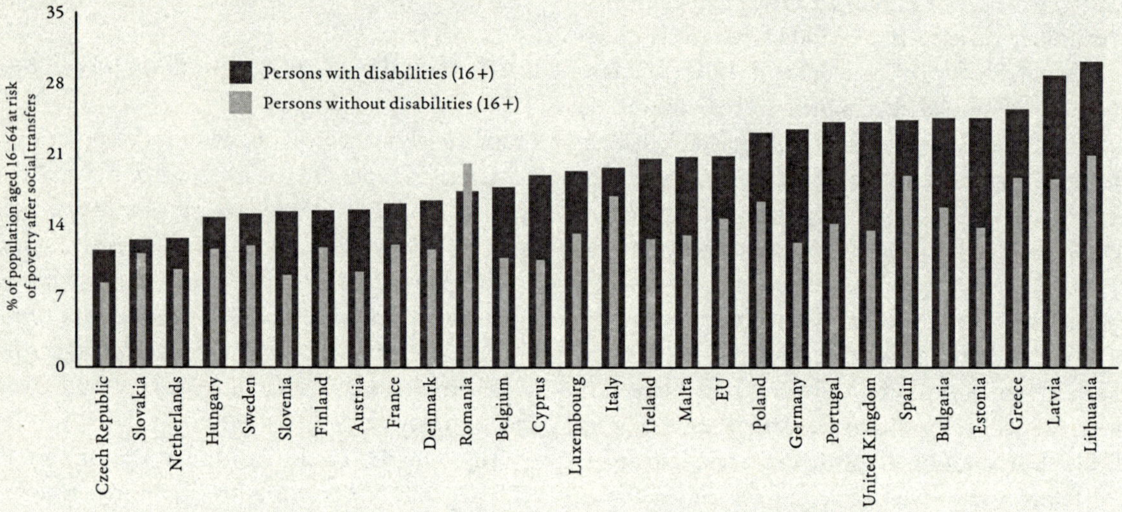

Source: Grammenos, 2013, based on EU-SILC data.

Link: http://www.social-protection.org/gimi/gess/RessourceDownload.action?ressource.ressourceId=42998.

Source: Based on Grammenos, 2013.

may appear low, but it should be noted that not all persons with a disability either need or are entitled to a benefit; benefits are normally provided to persons with disabilities that are severe enough to significantly affect their functional capacities, and thereby their earning capacity.

Nonetheless, persons with disabilities remain at higher risk of poverty than others (see box 3.10).

3.4.4 Recent developments and challenges

In recent years some countries have taken decisive steps to extend the coverage of disability benefits and enhance the adequacy of benefits (see box 3.11). Measures to extend the coverage of pension insurance to more groups of the population (e.g. self-employed, domestic workers) often include coverage for disability. The emergence of cash transfer programmes covering poor and vulnerable categories of the population is also of particular relevance, as the presence in the household of a person with a disability at a degree that affects his or her earning capacity is often one of the eligibility criteria of these programmes. Other existing non-contributory programmes have extended coverage by raising the means-testing threshold.

At the same time, disability benefits were not spared from fiscal consolidation measures introduced in the wake of the global crisis, some of which – adding to the more difficult labour market situation – significantly reduced income security for persons with disabilities (for examples, see box 3.11).

Some of the recent policy reforms continue a longer-standing trend to bring beneficiaries of disability

Box 3.11 Recent developments: Country examples

Some recent reforms in the area of disability benefits have aimed at extending coverage and better meeting the needs of persons with disabilities:

- In Paraguay, coverage was extended in 2013 to allow self-employed, female heads of household, and domestic workers, to enrol voluntarily in the disability insurance scheme (OASDI).
- South Africa extended the coverage for the disability grant in 2011 by applying a higher threshold for the means-test.
- In Ghana, the presence of a person with a severe impairment in a poor household is one of the eligibility criteria under the LEAP programme introduced in 2008.

Other recent reforms in the area of social protection for persons with disabilities include some fiscal consolidation measures:

- In Hungary, the disability pension was replaced in 2012 with a combination of a rehabilitation benefit (three years for retraining and re-entry in the labour force where feasible) and a significantly restricted disability benefit. The Government envisaged savings of around €800 million as a result.
- In Lithuania, between 2010 and 2012 both the Special Compensation for Care Expenses and the Special Compensation for Attendance Expenses were temporarily paid at 85 per cent of their normal value.
- In Ireland, disability benefits have been cut by about 5 per cent since 2008, including invalidity pensions for persons aged under 65, most long-term care cash benefits and the non-contributory disability allowance.

Sources: ISSA, 2013b; Eurofound European Working Conditions Observatory; Hauben et al., 2012; national sources.

Box 3.12 How social protection can help persons with disabilities gain access to employment

Measures to facilitate the transition from receiving benefits to performing work have been introduced in several countries. Examples include a requirement that employers provide occupational health services and support for reintegration and employment; and so-called "bridging arrangements", transitional arrangements which allow persons with disabilities who take up work to retain benefits until a certain wage threshold is reached, to resume receipt of benefits without delay should they lose their jobs, and to retain their right to benefits in kind – such as health care – for a specified period. This is the case in Australia, where, in order to encourage their greater participation in work, Disability Support Pension (DSP) recipients can now work for 30 hours per week before their benefit entitlements are affected. This change was combined with extra support for people with disability, including more employment services and financial incentives for employers to take on more persons with disabilities.

The Government in Ireland is committed to helping persons with disabilities to participate more fully in society, and to become more self-sufficient, by providing support to address financial and other barriers, as outlined in Department for Social Protection's disability sectoral plan. The Reasonable Accommodation Fund for the Employment of Disabled People functions as an umbrella covering a series of private sector employment support programmes to help persons with disabilities to access and progress in employment.

The Work Choice programme introduced in the United Kingdom in 2010 targets persons with disabilities facing complex barriers to employment to help them prepare to enter work, find a job, stay in work and progress into open, unsupported employment.

In Saudi Arabia, the Tawafuq programme was dedicated to the extension of jobseeking support to persons with disabilities, through an encompassing framework including six areas: regulations and frameworks; accessibility; stakeholder awareness; employment programmes; skills and training; and disability data.

The Government of the United States provides funding and technical support for states to develop their strategies for disability employment policy, and grants funds to states that improve education and employment outcomes of persons with disabilities.

In the Russian Federation, the introduction in 2013 of amendments to the Federal Law on the Social Protection of Persons with Disabilities was intended to fill a gap in the legal regulation of employment of persons with disabilities. Also in 2013, public organizations for persons with disabilities planned to offer assistance in finding employment and to create 692 jobs for persons with disabilities. The total amount of subsidies from the federal budget to support public organizations for persons with disabilities was set at 124.36 million roubles. Since 2010, more than 7,800 unemployed persons with disabilities have found employment at workplaces where employers have equipped their work spaces to meet their physical needs.

Source: Based on Aleksynska et al., 2013.

benefits into employment through measures that support the return to work and strengthen the employability of persons with disabilities (ILO and OECD, 2013; see also box 3.12). In OECD countries, most of the policy reforms prior to 2010 focused on contributory disability pensions, reducing levels of compensation and strengthening measures to bring beneficiaries (back) into employment (OECD, 2010b; ISSA, 2012). Some of these measures aimed to reverse the earlier trend of moving beneficiaries of unemployment benefits to disability benefit schemes: in several countries (e.g. Australia, Denmark, Luxembourg, the Netherlands and, more recently, Hungary), people with significant capacity for work are no longer eligible for partial disability benefits, but are supported in seeking part-time work through wage subsidies and other in-work benefits, or receive unemployment or other benefits. While in some countries such reforms have had a significant impact on eligibility conditions and benefit levels, they have had only limited success in increasing the proportion of persons with disabilities in employment. The reasons for this include an often unfavourable labour market situation and uneven implementation of effective rehabilitation, insertion and other measures intended to facilitate their (re-)integration into employment (OECD, 2010b).

This assessment highlights an ambiguity often found in activation policies. Effective measures that support persons with disabilities in finding and retaining quality employment are a key element of non-discriminatory and inclusive policies that help to realize their rights and aspirations as productive members of society. There is, however, a risk that such policies may restrict the rights of those who, for various reasons, are not able to find suitable employment, and for whom such reforms may result in a reduction of income security and potentially higher risk of poverty. Policy reforms should therefore pay special attention to finding the right balance between supporting engagement in employment and providing an adequate level of income security for persons with disabilities, and promoting their individual autonomy and independence, and their full and effective participation in society.

3.5 Maternity protection

KEY MESSAGES

- Effective maternity protection ensures income security for pregnant women and mothers of newborn children and their families, and also effective access to quality maternal health care. It also promotes equality in employment and occupation.
- Worldwide, less than 40 per cent of women in employment are covered by law under mandatory maternity cash benefit schemes; 57 per cent if voluntary coverage (mainly for women in self-employment) is included.
- Due to the ineffective enforcement and implementation of the law in some regions (Asia and the Pacific, Latin America and Africa in particular), effective coverage is even lower: only 28 per cent of women in employment worldwide are protected through contributory or non-contributory maternity cash benefits.
- An increasing number of countries are using non-contributory maternity cash benefits as a means to improve income security and access to maternal and child health care for pregnant women and new mothers, particularly for women living in poverty. However, significant gaps remain.
- Ensuring effective access to quality maternal health care is of particular importance, especially in countries where the informal economy accounts for a large proportion of employment.

3.5.1 Maternity protection: Ensuring income security, maternal health care and women's rights at work

Maternity protection is multidimensional. From a social security perspective, it includes protection against suspension or loss of income during maternity leave, and access to maternal health care (see ILO, 2010c). Maternity leave supported with cash benefits to fully or partially replace women's earnings during the final stages of pregnancy and after childbirth is of critical importance for the well-being of pregnant women, new mothers and their families. The absence of income security during the final stages of pregnancy and after childbirth forces many women, especially those in the informal economy, to return to work prematurely, thereby putting at risk their own and their children's health.

Box 3.13 International standards relevant to maternity protection

Maternity protection has long been regarded by the international community as an essential prerequisite for the achievement of women's rights and gender equality. Women's right to maternity protection is enshrined in a number of major human rights instruments. The Universal Declaration of Human Rights, 1948, notably states that motherhood and childhood are entitled to special care and assistance, as well as to social security. The International Covenant on Economic, Social and Cultural Rights, 1966, establishes the right of mothers to special protection during a reasonable period before and after childbirth, including paid leave or leave with adequate social security benefits. The Convention for the Elimination of All Forms of Discrimination Against Women, 1979, recommends that special measures be taken to ensure maternity protection, proclaimed as an essential right permeating all areas of the Convention.

The ILO has led the establishment of international standards on maternity protection, adopting the first international standard on this subject in the very year of its foundation: the Maternity Protection Convention, 1919 (No. 3). Since then, a number of more progressive instruments have been adopted in line with the steady increase in women's participation in the labour market in most countries worldwide. The current ILO maternity protection standards provide detailed guidance for national policy-making and action to enable women to successfully combine their reproductive and productive roles. To this end, the standards aim to ensure that women benefit from adequate maternity leave, income and health protection measures, that they do not suffer discrimination on maternity-related grounds, that they enjoy the right to nursing breaks and that they are not required to perform work prejudicial to their health or that of their child. In order to protect the situation of women in the labour market, ILO maternity protection standards specifically require that cash benefits be provided through schemes based on solidarity and risk-pooling, such as compulsory social insurance or public funds, while strictly circumscribing the potential liability of employers for the direct cost of benefits. At the same time, the relevant standards aim at ensuring that women have access to adequate maternal health care and services during pregnancy and childbirth, and beyond.

Convention No. 102 (Part VIII) sets minimum standards as to the population coverage of maternity protection schemes and for the provision of cash benefits during maternity leave, to address the suspension of earnings during this time (see Annex III, table AIII.7). The Convention also defines the medical care that must be provided free of charge at all stages of maternity, as required to maintain, restore or improve the health of the women protected and their ability to work, and to attend their personal needs. Maternal health care must be available not only to the women participating in a maternity protection scheme, but also to the wives of men covered by such schemes, at no cost to either.

The Maternity Protection Convention, 2000 (No. 183), and its accompanying Recommendation (No. 191), are the most up-to-date ILO standards on maternity protection. They set higher and more comprehensive standards on population coverage, health protection, maternity leave and leave in case of illness or complications, cash benefits, employment protection and non-discrimination, as well as breastfeeding.

Recommendation No. 202 calls for such benefits to be provided as part of the basic social security guarantees that make up social protection floors. These include access to essential health care, including maternity care, comprising a set of necessary goods and services, and basic income security for persons of active age who are unable to earn sufficient income due, inter alia, to maternity. Maternity medical care should meet criteria of availability, accessibility, acceptability and quality (United Nations, 2000); it should be free for the most vulnerable; and conditions of access should not be such as to create hardship or increase the risk of poverty for people in need of health care. Cash benefits should be sufficient to allow women and their children a life in dignity, out of poverty. Maternity benefits should be granted at least to all residents, with the objective of achieving universal protection; a variety of schemes can be used to achieve such coverage, including universal schemes, social insurance, social assistance and other social transfers, providing benefits in cash or in kind.

Another fundamental component of maternity protection is maternal health care, namely effective access to adequate medical care and services during pregnancy and childbirth, and beyond, to ensure the health of both mothers and children. As with health care in general (see Chapter 5), a lack of effective access to maternal health care coverage not only puts the health of women and children at risk, but also exposes families to significantly increased risk of poverty.

According to ILO standards (see box 3.13), maternity protection also includes the protection of women's rights at work during maternity and beyond, through measures that safeguard employment, protect women against discrimination and dismissals, and allow them to return to their jobs after maternity leave under conditions that take into account their specific circumstances (ILO, 2010c; ILO, 2013e; ILO, 2014e). It also includes occupational safety and health components that are essential to protect the health of pregnant and breastfeeding women and their babies, as well as women's reproductive capacity.

Box 3.14 Maternity protection: Collectively financed schemes vs employer's liability provisions

Maternity cash benefits can be provided by different types of schemes: contributory (e.g. social insurance), non-contributory, usually tax-financed (e.g. social assistance and universal schemes) and employer's liability provisions. Collectively financed schemes, funded from insurance contributions, taxation or both, are based on the principles of solidarity and risk-pooling, and therefore ensure a fairer distribution of the costs and responsibility of reproduction. Employer's liability provisions, on the other hand, oblige employers to bear the economic costs of maternity directly, which often results in a double burden (payment of both women's wages during maternity leave and costs of their replacement), although employers may be able to obtain commercial insurance to cover their liabilities. While some individual workers may obtain appropriate compensation under such provisions, employers may be tempted to adopt practices that deny women the income security to which they should be entitled in order to avoid the related costs and the financial hardship that they may entail for small businesses or in times of instability. Discrimination against women of childbearing age in hiring and in employment, and non-payment of due compensation by the employer, are more commonly evident in the absence of collective mechanisms to finance maternity protection. Pressure on women to resume work to the detriment of their health or that of their child may also be more prevalent where employers have to bear the costs of maternity leave.

In order to protect the situation of women in the labour market, Convention No. 183 states a preference for compulsory social insurance or publicly funded programmes as the vehicles for provision of cash benefits to women during maternity leave, confining individual employers' liability for the direct costs of benefits to a limited range of cases.[a] Where women do not meet qualifying conditions for entitlement to maternity cash benefits, Convention No. 183 requires the provision of adequate benefits financed by social assistance funds, on a means-tested basis.

Maternity cash benefits financed collectively have proved the more effective means of securing an income to women during maternity leave. In recent years, several countries have shifted from employer's liability provisions to collectively financed maternity benefits, a trend that represents an advance for the promotion of equal treatment for men and women in the labour market.

[a] According to Art. 6, para. 8, of Convention No. 183: "An employer shall not be individually liable for the direct cost of any such monetary benefit to a woman employed by him or her without that employer's specific agreement except where: (a) such is provided for in national law or practice in a member State prior to the date of adoption of this Convention by the International Labour Conference; or (b) it is subsequently agreed at the national level by the government and the representative organizations of employers and workers."

3.5.2 Types of maternity protection schemes

Maternity cash benefits are provided through schemes anchored in national social security legislation in 136 out of the 188 countries reviewed. A further two countries allow women to take maternity leave by law, but make no legal provision for replacement of their earned income.

Of those 188, 50 countries – 38 of them in Africa or Asia – have provisions in their labour legislation setting out a mandatory period of maternity leave and establishing the employer's liability for the payment of the woman's salary (or a percentage thereof) during that period (see box 3.14).

Most maternity cash benefit schemes and employer's liability provisions cover only women in formal employment. Consequently, in many low- and middle-income countries, where levels of formal employment are lower, maternity benefits are available only to a minority of women. Figure 3.21 shows the types of programmes existing in the 188 countries for which information is available. Social insurance schemes form the vast majority of these programmes, prevailing in 134 countries, of which 11 also operate social assistance schemes.[48]

3.5.3 Extent of legal coverage

Worldwide, the vast majority of women in employment are still not protected against loss of income in the event of maternity. Only 35.3 per cent of employed women benefit from mandatory coverage by law and thus are legally entitled to periodic cash benefits as income replacement during their maternity leave.[49] In 55 countries (67 countries when voluntary

[48] For more detailed characteristics of the schemes in place in different countries, see Annex IV, table B.5.

[49] When including voluntary coverage, legal coverage concerns nearly half of all women in employment (56.8 per cent), with the 20 additional percentage points concerning mainly the choice left to the self-employed to join (or not) the existing contributory scheme on a voluntary basis. In many countries, such voluntary provisions are taken up only sparsely; thus voluntary coverage may not reach the same level of protection as compared to mandatory coverage.

Figure 3.21 Maternity cash benefit schemes anchored in national legislation: Types of schemes, 2013

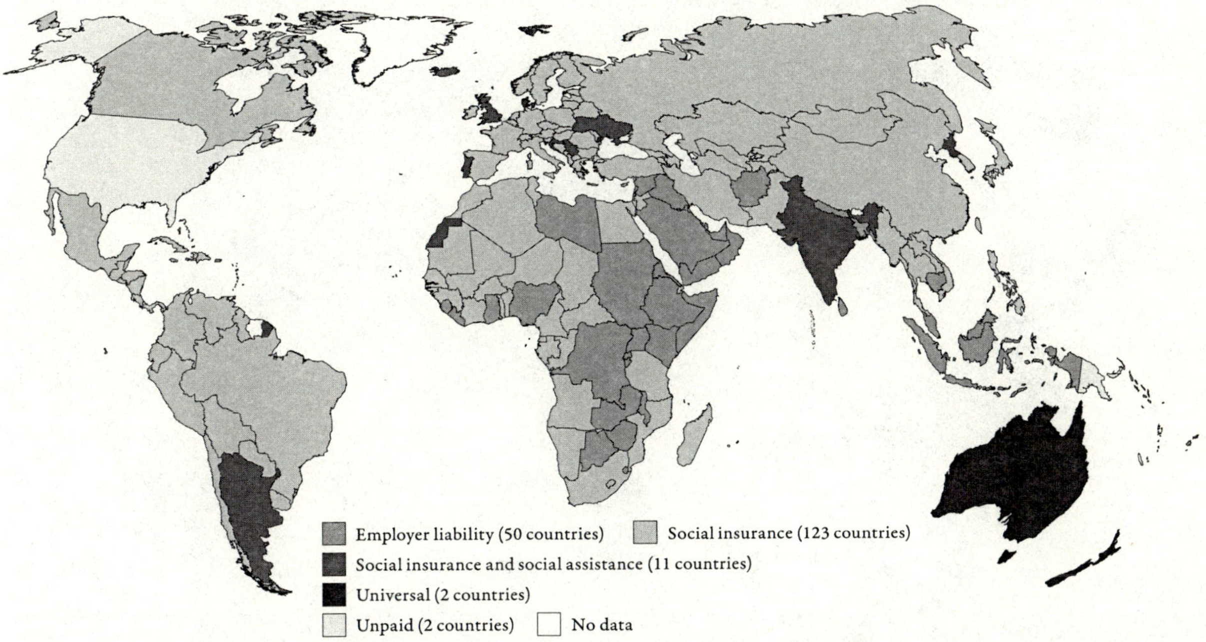

Note: In the United States there is no national programme. Under the Family and Medical Leave Act, 1993, maternity leave is unpaid as a general rule; however, subject to certain conditions accrued paid leave (such as vacation leave, personal leave, medical or sick leave, or paid medical leave) may be used to cover some or all of the leave to which a woman is entitled under the Act. A cash benefit may be provided at the state level. Provisions for maternity cash benefits exist in five states (New York, New Jersey, California, Hawaii and Rhode Island), under the class of temporary disability insurance for employees. Additionally, employers may offer paid maternity leave as a job benefit.

Sources: Based on ILO, 2014e; SSA and ISSA, 2012; SSA and ISSA, 2013a; SSA and ISSA, 2013b; SSA and ISSA, 2014; United Nations, 2013c. See also Annex IV, table B.5.

Link: http://www.social-protection.org/gimi/gess/RessourceDownload.action?ressource.ressourceId=37055.

Figure 3.22 Legal (mandatory) coverage for maternity cash benefits: Women in employment protected by law for loss of income during maternity (percentages)

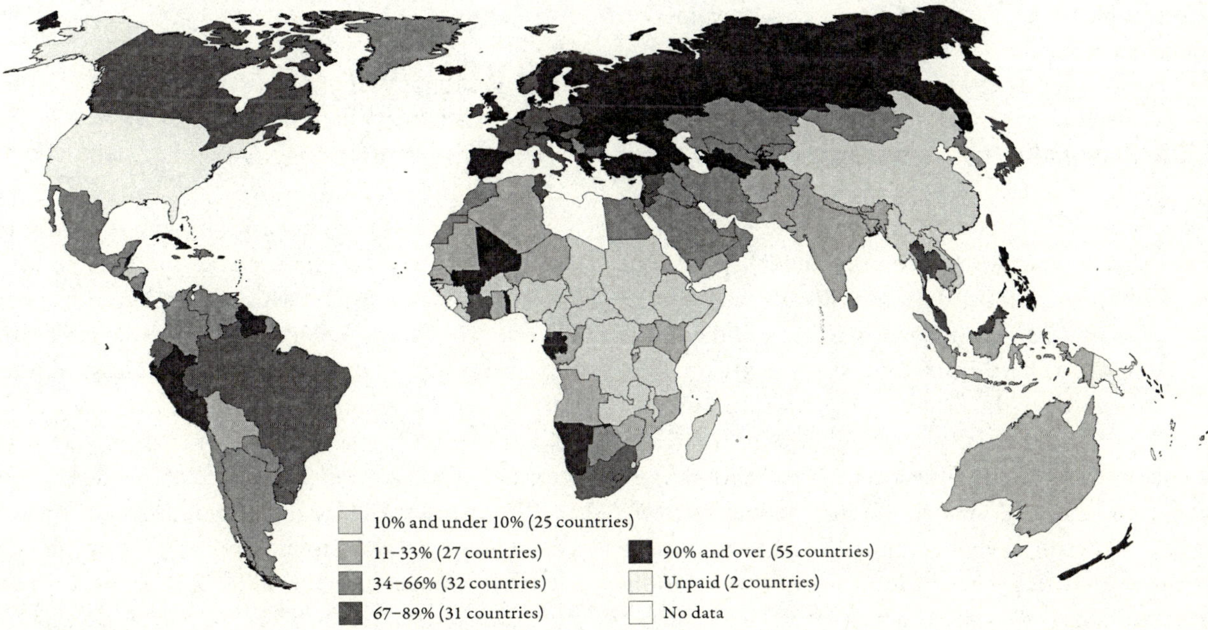

Note: Legal coverage refers to social security legislation as well as labour law.

Source: Based on data collected and indicators developed for ILO, 2014e.

Link: http://www.social-protection.org/gimi/gess/RessourceDownload.action?ressource.ressourceId=42477.

Figure 3.23 Effective coverage for maternity cash benefits: Women in employment contributing to maternity cash benefits schemes or otherwise entitled to such benefits (percentages)

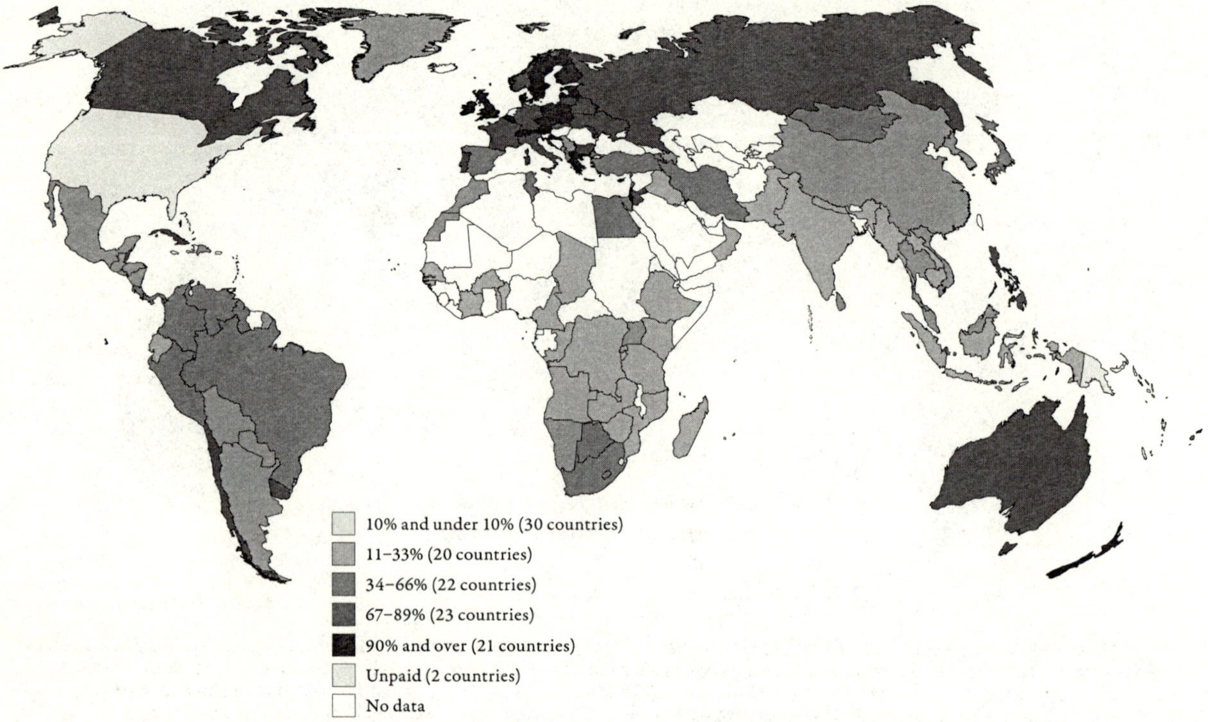

Sources: Based on ILO, 2014e. Original data from national sources and the ILO Social Security Inquiry.

Link: http://www.social-protection.org/gimi/gess/RessourceDownload.action?ressource.ressourceId=42478.

coverage is included), more than 90 per cent of women in employment enjoy a legal right to cash maternity benefits on a mandatory basis (see figure 3.22). At the other end of the spectrum, in 25 countries,[50] most of them in sub-Saharan Africa, under 10 per cent of women in employment are entitled to cash maternity benefits.

3.5.4 Extent of effective coverage

Irrespective of legal requirements, there may be obstacles that prevent women from receiving the benefits to which they are entitled. In fact, just above one-quarter (28.4 per cent) of employed women worldwide are effectively protected in maternity through contributory or non-contributory cash benefits. In much of Africa and South Asia, a small minority of women in employment (less than 10 per cent) are effectively protected through contributory or non-contributory forms of cash maternity benefits (figure 3.23). It is in many of these countries that employer's liability provisions (see figure 3.21) prevail, informal employment plays a prominent role in the economy, and maternal mortality ratios are still very high. Coverage of more than 90 per cent of employed women is reached in only 21 countries, most of them in Europe.

3.5.5 Adequacy of maternity benefits in ensuring income security during maternity leave

The adequacy of cash benefits provided during maternity leave to meet the needs of mothers and their babies can be assessed in terms of duration and amount. In order to allow women to fully recover after childbirth, 96 countries out of 188 provide at least 14 weeks' paid maternity leave, meeting the standards of Convention No. 183; of these, 31 countries provide 18–26 weeks, and ten more than 26 weeks (see figure 3.24). In 59 countries, the length of paid maternity leave is 12–13 weeks, which still meets the minimum standard set out in Convention No. 102. In 31 countries, maternity leave with cash benefits is less than 12 weeks.

---

[50] Twenty-one countries when including voluntary coverage.

Figure 3.24 Duration of paid maternity leave in national legislation, 2013 (weeks)

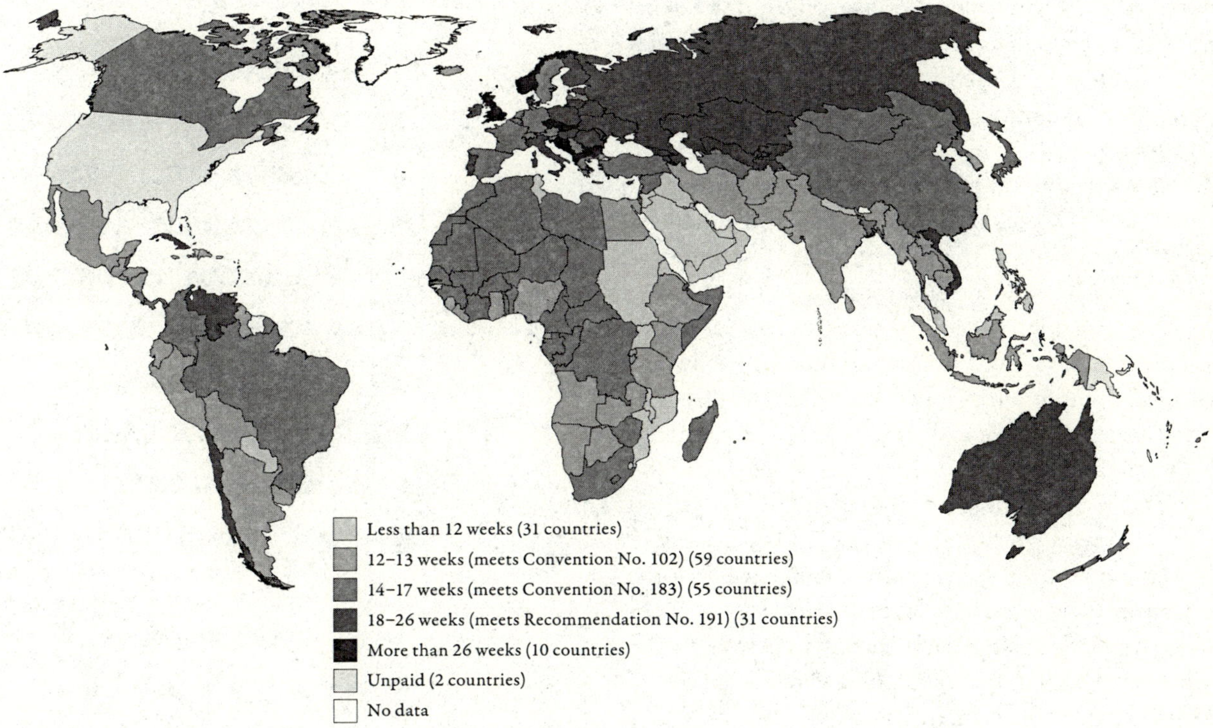

Sources: Based on ILO Working Conditions Laws database; ILO, 2014e; national legislation.

Link: http://www.social-protection.org/gimi/gess/RessourceDownload.action?ressource.ressourceId=37056.

Figure 3.25 Level of maternity cash benefits as a proportion of previous earnings, 2013 (per cent)

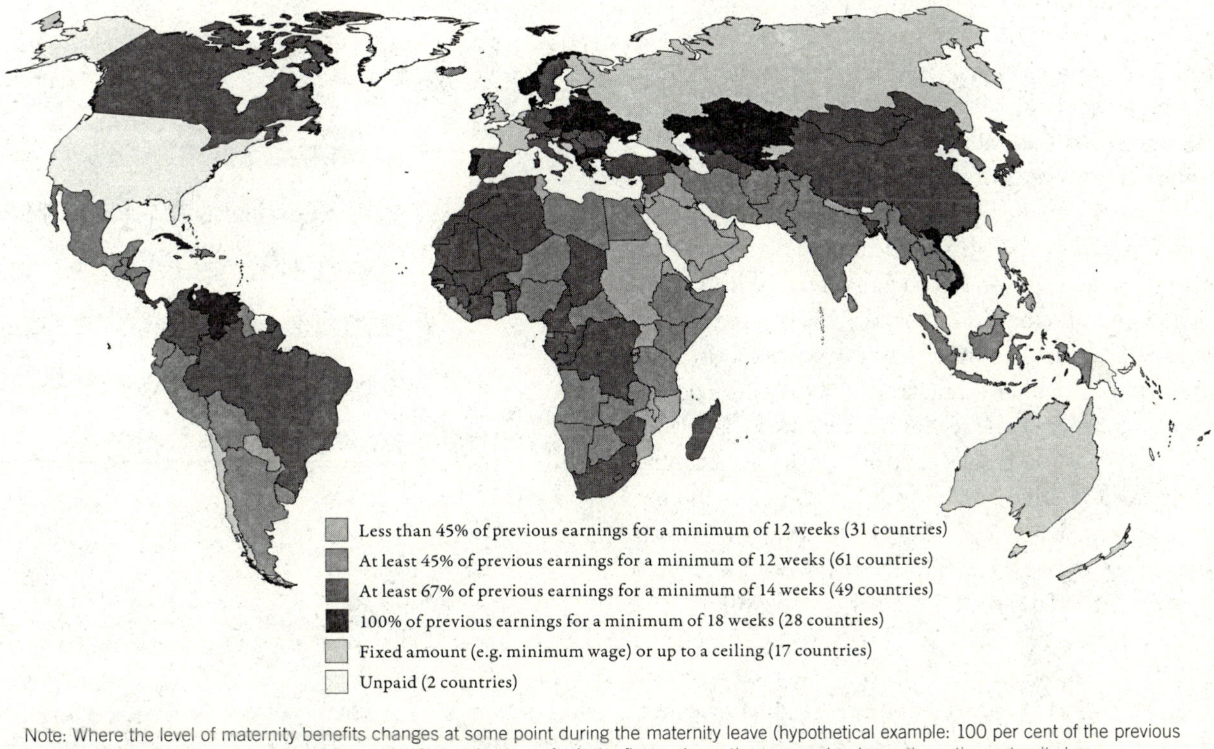

Note: Where the level of maternity benefits changes at some point during the maternity leave (hypothetical example: 100 per cent of the previous earnings for the first four weeks and 80 per cent for weeks thereafter), the figure shows the average level over the entire maternity leave.

Source: Based on ILO Working Conditions Laws database.

Link: http://www.social-protection.org/gimi/gess/RessourceDownload.action?ressource.ressourceId=42013.

The level of the maternity cash benefit, calculated as a proportion of women's previous earnings for a minimum number of weeks of paid maternity leave, varies widely from country to country (figure 3.25). In 77 out of the 188 countries, women are entitled to paid maternity leave of at least two-thirds of their regular salary for a minimum period of 14 weeks, meeting the benchmark of Convention No. 183. In 28 countries (nearly 15 per cent of the total reviewed), women are entitled to 100 per cent of their regular salary for at least 18 weeks, meeting the highest standard set out in Recommendation No. 191. An additional 17 countries provide benefit at a fixed level (for instance, the minimum wage). This leaves a large number of countries (61) in which women are entitled to benefit at a level lower than 67 per cent of previous earnings for a period of 12–13 weeks, which falls short of the benchmark of Convention No. 183 but is still in compliance with the minimum requirements of Convention No. 102. In 31 countries, the cash benefit corresponds to less than 45 per cent of the previous salary and/or the period of paid maternity leave is inferior to 12 weeks.

3.5.6 Access to maternal health care

Access to free, affordable and appropriate antenatal and post-natal health care and services for pregnant women and mothers with newborns is an essential component of maternity protection. Access to maternal health care is closely associated with access to health care in general, which is discussed in Chapter 5.

The importance of guaranteed access to maternal health care in safeguarding maternal and infant health is highlighted in the Millennium Development Goals, particularly MDG5 on improving maternal health and MDG3 on reducing child mortality. While remarkable progress has been achieved in many countries in reducing maternal and child mortality, some countries are still facing major challenges in this regard (UN, 2013b).

It is widely recognized that one of the key enabling factors for maternal and child health is access to antenatal care, which is still uneven and far from universal in many regions (see figure 3.26). According to the latest available data, while 84.2 per cent of childbearing women receive antenatal care provided by skilled personnel during at least one visit to a health facility, only 60.8 per cent of them were monitored during at least four visits. In sub-Saharan Africa, more than a quarter of childbearing women did not receive any antenatal care provided by skilled health personnel; the same is

Figure 3.26 Antenatal care coverage by region, latest available year (percentage of live births)

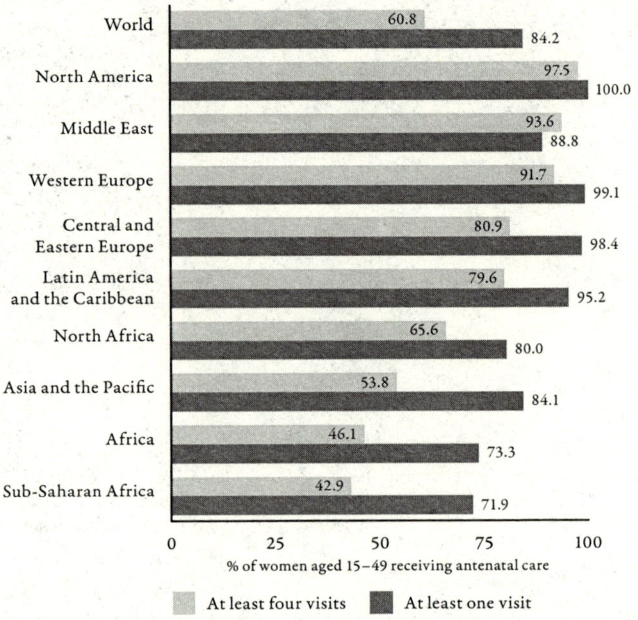

Notes: Antenatal care is measured by the percentage of women aged 15–49 with a live birth in a given time period who received antenatal care provided by skilled health personnel (doctors, nurses or midwives) at least once during pregnancy. Global average weighted by total population (UN, World Population Prospects, 2012 Revision; value for 2012).

Source: ILO calculations based on WHO Global Health Observatory (accessed Dec. 2013), various years.

Link: http://www.social-protection.org/gimi/gess/RessourceDownload.action?ressource.ressourceId=42481.

Figure 3.27 Access to antenatal care by health coverage, latest available year

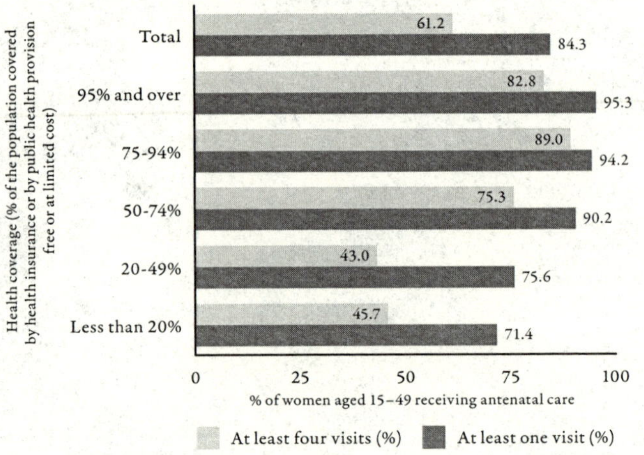

Notes: Access to antenatal care is measured by the percentage of women aged 15–49 with a live birth in a given time period who received antenatal care provided by skilled health personnel (doctors, nurses, or midwives) at least once during pregnancy. For health coverage, detailed information by country is available in Annex IV, table B.11. Global average weighted by total population (UN, World Population Prospects, 2012 Revision; value for 2012).

Sources: ILO calculations based on WHO Global Health Observatory, various years; national sources.

Link: http://www.social-protection.org/gimi/gess/RessourceDownload.action?ressource.ressourceId=37053.

true for one in five women in North Africa, and one in six women in Asia and the Pacific.

Health coverage is a key factor in facilitating access to maternal health care (figure 3.27). Access to antenatal care is high where health protection is available to the majority of the population, but lower where a large proportion of the population is not protected.

In many parts of the world, access to maternal health care is uneven and subject to significant disparities between urban and rural areas, and between poorer and more affluent groups of the population (see, e.g., Nawal, Sekher and Goli, 2013). In many developing countries, such disparities are closely associated with a lack of universal access to available and affordable health-care services of adequate quality, but the lack of financial protection that would allow women to benefit from existing services is also an important factor.

Inequalities in access to maternal health services (both antenatal care and medical care during and after childbirth) jeopardize further progress with respect to maternal and child health in both middle- and low-income countries. In most of these countries we observe significant levels of inequity in access to maternal health care across regions, and between residents of urban and rural areas, with urban populations tending to have better access to maternal health services. While inequalities are observed between urban and rural areas in countries in all parts of the world, the differential is much larger in Africa and in Asia and the Pacific than in other regions. These differentials are often associated with a lower density of health-care services in rural areas.

Another significant vector of inequality in access to maternity health protection is household wealth. In both low- and middle-income countries, only a small fraction of women in the lowest wealth quintile have access to maternal health protection, as compared to women in the highest wealth quintile (see figure 3.28). Such inequalities have detrimental effects on both maternal and child health, with often harmful long-term consequences for both individuals and societies.

Figure 3.29 illustrates the importance of providing quality maternal care services by showing the inverse correlation across countries between the percentage of births supervised by skilled birth attendants and the maternal mortality ratio.

Moreover, the available evidence suggests that income security also contributes to the well-being of pregnant women, new mothers and their children. Countries that have a higher level of coverage for maternity cash benefits also tend to achieve better results with respect to maternal mortality ratios. These results call for a comprehensive approach to maternity protection, combining maternal health care and income security, and also occupational safety and health measures, as stipulated in ILO maternity protection standards.

Figure 3.28 Inequities in access to maternal health services by wealth quintile and national income level, latest available year

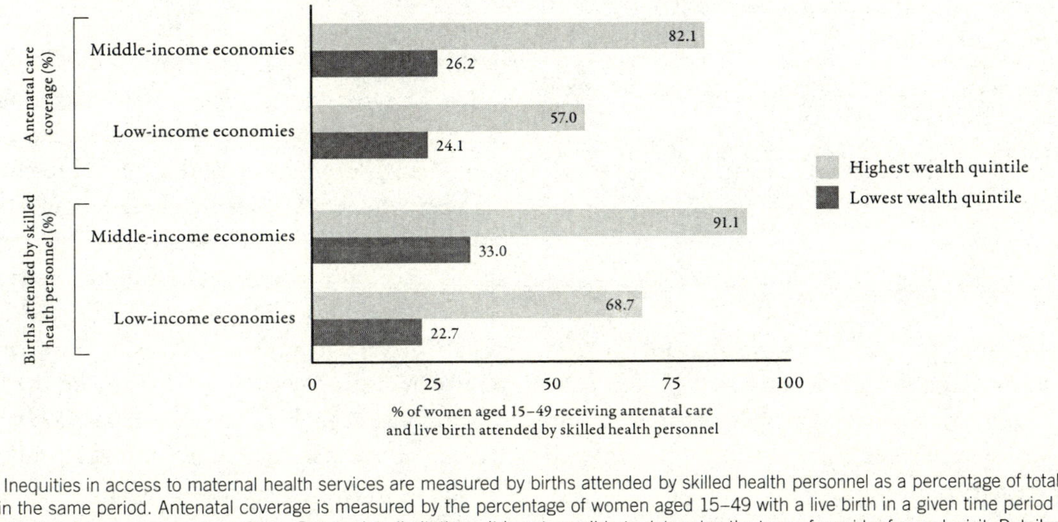

Notes: Inequities in access to maternal health services are measured by births attended by skilled health personnel as a percentage of total live births in the same period. Antenatal coverage is measured by the percentage of women aged 15–49 with a live birth in a given time period who received antenatal care four or more times. Due to data limitations, it is not possible to determine the type of provider for each visit. Detailed information and definitions are available in the Excel file (see link below). Global average weighted by total population (UN, World Population Prospects, 2012 Revision; value for 2012). Global averages should be considered with caution owing to the small sample size.

Source: ILO calculations based on WHO Global Health Observatory, various years.

Link: http://www.social-protection.org/gimi/gess/RessourceDownload.action?ressource.ressourceId=42882.

Figure 3.29 Maternal mortality ratio (per 100,000 live births) and live births attended by skilled health personnel, according to national income level, 2011

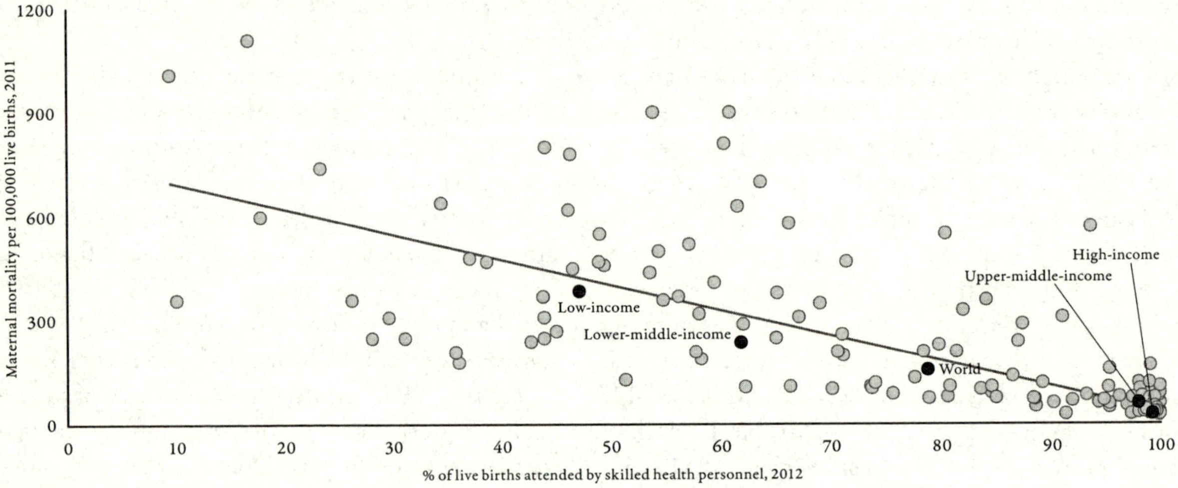

Note: R^2 = 0.6009.

Sources: Based on WHO Global Health Observatory and World Bank, World Development Indicators.

Link: http://www.social-protection.org/gimi/gess/RessourceDownload.action?ressource.ressourceId=42483.

3.5.7 Recent developments

Maternity protection is recognized globally as a crucial component of social protection – effectively, as an investment to secure each country's future human capital – as shown by the number and range of recent and continuing policy initiatives.

Changes in maternity protection schemes in different countries can be broadly classified as follows:

- extension of coverage, by enlarging the scope of existing schemes or introducing new contributory or non-contributory schemes;
- adjustments to the level of (cash) maternity benefits/allowances; or
- adjustments to the duration of benefits.

Extending maternity protection coverage

Many countries (for example, Australia, Jordan and South Africa) have enacted reforms that extend the scope of maternity coverage to categories of women who were previously unprotected. This has been achieved through a variety of measures (see box 3.15).

A number of countries, including Argentina, Bangladesh, the Plurinational State of Bolivia, India and Indonesia, have introduced or extended non-contributory maternity benefits to women workers in the informal economy or poor women in general. Non-contributory benefits are usually not directly associated with an interruption of employment in the form of maternity leave, but pursue a broader objective of providing pregnant women and new mothers with a predictable cash benefit during the final stages of their pregnancy and after childbirth.

Some of these programmes combine cash transfers with conditions relating to the utilization of maternal care services, with the aims of encouraging breastfeeding and improving nutrition. In some countries, pregnant women and new mothers are among the target groups in broader conditional cash transfer programmes. In others, there are specific programmes for maternity benefits. Many of these programmes explicitly aim at reducing maternal and child mortality in accordance with the MDGs and with national poverty reduction or social protection strategies. Some programmes explicitly aim at increasing the acceptance of family planning methods and reducing the incidence of child marriage. Benefits are usually provided only to women above a certain minimum age, and only for a certain number of pregnancies. Dedicated conditional cash transfer programmes have recently emerged in Bangladesh, Bolivia, India and Indonesia (see box 3.16).

Box 3.15 Maternity cash benefits: Some examples of recent expansion of coverage

A number of countries have extended coverage of maternity benefits to in recent years.

- Jordan established a new maternity benefit in 2011, covering workers in the private sector, financed through employer contributions of 0.75 per cent of assessable earnings. The scheme gives insured women the right to paid maternity leave at 100 per cent of previous earnings for a maximum of ten weeks. This benefit is expected to foster women's participation in the labour market and remove disincentives to the hiring of women.
- In Australia, the National Paid Parental Leave scheme, introduced in 2011, established an entitlement to 18 weeks of government-funded parental leave pay at the rate of the national minimum wage for eligible working parents (mothers and fathers). The scheme is subject to a (relatively generous) means test. Together with the "baby bonus" that is also paid to non-working parents and is subject to a stricter means test, the parental leave scheme reaches close to universal coverage.
- In South Africa, in 2003, domestic workers were brought under the Unemployment Insurance Fund, which is also responsible for the payment of maternity benefits.

Several countries introduced non-contributory benefits to extend the coverage of maternity benefits to those who are usually not covered by contributory schemes.

- Argentina introduced a universal birth allowance in 2011, which covers women from the 12th week of pregnancy to the birth or end of pregnancy. This non-contributory programme complements the birth allowance provided by the social insurance scheme. The programme covered 22 per cent of births in Argentina in 2011, covering on average more than 66,000 women per month between May 2011 and June 2012.

In some countries, the receipt of non-contributory maternity benefits is linked to the fulfilment of certain conditions with regard to antenatal and post-natal health care.

- In Bangladesh, the Maternity Allowance Programme for Poor Lactating Mothers, introduced in 2008, targets women aged 20 and over, living on a monthly income of less than 1,500 taka; it also covers mothers with a disability and women who are the breadwinners of poor families. If eligible, they one-time support during either the first or second pregnancy to the amount of 350 taka per month for a period of two years.
- In Bolivia, the Bono Madre Niño and Bono Juana Azurduy de Padilla benefits are targeted on poor women and their families without medical insurance or access to the breastfeeding grant. During pregnancy and the first two years of the life of the child, beneficiaries receive cash benefits on condition that they follow a schedule of regular health checkups for both mother and child.
- In India, the Indira Gandhi Matritva Sahyog Yojana (IGMSY) programme, introduced in 2010, provides cash benefits for pregnant women and lactating mothers in 52 pilot districts, covering approximately 1.38 million women. A daily benefit for all women aged 19 and over (limited to first two pregnancies; and excluding those who are covered through benefits provided to public sector employees) of approximately US$1.68 for approximately 40 days aims at providing partial compensation for wage loss to encourage women to take adequate rest before and after childbirth. In addition, all eligible women receive a cash incentive of 4,000 rupees in three instalments from the end of the second trimester of pregnancy until the child reaches six months of age, conditional upon compliance with various conditions pertaining to registration, medical check-ups, vaccinations and breastfeeding practice.
- In Indonesia, the Keluarga Haparan (PKH) conditional cash transfer programme provided regular cash benefits to 1.5 million poor households in 33 provinces in 2012; its conditions include the requirement that pregnant women and lactating mothers regularly visit health facilities for check-ups. The programme complements the Jampersal programme, introduced in 2011, which provides universal free delivery care, including prenatal and post-natal consultations.
- In Ghana, the Ghana Social Trust pilot programme, implemented in two districts from 2009, provides regular cash transfers every two months to poor women until the child reaches the age of five, on condition that women register themselves and their families with the National Health Insurance Scheme (under which registration fees and annual contributions are partially or fully subsidized), follow a schedule of ante- and post-natal care, child health care and vaccinations, have their babies delivered with the assistance of skilled health personnel and register the birth. In addition, women are encouraged to participate in health education sessions.

Sources: ADB, 2013; Aleksynska et al., 2013; Barrientos, Niño-Zarazúa and Maitrot, 2010; Ahluwalia, forthcoming; Fultz and Francis, 2013; national sources.

Box 3.16 Measures to facilitate parents' return to work

Supply-side measures to facilitate mothers' return to work after childbirth through help with training and job-search were implemented in Japan and the Russian Federation. In the latter, access to training programmes designed for jobseekers was extended to women on parental leave to care for a child under the age of three. In 2011, 26,200 women benefited from these programmes, out of which 15,700 found jobs. Additional measures included the introduction of flexible forms of work, self-employment programmes for women, and pre-school education for children aged 3–7. A Japanese programme supporting mothers of young children in their job search, for instance through nursing services, and information services was re-invigorated. In 2011, 69,000 women used the programme and successfully found a job.

In Italy, vouchers giving access to childcare services were introduced to promote female employment. Through this and other measures, takeup of formal child care was increased significantly, from 1 million children in 2011 to a projected 1.4 million in 2016/17, largely through direct financial assistance to families for childcare, and also through childcare support for parents receiving income transfers who are training or studying in order to find jobs. A one-day paid parental leave was introduced in 2012.

In Australia, Child Care Flexibility Trials and a Child Care Flexibility Fund were created to improve access to childcare, particularly outside standard hours, and hence allow women more flexible participation in the labour market. In addition to these supply-side measures, Australia also introduced parental leave pay at the national minimum wage and two weeks' payment for working fathers or partners. Since its implementation in January 2011, 240,000 individuals have benefited from this measure. Flexible childcare arrangements targeting families who require care outside standard working hours were also offered.

Sources: Based on ILO and OECD, 2013; Aleksynska et al., 2013.

Box 3.17 Recent contraction measures

Some recent reforms have resulted in a significant reduction of benefit levels for certain categories of beneficiaries.

- In the Czech Republic, the level of maternity benefit was temporarily reduced from 69 per cent to 60 per cent of the daily basis of assessment per calendar day in 2010, but has since been raised again.
- Germany reduced maternity benefits from 67 per cent to 65 per cent of previous salary for those with net earnings of more than €1,200 per month.
- Ireland reduced the maximum maternity benefit for new claimants from €262 to €230 per month as of January 2014 with the objective of saving €30 million. From 2013/14, maternity benefit is treated as taxable income. Consequently, around 48,000 women per year will be paying an average of €833 extra each in taxation, yielding savings of €40 million.
- In Latvia, the replacement rate of maternity benefit was reduced from 100 per cent to 80 per cent of insurable earnings in 2011. The Government also decided to extend the cap on the amount of sickness, maternity, paternity, parental and unemployed benefits paid until 31 December 2014. These measures are expected to save 25.83 million lat (LVL) in 2013 and LVL26.42 million in 2014.
- In Lithuania, the Law on Sickness and Maternity was amended in 2010 to temporarily reduce replacement rates of maternity/ paternity benefit from 100 per cent to 90 per cent of previous earnings.
- In Romania, a 15 per cent cut in maternity benefits was implemented as an emergency measure in 2010. The law enacting this reduction also changed the maternity benefits policy: benefits now amount to 75 per cent of previous earnings subject to a ceiling of 3,400 lei (RON) per month for a one-year period of leave, and of RON1,200 for a two-year leave. A bonus of RON500 per month is available to workers earning taxable income before the end of their one-year leave.
- In the United Kingdom, the conditional Health in Pregnancy grant of £190 for each expectant mother was abolished in 2011 in order to reduce the government deficit. It has been replaced with a £500 grant for first-time parents claiming other types of social benefits such as Income Support or Working Tax Credit.

Sources: Based on Gauthier, 2010; SSA and ISSA, 2012; SSA and ISSA, 2013a; SSA and ISSA, 2013b; SSA and ISSA, 2014; Labour Law Network; ILO Working Conditions Laws database, Leschke and Jepsen, 2011; Leschke and Jepsen, 2012; national sources.

Enhancing the duration and scope of maternity benefits

Several countries have extended the duration of paid maternity leave in law, following the adoption of Convention No. 183 in 2000. Although they have not yet ratified it, China, Colombia and Malta now meet the minimum benefit level requirements set by this Convention, and several countries, including Chile and the Bolivarian Republic of Venezuela, have gone further. A number of other countries (including Finland and Ireland) have increased the minimum rate of benefit levels and indexation mechanisms.

In addition, a number of countries have strengthened complementary provisions relating to assistance for mothers wishing to return to work (including Japan and the Russian Federation) and those relating to childcare facilities (including Australia and Italy; see box 3.16).

Contraction measures

In the context of the financial and economic crisis, several countries have taken measures that have reduced the level of maternity protection (see box 3.17). In countries including the Czech Republic, Germany, Ireland and the United Kingdom, the level of maternity benefits has been reduced. In addition, maternity benefits are now treated as taxable income in Ireland.

Some of these fiscal consolidation measures have significantly reduced the level of maternity protection available to certain groups of pregnant women and new mothers. Although in some countries measures have been taken to protect the levels of protection available to those on lower incomes, other groups may still have suffered marked reductions in the benefits they receive, jeopardizing their income security during this critical period of their lives. In addition, access to maternal health care may also have suffered from cuts within the health-care system (see Chapter 5). At a time when many European governments are considering or implementing measures to encourage higher birth rates, ill-designed fiscal consolidation measures may have unintended negative effects. It is thus necessary to carefully consider the short- and long-term impacts of policy reforms in this area.

Social protection for older women and men

4

Pensions and other non-health benefits

KEY MESSAGES

- The right to income security in old age, as grounded in human rights instruments and international labour standards, includes the right to an adequate social security pension. In many countries with high shares of informal employment, pensions are accessible only to a minority, and many older persons can rely only on family support.
- Nearly half (48 per cent) of all people over pensionable age do not receive a pension. For many of those who do receive a pension, pension levels are not adequate. As a result, the majority of the world's older women and men have no income security, have no right to retire and have to continue working as long as they can – often badly paid and in precarious conditions.
- Under existing laws and regulations, only 42 per cent of people of working age today can expect to receive contributory or non-contributory social security pensions from contributory schemes in the future, and effective coverage is likely to be even lower. This gap will have to be filled to a large extent by an expansion of non-contributory provisions.
- Many countries have recently made efforts to expand the coverage of contributory pension schemes and to establish non-contributory pensions to guarantee at least basic income security guarantee in old age to all.
- At the same time, there is a continuous global pressure which – under the guise of ensuring the sustainability of pensions in ageing societies and consolidating public finances – aims at reducing state responsibility for guaranteeing income security in old age and shifting large parts of the economic risks associated with pension provision on to individuals, thereby undermining the adequacy of pension systems and reducing their ability to prevent poverty in old age. In some countries, recent reversals of earlier reforms, including earlier privatizations of pension systems, have addressed these challenges, including the erosion of pension adequacy.
- The income security of older women and men depends also on their access to social services, including health care and long-term care.

4.1 The crucial role of pensions in ensuring income security and well-being of older persons

It is essential that persons are provided with reliable sources of income security throughout their old age. As people grow older, they can rely less and less on income from employment for a number of reasons: while highly educated professionals may often continue well-remunerated occupations until late in their life, the majority of the population is usually excluded from access to well-paid jobs at older ages. Private savings and assets (including housing ownership) make a difference, but for most people are usually not sufficient to guarantee an adequate level of income security until the end of their lives. Private, intra-family transfers may be important as an additional source of income security but are very often far from sufficient and not always reliable, in particular for families already struggling to live on a low income.

For all these reasons, in many countries public pension systems became a foundation on which at least basic income security has been built. Income security in old age depends also on the availability of and access to publicly provided social services – provided free or at low charge – including health care and long-term care. If secure and affordable access to such services is not provided, older persons and their families are pushed into extreme poverty.

4.2 Types of pension schemes

Public social security pensions have become important institutional solutions to guarantee income security in old age. Public pensions are usually supplemented in that task by publicly regulated private provision. In OECD countries, 59 per cent of household incomes of men and women aged 65 and over comes from public pension transfers (another 24 per cent comes from income from employment and self-employment, and 17 per cent from capital income – mainly private pensions) (OECD, 2013a; see figure 4.1).[1] This overall picture, however, hides large variations between and within countries. While in the majority of European countries public pensions are the source of more than 60 per cent of older person's incomes, in other regions – often due to limited public pension coverage – this share is much smaller. In many countries of the world, the pattern is similar to that evident in OECD countries such as the Republic of Korea, Mexico and Chile, where the majority of older persons' income comes from work.

In many OECD countries public pensions are the main source of income for older persons, particularly among the poorer part of the population: on average, public pensions account for more than 80 per cent of income for those in the lowest four deciles of the income distribution, while income from employment ranges between 5 and 9 per cent of the total income of these groups. On the other hand, in the top four deciles income from employment brings in between 20 and 40 per cent of all income of older persons. High earners in high-quality jobs are also usually in good health, fit and eager to continue their occupations, at least part time; those in low-quality and badly paid jobs often have to stop employment relatively early due to ill health or because they have been made redundant. Also, when older, they are excluded from earning opportunities which would supplement their low pensions.

Income from private pensions and other capital income constitutes less than 10 per cent of the total income of those in the lowest three deciles, after which this share grows with income to reach one-quarter in the top decile.

In some parts of the world outside the OECD, coverage by public pensions is low and pensions play a less prominent role as a source of income for less affluent groups of the population. The majority of older women and men in these countries work as long as they physically can – but this does not necessarily prevent them from being in poverty. In OECD countries, as figure 4.2 indicates, the greater the coverage by public pensions and – as a result – the greater the share of public pensions in older persons' incomes, the less poverty there is. In other countries, where the informal economy is large, the same pattern applies only where coverage by non-contributory pensions is at a high level (e.g. South Africa).

Housing wealth also has a significant impact on standards of living and the extent of poverty among older persons. Home ownership is usually much lower

[1] Income from work includes both earnings and income from self-employment. Capital income includes private pensions as well as income from returns on non-pension savings. Figure 4.1 shows the composition of incomes among individuals over 65 from work, capital and public transfers, focusing on those in the first decile of income (lowest), the fifth decile (middle) and the tenth decile (highest). For more information, see OECD, 2013a, p. 72.

Figure 4.1 Sources of income of people aged 65 and over, OECD countries

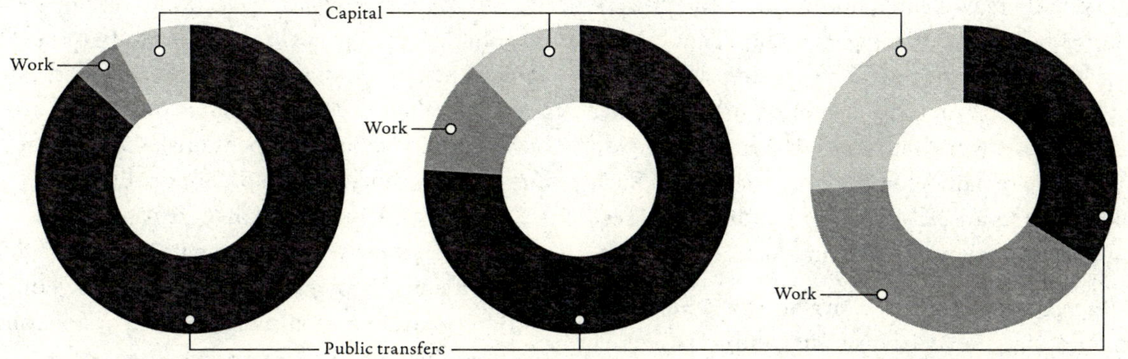

Notes: Composition of old people's (individuals) incomes from work, capital and public transfers considering, among people in old age, those in the first decile of income (lowest) and fifth decile (middle) and tenth decile (highest). Income from work includes both earnings (employment income) and income from self-employment. Capital income includes private pensions as well as income from returns on non-pension savings.

Source: Based on OECD, 2013a, Chapter 2.

Link: http://www.social-protection.org/gimi/gess/RessourceDownload.action?ressource.ressourceId=43157.

Figure 4.2 Correlation between greater public pension provision and lower poverty levels, OECD countries

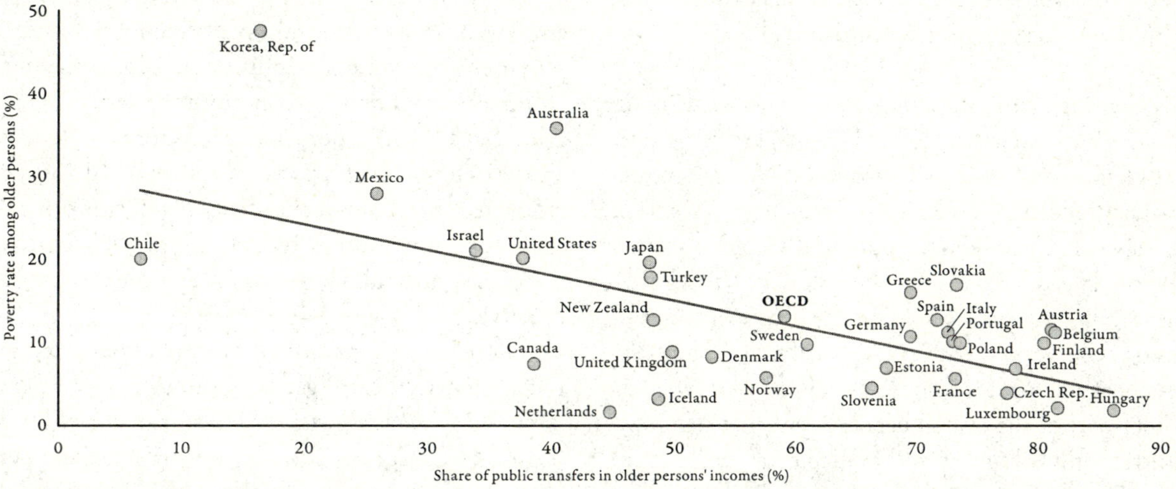

Note: $R^2 = 0.3952$.

Source: Based on OECD data.

Link: http://www.social-protection.org/gimi/gess/RessourceDownload.action?ressource.ressourceId=43158.

among lower-income households, and thus has only limited impact on the risk of poverty: in EU countries, for example, inclusion of estimates of so-called "imputed rent" (rent that the owners do not pay because they own their house) decrease the relative risk-of-poverty incidence by only 3.5 percentage points (OECD, 2013a, p. 104).

Whether cash income from pensions or other transfers is sufficient to ensure income security depends on many other factors, such as the need to pay for healthcare services, housing, long-term care, and other goods and services if needed. How provision of these services is secured and how are they financed also determine levels of income security in old age. An OECD study (OECD, 2013a, Chapter 2), shows, for example, that publicly provided in-kind services (including health care and long-term care) add on average 40 per cent to the value of monetary incomes of people aged 65 and over in OECD countries (compared to only 24 per cent for people of working age). In countries with wider access to quality public services, poverty in old age is also significantly lower. In most non-OECD countries, however, availability of and access to public services is often very limited and thus they do not play a similar role in the enhancing incomes of older persons and reducing poverty among them.

There exist a wide range of schemes providing different types of cash and in-kind benefits to older persons. In addition to the public social services mentioned above, in-kind benefits may include housing and energy subsidies, home help and care services, and residential care.

Cash benefits can be periodic payments awarded at reaching a specified age (and also often meeting other prescribed entitlement conditions) which are then paid throughout the remainder of the beneficiary's life. Such periodic payments are called pensions (or life annuities), and can be classified into two main types:

- Old-age pensions from contributory schemes of mandatory public social insurance and/or voluntary occupational or other private pension schemes.
- Old-age pensions from public non-contributory schemes, which can be (a) universal, covering all people above the eligible age who meet either a citizenship or minimum duration of residency condition; (b) pension tested;[2] or (c) means tested.[3] Most non-contributory schemes are national, but some are limited to certain geographical areas.[4]

Only pensions (that is, periodic payments: mainly life annuities but also means-tested benefits) are recognized by ILO standards such as Convention No. 102, or the Invalidity, Old-Age and Survivors' Benefits Convention, 1967 (No. 128), as benefits potentially able to protect individuals properly against the risk of outliving their own savings or assets. However, sometimes contributory pension schemes pay part of the benefit as a lump sum. In such situations it is important to make sure that the annuity part of the overall benefit is adequate. In many countries only a lump sum is available, or (as for example in Chile) people can opt at retirement for so-called "scheduled withdrawal" (under which their pensions are paid not as a life annuity but only for a limited number of years): such arrangements do not guarantee the level of security required by international standards.

The benefit expenditure data presented in this chapter attempt to cover, as far as evidence is available, all types of benefits provided by mandatory or quasi-mandatory (voluntary but with very wide coverage) schemes established by legislation, regulations or collective agreements. The indicators for the scope and extent of coverage take into account only coverage by any kind of cash periodic benefits (pensions); schemes providing lump-sum payments alone do not qualify.

The broad majority of countries (166 out of 178 countries for which information is available) provide pensions through at least one scheme, and often through a combination of different types of contributory and non-contributory schemes (see figure 4.3). The remaining 12 countries provide only lump-sum benefits through provident funds or similar programmes.

However, in 77 countries (over 43 per cent of the total number of countries but nearly 70 per cent of low-income countries) there exist schemes covering, on a contributory basis, only employees in the formal economy and exceptionally also certain groups of self-employed. In an equal number of countries, such employment-related contributory pension schemes are complemented by non-contributory schemes, either aimed at all older persons (27 countries) or at only those below a certain income threshold (50 countries). In only a small number are pensions provided on a non-contributory basis to all older people (nine countries) or to all those who pass a means test (three countries).

Globally, more than half of total public non-health social security expenditure, amounting to 3.3 per cent of global GDP, is allocated to income security for older persons (see figures 4.4 and 4.5).[5] Variations among regions are obviously influenced by differences in the demographic structure of the population, but also by variations in the policy mix between public and private provision for pensions and social services. Public non-health social protection expenditure for older persons takes the highest proportion of GDP in Western Europe, at 11.1 per cent, followed by 8.3 per cent of

[2] Non-contributory pensions of this type are provided to those older persons who do not receive a contributory pension at all, or whose contributory pension is below a certain minimum threshold; other types of incomes are not taken into account (as would be the case for means-tested pensions). Examples of this type of scheme include the Old Age Social Pension in Armenia and similar pensions in most CIS countries, as well as the "100 a los 70" scheme in Panama, the Old Age Allowance in Nepal, and the Allowance for Older People in Thailand.

[3] Means-tested pensions are provided only to those older persons whose pension and other income remains below a certain threshold. Means-tested pensions are not, strictly speaking, life annuities if designed and implemented in a way which includes all in need and at a level "sufficient to maintain the family of the beneficiary in health and decency" according to the requirements of ILO standards. The Older Persons' Grant in South Africa, for example, although means tested, effectively covers the majority of older people in the country and effectively prevents the recipients and their families from falling into poverty.

[4] For example, the Programa Colombia Mayor.

[5] While the data include not only pensions but, so far as possible, other cash and in-kind benefits for older persons, they do not usually include expenditure on long-term care, the cost of which in many countries is already significant and is likely to increase further in the future due to demographic change.

Figure 4.3 Overview of old-age pension schemes anchored in national legislation, by type of scheme, 2012/13

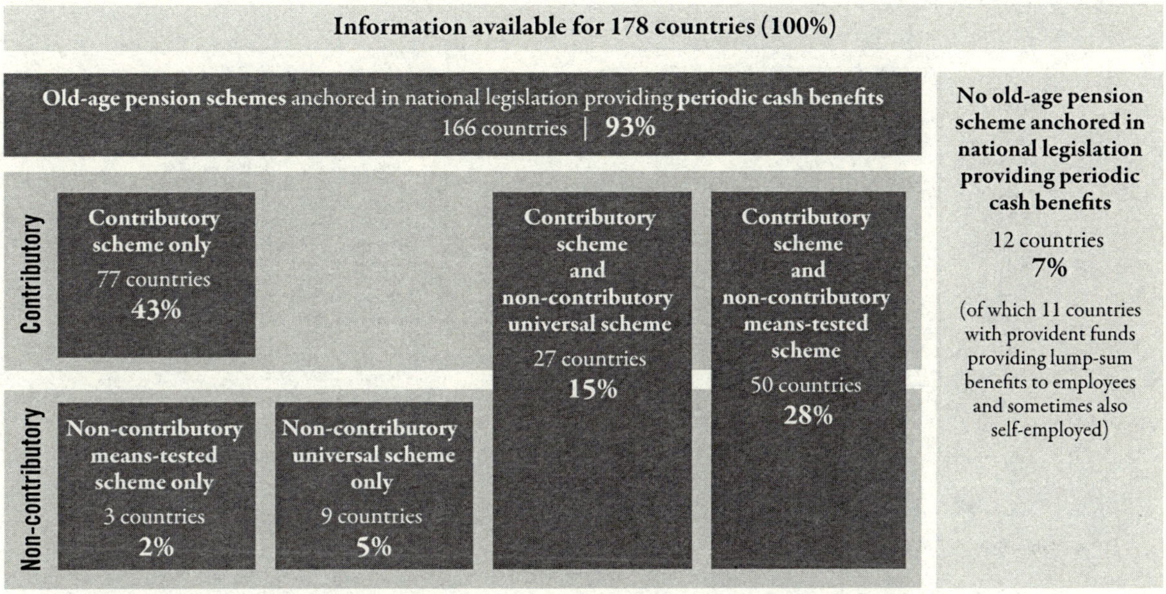

Sources: Based on SSA and ISSA, 2012; SSA and ISSA, 2013a; SSA and ISSA, 2013b; SSA and ISSA, 2014; European Commission, Mutual Information System on Social Protection (MISSOC).

Link: http://www.social-protection.org/gimi/gess/RessourceDownload.action?ressource.ressourceId=37157.

Figure 4.4 Non-health public social protection expenditure on pensions and other benefits for older persons, and share of older population (65 and above) in total population, 2010/11

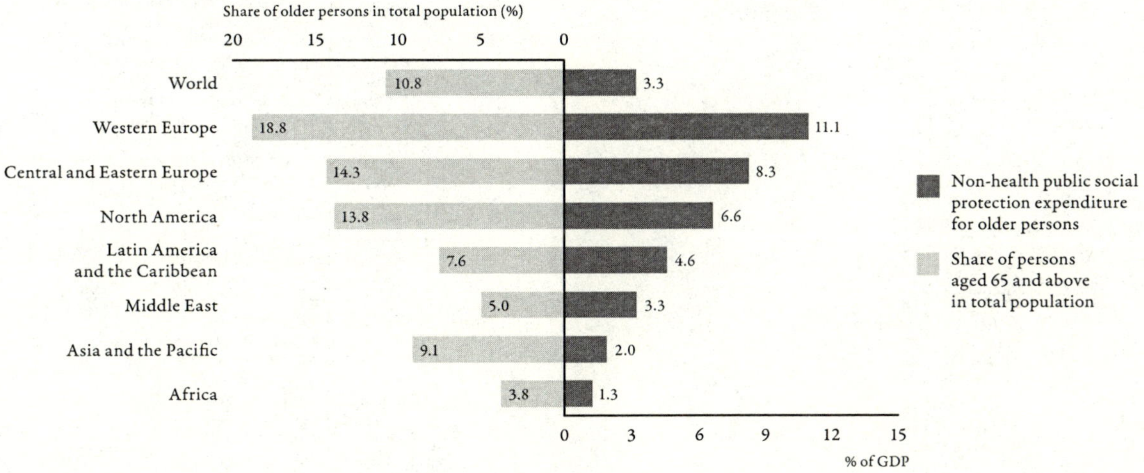

Sources: ILO Social Protection Department database. For detailed sources, see Annex IV, table B.13.

Link: http://www.social-protection.org/gimi/gess/RessourceDownload.action?ressource.ressourceId=39237.

GDP in Central and Eastern Europe and 6.6 per cent in North America, yet accounts for only 1.3 per cent of GDP in Africa, where the share of older persons in the total population is significantly lower. In Latin America and the Middle East, 4.6 per cent and 2.0 per cent of GDP respectively is allocated to the income security needs of older persons, while in Asia and the Pacific, where the share of the older population is significantly higher, only 2.0 per cent of GDP, or 52.8 per cent of total non-health social protection expenditure, is allocated to the older population. Considering that more than half of the world's older persons live in the Asia and Pacific region, and that their numbers are set to increase rapidly over the coming years, this figure suggests a disproportionately low (in relation to the size of the older population) allocation of resources to income security in old age, as one element of a wider need to invest more in social protection (UN, 2013e).

Figure 4.5 Non-health public social protection expenditure on pensions and other benefits for older persons, 2010/11 (percentage of GDP)

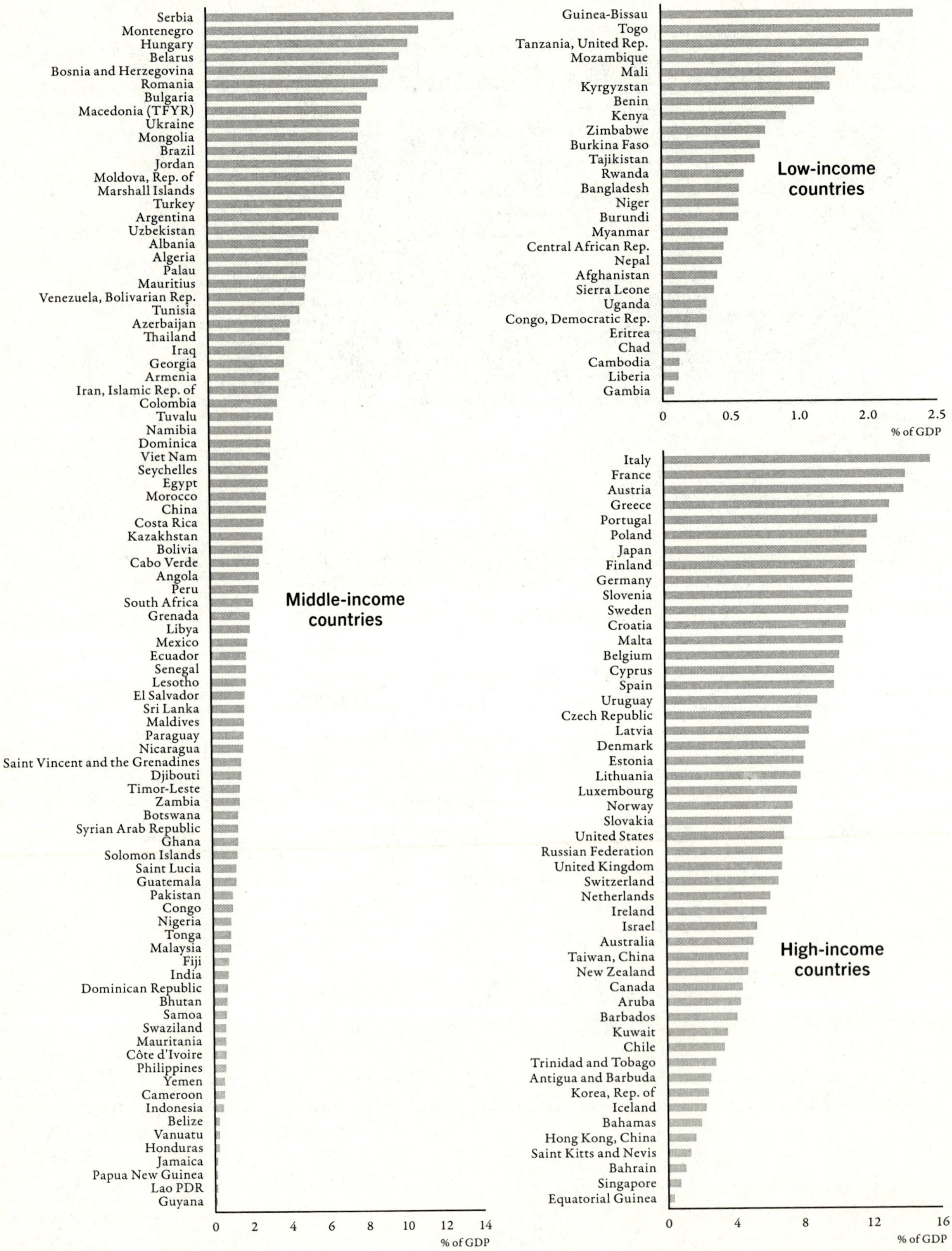

Sources: ILO Social Protection Department database. For more detail on sources, see Annex IV, table B.13.
Link: http://www.social-protection.org/gimi/gess/RessourceDownload.action?ressource.ressourceId=44419.

Box 4.1 International standards on old-age pensions

The rights of older persons to social security and to an adequate standard of living to support their health and well-being, including medical care and necessary social services, are laid down in the major international human rights instruments, the Universal Declaration of Human Rights (UDHR), 1948, and (in more general terms) the International Covenant on Economic, Social and Cultural Rights (ICESCR), 1966.[1] The content of these rights is further specified in the normative body of standards developed by the ILO, which provide concrete guidance to countries for giving effect to the right of older persons to social security, from basic levels to full realization.[2]

The Social Security (Minimum Standards) Convention, 1952 (No. 102), the Old-Age, Invalidity and Survivors' Benefits Convention, 1967 (No. 128), and its accompanying Recommendation No. 131, and the Social Protection Floors Recommendation, 2012 (No. 202), provide an international reference framework setting out the range and levels of social security benefits that are necessary and adequate for ensuring income maintenance and income security, as well as access to health care, in old age. The extension of coverage to all older persons is an underlying objective of these standards, with the aim of achieving universality of protection, as explicitly stated in Recommendation No. 202.

Conventions Nos 102 and 128 and Recommendation No. 131 make provision for the payment of pensions in old age, at guaranteed levels, upon completion of a qualifying period, and their regular adjustment to maintain pensioners' purchasing power. More particularly, Conventions Nos 102 and 128 envisage the provision of income security to people who have reached pensionable age through earnings-related contributory pensions (guaranteeing minimum benefit levels, or replacement rates, corresponding to a prescribed proportion of an individual's past earnings – in particular to those with lower earnings) and/or by flat-rate non-contributory pensions which can be either universal or means-tested. The guaranteed minimum levels for the latter should be a prescribed proportion of the average earnings of a typical unskilled worker, but the "total of the benefit and other available means … shall be sufficient to maintain the family of the beneficiary in health and decency" (Convention No. 102, Art. 67(a)).

Recommendation No. 202 completes this framework by calling for the guarantee of basic income security to all persons in old age, prioritizing those in need and those not covered by existing arrangements. Such a guarantee would act as a safeguard against poverty, vulnerability and social exclusion in old age, for people not covered by contributory pension schemes. It is also of high relevance to pensioners whose benefits are affected by the financial losses suffered by pension funds, whose pensions are not regularly adjusted to changes in the costs of living, or whose pensions are simply inadequate to secure effective access to necessary goods and services and allow life in dignity. ILO social security standards thus provide a comprehensive set of references and a framework for the establishment, development and maintenance of old-age pension systems at national level.

An important social policy challenge facing ageing societies is to secure an adequate level of income for all people in old age without overstretching the capacities of younger generations. In view of the financing and sustainability challenge faced by social security systems in the context of demographic change, the State has a vital role to play in forecasting the long-term balance between resources and expenditure in order to guarantee that institutions will meet their obligations towards older persons. The principle in ILO social security standards, strongly reaffirmed recently by Recommendation No. 202, of the overall and primary responsibility of the State in this respect will undoubtedly play an important role in how future governments are held accountable for the sustainability of national social security systems in view of, among other factors, demographic change.

[1] UDHR, Arts 22 and 25(1), and ICESCR, Art. 9. [2] See UN, 2008.

These regional variations in expenditure levels reflect the prevailing situation in actuality, in which most older persons in higher-income countries enjoy their rights to retirement and to income security in old age (see box 4.1), while in lower-income countries these rights are given only to a minority.

As clearly stated in Recommendation No. 202, national social protection floors should guarantee, in addition to income security, at a minimum "access to a nationally defined set of goods and services, constituting essential health care" (Part II, Para. 5(a)). This is particularly important for older persons, not just to ensure good health, but also because it has a role in protecting against health-related poverty, given that older persons generally have greater and specific health-care needs and may have to rely on long-term care. This concerns particularly older women, who in many countries tend to live alone in the later stages of their lives (Scheil-Adlung and Bonan, 2012). Thus, old-age pensions must be closely coordinated with other social protection provisions, especially in the areas of social health protection, long-term care (see box 4.2) and disability, in order to address the particular needs of older persons.

Box 4.2 The crisis of the care economy: Risks associated with inattention to long-term care needs in times of fiscal consolidation[1]

The need for long-term care is constantly growing as numbers of older persons everywhere increase. Across the world, at present such care is predominantly provided by relatives, mainly women. However, this work is often not sufficiently valued and not remunerated adequately, if at all. Over recent years the situation has become even worse, not only because of demographic ageing, leading to a growing number of older persons with chronic illnesses, but also because younger women are now more likely to participate in the labour market and thus less likely to be available for family care.

In the face of these changes in the health profile and lifestyle patterns of families, social protection provisions for long-term care are in many cases inadequate. However, the problem goes far beyond families and national policies; indeed, it amounts to a global crisis of the care economy. The lack of nurses and other care professionals to meet the growing need has resulted in an ever-increasing pull of labour from developing countries into developed countries. It is based on international "labour supply chains" involving mostly female migrant workers from poor families who provide care services to meet the physical and emotional needs of older persons. Often the wages, conditions of work and social security coverage of caregivers in recipient countries are insufficient, with a negative impact on the quality of care, resulting in discontent on the part of both caregivers and beneficiaries.

Debates are taking place in Thailand, Viet Nam and other countries on how to improve institutional and home care, often in the hope that volunteer caregivers and self-help groups can play a bigger role and that demands on public expenditure can be minimized by shifting the financial impact to the private sector (see e.g. HelpAge International, 2014). Similar approaches are being pursued in India and Singapore, and in China, where legislation has been implemented that imposes on adult children the responsibility to provide the care their parents need, under threat of jail or fines if they do not. In other regions of the world, such as Africa and Latin America, policies are also built on the assumption that private networks – communities or families – can shoulder the burden of care for older persons, sometimes overlooking limitations in the capacities of family carers (most of whom are women) and the impacts of such unpaid work on the quality of care, the income of care families, and the health and future employability of carers. The global inattention to the care needs of older persons reflects broader attitudes towards older persons and can also be observed in other social protection systems that should both prevent and meet long-term care needs. In health care, for example, the number of geriatricians is often insufficient to meet the need.

Only few countries have implemented specific schemes providing benefits for long-term care. Most of these are using tax-based financing, as is the case in Denmark, Norway and Sweden. Only a small number of countries, including Germany, Japan, the Netherlands and Taiwan (China), are using social insurance schemes to cover related costs. Given the complexity of both needs and the schemes in place, significant "long-term care literacy" is required from older persons when applying for the benefits they need. These benefits might be in cash – including those for financial support of family carers – or in kind, such as institutional care and home care. Eligibility criteria vary widely and are frequently means-, age- and needs-tested.

Generally, although public expenditure on long-term care remains very low compared to expenditure on health and old-age pensions, European Union projections – while admitting uncertainty regarding the magnitudes of fiscal consequences and considering a number of alternative scenarios – foresee at least a doubling of current expenditure levels by 2060 (figure 4.6).

Given the limited availability of public resources, all the existing schemes and systems are characterized by a strong reliance on co-payments from both public and private sources. As a result, out-of-pocket payments (OOP) for long-term care have a significant impact on the disposable income of older persons: recent ILO research (Scheil-Adlung and Bonan, 2012) has found that even in European countries OOP on long-term care amounts on average to 9.6 per cent of older persons' household income and can be as much as 25 per cent. The poor, women and the very old are particularly affected. In fact, the very old, aged 80 and over, face OOP up to seven times as high as those of beneficiaries aged between 65 and 79 years. In this context, given the variable availability of carers and affordability of services, it should be noted that statistics on OOP include only those who have effective access to such services, and excludes those who are too poor to purchase such services or cannot obtain them due to the lack of care workers.

[1] In this report, "fiscal consolidation" refers to the wide array of adjustment measures adopted to reduce government deficits and debt accumulation. Fiscal consolidation policies are often referred to as austerity policies.

Figure 4.6 Long-term care expenditure as a proportion of GDP, 2010 and projections for 2060 (percentages)

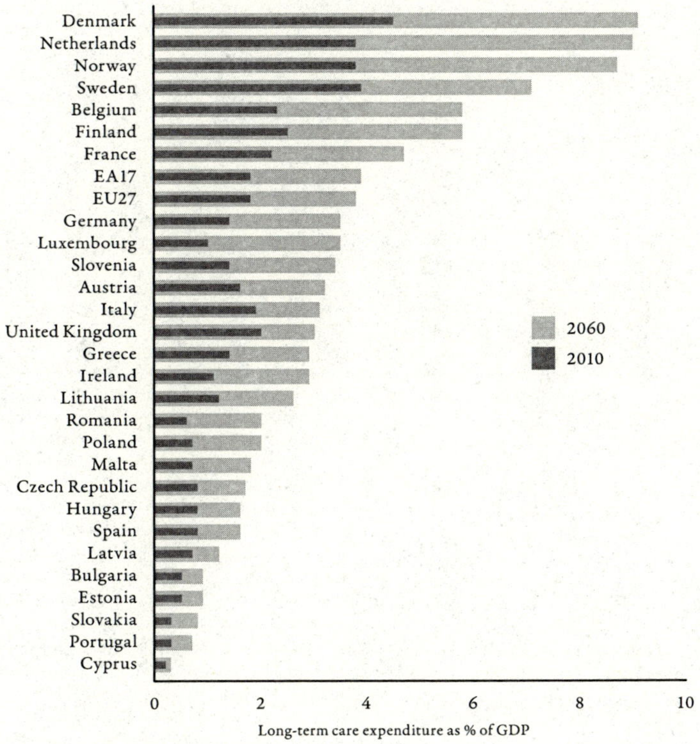

Source: Based on European Commission, 2012c.

Link: http://www.social-protection.org/gimi/gess/RessourceDownload.action?ressource.ressourceId=43302.

The twin objectives of protection are to reach all older persons in need and to do so at an appropriate monetary level of benefit provision. The available statistics allow much more detailed analysis of the former aspect (extent of coverage) than the latter (level of benefit), even though the assessment of income security in old age requires at the least consideration of these two dimensions. In simple terms, the available information provides some quantitative data by country as well as at the level of region (or other global grouping) on both coverage by social security laws and their effective implementation. Effective implementation can be translated into two distinct measures (and the complementary realities), namely the number of people of working age actually contributing to a pension scheme (focus on the contributory side of pension systems) and the proportion of older persons receiving a pension – either contributory or not – every month, or at least on a regular basis.

4.3 Extent of legal coverage

For most of the world's population, the right to income security in old age is unfulfilled, and considerable inequalities persist. Globally, 42.2 per cent of the working-age population is currently potentially covered by existing laws,[6] and will therefore receive an old-age pension once reaching the prescribed age, if these laws are properly implemented and enforced (see figure 4.7). Coverage for women is lower than for men: only one out of three women of working age has some form of legal coverage. Women's lower coverage rates for contributory schemes largely reflect their lower labour market participation rates, their over-representation among those working as self-employed or unpaid family workers, or in agriculture or other sectors frequently not covered by existing legislation, and their higher likelihood of having shorter and more often interrupted

[6] The extent of legal coverage for old age is defined as the proportion of the working-age population (or alternatively the labour force) covered by law with schemes providing periodic cash benefits once statutory pensionable age or other eligible age is reached. The population covered is estimated by using the available demographic, employment and other statistics to quantify the size of the groups covered as specified in the national legislation. Actual, effective coverage is often significantly lower than legal coverage where laws are not implemented fully or enforced. For additional details, see the glossary in Annex I, as well as Annex II.

Figure 4.7 Old-age pensions: Extent of legal coverage, by region, latest available year (percentages)

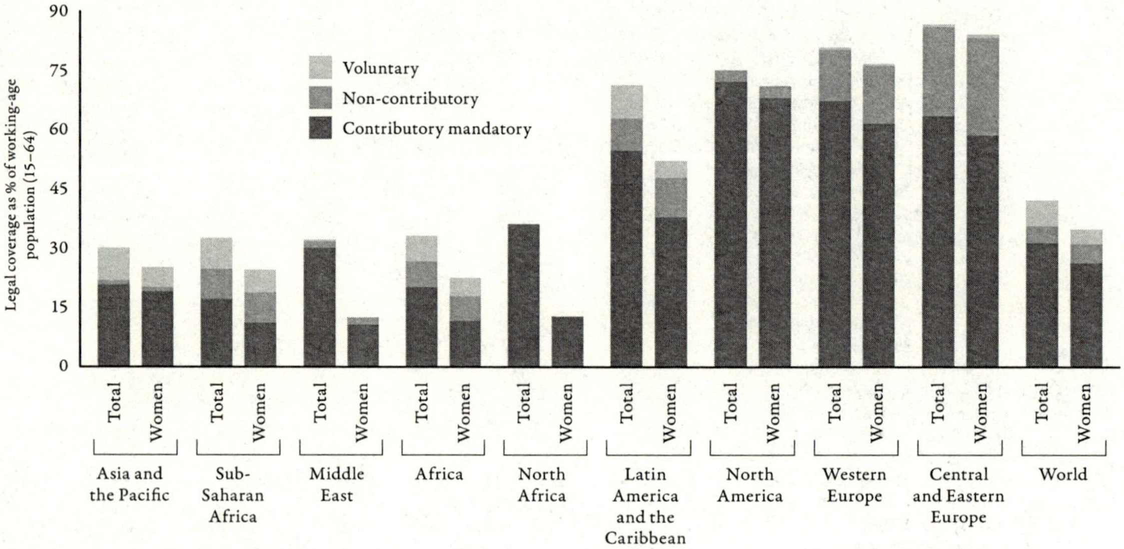

Note: Regional and global estimates weighted by total population. For more details on estimates of the extent of legal coverage by country, see Annex IV, table B.6.

Sources: ILO Social Protection Department, based on SSA and ISSA, 2012; SSA and ISSA, 2013a; SSA and ISSA, 2013b; SSA and ISSA, 2014; ILO LABORSTA; UN World Population Prospects; national legislative texts; national statistical data for estimates of legal coverage.

Link: http://www.social-protection.org/gimi/gess/RessourceDownload.action?ressource.ressourceId=37085.

careers in formal employment, which constrains their ability to contribute to social insurance (or other forms of pension insurance). Women whose husbands were covered by contributory schemes are in many countries entitled to survivors' pensions which often become their only source of income.

Overall, levels of legal coverage (mandatory and voluntary coverage taken together) range from about 30 per cent in Asia and the Pacific and 32.8 per cent in Africa – where informality and "unorganized sectors" predominate – to 76.4 per cent in North America and over 80 per cent in both Western and Central and Eastern Europe. Globally, 31.5 per cent of the working-age population is mandatorily covered by law and may receive in future old-age pensions from contributory schemes, and just over 4 per cent may become eligible to receive a non-contributory pension.[7] The corresponding rates of legal coverage for women are lower (26.4 per cent being covered by mandatory contributory schemes, and an additional 5 per cent potentially covered by universal or pension-tested non-contributory schemes). In addition, national laws may provide for voluntary coverage complementing the mandatory provisions.

4.4 Extent of effective coverage

Indicators of the extent of effective coverage attempt to measure the extent to which the existing statutory framework is actually implemented. Figure 4.8 presents global results for two (or rather three) parallel measures of effective coverage. The first measure ("beneficiary coverage ratio") shows the percentage of older persons above statutory pensionable age receiving contributory or non-contributory pensions. Focusing on contributory pensions, the second measure ("contributor coverage ratio"), in its two variants, provides some indication of future pension coverage: it shows the percentages of, respectively, those who are economically active ("contributor/labour force coverage ratio") and those of working age ("contributor/population coverage ratio") who contribute to existing contributory pension schemes.

[7] The estimation method adopted tends to underestimate potential legal coverage by non-contributory pension schemes.

Figure 4.8 Effective pension coverage ratios, by region, latest available year (percentages)

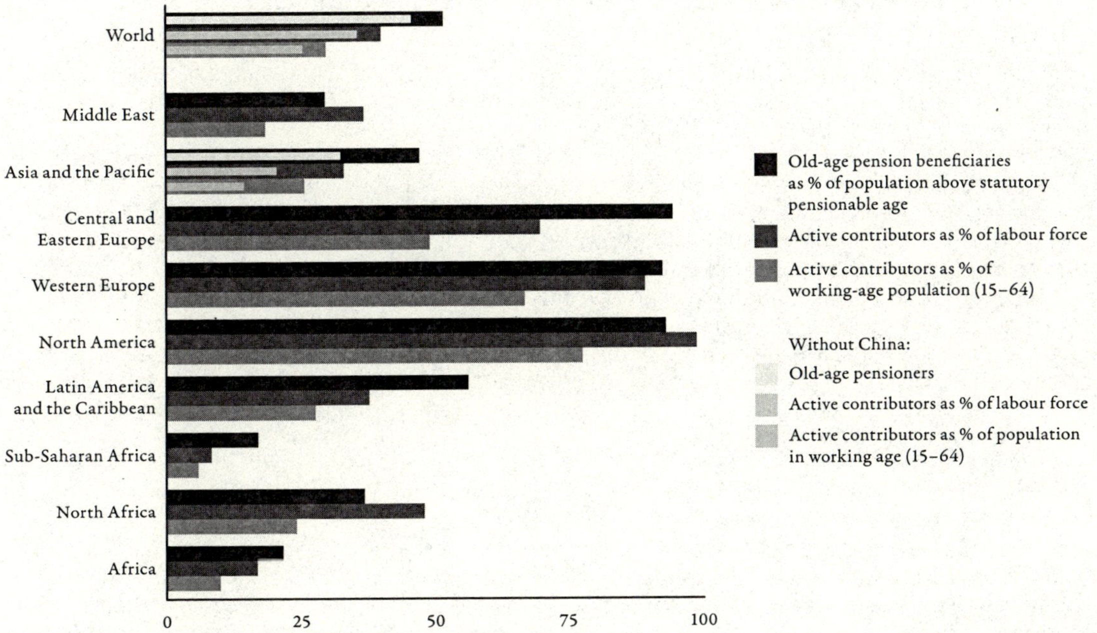

Note: The age range considered is 15–64 for the denominator and, as far as possible, also for the numerator in the case of active contributors. Weighted by total population.

Sources: ILO Social Protection Department, compilation of national available data collected in national social security pension schemes. Based on SSA and ISSA, 2012; SSA and ISSA, 2013a; SSA and ISSA, 2013b; SSA and ISSA, 2014; Eurostat Income and Living Conditions Database; UN World Population Prospects, 2012 revision.

Link: http://www.social-protection.org/gimi/gess/RessourceDownload.action?ressource.ressourceId=37158.

4.4.1 Income security in old age: A right still unfulfilled for many

On a global scale, only slightly more than half of older persons above statutory pensionable age (51.5 per cent) receive an old-age pension (i.e. periodic cash benefits),[8] and if China is excluded the proportion falls to 45.6 per cent (see box 4.3).[9] Despite an impressive extension of pension coverage in many countries (see below), significant inequalities persist. In sub-Saharan Africa, less than one in five older persons (16.9 per cent) receives an old-age pension which would provide him or her with a certain level of income security during old age. In the Middle East, 29.5 per cent of older persons receive a pension; the figure is 36.7 per cent in North Africa, 47.0 per cent in Asia and the Pacific (32.4 per cent excluding China), and 56.1 per cent in Latin America and the Caribbean. Regional coverage ratios of more than 90 per cent of older persons are achieved only in North America and Europe.

The contributor coverage ratio gives an indication of the proportion of the population – or the labour force – which will have access to contributory pensions in the future. Although this measure does not reflect access to non-contributory pensions, it still gives an important signal regarding future levels of coverage, taking into account that benefit levels in contributory pension schemes tend to be higher than those from non-contributory pension schemes. At the global level, less than one-third of the working-age population (30.9 per cent), just more than a quarter (25.4 per cent) excluding China, is contributing to a pension scheme (see figure 4.8). Effective coverage ratios range from 5.9 per cent of the working-age population in sub-Saharan Africa to 77.5 per cent of the working-age population in North America.

Focusing on those persons who are economically active, 41.4 per cent of the global labour force contribute to a pension insurance scheme, and can therefore expect to receive a contributory pension upon

[8] Weighted by total population.

[9] As the available data for many countries do not allow for a detailed age breakdown of old-age pensioners, the indicator is calculated as the total number of beneficiaries of old-age pensions as a proportion of the population above statutory pensionable age.

Box 4.3 Extension of social protection of older persons in China

Before 2009, only two institutional mechanisms for income security in old age existed in China: one for urban workers, based on social insurance principles, and one for civil servants and others of similar status, based on the employer's liability approach. Together, they covered under 250 million people (including pensioners), about 23 per cent of the population aged 15 and above in 2008.

In 2009 and 2011, two new old-age pension schemes were introduced for the rural population and urban residents otherwise not covered respectively. Participation is voluntary. To encourage people to join, the Government employed a number of measures, including contribution subsidies and immediate pension payments to the elderly parents of adults registered with a rural pension scheme. Pensions consist of two components: a social pension paid by the Government, and an individual savings account pension financed jointly by contributions from the insured persons, collective entities (if any) and the Government. A minimum level is set for the social pension, which can be higher if local governments so wish and are able to fund it: this provision partially explains the differences in the levels of pension payments across different regions. For contributions to the individual savings account, a minimum level of subsidy from the Government is fixed, and personal contribution scales are established to allow each of the insured to choose the level of contribution he or she wants to make.

At the end of 2013, 850 million people, nearly 75 per cent of the population aged 15 and above, were covered under the four pension schemes, of which 498 million were covered under the two new schemes, accounting for 59 per cent of the total number covered.

Essential expansion has also been made within the pension system for urban workers, in particular to cover rural-to-urban migrant workers, the overall number of whom exceeded 260 million in 2012.

To consolidate the progress achieved so far and to address issues of adequacy, equality, portability and sustainability in a more coherent, effective and efficient manner, in 2013 China began the process of overhauling the entire old-age pension system, now comprising the four components outlined above. The first outcomes of this review include the policies announced in early 2014 on the merging of the two new pension schemes to equalize their rights and opportunities; the portability of pension entitlements between the merged scheme and others; and the conversion of employers' liability for civil servants into a social insurance pension scheme.

Sources: Based on ISSA country reforms database and national sources; see also Ringen and Ngok, 2013.

retirement. Owing to the high proportion of informal employment in sub-Saharan Africa, only 8.4 per cent of the labour force contributes to pension insurance and earns rights to a contributory pension. In Asia and the Pacific, about one-third of the labour force (34.0 per cent) contributes; coverage ratios are slightly higher in the Middle East (37.1 per cent), Latin America and the Caribbean (38 per cent), and North Africa (47.4 per cent). Western Europe and North America reach coverage rates of 89.2 and 98.5 per cent respectively, followed by Central and Eastern Europe with 69.7 per cent of the labour force.

In lower-income countries, usually only a very small proportion of those employed are wage and salary earners with formal employment contracts, and are thus relatively easily covered by contributory pensions. Informality, evasion and inadequate enforcement of laws are also more prevalent in lower-income countries. That is why effective pension coverage seems to be strongly associated with a country's income level (see figure 4.9), although it is in fact labour market structures and law enforcement and governance that actually exert the crucial influence. While in high-income economies, 90.8 per cent of the labour force contribute to a pension scheme, this is the case for only 50.7 per cent in upper-middle-income economies, 15.2 per cent in lower-middle-income economies, and only 5.7 per cent in low-income economies. These low coverage ratios tend to be associated with a low degree of formality in the labour market. Unless effective non-contributory pensions are available, coverage gaps also show in the proportion of older persons effectively benefiting from a pension: beneficiary coverage ratios range from 18.1 per cent in low-income economies and 24.1 per cent in lower-middle-income economies to 71.0 per cent in upper-middle-income economies and 89.1 per cent in high-income economies.

With efforts to extend contributory schemes to all with some contributory capacity, and with the introduction of non-contributory pensions in a larger number of countries, coverage has been extended significantly to workers in informal employment, providing at least a minimum of income security in old age. These trends will be assessed in more detail in the following section.

Figure 4.9 Old-age pension beneficiaries as a proportion of the population above statutory pensionable age, latest available year (percentages)

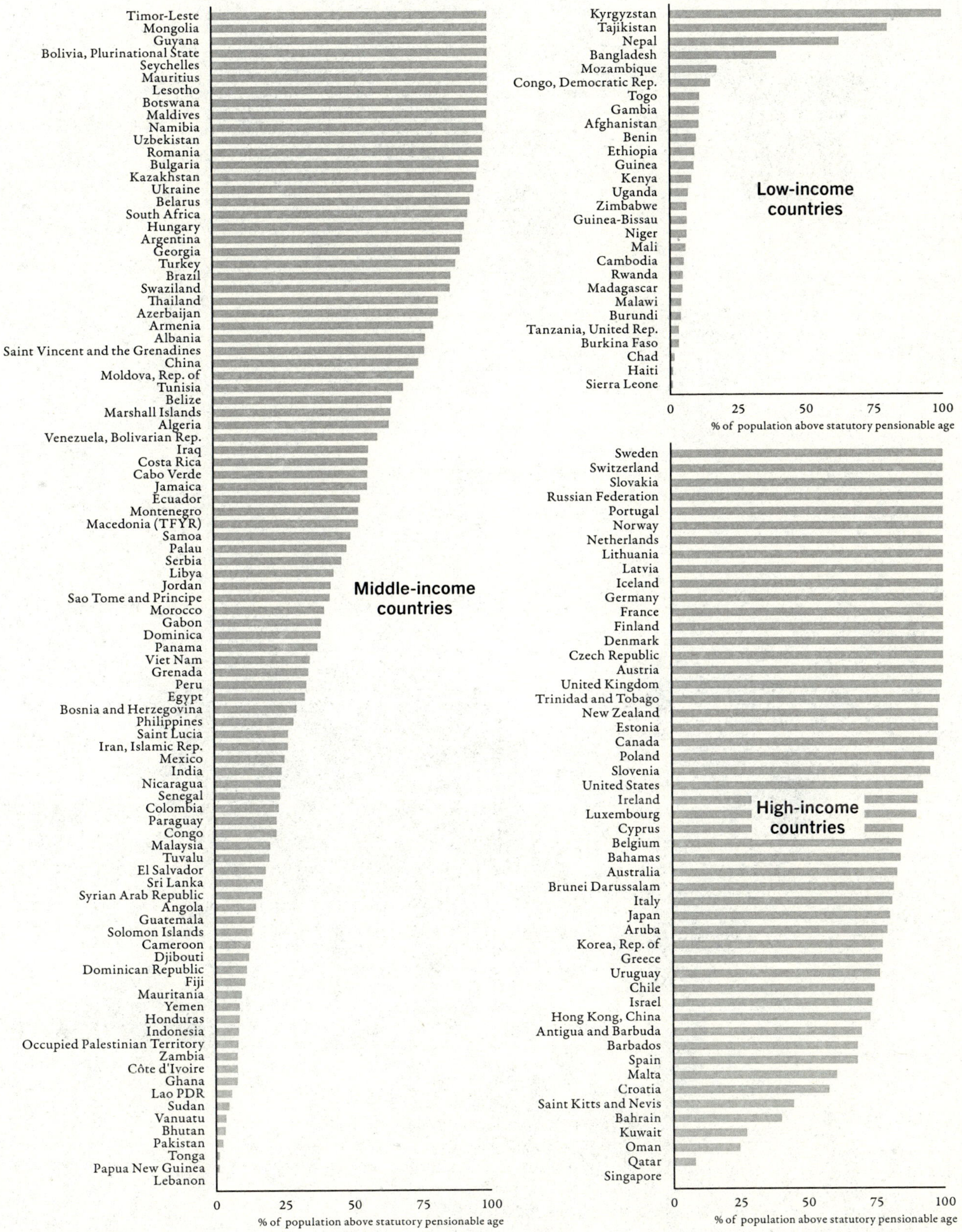

Sources: ILO Social Protection Department, compilation of national available data collected in national social security pension schemes. Based on SSA and ISSA, 2012; SSA and ISSA, 2013a; SSA and ISSA, 2013b; SSA and ISSA, 2014; Eurostat, Income and Living Conditions Database; UN World Population Prospects, 2012 Revision.

Link: http://www.social-protection.org/gimi/gess/RessourceDownload.action?ressource.ressourceId=44420.

Figure 4.10 Old-age pension beneficiaries as a proportion of the population above statutory pensionable age, 2000 and 2010–12 (percentages)

(a) 2000

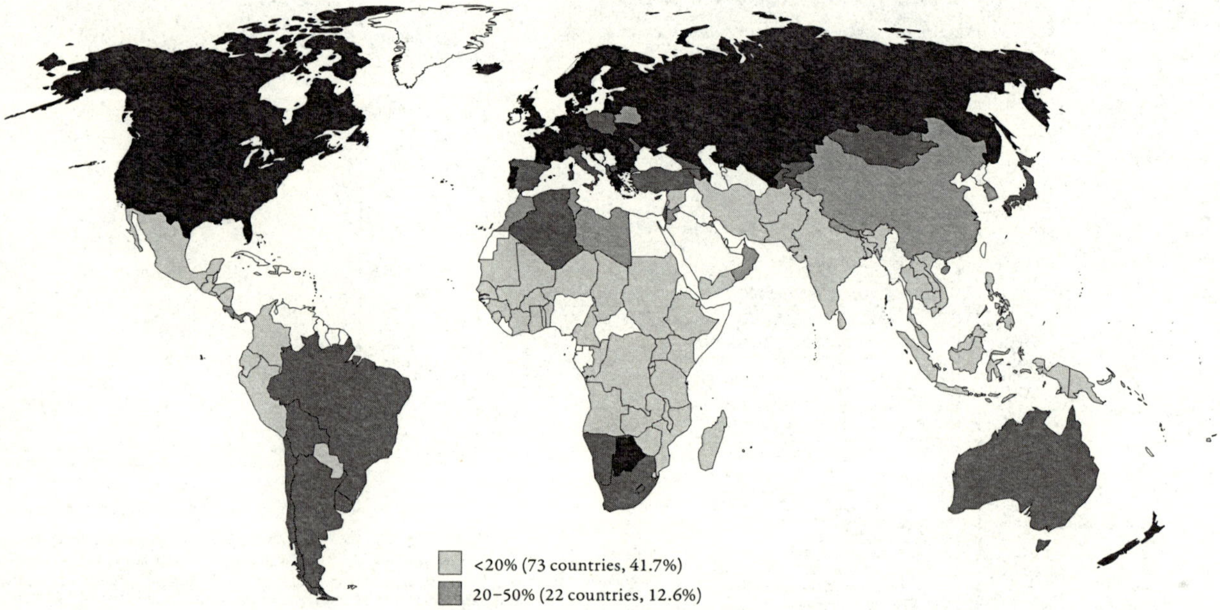

- <20% (73 countries, 41.7%)
- 20–50% (22 countries, 12.6%)
- Between 50–90 per cent (30 countries, 17.1%)
- >90% and over (34 countries, 19.4%)
- No data in 2000 compared to 2010–12 (16 countries, 9.1%)

(b) 2010–12

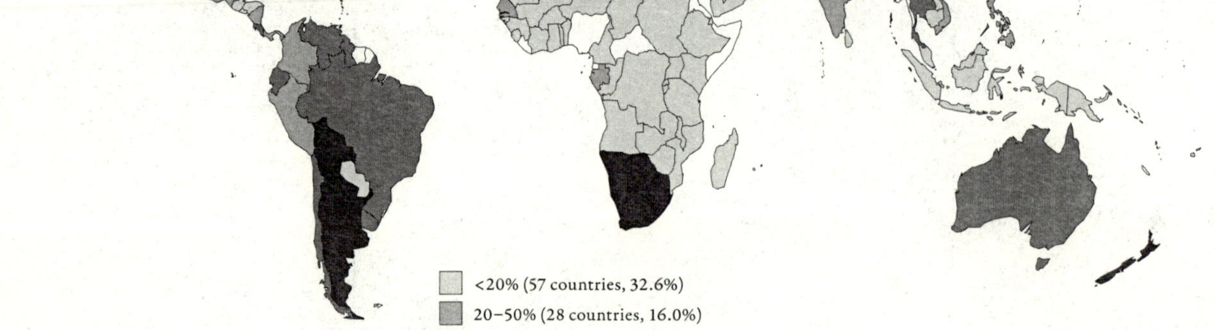

- <20% (57 countries, 32.6%)
- 20–50% (28 countries, 16.0%)
- 50–90% (45 countries, 25.7%)
- 90% and over (45 countries, 25.7%)

Note: Map (a) includes data for 2000 from 159 countries; map (b) includes data for 2010–12 from 175 countries. For individual country data with corresponding year, see Annex IV, table B.9.

Sources: ILO compilation of national available data collected in national social security pension schemes. Based on SSA and ISSA, 2012; SSA and ISSA, 2013a; SSA and ISSA, 2013b; SSA and ISSA, 2014; Income and Living Conditions Database; UN World Population Prospects, 2012 revision.

Links: 2000: http://www.social-protection.org/gimi/gess/RessourceDownload.action?ressource.ressourceId=42880; 2010–12: http://www.social-protection.org/gimi/gess/RessourceDownload.action?ressource.ressourceId=37159.

Figure 4.11 Comparison of the proportion of older persons receiving a pension, 2000 and 2010–12 (percentages)

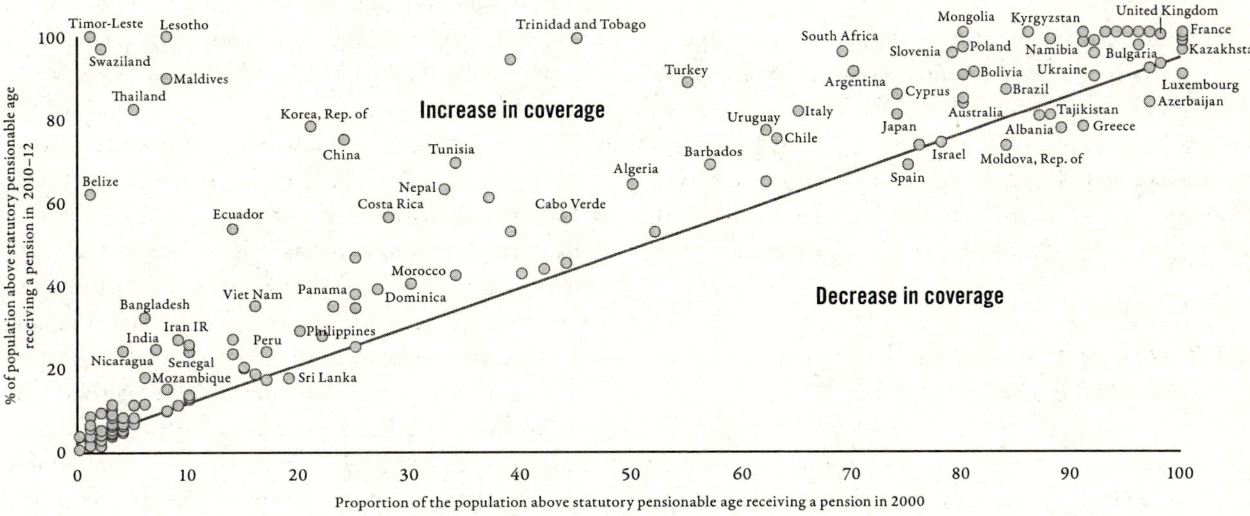

Sources: ILO Social Security Inquiry Database; Eurostat (based on national data sources; see Annex IV, table B.9).
Link: http://www.social-protection.org/gimi/gess/RessourceDownload.action?ressource.ressourceId=42999.

4.4.2 Changes in pension coverage across the world: Progress and regression

Although effective pension coverage ratios are still insufficient, significant progress has been achieved in recent years. Whereas in 2000, only 34 countries reached high coverage of more than 90 per cent of the population above statutory pensionable age, 45 countries fell into this category in 2010–12 (see figures 4.10 and 4.11). At the opposite end of the scale, those countries where pension provision reaches less than 20 per cent of older persons numbered 57, according to the more recent data, as compared with 73 countries in 2000. Overall, the data indicate visible improvement in coverage.

Many countries experienced a significant increase in coverage between 2000 and 2010. Bolivia increased the proportion of older persons receiving a pension from 80.7 to 90.5 per cent between 2000 and 2009, largely due to the reform of its Renta Dignidad programme, which replaced the Bonosol scheme in 2008. Lesotho's pension-tested old-age pension scheme, launched in 2004, now provides a pension to all people above the age of 70, a benefit available to only 8.4 per cent of older persons in 2000. Timor-Leste's universal Support Allowance for the Elderly, introduced in 2008, steeply increased coverage rates from 0.5 per cent to 100 per cent of people aged 60 and older between 2000 and 2011. The introduction of the pension-tested Old Age Grant in Swaziland in 2005 expanded coverage among people aged 60 and older from 1.8 per cent in 2000 to 96.3 per cent in 2010. By expanding the old-age allowance (introduced in 1993) to all those not in receipt of other pensions in 2009, Thailand increased coverage ratios from 5 per cent in 2000 to 81.7 per cent of people aged 60 and above in 2011. By lowering the age threshold of its Old Age Allowance (introduced in 1995) in 2008, Nepal increased its coverage ratio from 33 per cent to 62.5 per cent of people aged 58 and over between 2000 and 2010. China, after increasing potential future pension coverage from 24.4 per cent to 74.4 per cent of the population over statutory pensionable between 2000 and 2011, planned to extend its pension system further towards universal coverage with the decision in 2012 to expand the "new" rural pension scheme piloted in 2009 and the pilot social pension insurance for urban residents launched in 2011 to all counties, aiming at nearly doubling statutory pension insurance coverage by the end of 2015 (see box 4.3). Tunisia improved pension coverage for the self-employed, domestic workers, farmers, fishers and other low-income groups in 2002, helping to increase the proportion of pension beneficiaries among people aged 60 and over from 33.9 per cent in 2000 to 68.8 per cent in 2006. In many countries, the extension of coverage was made possible mainly through the establishment or extension of non-contributory pension schemes which provide at least a basic level of protection for many older persons, while others have combined the expansion of contributory schemes to previously uncovered groups of the population with other measures.[10]

The impressive extension of pension coverage in some parts of the world contrasts with a contraction in others between 2000 and 2010 (see figure 4.11). The latter include several countries, including Albania, Azerbaijan and Greece, which had previously achieved coverage rates close to 90 per cent or higher in 2000, and which suffered a significant decrease thereafter.

4.4.3 Persistent inequalities in access to income security in old age

Access to income security in old age is closely associated with existing inequalities in the labour market and in employment. Such inequalities become evident from examination of a disaggregation of coverage rates by gender and by area of residence (rural/urban), which are the focus of this section (see figures 4.12 and 4.13).[11]

Older women tend to face higher risk of poverty than men. There are many underlying reasons for this, not least the fact that the greater longevity of women results in predominance at the oldest ages of women with poor levels of support and livelihood (UNFPA and HelpAge International, 2012; UNRISD, 2010). This is because pension systems in many countries fail to meet the needs of men and women equitably: contributory pension coverage of women tends to be significantly lower than men's, and the amounts received by women on average tend to be lower (Razavi et al., 2012). While these inequities may be partly due to the gender-biased design of pension schemes (e.g. lower pensionable age for women, or the application of sex-specific mortality tables to calculate benefit levels which result in women receiving lower pensions than men with the same contribution record and retirement age), in many cases a more significant driver of gender inequality is found in the interaction between the results of discrimination against women in the labour market and the design of pension schemes, which does not compensate for differences deriving from labour market conditions and sometimes even magnifies them (Behrendt and Woodall, forthcoming). The fundamental problem is that for many women it is not possible to accrue pension rights on an equal basis with their male counterparts. Women's share in wage employment, particularly in formal wage employment, has historically been lower than men's and continues to be so in many part of the world (ILO, 2012d). Also, women who work in wage employment systematically earn less than men (ILO, 2014c), which also affects the level of their contributions to contributory pension schemes. As women tend to take on a greater share of family responsibilities, they are more likely to shorten or interrupt their employment careers, and face a higher risk of working in precarious and informal employment, which also affects their ability to build up pension entitlements. These factors lead to relatively low pension benefits where these are calculated on an earnings-related basis, unless effective measures are put in place to compensate for gender inequalities. Non-contributory pensions can play a key role in ensuring women's access to at least a basic pension, yet benefit levels are often not sufficient to fully meet their needs.

It is clear, too, that closing the gap in pension provision between women and men is closely linked to the issue of providing equitably for rural and urban residents (see figures 4.12 and 4.13). In many parts of the world, women are disproportionately represented among the rural population, where paid work, even if available, is likely to be relatively poorly paid, informal and insecure – reflecting, in part at least, the movement of men to cities in search of better-paid work at the more formalized end of the labour market spectrum. At the same time, the growing importance of non-contributory pensions in the provision of old-age income is clearly helping to bridge the coverage gap between men and women to some extent. For instance, in Cabo Verde, 41.4 per cent of women above retirement age are receiving the non-contributory pension (31.6 per cent of men); the proportions in rural areas are respectively 53.6 and 42.1 per cent. At the same time, women are less likely than men to receive a contributory pension (11.4 per cent compared to 28.2 per cent), especially in rural areas (8 per cent of women and 22.2 per cent of men).[12] In the case of the Plurinational State of Bolivia, the proportion of older women receiving the

[10] While the extension of coverage constitutes significant progress towards guaranteeing at least a basic level of income security for older persons, a remaining challenge is ensuring the adequacy of pension levels (see below).

[11] As part of the research undertaken to prepare this report, the Social Protection Department of the ILO produced a separate study on social protection for rural women, which includes more detailed discussion of their pension coverage and will be published separately.

[12] Based on an analysis of the Cabo Verde employment survey 2009 (proportion of people aged 60 and older receiving non-contributory pensions).

Figure 4.12 Proportions of women and men in employment contributing to a pension scheme, by area of residence (percentages)

Source: ILO calculations based on national household surveys.

Link: http://www.social-protection.org/gimi/gess/RessourceDownload.action?ressource.ressourceId=43318.

Figure 4.13 Proportions of women and men above statutory pensionable age receiving an old-age (or survivors') pension, by area of residence

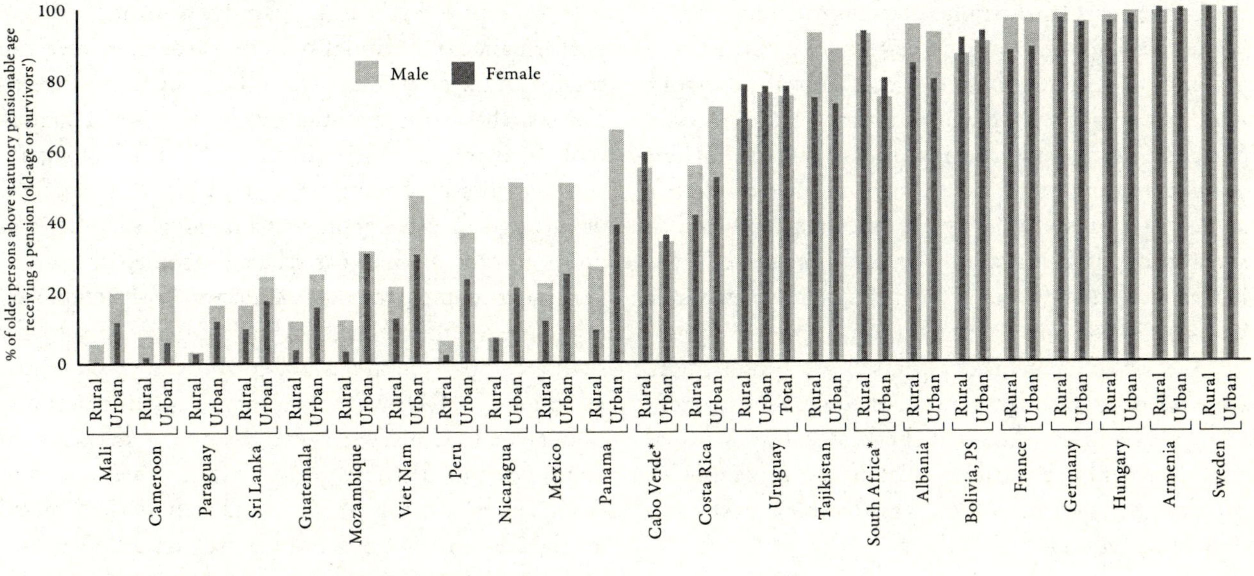

* Percentages based on non-contributory pension only.

Source: ILO calculations based on national household surveys.

Link: http://www.social-protection.org/gimi/gess/RessourceDownload.action?ressource.ressourceId=43317.

non-contributory Renta Dignidad only (as opposed to receiving a reduced level of Renta Dignidad in addition to a contributory pension) is significantly higher than that of men, both at a national level (83.3 per cent compared to 66.3 per cent of men), and in rural areas (90.6 per cent of women and 78.4 per cent of men).[13]

More optimistic prospects may nevertheless be seen in a number of nascent trends that address inequality

[13] ILO calculations based on Bolivian Household Survey 2009.

in pension coverage. There are efforts everywhere to expand the effective coverage of contributory schemes to at least some categories of self-employed and other workers with contributory capacity.[14] Measures to extend the coverage of contributory schemes to agricultural and rural workers in some countries (e.g. Brazil) have contributed to a further narrowing of the rural–urban gap in pension coverage, although significant inequalities persist. In addition, the establishment of large-scale non-contributory pension schemes in many countries has expanded the effective coverage and reduced inequalities, both between the genders and between rural and urban populations.

Gender equality considerations are gaining some ground in the public debate on pensions. Proactive policy measures have been implemented in some countries to reduce the effect of differentiated career patterns on old-age income security. The most obvious discriminatory elements and parameters of national pension schemes, such as the differential pension ages which were common until recently, are rapidly being eliminated, albeit in the context of general increases in pension ages for both women and men.

Other steps in the same direction include crediting pension accounts during maternity, paternity and parental leave, and a better recognition of care work undertaken by both women and men. Measures to facilitate a more equal sharing of care responsibilities between women and men contribute to addressing some of the inequalities in the labour market and in social protection more broadly, and may be reflected in a reduction of gender inequalities in labour markets and pension systems in the long run.[15]

As with so many other aspects of social protection, those relating to the promotion of equitable treatment of women and men must, if they are to be addressed effectively and in a spirit of social justice, be dealt with on a basis which fully integrates labour market and social protection policy-making.

4.5 The adequacy of pensions to provide genuine income security to older persons

In any society, what kind of retirement provisions are considered adequate depends on the prevailing attitudes on such matters as the distribution of responsibility between individuals and the State, redistribution and the support to be provided to the poor and vulnerable, and intergenerational solidarity. At what age retirement happens, what level of income security should be guaranteed and to whom, what degree of intergenerational solidarity should be expected in financing pensions – these are the issues which are usually agreed as underpinning partially implicit and partially explicit social contracts. These social contracts, and the attitudes behind them, evolve over time as social, cultural, demographic and economic conditions change. They are also reflected in international labour standards or human rights instruments.

4.5.1 Guaranteeing income replacement

Any attempt to make a comparative assessment of the performance of national pension systems in meeting their relevant objectives today is beset by many complications. The first is that it is very hard to find a comparable benchmark. One possible solution is to compare the average level of pensions received to the average level of earnings in the economy, as a national snapshot at a given point in time of the relative income situation of pensioners compared to the situation of the employed population. Unfortunately, while the data necessary for such a comparison are available and widely presented in various OECD and EU reports, it is still practically impossible to replicate the exercise on a wider scale for countries outside these groups, mainly due to lack of comparable earnings statistics as well as the limited availability of the household survey data that would enable such comparisons.[16]

Such estimates of income replacement rates provided by pension schemes after retirement are, however, important measures of the degree to which those

---

[14] Opening up the legal opportunity to contribute on a voluntary basis (as, for example, has been done in Indonesia, Mongolia, Thailand and Viet Nam, and in some countries in other regions of the world) does not in itself necessarily secure an effective increase in coverage. To ensure this, additional measures are necessary, including subsidizing the contributions of those with low incomes.

[15] For example, in the case of parental leave, measures to encourage a greater engagement of fathers (e.g. in Sweden or Germany) in sharing care responsibilities can help to reduce discrimination against women in the labour market, which may have a long-term effect on gender inequalities in access to adequate pensions.

[16] Also, such an indicator has a very narrow interpretation in countries where wage earners in the formal economy form only a minority of the population, and thus average wage levels have a very weak relationship with the much lower average household income.

schemes provide adequate benefits for those covered by them (see box 4.4). Other indicators may relate pension amounts to average household incomes, to GDP per capita or to poverty lines. The problem is that, while they may be useful in analysing the adequacy of pension systems within the respective countries, and in comparing the quality of coverage of different groups provided by different schemes, they are not comparable between countries with different extents and patterns of coverage. For this reason, and owing to the limitations in data availability, this report does not include global or regional estimates of the replacement rates and other aspects of quality of pension coverage beyond the OECD.[17]

Table 4.1 Indexation methods

Indexation method	Number of schemes
Price indexation	44
Wage indexation	27
Mixed price/wage	21
Regular, not specified	24
Ad hoc	4
No information	57
Total	177

Note: "no information" in most cases means "no indexation".

Source: ILO Social Protection Department, based on SSA and ISSA, 2012; SSA and ISSA, 2013a; SSA and ISSA, 2013b; SSA and ISSA, 2014.

4.5.2 Preventing erosion of the value of pensions over time: Ensuring regular adjustments

As old-age pensions are drawn for many years after they are initially calculated and awarded, the questions of what happens over the years to their purchasing power and real value, how much those retired have to reduce their standards of living the longer they live after the moment of retirement, what their income position is relative to other groups of the society, and what are the risks of their falling into poverty, are extremely important. Mechanisms to protect the value of pensions in payment through more or less regular pension increases are sometimes referred to as "cost-of-living" adjustments or indexation, and how this is done effects greatly the standard of living of long-term pensioners.

Conventions Nos 102 and 128 both call for levels of benefits in payment to be reviewed following substantial changes in levels of earnings or of costs of living, while Recommendation No. 131 explicitly stipulates that benefit levels should be periodically adjusted taking into account changes in the general level of earnings or costs of living. Recommendation No. 202 requires social protection floor guarantee levels to be reviewed regularly through a transparent procedure that is established by national laws, regulations or practice.

The practice of indexation varies across countries and schemes, as shown in table 4.1.

While wage indexation was more popular in the past, nowadays more and more schemes guarantee at the best only increases in line with cost of living increases. The choice of an indexation method may appear to be a technical detail, but can have a significant impact on the level of pensions, and as a consequence, expenditure on pensions. Where wages increase faster than prices, the change from wage-based indexation to price-based indexation offers significant reductions in pension expenditure, but also leads to the decoupling of pensioners' living standards from those of the working population. The evolution of indexation in Hungary can be taken as an example of a more general trend: in the 1990s indexation of pensions moved from wage indexation to a 50:50 mix of price and wage indices, and recently during the crisis was shifted further to pure wage indexation. Other countries have changed their indexation policy for pensions in payment in a less generous direction: Finland (from 50:50 between earnings and prices to 80 per cent prices and 20 per cent earnings), France (wages to prices), Poland (various changes, most recently from 20:80 earnings:prices to 100 per cent prices) and Slovakia (100 per cent wages to 50:50 wages and prices) (OECD, 2012a, p. 58). Spain decided in 2013 to delink pension adjustment from any standard of living indices and will not allow benefit adjustments higher than 0.25 per cent per annum for a certain time.

[17] The OECD in collaboration with the World Bank has made some attempts to calculate replacement indicators beyond EU and OECD countries, specifically regarding replacement rates provided by pension systems in different countries for hypothetical individuals with different levels of earnings and contributory past service (see Whitehouse, 2012); however, these are not yet included in the World Bank Pension Database. HelpAge's Global AgeWatch Index (HelpAge International, 2013) looks at the overall income situation of older people, not specifically at the levels of protection provided by existing pension systems. Within the AgeWatch Index, income security of older persons is measured by three indicators: percentage of older persons receiving pensions, relative poverty rates of the elderly, and relative income position of the elderly (average incomes of those over 60 as a proportion of average incomes of the rest of the population).

Figure 4.14 Pensioners' declining relative standard of living as a result of price indexation or no indexation (compared to standard of living with wage indexation = 100)

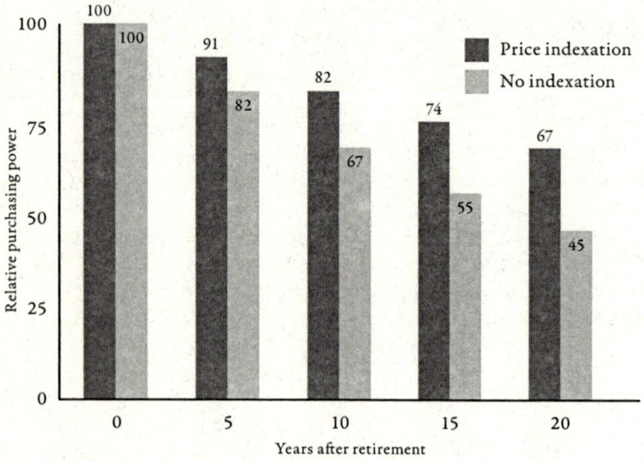

Note: These calculations are based on the assumption that both real wages and prices increase by 2 per cent per year.

Source: ILO calculations based on Hirose, 2011.

Link: http://www.social-protection.org/gimi/gess/RessourceDownload.action?ressource.ressourceId=43319.

Other schemes, including many in Africa, have provided at the best only occasional, ad hoc increases. This results, particularly in inflationary environments, in a majority of pensioners eventually receiving only a minimal pension, and many of them falling into poverty even though before retirement they were high-earning professionals.

Figure 4.14 shows how pensions in payment lose their relative purchasing power if not increased at the same rate as wages under conditions of real wage growth (assuming moderate real wage growth of 2 per cent and inflation of only 2 per cent[18]).

Reducing the frequency of adjustments, or suspending them totally, severely and immediately affects the standard of living of pensioners and their families. Unless pensions are adjusted in line with increases in real wages or some other measure of overall living standards, the further men and women are beyond the moment of retirement, the larger the gap between their living standards and those of people who are still economically active. This widening gap may exacerbate the economic and social exclusion of older persons as it may mean, among other things, that they cannot afford

[18] In many countries, rates of inflation are much higher than this and, as a result, the erosion of pensions' absolute purchasing power progresses much faster in the absence of regular and adequate indexation. In some countries, the majority of beneficiaries receive pensions at the minimum pension level a few years after retirement.

Box 4.4 Trends in replacement rates and adequacy of pension payments

One of the great achievements of pension policies in many European countries and in some other parts of the world in the years following the Second World War was to dramatically reduce poverty in old age. However, recent developments in the labour market, as well as some policy reforms, increase the risk of a resurgence of old-age poverty.

While most countries protected the income of older persons relatively well during the recent crisis, there are exceptions. Countries that either continuously adjust pensions (including the lowest ones) at a significantly lower rate than the increase in wages or average incomes (e.g. Poland, where pensions are adjusted at only 20 per cent of real wage growth) or suspend pension adjustments (as Sweden did during the crisis as a result of its automatic balancing mechanism) experienced an increase in relative poverty of their older populations. Between 2005 and 2012, poverty rates among retired people increased from 10 to 18 per cent in Sweden and from 7 to 14 per cent in Poland.

This trend may spread in the future to other countries as well. Many pension reforms undertaken to stabilize future costs of pension systems will result in much lower benefits. Figure 4.15 presents changes in future replacement rates of public pension schemes in EU countries. In some countries the expected decrease in replacement rate is very significant. In addition, as many reforms removed redistributive mechanisms from contributory schemes, these lower replacement rates will apply also to those with low earnings throughout their working lives.

According to Eurostat, in 2010 17 per cent of employees in the EU (over 21 per cent of women and over 13 per cent of men) had earnings below the "low-earnings" threshold (defined as two-thirds of median earnings). The highest proportions of low-wage-earners were in Latvia (27.8 per cent), Lithuania (27.2 per cent), Romania (25.6 per cent), Poland (24.2 per cent) and Estonia (23.8 per cent), while the lowest were in Sweden (2.5 per cent, Finland (5.9 per cent), France (6.1 per cent), Belgium (6.4 per cent) and Denmark (7.7 per cent).[1]

What minimum replacement rates would guarantee those low-wage-earners a future pension income above the poverty line? As figure 4.16 shows, countries would need to provide replacement rates of between 50 and 90 per cent of previous earnings to prevent poverty in old age for those on low-incomes.

In what are often considered "old-fashioned" defined-benefit social security pension schemes, redistributive benefit formulas (usually with a flat rate component or equivalent) used to guarantee such higher replacement rates for low-wage-earners. →

Today, many countries have removed those redistributive formulas when introducing either defined-contribution or notional defined contribution (NDC) components or converting defined-benefit schemes into purely earnings-related schemes. In this situation, securing a sufficient level of benefits for low-paid workers would require strengthening minimum benefit provisions, by means including various forms of non-contributory minimum income guarantees.

[1] Calculations based on Eurostat Structure of Earnings Survey 2010.

Figure 4.15 Average replacement rates at retirement in public pension schemes in 2010 and projected for 2060, selected European countries (percentages)

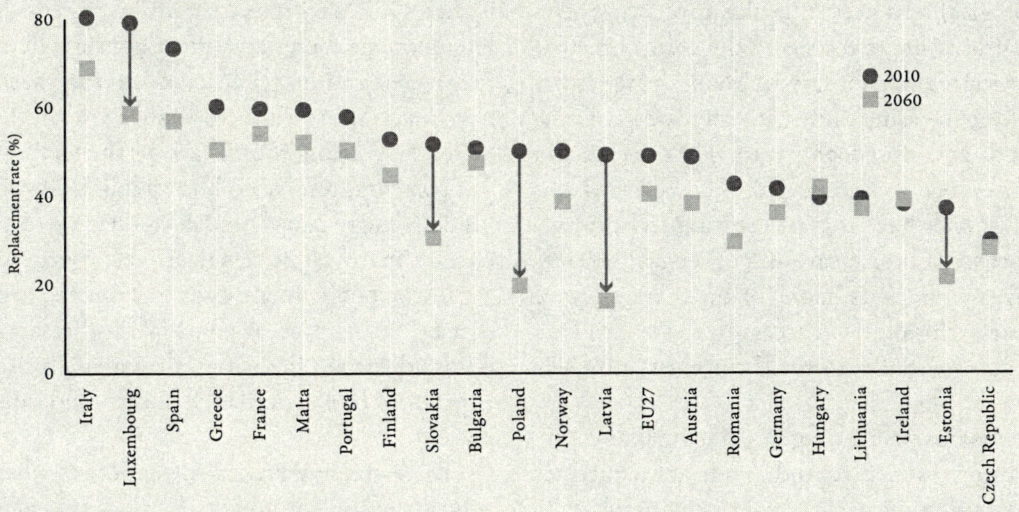

Source: Based on European Commission, 2012c.

Link: http://www.social-protection.org/gimi/gess/RessourceDownload.action?ressource.ressourceId=43003.

Figure 4.16 Minimum replacement rates necessary to guarantee pension income above the poverty threshold

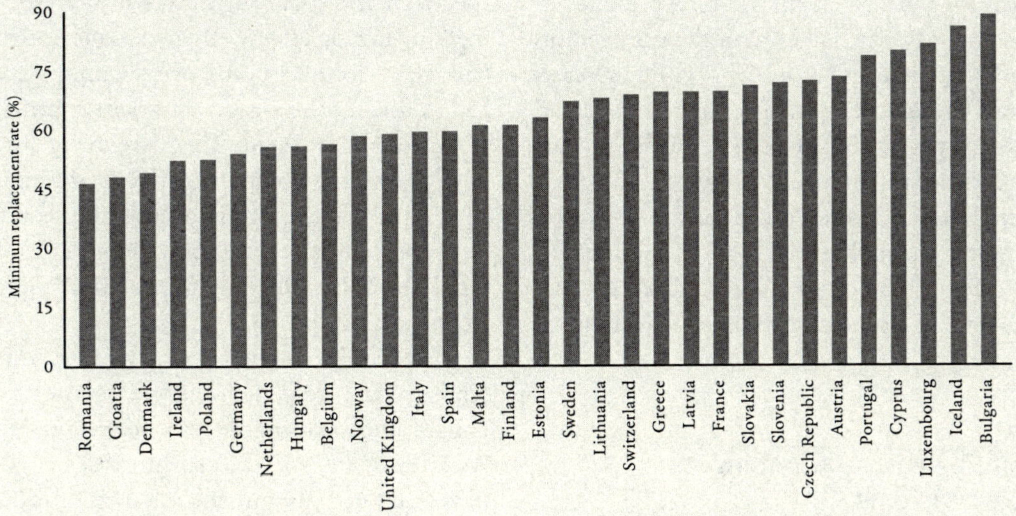

Source: ILO calculations using Eurostat data.

Link: http://www.social-protection.org/gimi/gess/RessourceDownload.action?ressource.ressourceId=43002.

Source: Based on information from Eurostat.

to access new, modern technologies and new goods and services changing the lives of more affluent groups in society. In cases where pensions are not even fully adjusted to inflation – which is quite common globally – the absolute purchasing power of older persons deteriorates and they are pushed into poverty.

The effects of incomplete adjustments of pensions that prevent older persons from keeping up with rising overall living standards are rendered more dramatic by the technological advances in health care that everywhere are pushing up its costs, and the costs of related goods and services, at a faster pace than average inflation – while at the same time, with increasing age the need for more (and more sophisticated) health care and related services increases dramatically. As older persons in many countries have to pay a substantial proportion of the costs of health care and other care services out of their own pockets, many of them are at grave risk of either exclusion from access to the health care they need or financial ruin for themselves and their families.

Nonetheless, as suspending or delaying indexation of benefits brings immediate and significant reductions in public spending, in particular in demographically "old" countries with matured pension systems and large numbers of pensioners, it is often seen and used by governments as one of the instruments to contain public spending. The OECD noted that "governments frequently override indexation rules ... in a pro-cyclical way: pension increases are larger than the rules require when the public finances are healthy while increases are postponed or reduced in times of fiscal constraint" (OECD, 2012a, pp. 59–60). Several countries (including Canada, Germany, Japan, Portugal and Sweden) have explicitly linked indexation to certain indicators of sustainability. The problem is that – as became clear during the recent economic and financial crisis – such mechanisms may result even in absolute benefit cuts in times of crisis.

4.6 Reforming and re-reforming pension systems

ILO social security standards provide guidelines respecting different dimensions of benefit adequacy (age of eligibility and other entitlement conditions, benefit levels and protection of purchasing power) and at the same time require careful monitoring of the long-term financial situation of pension schemes through actuarial valuations undertaken both regularly and whenever any important parameters of the scheme change. Policy decisions to adjust and reform schemes and systems are, however, left to governments and their social partners.

Unfortunately, practice in many countries shows that even if actuarial valuations are undertaken on a regular basis and lead to recommendations for reform, actual reforms are often significantly delayed or do not happen at all. One of the main reasons for this is that while decisions on pension systems have a very long-term character and affect not only living but also future generations, politicians taking these decisions have much shorter time horizons within the electoral cycle. In addition, there is always the temptation to use pension fund reserves – both public and private – as a kind of "piggy bank", which can be raided – as experience in many countries over recent years shows – to repair the public finances or bail out the private sector (Casey, 2014). Use of pension fund reserves for purposes other than financing current and future pensions is proof of bad governance and should not be taking place.

There are, however, many countries where effective solutions were found which allow the adequacy and sustainability of pension systems to be held in balance through democratic policy dialogues well informed by independent expertise, and where reforms are implemented with a broad consensus across the political spectrum and spanning different interests, guaranteeing long-lasting effects. There is no recipe to be identified which would work in every country; each country has to find a solution which fits its specific social and political environment. There are many studies by the ILO and others analysing different solutions and processes and identifying good practice as well as problems and challenges (e.g. Eurofound, 2013; Sarfati and Ghellab, 2012; Ghellab, Varela and Woodall, 2011; Reynaud, 2000).

Conversely, in many countries in Europe and elsewhere over recent decades the balance between adequacy and sustainability concerns was endangered. Assertions of a "social security crisis" or "old-age crisis" have been used as a justification to introduce reforms which substantially reduce the future adequacy of benefits and significantly increase the risk of poverty in old age for future generations of retirees (see European Commission, 2012d; OECD, 2013a). Pressures of tax competition and global financial markets limit governments' ostensibly sovereign power to introduce increases in social security contributions and taxes where necessary to prevent benefit cuts. Lobbying by the international financial services sector was successful in pushing for large-scale privatizations of social security pensions (Hagemejer and Scholz, 2004; Hagemejer, 2005) – though these were reversed in a number of countries in the wake of the financial and economic crisis (see box 4.5). Social dialogue mechanisms failed in a number of cases to reach a consensus with the social partners on how and to what extent to bring about increases in the (effective average) age at which individuals start to draw pension benefits, and on how labour markets should be reorganized and regulated so as to better meet the needs of increasing numbers of those older persons who wish to, or indeed need to, continue in employment to significantly greater ages than previously considered appropriate.

These failures to agree on necessary reforms through social dialogue and implement them through well-informed and deliberate policy-making has led many countries to adopt too readily a "hands-off" approach to their governance of the pension system (Woodall and Hagemejer, 2009), through partial privatization but also through various "automatic balancing mechanisms". These include linking accrual rates used to calculate pensions in social security schemes automatically to life expectancy at retirement (as in countries which introduced NDC schemes, but also in Brazil in the case of early-retirement pensions, as well as in many other countries), or automatically linking the age of pension eligibility to life expectancy (as in Denmark, France, Greece and Italy). This took most extreme form in Sweden, where changes in value of one indicator ("balance ratio") deemed to reflect the long-term financial position of the pension scheme not only affect the future pension entitlements of contributors, but may also lead to reductions in the amounts of pension paid to current pensioners (as happened in the middle of the financial and economic crisis).

"Solutions" of this kind would automatically, without intervention of policy-makers and without discussions among the social partners, adjust benefit levels, indexation formulas, retirement ages and numbers of years of contributions required to receive a full pension, according to certain selected statistical indicators (linked to life expectancy at retirement or to certain ratios between revenue or assets of a scheme and its expenditure or liability). One of the ways to achieve such automatic (downward) adjustments of benefit levels to the changing demographic and economic conditions is to expand the defined contribution components of pension systems, as has happened in many countries across the world. Such "automatic pilots" are however also built in into "notional" defined-contribution schemes in countries including Italy, Latvia, Norway, Poland and in particular Sweden, where the "automatic balancing mechanism" in addition regulates the pace of indexation of benefits and the valorization of past contributions. They are also present in the form of various "sustainability factors" in different "point" schemes (such as those in Germany and France, and outside Europe in Canada or Japan). Some countries, including Denmark, France, Greece and Italy, have linked future increases in the pensionable age to future changes in life expectancy.

Most of these automatic mechanisms lead ultimately to downward adjustments of benefit levels to ensure financial sustainability. In only two OECD countries (Canada and Germany) are there mechanisms that may result in an increase of the effective contribution rate (Di Addio and Whitehouse, 2012). Apart from minimum pension guarantees – where they exist – there are no similar automatic mechanisms which would adjust the system to ensure that benefits are adequate. Even automatic adjustments of benefits in payment to price changes are reduced or totally eliminated.

These automatic mechanisms focus solely on the objective of ensuring the long-term financial sustainability of pension systems, while at the same time trying to sidestep open policy debates and social dialogue, which are seen as obstacles preventing timely adoption of necessary policy changes. The consequences of this approach are very severe, as the absence of any corresponding automatic mechanisms to secure desired levels of adequacy undermines the necessary balance between adequacy and sustainability concerns. In addition, in the short term some of these mechanisms cause pro-cyclical change in the amounts of benefits paid. Joseph Stiglitz drew attention to this phenomenon in 2009:

> When the economy gets weaker, spending on social protection and unemployment schemes should automatically go up, helping to stabilize the economy. However, ... one of the sad facts of the so-called reforms in recent decades is that we have been weakening these important automatic stabilizers. The extent of progressivity in tax systems has been lowered, and we have moved from defined benefit systems to defined contribution retirement systems, again weakening the automatic stabilizers of the economy and in some cases converting them into automatic destabilizers (Stiglitz, 2009, pp. 4–5).

Box 4.5 Re-reforms and "un-privatizations" of pension systems in Latin America and Central and Eastern Europe

Between 1981 and 2008, 11 Latin American countries completely or partially privatized their public pay-as-you-go pension systems. Such reforms also spread at the end of the 1990s and the beginning of the new millennium in most of the countries of Central and Eastern Europe, where a proportion of social security contributions (in some countries, such as Hungary, Poland and Slovakia, up to one-third) were channelled out of public social security pensions into mandatory, privately managed individual accounts. However, during the past few years these privatizations have come to a halt, and in some countries have been reversed, while public provision was reintroduced or strengthened.

In Chile, where the "new paradigm" was introduced as early as 1981, enough time elapsed to show that the new system not only did not enhance coverage and compliance as expected but was also unable to provide adequate income security in old age, especially to those with low earnings and shorter, broken careers (and in particular to women). Chile was thus also the first country to initiate a re-reform. In 2008 the existing mandatory, privately managed fully funded scheme was complemented by two new public schemes: a basic universal pension for the 60 per cent of the population on lower incomes without pension provision (Pensión Básica Solidaria, PBS) and, alternatively, a government-funded supplement to those with very low pensions (Aporte Previsional Solidario, APS). Moreover, President Bachelet is creating a Public AFP (pension fund). To reduce the administration costs of the private pension tier, public supervision was strengthened and greater competition among pension fund administrators was encouraged.

Other countries in the region have also implemented substantial re-reforms of their pension systems: Argentina in 2008, the Plurinational State of Bolivia in 2010 and Uruguay in 2013. While the first two countries completely eliminated the private pillar, Uruguay, like Chile, retained it, but improved supervision and strengthened the public pillar. The main objectives of all these reforms are to improve coverage and adequacy by expanding (Argentina), universalizing (Plurinational State of Bolivia) or introducing (Chile) non-contributory schemes.

One of the aspects of the re-reforms was to scale down the size of mandatory individual account schemes. This scaling down has two main objectives: first, to make pensions more secure again, and, second, to ease the pressure on the public finances from the need to fill the gap in funding for public provision after a proportion of contributions was channelled into private funds.

Full or partial renationalizations of assets accumulated in mandatory private pension schemes took place in Argentina and the Plurinational State of Bolivia in Latin America, and elsewhere in Hungary, Kazakhstan and Poland. A number of countries (including Lithuania, Poland, the Russian Federation, Slovakia and, for some categories of workers, Uruguay) made the privately managed sector voluntary, allowing people to opt out and go back to public provision. During the years of the crisis, most countries with mandatory private pension schemes in Europe either temporarily or permanently reduced or froze the stream of contributions allocated to private pension funds, keeping them for the public system, which was in most cases in significant deficit.

While the Chilean re-reform was clearly done with the objective of building a floor of protection so that everybody on reaching old age will have a guarantee of at least minimum income security (an objective that also played a strong role in the Plurinational State of Bolivia), other countries, in particular those of Central and Eastern Europe, were to a large extent motivated by public finance concerns, with a view to reducing budgetary deficits and public debt. In countries such as Poland, Hungary and Slovakia, privatization of social security pensions has been adding about 1.5 per cent of GDP every year to national deficits. As private pension funds invested most of their assets in bonds issued by governments to cover – among other things – deficits caused by channelling contributions to private pension funds, one can understand the radical decisions taken by some governments to stop this circular flow of money which seemed to benefit only the incomes of private pension administrators. The Polish Government, for example, not only cut contributions to the funded tier from 7.3 per cent to 2.9 per cent of wages and made participation voluntary (and required current members to reconfirm they want to continue rather than be transferred, with their assets, to the public tier), but in 2014 is transferring all assets kept in government bonds to a social insurance institution and banning any further investments by the remaining funded tier.

Sources: Based on Mesa-Lago, 2012; Hirose, 2011; Calvo, Bertranou and Bertranou, 2010; ILO, 2010e; Bertranou et al., 2012.

4.7 Ensuring income security for older persons: The continuing challenge

Today, the majority of the world's older persons live in developing countries, where retirement is a privilege of public and private sector workers who are fortunate to work in the formal economy. Globally, the broad majority of older persons do not benefit from publicly provided minimum income guarantees, have to work as long as they are physically able to for their survival, and have to rely on kinship and charity which are often insufficient to provide even basic income security. This situation stands in sharp contrast with the global social contract embodied in human rights instruments and international labour standards, under which everybody has a right to at least minimum income security in old age.

Fortunately, attitudes are changing and are followed by policy actions: more and more countries across the world are seeking to expand their contributory pensions to those who are not currently covered but potentially have sufficient contributory capacity to participate. Many countries are also expanding non-contributory provisions in the form of so-called "social pensions", available either universally to all who reach a certain age threshold or to those who have no or insufficient pension or other income, which provide at least a modest regular income to older persons.

There are of course questions to be addressed relating to the balance between the adequacy of benefits and their affordability, and to the long-term financial and fiscal sustainability of pension schemes. Establishing a pension system is a long-term commitment, and long-term balances between future benefit costs and available means of financing have to be regularly monitored (as, indeed, has been explicitly required from the outset by international labour standards). If people live longer but pensionable age is not proportionally adjusted (that is, if the duration of retirement and of the period during which pensions are received increases relative to the duration of economic activity and of contributory period), the costs of pensions will unavoidably increase unless benefit levels are cut.

Affordability depends on the existence of policy space for the objective of guaranteeing income security in old age: if such space exists (that is, if there is a political willingness to implement such guarantees), the way is usually open to create the necessary fiscal space as well (after assessing the opportunity costs of allocating resources to this and not to other ends). However, support for pension financing, the ensuing policy choices, and the corresponding fiscal space may erode over time if coverage and benefits cease to be perceived as adequate and just, or if governance and delivery fail.

As noted above, the sustainability of pension systems seems to be quite well guarded in many countries. However, what is missing is an equally careful monitoring of benefit adequacy, and of the social and economic impacts of ongoing benefit reductions. The conclusions and recommendations that arise from such monitoring should feed into policy dialogue involving all stakeholders, and should also lead to changes in the application of "automatic pilots" if they put the system on the wrong track.

Adequacy and sustainability are two sides of the same coin: promises of generous pensions not balanced by sustainable financing will never materialize, while, on the other hand, if a low-cost pension system is not accepted as adequate, the willingness to pay the taxes and contributions necessary to finance it will erode. What is needed vmeasures that ensure a genuine balance between adequacy and sustainability – a balance which can only be achieved through real and democratic social dialogue resulting in a renewed and reinvigorated social contract on pensions.

Towards universal coverage in health

5

KEY MESSAGES

- The ILO's pioneering role in the foundation of universal coverage in health protection dates back to 1944, when the Declaration of Philadelphia and the Medical Care Recommendation, 1944 (No. 69), were adopted. Most recently, the ILO was requested, along with the WHO and other UN agencies, to give high priority to working jointly towards universal health coverage, and towards the associated goal of establishing social protection floors, by the UN General Assembly.
- The urgency of striving for universal coverage in health is illustrated by the fact that more than 90 per cent of the population living in low-income countries remains without any right to coverage in health. Globally, about 39 per cent of the population is lacking such coverage. As a result, about 40 per cent of global health expenditure is shouldered directly by the sick.
- Despite coverage, health care is frequently neither available nor affordable, and access to needed services can lead to poverty. As a result, much of the coverage that exists is illusory. Often, even people who are legally covered experience limited health benefits, high out-of-pocket payments and a lack of the health workers needed to deliver services.
- The ILO estimates that there is a global shortfall of 10.3 million health workers required to ensure that all in need receive quality health services. This gap, and the often close-to-poverty wages of health workers, are blocking progress towards universal health coverage.
- Globally, 88 countries in all regions have proved that it is possible to close the gaps in health coverage. Many of them began the process of reform at lower levels of national income and invested in times of economic crisis. Further, they have shown that countries can achieve high coverage rates and even universal coverage irrespective of the financing mechanisms chosen.
- Investing in health protection, including paid sick leave, yields returns. However, public expenditure on health protection is at present too low to be sufficiently effective: the potential economic returns from increased productivity and employment cannot be realized while gaps in coverage persist. Closing these gaps would lead to the highest rates of return in the world's poorest countries.
- Fiscal consolidation measures have sharpened inequities in access to health care and increased exclusion by shifting the burden from the public purse to private households. Further, fiscal consolidation measures have blocked economic recovery by reducing the effectiveness and efficiency of health protection.
- Significant investments in health protection and coherent policy approaches across the health, social and economic sectors are needed to address inequities in access to health care and realize the potential of health protection as an economic stabilizer.

5.1 The crucial role of universal health coverage for individuals and the economy

Health coverage, and particularly access to health care when it is needed, is crucial for human well-being. In addition, of all the elements of social protection, health care is most essential to the economy as a whole and to economic recovery in particular. In developing countries the economic returns on investing in health are estimated at 24 per cent of economic growth between 2000 and 2011, taking into account increases in both national income and life years gained (The Lancet Commission, 2013). The economic impacts of investments in health care may be summarized as follows:

- development and economic growth, through increased labour productivity; a growing labour force due to reductions in disability, mortality and life expectancy; the contribution of the health sector itself to economic activity; increased household consumption opportunities as a result of reduced out-of-pocket expenditure;
- productivity increases through reduced absenteeism;
- employment effects and job growth arising from the improved physical capacities of workers and from both direct employment in the health sector and multiplier effects in industry, local businesses and other sectors;
- stabilization of the economy in times of crises, by cushioning the impacts of economic crises on individual health and ensuring continued employment for those in the health sector and related sectors;
- income generation, based on increased ability to work;
- poverty alleviation, through minimizing the private health expenditure of those who are poor or near to poverty.

In the longer term, growing tax bases arising from the indirect economic effects of investments in health will generate more public funds at national level, particularly in low- and middle-income countries.

Against this background, health protection schemes and systems that are well designed and implemented, and are embedded in appropriate economic and labour market policies, have the potential to recover large parts of their costs at the national level. Thus, both the (working) population and the economy are beneficiaries of investments in social health protection.

5.2 The foundation of universal coverage in health in international labour standards

Given the critical importance of human health both to individuals and to social and economic development, it is important that countries and development partners across the world be aligned in support of the objective of establishing universal coverage. In recognition of this imperative, health coverage has been at the core of the ILO mandate since its foundation in 1919 (see box 5.1). The extension of such coverage to all in need has been a priority since 1944, as stated in the Declaration of Philadelphia. The first formulation of guidance to achieve universal coverage dates back to the same year, when ILO constituents adopted the Medical Care Recommendation, 1944 (No. 69), which states: "The medical care service should cover all members of the community, whether or not they are gainfully occupied" (Para. 8).

Since then, this objective and the specific means for its realization have been spelled out in numerous ILO Conventions and Recommendations, most recently in the Social Protection Floors Recommendation, 2012 (No. 202), which emphasizes that in each country, all residents and children should be guaranteed access to health care, and that this should include at least essential health care, prevention and maternal care, financed through social protection systems and schemes so as to avoid financial access barriers, e.g. through excessive out-of-pocket payments.

Recommendation No. 202 specifies the need for:

- *legal health coverage* by a health protection system or scheme, e.g. through entitlements to benefits prescribed by national law; that is, rights-based protection (in contrast to charitable provision, for instance) through national health services and/or national, social or private health insurance schemes operated in line with certain conditions; and
- *guaranteed access* to at least essential health care that meets the criteria of availability, accessibility, acceptability and quality (AAAQ),[1] without risk of hardship or increased risk of poverty due to the financial consequences of gaining such access.

[1] These criteria have been set out in UN, 2000.

Box 5.1 Approaching universal coverage in health: Anchored in ILO Conventions and Recommendations and further international standards

The Universal Declaration of Human Rights (UDHR, 1948) and the International Covenant on Economic, Social and Cultural Rights (ICESCR, 1966) set out:

- the right to the "highest attainable standard of physical and mental health" (ICESCR, Art. 12(1)) and to "a standard of living adequate for the health and well-being of himself and his family, including ... medical care" (UDHR, Art. 25(1));
- the right to "social security, including social insurance" (ICESCR, Art. 9), "in the event of ... sickness, disability ... or other lack of livelihood in circumstances beyond his control" (UDHR, Art. 25(1)); and
- the right to "conditions which would assure to all medical service and medical attention in the event of sickness" (ICESCR, Art. 12(2d)).

The ILO Medical Care Recommendation, 1944 (No. 69), emphasizes that "medical care service should cover all members of the community, whether or not they are gainfully occupied" (Para. 8) and provides comprehensive guidelines for the provision and delivery of medical care, particularly the essential features of a medical care service, the entitlement of persons covered, as well as the scope, organization, quality, funding and administration of medical care.

The Social Security (Minimum Standards) Convention, 1952 (No. 102), states that medical care needs to be provided "in respect of a condition requiring medical care of a preventive or curative nature" (Art. 7), in cases of "morbid condition", that is, ill health (Art. 8), and in maternity (Art. 8). Medical care benefits should include:

- general practitioner care, including domiciliary visiting;
- specialist care at hospitals for inpatients and outpatients, and such specialist care as may be available outside hospitals;
- essential pharmaceutical supplies, as prescribed by medical or other qualified practitioners;
- hospitalization where necessary; and,
- pre- and post-natal care for pregnancy and childbirth and their consequences, either by medical practitioners or by qualified midwives, and hospitalization where necessary.

The Medical Care and Sickness Benefits Convention, 1969 (No. 130), and its accompanying Recommendation (No. 134), outline a more advanced set of standards for medical care than Convention No. 102, extending the benefit package to include dental care, medical rehabilitation (prosthetics), medical aids such as eyeglasses, and services for convalescents. Convention No. 130 also mandates those member States that have ratified the Convention to increase the number of persons protected, extend the range of medical care provided and extend the duration of sickness benefit.

The Social Protection Floors Recommendation, 2012 (No. 202), stipulates that national social protection floors should be established consisting of basic guarantees ensuring at a minimum that, over the life cycle, all in need have access to essential health care and to basic income security (Paras 4 and 5), including sickness benefits. According to the Recommendation:

- the principles of universality and entitlement to benefits prescribed by national law should apply (Para. 3);
- all residents and children should be entitled to "access to a nationally defined set of goods and services, constituting essential health care, including maternity care, that meets the criteria of availability, accessibility, acceptability and quality", without risk of "hardship and an increased risk of poverty due to the financial consequences of accessing essential health care" (Paras 5, 6 and 8);
- social protection floors should be established by member States with a view to "building comprehensive social security systems" incorporating "the range and levels of benefits set out in the Social Security (Minimum Standards) Convention, 1952 (No. 102), or in other ILO social security Conventions and Recommendations setting out more advanced standards" (Para. 17).

Universality of health coverage implies that in all countries, rights-based approaches, anchored and framed in legislation, should exist to cover the whole population, including workers in the formal and informal economy and their families. The implementation and enforcement of these approaches is a prerequisite for access to health care when needed.

According to Recommendation No. 202, universal health coverage further requires effective access to at least essential health care as defined at national level and also income replacement during periods of sickness, provided equally to all in need. This necessitates the availability of acceptable quality care, which entails a sufficient number of skilled health workers for service delivery and adequate funds e.g. for drugs and infrastructure. In addition, it is necessary that co-payments, user fees and other costs involved in taking up care are affordable and that financial protection is provided in order to avoid hardship or impoverishment. Finally, effective access requires good governance of schemes and systems, which should be based on accountability, including participatory processes such as social and national dialogue.

Thus, the Recommendation defines a concept of universal coverage in health that entails taking into account both legal coverage and access to health care: only the combination of both will lead to meaningful protection for the population and ensure equitable access as a matter of right to services that meet the AAAQ criteria. The ILO has developed tools and indicators for measuring the status quo and progress towards universal health coverage on both dimensions.

The notion of universal health coverage was also developed over the years in other UN agencies, particularly the World Health Organization (WHO), which referred to it in, for example, a resolution of the World Health Assembly (WHO, 2011b) encouraging countries to aim for universal coverage. Today, the principle of universal health coverage has gained momentum and the UN General Assembly has asked the WHO and other UN agencies, including the ILO, to give high priority to working jointly towards universal health coverage in the context of wider approaches to social protection, in consultation with UN member States (UN, 2012c).

5.3 Coverage deficits, especially in low-income countries

The ILO's work towards establishing universal coverage in health is supported by specific databases that reveal health coverage and access deficits. In line with Recommendation No. 202, data have been gathered and analysed on both key aspects of coverage: legal health coverage, defined as affiliation to a health system or scheme and access to health care that meets specific criteria which are measured by proxy indicators.[2] While these data are subject to limitations including reliance on published secondary data and gaps in availability, the ILO considers the aggregate data to be reliable.

These data reveal that nearly four-tenths (38.9 per cent) of the world's population are without any form of legal health coverage. The largest coverage gaps are in Africa, particularly in sub-Saharan Africa, where some 80 per cent of the population is excluded from legal coverage, and in Asia: for example, in India, more than 80 per cent of the population is not legally covered (figure 5.1).

In 44 countries across the world more than 80 per cent of the inhabitants remain without coverage as they are not affiliated to any health system or scheme (figure 5.2). These countries include Azerbaijan, Bangladesh, Burkina Faso, Cameroon, Haiti, Honduras, India and Nepal.

Figure 5.1 Health coverage by region: Proportion of population affiliated to national health services, social, private or micro-insurance schemes, latest available year (percentages)

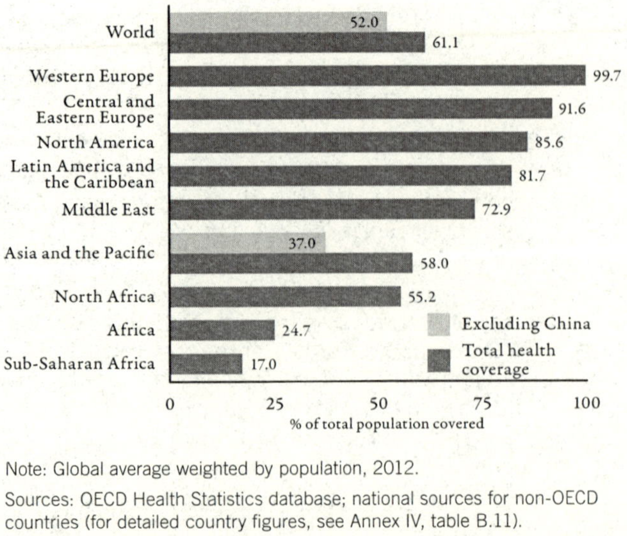

Note: Global average weighted by population, 2012.

Sources: OECD Health Statistics database; national sources for non-OECD countries (for detailed country figures, see Annex IV, table B.11).

Link: http://www.social-protection.org/gimi/gess/RessourceDownload.action?ressource.ressourceId=36977.

[2] Detailed descriptions of definitions and indicators are available in Annex IV.

Figure 5.2 Global health coverage: Proportion of population affiliated to national health services, social, private or micro-insurance schemes, latest available year (percentages)

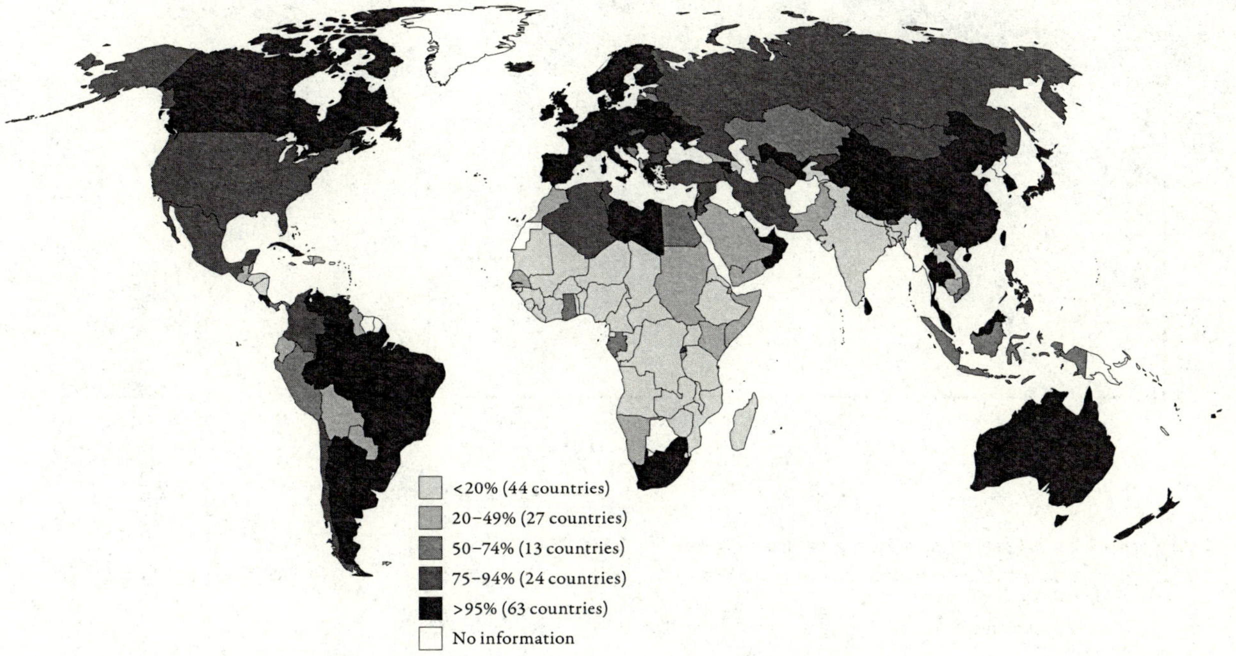

Sources: OECD Health Statistics database; national sources for non-OECD countries (for detailed country figures, see Annex IV, table B.11).
Link: http://www.social-protection.org/gimi/gess/RessourceDownload.action?ressource.ressourceId=38197.

Further analyses disclose that the most significant gaps in legal health coverage are found in those countries with the highest poverty levels among the population, whereas the highest coverage rates are achieved in countries with low poverty levels, such as those of Western Europe (figure 5.3). A close relationship between coverage rates and income levels of countries is also apparent: the lower a country's income, the more likely it is to experience coverage gaps in social health protection.

The global deficit in legal health coverage is compounded by gaps in effective access to health care, as revealed by the access deficit indicators chosen to assess performance against the AAAQ criteria, namely the deficits in the number of health workers needed to deliver services, per capita health spending, OOP and as indicator for quality and overall health-system outputs the maternal mortality rate. Related thresholds used to identify the deficits are based on data from countries that are considered low vulnerability.[3] Figure 5.4 provides a comprehensive overview of the situation at the global level, revealing deficits in effective access to health care in countries grouped by income level.

The figure shows that across low-income countries:

- more than 90 per cent of the population remains without any legal health coverage to provide access to the most essential health care;
- more than 80 per cent of the population lacks access to health care due to the absence of health workers needed to provide such services;[4]
- with OOP accounting for more than 45 per cent of total health expenditure, the affordability of health services and financial protection is a grave problem and financial hardship as a result of private health expenditure is assumed to be very prevalent.

Significant gaps in the funding of health care are also apparent in this group of countries. The threshold required to provide quality health care is estimated by the ILO at US$239 per person per year.[5] The current financial deficit in low-income countries exceeds 90 per cent of necessary expenditure to cover the costs of at least essential health care. The global average annual per capita spending on health is US$948; the country with

[3] Details of indicators and definitions are described in Annex IV, table B.11.

[4] This assessment is based on the ILO threshold of 41.1 health workers per 10,000 population (for further details, see Annex IV, table B.11).

[5] Based on median value of expenditure in low vulnerable countries. See Annex IV, table B.11.

Figure 5.3 Legal health coverage and poverty, latest available year (percentages)

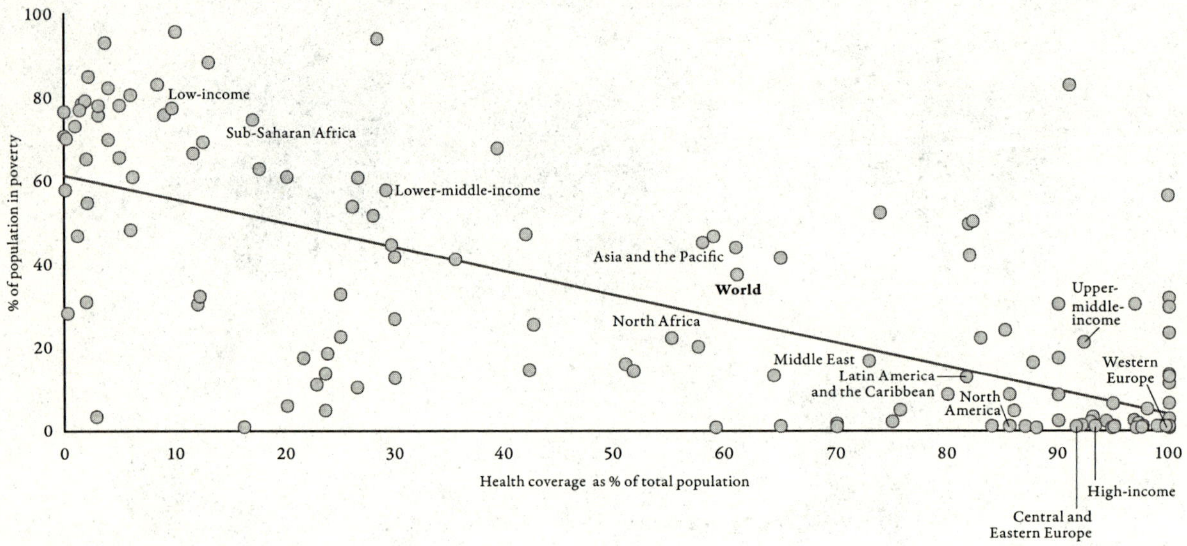

Note: Poverty is defined as daily per capita income of US$2 or less. $R^2 = 0.5684$

Sources: Social health protection coverage data from the ILO Social Protection Department database; poverty data from World Bank, World Development Indicators; OECD; ADB.

Link: http://www.social-protection.org/gimi/gess/RessourceDownload.action?ressource.ressourceId=36980

Figure 5.4 The global deficit in effective access to health services, 2011/12, by level of country income

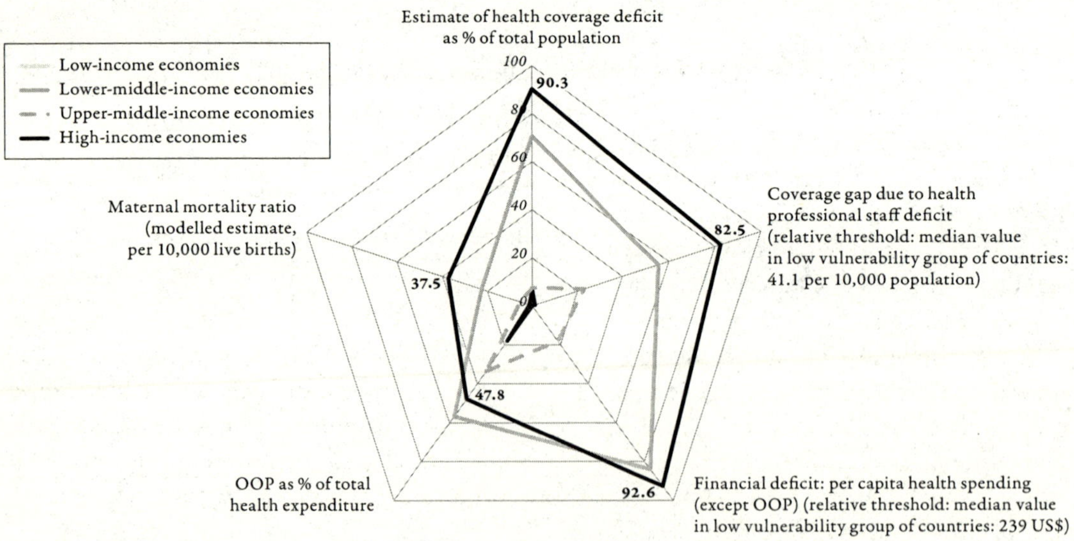

Notes: OOP = out-of-pocket payments. Regional averages weighted by total population 2012. For the multiple dimensions of health coverage, and definitions of the health staff deficit and financial deficit indicators, see Annex IV, table B.11.

Sources: ILO calculations based on WHO Global Health Observatory, 2011 data; OECD; national sources; UN World Population Prospects, 2012 Revision.

Link: http://www.social-protection.org/gimi/gess/RessourceDownload.action?ressource.ressourceId=41717.

the lowest total spending per year on health, Eritrea, spends just US$12 (WHO, 2012).

The maternal mortality ratio is estimated to be as high as 37.5 deaths per 10,000 live births in low-income countries, and is often directly related to gaps in the availability of skilled health workers, particularly midwives.

In addition to these deficits in effective access to health care, it should be noted that in most countries certain groups, such as the rural population, women, the elderly, minorities and people with special needs such as those affected by HIV/AIDS, are even more likely to face barriers to access than the general population (Scheil-Adlung and Kuhl, 2012).

Further, when comparing different groups of countries, or different schemes within countries, it is important to be aware that the scope of benefits provided by the various systems and schemes may vary significantly. Depending on economic, financial, epidemiological and social conditions, the scope of benefits might range from providing a limited number of public health and clinical interventions in primary care facilities to comprehensive benefit packages limited only by the exclusion of some services. Thus figure 5.4 does not reflect the wide disparities in effective access to care both within and across countries.

In countries characterized by significant coverage and access deficits, social health protection cannot play the roles mentioned above in terms of enhancing productivity, employment, income generation and poverty alleviation. Frequently, workers and their families will not be protected during periods of sickness, jobs and incomes may be lost due to sickness, and economic downturns will not be counterbalanced by the positive productivity and employment impacts of social health protection but will, on the contrary, be aggravated by its absence.

5.4 Affordability and risk of impoverishment

In nearly all countries throughout the world, OOP is involved when seeking health care. Such payments of course are frequent where legal health coverage is absent, but are also common in countries that have not fully implemented and enforced existing legislation or have failed to link eligibility and affordability of health care when designing health systems and schemes – for example, if the scope of the benefits provided is too limited or co-payments, user fees and others costs associated with taking up health care are high. Where OOP is significant, even to the extent of being impoverishing, it creates financial barriers preventing access to health care when needed. In these cases legal health coverage is an illusion, masking a lack of effective access.

An overview of the extent of legal health coverage, and OOP, in selected African countries is presented in figure 5.5. It reveals that in some countries with relatively high legal coverage rates, such as Mauritius and Egypt, OOP still exceeds 50 per cent of total health expenditure.

Often, even the most basic care involves OOP. This includes facility-based maternity care in countries where most of the population earns less than US$1 a day: for example, in Kenya, where nearly 100 per cent of women had to pay fees amounting to more than US$18, and in Burkina Faso, where 92.5 per cent of women reported paying fees.

Also, when evaluating the impacts of OOP, it should be kept in mind that those living in poverty are more often affected by sicknesses incurring higher OOP than other groups of the population. This is the case for many non-communicable diseases, such as

Figure 5.5 Legal health coverage and out-of-pocket payments in selected African countries, 2011 (percentages)

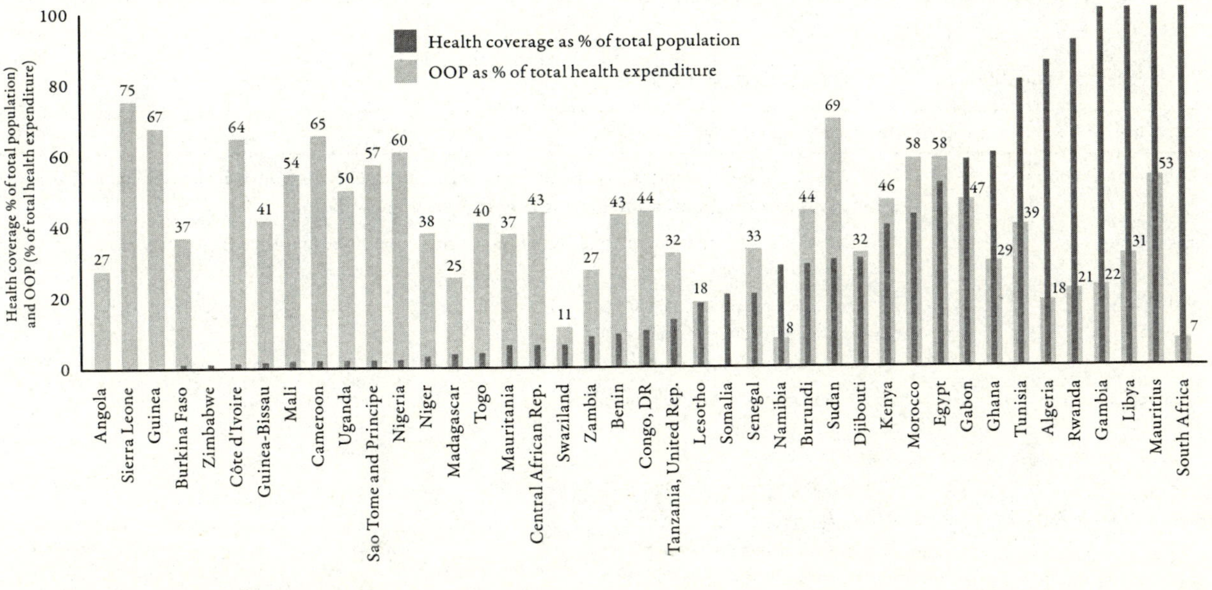

Sources: Health coverage: OECD and national sources; OOP: WHO.

Link: http://www.social-protection.org/gimi/gess/RessourceDownload.action?ressource.ressourceId=43300.

chronic conditions often prevalent among older persons, and lifestyle-related diseases such as obesity, which is often due to the unavailability of healthy food at low prices (FAO, 2004) and the difficulty of taking exercise in the absence of public recreational facilities. As a result, the poor often suffer from both worse health and higher OOP than the rich, a combination that frequently results in increased levels of poverty.

In many countries, women are affected more severely than men by OOP; this applies particularly to poor women, whose health-care needs tend to be greater than those of men, including those related to HIV/AIDS, which is more prevalent among women than men (Scheil-Adlung and Kuhl, 2012).

5.5 Protection from income loss: The benefits of paid sick leave

In addition to protecting against OOP, financial health protection involves the provision of sickness benefits that aim to replace loss of income and of sick leave during periods of ill health. Sickness benefits and sick leave are crucial to addressing deteriorating health, health-related poverty and loss of productivity. The financing mechanisms for paid sick leave are usually similar to those for health care, involving some form of taxes, including tax subsidies and contributions/payroll taxes and premiums. In a few countries, specific employer funds apply. Provisions include both time off work and wage replacement during sickness.

While paid sick leave legislation exists for formal sector workers in 145 of about 190 countries globally, the benefits provided differ widely with regard to definition of work, wages covered, level of income replacement, duration of payments and other specific conditions (table 5.1).

Income replacement rates vary between lump sums (in 14 per cent of all countries) and 100 per cent of wages (in 21 per cent of all countries). More than half of countries provide for replacement rates of between 50 and 75 per cent of wages. The wage replaced also varies, and may be limited, for example by a ceiling or the exclusion of supplements. The wage replacement might further be subject to means testing and waiting times. The period of leave also varies widely: out of a total of 145 countries reviewed, 102 countries provide for one month or more, while seven provide under seven days (Scheil-Adlung and Bonnet, 2011).

Where legislation exists, coverage is usually strongly skewed to formal sector workers. In most countries, workers in the informal economy are totally excluded from income replacement during sickness. Even those who are covered frequently face barriers to accessing paid sick leave, given the fear of losing their jobs, particularly in times of economic crisis and/or high unemployment (Scheil-Adlung and Sandner, 2010).

In fact, paid sick leave offers ample returns in the form of gains in health and economic productivity for employers, workers and the economy at large. Paid sick leave allows workers to recuperate rapidly, prevents more serious illness and disability developing, and reduces the spreading of diseases to co-workers and beyond, whereas working while sick incurs high economic costs, due to higher number of people to be treated for more severe signs of ill health (Economist

Table 5.1 Global variations in sickness and sick leave benefits

Aspect of benefit	Variations in provision/eligibility
Definition of work applied	• Exclusion of work not provided under employment contract e.g. domestic work and self-employment • Limitations regarding minimum working hours per week/month
Wages covered	• Effective wages received before the period of leave, with or without supplements for dependants; average earnings; wage ceilings
Period of leave	• Between one day and two years • Minimum and maximum periods • Often limited to a single disease
Income replacement rates	• Vary from lump sum to 100% of wages • Means testing • Waiting times • Differences for short-term and long-term sickness
Other specific conditions	• Waiting periods • Previous contribution payments • Medical certificates

Source: Scheil-Adlung and Sandner, 2010.

Intelligence Unit, 2014). Also, the lower productivity of sick workers has been found to slow down growth and development; thus the absence of sick leave creates economic costs and avoidable health expenditure (Scheil-Adlung and Sandner, 2010).

5.6 Financing mechanisms for universal coverage in health

Generally, countries that have achieved high health coverage rates have used revenue-collection and risk-pooling mechanisms, mainly taking the form of state-financed national health services or contribution-financed national, social or private health insurance schemes.

A schematic overview of financing mechanisms currently in place, showing the various sources and funding flows used for financing health coverage, is provided in figure 5.6. It distinguishes between the use of government revenues to fund national health services, such as that in Canada, and other tax-funded programmes, e.g. maternity vouchers in Kenya or conditional cash transfers in Nicaragua. In other countries, government revenues are used to subsidize schemes funded through income-related contributions, particularly social health insurance schemes where contributions are made by both employers and employees (as in Germany and Austria) and national health insurance schemes where the contributions of those without formal employment are supported by state subsidies (as in Ghana).

The figure also includes private direct funding – OOP – as it is found to various extents in all countries, despite the fact that it should not be considered as a health financing mechanism given its regressive and potentially impoverishing impacts, and the absence of burden-sharing it implies. Resort to OOP should be restricted to the provision of cost control incentives only.

Countries that have achieved universal coverage in health for many decades using tax and contribution-based financing mechanisms include the United Kingdom, with its National Health Service, and Germany, using a social health insurance scheme. More recently, universal coverage schemes and systems based on both

Figure 5.6 Schematic overview of health-care financing mechanisms currently in use

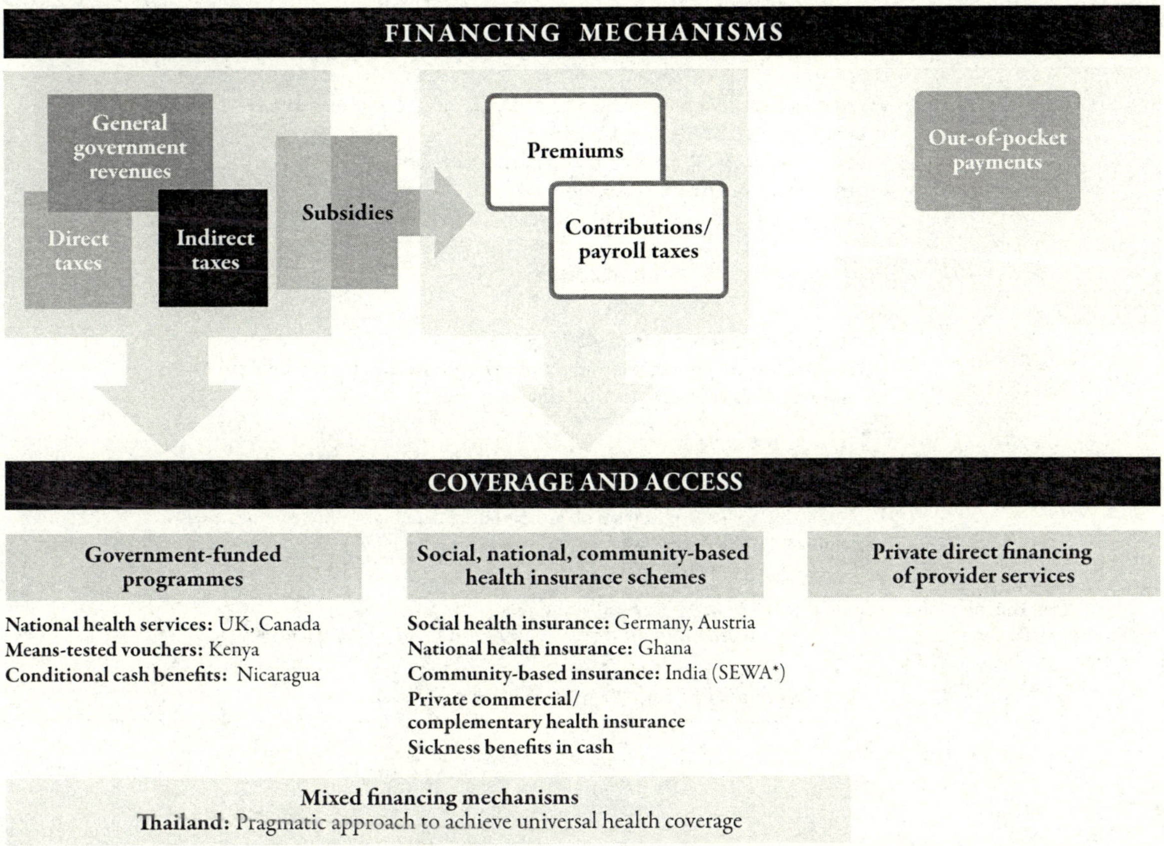

* Self-Employed Women's Association.

Link: http://www.social-protection.org/gimi/gess/RessourceDownload.action?ressource.ressourceId=43299.

Table 5.2 Key aspects of performance associated with various health coverage and financing mechanisms

Coverage/financing mechanism	Key aspects of performance
Mainly tax funding	**National health systems** **Pro** • Risks are pooled for the whole population on a national or sometimes subnational level in fiscally decentralized settings • Good potential for administrative efficiency and cost control • Redistributes between high- and low-risk and high- and low-income groups in the population covered **Con** • Risks of unstable funding and underfunding due to competing claims on public expenditure • Inefficient if no incentives and no effective supervision established • Often perceived low quality of services
Mainly employers'/employees' contributions (payroll taxes) and premiums to health insurance schemes	**Social and national health insurance** **Pro** • Generates stable revenues • Often strong support from the population given perceived high quality of services • Usually involves tax subsidies – particularly in national health insurance schemes – to cover the poor and/or other vulnerable groups • Involvement of social partners and voice representation • Redistributes between high- and low-risk and high- and low-income groups in the population covered **Con** • Limited to formal sector workers and their families if no subsidies for informal sector workers and other parts of the population are provided • Payroll contributions can reduce competitiveness and lead to higher unemployment • Complex to manage; governance and accountability may be problematic • Can lead to cost escalation unless effective contracting mechanisms are in place **Community-based health insurance** **Pro** • Can reach out to workers in the informal economy and poorer segments of the population **Con** • Coverage usually only extended to a small percentage of the population • Poor may be excluded unless subsidized • May be financially vulnerable if not supported by national subsidies • Strong incentive to adverse selection • May be associated with lack of professionalism in governance and administration **Private commercial health insurance** **Pro** • Preferable to out-of-pocket expenditure • Increases financial protection and access to health services for those able to pay • Encourages better quality and cost efficiency **Con** • High administrative costs • Ineffective in reducing cost pressures on public health systems • Inequitable without subsidized premiums or regulated insurance content and price • Requires administrative and financial infrastructure and capacity
Mixed mechanisms: Using a mix of taxes, contributions and premiums to social and micro health insurance schemes for various groups of the population	**Pro** Potential to cover the whole population Generate more domestic funds than a single health-financing mechanism **Con** Risk of fragmentation if not well designed and coordinated

financing mechanisms have been implemented successfully: for example, in Thailand various systems and schemes exist alongside one another, and are well coordinated to avoid fragmentation.

For other countries, achieving universal coverage required that existing gaps be closed by removing barriers within the health-care system and tackling the root causes of inequities in access to health care, many of which reside outside health systems themselves. Key issues to be addressed within the health sector frequently include gaps in legislation and/or implementation, resulting in fragmentation, inequitable access due to deficits in financial protection, affordability of services, and absence of paid sick leave; inadequate availability of services due to a lack of trained health personnel, and related low quality of services; and the underfunding of social health protection. Causes that lie beyond the health sector often relate to poverty; the structure of employment and the labour market (e.g. the prominence of the informal economy); inequities relating to e.g. gender, age, minority status; gaps in income support through social protection; and individual life circumstances (e.g. migration). If sustainable progress is to be made in extending health coverage, both types of issue need to be addressed simultaneously, with particular attention paid to poverty alleviation and labour market policies in order to cut the reciprocal relationship of poor health and poverty across the social, economic and health sectors.

There are positive and negative aspects to each of the different financing mechanisms outlined here, and there is no one model that serves all social and economic contexts. Many countries have developed mixed mechanisms, either within a single scheme – e.g. state subsidization of contributions for the poor in insurance-based schemes, or introduction of insurance features in a national health service – or by maintaining State and insurance schemes alongside one another. The reasons for mixed solutions are often linked to the desire to generate sufficient funds from different sources and to make best use of the respective advantages of the different mechanisms, such as large risk pools, generation of stable revenues, and reaching out to populations in remote areas. An overview of observations on some key aspects of performance of these coverage and financing mechanisms is provided in table 5.2.

When developing mixed mechanisms, it is of particular importance to avoid a large number of uncoordinated schemes and systems using different financing mechanisms for various population groups and providers. Such fragmentation reduces the positive impacts of risk-pooling and cross-subsidization. Thus, mixed mechanisms require close coordination of all schemes and systems in a country with an overall view to achieving universal coverage.

Countries that have recently made efforts to reduce coverage gaps and fragmentation include Cambodia, where some 50 health equity funds now provide access to free health-care services to more than half of the country's poor people; Indonesia, where the Government committed itself to achieving universal coverage by 2019 through a coordinated approach of contributory and non-contributory schemes; and the Lao People's Democratic Republic, which is currently implementing a national health insurance merging the existing four fragmented schemes with a view to increasing risk-pooling and efficiency.

Across all regions, 88 countries have currently achieved high legal coverage rates of at least 80 per cent of the population. Some countries achieved universal coverage in a relatively short period (about ten years in the case of Thailand) and started reforms at low levels of national income and during times of economic crisis (Evans et al., 2012).

As shown in figure 5.7, the majority of countries (45) that have achieved high legal coverage rates of 80 per cent or more of the population did so using mainly state coverage mechanisms, whereas 28 countries used mainly insurance mechanisms and the remaining 15 countries applied both mechanisms in unspecified combinations. Analysis of the available information by region indicates a preference for state mechanisms among countries with high coverage rates in Asia and

Figure 5.7 Coverage mechanisms used by countries with legal health coverage rates of 80 per cent of the population or over, 2014 or latest available year

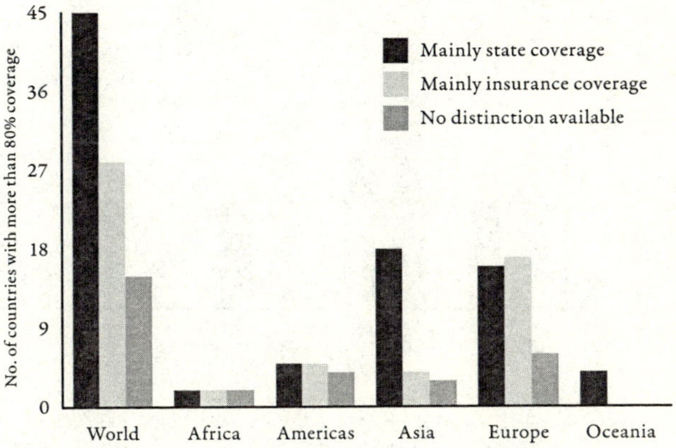

Source: ILO Social Protection Department database, see Annex IV, table B.11.

Link: http://www.social-protection.org/gimi/gess/RessourceDownload.action?ressource.ressourceId=43320.

the Pacific, whereas in Europe, Africa and the Americas there is approximately equal inclination towards state and insurance mechanisms.

These data suggest that, given a strong role and commitment on the part of the Government, countries can achieve high or even universal health coverage irrespective of the coverage mechanism(s) chosen if the systems and schemes are well designed and the pros and cons of different mechanisms are balanced with a view to avoiding fragmentation. More important than which mechanism is chosen is for the decision to be taken on the basis of what is most appropriate to the social, economic, historical and cultural context of the particular country concerned. Further, it is most important that the overall and primary responsibility for health coverage lies with the State and is based on certain key principles, such as solidarity and burden-sharing in financing. Achieving progress in both legal health coverage and access to health care requires strong government commitment to regulation to maximize the efficiency and effectiveness of health protection schemes and systems. Guidance to governments in tackling this task is available through various international legal instruments, ranging from the UDHR to ILO Conventions and Recommendations in the area of health protection, especially Convention No. 102 and Recommendation No. 202 (see box 5.1 above).

5.7 Levels of public and private health expenditure

Globally, public expenditure on health protection as a share of GDP more or less equals private health expenditure. A similar picture can be observed at regional level, where we find equal public and private shares in Asia and the Pacific and in Africa, Latin America and the Caribbean, and the Middle East (figure 5.8). Thus more than 40 per cent of the global burden of health expenditure is borne by private households in the form of OOP. This is an alarming statistic, given that OOP has the potential to create access barriers, inequities and impoverishment, and, being regressive in character and lacking any element of risk-pooling, runs counter to the key principle of solidarity in financing.

Generally, private OOP is a particularly dominant source of health-care funding in the poorest countries of the world, despite its regressive impact on income: In Africa, private expenditure even exceeds public expenditure and amounts to nearly 3 per cent of GDP.

In fact, there exists a positive correlation between poverty rates and shares of OOP in total health expenditure: the extent of impoverishing OOP in a country increases with the level of the population living below the poverty line. In countries where less than 2 per cent of the population are living on US$2 day, about 20 per cent of total health expenditure derives from OOP; in countries where more than 50 per cent of the population are living on US$2 a day, it amounts to around

Figure 5.8. Sources of health-care financing, by region, 2011 (percentage of GDP)

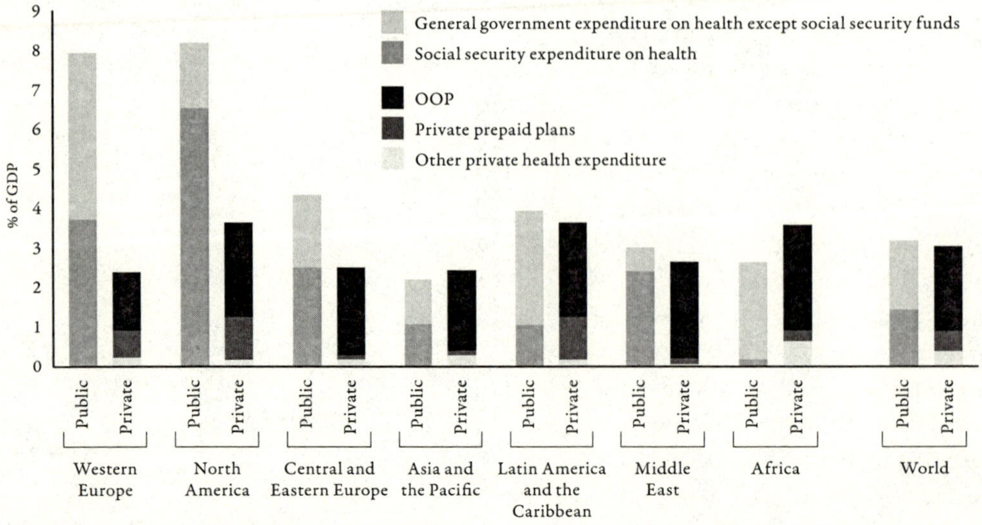

Note: Regional averages weighted by total population.

Sources: ILO calculations based on WHO Global Health Observatory, 2011 data. Population: UN World Population Prospects, 2012 Revision.

Link: http://www.social-protection.org/gimi/gess/RessourceDownload.action?ressource.ressourceId=41677.

Figure 5.9 Share of OOP in total health expenditure, by proportion of the population living on less than US$2 a day PPP, 2011 (percentages)

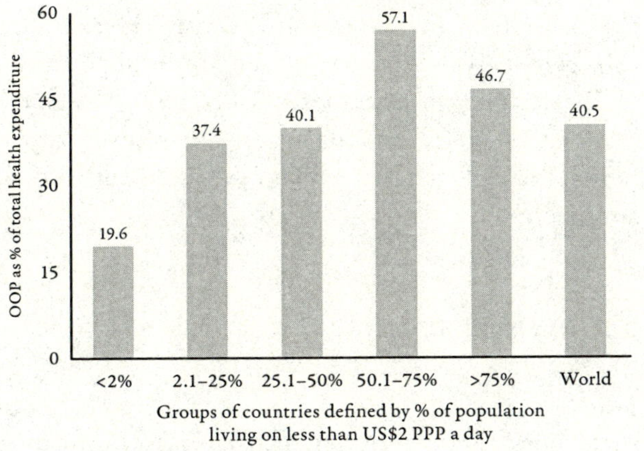

Note: Weighted by total population.

Sources: ILO calculations based on WHO data; poverty data: World Bank, ADB and CEPAL data.

Link: http://www.social-protection.org/gimi/gess/RessourceDownload.action?ressource.ressourceId=42859.

Table 5.3 Numbers of medical personnel per 10,000 people, selected countries, latest available year

Country	No. of health workers per 10,000 of population
Niger	1.56
Sierra Leone	1.88
Central African Republic	2.95
Haiti	3.60
Mozambique	3.67
Senegal	4.79
Bangladesh	5.74
Gambia	9.72
Norway	196
Switzerland	216
Finland	269

Source: Based on WHO Global Health Observatory.

50 per cent. Thus it is the poorest, who are also the most in need, who suffer most from OOP and related inequities (figure 5.9).

5.8 The global shortage of health workers

The low level of public health financing is also reflected in the low number of health workers. Skilled health workers are the backbone of any health system (Global Health Workforce Alliance and WHO, 2014): indeed, professional health staff – physicians, nurses and midwifery personnel as defined by the WHO – are a prerequisite for the delivery of quality care services to those in need. However, the health workforce is experiencing a global crisis: it is much too small in numbers to deliver the services needed, unequally distributed and often lacking decent working conditions. According to the latest available data, in numerous countries – including, for example, Haiti, Niger, Senegal and Sierra Leone – as many as 10,000 people have to rely on services provided by five or fewer health workers. By contrast, in a high-income country such as Finland there are 269 health workers for 10,000 people (table 5.3).

As a result, in many countries health workers are stretched to their limits and seek jobs elsewhere; this in turn often further reduces the availability of health services, especially in rural areas, and contributes to a "brain drain" of skills and experience. At the global level, health-worker migration from poorer to richer countries is constantly increasing: for example, between 2007 and 2012 more than 230,000 migrant health workers took up job opportunities in health-care services in the United States (OECD, 2013c).

At the same time, pay cuts for civil servants, including health workers, are under consideration in many countries, both at lower-middle-income level (for example, Mongolia) and also at higher-income level, mainly to achieve cost savings (Ortiz and Cummins, 2013).

Only a few countries have indicated that they plan to increase the number of their health workers, ensure training of existing health workers or improve the important coordination between education, the labour market and the health sector. However, according to a recent review of IMF country reports, general increases in the number of civil servants including health workers are under consideration in some countries, including the Central African Republic, Gambia and Mozambique (Ortiz and Cummins, 2013). Timor-Leste aims to increase its number of medical staff by retaining trained doctors from Cuba (Asante et al., 2014).

The ILO estimates that 41.1 health workers per 10,000 population are necessary to provide at least essential services to all in need.[6] This target is met or exceeded

[6] This figure is based on calculations of median value of the density of health workers in countries where socio-economic conditions and health financing characteristics are conducive to universal coverage. Statistical details of the ILO Access Deficit Indicator and the assessment of deficits are presented in Annex IV, table B.11.

Figure 5.10 Number of skilled health workers required to close global and regional gaps in universal health coverage, ILO estimate, 2014

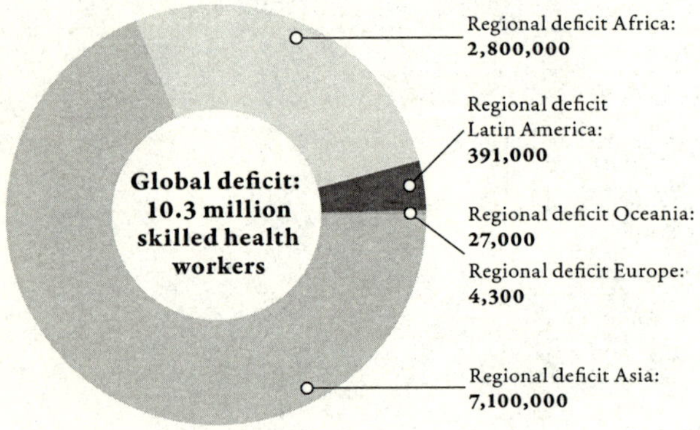

Source: ILO calculations based on WHO Global Health Observatory.

Link: http://www.social-protection.org/gimi/gess/RessourceDownload.action?ressource.ressourceId=44517.

not only by high-income countries but also by some low- and lower-middle-income countries, including Armenia, Kyrgyzstan, Mongolia and Swaziland. However, across the globe 10.3 million additional health workers are required to close the current gaps and ensure the delivery of health services to all in need. The majority of these are needed in developing countries, mainly in Asia (7.1 million) and Africa (2.8 million) (figure 5.10).

Investment in the development of the health workforce is an essential condition of progress towards universal health coverage and addressing the global health access deficit. Such investment is now timely, given that the share of total health expenditure devoted to remuneration of the health workforce has fallen over the past ten years while other elements of health expenditure have increased significantly (Hernandez-Pena et al., 2013). Furthermore, and most importantly, such investment has the potential to boost the global economy, promote equitable economic recovery at national level and generate much-needed decent work at fair incomes.

5.9 Inadequate levels of pay for health workers

In the quest for progress in health coverage, the increase in numbers of health workers must go hand in hand with the creation of decent working conditions, including adequate wages.

In recent years, the wage bills of health workers have fallen, sometimes dramatically: in the Democratic Republic of Congo and Myanmar, for example, they declined by about 40 per cent during economic crises between 2007 and 2009 (UNICEF, 2010). In fact, the wages are often so poor that the workers in the lowest-paid categories are faced with the risk of impoverishment: In countries such as Sudan, Egypt and Myanmar, health-sector wages are only 1 per cent above the poverty line of US$2 a day.[7] In other countries, while the wage bills of health workers were stable in nominal terms, they declined in real terms as a result of falling purchasing power.

Figure 5.11 Yearly change in health workers' remuneration as proportion of total health expenditure and GDP, by national income level, 2000–10 (percentages)

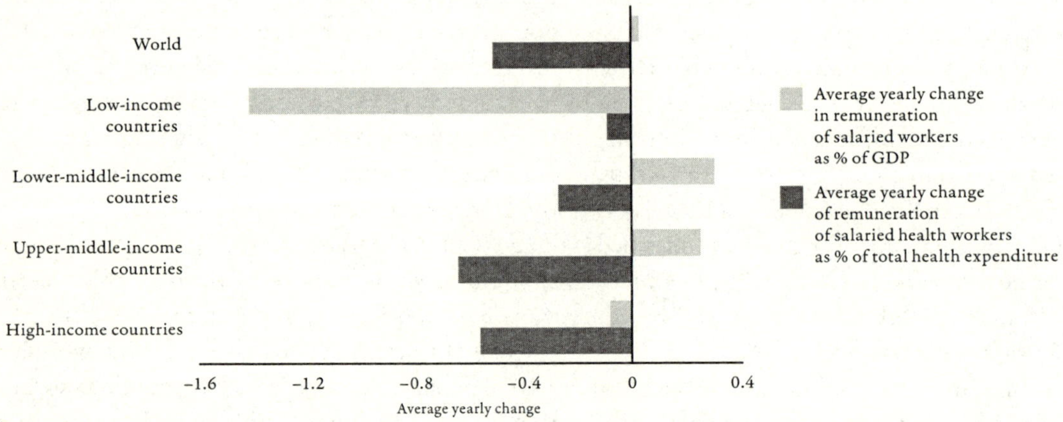

Source: Based on Hernandez-Pena et al., 2013.

Link: http://www.social-protection.org/gimi/gess/RessourceDownload.action?ressource.ressourceId=43298.

[7] US$ PPP, 2009.

Over the first decade of this century, the remuneration of salaried health workers as a proportion of GDP remained nearly unchanged globally and decreased in terms of total health expenditure (figure 5.11). In addition, delays in payment are frequent in many countries. The consequences include absenteeism, requests for informal payments and a brain drain of workers seeking better wages outside their home countries.

5.10 Fiscal consolidation measures: Drivers of economic recovery or part of the problem?

During the recent crisis, only a few countries managed to increase legal health coverage. Universal health insurance schemes were introduced in Benin and Gabon (ISSA, 2013b); legal coverage was expanded in the United States (for young people and those with pre-existing conditions) under the 2010 Affordable Care and Patient Protection Act, in the Philippines under the Aquino Health Agenda for Achieving Universal Coverage in 2010, and in China for both urban and rural residents (SSA and ISSA, 2012; SSA and ISSA, 2013a). Other countries, such as Uruguay, aimed at both expanding coverage and also reducing fragmentation and segmentation (EsSalud and ILO, 2013).

At the same time, many countries implemented fiscal consolidation measures,[8] with the aim of achieving economic recovery primarily through the reduction of fiscal deficits. Among these measures were structural reforms and quantitative adjustments in the public sector. In the health sector, these frequently take the form of budget cuts with negative effects on the availability and affordability of health services and of essential drugs such as antibiotics, and the creation and maintenance of infrastructure. Thus per capita health spending fell significantly between 2009 and 2011 in 11 OECD countries, notably in Greece and Ireland (11.1 and 6.6 per cent respectively) (OECD, 2013c).

Table 5.4 provides an overview of some recent announcements of fiscal consolidation policies in the area of health protection, along with the actual or projected fiscal savings arising.

These announcements reveal both general budget cuts for government health ministries and severe cutbacks in public health expenditure on a per capita basis. Such cuts have resulted in reduced supply of health care in a range of areas, from preventive care to non-emergency care for undocumented migrants in Spain. Reductions in public expenditure also affected the wages of the health workforce (table 5.5); caused the postponement of important reforms improving and extending legal health coverage, e.g. the national health insurance system in Cyprus; imposed volume limits on some services; and led to reduced benefits and the removal of preventive care. Meanwhile, OOP increased markedly in several countries, while public health expenditure contracted or remained more or less constant (table 5.6).

The shift of the burden for paying health care from the public purse to individuals and households is having a particularly severe effect on lower income groups, given the regressive impact of OOP. As a result, gaps in coverage and access between rich and poor are widening. Thus fiscal consolidation policies combined with growing poverty due to the recession are likely to increase inequities within countries.

In addition, job and wage cuts for health workers significantly reduced access to health services. Table 5.5 outlines the most recently announced cuts in wages of public sector workers, including health workers, in European countries that were particularly badly hit by the financial crises: in Greece, cuts have reduced public wages since 2010 by some 30 percentage points, while in Portugal and Spain reductions of 5 percentage points have occurred.

At just the same time as fiscal consolidation measures were resulting in reductions in the numbers and wages of health workers, an increased demand for public health services was apparent in countries such as Greece and Cyprus. Even though public hospital admissions were rising and private hospital admissions falling (Kentikelenis et al., 2011), the Government of Cyprus decided to postpone the implementation of the planned national health insurance scheme (WHO, 2012), which led to further inequities and gaps in access.

Overall, the impact of fiscal consolidation measures taken in response to the crisis has been to stall or even reverse progress towards universal health coverage by sharpening inequities in access to health care, increasing the financial burden on private households, reducing benefits and thus increasing exclusion.

---

[8] In this report, fiscal consolidation refers to the wide array of adjustment measures adopted to reduce government deficits and debt accumulation. Fiscal consolidation policies are often referred to as austerity policies.

Table 5.4 Announced fiscal consolidation policies and associated fiscal savings, selected countries, 2007–14

Country	Year	Reform	Fiscal savings
Botswana	2007–11	Reduction in government per capita expenditure on health of 14.4% in constant US$	
Bulgaria	2009	Budget of Ministry of Health reduced	Budget reduced from 713 million lev (BGN) in 2008 to BGN537 million in 2009 and BGN570 million in 2010 (total reduction of US$100 million)
Cyprus	2011	Postponement of implementation of new national health insurance system	
Czech Republic	2010	Ministry of Health budget reduced by about 30% in 2010 compared to 2008	US$107.18 million
Hungary	2010	Volume limits to inpatient services Increased user charges	1.3% average annual drop in government expenditure on health, from US$476.6 to US$452.0 per capita
Estonia	2009	Estonian Health Insurance Fund (EHIF) budget reduced. Health insurance budget reduced by 1% and Ministry of Health expenditure reduced by 24% between 2008 and 2009	EHIF spending reduced by 263,699,000 EEK (US$22.48 million)
Greece	2011	Removal of certain preventive care provisions Agreement to reduce public health expenditure in 2012 from 1.9 to 1.33% of GDP as part of request for support from IMF 3.7% average annual drop in government expenditure on health, from US$1 281.2 to US$1 100.9 per capita	Health budget for 2011 reduced by €1.4 billion
Lithuania	2010	Law on Sickness and Maternity amended to reduce maternity benefit from full pay to 90% of pay	
Malawi	2011	Suspension of UK aid to Malawi Government, much of which funded the health sector	IRIN (UN service for coordination of humanitarian affairs) estimates that before cuts US$49 million worth of UK DFID aid to Malawi went to health sector
Mongolia	2009	Amendment to health budget reduced public salaries by 3%, spending on staff training by 55%, allocation for medicines and vaccines by 20%, other goods and services by 17%, and domestic investment for capital projects by 20%	Health sector budget decreased by 23 billion tughrik (US$13.5 million)
Romania	2008–11	Ministry of Health budget reduced by 4,969 million new leu (RON) in 2008 to RON 4,417 million in 2011	US$171 million
Slovenia	2010	Reductions in non-acute spa treatment, certain medicines, non-urgent ambulance services, dental prostheses and some ophthalmologic appliances	
Sri Lanka	2007–11	Government expenditure raised by 0.7%; average annual OOP increased by 5.6% (constant US$ per capita)	
Tanzania, United Rep.	2007–11	Government expenditure reduced by 2.6%; average annual OOP increased by 34.6% (constant US$ per capita)	
Ukraine	2007–11	Government expenditure increased by 0.4%; average annual OOP increased by 7.8% (constant US$ per capita)	
United Kingdom	2010	Health in Pregnancy Grant of £190 for each expectant mother cut from Jan. 2011	Parliament estimates savings of £40 million in costs in 2010/11 and £150 million in each succeeding year
	2012	Health and Social Care Act 2012 "cuts the number of health bodies"	Exact savings unknown; Government cites goal as NHS making "up to £20 billion worth of efficiency savings by 2015"

Source: ILO Social Protection Department database on measures adopted in response to the crisis since 2007/8.

Table 5.5 Announced cuts in public wages, selected European countries, 2010–13 (percentages)

Country	2010	2011	2013
Greece	14		17
Portugal	0 (freeze)	5	0 (freeze)
Spain	5		

Source: Based on Busch et al., 2013.

Table 5.6 Average annual increase in OOP, selected countries, 2007–11 (percentages)

Country	Average annual increase in OOP, 2007–11 (%, constant US$ per capita)
Tanzania	34.6
Equatorial Guinea	32.2
Turkmenistan	16.7
Paraguay	15.1
Cambodia	12.1
Russian Federation	9.2
China	7.2
Sri Lanka	5.6
Rwanda	5.3

Source: WHO, National Health Accounts, 2013, see Annex IV, table B.11.

As for their impact on the economy, it can be concluded that, rather than curing the symptoms of debts and deficits, fiscal consolidation measures in the area of health protection have acted as barriers to economic recovery and worsened the effects of the economic crisis by weakening the productivity of the workforce and reducing employment of much-needed health workers. In addition, these measures have had a negative impact on the right to work and on adequate standards of living, particularly those of the most vulnerable segments of the population that have been hit hardest by budget cuts and increased OOP.

5.11 Addressing the challenges: Achieving sustainable progress in access to health care

The recent economic and financial crisis strained households' and governments' budgets in many countries. It led to preventable negative impacts on health through the reduced availability and affordability of quality health care, and contributed to increased inequities in access to health care. Furthermore, the economic recovery was hampered by the fiscal consolidation measures taken to address it. There is now an urgent need to act in pursuit of sustainable progress.

Scaling up global and national health coverage rates and providing access to necessary health benefits, particularly in low- and middle-income countries, will end the downward spiral of ill health and poverty and contribute to economic recovery. However, to achieve sustainable progress it will be necessary to rethink policies and consider lessons learnt.

In recent decades, the importance of health coverage to the economy has often been insufficiently taken into account by policy-makers, who accepted the existence of huge access deficits that in some countries have left up to 80 per cent of the population – often those most in need – without any legal health coverage. In addition, the erroneously assumed trade-off between costs of universal coverage in health and economic growth led to potential gains in productivity, employment and development more generally being overlooked. As a result, ill health was frequently understood as a private matter, ignoring the complex social and economic relationships that link poverty, employment, gender and socio-economic stratification in excluding people from effective access to health care.

A contemporary concept of providing access to health care through social protection places health within a framework based on human rights. ILO Recommendation No. 202 connects the right to health with the underlying social and economic determinants and addresses these links at the systemic level, both within and beyond the health sector, rather than pointing to the individual level and advising short-term remedies without seeing the big picture.

Such an approach aims at sustainable progress through investments in social health protection structures and institutions, backed up by political commitment and technical knowledge. It requires an explicit acknowledgement of the need for *both* legal health coverage *and* accessibility of at least essential health care that is available, of acceptable quality, and affordable without financial hardship. Such provision contributes to equity, reducing exclusion as well as poverty. Further, a contemporary concept of universal health coverage involves fair financing based on burden-sharing, using taxes (e.g. for national health services), contributions/payroll taxes and/or premium-based financing (for various forms of social, national or private insurances). OOP does not feature as a means of health financing but may be used in a minimal capacity for other purposes, such as incentives. The obligation to meet the core content of the right to health through

Table 5.7 Key aspects of social protection floor policies aiming at achieving universal coverage in health, based on Recommendation No. 202

Objectives	Policy principles	Key components of essential health benefits	Financing	Complementary policies
• Universal coverage providing access to a nationally defined set of goods of services for essential health care, including preventive and maternal care • Meeting the criteria of availability, accessibility, acceptability and quality • Aiming at achieving higher levels of protection as outlined in Convention No. 102 • Achieving policy coherence	• Universality (access to quality services for all in need) • Rights-based approach • Social inclusion • Non-discrimination • Responsiveness to basic and special needs • Participation including social dialogue	• In-kind benefits, including curative, preventive and maternal care based on an adequate level of quality health services (inpatient/outpatient) and drugs • Cash benefits providing financial protection (e.g. transport costs, and reduction/abolition of impoverishment due to health expenditure)	• Solidarity in financing by increasing risk-pooling and minimizing unpooled private health expenditure, e.g. due to user fees, constrained benefit packages, low quality • Diversity of financing mechanisms and delivery, including tax- and contribution/premium-based systems	• Analysing gaps in social protection coverage, benefits and services with a view to poverty alleviation • Developing fiscal space, ensuring financial and economic sustainability and monitoring progress • Coherence with social, economic and employment policies such as promoting formal employment • Strengthening capacities and monitoring of the social security system

health service delivery must be met irrespective of the financing mechanism chosen.

ILO Recommendation No. 202 offers guidance on related policies that are necessary to fully realize the positive impacts and sustainability of investments in health and achieve universal health coverage (table 5.7). According to this Recommendation, access to needed health care should be enshrined in legislation that protects the affordability of services and ensures access to care in terms of the availability of services and facilities that are of adequate quality and delivered by skilled staff. The aim should be universal coverage based on the provision of, at a minimum, essential health care benefits. Such benefits are to be defined at national level with a view to meeting vital medical needs and demand for maternal and preventive care, and providing financial protection. The progressive development of essential health care towards more comprehensive benefit packages is recommended.

The availability of quality services necessitates that a *sufficient number of health workers* be trained, recruited, provided with decent working conditions and distributed in an equitable way within countries, particularly in rural and urban slum areas. In this context, it is essential that governments balance supply and demand within national labour markets through improved working conditions, including wages. Further, it is important to address wage disparities across regions, and between general practitioners and specialists. Improving working conditions and wages for health-care workers is crucial for overcoming the lack of labour supply in all branches of the sector. This requires the right to organize and bargain for all health-care workers. Collective bargaining is the best way to negotiate workplace arrangements that attract the necessary number and quality of health-care workers. Further, public authorities need to be exemplary employers and procurers. Thus, expenditure of public funds and any contract for health-care provision must include clauses ensuring decent wages.[9] Key instruments to achieve the necessary conditions include laws and regulations, collective agreements and other mechanisms for negotiation between employers' and workers' representatives, and arbitration awards. Finally, as regards migration of health workers, bilateral and multilateral arrangements are needed with a view to compensate for training costs and avoiding brain drain.

Generating sufficient funds for universal health protection involves exploring the pros and cons of all existing financing mechanisms and efficiently coordinating various approaches in a way that is perceived as fair, avoids fragmentation and tax evasion, and combats corruption. Most important for allocating sufficient funds is political will, as shown most recently in Thailand, where universal health coverage was achieved within a decade and reform efforts started in conditions of relatively low per capita income and a large informal economy (Evans et al., 2012). Further, fiscal policies should

[9] Labour Clauses (Public Contracts) Convention, 1949 (No. 94).

be systematically used with a view to closing funding gaps and addressing the reciprocal relationship between ill health and poverty through various social protection measures. In this context, returns on investments in health in terms of productivity, employment and development should be taken into account when assessing the cost of extending social health protection.

Many of the problems outlined in this chapter may be diagnosed as resulting at least in part from inefficient and ineffective governance and administration of national systems of health protection. This raises broad issues such as the absence of political and institutional commitment as well as the importance of regular *monitoring, feedback and support through tripartite national and social dialogue*. Monitoring advances in equitable access against thresholds is a prerequisite of sustainable progress. Thresholds should be set with a view to measuring both affordability and availability of quality care and financial protection for all in need, and should include universal population coverage in terms of legislation, limitations on OOP to rule out impoverishment or rise above 40 per cent of household income (net of subsistence), and a threshold of 41.1 health workers, enjoying decent working conditions, per 10,000 population.

Further, social dialogue, fundamentally on a tripartite basis, is essential in addressing inefficiencies – whether they are of an administrative or managerial nature within a scheme or system, or result from incoherent policies at the national, regional or community level. The need for social dialogue has been reinforced in Recommendation No. 202, which mandates "tripartite participation with representative organizations of employers and workers, as well as consultation with other relevant and representative organizations of persons concerned" (Para. 3(r)). In facilitating progress in health protection it is of paramount importance to establish regular tripartite social dialogue between relevant stakeholders under the leadership of national governing bodies, and to ensure proper governance and administration of health systems and policies.

In addressing equally the needs for essential health care and income support, the policies suggested in table 5.7 provide ample scope for tackling the root causes of inequities in access to health care and contributing to universal coverage of social protection in health. When implementing coherent policies across the social, economic and health sectors, governments should emphasize poverty alleviation and labour market policies in order to avoid unintended increases in inequality and to realize the economic spillover effects.

These policies have the potential to achieve both universal health coverage and economic returns – in all countries, and at all levels of national income. They entail:

- a political vision of universality based on an inclusive framework that is supported by a committed government, social partners and civil society and incorporates an evidence-based system and/or scheme design applying technical expertise and global best practices;
- objectives that match expectations of the population in terms of availability, affordability and quality of services;
- realizing the potential of social protection floor policies, created, implemented and monitored on the basis of solid assessment and impact analyses, to create fiscal space and generate domestic funds for health protection;
- institutions characterized by good governance that have the capacity and means to implement necessary reforms based on efficient and effective strategies aimed at coordinating existing schemes and systems, addressing gaps in the health workforce and striving to ensure that people receive the care they expect wherever they live.

Expanding social protection

Key to crisis recovery, inclusive development and social justice

6

KEY MESSAGES

- The global financial and economic crisis has forcefully underlined the importance of social security as a human right, and as an economic and social necessity, as set out in the ILO Social Protection Floors Recommendation (2012), No. 202.
- In the first phase of the crisis (2008–09), social protection played a strong role in the expansionary response. About 50 high- and middle-income countries announced fiscal stimulus packages totalling US$2.4 trillion, of which approximately a quarter was invested in counter-cyclical social protection measures.
- In the second phase of the crisis (2010 onwards), many governments embarked on fiscal consolidation and premature contraction of expenditure, despite an urgent need of public support among vulnerable populations. In 2014, the scope of public expenditure adjustment is expected to intensify significantly; according to IMF projections, 122 countries will be contracting expenditures in terms of GDP, of which 82 are developing countries. Further, a fifth of countries are undergoing fiscal consolidation, defined as cutting public expenditures below pre-crisis levels.
- Contrary to public perception, fiscal consolidation measures are not limited to Europe; many developing countries have adopted adjustment measures, including the elimination or reduction of food and fuel subsidies; cuts or caps on wages, including for health and social care workers; more narrow targeting of social protection benefits; and reforms of pension and health care systems. Many governments are also considering revenue-side measures, for example increasing consumption taxes such as value added tax (VAT) on basic products that are consumed by poor households.
- In developing countries, some of the proceeds of these adjustments, e.g. from the elimination of subsidies, have been used to design narrowly targeted safety nets, as a compensatory mechanism to the poorest. However, given the large number of vulnerable low-income households in developing countries, more efforts are necessary to meet the social protection needs of the population.
- Of particular significance are the divergent trends in richer and poorer countries: while many high-income countries are contracting their social security systems, many developing countries are expanding them. →

- High-income countries have reduced a range of social protection benefits and limited access to quality public services. Together with persistent unemployment, lower wages and higher taxes, these measures have contributed to increases in poverty or social exclusion, now affecting 123 million people in the European Union, 24 per cent of the population, many of them children, women and persons with disabilities. Future old-age pensioners will receive lower pensions in at least 14 European countries. Several European courts have found cuts unconstitutional. The cost of adjustment has been passed on to populations, who have been coping with fewer jobs and lower income for more than five years. Depressed household income levels are leading to lower domestic consumption and lower demand, slowing down recovery. The achievements of the European social model, which dramatically reduced poverty and promoted prosperity and social cohesion in the period following the Second World War, have been eroded by short-term adjustment reforms.
- Most middle-income countries are boldly expanding their social protection systems, thereby contributing to their domestic demand-led growth strategies: this presents a powerful development lesson. China, for instance, has achieved nearly universal coverage of pensions and increased wages; Brazil accelerated the expansion of social protection coverage and minimum wages since 2009. Continued commitment is necessary to address persistent inequalities.
- Some lower-income countries have extended social protection mainly through narrowly targeted temporary safety nets with very low benefit levels. However, in many of these countries debates are under way on building social protection floors as part of comprehensive social protection systems. There are options available to governments to expand fiscal space for social protection even in the poorest countries.
- The case for social protection is compelling in our times. Social protection is both a human right and sound economic policy. Social protection powerfully contributes to reducing poverty, exclusion, and inequality – while enhancing political stability and social cohesion. Social protection also contributes to economic growth by supporting household income and thus domestic consumption; this is particularly important during this time of slow recovery and low global demand. Further, social protection enhances human capital and productivity, so it has become a critical policy for transformative national development. Social protection and specifically social protection floors are essential for recovery, inclusive development and social justice, and must be part of the post-2015 development agenda.

Social protection systems have undergone profound changes in recent years. While many emerging economies have taken bold measures to expand social protection to promote economic and social development, other parts of the world, including many high-income countries, have been grappling with fiscal consolidation[1] and adjusting their social protection systems to make for cost savings. These divergent policy trends and their implications are the focus of this chapter. In particular, the chapter identifies the rationale and impact of, respectively, fiscal consolidation measures and expansionary policies on recovery efforts in high-, middle- and low-income countries. The chapter concludes by setting out the positive developmental impacts of social protection in the drive to promote sustainable and inclusive growth, to build human capital, and to achieve political stability, together constituting a set of powerful reasons why social protection must be part of the post-2015 development agenda.

[1] In this report, "fiscal consolidation" refers to the wide array of adjustment measures adopted to reduce government deficits and accumulated debt. Fiscal consolidation policies are often referred to as austerity policies.

6.1 Grappling with recession and slow growth: Social protection and the global crisis

6.1.1 Social protection in the first phase of the global crisis: Expansion and fiscal stimulus (2008–09)

As the crisis bit in 2008–09, the vast majority of governments in countries immediately affected scaled up public social expenditure in order to sustain growth and protect their populations from the adverse effects of the food, fuel and financial shocks. A total of 145 countries ramped up public expenditure during this first phase of the crisis. At least 48 countries announced fiscal stimulus packages totalling US$2.4 trillion, of which approximately a quarter was invested in social protection measures (figure 6.1). An ILO survey of fiscal stimulus plans in 54 developing and developed countries (ILO, 2009b) indicated that 54 per cent of governments boosted cash transfers, 44 per cent supported old-age pensions and 37 per cent increased access to health benefits. Additionally, 16 per cent of governments introduced food subsidies.

Social protection played a key role in attenuating the immediate negative effects of the crisis on households in this first phase. One of the key lessons from these initial crisis responses is that social protection can function as an automatic stabilizer most effectively if the relevant schemes and programmes are implemented before crisis conditions take hold (ILO, 2010c; ILO and World Bank, 2012; Bonnet, Saget and Weber, 2012; Behrendt et al., 2011). In the absence of such social protection measures, the effect of the crisis on unemployment, households' disposable income and poverty rates in 2009–10 would have been much higher (ILO, 2011a).

6.1.2 Social protection in the second phase of the global crisis: Fiscal consolidation (2010 and after)

These Keynesian counter-cyclical measures were short-lived. As the crisis moved into a second phase from 2010 onwards, rising concerns over sovereign debt levels and fiscal deficits led governments to abandon fiscal stimuli and introduce fiscal consolidation measures. According to the IMF's projections of government expenditure in the *World Economic Outlook* database (October 2013), 106 of the 181 countries for which data were available moved to contract public spending in 2010.

In 2014, the scope of public expenditure contraction is expected to intensify significantly, with impacts in 122 countries, and then steadily increase to affect 125 countries in 2015. The latest IMF forecast suggests that governments will continue on this contractionary trend at least through 2016 (figure 6.2, panel (a)).[2] It is

Figure 6.1 Social protection in stimulus packages, 2008–09 (percentage of total announced amount)

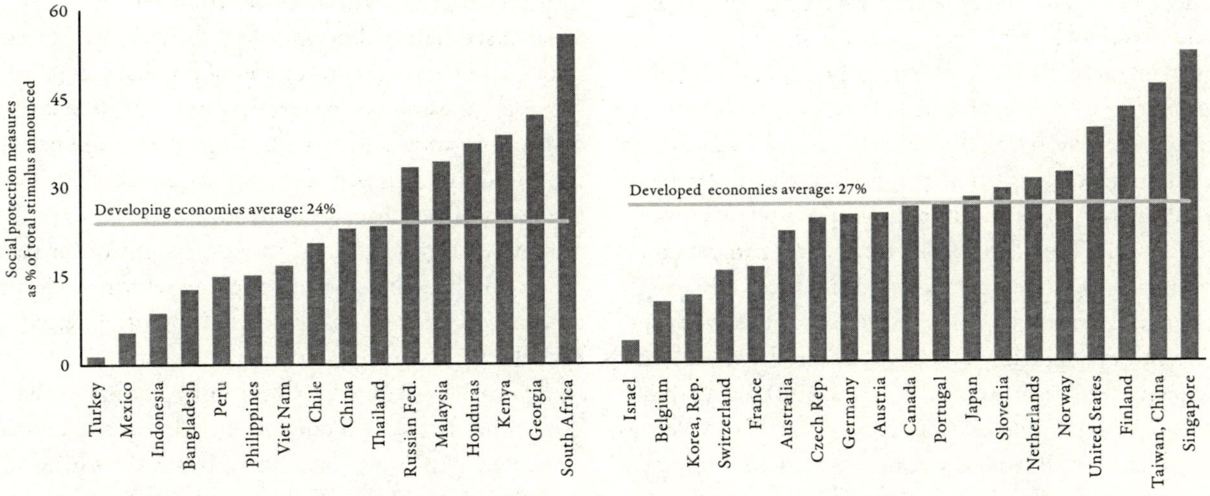

Source: Ortiz and Cummins, 2013, based on UNDP, 2010 and IMF country reports.

Link: http://www.social-protection.org/gimi/gess/RessourceDownload.action?ressource.ressourceId=43337.

[2] IMF expenditure projections change significantly; this section is an update of earlier work (Ortiz and Cummins, 2012; Ortiz and Cummins, 2013) in which the authors applied the same methodology to understand the scope of austerity, using the same data source – the expenditure projections contained in the IMF's *World Economic Outlook*, updated every six months. Any divergence in results is due to changes in IMF forecasts.

Figure 6.2 Number of countries contracting public expenditures (year on year), 2008–16, (a) relative to GDP and (b) in real terms

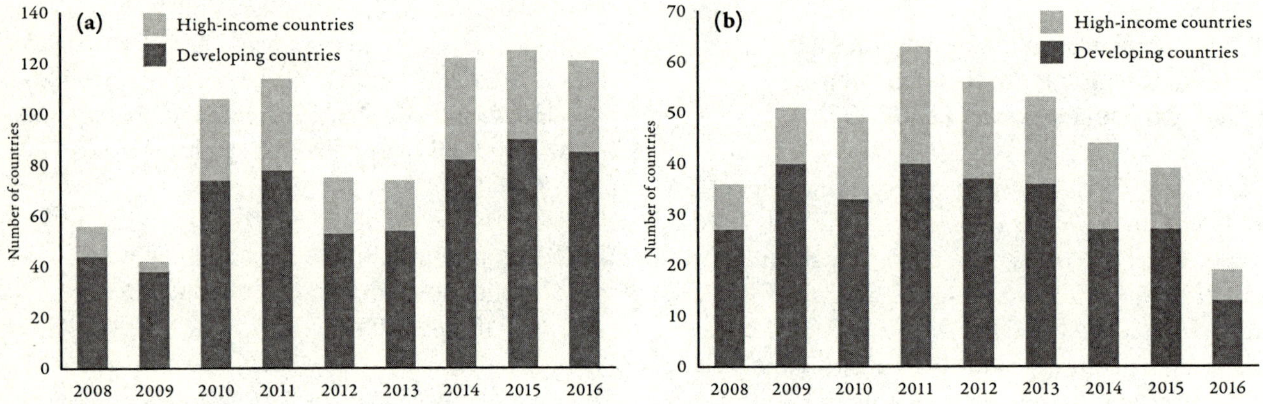

Source: ILO calculations based on the IMF's *World Economic Outlook* database (Oct. 2013).

Link: http://www.social-protection.org/gimi/gess/RessourceDownload.action?ressource.ressourceId=43338

important to note that this trend is observed across countries with different levels of income. Specifically, during 2010 public expenditure contraction affected 13 low-income, 28 lower-middle-income, 33 upper-middle-income and 32 high-income countries. In 2014, according to IMF fiscal projections, as many as 82 developing and 40 high-income countries are expected to contract public expenditures.[3]

In terms of real spending growth, a more conservative measure, IMF fiscal data reveal a peak contraction in 2011, with more than 60 countries contracting, but thereafter an easing from 2012 onwards (figure 6.2, panel (b)). Again, the incidence is larger in developing countries than in high-income economies.

Compared with the pre-crisis period, an alarming number of countries in 2013–15 appear to be undergoing excessive fiscal contraction, defined as cutting public expenditures below pre-crisis levels.[4] In terms of GDP, analysis of expenditure projections reveals that in 37 countries (one-fifth of the total), governments may be cutting their budgets excessively during 2013–15 (figure 6.3, panel (a)). These include countries with significant development challenges, such as Eritrea, Sudan, Iraq, Guinea-Bissau, Yemen, Sri Lanka, Ethiopia, Madagascar, Jamaica, Kazakhstan, Botswana, Cabo Verde, Turkmenistan, Burundi, Lebanon and the Philippines, among others. Nearly half (18) of these countries are expected to reduce spending by more than 3.0 per cent of GDP, on average, during this latest phase of the crisis when compared to expenditure levels during the pre-crisis period. In real terms, 17 governments are forecast to have fiscal envelopes in 2013–15 that are smaller, on average, than those of 2005–07 (figure 6.3, panel (b)). This is a dramatic situation, especially for developing countries where social spending is already very limited to start with.

How have governments been adjusting public expenditures since 2010? A review of 314 IMF country reports in 174 countries published between January 2010 and February 2013 (Ortiz and Cummins, 2013) indicates that governments are considering a combination of six main policy options (table 6.1), which relate strongly to the social protection of populations (see also box 6.1): phasing out or eliminating subsidies; cutting or capping wage bills; increasing taxes on consumption; undertaking pension reforms aimed at reducing the costs of pension systems; rationalizing and more narrowly targeting social assistance and other social protection benefits; and introducing reforms to healthcare systems aimed at cost containment. These fiscal consolidation strategies are not limited to Europe, and, in fact, are prevalent in developing countries. Many governments are also considering revenue-side measures that can have adverse impacts on vulnerable populations, mainly the introduction or extension of consumption taxes such as VAT, on basic products that

[3] For a more detailed analysis of public expenditure trends worldwide between 2005 and 2015, see Ortiz and Cummins, 2013.

[4] For the purposes of this report, excessive fiscal contraction is defined as reducing government expenditure below pre-crisis levels (average spending values during 2005–07). The analysis does not make a judgement about the adequacy or not of pre-crisis spending levels, it merely uses expenditures in 2005–07 to establish a baseline.

Figure 6.3 Excessive fiscal contraction: Projected decline in total government expenditure relative to GDP, and in real government expenditure (2013–15 average over 2005–07 average, percentages)

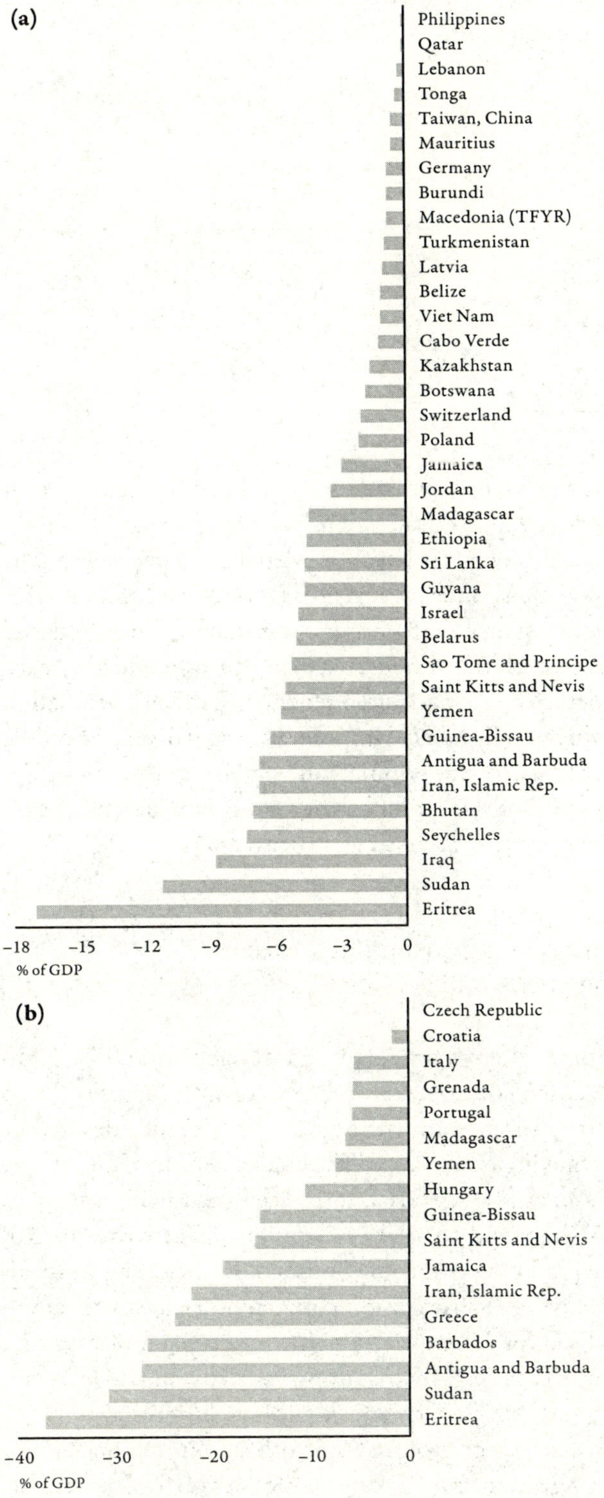

Note: Excessive fiscal consolidation is defined here as a cut of expenditures below pre-crisis levels.

Source: ILO calculations based on IMF, World Economic Outlook database (Oct. 2013).

Link: http://www.social-protection.org/gimi/gess/RessourceDownload.action?ressource.ressourceId=43339.

Box 6.1 From fiscal stimulus to fiscal consolidation – Implications for social protection

In 2008–09 there was a global counter-cyclical policy consensus, whereby countries coordinated policies to combat the negative social and economic impacts of the crisis with the aim of maintaining demand and growth. The IMF spelled out the need for global fiscal stimulus: "In normal times, the Fund would indeed be recommending to many countries that they reduce their budget deficit and their public debt. But these are not normal times … if no fiscal stimulus is implemented, then demand may continue to fall … what is needed is … a commitment by governments that they will follow whatever policies it takes to avoid a repeat of a Great Depression scenario" (Blanchard, 2008).

Early in 2010, IMF advice underwent a major change (later to be supported by the OECD), and ultimately also by the G20. Two IMF Board papers approved in February 2010 – *Exiting from crisis intervention policies* and *Strategies for fiscal consolidation in the post-crisis world* – called for large-scale fiscal adjustment "when the recovery is securely underway" and for structural reforms in public finance to be initiated immediately "even in countries where the recovery is not yet securely underway" (IMF, 2010a; IMF, 2010b). Reforms of pension and health entitlements were called for, accompanied by strengthened "safety nets" for the poorest (IMF, 2010a, pp. 15–32). On the composition of fiscal adjustment, it was advised that most of it could come from:

1. unwinding the previously adopted fiscal stimulus packages;
2. reforming pension and health entitlements to reduce the long-term financial obligations of the state by way of avoiding "a rise in spending as a share of GDP" (IMF, 2010a, p. 16);
3. containing other spending, by means such as eliminating subsidies;
4. increasing tax revenues.

All these suggested reforms became mainstream policy advice in a majority of countries around the world after 2010 and shaped the direction embraced by the economic adjustment programmes agreed with countries facing a sovereign debt crisis. The OECD 2010 *Economic Outlook* (OECD, 2010d) also focused on the urgent need for fiscal consolidation and structural reforms (in, for example, labour and product markets), pointing out that in both OECD and non-OECD countries the economic slack was disappearing rapidly. While these documents generally focused on higher-income countries, they also urged fiscal adjustment in developing countries, given that the risk of debt distress was increasing there too. These documents thus represented the first signs of a worldwide policy reversal. However, it turned out that economic slack did not disappear and instead a slow growth pattern risks becoming entrenched, partly due to fiscal consolidation itself.

Table 6.1 Main adjustment measures by region, 2010–13 (number of countries)

	Eliminating subsidies	Wage bill cuts/caps	Increasing consumption taxes	Pension reforms	Rationalizing and targeting social assistance	Health reforms
East Asia and the Pacific	12	13	8	4	9	0
Eastern Europe and Central Asia	9	15	13	16	15	9
Latin America and the Caribbean	11	14	13	12	11	0
Middle East and North Africa	9	7	7	5	5	3
South Asia	6	4	4	1	4	0
Sub-Saharan Africa	31	22	18	9	11	0
Developing countries	78	75	63	47	55	12
High-income countries	22	23	31	39	25	25
All countries	**100**	**98**	**94**	**86**	**80**	**37**

Source: Ortiz and Cummins, 2013, based on IMF country reports (Jan. 2010 to Feb. 2013).

are disproportionately consumed by poor households. All of the different adjustment approaches pose potentially serious consequences for vulnerable populations, as summarized below.

Eliminating or reducing subsidies

Overall, 100 governments in 78 developing and 22 high-income countries appear to be reducing or removing subsidies, predominately on fuel, but also on electricity, food and agriculture. While energy subsidies are being scaled back across all regions, this policy choice appears to be especially dominant in the Middle East and North Africa, South Asia and sub-Saharan Africa. The removal of public support for food and agriculture is also most frequently observed in the Middle East and North Africa, and in sub-Saharan Africa. These adjustment measures are being implemented at a time when food and energy prices are hovering near record highs; if basic subsidies are withdrawn without compensation being provided through adequate social protection mechanisms, food and energy may become unaffordable for many households, in particular, but not only, the poorest ones. The lack of proper compensation has led to a significant number of public demonstrations, reported in 60 countries (Ortiz et al., 2013; Zaid et al., 2014).

Wage bill cuts/caps

As recurrent expenditures such as the salaries of civil servants (particularly of social sector workers) tend to be the largest component of national budgets, an estimated 98 governments in 75 developing and 23 high-income countries have considered reducing their public wage bills, often as a part of civil service reforms. This policy stance may translate into salaries being reduced or eroded in real value, payments being made in arrears, hiring freezes and/or employment retrenchment, all of which have adverse impacts on the delivery of public services to the population. Health authorities have warned of the health hazards caused by such fiscal consolidation in Europe and other regions.

Increasing consumption taxes on goods and services

Some 94 governments in 63 developing and 31 high-income countries have been considering options to boost revenue by raising rates of VAT or sales tax, or removing exemptions. The consequent increases in the costs of basic goods and services are usually regressive, as they tend to affect more significantly the costs of living of lower-income households, including those already in poverty, unless compensatory measures are in place, for example through the provision of cash and near-cash (e.g. food stamps) benefits, or the distribution of basic goods and services at subsidized prices to lower income groups. Some other countries are considering alternative tax approaches, involving for example the expansion of usually more progressive taxes, such as those on income, inheritance, property and corporations, including taxes on the financial sector.

Reforming pension and health systems

Approximately 86 governments in 47 developing and 39 high-income countries have been considering a variety of changes to their contributory pension systems, by means such as making eligibility conditions stricter or raising the statutory pensionable age, so that people have to work longer to receive a full benefit, lowering benefit replacement rates, or eliminating minimum pension guarantees for less fortunate workers. Another 37 countries are also discussing reforming their health-care systems with a focus on cost containment, generally by increasing fees and co-payments made by patients along with cost-saving measures in public health centres. These adjustment measures have immediate negative effects on the poor, increase poverty risks for others, and may lead to the effective exclusion of many from the receipt of benefits or critical assistance at a time when their incomes are decreasing and their social needs are greatest.

Rationalizing and more narrowly targeting social assistance and other social protection benefits

Overall, 80 governments in 55 developing and 25 high-income countries have been considering rationalizing their social spending, often by revising eligibility criteria and targeting benefits more narrowly on the very poorest, which implies a de facto reduction of social protection coverage and a more limited role for social protection systems in preventing poverty. A more narrow targeting on the poorest has been discussed by governments in 25 high-income and 55 developing countries, including low-income countries such as the Gambia, Haiti, Mali, Mauritania, Nicaragua, Senegal, Sudan, Timor-Leste, Togo and Zambia, where on average about half of the population is below the national poverty line. In such places, the rationale for targeting assistance on the poorest of the poor is weak. This policy approach runs a high risk of excluding large segments of vulnerable populations at a time of economic crisis and hardship. Rather than targeting and scaling down social protection programmes to achieve cost savings over the short term, there is a strong case for scaling them up in times of crisis and building rights-based social protection floors.

Contrary to public perception, fiscal consolidation measures are not limited to Europe; in fact, most of the adjustment measures summarized here feature most prominently in developing countries, particularly subsidy reduction, wage bill cuts/caps, and more and more "rationalization" of existing social protection programmes. The main risk of these expenditure-contracting measures is that, when taken without due recognition of their negative consequences, they result in often large vulnerable groups being excluded from receiving benefits or critical assistance.

Ill-designed fiscal consolidation measures threaten not only the human right to social security, but also the rights to food, health, education, and other essential goods and services (Sepúlveda, 2012; UN, 2012b). In many contexts, fiscal consolidation policies are driven by a cost-saving logic, and their negative social impacts on women, children, older persons, the unemployed, immigrants or persons with disabilities, are viewed as unavoidable collateral damage in the quest for fiscal balances and debt service (CESR, 2012). The UN High Commissioner for Human Rights has warned that "austerity measures endanger social protection schemes, including pensions, thereby dramatically affecting the enjoyment of the rights to social security and to an adequate standard of living" (OHCHR, 2013, para. 36), particularly for vulnerable and marginalized groups, pointing to States' positive obligation to ensure adequate financial regulation, as necessary to safeguard human rights, as well as the obligation to ensure the satisfaction, at the very least, of minimum essential levels of all economic, social and cultural rights, including the right to social security (OHCHR, 2013, esp. paras 36–71).

6.1.3 Divergent trends across countries

Generally, the latest available complete data (2011) show a worldwide decline in social protection expenditure in terms of GDP, particularly for middle-income and high-income countries (figure 6.4).[5] Only low-income countries have increased public social protection expenditure as a percentage of GDP. The level of social expenditure has not risen sufficiently to keep up with the increases in unemployment and poverty.

The four panels of figure 6.4 show trends in per capita real government social protection expenditure in

[5] At the time of writing of this report, comparable worldwide data on social security expenditure trends for 2012–14, and measurements of their more recent effects on inequalities and poverty, are limited.

Figure 6.4 Public social protection expenditure as a percentage of GDP, real GDP and real social protection expenditure (index 100 = 2007): (a) world; (b) high-income countries; (c) middle-income countries; (d) low-income countries

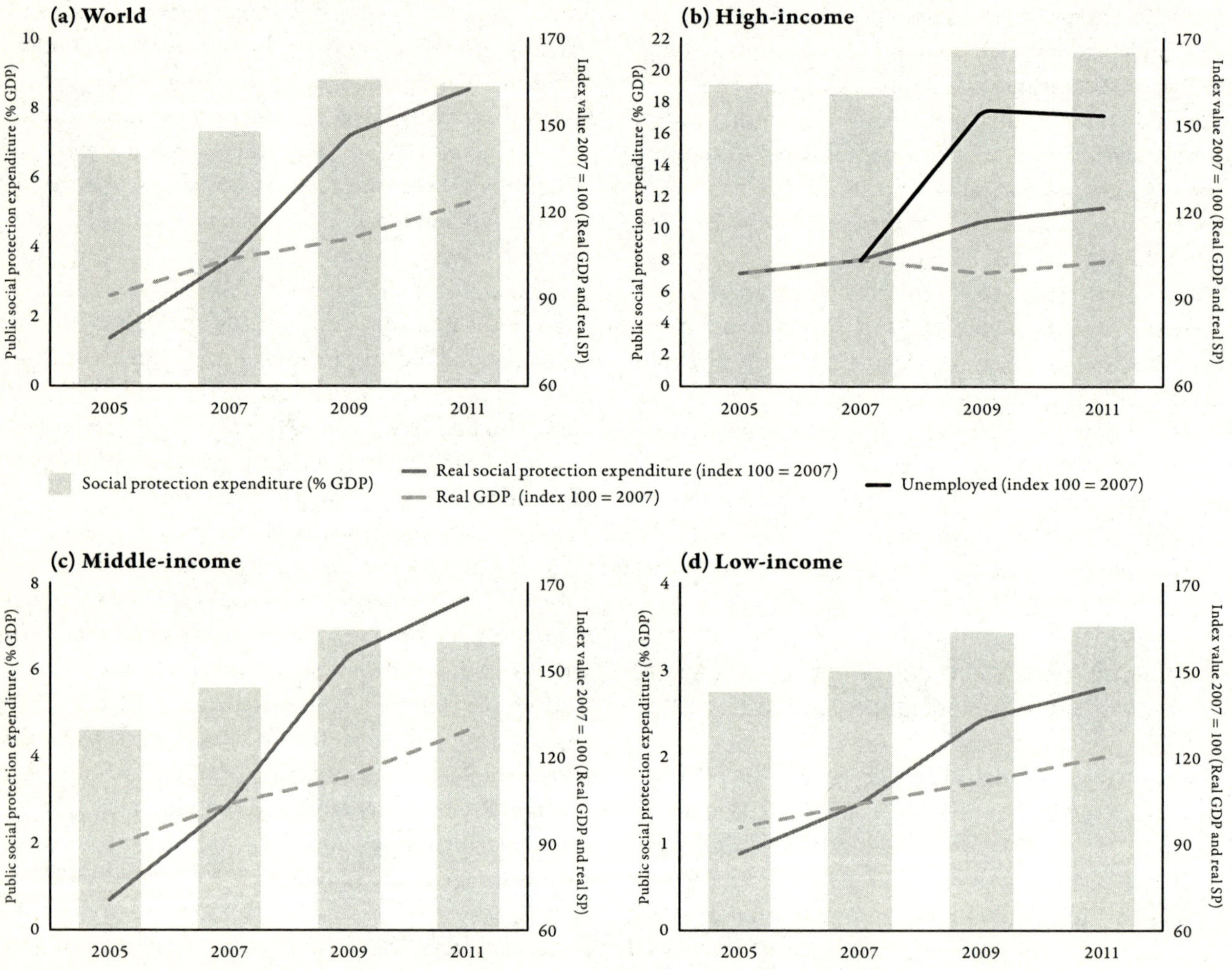

Note: The panel on high-income countries excludes the Russian Federation. The left (vertical) scale differs between income groups.

Sources: ILO calculations based on ILO, OECD, Eurostat, CEPAL, ADB, World Bank, IMF and national data.

Link: http://www.social-protection.org/gimi/gess/RessourceDownload.action?ressource.ressourceId=43321.

the two phases of the crisis. It is clear that, despite the significant contraction in 2011, a large number of countries (mostly in the developing world) were at that point still expanding social security. It must be noted that in many of these developing countries such expansion is being partly financed using the cost savings resulting from fiscal consolidation and adjustment measures such as reducing or eliminating subsidies (including food and fuel subsidies). The net social outcome effects remain to be studied and will inevitably vary from country to country.

While a significant number of governments have adjusted their social protection systems since 2010, many developing countries have taken bold measures to extend social protection coverage and enhance at least the social assistance provided to the poorest segments of their populations (see figures 6.5 and 6.6). The strong push for the expansion of social protection started well before the onset of the global crisis, but has accelerated since 2009, sometimes as part of short-term fiscal stimulus measures, often as part of longer-term structural policies aiming at promoting human and economic development, as well as political stability.

Figure 6.5 Trends in government and public social protection expenditure per capita (in constant prices): (a) 2007–09; (b) 2009–11

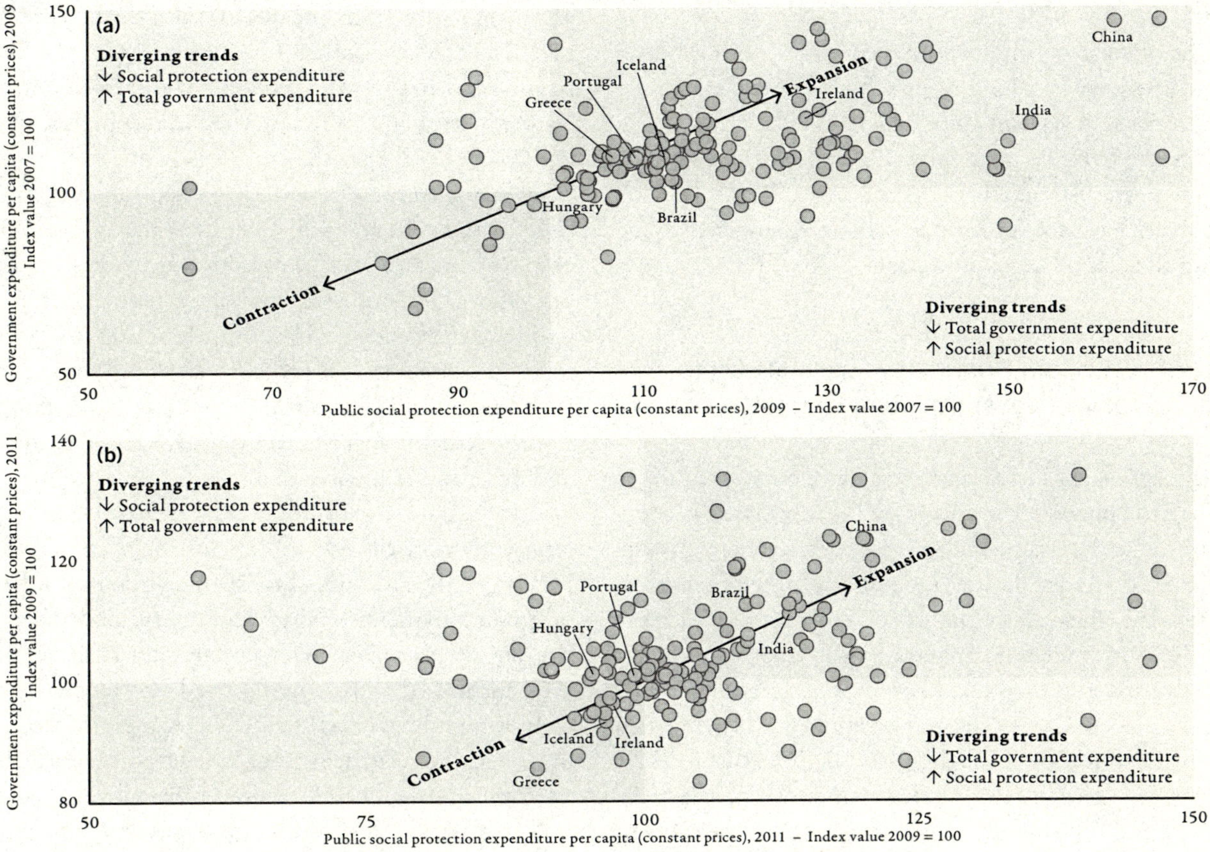

Sources: ILO calculations based on ILO, OECD, Eurostat, CEPAL, ADB, World Bank, IMF and national data.

Link: http://www.social-protection.org/gimi/gess/RessourceDownload.action?ressource.ressourceId=43322.

Figure 6.6 Expansion of social protection in middle- and low-income countries: Selected examples of new and expanded programmes, 2000–13

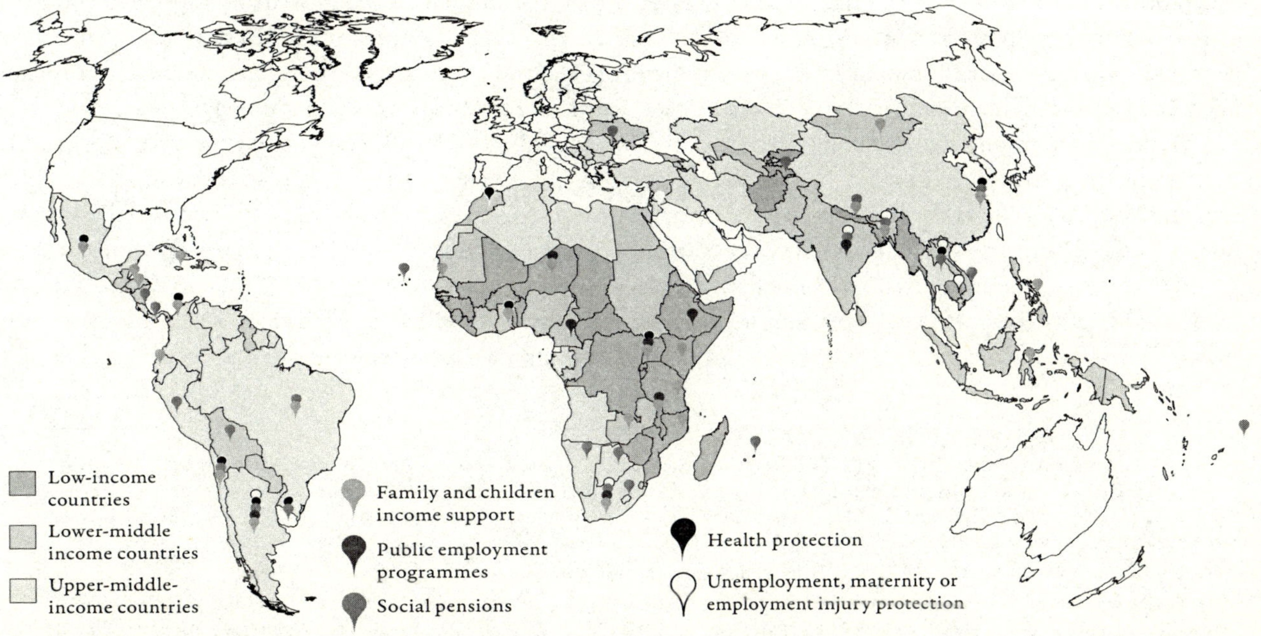

Source: ILO compilation.

Link: http://www.social-protection.org/gimi/gess/RessourceDownload.action?ressource.ressourceId=43519.

6.2 High-income countries: Fiscal consolidation and its effects

The majority of high-income countries (HICs)[6] have been engaged in long-term reforms of social protection pension systems since long before the crisis, under pressure from demographic change and the search for long-term sustainability. The recent fiscal consolidation policies have accelerated such changes, however, affecting all areas of social protection.

6.2.1 Overview: Prioritizing financial sector recovery over social protection

The significant increases in social protection spending in the early phase of the crisis were broadly aimed at countervailing the exceptional severity of the economic downturn. There were, however, significant differences across countries: in late 2008 and 2009, while among European HICs such increases amounted to around 7 per cent in real terms, they exceeded 10 per cent in the entire OECD and reached 15 per cent in the United States, with their effect continuing through 2010 (OECD, 2012b). These increases crucially contributed to minimizing the social costs and limiting the economic impact of the crisis by avoiding a collapse of consumption and maintaining economic activity (see section 6.2.2 below).

The second phase of the crisis, beginning in 2010, saw a total policy reversal: annual spending growth slowed significantly, followed by a contraction in social expenditure in 2011 for many HICs. This reflected not a reduction in social protection needs, but rather a 180-degree shift in governments' public expenditure policy from 2010 onwards. The sovereign debt crisis in Europe turned public attention to government spending, as if it were this that had caused the crisis. However, government debt and deficits were symptoms of the crisis, not its cause. Rising debts and deficits at this point resulted from bank bailouts to rescue the financial sector from bankruptcy, stimulus packages, and lower government revenues due to the slowdown in economic activity (figure 6.7). Yet fiscal consolidation focused on deep cutbacks to public policies and shrinking the State as the main way to fix the deficit, calm the markets and revitalize the economy; following this logic, the European social model was depicted as unaffordable and burdensome, which ultimately reduced competitiveness and discouraged growth.

When government policies shifted highest priority to servicing debt and achieving fiscal balances in 2010, employment and social protection became secondary priorities. Decisions were taken to reduce public expenditures in most HICs, despite rising unemployment and poverty (see table 6.1 above). Public social expenditure in HICs has not kept pace with populations' needs for income security and access to health and other social services.

Overall, unemployment rose by more than 45 per cent, with more than 44 million unemployed in OECD HICs in 2013 compared to 2008, while expenditure on unemployment benefits and tax-funded social assistance was initially increased but later reduced, with around half of those unemployed not receiving unemployment benefits (ILO, 2014a; Annex IV, table B.3 in this report). At the time of writing this report, there are large groups of people, many of them formerly in the middle class, living in conditions of poverty or near-poverty in HICs; this situation is most evident in the crisis-affected countries of Europe, where in 2012 there were 9.5 million more poor people than in 2008, and child poverty was reported to be increasing at an alarming rate[7] (figure 6.8). Rising unemployment and increased poverty on such a scale in so many European countries should have prompted measures to further strengthen social protection expenditure rather than curtailments informed by fiscal consolidation objectives.

Reductions in social protection were most severe in those HICs with the highest budget deficits, which were also those with the most limited social assistance programmes in place (Greece, Portugal and Ireland) (Vaughan-Whitehead, 2014).[8] According to a recent OECD survey across more than 30 OECD countries, around half have been considering fiscal consolidation

[6] This section focuses mostly on HICs which are members of the OECD. The situation of other HICs is not discussed here as it mostly relates to countries where social protection developments resemble those of middle-income countries: for example, Bahrain, Qatar, Saudi Arabia and the United Arab Emirates, where aggregate social protection expenditure is less than 5 per cent of GDP (with the exception of Kuwait, where it amounts to 12 per cent of GDP), in comparison to an average of 22 per cent of GDP in OECD countries.

[7] Eurostat data for 2012, except Ireland (2011); based on fixed poverty line as of 2008.

[8] Greece reduced public spending by more than €30 billion or the equivalent of 10 per cent of GDP between 2009 and 2011, and an additional 8 per cent is expected to be saved by 2015 (Hermann, 2013; OECD, 2012c).The Irish austerity programme is also intended to save approximately 18 per cent of GDP by 2015, while Spain, Portugal, the United Kingdom and Hungary aim at 7–8 per cent of savings at least (Vaughan-Whitehead, 2014).

Figure 6.7 Support for the financial sector, fiscal stimulus packages and public debt increases, selected HICs, 2008–10 (US$ billions)

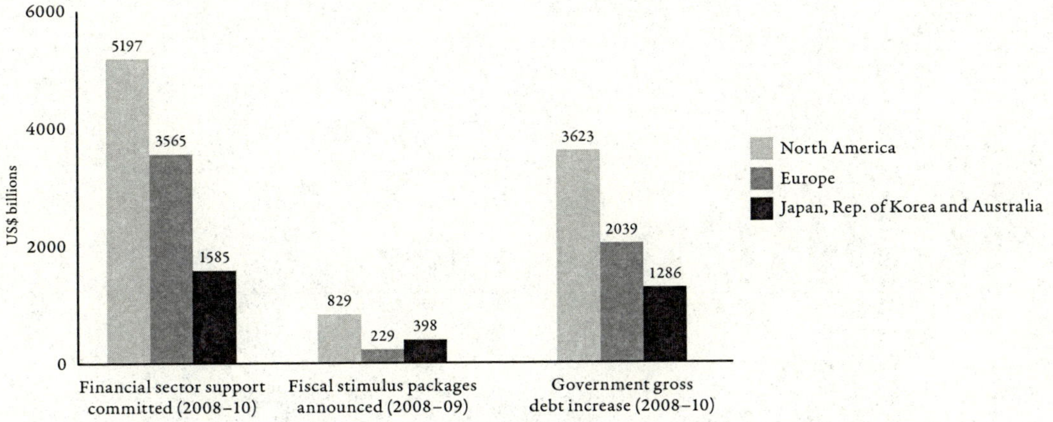

Note: North America includes United States and Canada; Europe includes Austria, Belgium, Finland, France, Germany, Greece, Ireland, the Netherlands, Poland, Portugal, Spain, Sweden and the United Kingdom.

Sources: IMF, 2010c; IMF, 2013a; Stolz and Wedow, 2010; UNDP, 2010.

Link: http://www.social-protection.org/gimi/gess/RessourceDownload.action?ressource.ressourceId=43679.

Figure 6.8 Increase in the proportion of the population at risk of poverty in 18 European countries between 2008 and 2012

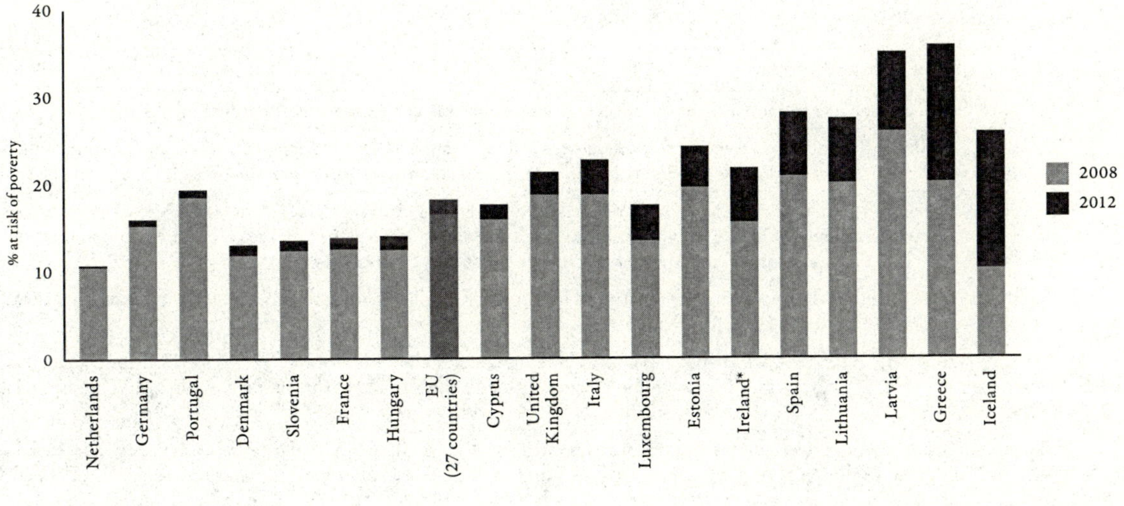

* Data for 2011.

Note: This graph is based on an at-risk-of-poverty line of 60 per cent of median equivalized income anchored at a fixed moment in time (2008).

Source: Eurostat.

Link: http://www.social-protection.org/gimi/gess/RessourceDownload.action?ressource.ressourceId=43342.

plans requiring adjustments of more than 5 per cent of GDP from 2009 to 2015, with a high predominance of direct spending cuts as opposed to revenue-side measures (figure 6.9). The survey indicates that the current fiscal consolidation plans are leading to a decline in social transfers in cyclically adjusted terms in about half of OECD countries, while adjusted household taxes are expected at the same time to increase in most OECD countries.[9]

Social protection has frequently been targeted for expenditure reductions or freezes, in particular in the areas of unemployment benefits, health care, pensions and social assistance (see table 6.2). On the revenue side, measures have often aimed at increasing indirect taxes, such as VAT, which is reported to have increased on average by 1.8 percentage points in European Union member countries.[10] Such increases in indirect taxes

[9] This result is based on an OECD survey of the consolidation strategies of over 30 governments between 2009 and 2015. Most governments reported plans to improve their public budgets primarily via spending restraints (Rawdanowicz, Wurzel and Christensen, 2013).

[10] According to Eurostat, the average VAT rate in the EU was 19.4 per cent in 2008; by 2012, it had increased to 21.0 per cent.

Figure 6.9 Distribution of expenditure-based versus revenue-based fiscal consolidation plans in 30 OECD countries, 2009–15

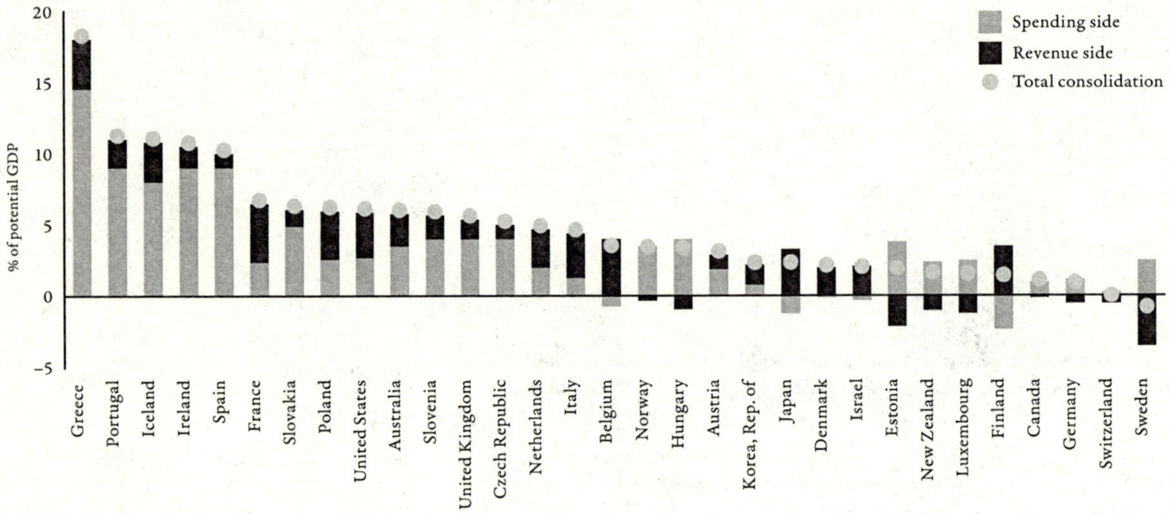

Sources: Based on OECD, 2012c; Rawdanowicz, Wurzel and Christensen, 2013. Link to original graph: http://www.oecd-ilibrary.org/governance/restoring-public-finances-2012-update_9789264179455-en [accessed 30 Apr. 2014].

Link: http://www.social-protection.org/gimi/gess/RessourceDownload.action?ressource.ressourceId=43477.

Table 6.2 Selected fiscal consolidation measures recently adopted or under discussion in high-income countries

Country	Measures adopted or under discussion
Denmark	Freeze in several social benefits, reduction of duration of unemployment benefits, introduction of a ceiling on family benefits
Estonia	Increases in VAT (to 20 per cent) and excise taxes, decreases in social benefits (health, pensions), operating spending cuts, (temporary) adjustment in second pillar pension contributions, land sales, discretionary spending cuts
France	Cuts in public pensions, health care and public administration; increase of retirement age (from 60 years to 62 years by 2018); increased taxes on capital; increase in top income tax rate by 1 percentage point; plans to increase required contribution record to receive a full pension (de facto increasing further the retirement age for future generations)
Germany	Additional taxes, cuts in spending on social security and labour market policies, adjustments to unemployment insurance provisions, cuts in military and administrative expenditure
Greece	10 per cent reduction in general government expenditure on salaries and allowances, public sector recruitment freeze, drastic structural reform to social protection system and drastic reduction in the number of the public bodies/entities linked to local authorities
Hungary	Cuts to the public sector (reduction of wages, elimination of certain benefits), six-year tax for financial institutions, increase in VAT to 27 per cent, reduction of bureaucracy for investors, ban on foreign exchange mortgages and partial reversal of pension reform
Ireland	Tax increases, spending cuts (public sector wages, social welfare benefits)
Italy	Public sector hiring freeze and public sector wage cuts, curtailments in health-care spending, reduction in transfers from central to regional and local governments, drastic adjustments to public pension system
Latvia	Increase in VAT from 18 to 21 per cent, introduction of capital income tax, increase of personal income flat tax rate by 3 percentage points and adjustments to public pension system
Portugal	Reduction in public sector pay and hiring, increase in VAT to 23 per cent, taxes on high income earners and drastic adjustments to public pensions
Romania	25 per cent reduction in public sector wages, 15 per cent reduction in pensions and unemployment benefits, other adjustments to social protection system, increase in VAT from 19 to 24 per cent
Spain	Cuts in public sector jobs and pay, introduction of new income tax, increase in VAT to 21 per cent, cuts in public pension provision including the suspension of pension indexing to inflation
United Kingdom	Abolition of child trust fund, cuts in employment programmes, civil service recruitment freeze, increase in VAT from 17.5 to 20 per cent.
United States	Freeze of non-security discretionary funding for three years by cutting/reducing 120 programmes deemed ineffective, public sector pay freeze, reduction in duration of unemployment insurance, restrictions to food assistance system, introduction of a national health insurance programme.

Sources: Based on ILO, EU and IILS, 2011, and national sources.

Box 6.2 Using sovereign pension reserve funds to fund bailouts

Sovereign pension reserve funds, normally established to support governments in funding future pension liabilities by complementing the accumulated funds from employers' and workers' contributions, have been tapped to a substantial extent during the course of the global crisis to help ease the strain on national public finances. In some cases they have been used them to finance interventions directly; in others, to support specific economic sectors facing difficulties or to guarantee loans.

For example, the Irish National Pension Reserve Fund was used to recapitalize the Irish banking system as one of the solicited national contributions under the economic adjustment programme for Ireland. Another example is the Australian Future Fund, which received its last financial allocation from the government in 2008, as a result of which its asset level is now considered to fall below its target level as determined by Australia's Government Actuary. The New Zealand Superannuation Fund, meanwhile, has increased its exposure to New Zealand's domestic economy in response to the government's advice to consider attractive investment opportunities in New Zealand. Here too, the government reduced the transfer of funds from the government budget to the Fund in 2009/10 and suspended it in 2010/11; it is scheduled to resume in 2020/21.

Source: ILO, 2011a; Casey, 2014; national sources.

Figure 6.10 The social and economic risks of fiscal consolidation

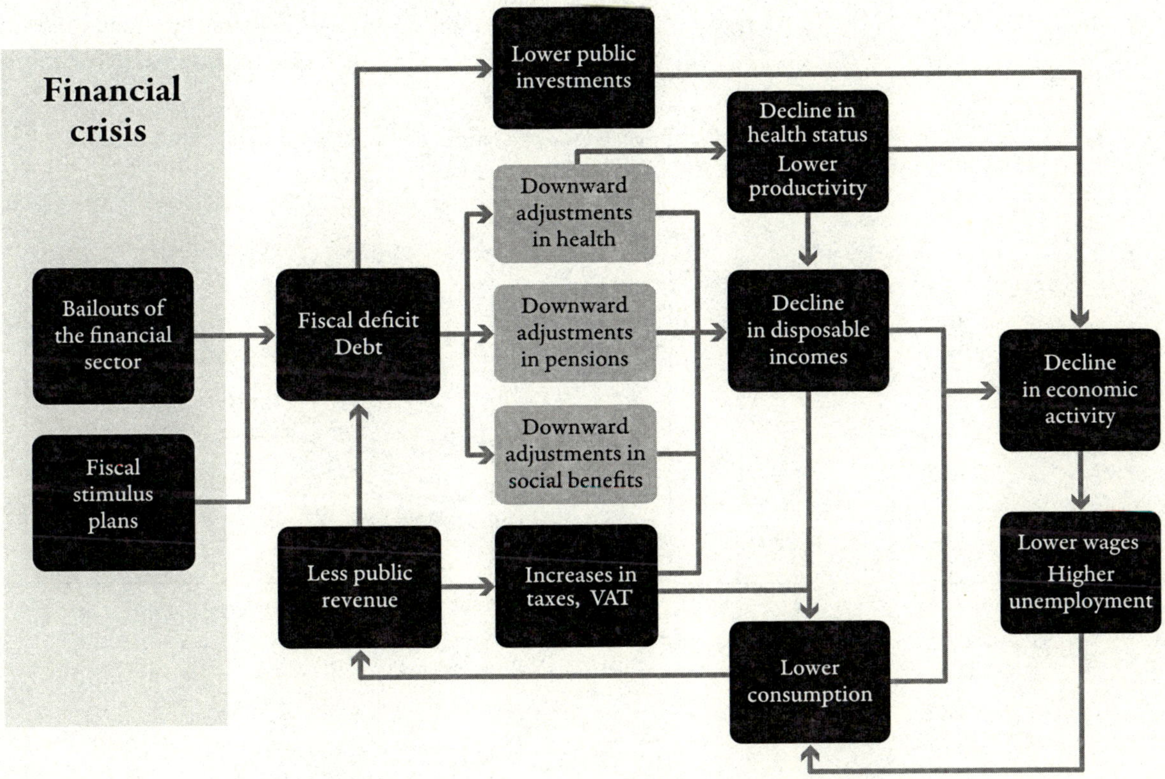

Source: ILO.

Link: http://www.social-protection.org/gimi/gess/RessourceDownload.action?ressource.ressourceId=43680.

disproportionately affect low income groups (Thomas and Picos-Sánchez, 2012).

In addition to these measures, some governments have had to look at available sources of funding to finance bailouts of financial institutions in trouble. The use of national pension funds, either through explicit loans and investment decisions or through non-explicit loan guarantees (see box 6.2), is cause for concern, as such funds are subject to rigorous performance objectives and targets as well as strict governance rules which now appear to be being sidestepped. Such pension assets usually represent the accumulated contributions of workers and employers towards guaranteeing their social security in old age, a demand ever more pressing as these societies age.

Overall, the deployment of vast public resources to rescue private institutions considered "too big to fail" and, to a lesser degree, to fund fiscal stimulus plans, caused sovereign debt to increase, forced taxpayers to absorb the losses and, ultimately, hindered economic growth (figure 6.10). Many governments have curtailed government consumption and investment and also reduced social benefits, thus creating a vicious circle: reductions in infrastructure investment and public sector wages, as well as cuts in social security, further depressed aggregate demand in the economy, in consequence reducing the demand for labour, and thus in turn increasing unemployment, reducing revenues from income taxation and narrowing the available fiscal envelope, thereby adding pressure to further reduce social transfers. The cost of adjustment has been passed on to populations, who have now been attempting to cope with fewer jobs, lower income and reduced access to public goods and services for more than five years.

6.2.2 First phase of the crisis: Scaling up social protection to sustain households' disposable income and domestic demand (2008–09)

The automatic provision of unemployment insurance benefits in the early phase of the crisis demonstrated the counter-cyclical role of such schemes, where funded from accumulated contributions with a view to meeting increased benefit expenditures during economic downturns. In a number of countries, these schemes were scaled up to facilitate access to benefits in the face of massive unemployment. For example, the United States extended the maximum duration for paying benefits as job opportunities were too few to accommodate the increased numbers of unemployed. Other countries, such as Germany, adjusted their legal frameworks to allow companies in certain sectors to introduce a temporary reduction in working time, compensated for by social protection benefits, in order to avoid job cuts.

Figure 6.11 Trends in real per capita public social protection expenditure, GDP, consumption and unemployment, 2007–2012/13: (a) United States; (b) Japan; (c) France; (d) Germany

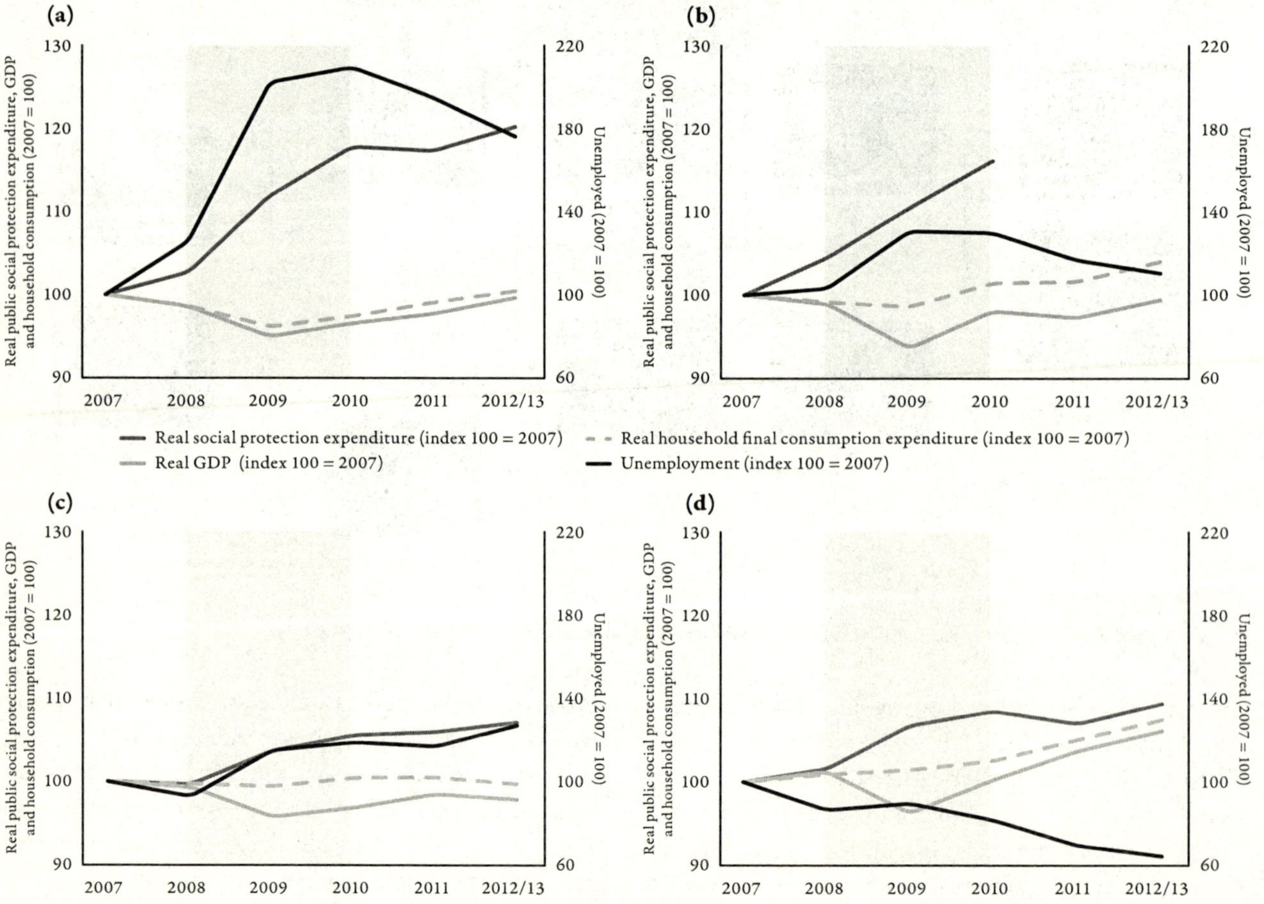

Note: Indexed levels, 2007 =100.

Sources: ILO, OECD, Eurostat, IMF.

Link: http://www.social-protection.org/gimi/gess/RessourceDownload.action?ressource.ressourceId=43323.

Figure 6.12 Contributions of various components to the growth of nominal gross disposable income of households, European Area 17 countries, 2000–12 (percentages)

Notes: Annual percentage change and percentage point contributions. Labour income includes compensation of employees, gross operating surplus and mixed income (compensation of self-employed).

Source: Eurostat/European Central Bank.

Link: http://www.social-protection.org/gimi/gess/RessourceDownload.action?ressource.ressourceId=43324.

Other examples of good practice include special stimulus packages incorporating urgently needed social assistance benefits for the growing number of poor. These and other such short-term adjustments limited the fall in citizens' purchasing power and thus also the decline in global aggregate demand.

Data from the United States, Japan, France and Germany from 2009 to early 2010 provide evidence of the counter-cyclical automatic economic and social stabilizer function of social protection expenditure, especially of the role played by special fiscal stimuli to scale up short-term benefits for the unemployed and the poor in reversing the downward trend of private consumption expenditure (figure 6.11).[11]

Further evidence of the counter-cyclical effect of social protection is provided by analysis of different components of growth in private disposable income over time. Before the crisis, labour income, net social benefits, taxes and property income varied across economic cycles such that gross disposable real income increased by around 4 per cent annually in the European Area up to 2008 (figure 6.12). Then, in 2009 and early 2010, populations in a majority of countries experienced significant declines in their incomes from earnings and other sources of market income, due to increased unemployment, reductions in working time and earnings, and declining profits and other capital incomes.

On average, incomes from earnings and capital (market incomes) dwindled by 1.9 per cent per year in real terms across the OECD over this period; however, in some countries, such as Greece, Iceland and New Zealand, market incomes dropped by more than 7 per cent per year (figure 6.13). Increased social transfers and other elements of the special fiscal stimuli played a particularly strong role in cushioning the effects of a reduction of market incomes in countries such as Estonia, Ireland, New Zealand and Spain. In other countries, where regular and adequate social protection benefits were not available, no such cushioning effect against the drastic falls in households' disposable income could be observed. From 2010 up to early 2012, the earnings component added on average 2 percentage points to growth of disposable incomes, while changes in reduced social benefits clearly worked in the opposite direction.

However, the evidence of the counter-cyclical automatic economic and social stabilizer function of

[11] In Germany, where 26 per cent of GDP was spent on public social protection in 2012, four stimulus packages were introduced from 2008, with the main aim of preserving jobs. Their cost as of 2011 amounted to about 4 per cent of 2008 GDP (compared to 19.8 per cent spent on the rescue of the financial sector). In France, where 32 per cent of GDP in 2012 was spent on social protection, extraordinary fiscal rescue efforts were more modest, representing (as of 2011) 1.6 per cent of 2008 GDP (compared to 19.0 per cent spent on the rescue of the financial sector). In the United States, where 20 per cent of GDP in 2012 was spent on social protection, there was one main extraordinary stimulus package in 2008 and some lesser ones afterwards. As of 2011, their cost amounted to about 5.6 per cent of the 2008 GDP (compared to 5.1 per cent spent on the rescue of the financial sector).

Figure 6.13 Annual changes in disposable income, 2007–10, by income component, selected OECD countries (percentages)

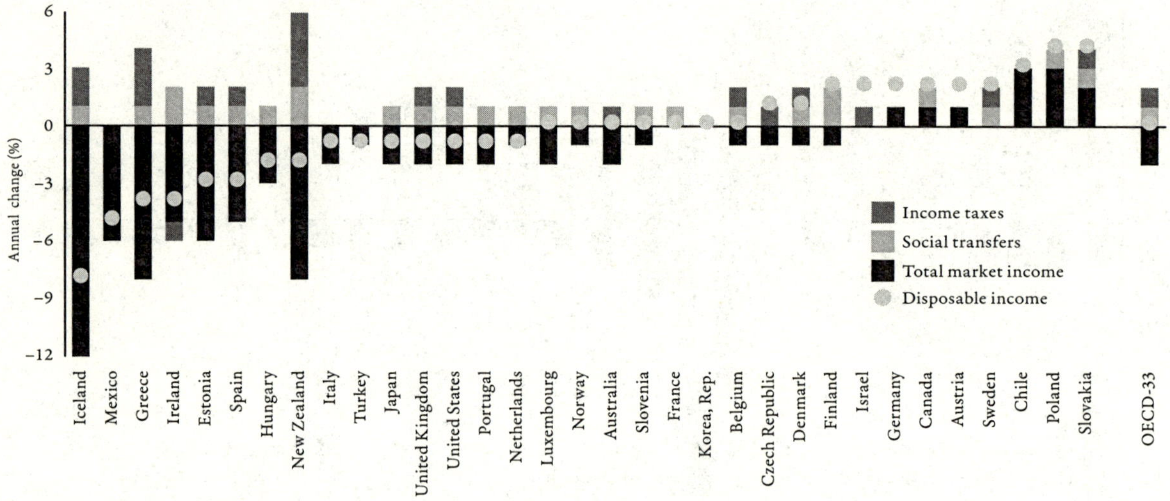

Notes: 2007 figure refers to 2006 for Chile and Japan; 2008 figure for Australia, Finland, France, Germany, Israel, Italy, Mexico, New Zealand, Norway, Sweden and the United States. Figure for 2010 refers to 2009 for Hungary, Japan, New Zealand and Turkey; 2011 for Chile. Data for 2010 based on the European Union Statistics on Income and Living Conditions (EU-SILC) surveys are provisional for Austria, Belgium, Czech Republic, Estonia, Finland, Greece, Iceland, Ireland, Italy, Luxembourg, Poland, Portugal, Spain, Slovakia and Slovenia. Household incomes are adjusted for household size. Market incomes are reported net of taxes in Hungary, Mexico and Turkey.

Source: Based on OECD Income Distribution database; see OECD, 2013b.

Link: http://www.social-protection.org/gimi/gess/RessourceDownload.action?ressource.ressourceId=43417.

social protection expenditure observed in 2009 and early 2010 was not enough to contain the pressure from financial markets, ratings agencies and orthodox approaches to adopt adjustment measures in social protection programmes from 2010. Instead of joining with social partners in looking for alternative responses to the crisis that could have enabled them to accommodate structural reform without undermining social rights or exacerbating the hardship experienced by enterprises, the governments of most HICs adopted fiscal consolidation policies, including reductions in benefit entitlements and durations. Negative outcomes during this deep and protracted economic downturn are seen not only in increased poverty but also in the gradual economic effects of reduced aggregate private consumption (see section 6.2.3).

Despite the cushioning and consumption-stabilizing effects of taxes and transfers, the crisis effectively depressed disposable incomes in many OECD countries, with in many cases negative knock-on effects on private consumption and aggregate demand. Overall, between 2007 and 2010 private households suffered an annual decline in their disposable incomes of as much as 8.4 per cent in Iceland and between 2 and 4 per cent in Estonia, Greece, Hungary, Ireland, Mexico, New Zealand and Spain (figure 6.13). This effect was further sharpened by the internal devaluations pursued in some countries of the eurozone.

6.2.3 Second phase of the global crisis: Fiscal consolidation, 2010 onwards

The turn towards fiscal consolidation measures in the second phase of the crisis, from 2010 onwards, reversed the expansionary stance typical of responses to the first phase and included various measures to reduce benefits. This coincided with the policy reversal adopted by the IMF Board and endorsed by the OECD and the G20 (box 6.1). More recently, IMF Chief Economist Olivier Blanchard has admitted serious underestimation of fiscal multipliers with respect to the depth of the economic contraction in the design of fiscal consolidation policies (Blanchard and Leigh, 2013); also, IMF research has acknowledged that fiscal consolidation has adverse effects on both short- and long-term unemployment, private demand and GDP growth, with wage earners hurt disproportionately more than profit- and rent-earners (Guajardo, Leigh and Pescatori, 2011; Ball, Leigh and Loungani, 2011), and that policies that sustain aggregate demand are still critically important (Blanchard, Jaumotte and Loungani, 2013). Nevertheless, at the time fiscal consolidation policies were adopted across HICs, with spending cuts targeted in particular on short-term benefits, such as unemployment benefits, family benefits and family support programmes, thus making it more difficult for households to maintain a life in dignity with at least a minimum income security, especially for many families with children. Following recent reforms, some European countries may no longer be compliant with the requirements of the ILO's Social Security (Minimum Standards) Convention, 1952 (No. 102), which most of them have ratified. Table 6.2 provides an overview of some of the main measures adopted during the global crisis.

Unemployment benefits

Access to unemployment benefits, and the levels and maximum duration of payments, were reduced starting in 2010 (see also Chapter 3, section 3.2). Increases in poverty have been attributed in part to such reductions in protection: one recent study, for example, argues that increases in poverty in the United States stem directly from cuts to unemployment benefits (CBPP, 2014).

In countries with advance-funding approaches, unemployment benefits from 2008 to early 2010 were financed from current contributions and reserve funds accumulated under unemployment insurance (UI) schemes. However, as high unemployment rates persisted beyond 2010, UI reserve funds started to run out. Increases to UI contribution rates were then considered, although there was reluctance from employers, who argued on the contrary for pro-cyclical support in the form of lower social security contributions. This highlights the importance of promoting counter-cyclical UI funding in countries without advance-funding policies to ensure the availability of reasonable UI funds during future economic downturns. The advance funding of unemployment benefits in reasonable proportions and within a well-governed framework could help to ease the pressure on public budgets during downturns, when needs are high and revenues are falling, and when the business sector is less receptive to possible contribution increases.

Health

Most governments have initiated reforms in health protection systems, such as rationalizing the costs of public health facilities, introducing patient co-payments and cutting wage bills for medical staff. Increased out-of-pocket expenditures for health add further pressure on governments to increase pensions and other social protection benefits to cover the additional cost for households of seeking necessary health care. Meanwhile, a lower quality of health service provision leads to worse health outcomes (e.g. Karanikolos et al., 2013; Mladovsky et al., 2012). Weakened mental health, increased substance abuse and higher suicide rates have all been linked with fiscal consolidation measures (WHO, 2011a; Stuckler and Basu, 2013). The European Centre for Disease Control warned that serious health hazards are emerging because of the fiscal consolidation measures introduced since 2008.[12] More specifically, in Greece, Spain and Portugal citizens' access to public health care services has been seriously constrained, to the extent that there are reported increases in mortality and morbidity. *The Lancet* speaks of "a Greek public health tragedy" in which citizens are subject to one of the most radical programmes of welfare state retrenchment in recent times (Kentikelinis et al., 2014).

Social benefits

The vast array of tax-financed allowances such as child allowances, disability benefits and housing support have been rationalized during the crisis in the search for cost savings. The negative effects of fiscal consolidation on poverty have been most noticeable in countries where the basic system of social assistance is weak or has been recently weakened, as in some of the crisis-hit Baltic States and the European countries under ratified economic adjustment programmes. The Government in Greece, for instance, is planning drastic structural changes to replace a large number of existing social benefits, such as disability and family benefits, as well as the minimum pension provided under social insurance schemes, with a safety net for the poorest, a single targeted guaranteed minimum income scheme providing a relatively low benefit. Ireland is also replacing a universal child benefit by a means-tested allowance to low-income families. The introduction of means testing for previously universal benefits, and the more narrow targeting of benefits on people living in poverty, erodes the principles of universal protection which used to be

---

[12] In January 2013, doctors from Portugal, Spain, Ireland and Greece sent an open letter to European political leaders and health authorities in which they deplored the effects that financial and economic decisions adopted as a response to the economic crisis were having on the health of the populations of their countries and called for immediate action to reverse this situation: http://www.epha.org/spip.php?article5563 [accessed 1 May 2014].

part of the social contract in many European countries, based on legal rights. For instance, fiscal consolidation measures have restricted the access of persons with disabilities to community living, education, primary care and assistance. Cuts in gender equality programmes, child-care services, parental and child benefits, services to victims of violence and legal aid affect women in particular (EU Commissioner for Human Rights, 2013).

Pensions

Common pension reforms include raising the retirement age, reducing benefits, increasing contribution rates and reducing pension tax exemptions, as well as the structural reforms introduced in some countries. Most countries were introducing changes to their pension systems prior to the crisis, in view of the demographic ageing of populations, but fiscal consolidation precipitated drastic cost-saving measures adopted without adequate consideration of their social impacts. Some of these reforms have been contested in national constitutional courts. A good measure by which to grasp the effect of reforms is the gross theoretical replacement rate for public (statutory) pensions. Simulations show future pensioners receiving lower pensions in at least 14 European countries, with a projected decline by more than 10 percentage points in eight countries (figure 6.14).[13]

Most structural pension reforms in HICs that have introduced the principle of individual savings have removed the de facto minimum pension guarantees that used to be explicitly provided under traditional "defined benefit" pension systems (some of which are still in existence). In addition, numerous reforms have further eroded the purchasing power of pensions through indexation measures limiting their adjustment to a level below changes in prices and wages: Spain, for instance, stopped indexing pensions to price inflation in 2013.[14] These changes result in more older persons not having sufficient income security: pensioners become poorer and poorer as they grow older and the real value of their pension dwindles in the absence of adequate indexation mechanisms. In Sweden and Poland, for instance, poverty rates for older persons have nearly doubled, from 10 to 18 per cent and from 7 to 14 per cent respectively

Figure 6.14 Reduction in gross theoretical replacement rates of statutory pensions for average wage workers retiring at age 65 after 40 years of contributions, 2010–50 (percentage points of theoretical average wage)

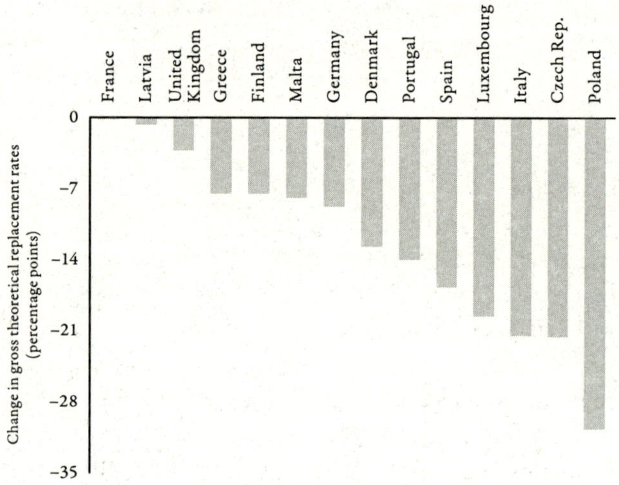

Source: Based on European Commission, 2012c; European Commission, 2012d.

Link: http://www.social-protection.org/gimi/gess/RessourceDownload.action?ressource.ressourceId=43721.

between 2005 and 2012 (see Chapter 4). There is a need to revisit pension provisions to ensure that explicit provision is made for minimum benefit guarantees through contributory pension systems or via coordinated policies with non-contributory social assistance benefits.

Overall, the ILO expects that more and more workers will have to resort to tax-financed social assistance or guaranteed minimum income schemes in their old age as a result of the pension reforms of the past decade or so. Some national pension systems will no longer meet the adequacy requirements they are required to fulfil in countries that have ratified the European Code of Social Security and the ILO's Convention No. 102 – which is the case for a majority of European countries.

Erosion of the European social model

In 2012, 123 million people in the then 27 Member States of the European Union, representing 24 per cent of the population, were at risk of poverty or social exclusion, compared to 116 million in 2008, and as many as

[13] Since these projections were made, Portugal, Spain, Greece and Italy have adopted further austerity measures to reduce future pension entitlements under their public systems (EU Social Protection Committee, 2009; European Commission, 2012c).

[14] Ley 23/2013 Reguladora del Factor de Sostenibilidad y del Índice de Revalorización del Sistema de Pensiones de la Seguridad Social, *Boletín Oficial del Estado*, 26 Dec. 2013.

800,000 more children than in 2008 were living in poverty.[15] These figures raised alarm across Europe. Some estimates foresee an additional 15–25 million people facing the prospect of living in poverty by 2025 if fiscal consolidation continues (Oxfam, 2013). Higher poverty and inequality are the results not only of the severity of the global recession, but also of specific policy decisions curtailing social transfers and limiting access to quality public services. The achievements of the European social model,[16] which dramatically reduced poverty and promoted prosperity in the period following the Second World War, have been eroded during and since the crisis by a series of adjustment reforms that have led to a resurgence of poverty in Europe and a loss of prosperity for the middle classes. The long-accepted concept of universal access to decent living conditions for all citizens has been threatened by a widening gulf between more narrowly targeted programmes for those at the lower levels of the income distribution and a stronger emphasis on individual savings for the middle and upper income groups. This fragmentation of social security systems limits the potential for a collective pooling of risk, erodes social solidarity, limits the responsibility of the State to the care of only the extremely poor, and changes the terms of the social contract that has been at the very basis of the European social model. The weakening of collective bargaining and social dialogue, along with the deregulation and "flexibilization" of labour markets, has further compounded this erosion (ILO, 2013b; IILS, 2012; Vaughan-Whitehead, 2013).

Furthermore, while cost savings from fiscal consolidation measures may have assisted in servicing debt, they have not supported economic growth. In Ireland, Greece, Portugal and Cyprus, where some of the boldest structural reforms have taken place as part of the terms agreed under the different economic adjustment programmes adopted by these countries since 2008, disposable household incomes have declined in consequence, as a result of high unemployment, lower wages and social protection expenditure cuts, and this in turn has led to lower consumption (figure 6.15). For example, in Greece the reform of the social protection system limits the responsibility of the State to a guaranteed minimum income benefit targeted on the poor, which is provisionally set at a low level equivalent to 75 per cent of the current average minimum pension guarantee. The reform foresees that supplementary pensions will likely become the responsibility of individuals and employers (through a system of individual accounts); this replaces a system, albeit a very fragmented one, of dubious sustainability, under which in the past nearly every person could count on having at least a minimum old-age pension. As salaries decreased by nearly 35 per cent and unemployment increased to 28 per cent between 2008 and the end of 2013, the revenues from contributions to the social security system have dwindled. Continuing to pay social security benefits would have required deficit financing, but this was not prioritized. Instead, curtailments informed by fiscal consolidation objectives have reduced social protection expenditure by more than 12 per cent in real terms since 2008, and private consumption followed the same downward path (figure 6.15, panel (b)). Inevitably, poverty in Greece rose to a historically high level, exceeding 35 per cent of the population in 2013, inflicting intense human suffering as many families found themselves unable to access any longer the basic necessities for a life in dignity. Trade union activists speak of "a programmed impoverishment of the population".[17]

Other countries under severe pressure from financial markets, such as Italy and Spain, also introduced reforms that were more far-reaching than in countries where the debt crisis was less acute, such as France or Belgium, or marginal, as in Germany. While some reforms were aimed at making necessary improvements in administrative efficiency, others represented a shift away from an approach focusing on the *prevention* of poverty and of income insecurity for the entire population towards an approach limited to poverty *alleviation* ("safety nets"). Such reforms have disproportionately emphasized the fiscal objective of balancing public budgets without due consideration to the objective of adequate benefits to all people, as promulgated in various international instruments – including, among others, ILO Convention No. 102,

---

[15] According to Eurostat, "at risk of poverty or social exclusion" means that they were at risk of poverty (set at 60 per cent of the national median equivalized disposable income, after social transfers), severely materially deprived and/or living in households with very low work intensity (Eurostat, 2013).

[16] Recent ILO research identifies the following key features of the European social model: (1) increased minimum rights on working conditions, (2) universal and sustainable social protection systems, (3) inclusive labour markets, (4) strong and well-functioning social dialogue, (5) public services and services of general interest, and (6) social inclusion and social cohesion (Vaughan-Whitehead, 2013).

[17] Mr Rompolis, Greek Confederation of Trade Unions (GSEE), Geneva, 14 Jan. 2014.

Figure 6.15 Real public social protection and real household final consumption expenditure, unemployment and real GDP: Recent developments in the four EU countries under economic adjustment programmes, 2008–13: (a) Ireland; (b) Greece; (c) Portugal; (d) Cyprus

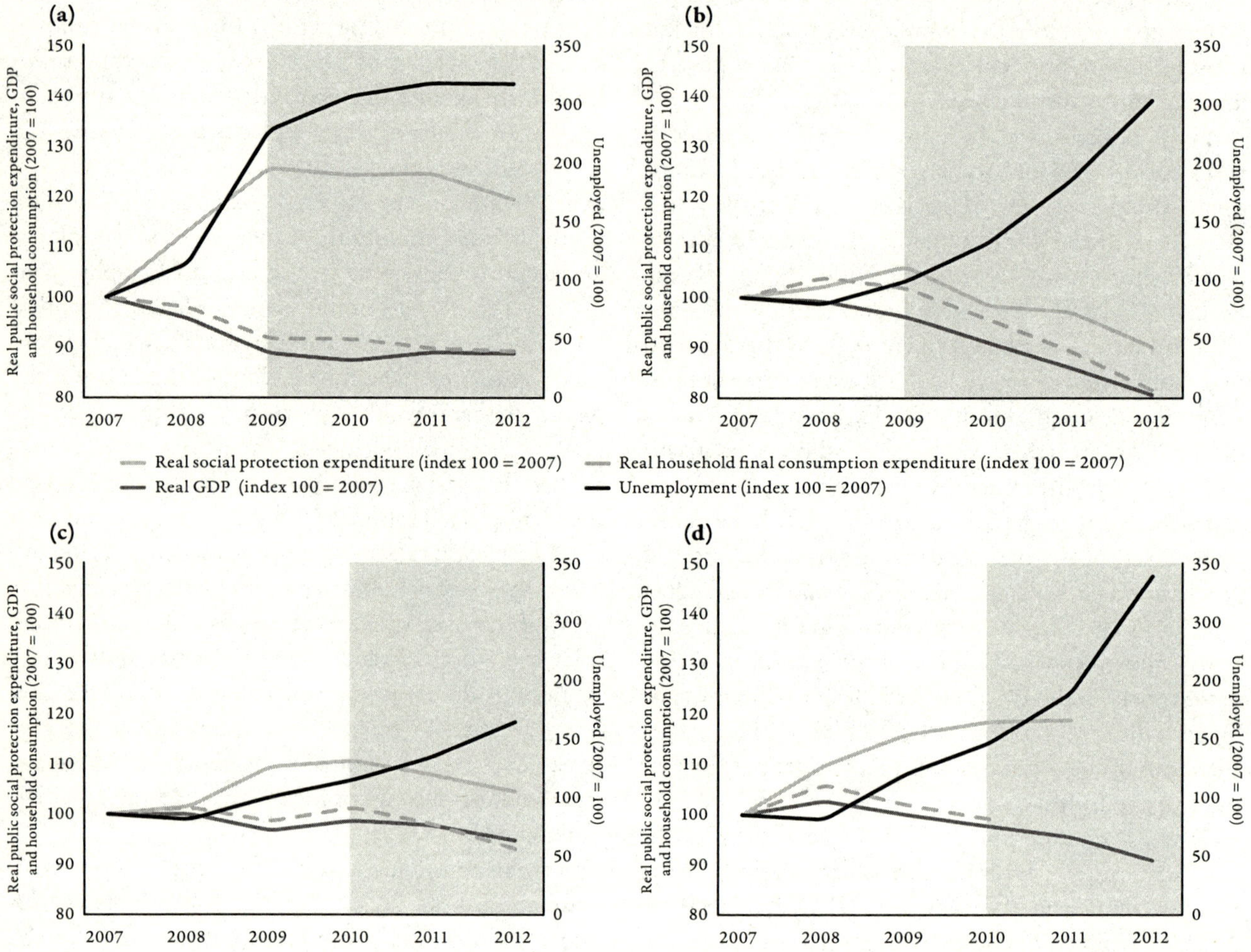

Note: Indexed levels, 2007 =100.

Sources: ILO, OECD, Eurostat, IMF.

Link: http://www.social-protection.org/gimi/gess/RessourceDownload.action?ressource.ressourceId=4320.

the Invalidity, Old-Age and Survivors' Benefits Convention, 1967 (No. 128), and the Social Protection Floors Recommendation, 2012 (No. 202). Such disequilibrium constitutes a significant danger for social cohesion and social justice, and contributes to the erosion of the European social model.

In some European countries, courts have reviewed the constitutional validity of fiscal consolidation measures. In 2013, the Portuguese constitutional court ruled that four fiscal consolidation measures in the budget, mainly affecting civil servants and pensioners, were unlawful and in breach of the country's constitution. In Latvia, the 2010 budget proposed new spending cuts and tax increases, including a 10 per cent cut in pensions and a 70 per cent decrease for working pensioners; the constitutional court ruled that the pension cuts were unconstitutional on the grounds that they violated the right to social security, and the cuts had to be reversed. In Romania, 15 per cent pension cuts proposed in May 2010 were also declared unconstitutional; although pensions partly funded by worker contributions are constitutionally protected, the Government had circumvented this protection on the grounds of a separate constitutional article allowing the temporary limitation of certain rights in order to defend national security (UNDP and RCPAR, 2011; OHCHR, 2013). More recently, the European Parliament has launched an inquiry into the democratic legitimacy of adjustment reforms and their social impacts in Ireland, Cyprus, Spain, Slovenia, Greece, Portugal and Italy (European Parliament, 2014a; European Parliament, 2014b).

6.2.4 Adequate transfers, taxes and social dialogue: Key elements of a socially responsive recovery

Social protection plays a role in preventing as well as reducing poverty in all societies, although the potential of different social protection systems to prevent and reduce poverty varies. For example, without social protection transfers and tax measures, 32.2 per cent of the people of Finland would have found themselves in poverty in 2010, as opposed to the 7.3 per cent of the population who actually were in poverty that year. Figure 6.16 sets out the effective poverty prevention and reduction capacity of national transfers and tax systems in OECD countries. It shows quite significant differences between countries, even for those at a similar level of economic development and potential fiscal resources, illustrating the point that it is the political will of each society that sets the framework for its social protection system.

Social protection supports growth and structural change in the labour market. It also supports household income, essential to sustain consumption and domestic demand. Adequate levels of social protection are an important element of an inclusive growth strategy, as outlined in the various sections of this report.

Integrating social protection, employment and taxation policies is key to a socially responsive recovery. The increase in poverty and inequalities reflects to a large extent not just the recent crisis, but a longer-term trend weakening the State's developmental role and redistributive capacity (e.g. OECD, 2008; OECD, 2011a; UNRISD, 2010). Global imbalances may be further exacerbated as households increase their precautionary savings because they have lost trust in the capacity and/or willingness of the public system to provide for their long-term income security. This situation calls for effective coordination of social protection, employment and fiscal policies to better address emerging circumstances in the labour market and to avert lasting damage to their knock-on effects on current and future levels of social protection for all, including not only the poorer segments of society but also the middle class. Countries are encouraged to make better use of their social protection systems in order to avoid a rupture in solidarity across generations and income groups, and to achieve social peace.

National dialogue and consultations on alternative policy options can achieve an optimal balance between adequacy and sustainability. ILO country surveys in Europe have indicated that most reforms adopted during the crisis have been introduced without due regard to consultations with social partners and key stakeholders in civil society (e.g. Guardiancich, 2012). As a result, those reforms tend to be unbalanced, overemphasizing the cost-effectiveness dimension with a view to restoring public finances, while overlooking the social outcomes in terms of poverty and inequality. National dialogue is essential to secure adequate social protection measures, particularly with regard to protecting children and older persons from poverty and vulnerability, and to ensure that necessary adjustments are based on a fair and viable balance between adequacy and sustainability, as part of the core social contract on which modern societies are based.

The Social Protection Committee of the European Commission stressed in late 2013 that lessons must be learnt from recent reform experiences, that policy corrections must be considered on the basis of robust social impact assessments of both short- and long-term effects

Figure 6.16 Poverty rates in OECD countries before and after taxes and social protection transfers, latest available year

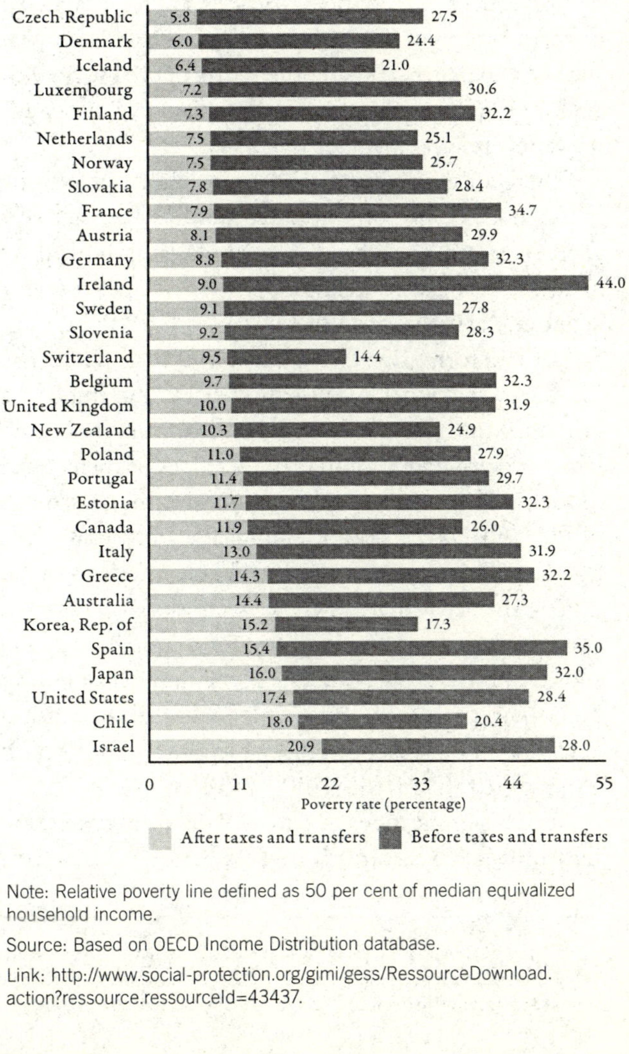

Note: Relative poverty line defined as 50 per cent of median equivalized household income.

Source: Based on OECD Income Distribution database.

Link: http://www.social-protection.org/gimi/gess/RessourceDownload.action?ressource.ressourceId=43437.

Box 6.3 Iceland: A socially responsive recovery from the crisis

Iceland repudiated private debt to foreign banks and did not bail out its financial sector, pushing losses on to bondholders instead of taxpayers. This was not a sovereign debt issue; according to the IMF, this debt was a result of privatization and deregulation of the banking sector, facilitated by easy access to foreign funding; the growing imbalances were not detected by Iceland's financial sector supervision. Two national referendums, held in 2010 and 2011, allowed citizens to vote on whether and how the country should repay a nationalized private debt; Icelandic voters delivered a resounding "no" to the orthodox policies that would have accompanied such a debt repayment plan. Despite the pressures and threats elicited by Iceland's heterodox policies – debt repudiation, capital controls and currency depreciation – the country is recovering well from the crisis (Krugman, 2012). It has regained access to international capital markets while preserving the welfare of its citizens, with support from the IMF. In 2012, Iceland's credit rating was much higher than Greece's. As Iceland's IMF Article IV Consultation stated:

> A key post crisis objective of the Icelandic authorities was to preserve the social welfare system in the face of the fiscal consolidation needed. Wage increases, agreed among the social partners in May 2011, led to a rise in nominal wages of 6 per cent and the unemployment rate fell to about 7 per cent in 2012. ...
>
> ... In designing fiscal adjustment, the authorities introduced a more progressive income tax and created fiscal space to preserve social benefits. Consequently, when expenditure compression began in 2010, social protection spending continued to rise as a per cent of GDP, and the number of households receiving income support from the public sector increased. These policies led to a sharp reduction in inequality. Iceland's Gini coefficient – which had risen during the boom – fell in 2010 to levels consistent with its Nordic peers (IMF, 2012, pp. 5–6).

and, above all, that such analysis should be available before policies are adopted.[18] The ILO encourages all countries to re-establish national policy dialogue with the social partners and all other parts of civil society to explore the optimal policy options that effectively address poverty and inequalities.

There are examples of good approaches. The Nordic social model is not only resilient but has been actively used in crises. Finland, for example, ring-fenced its health and social protection system during the major economic crisis it faced in the 1990s after the downfall of the former Soviet Union, at a time when the Nordic social model was heavily criticized for impeding growth. More recently, Nordic countries have reformed while preserving the fundamental values of their social model, and are now well placed to face the aftermath of the global crisis, both economically and socially (see box 6.3). Other good examples include measures taken during the early phase of the crisis to scale up targeted assistance: in the United States, for example, the food subsidies for the poor which cut the number of households living in extreme poverty by half, and the Affordable Health Care Act of 2013 which introduced health coverage for all citizens (CBPP, 2014).

Other significant examples include social protection measures that were already in place before the crisis and could be easily scaled up when conditions dramatically worsened, such as the unemployment insurance scheme in Germany, which could provide adapted benefits to help limit lay-offs, or the French reforms to provide firms with incentives for retaining older workers while also hiring younger workers.

6.3 Middle-income countries: Inclusive growth through social protection

6.3.1 Significant extension of social protection coverage

In many middle-income countries, the dominant trend of recent years, starting well before the global crisis of 2008, has been that of an expansion of social protection coverage, yet with wide cross-national variation. Many social protection policy reforms explicitly acknowledged the importance of investments in health, education and social protection, in order to foster inclusive growth and poverty reduction in the short term, and to build human capital and human capacities in the longer term. In many ways, these policies mark a clear break with some of the policies of the 1980s and 1990s, which emphasized cutbacks to the public sector, the introduction

[18] The EU Social Protection Committee concluded in September 2013 that "social impact assessments must become part of the Economic Adjustment Programmes in order to choose the most appropriate path of reforms and adjust the resulting distribution impact across income and age groups" (EU Social Protection Committee, 2013, p. 26).

of user fees for health, education and other public services, and the privatization of pensions. The experience of the fiscal and economic crises of the late 1990s in Asia and Latin America prompted many countries to reconsider their economic models. The new policies recognize a more active role of the State in fostering social and economic development and strengthening domestic demand. The strong emphasis on social protection policies in many middle-income countries is a powerful testimony to the premise that sustainable and equitable growth cannot be achieved in the absence of strong social protection policies and the progressive extension of social security coverage to much larger groups of the population (ILO, 2010b; ILO, 2011a; ILO, 2012a).

Several middle-income countries, including Argentina, Brazil, China, India, Indonesia, Mexico, Namibia, South Africa and Thailand, have significantly extended various elements of their social protection systems, particularly since the early 2000s, with remarkable outcomes (see, e.g. Fiszbein and Schady, 2009; ILO, 2010b; ISSA, 2013). These efforts were temporarily disrupted in some parts of the world by the global crisis, the effects of which compounded those the food and fuel crises in various ways. Some countries rebounded after 2010 in terms of economic growth, but still saw an increase in vulnerable and informal employment, and their economic positions remain exposed to the uncertain recovery of global demand.

Several countries, which recently joined the ranks of middle-income countries or graduated from least developed country status, such as Cabo Verde, Ghana, Lesotho and Zambia, have implemented distinct social protection policies aiming at gradually extending social protection to larger groups of the population, in so far as available national and external resources allow, as part of their development strategies.

Many reforms have focused on non-contributory schemes and programmes, such as conditional or unconditional cash transfers for children and families, social pensions, and/or employment guarantee schemes. Many countries have also rendered their social insurance programmes more equitable, more effective and more sustainable, although many are also still struggling to bring the majority of informal workers, especially in rural areas into the formal economy. These reforms contributed to further extension of national social protection systems, while ensuring that at least a minimum level of social security is guaranteed in the form of a national social protection floor.

Table 6.3 and the map in figure 6.6 above illustrate the wide range of recent efforts to extend social protection in middle-income countries, both through the introduction of new schemes and programmes and the significant expansion of existing ones.

The large number of middle-income countries that have extended social protection demonstrates a significant prioritization of social protection policies in this group of countries in recent years, highlighted by the fact that many middle-income countries have also significantly expanded the envelope of resources allocated to social protection.

Good rates of economic development have contributed to the observed significant increases in social protection expenditure ratios in many middle-income countries, although a wide variation in expenditure levels persists. Since 2000, 14 out of the 32 countries

Table 6.3 Selected recent examples of the extension of social protection in middle-income countries*

Type of programme	Countries in which programmes/schemes have recently been introduced or significantly expanded
Child and family benefits	Argentina, China, Mongolia, Senegal, South Africa
Cash transfers with human development focus	Argentina, Brazil, Colombia, Ecuador, Ghana,** Honduras, Indonesia, Jamaica, Mexico, Mongolia, Nicaragua, Philippines, United Republic of Tanzania
Household minimum income support	Chile, China, Ghana,** Zambia**
Public employment programmes	Argentina, Cameroon, Ghana,** India, Indonesia, South Africa
Maternity protection	Argentina, Plurinational State of Bolivia, Ghana,** India,** Indonesia,** Jordan, South Africa
Unemployment protection	Jordan, Saudi Arabia, South Africa, Thailand, Viet Nam
Social pensions	Argentina, Plurinational State of Bolivia, Botswana, Brazil, Cabo Verde, Chile, China, Costa Rica, India, Lesotho, Mauritius, Republic of Moldova, Namibia, Panama, Peru, Samoa, South Africa, Thailand, Viet Nam
Health coverage expanded	Argentina, Brazil, Chile, China, Colombia, Ghana, Lao PDR, Indonesia, Mexico, Morocco, Thailand

* Inevitably, this table cannot provide a full account of recent reforms and initiatives, but presents only a selection for illustration purposes.
** Pilot programme.
Source: ILO compilation.

Figure 6.17 Increase in public social protection expenditure, selected middle-income countries, 2000 to latest year (percentage of GDP)

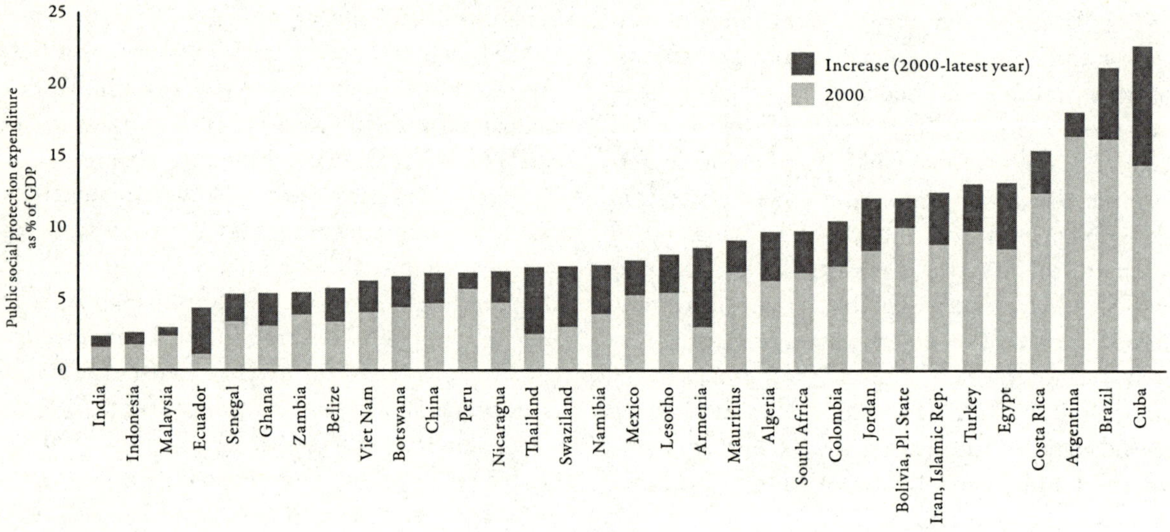

Source: See detailed sources in Annex IV, table B.12.

Link: http://www.social-protection.org/gimi/gess/RessourceDownload.action?ressource.ressourceId=43537.

included in figure 6.17 have increased the proportion of GDP invested in public social protection (including health) by more than 3 per cent of GDP.

6.3.2 Towards more inclusive growth

Many middle-income countries have enjoyed relatively high rates of economic growth since 2000. This growth has helped to enlarge fiscal space, broaden the revenue base of the State and facilitated the strengthening of public administrations, all of which are conducive to the extension of social protection. Taking advantage of this opportunity, some Latin American and Asian economies, having learnt from the financial crises they faced in the 1980s, late 1990s and again in the early 2000s, have been expanding social protection mechanisms to better protect the most vulnerable groups of their population, and to enable the population to better cope with social risks and contingencies.

Most importantly, the crisis has triggered a shift in the way developing countries see the relationship between growth and social protection. When emerging economies found demand for their exports falling, policy-makers started questioning unsustainable export-led growth models and moving instead towards recovery strategies centred on building up domestic consumption and internal markets. One way to raise household income and thereby domestic consumption is through improved social protection systems.

With the aim of moving economies on to a more sustainable development path, the extension of social protection has been seen as an investment to foster a healthier, better educated and more highly skilled workforce capable of responding to new demands and to support the transition to the higher levels of productivity necessary to sustain economic growth (ILO, 2011a; ILO, 2014b; see also figures 6.23 and 6.24 below). Such measures can contribute to overcoming a "middle income trap" of stagnating growth due to unbalanced growth trajectories (IMF, 2013c; Aiyar et al., 2013). The expansion of effective social protection mechanisms for the whole population, particularly for the middle classes, is also considered to be an effective way to counter disproportionately high precautionary savings rates, which can hold back aggregate domestic demand and contribute to global imbalances (Padoan, 2010; Social Protection Floor Advisory Group, 2011).

In fact, many middle-income countries have pursued the expansion of their social protection systems explicitly with the objective of investing in human capital and human capabilities, with a view to achieving more sustainable and inclusive growth.

The expansion of social protection coverage in Brazil (see box 6.4), China (see box 6.5) and Thailand are particularly instructive examples, as in these cases the extension of social security coverage was embedded in a broader approach aimed at moving the economy to a more inclusive and more sustainable growth pattern, which included also measures to reform minimum

Box 6.4 The role of social protection in the Brazilian model of domestic demand-led growth

When the financial crisis hit Brazil in 2008, the Brazilian economy, which had hitherto benefited greatly from favourable terms of trade and growing exports of commodities, suffered severely from a sharp decline in exports and a credit crunch among private Brazilian banks. This resulted in a loss of 695,000 formal jobs in November and December 2008 (see CAGED/IPEADATA) and a fall in GDP of 4.4 per cent in the fourth quarter of 2008 (Berg and Tobin, 2011, p. 5). To counterbalance the decline in exports, the government responded with a strategy of domestic demand-led growth. This strategy had two pillars: boosting domestic consumption by increasing family incomes and stimulating domestic investments. To the latter end, a fiscal stimulus package of US$20 billion (1.2 per cent of GDP) was launched, focusing on investments in infrastructure and the establishment of credit lines for sectors experiencing difficulties. To support domestic demand, tax cuts for middle-income households and social policies focusing on the poorest were financed through the stimulus package. Besides guaranteeing the maintenance of the existing social protection programmes and compliance with previous commitments, the Government extended the conditional cash transfer programme Bolsa Família to 1.3 million additional extremely poor families; in addition, the duration of unemployment insurance payments was extended by two months for people who had been working in sectors strongly hit by the crisis, benefiting some 310,000 people. Although quantitatively the investments in social protection seem comparably small, accounting for only 2.4 per cent of the stimulus package, the existing comprehensive network of social policies allowed for a quick reaction at low cost by means of scaling up relevant programmes; this had a very significant impact, reaching over 1.6 million of the most vulnerable people. Outside the stimulus package, the Government also maintained the real increases in the official minimum wage scheduled for February 2009 and January 2010. It is estimated that in 2009 this affected more than 20 per cent of the population, principally those on lower incomes.

Social policies and increases in the minimum wage thus helped to maintain or even increase the incomes of the poorest, and this in turn contributed to domestic demand growth. Despite a decrease in GDP in 2009 of 0.6 per cent, private consumption remained stable and in the second half of 2009 was already beginning to grow again (Berg and Tobin, 2011, p. 7). This had multiplier effects on the economy, boosting employment and incomes and contributing substantially to its recovery. By 2010, GDP had grown again by an impressive 7.5 per cent (IMF, 2013a). The stronger accent on domestic-led growth has not broken the prevailing trend in reducing inequality, as shown by the continued drop of the Gini index from 0.54 in 2008 to 0.526 in 2012 (IPEA, 2013, p. 11). Thus, by boosting the incomes of the lower and middle classes, social protection helped mitigate the impact of the crisis on the most vulnerable and functioned as an important element of the domestic demand-led growth policy implemented by the Brazilian Government as a response to the crisis. The case of Brazil also proves that income policies can promote economic growth while reducing poverty and inequality.

Sources: Based on Berg and Tobin, 2011; IILS, 2011b; IPEA, 2013; IMF, 2013a; CAGED/IPEADATA database.

wages. These countries have implemented a package of economic and social policies combining contributory and non-contributory programmes to reinforce their national social protection floors and strengthen their social security systems. These have been coordinated with employment policies, and particular emphasis has been placed on making the benefits and services accessible to the population through an integrated approach. These governments have not focused exclusively on reducing poverty by targeting social protection measures on the poorest, but have pursued a broader strategy, which also helped low income earners and the middle classes to improve their living standards sustainably. These cases highlight the importance of coherent strategies that embed social policies in a wider range of coordinated employment, labour market, fiscal and macroeconomic policies.

While some middle-income countries have managed to reduce inequalities significantly, more efforts are necessary in this area (UNDP, 2014; UN, 2013b). Here the social protection system plays a particularly important role as one of the channels through which the benefits of growth can be shared in a more equitable way: not only in its direct impact on redistribution through social transfers and contributions, but also in more indirect ways by facilitating access to health and education. Investing in the extension of social protection, as many middle-income countries have done, helps to contain inequality and its negative effects on growth, and allow countries to follow a more equitable and more sustainable growth path (e.g. Berg and Ostry, 2011; Ostry et al., 2014). Such an approach is, indeed, particularly relevant for middle-income countries, which now are the home of the majority of the world's poor (Sumner, 2010). In this context, social protection mechanisms play a particularly important role in reducing and preventing poverty, containing inequality, ensuring equitable life chances and fostering social inclusion.

Box 6.5 Strengthening domestic demand-led growth in China through increased wages and an expansion of social protection benefits

Since the middle of the century's first decade, China's five-year plans have recognized the need to address rapidly growing income inequalities and to provide income security to all the people of China, who place great trust in the public social security system.

Income disparities between the rural and urban populations, between its more developed and less developed regions, among various groups of the population and among different sectors of the economy have been a recurrent concern of the national authorities. The other key social challenges in China are providing for income security, ensuring equal and affordable access to health, education and housing, and generating enough employment for both urban and rural populations. From the economic perspective, strengthening aggregate domestic demand and consumption has become one of the national priorities since the start of the global economic crisis, given the consequent lower demand for Chinese exports.

The Government has clearly seen the links between these economic and social challenges and decided to address them as closely as possible. The rapid economic growth China has experienced since the late 1970s has built up the country's economic and fiscal capacity for the expansion of its social security system. Accordingly, alongside the economic expansion strategy, priority has been given to the following initiatives, among others:

- In 2003 and 2007, two new social health insurance schemes were established for, respectively, the rural population and the previously uninsured part of the urban population. These, together with other existing health insurance schemes, now cover a total of 1.34 billion people, more than 96 per cent of the population.
- The adequacy of health insurance benefits was improved to ensure equal and effective access to health care. This took several forms, such as increasing reimbursement rates, extending the range of reimbursable items, raising the cap for reimbursement, introducing insurance for high out-of-pocket payments, reforming the public health sector, and investing more in rural health facilities and urban community-based health centres.
- In 2009 and 2011, two new old-age pension schemes were introduced, again for the rural population and uninsured urban residents. The goal was to achieve universal coverage by 2020; in fact, this was already reached in 2012. The total number of those insured under these two new schemes was 498 million at the end of 2013, including 138 million pensioners. Together with those covered under the existing schemes, the overall number of insured (including beneficiaries) amounted to 820 million, more than 80 per cent of the population over 18 years old.
- Both the new health and the new pension schemes are highly subsidized by the Government. For instance, the annual fiscal contribution to health insurance for uninsured urban residents was raised from 40 yuan renminbi (CNY) per person in 2007 (as against CNY60 for the insured) to CNY280 in 2013, and is planned to rise again to CNY320 for 2014.
- The level of pension paid under the urban workers' pension system has been increased consecutively for ten years (2005–14) at an annual rate of 10 per cent to secure its purchasing power.
- The overall amount of social insurance benefits paid out in 2013 amounted to CNY2.8 trillion –a nearly threefold increase from its 2007 level – representing a major contribution to domestic-led growth.
- The minimum living standard guarantee programme has achieved the goal of universal coverage since 2007, making an essential contribution to the reduction of poverty and inequality.

As a result of these and other initiatives, social security expenditure has grown constantly, contributing to increases in disposable income for millions of households and supporting China's sustainable economic development.

Sources: Based on ADB, 2010; ILO, 2012f; ISSA, 2013; national sources.

Given the slowing rates of economic growth in many middle-income countries (IMF, 2013a) and the potentially detrimental effects of ill-designed fiscal consolidation policies, continued efforts are essential to strengthen social security systems and expand them in two dimensions: guaranteeing at least basic levels of social security to all through national social protection floors, and progressively reaching higher levels of social security that effectively prevent vulnerability and respond to the social security needs of the middle classes, which are often neglected by conventional poverty reduction policies (e.g. Birdsall, 2010).

6.4 Low-income countries: Beyond safety nets, towards social protection floor guarantees

6.4.1 Against the odds: Extending social protection coverage in low-income countries

Low-income countries face stronger constraints in extending social protection coverage than middle- and high-income countries. Typically, they face higher levels of poverty and destitution that have to be addressed with fewer financial resources, through weaker institutional capacities and within often fragile contexts. Nonetheless, a number of low-income countries have also taken decisive steps towards the extension of social protection in various areas (see figure 6.6 above and table 6.4). Rwanda, for example, thoroughly reformed its health system in order to ensure effective access for more than 90 per cent of the population to health services and improved the quality of health services provided; this has contributed to a rapid decrease in maternal and child mortality (Sekabaraga et al., 2011). Bangladesh, Kenya and Malawi are among the countries that have introduced conditional cash transfer programmes, which contributed to enhancing income security and access to education for the targeted vulnerable households in difficult contexts where public services and delivery capacities were sometimes too limited even to meet food security emergencies (García and Moore, 2012; Monchuk, 2014). In Nepal, the extension of social pension coverage has enhanced income security for older women and men. In Mozambique, a large cash transfer programme has improved income security for vulnerable households, many of which include older persons and children (Cunha et al., 2013). In Ethiopia, Malawi and Niger, among other countries, public employment programmes contribute to enhancing income security for workers in rural areas during the lean season (McCord, 2012; Lieuw-Kie-Song, 2011). Although the coverage of some of these programmes is limited to certain geographic areas or narrowly defined groups of the population, they constitute an important investment in the health, nutrition, education and productive capacities of the population, and have generated significant effects in reducing poverty and vulnerability and improving living standards.

Figure 6.18 Increase in public social protection expenditure, selected low-income countries, 2000 to latest year (percentage of GDP)

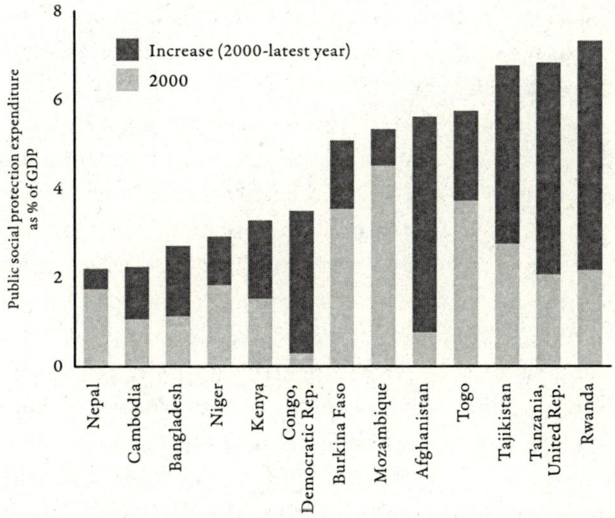

Note: Some donor-financed expenditure on social protection programmes may not be fully reflected in this figure.

Source: For details, see Annex IV, table B.12.

Link: http://www.social-protection.org/gimi/gess/RessourceDownload.action?ressource.ressourceId=43578.

Table 6.4 Selected recent examples of the extension of social protection in low-income countries*

Type of programme	Countries in which programmes/schemes have recently been newly introduced or significantly expanded
Child and family benefits	Mozambique, Nepal, Niger**
Cash transfers with human development focus	Bangladesh, Kenya,** Malawi**
Household minimum income support	Mozambique, Rwanda, Uganda**
Public employment programmes	Benin, Ethiopia, Malawi, Niger, Rwanda, United Rep. of Tanzania
Maternity protection	Bangladesh**
Social pensions	Bangladesh,** Kyrgyzstan, Nepal, Sierra Leone, Tajikistan, United Rep. of Tanzania**
Health coverage expanded	Burundi, Cambodia, Rwanda

* As it is not possible to provide a full account of recent reforms and initiatives worldwide, this table presents a selection for illustration purposes.
** Pilot programme.

Source: ILO compilation from various sources.

As a result of these efforts, many low-income countries have significantly increased the share of GDP that they invest in social protection (including health) (see figure 6.18). This reflects an important shift in development priorities towards a stronger emphasis on human development.

Poor households, including the working poor, face insecurity in countries that provide no basic guarantee of income security and health care through social protection mechanisms. Many poor people work in the rural informal economy, where they depend largely on the income they can earn from selling their crops. From an economic perspective, the lack of social protection coverage leads to inefficient use of resources, forcing poor rural households to opt for low-risk, low-return crops, to hold liquid but less productive assets, and/or to withdraw children from school in response to crises.[19] The absence of insurance or other forms of protection can thus lead to chronic poverty, or to a situation in which people can easily fall back into poverty in the event of shocks and thus are not in a position to improve their situation in a sustainable manner. Social transfers can contribute to improving household income security by stabilizing and protecting consumption, which in turn can facilitate investment (ILO, 2010b).

In recent years, social protection policies have been actively promoted in low-income countries, in recognition of their role in reducing chronic poverty and vulnerability, and in contributing to the attainment of economic and social development objectives. Emphasis has been placed on the role of social protection in enhancing nutrition, health and education outcomes, particularly for children, and in strengthening human resources and capabilities (see figures 6.23 and 6.24 below). More recently, stress has also been placed on the economic role of social protection in stabilizing household consumption, boosting aggregate demand and stimulating local markets, particularly in remote areas. Simulations of cash transfers in Ethiopia and Kenya demonstrate that the aggregate real benefit to the local economy is significantly higher than the actual amount of the transfer itself (FAO, 2014; Taylor, Thome and Davis, 2013). For many low-income countries, a particular challenge remains in shifting spending from security to social protection: a recent IMF study on Afghanistan found that there is a balance to be achieved between security and social spending in order to optimize the chances of establishing and maintaining social peace (Aslam, Berkes and Fukač, 2013).

These developments have shifted perceptions of social protection policies in low-income countries away from the assumption that they represent a cost (often assumed to be unaffordable) to an understanding that they constitute an "investment in people" that is in fact indispensable for future development (Cichon et al., 2006; ILO, 2008a; Monchuk, 2014). As a result of this shift, recent policies have placed a stronger emphasis on social and human development, with a focus on reducing extreme poverty and promoting "pro-poor growth" (e.g. OECD, 2009a); some concentrated attention on targeted safety-net approaches, while others have gone further to promote inclusive growth (e.g. ILO, 2011a).

Integrated development policies are crucial to foster synergies between the provision of cash transfers, access to health and other social services, and public investment. For example, a number of French-speaking African countries have implemented measures to ensure universal effective access to health care for children and young mothers. While these have had a notable impact, they could have been even more successful if they had been coupled with more effective measures to improve and scale up the supply, and improve the accessibility and quality, of health services. Such measures could include the strengthening of public health infrastructure through public employment programmes that also provide employment opportunities and strengthen income security for vulnerable populations.

6.4.2 Expanding social protection using proceeds from fiscal consolidation and adjustment measures

The expansion of social protection in developing countries began well before the global financial and economic crisis, and then gathered pace as the crisis led to an acceleration of investments in social protection. This was possible in part because some countries had benefited from the recent boom in commodity prices; however, many developing countries financed expansion of social protection from the proceeds of adjustment measures such as the reduction of subsidies, increased taxes on consumption taxes, such as VAT, and

[19] See e.g. Barrientos, 2007; Barrientos, 2013; Morduch, 1995; Dercon, 2003; ILO, 2010b; ILO, 2013b; Social Protection Floor Advisory Group, 2011.

cost savings from reforms in the pension and social protection systems, as set out in section 6.2.2 above. The net welfare effects vary from country to country and have not yet been adequately studied.

During the food and fuel crisis, many developing countries increased subsidies or cut taxes on food and/or fuel (IMF, 2008); however, more recently 78 developing countries started to reverse food and energy subsidies, despite the lack of any clear indication that local food and energy prices had fallen or that any compensatory social protection floor had been successfully put in place. This trend was largely driven by the orthodox logic that generalized subsidies can be ineffective and costly, and that replacing them with targeted safety nets can remove market distortions and support vulnerable groups more cost-effectively (Coady et al., 2010). Thus the IMF standard strategy recommended reducing energy subsidies (IMF, 2013b), a policy which in principle can have positive environmental impacts – one reason why UN agencies have supported this policy in countries such as Mozambique (see box 6.6).

There are, however, some important policy implications that must be taken into account when considering a focus on subsidy removal and benefits targeted on the poorest.

- While subsidies can be removed overnight, developing a social protection system takes a long time, particularly in countries where institutional capacity is limited. Thus there is a high risk that subsidies may be withdrawn and populations left unprotected, without compensation through adequate social protection mechanisms, so that food and energy become unaffordable for many households, in particular, but not only, the poorest ones.

Box 6.6 Mozambique: Using a fuel subsidy to extend social protection

In Mozambique, the Government has worked together with the ILO, the IMF, UNICEF, other UN agencies and the World Bank to reprioritize expenditure and to ensure sufficient resources are available for the building of a national social protection floor. A joint ILO–IMF study (Cunha et al., 2013) concluded that progressively expanding a social protection floor did not present a threat to fiscal sustainability. The study recommended that the ill-targeted fuel subsidy be replaced by a more effective social protection system. Revenues from the booming natural resource sector have the potential to widen the available fiscal space for such provision. The Government envisages making a budget allocation of around 0.8 per cent of GDP for the social protection floor over 2014–16.

- Targeting the poor excludes other vulnerable households and may lead to poor developmental outcomes. Designing a safety net for the poor alone may leave unprotected many non-wealthy households that benefited from subsidies. The removal of fuel subsidies and consequent increases in energy prices to unaffordable levels have sparked protests in many countries, e.g. Algeria, Cameroon, Chile, India, Indonesia, Kyrgyzstan, Mexico, Mozambique, Nicaragua, Niger, Nigeria, Peru, Sudan and Uganda (Ortiz et al., 2013; Zaid et al., 2014). Recent studies, including some by the IMF, point out that income inequality is a gross obstacle to development, especially while global recovery remains fragile and many developing countries are trying to develop their internal markets to encourage national demand. A safety net for the poorest is by no means a sufficient response to these challenges.

- The large cost savings resulting from reductions in energy subsidies should allow countries to develop comprehensive social protection systems: fuel subsidies are large, but new safety nets tend to be small in scope and cost. For example, in Ghana, the eliminated fuel subsidy would have cost over US$1 billion in 2013, whereas the well-targeted LEAP programme costs about US$20 million per year.

- Subsidy reforms are complex and their social impacts need to be properly assessed, and discussed within the framework of national dialogue, so that the net welfare effects are understood and reforms are agreed before any subsidies are removed.

6.4.3 Beyond safety nets: Towards national social protection floors

The extension of social protection programmes in low-income countries has contributed greatly to accelerating social and economic development, and to progress towards the achievement of the MDGs (UN, 2013b). In addition, greater recognition is now given to the wider functions of social protection with regard to the realization of human rights, the containment of inequality and income insecurity, and the promotion of social cohesion. At the same time, low-income countries face certain specific constraints, including limited fiscal space, the unpredictability of external aid and weak institutional capacity, including with regard to tax systems. Economists often counsel governments in these countries to target social protection more narrowly as a way to reconcile poverty reduction with fiscal consolidation (Ravallion, 1999), a line of advice that has been particularly prevalent in the current recession and slow growth period. As a result, social protection programmes are often implemented in the form of temporary, small-scale safety net programmes, often narrowly targeted and/or limited to certain geographical areas. Allocating scarce resources to respond to the social protection needs of the population in a context of widespread poverty is a challenge, particularly with regard to establishing eligibility criteria that are equitable and transparent, and protect the dignity of the intended beneficiaries. It is important to bear in mind that people who manage to climb out of poverty are at high risk of falling back into poverty. In rural Ethiopia, between 1999 and 2009, less than 40 per cent of those who escaped poverty managed to remain above the poverty line (Chronic Poverty Advisory Network, 2014, p. 77).

While programmes of the safety-net type initially offer social protection to those targeted, their effectiveness is often hampered by their lack of foundations in national legislation and of stable, reliable sources of funding. Few low-income countries provide rights-based entitlements with clear definitions of eligibility criteria and type and level of benefits. Targeting social programmes on the extreme poor, excluding most of the poor and vulnerable households who are also in need of public assistance, is a politically difficult and administratively complicated enterprise.

In many countries, there is a marked cleavage between contributory and non-contributory schemes. Whereas social insurance schemes are often perceived as catering to the interests of the (often small) number of employees in the formal economy, non-contributory schemes (means tested or not) tend to be considered as part of poverty reduction policies. By better coordinating and combining contributory and non-contributory programmes, countries can find more effective ways not only to reduce poverty, but also to prevent impoverishment, keep those who escape poverty from falling back into it, and enhance economic security for the entire population. Comprehensive and well-coordinated social protection systems are therefore a major component of an integrated policy package to address chronic and recurrent poverty.

Some low-income countries have made great strides in improving coordination of existing social protection programmes, bringing them under a common strategic framework owned by the Government and developed with the participation of key stakeholders, and strengthening national legal, institutional and fiscal frameworks, so as to render national social security systems more effective, efficient, equitable and sustainable. Such efforts reach beyond a narrow focus on (often fragmented) safety nets, and aim at building national social protection floors and social security systems (ILO, 2012a).

During times of crisis, it is important to scale up, rather than scale down, social investments, and narrowly targeted safety nets tend to represent a de facto reduction in coverage. Given the critical importance of supporting households in times of hardship, and of raising people's incomes in order to encourage socio-economic recovery, a strong case can be made for the progressive extension of universal transfers to (for example) families with children, older persons, persons with disabilities and other groups. Targeting social protection on the poorest and excluding vulnerable populations as a conscious decision in policy design is inconsistent with the United Nations Charter, the Millennium Declaration the Universal Declaration of Human Rights (according to which everyone is entitled to minimum standards of living, including food, clothing, education and social security), and conventions that have been signed by virtually every government across the world (e.g. UN, 2008; Sepúlveda, 2014; Sepúlveda and Nyst, 2012).

A progressive expansion of social security provision requires, among other things, a strengthening of legal frameworks and institutional capacities, as well as a sustainable resource base, which in many cases will be based on a combination of domestic and external sources. Robust tax policies and tax administration are essential for ensuring that governments can rely on a sustainable and equitable resource base for their economic and social development policies. This is particularly important in resource-rich countries, in order to ensure that the benefits of growth are equitably shared and serve the needs of their populations (OECD, 2014a; Hujo and McClanahan, 2009; Hujo, 2012).

An approach that focuses on nationally owned and rights-based solutions emphasizes the importance of effective national social protection policies that can support inclusive growth and sustainable social and economic development, and contribute to the realization of human rights. In doing so, this approach reaches beyond external development aid and short-term safety-net policies, and contributes to ensuring coherence between economic, employment and social policies within a strong and sustainable legal and institutional framework (Townsend, 2009; Behrendt et al., 2009). Such dedicated and nationally owned efforts to strengthen institutional capacities have contributed to enhancing development outcomes, for example in Ethiopia and Rwanda. In other countries, particularly those considered as fragile States, these challenges may be even greater; however, social protection is among the policy areas that can potentially contribute to strengthening the "social contract", fostering national dialogue and enhancing trust in the government and public institutions in general (e.g. Hickey, 2010).

If governments and other national actors pursue these policies with commitment and in good faith, the establishment and strengthening of national social protection floors will not only have an immediate impact on people's lives, but will also contribute to building more inclusive societies and economies in the longer term.

6.5 Fiscal space for social protection floors

It is often argued that social protection is not affordable or that government expenditure cuts are inevitable during adjustment periods. But there are alternatives, even in the poorest countries. Finding fiscal space for critical economic and social investments is essential if sustained and equitable development is to be achieved, particularly during a recession and periods of slow growth.

It is important to understand at the outset that governments' options in respect of revenue and spending vary widely across the globe. It is a matter of political choice (ILO, 2008a; Hall, 2010). Some countries opt to spend more or less, as part of their social contract, as shown in figure 6.19. As in spending decisions, there is a similar disparity in how governments raise resources for social and economic development. By utilizing all possible options to expand fiscal space and invest in their people, countries can achieve a virtuous circle of sustained growth and social development, and avoid the risk of a slow growth and weak human development trap (Ryder, 2013; ILO, 2012e).

Today, the need to create and maintain fiscal space for socio-economic investments has never been greater. Given the significance of public investment in enhancing the prospects for equitable, inclusive economic growth and social development, it is critical that governments explore options to increase social spending and employment-generating economic investments. Even the IMF Managing Director, recognizing the risk that fiscal consolidation may jeopardize global recovery efforts, has called for "aggressive exploration of all possible measures that could be effective in supporting short-term growth" (Lagarde, 2011).

There are options available to governments to expand fiscal space for a socially responsive recovery even in the poorest countries – options that are all supported by policy statements of the United Nations and international financial institutions (IMF and World Bank, 2006; ILO, 2009a; ILO, 2011a; ILO, 2012a; OECD, 2014a; UNDP, 2007; UN, 2009b; UN, 2013c). These

Figure 6.19 Total government expenditures in selected countries, 2013 (percentage of GDP)

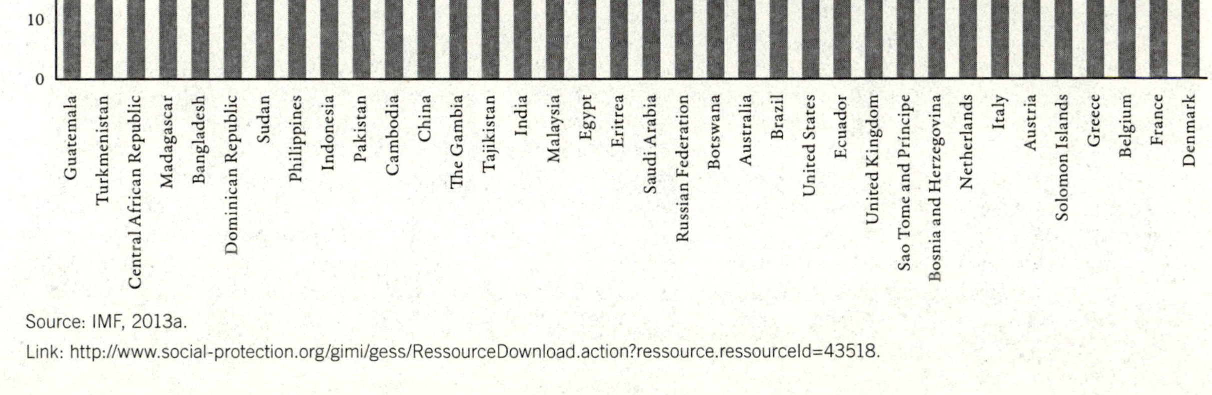

Source: IMF, 2013a.

Link: http://www.social-protection.org/gimi/gess/RessourceDownload.action?ressource.ressourceId=43518.

include: (1) reallocating public expenditures, (2) increasing tax revenues, (3) extending social security contributions, (4) borrowing or restructuring existing debt, (5) curtailing illicit financial flows, (6) drawing on increased aid and transfers, (7) tapping into fiscal and foreign exchange reserves and/or (8) adopting a more accommodating macroeconomic framework (Hujo and McClanahan, 2009; Durán-Valverde and Pacheco, 2012; Ortiz and Cummins, 2012). Normally a government would carve out its own fiscal space from a few of these options. The uniqueness of each country requires that the range of options be carefully examined at the national level and the selection based on effective social dialogue and a sound approach to political economy (ILO, 2012a).

6.5.1 Option 1: Reallocating current public expenditures

This is the most orthodox option, which includes assessing ongoing budget allocations, replacing high-cost, low-impact investments with those that can generate larger socio-economic impacts, eliminating spending inefficiencies and/or tackling corruption. Reprioritization requires that governments be prepared to reconsider what areas of public policy require most support. For example, governments in Cambodia, Costa Rica, Mauritius and Sri Lanka have reduced expenditures in the defence and security sectors in favour of increased spending in social sectors. One area of expenditure with great potential in creating fiscal space is subsidies. Removing subsidies has allowed expansion of social

Box 6.7 Financing social protection from subsidy removal

Since 2010, 100 governments have been considering removing food and fuel subsidies and replacing them with safety nets targeted on the poor, including 31 countries in sub-Saharan Africa, 22 in HICs, 12 in East Asia and the Pacific, 11 in Latin America, nine in the Middle East and North Africa, and six in South Asia. The IMF's standard policy advice is to phase out energy subsidies (IMF, 2013b), a course of action that in principle has positive environmental externalities. However, the quick removal of subsidies – a main element of fiscal consolidation in developing countries – has led to significant protests against the resulting in higher food and fuel prices (Ortiz et al., 2013). For example, in Nigeria, where the majority of the population lives on less than US$2 per day, cheap petrol is viewed by many as the only tangible benefit they receive from the State: hence the massive protests in 2012 when the Government removed a fuel subsidy that kept food and transportation costs low.

There are three key lessons that Governments contemplating subsidy removal need to consider: (1) subsidy reforms are complex; there is no "one-size-fits-all" option, and the net welfare effect of any reform it its national context must be properly understood and discussed in national dialogue. (2) designing a meagre safety net for the poorest alone is an insufficient compensation mechanism if other households were also benefiting from subsidies; the huge public savings reaped from cancelling energy subsidies should allow governments to consider adequate universal social protection systems and other necessary development policies that work for all citizens, not just for a few. (3) As food and energy prices hover near record highs, scaling back subsidies should be avoided unless a well-functioning social protection system is already in place that can protect households; such a system takes time to be developed, and if subsidies are withdrawn overnight, populations will be left unprotected during a period of exceptional vulnerability, as shown by recent claims by civil society (Zaid et al., 2014).

Box 6.8 Taxing mineral and natural resource extraction to generate fiscal space for social protection

Taxing natural resource extraction offers great potential for many developing countries. While Norway's approach of taxing oil profits and storing the revenues in the Government Pension Fund Global is perhaps the best-known case, developing countries offer several innovative examples of channelling natural resource revenue streams for social protection (Hujo, 2012; OECD, 2014a). For instance, Mongolia is financing a universal rights-based child benefit from taxation on copper exports. When copper prices dropped with falling demand in 2009, Mongolia was advised to target its universal child benefit; this it refused to do, when in 2010/11 copper prices rise again. Given the volatile nature of primary commodity prices, many governments have created "stabilization funds" based on windfall taxes. Such funds allow governments to smooth their income and expenditure, saving the proceeds bonanza years for "rainy days" when prices of commodity exports may be low, and hence ensuring that investments in social and economic development remain constant. Examples include Chile's Copper Stabilization Fund, Iran's Oil Stabilization Fund and Papua New Guinea's Mineral Resources Stabilization Fund. During the recent economic downturn, a number of countries have drawn on these funds to finance stimulus measures for national growth and increase social protection.

protection schemes in a number of countries, including Mozambique and Ghana, though the net welfare effect of any reform must be properly understood prior to removing subsidies (box 6.7).

6.5.2 Option 2: Increasing tax revenues

This may be achieved by altering various types of tax rates, by strengthening the efficiency of tax-collection methods, and by improving overall compliance. As noted above, 94 countries are already increasing consumption taxes such as VAT, which are generally regressive as they cover products that the poor consume. The focus should be shifted instead to other taxes, such as those on corporate profits, financial activities, personal income, property, imports or exports, which tend to be progressive. Progressive taxation – the principal redistribution tool available to policy-makers – should be prioritized on grounds of both fiscal space and equity in order to enlist the political support of citizens and promote socio-economic recovery (IMF, 2010c; Ostry et al., 2014).

6.5.3 Option 3: Extending social security contributions

Generating funding through social contributions is by its nature associated with the extension of contributory social security schemes. Many countries in recent years have increased social protection financing significantly by this means, including Brazil, China, Costa Rica, Lesotho, Namibia, South Africa and Thailand. In most countries, these initiatives are closely associated with the introduction of new measures to bring more workers into formal employment and to expand the coverage of contributory social security schemes.

6.5.4 Option 4: Borrowing or restructuring existing debt

Some countries have potential capacity to borrow (through loans or bond issues); other already have large debts and need better debt management. Debt restructuring is the process of reducing existing levels of debt or debt service charges. For those countries suffering from high levels of debt, restructuring existing debt may be possible and justifiable if the legitimacy of the debt is questionable (e.g. nationalized private sector debts) and/or the opportunity cost in terms of worsening growth and living standards is high (box 6.9). Five main options are available to governments seeking to restructure sovereign debt: (1) renegotiating debt (as more than 60 countries have done since the 1990s), (2) achieving debt relief/cancellation (e.g. under the Heavily Indebted Poor Countries Initiative or HIPC, introduced in 1996), (3) entering into debt swaps/conversions (as done by more than 50 countries since 1980s), (4) repudiating debt (as Iraq and Iceland have done), or (5) defaulting (done by more than 20 countries since 1999, including Argentina and the Russian Federation). There is ample experience of governments

Box 6.9 Ecuador: Using resources freed up by debt restructuring for social protection

Some developing countries have re-examined accumulated debts dating back to the 1970s in order to decrease their outstanding obligations. In 2008, Ecuador became the first country to hold an official audit to assess the legitimacy of its sovereign debt. The government-commissioned, two-year-long investigation concluded that some of its foreign debts (mostly private sector debts nationalized by former governments) had broken multiple principles of international and domestic law and were therefore "illegitimate". While Ecuador respected all of the debt that had contributed to the country's development – the so-called "legitimate" debt – it defaulted on its alleged illegitimate debt in November 2008 and bought it back at 35 cents to the dollar just a few weeks later.

On the basis of the Ecuadorean (and also the Norwegian) experience, a special United Nations Commission of Experts on Reforms of the International Monetary and Financial System came out in support of public debt audits as a mechanism for transparent and fair restructuring of debts (UN, 2009b). The public resources freed up in Ecuador by this method were invested in human development, which included doubling education spending between 2006 and 2009, nearly doubling housing assistance programmes for low-income families and expanding its main social protection programme, the cash transfer Bono de Desarrollo Humano (human development bond). The results are impressive: poverty fell from a recession peak of 36.0 per cent to 28.6 per cent, unemployment dropped from 9.1 per cent to 4.9 per cent and school enrolment rates rose significantly (Ray and Kozameh, 2012).

restructuring debt or reducing debt service payments, often against opposition from creditors. The IMF has proposed a Sovereign Debt Restructuring Mechanism (Kruger, 2002; IMF, 2003), and the United Nations has also called for a mechanism for the reduction of sovereign debt that deals fairly with lenders and borrowers alike (UN, 2009b; UN, 2010b).

6.5.5 Option 5: Curtailing illicit financial flows

Curtailing illicit financial flows (IFFs) also has the potential to generate large amounts of additional resources for socio-economic investments, including social protection. IFFs involve capital that is illegally earned, transferred or used and include, inter alia, traded goods that are mispriced to avoid higher tariffs, wealth funnelled to offshore accounts to evade income taxes and unreported movements of cash (UNDP, 2011). It is estimated that in 2009 US$1.3 trillion in IFFs moved out of developing countries, mostly through trade mispricing, of which nearly two-thirds ended up in high-income countries; this amounts to more than ten times the total amount of aid received by developing countries (figure 6.20).

Figure 6.20 Illicit financial flows (IFF) versus official development assistance (ODA), 2000–09 (current US$ billions)

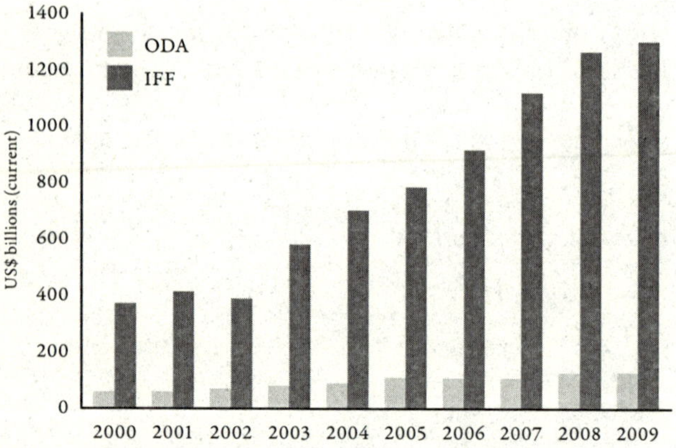

Sources: Kar and Curcio, 2011; World Bank, World Development Indicators, 2011.

Link: http://www.social-protection.org/gimi/gess/RessourceDownload.action?ressource.ressourceId=43517.

6.5.6 Option 6: Drawing on increased aid and transfers

This requires either engaging with different donor governments in order to increase North–South or South–South transfers, or reducing South–North transfers, such as IFFs, which are significantly larger (see above). As a result of the fiscal consolidation policies adopted in most donor countries, development aid fell by 4 per cent in real terms in 2012, following a 2 per cent fall in 2011 (OECD, 2013e). In 2012, the United Nations Special Rapporteurs for the Right to Food, and for Extreme Poverty and Human Rights, called for a global fund for social protection to redress the balance (De Schutter and Sepúlveda, 2012).

6.5.7 Option 7: Using fiscal and central bank foreign exchange reserves

This includes drawing down fiscal savings and other state revenues stored in special funds, such as sovereign wealth funds, and/or using excess foreign exchange reserves in the central bank for domestic and regional development. A more detailed discussion of this option can be found in Ortiz and Cummins, 2012; here there is space only to highlight the case of sovereign wealth funds (SWFs), which can potentially be used for national socio-economic development and social protection. The logic behind SWFs – such as the Abu Dhabi Investment Authority, Norway's Government Pension Fund Global, and Singapore's Temasek Holdings and Government of Singapore Investment Corporation – is to maximize financial returns on investment, usually in international capital markets. While creating an SWF is an option available to most governments, many have questioned the logic of investing earned public income for capital market growth when those resources could be invested in social and economic goods and services urgently needed at home. The Bolivarian Republic of Venezuela, for example, has used its fiscal reserves to finance a number of development objectives both domestically and regionally. On the other hand, Timor-Leste, a country with very low scores on human indicators of development and a high proportion of people living in poverty (50 per cent in 2007, up from 36 per cent in 2001), has an estimated US$6.3 billion stored in an SWF investing overseas. The key point is that governments have multiple options in how to use their reserves for socio-economic development, and the alternatives should be carefully evaluated (see box 6.8).

6.5.8 Option 8: Adopting a more accommodating macroeconomic framework

This entails allowing for higher budget deficits and higher levels of inflation without jeopardizing macroeconomic stability (e.g. through quantitative easing in the United States). The goals of macroeconomic policy are multiple, from supporting growth, price stabilization or inflation control to smoothing economic cycles, reducing unemployment and poverty, and promoting equity. In recent decades, macroeconomic frameworks have placed strong emphasis on short-term stabilization measures, such as controlling inflation and fiscal deficits, as part of broader efforts aimed at liberalizing economies, integrating them into global markets and attracting investment. While these macroeconomic objectives are not necessarily unsound, there is an increasing risk in many developing countries that other important objectives, such as employment-generating growth and social protection, lose priority and come to be underemphasized. It is important to underscore that there are diverse views on what constitutes an "acceptable" level of inflation or fiscal deficits, and that, as part of the crisis response, there has been a growing recognition of the need to ease budget constraints and allow for an increasing degree of deficit spending, especially to support socially relevant investments and employment-generating economic growth (IMF, 2009; Epstein, 2009; Pollin, Epstein and Heintz, 2008; Islam and Chowdhury, 2010a; Islam and Chowdhury, 2010b; UNCTAD, 2011; UNCTAD, 2012; UNCTAD, 2013).

In summary, there are ample opportunities for countries to increase fiscal space for social protection through a combination of tailored strategies. Usually it is appropriate for governments to consider a mix of the different strategies, as in the examples presented in table 6.5. Each country is unique, and the full range of available fiscal space options should be carefully examined – with close attention to the potential risks and trade-offs associated with each opportunity – at the national level through an inclusive dialogue to ensure a socially responsive recovery. All of the fiscal space options described in this report are supported by policy statements of the United Nations and international financial institutions. ILO Recommendation No. 202 emphasizes the responsibility of national governments in financing national social protection floors, and in mobilizing the necessary resources to ensure the financial, fiscal and economic sustainability of these arrangements. The Recommendation also notes explicitly that national resource mobilization strategies may include the effective enforcement of tax and contribution obligations, reprioritizing expenditure, and/or a broader and sufficiently progressive revenue base. The Recommendation further states that countries whose economic and fiscal capacities are insufficient to implement the guarantees may seek international cooperation and support to complement their own efforts (Paras 11–12; see also ILO, 2012a).

Table 6.5 Fiscal space strategies: Country examples

Strategy	Pl. State of Bolivia	Botswana	Brazil	Costa Rica	Lesotho	Iceland	Namibia	South Africa	Thailand
Reallocating public expenditures				×	×	×		×	×
Increasing tax revenues	×	×	×		×	×			×
Expanding social security contributions			×	×	×		×	×	×
Reducing debt/debt service	×	×	×	×	×	×		×	×
Curtailing illicit financial flows						×	×		
Increasing aid							×		
Tapping into fiscal reserves	×	×	×						
More accommodating macroeconomic framework	×		×			×			

Sources: Adapted from Durán-Valverde and Pacheco, 2012; Ortiz and Cummins, 2012.

6.6 Why social protection floors are key to recovery and must be part of the post-2015 development agenda

As the global community struggles to emerge from recession and slow growth, and assesses the current development agenda and the progress made towards the achievement of the Millennium Development Goals, it is high time to recall the three main reasons why social protection is one of the necessary conditions for sustainable development. First, it is a *human right* and a core element of labour rights. It is also a *social and political necessity*, as States need a capacity to intervene where markets have failed; effective national social protection systems are powerful tools to provide income security, to prevent and reduce poverty and inequality and to build inclusive society; thus they strengthen social cohesion and contribute to establishing and maintaining social peace. Social protection is also an *economic necessity* to sustain domestic consumption and demand by raising household income. Adequate social protection enhances productivity and human development, enables workers to adapt to change, and facilitates equitable and inclusive structural change. Investing in social protection is investing in a healthy, productive and equitable society.

6.6.1 Social protection floors reduce poverty and inequalities

Social protection reduces poverty and social exclusion

Social protection is a crucial instrument in addressing all forms of poverty. Cash transfer schemes have successfully reduced poverty in Africa, Asia, Central and Eastern Europe, and Latin America, potentially delivering much faster results than those expected from the "trickle-down" effects of economic policies. Although in practice benefits have tended to be lower than needed, a cash transfer at an adequate level can bring people out of poverty overnight. Equally importantly, cash transfers have had even larger effects on reducing the depth of poverty. For example, South Africa's non-contributory grants have reduced the poverty gap by more than one-third (Woolard, Harttgen and Klasen, 2010), the Oportunidades programme in Mexico has reduced the numbers living in poverty by 10 per cent and the poverty gap by 30 per cent (Skoufias and Parker, 2001), and Kyrgyzstan's Social Protection Programme has reduced the number of people living in extreme poverty by 24 per cent and the poverty gap among beneficiaries by 42 per cent (World Bank, 2003). The expansion of food assistance in the United States is reported to have reduced the number of households in extreme poverty by half (CBPP, 2014). Overall, social transfers and

Figure 6.21 Public social protection expenditure (percentage of GDP) and proportion of the population in poverty

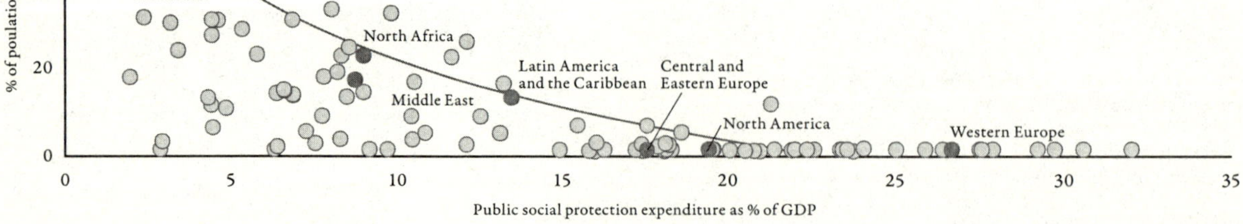

Notes: R2 = 0.5326. The relationship between public social protection expenditure and poverty outcomes is complex, involving a variety of factors. It should be noted in particular that US$2 PPP per day does not represent a meaningful absolute poverty line in high-income countries; this cut-off point was selected for the purpose of the graph to ensure international comparability.

Sources: Public social protection expenditure: Based on data from IMF, OECD, Eurostat, ILO, CEPALSTAT, ADB and national sources. Poverty headcount: World Bank, World Development Indicators (accessed April 2013). For more details see Annex IV, table B.12.

Link: http://www.social-protection.org/gimi/gess/RessourceDownload.action?ressource.ressourceId=38559.

Figure 6.22 Public social protection expenditure (percentage of GDP) and income equality (Gini coefficient), latest available year

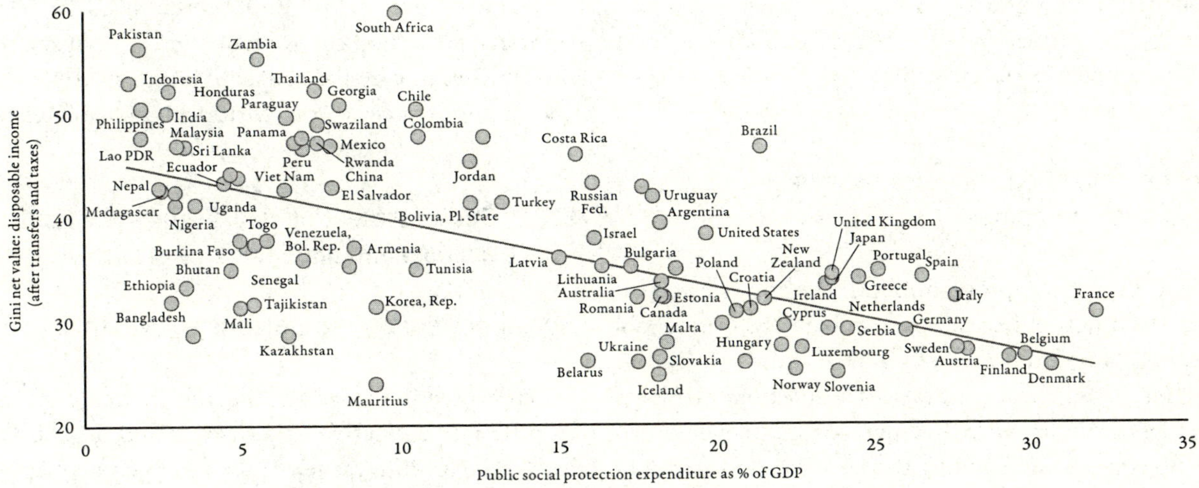

Notes: $R2 = 0.3893$. Again, the relationship between social protection policies (measured here by expenditure) and inequality (here measured by Gini coefficient) is much more complex than can be captured here. Well-designed social protection policies address not only income inequality, but also various other dimensions of inequality (see e.g. UNRISD, 2010; OECD, 2011b; UNDP, 2014).

Sources: Public social protection expenditure: based on data from IMF, OECD, Eurostat, ILO, CEPALSTAT, ADB and national sources (see Annex IV, table B.12). Gini index: World Bank, World Development Indicators (accessed Jan. 2014); ADB, CEPAL; Solt, 2009; Solt, 2013).

Link: http://www.social-protection.org/gimi/gess/RessourceDownload.action?ressource.ressourceId=42217.

taxation have reduced poverty by more than 50 per cent in most European countries (see figure 6.16 above).

Social protection expenditure has a prominent role in reducing and preventing poverty, containing inequality and addressing social exclusion. Particularly crucial is its capacity to ensure that people can escape poverty for good: the risk of falling back into poverty is very high where effective social protection mechanisms do not exist (Chronic Poverty Advisory Network, 2014). Social protection is essential in addressing not only monetary poverty but also social exclusion (Babajanian and Hagen-Zanker, 2012). Indeed, social protection constitutes one of the essential channels through which governments can distribute and redistribute income and resources, and share the benefits of growth, reinforcing the democratic mandates granted them on election to fulfil societal expectations. The key role of social protection in inclusive growth is now widely recognized (e.g. OECD, 2009a). It is therefore not surprising that higher levels of social protection expenditure are associated with lower levels of poverty (see figure 6.21).

Social protection reduces income inequality

The role of social protection reaches far beyond a mere reduction of income poverty. While debate has for some time focused narrowly on poverty reduction and the efficiency of targeting, it is increasingly acknowledged that the reduction of poverty is not sufficient to promote inclusive growth (UNDP, 2013; UN, 2013d; UN, 2013e). Broader social protection policies encompassing approaches such as extending social insurance are needed to help prevent poverty and insecurity and to contain inequality (figure 6.22). The correlation between public social protection expenditure and inequality (as expressed by the Gini coefficient) is less strong than for poverty, but there is still a distinct relationship, suggesting that higher levels of social protection expenditure are associated with lower levels of inequality.

Social protection contributes to human capital development, reduces hunger and contributes to food security

There is strong evidence of the positive impacts of social protection on hunger and nutrition. In Africa, Asia and Latin America, cash transfers have been shown to improve both the quantity and the diversity of food consumption, and to protect food consumption during shocks or lean periods. Better nutrition also contributes to better physical development: programmes in Mexico, Malawi, and Colombia all demonstrate reductions in the numbers of children with stunted growth (Yablonski and O'Donnell, 2009; Tirivayi, Knowles and Davis, 2013), while children in South African households receiving a pension grow on average 5 centimetres taller than those in households without a pension (Case, 2001).

Social protection supports positive education outcomes

Social protection programmes, including cash transfers, the supply of free tuition and materials, and school feeding programmes, have all been shown to lead to higher school enrolment rates, fewer school dropouts and less child labour by removing demand-side barriers to education, including the need for poor families to rely on children for income-earning and care work. Transfer programmes in Bangladesh, Brazil, Cambodia, Ecuador, Ethiopia, Malawi, Mexico, Nicaragua, Pakistan, South Africa, and Turkey have all demonstrated significant increases in children's school enrolment and/or attendance (Adato and Bassett, 2008).

Social protection supports positive health outcomes

Social protection can contribute to better and more equal health outcomes in various ways. Investments in health infrastructure, staff and drugs are most urgently needed where the burden of illness is heaviest. Financial support is also needed to prevent families falling into poverty because of heavy out-of-pocket health expenditures. A WHO cross-country study showed this can be done by reducing the health system's reliance on OOP and providing more financial risk protection (Xu, Evans and Kawabata, 2003). Thailand's commitment to achieving universal access to health care led to significant improvements in health outcomes on a number of measures, including take-up of services and the rate of health-related impoverishment (Evans et al., 2012; Tangcharoensathien et al., 2009). The Oportunidades programme in Mexico combined cash transfers and free health services with improvements in the supply of health services, leading to a 17 per cent decline in rural infant mortality over a three-year period and an 11 per cent reduction in maternal mortality rates (Barham, 2010; Adato and Bassett, 2008). In Ghana, user fee exemptions for pregnant women led to a significant reduction in the maternal mortality rate (Witter et al., 2007). More recently, there is evidence on the usefulness of broader social protection interventions in HIV and AIDS prevention, treatment, and care and support (ILO, 2008b; Temin, 2010). Cash transfers, for example, were found effective in supporting families to care for people living with HIV/AIDS and in improving access to treatment and adherence.

6.6.2 Social protection floors promote decent employment and inclusive growth

Social protection promotes employment

Social protection plays a major role in creating access to full and productive employment and decent work for all, including women and young people, through cash transfers, active labour market measures, health insurance and family support policies. These have been shown to encourage labour market participation in low- and middle-income countries by guaranteeing public work opportunities, covering the costs of jobseeking and supporting those with childcare responsibilities – with particularly strong effects for women. In South Africa, labour market participation among those receiving cash transfers was 13–17 per cent higher than in similar non-recipient households, with the greatest difference among women (Economic Policy Research Institute, 2004). For young people who are structurally unemployed or at high social risk, the Joven programme in Chile combines work experience, training and apprenticeships; this model has been replicated in other South American countries (World Bank, 2003). In other countries, such as India and Uganda, cash transfers have been used to provide employment for local youth and poor people. Cash transfers can also provide critical resources for funding job search, supporting quality training and skills development, increasing access to credit and bolstering the resilience of agricultural smallholders in maintaining production. Public employment programmes can also be linked to green jobs and environmental improvements, as for example in Brazil and the Philippines. A recent study from the United States indicates that giving food assistance to the children of poor families increases their average annual earnings in the long run by as much as US$3,000, and their average number of hours of work by 150 annually (CBPP, 2014).

Many countries in Asia, Africa and Latin America have developed ways of coordinating social protection mechanisms with labour market policies and services, thereby strengthening opportunities for the unemployed to return to the market. One particularly interesting finding is that adult participants in a number of the Latin American cash transfer programmes mentioned above, as well as beneficiaries of similar schemes in South Africa, were able to increase their rate of economic activity, finding their employability boosted through simple investments in and access to training and employment services, and to look for work more effectively with the costs of job searching boosted through the modest cash transfers received by families.

Social protection promotes economic growth

Social protection schemes contribute to sustainable economic growth by raising labour productivity and empowering people to find decent jobs. Injecting money into rural communities can have important multiplier effects on the local economy, stimulating trade in goods and services and encouraging more dynamic local development based on both agricultural and off-farm activities (Tirivayi, Knowles and Davis, 2013; Alderman and Yemtsov, 2012). Social protection represents an investment in a country's "human infrastructure" no less important than investments in its physical infrastructure. Only a population that is healthy, well nourished and well educated can realize its potential for productive employment. The positive impacts of cash transfers on children's nutrition, and on access to health and education, have been well recorded around the world. Well-designed social protection systems thus enable a country to unlock its full productive potential and to promote inclusive growth (ILO, 2014d).

There are multiple channels through which social protection systems can support such investments in people (see ILO, 2010b; Social Protection Floor Advisory Group, 2011; Behrendt, 2013), with beneficial effects in both the short and the longer term. In the short term, social protection can help to improve the health of the population, stabilize aggregate consumption, enable people to take more risky decisions and to engage in more productive economic activities, preserve and promote human capital and enhance the functioning of the labour market (see figure 6.23). It thereby contributes to supporting structural changes in the labour market and the economy, and also exercises its much-needed counter-cyclical function in economic downturns, such as that caused by the recent global crisis.

In the longer term, the effects of better access to food, better nutritional status and better health will

Figure 6.23 Schematic representation of some of the positive impacts of the extension of social protection on inclusive growth (short term)

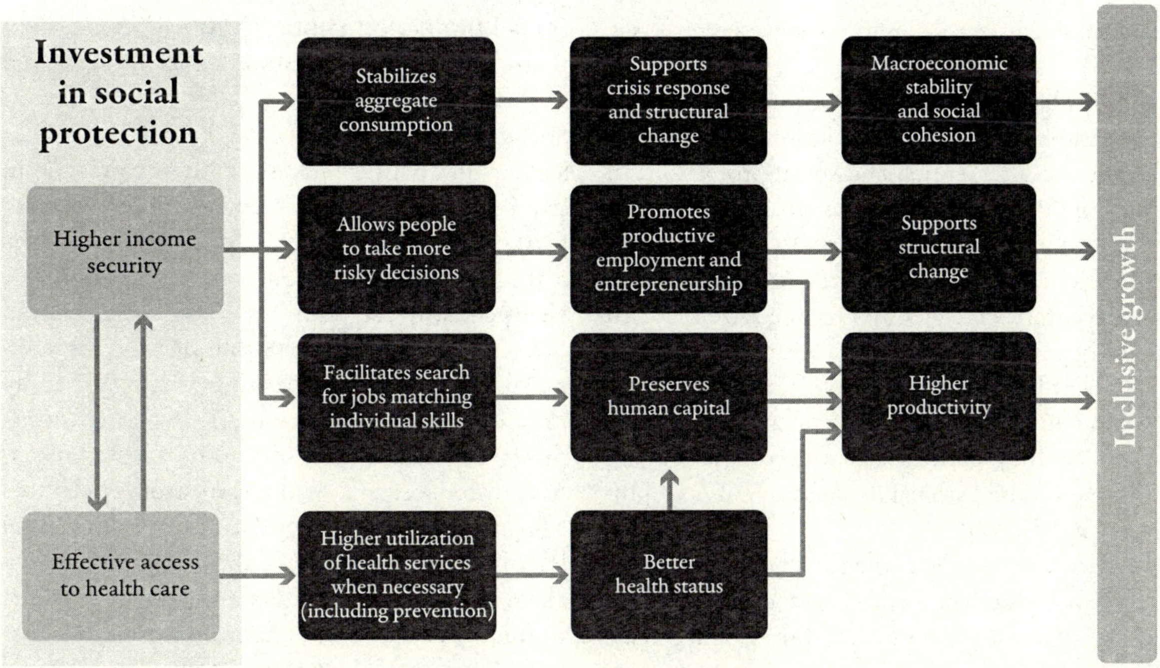

Source: Based on Behrendt, 2013.

Link: http://www.social-protection.org/gimi/gess/RessourceDownload.action?ressource.ressourceId=43579.

Figure 6.24 Schematic representation of some of the positive impacts of the extension of social protection on inclusive growth (longer term)

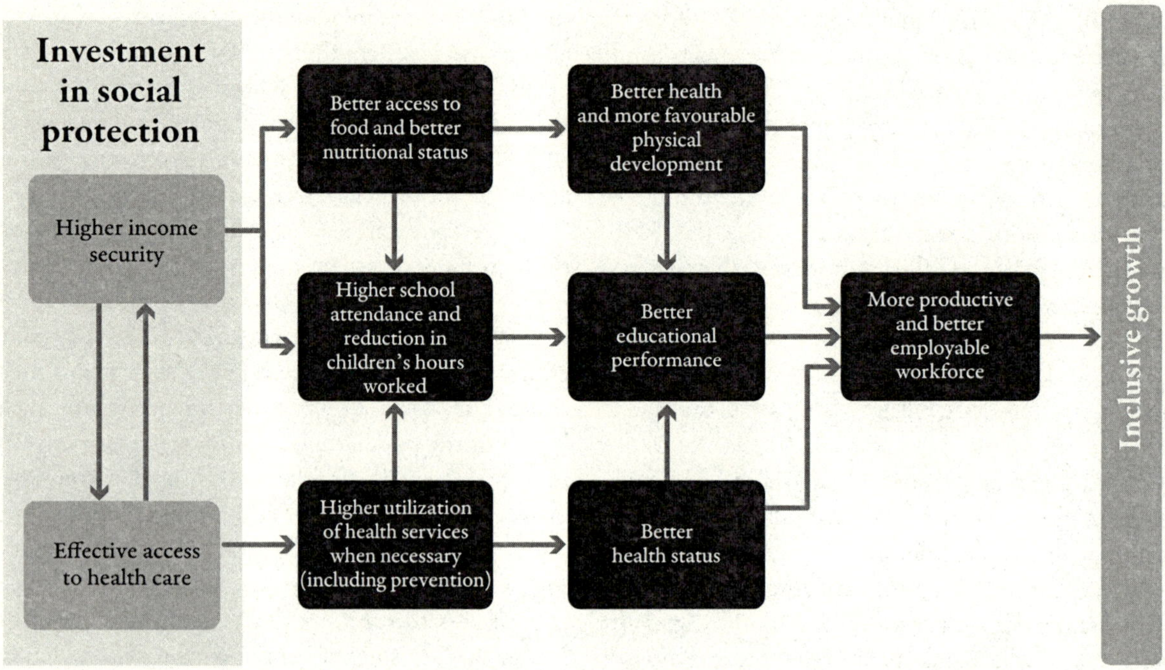

Source: Based on Behrendt, 2013.

Link: http://www.social-protection.org/gimi/gess/RessourceDownload.action?ressource.ressourceId=43580.

contribute to the better physical and mental development of the population. The effects of enhancing access to education and improving educational performance also contribute to fostering a more productive and more readily employable workforce, which is one of the preconditions of sustained and inclusive growth (see figure 6.24).

The crisis has triggered a shift in the way the international community sees the relationship between growth, public intervention and social protection. In Asia and the Pacific, for example, policy-makers are increasingly moving away from export-led growth approaches alone towards more inclusive employment-intensive recovery strategies which emphasize the need to reduce high domestic savings rates and improve the region's underdeveloped social protection programmes (Ortiz and Cummins, 2013). China is a good example, having massively expanded social protection schemes in recent years to raise national living standards and promote national demand.

In Africa and elsewhere, the food price crisis highlighted the limitations of family- and community-based traditional support systems in responding to aggregate shocks and spurred efforts to strengthen local agriculture. At the global level, there is now an awareness of the need to raise household incomes, expand internal markets and prepare better for future shocks by building up stronger systems during the current crisis recovery period.

Social protection supports social peace, political stability and state-building

Social protection is not only a human right; it is also a social and political necessity. There can be no inclusive and cohesive society where the poor and rich drift further and further apart. While the sources of political conflict vary from one country to another, conflict generally originates in severe social grievances, often rooted in the perception of inequality among social, ethnic, religious or other groups. Social protection measures have a central role to play in easing and preventing such sources of conflict. Governments that have introduced and maintained strong social security systems have not only significantly reduced inequality, but also earned the trust of their citizens by providing them with reliable benefits and quality services, delivered by efficient and trustworthy institutions (e.g. GIZ, 2012). Social protection thus plays a key role in state building, institution building and fostering social peace and social justice.

6.6.3 Leaving no one behind: Social protection floors to change people's lives by 2030

Social protection works. This is a key conclusion from this *World Social Protection Report*. The extension of social protection in many developing countries in recent years has successfully realized the right to social security for larger proportions of the population. More children and families receive cash benefits to enhance their income security, and these greatly facilitate access to nutrition, health and education. More older women and men can now rely on a regular source of income from a pension, even if levels are still modest. More people, especially those in rural areas, are benefiting from having the right to guaranteed employment for a certain number of days during lean seasons, and thus enhanced income security round the year. More children and adults have access to health services because governments have extended health insurance coverage and subsidized contributions for those who would not be able to afford them otherwise, and have improved the quality and accessibility of public health services. These significant investments in social protection also enable workers to engage in more productive employment, and strengthen aggregate consumption. A social protection benefit can make an enormous difference in the life of a single person, and of an entire country.

Despite these positive efforts, 73 per cent of the global working-age population, and their families, are still not sufficiently covered in comprehensive social security systems. More efforts are needed to accelerate the extension of social security to adequate levels. Governments, with the participation of social partners and other stakeholders, have a responsibility to fill the remaining gaps in social protection and to progressively ensure adequate levels of social security for their populations. Social protection floors address the daily concerns of families and households, and are linked to the realization of all people's rights – those of children, of women and men of working age, of persons with disabilities, of older persons. Rio+20's *The Future We Want* recognized "the need to provide social protection to all members of society, fostering growth, resilience, social justice and cohesion" and encouraged "initiatives aimed at providing social protection floors for all citizens" (UN, 2012a, p. 29). Looking beyond 2015, it is essential that social protection floors and social security systems be included among the new Sustainable Development Goals.

Annex I
Glossary

This glossary focuses on the basic concepts, definitions and methodology guiding the analytical work of the ILO on social security or social protection.[1] It does not set out to assert any universal definitions; its purpose is rather simply to clarify terms and concepts as they are used in this report and in the ILO.

Cash transfer programme. Non-contributory scheme or programme providing cash benefits to individuals or households, usually financed out of taxation, other government revenue, or external grants or loans. Cash transfer programmes[2] may or may not include a means test.

Cash transfer programmes that provide cash to families subject to the condition that they fulfil specific behavioural requirements are referred to as conditional cash transfer programmes (CCTs). This may mean, for example, that beneficiaries must ensure their children attend school regularly, or that they utilize basic preventative nutrition and health-care services.

Contributory scheme. Scheme in which contributions made by protected persons directly determine entitlement to benefits (acquired rights). The most common form of contributory social security schemes is a statutory social insurance scheme, usually covering workers in formal wage employment and, in some countries, the self-employed. Other common types of contributory schemes, providing – in the absence of social insurance – a certain level of protection include national provident funds, which usually pay a lump sum to beneficiaries when particular contingencies occur (typically old age, invalidity or death). In the case of social insurance schemes for those in waged or salaried employment, contributions are usually paid by both employees and employers (though in general, employment injury schemes are fully financed by employers). Contributory schemes can be wholly financed through contributions, but often are partly financed from taxation or other sources; this may be done through a subsidy to cover the deficit, or through a general subsidy supplanting contributions altogether, or by subsidizing only specific groups of contributors or beneficiaries (e.g. those not contributing because they are caring for children, studying, in military service or unemployed, or have too low a level of income to fully contribute, or receive benefits below a certain threshold because of low contributions in the past).

Employment guarantee scheme. Public employment programme which provides a guaranteed number of workdays a year to poor households, generally providing wages at a relatively low level (typically at the minimum wage level if this is adequately defined).

---

[1] The glossary largely draws on the definitions, concepts and methods provided in the first edition of the *World Social Security Report* (ILO, 2010a), with a number of important updates to reflect the provisions of the Social Protection Floors Recommendation, 2012 (No. 202), and other recent developments.

[2] Strictly speaking, this term would encompass all social transfers provided in cash, including fully or partially contributory transfers, yet it is usually understood as limited to non-contributory transfers.

Means-tested scheme. A scheme that provides benefits upon proof of need and targets certain categories of persons or households whose means fall below a certain threshold, often referred to as *social assistance schemes*. A means test is used to assess whether the individual's or household's own resources (income and/or assets) are below a defined threshold and determine whether the applicants are eligible for a benefit at all, and if so at what level benefit will be provided. In some countries, proxy means tests are used: that is, eligibility is determined without actually assessing income or assets, on the basis of other household characteristics (proxies) that are deemed more easily observable. Means-tested schemes may also include entitlement conditions and obligations, such as work requirements, participation in health checkups or (for children) school attendance. Some means-tested schemes also include other interventions that are delivered on top of the actual income transfer itself.

Non-contributory schemes. Non-contributory schemes, including non-means-tested and means-tested schemes, normally require no direct contribution from beneficiaries or their employers as a condition of entitlement to receive relevant benefits. The term covers a broad range of schemes, including universal schemes for all residents (such as a national health services), categorical schemes for certain broad groups of the population (e.g. for children below a certain age or older persons above a certain age), and means-tested schemes (such as social assistance schemes). Non-contributory schemes are usually financed through taxes or other state revenues, or, in certain cases, through external grants or loans.

Public employment programme. Government programme offering employment opportunities to certain categories of persons who are unable to find other employment. Public employment programmes include employment guarantee schemes and "cash for work" and "food for work" programmes (see box 3.2).

Social assistance scheme/programme. A scheme that provides benefits to vulnerable groups of the population, especially households living in poverty. Most social assistance schemes are means-tested.

Social insurance scheme. Contributory social protection scheme that guarantees protection through an insurance mechanism, based on: (1) the prior payment of contributions, i.e. before the occurrence of the insured contingency; (2) risk- sharing or "pooling"; and (3) the notion of a guarantee. The contributions paid by (or for) insured persons are pooled together and the resulting fund is used to cover the expenses incurred exclusively by those persons affected by the occurrence of the relevant (clearly defined) contingency or contingencies. Contrary to commercial insurance, risk-pooling in social insurance is based on the principle of solidarity as opposed to individually calculated risk premiums.

Many contributory social security schemes are presented and described as "insurance" schemes (usually "social insurance schemes"), despite being in actual fact of mixed character, with some non-contributory elements in entitlements to benefits; this allows for a more equitable distribution of benefits, particularly for those with low incomes and short or broken work careers, among others. These non-contributory elements take various forms, being financed either by other contributors (redistribution within the scheme) or by the State.

Social protection. The term "social protection" is used in institutions across the world with a wider variety of meanings than "social security". It is often interpreted as having a broader character than social security (including, in particular, protection provided between members of the family or members of a local community), but it is also used in some contexts with a narrower meaning (understood as comprising only measures addressed to the poorest, most vulnerable or excluded members of society). Thus, in many contexts the two terms, "social security" and "social protection", may be largely interchangeable, and the ILO certainly uses both in discourse with its constituents and in the provision of relevant advice to them. In this report, reference is made to "social protection" both as an alternative expression for "social security" and to denote the protection provided by social security in case of social risks and needs.

Social protection floor. ILO Recommendation No. 202 sets out that member States should establish and maintain national social protection floors as a nationally defined set of basic social security guarantees which secure protection aimed at preventing or alleviating poverty, vulnerability and social exclusion (ILO, 2012a). These guarantees should ensure at a minimum that, over the life cycle, all in need have access to at least essential health care and basic income security. These together ensure effective access to essential goods and services defined as necessary at the national level. More specifically, national social protection floors should comprise at least the following four social security guarantees, as defined at the national level:

(a) access to essential health care, including maternity care;

(b) basic income security for children, providing access to nutrition, education, care and any other necessary goods and services;

(c) basic income security for persons in active age who are unable to earn sufficient income, in particular in cases of sickness, unemployment, maternity and disability; and

(d) basic income security for older persons.[3]

Such guarantees should be provided to all residents and all children, as defined in national laws and regulations, and subject to existing international obligations.

Recommendation No. 202 also states that basic social security guarantees should be established by law. National laws and regulations should specify the range, qualifying conditions and levels of the benefits giving effect to these guarantees, and provide for effective and accessible complaint and appeal procedures.

Social protection floors correspond in many ways to the existing notion of "core obligations", to ensure the realization of, at the very least, minimum essential levels of rights embodied in human rights treaties (OHCHR, 2013).

Social protection programme/scheme (social security programme/scheme). Distinct framework of rules to provide social protection benefits to entitled beneficiaries. Such rules would specify the geographical and personal scope of the programme (target group), entitlement conditions, the type of benefits, benefit amounts (cash transfers), periodicity and other benefit characteristics, as well as the financing (contributions, general taxation, other sources), governance and administration of the programme.

While "programme" may refer to a wide range of programmes, the term "scheme" is usually used in a more specific sense referring to a programme that is anchored in national legislation and characterized by at least a certain degree of "formality".

A programme/scheme can be supported by one or more social security institutions governing the provision of benefits and their financing. It should, in general, be possible to draw up a separate account of receipts and expenditure for each social protection programme. It is often the case that a social protection programme provides protection against a single risk or need, and covers a single specific group of beneficiaries. Typically, however, one institution will administer more than one benefit programme.

Social security. The fundamental right to social security is set out in the Universal Declaration on Human Rights (1948) and other international legal instruments. The notion of social security adopted here covers all measures providing benefits, whether in cash or in kind, to secure protection, inter alia, from

- lack of work-related income (or insufficient income) caused by sickness, disability, maternity, employment injury, unemployment, old age, or death of a family member;
- lack of (affordable) access to health care;
- insufficient family support, particularly for children and adult dependants;
- general poverty and social exclusion.

Social security thus has two main (functional) dimensions, namely "income security" and "availability of medical care", reflected in the Declaration of Philadelphia (1944), which forms part of the ILO's Constitution: "social security measures to provide a basic income to all in need of such protection and comprehensive medical care" (III(f)).[4] Recommendation No. 202 sets out that, at least, access to essential health care and basic income security over the life cycle should be guaranteed as part of nationally defined social protection floors, and that higher levels of protection should be progressively achieved by national social security systems in line with Convention No. 102 and other ILO instruments.

[3] Recommendation No. 202, Para. 5.

[4] These two main dimensions are also identified in the ILO Income Security Recommendation, 1944 (No. 67), and the Medical Care Recommendation, 1944 (No. 69), respectively, as "essential element[s] of social security". These Recommendations envisage that, first, "income security schemes should relieve want and prevent destitution by restoring, up to a reasonable level, income which is lost by reason of inability to work (including old age) or to obtain remunerative work or by reason of the death of a breadwinner" (Recommendation No. 67, Guiding principles, Para. 1); and, second, that "a medical care service should meet the need of the individual for care by members of the medical and allied professions" and "the medical care service should cover all members of the community" (Recommendation No. 69, Paras 1 and 8). Recommendation No. 202 also reflects these two elements in the basic social protection guarantees that should form part of national social protection floors (for more detail, see box 1.1).

Access to social security is essentially a public responsibility, and is typically provided through public institutions, financed from either contributions or taxes or both. However, the delivery of social security can be and often is mandated to private entities. Moreover, there exist many privately run institutions (of an insurance, self-help, community-based or mutual character) which can partially assume selected roles usually played by social security, such as the operation of occupational pension schemes, that complement and may largely substitute for elements of public social security schemes. Entitlements to social security are conditional either on the payment of social security contributions for prescribed periods (contributory schemes, most often structured as social insurance arrangements) or on a requirement, sometimes described as "residency plus", under which benefits are provided to all residents of the country who also meet certain other criteria (non-contributory schemes). Such criteria may make benefit entitlements conditional on age, health, labour market participation, income or other determinants of social or economic status and/or even conformity with certain behavioural requirements.

Two main features distinguish social security from other social arrangements. First, benefits are provided to beneficiaries without any simultaneous reciprocal obligation (thus it does not, for example, represent remuneration for work or other services delivered). Second, it is not based on an individual agreement between the protected person and the provider (as is, for example, a life insurance contract); the agreement applies to a wider group of people and so has a collective character.

Depending on the category of applicable conditions, a distinction is also made between non-means-tested schemes (where the conditions of benefit entitlement are not related to the total level of income or wealth of the beneficiary and her or his family) and means-tested schemes (where entitlement is granted only to those with income or wealth below a prescribed threshold). A special category of "conditional" schemes includes those which, in addition to other conditions, require beneficiaries (and/or their relatives or families) to participate in prescribed public programmes (for example, specified health or educational programmes).

Social security system/social protection system. Totality of social security/protection schemes and programmes in a country, taking into account that the latter term is often used in a broader sense than the former.

All the social security schemes and institutions in a country are inevitably interlinked and complementary in their objectives, functions and financing, and thus form a national social security system. For reasons of effectiveness and efficiency, it is essential that there is close coordination within the system, and that – not least for coordination and planning purposes – the receipts and expenditure accounts of all the schemes are compiled into one social security budget for the country so that its future expenditure and financing of the schemes comprising the social security system are planned in an integrated way.

Social transfer. All social security benefits comprise transfers, either in cash or in kind: i.e. they represent a transfer of income, goods or services (e.g. health-care services). This transfer may be from the active to the old, the healthy to the sick, or the affluent to the poor, among others. The recipients of such transfers may be in a position to receive them from a specific social security scheme because they have contributed to such a scheme (contributory scheme), or because they are residents (universal schemes for all residents), or because they fulfil specific age criteria (categorical schemes), or specific resource conditions (social assistance schemes), or because they fulfil several of these conditions at the same time. In addition, it is a requirement in some schemes (employment guarantee schemes, public employment programmes) that beneficiaries accomplish specific tasks or (conditional cash transfer programmes) adopt specific behaviours. In any given country, several schemes of different types generally coexist and may provide benefits for similar contingencies to different population groups.

Targeted scheme/programme. See *social assistance scheme*.

Universal scheme/categorical scheme. Strictly speaking, universal schemes provide benefits under the single condition of residence. However, the term is also often used to describe categorical schemes that provide benefits to certain broad categories of the population without a means-test. The most frequent forms of those schemes are those that transfer income to older persons above a certain age or children below a certain age. Some categorical schemes also target households with specific structures (one-parent households, for example) or occupational groups (such as rural workers). In some schemes, entitlement to benefits may be conditional on performing or accomplishing certain tasks. Most categorical schemes are tax-financed.

Annex II

Measuring social security coverage

Measuring social security coverage is a complex task. Several dimensions need to be considered in order to arrive at a complete assessment. In practice, few countries have available the full range of statistical data necessary for a complete assessment of social security coverage; nevertheless, partial information is available for a large number of countries. Many countries have acknowledged the need to undertake better regular monitoring of social security coverage and are stepping up their efforts to improve data collection and analysis.

Social security coverage is a multidimensional concept with at least three dimensions:

- *Scope.* This is measured here by the range (number) and type of social security areas (branches) to which the population of the country has access. Population groups with differing status in the labour market may enjoy different scopes of coverage, and this factor must be taken into account in assessing scope.
- *Extent.* This usually refers to the percentage of persons covered within the whole population or the target group (as defined by e.g. gender, age or labour market status) by social security measures in each specific area.
- *Level.* This refers to the adequacy of coverage by a specific branch of social security. It may be measured by the level of cash benefits provided, where measurements of benefit levels can be either absolute or relative to selected benchmark values such as previous incomes, average incomes, the poverty line, and so on. Measures of quality are usually relative and may be objective or subjective – for example, the satisfaction of beneficiaries measured against their expectations.

In measuring coverage, a distinction is made between legal coverage[1] and effective coverage in each of the above three dimensions, and for each social security area. Effective coverage is usually different from legal coverage; it is often lower, largely due to various governance problems in implementing the legal provisions and also to gaps in funding. Table AII.1 summarizes these various dimensions of coverage.

Legal coverage

Estimates of the *scope of legal coverage* usually measure the number of social security areas (branches) by which – according to existing national legislation – a population or its specific groups is covered. The list of the nine branches covered by ILO Convention No. 102 is used as guidance.

Estimates of the *extent of legal coverage* use both information on the groups covered by statutory schemes for a given social security area (branch) in national legislation, and available statistical information quantifying the number of persons concerned at the national

[1] Legal coverage is sometimes referred to as "statutory coverage", taking into account that provisions may be rooted in statutory provisions other than laws.

Table AII.1 Multiple dimensions of coverage: Examples of questions and indicators

Dimension of coverage	Legal coverage	Effective coverage
Scope	Which social security areas are addressed by the national legislation? For a given group of the population: for which social security area(s) is this group covered according to the national legislation?	Which social security areas are actually covered (actual implementation)? For a given group of the population: for which social security areas is this group effectively covered (benefits are actually available)?
Extent	For a given social security area (branch): which categories of the population are covered according to the national legislation? What percentage of the population or labour force is covered according to the national legislation?	For a given social security area (branch): which categories of the population are effectively covered, that is, enjoy actual access to benefits in case of need (currently or in the future)? The "beneficiary coverage ratio": for a given social security area, what percentage of the population affected by the contingency receives benefits or services (e.g. percentage of older persons receiving an old-age pension; percentage of unemployed receiving unemployment benefits)? The "contributor coverage ratio": for a given social security area, what percentage of the population contributes to the scheme, or is otherwise affiliated to the scheme, and can thus expect to receive benefits when needed (e.g. percentage of working-age population or of the labour force contributing to a pension scheme)? By extension, the "protected person coverage ratio" includes people potentially entitled to non-contributory benefits.
Level	For a given social security area: what is the level of protection provided according to the national legislation? For cash benefits: what is the prescribed amount or replacement rate according to the national legislation?	For a given social security area: what is the level of protection actually provided (e.g. for cash benefits, average level of benefit as a proportion of median income, minimum wage or poverty line)?

Source: Based on ILO, 2010a.

level. A population group can be identified as legally covered in a specific social security area (e.g. old age, unemployment protection, maternity protection) if the existing legislation sets out that this group is mandatorily covered by social insurance; or that this group will be entitled to specified non-contributory benefits under certain circumstances – for instance, to an old-age state pension on reaching the age of 65, or to income support if income falls below a specified threshold. A legal coverage ratio for a given branch of social security is the ratio between the estimated number of people legally covered and – as appropriate – the total population or labour force in the relevant age bracket, the total number of employees (that is, waged and salaried workers) or the total number of employed persons (including employees and the self-employed). For example, since Convention No. 102 allows a ratifying country to provide coverage through social insurance, through universal or means-tested benefits, or a combination of both, it also formulates alternatives to minimum requirements for the extent of coverage, as follows: (a) prescribed classes of employees, constituting not less than 50 per cent of all employees; or (b) prescribed classes of the economically active population, constituting not less than 20 per cent of all residents; or (c) all residents whose means during the contingency do not exceed prescribed limits.

The *level of legal coverage* for specific branches of social security is usually measured (for cash benefits) by benefit ratios or replacement ratios calculated for specified categories of beneficiaries, using benefit formulas or benefit amounts specified in the legislation. For example, Convention No. 102 sets minimum replacement rates for cash benefits in seven of its nine branches (see tables in Annex III below). It specifies that such minimum rates should apply to a defined "standard" beneficiary meeting qualifying conditions, and be guaranteed at least to those with earnings up to a certain prescribed selected level.

Effective coverage

Measurements of effective coverage should reflect how in reality the legal provisions are implemented. Effective coverage is usually different from legal coverage (and usually lower) because of non-compliance, problems with enforcement of legal provisions or other deviations of actual policies from the text of the legislation. In order to arrive at a full coverage assessment, measures of legal and effective coverage need to be used in parallel.

Measurements of the scope of *effective coverage* in a country reveal the number of social security areas (branches) for which there is relevant legislation that is actually enforced: that is, whether in all such areas the majority of the population legally covered is also effectively covered (as measured by the extent of effective coverage; see below).

When measuring the extent of effective coverage a distinction has to be made between coverage measured in terms of *protected persons* and in terms of *actual beneficiaries*. Protected persons are those who have benefits guaranteed but are not necessarily currently receiving them – for example, people who actively contribute to social insurance and are thus guaranteed benefits for a specified contingency, e.g. an old-age pension on reaching retirement age or people entitled to non-contributory benefits if needed.

In respect of *protected persons*, the *contributor coverage ratio* reflects, in the case of contributory schemes, the number of those protected should they be affected by the contingency covered now or in the future. That is, the share of the employed population (or alternatively the population of working age or in the labour force) which contributes directly or indirectly to social insurance in a given social security area and is thus likely to receive benefits when needed. An example is the percentage of employed persons contributing to a pension scheme. By extension, the *protected person coverage ratio* includes people entitled to non-contributory benefits.

In respect of actual beneficiaries, the *beneficiary coverage ratio* describes the proportion of the population affected by a certain contingency (e.g. older persons, unemployed) who actually benefit from the appropriate social security benefits (e.g. old-age pensions, unemployment benefits). This ratio reflects the number of those actually receiving benefits, such as the number of beneficiaries of any pension benefits among all residents over the statutory pensionable age, or the number of beneficiaries of some kind of income support among all those unemployed or all below the poverty line.

Measurements of the *level of effective coverage* would identify the levels of benefits (usually related to certain benchmark amounts) actually received by beneficiaries, such as unemployment benefits or pensions paid, compared to average earnings or to the minimum wage or the poverty line. In the case of contributory pension schemes, the effective level of coverage may also relate to future benefit levels.

When assessing coverage and gaps in coverage, distinctions need to be made between coverage by (1) contributory social insurance, (2) universal schemes covering all residents (or all residents in a given category[2]), and (3) means-tested schemes potentially covering all those who pass the required test of income and/or assets. In the case of social insurance it makes sense to look at the numbers of those who are actually members of and contributors to such schemes and who thus potentially enjoy – sometimes with their dependants – coverage in the event of any of the contingencies covered by their social insurance. These people fall into a category of persons "protected" in the event of a given contingency. The concept of protected persons may also apply where people are covered by universal or categorical programmes: if there is legislation specifying that all residents, or all residents in a given (e.g. age) category, are entitled to certain benefits or to free access to social services, it can be said that all those specified by law are "protected" in the event of the given contingency. It is, however, rather difficult to specify who is in fact "potentially protected" in the case of income or means-tested benefits or conditional cash transfers.

The above measures of extent and level of coverage are specifically applied to certain areas (branches) of social security (and sometimes even only to specific schemes or types of scheme), not to attempt to provide a generic measure of social security coverage. Ensuring the specificity of coverage indicators by area is essential to arrive at a meaningful analysis and ensure its relevance for policy development.

As an aggregate measure of coverage, the report uses the estimated proportion of the population enjoying comprehensive social security protection.[3] Those enjoying only a basic level of income security (income security at the level of a nationally defined threshold, such as the poverty line) at all stages of the life cycle as well as access to essential health care (as nationally defined) are considered to benefit from basic social protection (the social protection floor, as defined in

[2] Such schemes are also referred to as categorical schemes.

[3] This estimate is based on the number of persons of working age who enjoy comprehensive social security coverage, i.e. are covered by law in all eight areas (sickness, unemployment, old-age, employment injury, family responsibilities, maternity, invalidity, survivorship) in line with Convention No. 102. Health is not included for methodological reasons.

Recommendation No. 202). Those benefiting from coverage (basic or comprehensive) in some of the areas are considered to enjoy only partial basic or partial comprehensive coverage. The ultimate objective of all ILO standards is to provide as many people as possible with comprehensive protection; the intermediate objective is to provide all people with at least a basic level of protection.

Coverage in health

As regards coverage in health, dimensions similar to those used for other branches apply; however, approaches and indicators need to be adjusted, particularly with regard to the provision of medical benefits in kind. For example, the provision of quality medical care requires considering the availability of skilled health workers. Another difference from other branches relates to the fact that taking up health-care benefits often requires private expenditure, even if affiliation to a health system or scheme exists. Thus, implementing social protection rights to health care requires ensuring access to health care if needed and avoiding impoverishment arising from ill health.

Coverage in health has several dimensions:

- **Legal health coverage:** identification of the *proportion of the population that is protected by legislation* or otherwise affiliated to a health system or scheme. It is measured by one indicator, as explained below.
- **Affordability, availability and financial protection of quality benefits:** the scope of quality medical benefits that is available, given e.g. the existence of a sufficient number of skilled health workers that can be accessed when in need without involving financial hardship or impoverishment. It is measured by four proxy indicators, as explained below.

Against this background, assessing coverage in health requires all dimensions to be taken into account simultaneously, using five proxy indicators. They should measure deficits regarding specific thresholds. Only when data are considered from all five indicators *together* are insights provided into the status quo and/or progress towards universal coverage in health.

The indicator for legal health coverage measures the share of a population (percentage of total population) or its specific groups effectively affiliated to or registered in a public or private health system or scheme: mainly national health services, or social, national, private or micro/community-based schemes. It is usually measured as a deficit compared to 100 per cent of the population in a given country and provides information on the current status and progress of population coverage in terms of affiliation for each country and region, and at the global level.

The indicators for affordability, availability and financial protection of quality benefits are:

1. *Extent of out-of-pocket payments (OOP) as a percentage of total health expenditure:* The direct outlays of households, including gratuities and payments in kind, made to health practitioners and suppliers of pharmaceuticals, therapeutic appliances and other goods and services, whose primary intent is to contribute to the restoration or to the enhancement of the health status of individuals or population groups. It includes household payments to public services, non-profit institutions and non-governmental organizations, and non-reimbursable cost-sharing, deductibles, co-payments and fees-for-service, but excludes payments made by companies that deliver medical and paramedical benefits, whether required by law or not, to their employees. It excludes payments for overseas treatment.

2. *Coverage gap due to health professional staff deficit.* This indicator reflects both the supply side of access in terms of availability of health care and the proportion of the population not having access to health care due to the absence of a sufficient health workforce.

The element first focuses on the availability of human resources at a level that guarantees at least basic, but universal, effective access for everybody. To estimate access to the services of skilled medical professionals (physicians and nursing and midwifery personnel), it uses as a proxy the relative difference between the density of health professionals in a given country and its median value in countries with a low level of vulnerability (population access to services of medical professionals in countries with low vulnerability is thus used as a threshold for other countries).

The relative ILO threshold corresponds to the median value in the group of countries assessed as "low vulnerability". Countries have been classified in four groups according to their level of vulnerability: very low, low, high and very high vulnerability (see table AII.1). The classification is based on three criteria: level of poverty, extent of informal economy and fairness of health-financing mechanisms. Proxies used are (1) the incidence of poverty, based on the international poverty line of income or consumption at or below US$2 PPP

Table AII.1 Composition of groups defined by the level of vulnerability

Very low vulnerability	Low vulnerability	High vulnerability	Very high vulnerability
Andorra, Argentina, Australia, Austria, Bahamas, Belarus, Belgium, Bosnia and Herzegovina, Bulgaria, Canada, Croatia, Cyprus, Czech Republic, Denmark, Estonia, Finland, France, Germany, Hungary, Iceland, Ireland, Isle of Man, Israel, Italy, Japan, Jordan, Kazakhstan, Republic of Korea, Republic of, Latvia, Liechtenstein, Lithuania, Luxembourg, Malta, Mauritius, Montenegro, Netherlands, New Zealand, Norway, Occupied Palestinian Territory, Poland, Portugal, Romania, Russian Federation, Serbia, Seychelles, Singapore, Slovakia, Slovenia, Spain, Sweden, Switzerland, Taiwan (China), Ukraine, United Kingdom, United States, Uruguay.	Albania, Algeria, Armenia, Belize, Bolivia, Brazil, Chile, Colombia, Costa Rica, Dominican Republic, Ecuador, Egypt, El Salvador, Fiji, Gabon, Guyana, Iran, Islamic Republic of Iraq, Jamaica, Kyrgyzstan, Malaysia, Maldives, Mexico, Republic of Moldova, Morocco, Panama, Paraguay, Peru, South Africa, Suriname, Syrian Arab Republic, Thailand, The former Yugoslav Republic of Macedonia, Trinidad and Tobago, Tunisia, Turkey, Bolivarian Republic of Venezuela.	Azerbaijan, Bhutan, Botswana, Cambodia, Cameroon, Cabo Verde, China, Côte d'Ivoire, Djibouti, Georgia, Guatemala, Honduras, Indonesia, Kenya, Lesotho, Mauritania, Mongolia, Namibia, Nicaragua, Pakistan, Philippines, Saint Lucia, Sao Tome and Principe, Sri Lanka, Sudan, Swaziland, Tajikistan, Timor-Leste, Turkmenistan, Viet Nam, Yemen.	Angola, Bangladesh, Benin, Burkina Faso, Burundi, Central African Republic, Chad, the Congo, Democratic Republic of the Congo, Ethiopia, Gambia, Ghana, Guinea, Guinea-Bissau, Haiti, India, Lao People's Democratic Republic, Liberia, Madagascar, Malawi, Mali, Mozambique, Nepal, Niger, Nigeria, Papua New Guinea, Rwanda, Senegal, Sierra Leone, Somalia, Togo, Uganda, United Republic of Tanzania, Zambia, Zimbabwe.

a day; (2) non-waged employment as a proxy indicator of informal employment; and (3) with regard to countries with low vulnerability, health expenditure not financed by OOP to a level above 40 per cent of total health expenditure. The population-weighted median number of skilled health workers (physicians and nursing and midwifery personnel) in countries considered to be at low vulnerability serves as the threshold. Given the socio-economic characteristics of these countries and the health-financing mechanisms applied, these countries are considered to be in a position to provide universal access through a sufficient number of health workers enjoying decent working conditions. In 2014, the threshold stands at 41.1 physicians, nursing and midwifery personnel per 10,000 population. Individual countries' deficits are calculated using this threshold and the actual number of health workers.

Another way to look at the indicator is to refer to population not covered due to a deficit from the supply side. In this context, the ILO staff access deficit indicator estimates the dimension of the overall performance of health-care delivery as a percentage of the population that has no access to health care if needed.

3. *Financial deficit*, calculated as per capita expenditure (except OOP) using the relative threshold of the median expenditure in low vulnerability countries as defined under (2) above. In 2014, the threshold stands at US$239 per capita.

4. *Maternal mortality* ratio per 10,000 live births.

Further considerations

The main sources of this information are: country legislation; data on protected persons, beneficiaries, benefits provided, costs and financing from the registers and accounts of the institutions administering the various social security schemes; and household survey data from regular labour force surveys, household income and expenditure surveys, household budget surveys or surveys of similar type, or from surveys specially designed to monitor the coverage and impacts of social security.

To summarize, a number of issues have to be taken into account when measuring coverage:

- Social security coverage can be directly measured only separately for each of the specific branches such as health care, old age or unemployment, or even for a group of specific schemes within each branch. Aggregate coverage measures such as the ADB Social Protection Index can be built only by aggregating the separate coverage indicators for all social security branches.
- Coverage by social security schemes against specific social risks and contingencies can be understood in two ways: potential coverage, measured by the number of persons protected if a given contingency occurs (for example, those covered by social insurance schemes, or contributors to such schemes), and actual coverage, measured by the number of beneficiaries actually receiving benefits or utilizing

services. These two concepts are complementary to each other and should be assessed separately.

- Legal and effective coverage are distinct and must be measured separately. Though people may be legally covered, enforcement of the legal provisions may be incomplete, so that effective coverage is usually lower than legal coverage.
- In measuring the extent of coverage it is important to choose the right numerator and denominator. Ideally, the absolute number of persons covered for a specific risk is divided by the size of the population group targeted by the specific policy or benefit. For example, to measure the extent of actual coverage by old-age pensions, the number of pensioners should be related to the total number of older persons, where both numerator and denominator can be restricted to a given age bracket, such as those over 65 (or above any other statutory pensionable age).
- There is a trade-off between specificity of national circumstances (and relevance of the indicator at the national level regarding, for example, the retirement age) and international comparability.
- Both administrative and survey data are necessary to arrive at a full assessment of coverage. Administrative data are needed to assess potential and actual effective coverage rates. However, the availability and quality of such data vary across countries, and across schemes within countries. Very often, administrative data trace certain administratively registered events (such as payment of contributions or benefits) rather than the people behind such events. This leads to double counting, in particular when aggregating administrative data, as one individual can be contributing to the same scheme from more than one job, or to more than one scheme covering the same contingency, or be receiving similar types of benefit from more than one source.
- Household survey data are particularly important in assessing the level and quality of coverage and its impacts. Also, only household survey data can help to assess the nature of coverage gaps, the characteristics of population groups not covered, and in particular the consequences of their lack of coverage and their need for specific types of coverage. Unfortunately, many regular household surveys still either lack information relevant to assessing coverage, or pose questions that are so various that international comparisons are not possible. Special surveys, too, are rare and also not internationally standardized.

This annex has presented a recommended approach to measuring coverage. Unfortunately, as the data actually available are still limited, it has proved difficult to follow the recommended approach fully in compiling the present report. In consequence, the report is limited to a detailed assessment of coverage in selected social security areas, and does not fully measure all dimensions of coverage; moreover, data are available for too few countries for an assessment of the level and quality of coverage in most of the social security branches to be made. This report therefore presents regional estimates for selected indicators of coverage on the basis of available data. These regional estimates are calculated when data availability ensures that countries included represent at least three quarters of the total population for a given region. Regional averages are weighted, depending on the indicator, by total population, the working-age population, persons in the labour force or in employment. Owing to the limitations in data availability, most of these regional estimates are calculated for the latest available year, which is not necessarily the same for all the countries included. While data availability has already improved since the first edition of this report, it is hoped that further progress in improving national and subnational statistics on social security will further enhance the accuracy of global and regional estimates.

Annex III

Minimum requirements in ILO social security standards: Overview tables

ILO social security standards serve as key references, guiding all ILO policy and technical advice in the field of social security. They also give meaning and definition to the content of the right to social security as laid down in international human rights instruments (notably the Universal Declaration of Human Rights, 1948, and the International Covenant on Economic, Social and Cultural Rights, 1966), thereby constituting essential tools for the realization of this right and the effective implementation of a rights-based approach to social protection.

The ILO's normative social security framework consists of eight up-to-date Conventions and Recommendations. The most prominent of these are the Social Security (Minimum Standards) Convention, 1952 (No. 102), and the Social Protection Floors Recommendation, 2012 (No. 202).[1] Convention No. 102 is unique among international standards in regrouping the nine classical social security contingencies (medical care, sickness, unemployment, old age, employment injury, family responsibilities, maternity, invalidity, survivorship) into a single comprehensive and legally binding instrument. It sets qualitative and quantitative benchmarks for each of these contingencies, which together determine the minimum standards of social security protection to be provided by social security schemes with regard, inter alia, to:

- definition of the contingency (what must be covered?)
- persons protected (who must be covered?)
- type and rate of benefits (what should be provided?)
- entitlement conditions, including qualifying period (what should a person do to get the right to a benefit?)
- duration of benefit and waiting period (how long must the benefit be paid/provided for?)

In addition, it establishes common rules of collective organization, financing and management, and lays down principles for good governance, including the general responsibility of the State for the due provision of benefits and proper administration of social security systems, participatory management, guarantee of defined benefits, adjustment of pensions, right of appeal and complaint, collective financing and risk-pooling, and periodical actuarial valuations. Convention No. 102 continues to serve as a yardstick and reference in the gradual development of comprehensive social security coverage at the national level and as a means to prevent the levelling down of social security systems worldwide, as confirmed by the International Labour Conference in 2011 (ILO, 2012a).

Tables AIII.1–AIII.9 below provide a summary overview of some of the key requirements set out in ILO standards.

[1] Convention No. 102 has been ratified to date by 50 countries, most recently by Brazil (2009), Bulgaria (2008), Honduras (2012), Jordan (2014), Romania (2009) and Uruguay (2010), and provides guidance for all 185 ILO member States. ILO Recommendations are not open for ratification.

Table AIII.1 Main requirements: ILO social security standards on health protection

	Convention No. 102 **Minimum standards**	**Convention No. 130a and Recommendation No. 134b** **Higher standards**	**Recommendation No. 202** **Basic protection**
What should be covered?	Any ill health condition, whatever its cause; pregnancy, childbirth and their consequences	The need for medical care of curative and preventive nature	Any condition requiring health care, including maternity
Who should be covered?	At least: • 50% of all employees, and wives and children; *or* • categories of the economically active population (forming not less than 20% of all residents, and wives and children); *or* • all residents with means under prescribed threshold	**C.130:** All employees, including apprentices, and their wives and children; *or* • categories of the active population forming not less than 75% of whole active population, and the wives and children); *or* • prescribed class of residents forming not less than 75% of all residents **R.134:** In addition: persons in casual employment and their families, family businesses, all economically active persons and their families, all residents	Universality of protection, through progressive realization; at least all residents and children should benefit from basic guarantee of access to at least essential health care; non-residents should also be in line with the country's international obligations
What should the benefit be?	In case of ill health: general practitioner care, specialist care at hospitals, essential medications and supplies, hospitalization if necessary In case of pregnancy, childbirth and their consequences: prenatal, childbirth and post-natal care by medical practitioners and qualified midwives, hospitalization if necessary	**C.130**: The medical care required by the person's condition, with a view to maintaining, restoring or improving health and ability to work and attend to personal needs, including at least: general practitioner care, specialist care at hospitals, allied care and benefits, essential medical supplies, hospitalization if necessary, dental care and medical rehabilitation **R.134**: Also the supply of medical aids (e.g. eyeglasses) and services for convalescence	Goods and services constituting essential health care, including maternity care, meeting accessibility, availability, acceptability and quality criteria; free prenatal and post-natal medical care for the most vulnerable; higher levels of protection should be provided to as many people as possible, as soon as possible
What should the benefit duration be?	As long as ill health, or pregnancy and childbirth and their consequences, persist. May be limited to 26 weeks in each case of sickness. Benefit should not be suspended while beneficiary receives sickness benefits or is treated for a disease recognized as requiring prolonged care.	**C.130:** Throughout the contingency. May be limited to 26 weeks where a beneficiary ceases to belong to the categories of persons protected, unless he/she is already receiving medical care for a disease requiring prolonged care, or as long as he/she is paid a cash sickness benefit **R.134:** Throughout the contingency	As long as required by the health status
What conditions can be prescribed for entitlement to a benefit?	Qualifying period may be prescribed as necessary to preclude abuse.	**C.130:** Qualifying period may be prescribed as necessary to preclude abuse **R.134:** Right to benefit should not be subject to qualifying period	Persons in need of health care should not face hardship and an increased risk of poverty due to financial consequences of accessing essential health care Should be defined at national level and prescribed by law, applying principles of non-discrimination, responsiveness to special needs and social inclusion, and ensuring the rights and dignity of people

[a] Medical Care and Sickness Benefits Convention, 1969.b Medical Care and Sickness Benefits Recommendation, 1959.

Table AIII.2 Main requirements: ILO social security standards on sickness benefits

	Convention No. 102 Minimum standards	Convention No. 130 and Recommendation No. 134 Higher standards	Recommendation No. 202 Basic protection
What should be covered?	Incapacity to work resulting from illness that results in the suspension of income	**C.130**: Incapacity to work resulting from sickness and involving suspension of earnings **R.134**: Also covers periods of absence from work resulting in loss of earnings due to convalescence, curative or preventative medical care, rehabilitation or quarantine, or due to caring for dependants	Basic income security for those who are unable to earn a sufficient income due to sickness
Who should be protected?	At least: • 50% of all employees; *or* • categories of the economically active population (forming not less than 20% of all residents); *or* • all residents with means under a prescribed threshold	**C.130:** All employees, including apprentices; *or* • categories of economically active population (forming not less than 75% of whole economically active population); *or* • all residents with means under prescribed threshold **R.134**: Extension to persons in casual employment, family businesses, all economically active persons, all residents	At least all residents of active age, subject to international obligations
What should be the benefit?	Periodic payments; at least 45% of reference wage	**C. 130**: Periodic payments: at least 60% of reference wage; in case of death of the beneficiary, benefit for funeral expenses **R.134:** Benefit should be 66.66% of reference wage	Benefits in cash or in kind at a level that ensures basic income security, so as to secure effective access to necessary goods and services; prevents or alleviates poverty, vulnerability and social exclusion; and enables life in dignity
What should the benefit duration be?	As long as the person remains unable to engage in gainful employment due to illness; possible waiting period of max. three days before benefit is paid; benefit duration may be limited to 26 weeks in each case of sickness	**C. 130:** As long as the person remains unable to engage in gainful employment due to illness; possible waiting period of max three days before benefit is paid; benefit duration may be limited to 52 weeks in each case of sickness **R.134**: Benefit should be paid for full duration of sickness or other contingencies covered	As long as the incapacity to earn a sufficient income due to sickness remains
What conditions can be prescribed for entitlement to a benefit?	Qualifying period may be prescribed as necessary to prevent abuse	**C. 130**: Qualifying period may be prescribed as necessary to prevent abuse	Should be defined at national level, and prescribed by law, applying principles of non-discrimination, responsiveness to special needs and social inclusion, and ensuring the rights and dignity of people

Table AIII.3 Main requirements: ILO social security standards on unemployment protection

	Convention No. 102 **Minimum standards**	**Convention No. 168[a] and Recommendation No. 176[b]** **Higher standards**	**Recommendation No. 202** **Basic protection**
What should be covered?	Suspension of earnings due to inability to find suitable employment for capable and available person	**C.168**: Loss of earnings due to inability to find suitable employment for capable and available person actively seeking work. Protection should be extended to loss of earnings due to partial unemployment, suspension or reduction of earnings due to temporary suspension of work, part-time workers seeking full-time work **R.176**: Provides guidance for assessing suitability of potential employment	Basic income security for those who are unable to earn sufficient income in case of unemployment
Who should be protected?	At least: • 50% of all employees; *or* • all residents with means under prescribed threshold.	**C.168**: At least 85% of employees, including public employees and apprentices; all residents with means under prescribed threshold. Coverage should be extended to persons seeking work who have never been, or have ceased to be, recognized as unemployed or covered by unemployment protection schemes **R.176:** Coverage should be extended progressively to all employees as well as to persons experiencing hardship during waiting period	At least all residents of active age, subject to international obligations
What should be the benefit?	Periodic payments; at least 45% of reference wage	**C.168:** Periodic payments: at least 50% of reference wage; *or* total benefits must guarantee the beneficiary healthy and reasonable living conditions **R.176:** For partial employment: total benefit and earnings from the part-time work should reach the sum of previous earnings from full-time work and the amount of full unemployment benefit	Benefits in cash or in kind at a level that ensures basic income security, so as to secure effective access to necessary goods and services; prevents or alleviates poverty, vulnerability and social exclusion; and enables life in dignity
What should the benefit duration be?	For schemes covering employees: at least 13 weeks of benefits within a period of 12 months For means-tested (non-contributory) schemes: at least 26 weeks within a period of 12 months Possible waiting period of max seven days	**C. 168**: Throughout the unemployment period; possibility to limit initial duration of payment of the benefit to 26 weeks in case of unemployment or 39 weeks over any period of 24 months; possible waiting period of max seven days **R.176**: Benefit duration should be extended until pensionable age for unemployed persons who have reached a prescribed age	As long as the incapacity to earn a sufficient income remains
What conditions can be prescribed for entitlement to a benefit?	Qualifying period may be prescribed as necessary to prevent abuse	**C.168:** Qualifying period may be prescribed as necessary to prevent abuse **R.176**: Qualifying period should be adapted or waived for new jobseekers	Should be defined at national level, and prescribed by law, applying principles of non-discrimination, responsiveness to special needs and social inclusion, and ensuring the rights and dignity of people

[a] Employment Promotion and Protection against Unemployment Convention, 1988. [b] Employment Promotion and Protection against Unemployment Recommendation, 1988.

Table AIII.4 Main requirements: ILO social security standards on income security in old age (old-age pensions)

	Convention No. 102 **Minimum standards**	**Convention No. 128a and Recommendation No. 131b** **Higher standards**	**Recommendation No. 202** **Basic protection**
What should be covered?	Survival beyond a prescribed age (65 or higher according to working ability of elderly persons in country)	**C. 128**: Same as C.102; also, the prescribed age should be lower than 65 for persons with occupations deemed arduous or unhealthy **R. 131**: In addition, the prescribed age should be lowered based on social grounds	Basic income security for older persons
Who should be protected?	At least: • 50% of all employees; *or* • categories of active population (forming not less than 20% of all residents); *or* • all residents with means under prescribed threshold	**C. 128**: All employees, including apprentices; *or* • categories of economically active population (forming not least 75% of whole economically active population); *or* • all residents or all residents with means under prescribed threshold **R.131**: Coverage should be extended to persons whose employment is of casual nature; *or* all economically active persons	All residents of a nationally prescribed age, subject to international obligations
What should be the benefit?	Periodic payments: at least 40% of reference wage; adjustment following substantial changes in general level of earnings and/or cost of living	**C.128**: Periodic payments: at least 45% of reference wage; adjustment following substantial changes in general level of earnings and/or cost of living **R.131:** at least 55% of reference wage; minimum amount of old-age benefit should be fixed by legislation to ensure a minimum standard of living; level of benefit should be increased if beneficiary requires constant help	Benefits in cash or in kind at a level that ensures basic income security, so as to secure effective access to necessary goods and services; prevents or alleviates poverty, vulnerability and social exclusion; and enables life in dignity Levels should be regularly reviewed
What should the benefit duration be?	From the prescribed age to the death of beneficiary	From the prescribed age to the death of beneficiary	From the nationally prescribed age to the death of beneficiary
What conditions can be prescribed for entitlement to a benefit?	30 years of contribution or employment (for contributory schemes) or 20 years of residence (for non-contributory schemes) Entitlement to a reduced benefit after 15 years of contribution or employment	**C.128**: Same as C.102 **R.131:** 20 years of contributions or employment (for contributory schemes) *or* 15 years of residence (for non-contributory schemes) Periods of incapacity due to sickness, accident or maternity, and periods of involuntary unemployment, in respect of which benefit was paid, and compulsory military service, should be assimilated to periods of contribution or employment for calculation of the qualifying period fulfilled	Should be defined at national level and prescribed by law, applying the principles of non-discrimination, responsiveness to special needs and social inclusion, and ensuring the rights and dignity of older persons

[a] Invalidity, Old-Age and Survivors' Benefits Convention, 1967. [b] Invalidity, Old-Age and Survivors' Benefits Recommendation, 1967.

Table AIII.5 Main requirements: ILO social security standards on employment injury protection

	Convention No. 102 Minimum standards	Convention No. 121[a] and Recommendation No. 121[b] Higher standards	Recommendation No. 202 Basic protection
What should be covered?	Ill health; and incapacity for work due to work-related accident or disease, resulting in suspension of earnings; total loss of earning capacity or partial loss at a prescribed degree, likely to be permanent, or corresponding loss of faculty; loss of support for the family in case of death of breadwinner	**C.121**: Same as C.102.	Basic income security for those who are unable to earn a sufficient income due to employment injury
Who should be protected?	At least 50% of all employees and their wives and children	**C. 121**: All public and private sector employees including members of cooperatives and apprentices; in case of death, spouse, children and other dependants as prescribed **R.121**: Coverage should be extended progressively to all categories of employees and other dependent family members (parents, brothers and sisters, and grandchildren)	At least all residents of active age, subject to international obligations
What should the benefit be?	*Medical care and allied benefits:* general practitioner, specialist, dental care, nursing care; medication, rehabilitation, prosthetics etc., with a view to maintaining, restoring or improving health and ability to work and attend to personal needs *Cash benefits:* • Periodic payments: at least 50% of reference wage in cases of incapacity to work or invalidity; at least 40% of reference wage in cases of death of breadwinner • Adjustment of long-term benefits following substantial changes in general level of earnings and/ or cost of living • Lump sum if incapacity is slight and competent authority is satisfied that the sum will be used properly	**C.121**: *Medical care:* Same as C. 102; also at the emergency and follow-up treatment at place of work *Cash benefits:* Periodic payments: at least 60% of reference wage in cases of incapacity for work or invalidity; at least 50% of reference wage in case of death of breadwinner Lump sum: same conditions as C.102, plus consent of injured person required **R.121**: Costs of constant help or attendance should be covered when such care is required Cash benefit: not less than 66.67% of previous earnings; adjustment of long-term benefits taking into account general levels of earnings or cost of living Lump sum allowed where degree of incapacity is less than 25%; should bear an equitable relationship to periodic payments and not be less than periodic payments for three years	Benefits in cash or in kind at a level that ensures basic income security, so as to secure effective access to necessary goods and services; prevents or alleviates poverty, vulnerability and social exclusion; and enables life in dignity Levels should be regularly reviewed
What should the benefit duration be?	As long as the person is in need of health care or remains incapacitated No waiting period except for temporary incapacity to work for a maximum of three days	**C.121**: As long as the person is in need of health care or remains incapacitated **R.121**: In addition, cash benefits should be paid from first day in each case of suspension of earnings	As long as the incapacity to earn a sufficient income remains
What conditions can be prescribed for entitlement to a benefit?	No qualifying period allowed for benefits to injured persons For dependants, benefit may be made conditional on spouse being presumed incapable of self-support and children remaining under a prescribed age	**C.121**: Same as C.102	Should be defined at national level and prescribed by law, applying the principles of non-discrimination, responsiveness to special needs and social inclusion, and ensuring the rights and dignity of the injured people

[a] Employment Injury Benefits Convention, 1964. [b] Employment Injury Benefits Recommendation, 1964.

Table AIII.6 Main requirements: ILO social security standards on family/child benefits

	ILO Convention No. 102 **Minimum standards**	**ILO Recommendation No. 202** **Basic protection**
What should be covered?	Responsibility for child maintenance	Basic income security for children
Who should be protected?	At least 50% of all employees; *or* • categories of active population (forming not less than 20% of all residents; *or* • all residents with means under prescribed threshold	All children
What should the benefit be?	• Periodic payments; or • provision for food, clothing, housing, holidays or domestic help; *or* • combination of both Total value of benefits calculated at a *global* level: • at least 3% of reference wage multiplied by number of children of covered people; or • a least 1.5% of reference wage multiplied by number of children of all residents	Benefits in cash or in kind providing access to nutrition, education, care and other necessary goods and services for children
What should the benefit duration be?	At least from birth to 15 years of age or school-leaving age	For the duration of childhood
What conditions can be prescribed for entitlement to a benefit?	• Three months' contributions or employment (for contributory or employment based schemes); • one year's residence (for non-contributory schemes)	Should be defined at national level and prescribed by law, applying the principles of non-discrimination, responsiveness to special needs and social inclusion, and ensuring the rights and dignity of children

Table AIII.7 Main requirements: ILO social security standards on maternity protection

	ILO Convention No. 102 Minimum standards	ILO Convention No. 183a and Recommendation No. 191b Higher standards	ILO Recommendation No. 202 Basic protection
What should be covered?	Medical care required by pregnancy, confinement and their consequences; resulting lost wages	**C. 183**: Medical care required by pregnancy, child birth and their consequences; resulting lost wages **R.191**: Same as **C.183.**	Goods and services constituting essential maternity health care Basic income security for those who are unable to earn a sufficient income due to maternity
Who should be protected?	At least: • 50% of all women employees; *or* • all women in categories of the active population (forming not less than 20% of all residents); *or* • all women with means under prescribed threshold	**C. 183**: All employed women including those in atypical forms of dependant work **R.191**: Same as **C.183.**	At least all women who are residents, subject to international obligations
What should the benefit be?	*Medical benefits:* At least: • prenatal, confinement and post-natal care by qualified practitioners; • hospitalization if necessary *Cash benefits:* periodic payment: at least 45% of the reference wage	**C. 183**: *Medical benefits:* At least prenatal, childbirth and post-natal care by qualified practitioners; hospitalization if necessary Daily remunerated breaks or reduced hours for breastfeeding *Cash benefits:* At least 66.67% of previous earnings; should maintain mother and child in proper conditions of health and a suitable standard of living **R.191**: Cash benefits should be raised to the full amount of the woman's previous earnings	*Medical benefits:* should meet criteria of availability, accessibility, acceptability and quality; free prenatal and post-natal medical care should be considered for the most vulnerable *Benefits in cash or in kind:* should ensure basic income security, so as to secure effective access to necessary goods and services, and be at a level that prevents or alleviates poverty, vulnerability and social exclusion and allows life in dignity. Levels should be regularly reviewed
What should the benefit duration be?	At least 12 weeks for cash benefits	**C. 183**: 14 weeks' maternity leave, including 6 weeks' compulsory leave after childbirth; additional leave before or after maternity leave in case of illness, complications or risk of complications arising from pregnancy or childbirth **R.191**: 18 weeks' maternity leave Extension of the maternity leave in the event of multiple births	As long as the incapacity to earn a sufficient income remains
What conditions can be prescribed for entitlement to a benefit?	As considered necessary to preclude abuse	**C.183**: Conditions must be met by a large majority of women; those who do not meet conditions are entitled to social assistance **R.191**: Same as C.183	Should be defined at national level and prescribed by law, applying the principles of non-discrimination, responsiveness to special needs and social inclusion, and ensuring the rights and dignity of women

[a] Maternity Protection Convention, 2000. [b] Maternity Protection Recommendation, 2000.

Table AIII.8 Main requirements: ILO social security standards on disability benefits

	ILO Convention No. 102 Minimum standards	ILO Convention No. 128 and Recommendation No. 131 Higher standards	ILO Recommendation No. 202 Basic protection
What should be covered?	Inability to engage in any gainful activity, likely to be permanent, or that persists beyond sickness benefit (total invalidity)	**C.128**: Incapacity to engage in any gainful activity, likely to be permanent, or that persists beyond temporary or initial incapacity (total invalidity) **R.131**: Incapacity to engage in an activity involving substantial gain (total and partial invalidity)	Basic income security for those who are unable to earn a sufficient income due to disability
Who should be protected?	At least: • 50% of all employees; *or* • categories of the active population (forming not less than 20% of all residents); *or* • all residents with means under prescribed threshold	**C.128:** All employees, including apprentices; *or* • at least 75% of economically active population; *or* • all residents *or* all residents with means under prescribed threshold **R.131:** Coverage should be extended to persons in casual employment and all economically active persons	At least all residents, subject to international obligations
What should the benefit be?	Periodic payment: at least 40% of reference wage Adjustment following substantial changes in general level of earnings and/or cost of living	**C.128:** Periodic payment: at least 50% of reference wage **R.131**: Reduced benefit for partial invalidity	Benefits in cash or in kind at a level that ensures basic income security, so as to secure effective access to necessary goods and services; prevents or alleviates poverty, vulnerability and social exclusion; and enables life in dignity
What should the benefit duration be?	As long as the person remains unable to engage in gainful employment or until old-age pension is paid	As long as the person remains incapacitated or until old-age pension is paid	As long as the incapacity to earn a sufficient income remains
What conditions can be prescribed for entitlement to a benefit?	15 years of contributions or employment (for contributory schemes) or 10 years of residence (for non-contributory schemes); entitlement to a reduced benefit after five years of contributions or three years of residence.	**C.128:** 15 years of contributions (for contributory schemes) or employment, *or* 10 years of residence (for non-contributory schemes) Entitlement to a reduced benefit after five years of contributions or three years of residence **R.131**: Five years of contributions, employment or residence; qualifying period should be removed (or reduced) for young workers or where invalidity is due to an accident Periods of incapacity due to sickness, accident or maternity and periods of involuntary unemployment, in respect of which benefit was paid, and compulsory military service, should be assimilated to periods of contribution or employment for calculation of the qualifying period fulfilled	No specific indication; entitlement conditions should be defined at national level, applying the principles of non-discrimination, responsiveness to special needs and social inclusion and ensuring the rights and dignity of persons with disabilities; they should be prescribed by law

Table AIII.9 Main requirements: ILO social security standards on survivors' benefits

	ILO Convention No. 102 Minimum standards	ILO Convention No. 128 and Recommendation No. 131 Higher standards	ILO Recommendation No. 202 Basic protection
What should be covered?	Widow's or children's loss of support in the event of death of the breadwinner	**C.128**: Widow's or children's loss of support in case of death of breadwinner **R.131**: Same as C.128	Basic income security for those who are unable to earn a sufficient income due to the absence of family support.
Who should be protected?	Wives and children of breadwinners representing at least 50% of all employees; *or* • wives and children of members of economically active persons representing at least 20% of all residents; *or* • all resident widows and children with means under prescribed threshold	**C.128**: Wives, children and other dependants of employees or apprentices; *or* • wives, children and other dependants forming not less than 75% of active persons; *or* • all widows, children and other dependants who are residents *or* who are residents *and* whose means are under prescribed threshold. **R.131**: In addition, coverage should progressively be extended to wives and children and other dependants of persons in casual employment or all economically active persons. Also, an invalid and dependent widower should enjoy same entitlements as a widow	At least all residents and children, subject to international obligations
What should the benefit be?	Periodic payment: at least 40% of reference wage Adjustment following substantial changes in general level of earnings and/or cost of living	**C. 128**: At least 45% of reference wage. Rates must be adjusted to cost of living **R. 131**: Benefits should be increased to 55% of reference wage; a minimum survivors' benefit should be fixed to ensure a minimum standard of living	Benefits in cash or in kind should ensure basic income security so as to secure effective access to necessary goods and services at a level that prevents or alleviates poverty, vulnerability and social exclusion and allows life in dignity. Levels should be regularly reviewed
What should the benefit duration be?	Until children reach active age; no limitation for widows	**C.128 and R.131**: Until children reach active age or longer if disabled; no limitation for widows.	As long as the incapacity to earn a sufficient income remains
What conditions can be prescribed for entitlement to a benefit?	15 years of contributions or employment (for contributory or employment based schemes) or 10 years of residence (for non-contributory schemes); entitlement to a reduced benefit after five years of contributions For widows, benefits may be conditional on being incapable of self-support; for children, until 15 years of age or school-leaving age	**C.128:** same as C.102; In addition, possible to require a prescribed age for widow, not higher than that prescribed for old-age benefit. No requirement of age for an invalid widow or a widow caring for a dependent child of deceased. **R.131**: same as **C.128;** Periods of incapacity due to sickness, accident or maternity and periods of involuntary unemployment, in respect of which benefit was paid and compulsory military service, should be assimilated to periods of contribution or employment for calculation of the qualifying period fulfilled.	Should be defined at national level and prescribed by law, applying the principles of non-discrimination, responsiveness to special needs and social inclusion, and ensuring the rights and dignity of people.

Annex IV
Statistical tables

Part A. The demographic, economic and labour market environment

For the tables in Part A, see: http://www.social-protection.org/gimi/gess/ShowTheme.do?tid=3985

Demographic indicators
- Table A.1. Demographic trends: Dependency ratios
- Table A.2. Demographic trends: Ageing
- Table A.3. Fertility, child and maternal mortality, life expectancy at birth
- Table A.4. Life expectancy at 20, 60, 65 and 80 years old, exact age, both sexes (in years)

Labour force and employment indicators
- Table A.5. Labour force to population ratios at ages 15–64
- Table A.6. Labour force to population ratios at ages 65+
- Table A.7. Employment to population ratio at ages 15–24
- Table A.8. Employment to population ratios at age 15+
- Table A.9. Status in employment (latest available year)
- Table A.10. Unemployment as a percentage of the labour force

Economic and poverty indicators
- Table A.11. Poverty and income distribution
- Table A.12. GDP and Human Development Index (HDI), various years

Part B. Social security coverage and expenditure

- Table B.1. Ratification of ILO social security Conventions, by region
- Table B.2. Overview of national social security systems

Unemployment
- Table B.3. Unemployment: Indicators of effective coverage. Unemployed who actually receive benefits (percentages)
- Table B.4. Employment injury: Key features of main social security programmes

Maternity
- Table B.5. Maternity: Key features of main social security programmes (cash benefits)

Old age
- Table B.6. Old-age pensions: Key features of main social security programmes
- Table B.7. Non-contributory pension schemes: Main features and indicators
- Table B.8. Old-age effective coverage: Active contributors (latest available year)
- Table B.9. Old-age effective coverage: Old-age pension beneficiaries

Health-specific indicators
- Table B.10. Total (public and private) health-care expenditure not financed by private households' out-of-pocket payments (percentage)
- Table B.11. The multiple dimensions of health coverage

Social protection expenditure
- Table B.12. Public social protection expenditure, 1990 to latest available year (percentage of GDP)
- Table B.13. Public social protection expenditure by guarantee, latest available year (percentage of GDP)

Table B.1 Ratification of ILO social security Conventions, by region

Country	Branch								
	Medical care C.102 C.130	Sickness C.102 C.130	Unemployment C.102 C.168	Old age C.102 C.128	Employment injury C.102 C.121	Family C.102	Maternity C.102 C.183	Invalidity C.102 C.128	Survivors C.102 C.128
Africa									
Benin							C.183 (2012)		
Burkina Faso							C.183 (2013)		
Democratic Republic of the Congo				C.102 (1987)	C.121 (1967)	C.102 (1987)		C.102 (1987)	C.102 (1987)
Guinea					C.121 (1967)				
Libya	C.102 (1975) C.130 (1975)	C.102 (1975) C.130 (1975)	C.102 (1975)	C.102 (1975) C.128 (1975)	C.102 (1975) C.121 (1975)	C.102 (1975)	C.102 (1975)	C.102 (1975) C.128 (1975)	C.102 (1975) C.128 (1975)
Mali							C.183 (2008)		
Morocco							C.183 (2011)		
Mauritania				C.102 (1968)	C.102 (1968)	C.102 (1968)		C.102 (1968)	C.102 (1968)
Niger				C.102 (1966)	C.102 (1966)	C.102 (1966)	C.102 (1966)		
Senegal					C.102 (1962) C.121 (1966)	C.102 (1962)	C.102 (1962)		
Togo (not in force)				C.102 (2013)		C.102 (2013)	C.102 (2013)		C.102 (2013)
Americas									
Barbados		C.102 (1972)		C.102 (1972) C.128 (1972)	C.102 (1972)			C.102 (1972) C.128 (1972)	C.102 (1972)
Belize							C.183 (2005)		
Bolivia (Plurinational State of)	C.102 (1977) C.130 (1977)	C.102 (1977) C.130 (1977)		C.102 (1977) C.128 (1977)	C.102 (1977) C.121 (1977)	C.102 (1977)	C.102 (1977) C.183 (1977)	C.102 (1977) C.128 (1977)	C.102 (1977) C.128 (1977)
Brazil	C.102 (2009)	C.102 (2009)	C.102 (2009) C.168 (1993)	C.102 (2009)	C.102 (2009)	C.102 (2009)	C.102 (2009)	C.102 (2009)	C.102 (2009)
Chile					C.121 (1999)				
Costa Rica	C.102 (1972) C.130 (1972)	C.130 (1972)		C.102 (1972)	C.102 (1972)	C.102 (1972)	C.102 (1972)	C.102 (1972)	C.102 (1972)
Cuba							C.183 (2004)		
Ecuador	C.130 (1978)	C.102 (1974) C.130 (1978)		C.102 (1974) C.128 (1978)	C.102 (1974) C.121 (1978)			C.102 (1974) C.128 (1978)	C.102 (1974) C.128 (1978)
Honduras	C.102 (2012)	C.102 (2012)		C.102 (2012)			C.102 (2012)	C.102 (2012)	C.102 (2012)
Mexico	C.102 (1961)	C.102 (1961)		C.102 (1961)	C.102 (1961)		C.102 (1961)	C.102 (1961)	C.102 (1961)

Table B.1 Ratification of ILO social security Conventions, by region

Country	Branch								
	Medical care C.102 C.130	Sickness C.102 C.130	Unemployment C.102 C.168	Old age C.102 C.128	Employment injury C.102 C.121	Family C.102	Maternity C.102 C.183	Invalidity C.102 C.128	Survivors C.102 C.128
Peru	C.102 (1961)	C.102 (1961)		C.102 (1961)			C.102 (1961)	C.102 (1961)	
Uruguay	C.102 (2010) C.130 (1973)	C.130 (1973)	C.102 (2010)	C.128 (1973)	C.121 (1973)*	C.102 (2010)	C.102 (2010)	C 128 (1973)	C.128 (1973)
Venezuela, Bolivarian Republic of	C.102 (1982) C.130 (1982)	C.102 (1982) C.130 (1982)		C.102 (1982) C.128 (1983)	C.102 (1982) C.121 (1982)		C.102 (1982)	C.102 (1982) C.128 (1983)	C.102 (1982) C.128 (1983)
Middle East									
Israel				C.102 (1955)	C.102 (1955)				C.102 (1955)
Jordan (not in force)				C.102 (2014)	C.102 (2014)			C.102 (2014)	C.102 (2014)
Asia									
Azerbaijan							C.183 (2010)		
Japan		C.102 (1976)	C.102 (1976)	C.102 (1976)	C.102 (1976) C.121 (1974)*				
Kazakhstan							C.183 (2012)		
Europe									
Albania	C.102 (2006)	C.102 (2006)	C.102 (2006) C.168 (2006)	C.102 (2006)	C.102 (2006)		C.102 (2006) C.183 (2004)	C.102 (2006)	C.102 (2006)
Austria	C.102 (1969)		C.102 (1978)	C.102 (1969) C.128 (1969)		C.102 (1969)	C.102 (1969) C.183 (2004)		
Belarus							C.183 (2004)		
Belgium	C.102 (1959)	C.102 (1959)	C.102 (1959) C.168 (2011)	C.102 (1959)	C.102 (1959) C.121 (1970)	C.102 (1959)	C.102 (1959)	C.102 (1959)	C.102 (1959)
Bosnia and Herzegovina	C.102 (1993)	C.102 (1993)	C.102 (1993)	C.102 (1993)	C.102 (1993) C.121 (1993)		C.102 (1993) C.183 (2012)		C.102 (1993)
Bulgaria	C.102 (2008)	C.102 (2008)		C.102 (2008)	C.102 (2008)	C.102 (2008)	C.102 (2008) C.183 (2001)		C.102 (2008)
Croatia	C.102 (1991)	C.102 (1991)	C.102 (1991)	C.102 (1991)	C.102 (1991) C.121 (1991)		C.102 (1991)		C.102 (1991)
Cyprus		C.102 (1991)	C.102 (1991)	C.102 (1991)	C.102 (1991) C.121 (1966)		C.183 (2005)	C.102 (1991)	C.102 (1991) C.128 (1969)
Czech Republic	C.102 (1993) C.130 (1993)	C.102 (1993) C.130 (1993)		C.102 (1993) C.128 (1993)		C.102 (1993)	C.102 (1993)	C.102 (1993)	C.102 (1993)

Table B.1 Ratification of ILO social security Conventions, by region

Country	Branch								
	Medical care C.102 C.130	Sickness C.102 C.130	Unemployment C.102 C.168	Old age C.102 C.128	Employment injury C.102 C.121	Family C.102	Maternity C.102 C.183	Invalidity C.102 C.128	Survivors C.102 C.128
Denmark	C.102 (1955) C.130 (1978)	C.130 (1978)	C.102 (1955)	C.102 (1955)	C.102 (1955)			C.102 (1955)	
Finland	C.130 (1974)	C.130 (1974)	C.168 (1990)	C.128 (1976)	C.121 (1968)*			C.128 (1976)	C.128 (1976)
France	C.102 (1974)		C.102 (1974)	C.102 (1974)	C.102 (1974)	C.102 (1974)	C.102 (1974)	C.102 (1974)	
Germany	C.102 (1958) C.130 (1974)	C.102 (1958) C.130 (1974)	C.102 (1958)	C.102 (1958) C.128 (1971)	C.102 (1958) C.121 (1972)	C.102 (1958)	C.102 (1958)	C.102 (1958) C.128 (1971)	C.102 (1958) C.128 (1971)
Greece	C.102 (1955)	C.102 (1955)	C.102 (1955)	C.102 (1955)	C.102 (1955)		C.102 (1955)	C.102 (1955)	C.102 (1955)
Hungary							C.183 (2003)		
Iceland				C.102 (1961)		C.102 (1961)		C.102 (1961)	
Ireland		C.102 (1968)	C.102 (1968)		C.121 (1969)				C.102 (1968)
Italy				C.102 (1956)		C.102 (1956)	C.102 (1956) C.183 (2001)		
Latvia							C.183 (2009)		
Lithuania							C.183 (2003)		
Luxembourg	C.102 (1964) C.130 (1980)	C.102 (1964) C.130 (1980)	C.102 (1964)	C.102 (1964)	C.102 (1964) C.121 (1972)	C.102 (1964)	C.102 (1964) C.183 (2008)	C.102 (1964)	C.102 (1964)
Moldova, Republic of							C.183 (2006)		
Montenegro	C.102 (2006)	C.102 (2006)	C.102 (2006)	C.102 (2006)	C.102 (2006) C.121 (2006)		C.102 (2006) C.183 (2012)		C.102 (2006)
Netherlands	C.102 (1962) C.130 (2006)	C.102 (1962) C.130 (2006)	C.102 (1962)	C.102 (1962) C.128 (1969)	C.102 (1962) C.121 (1966)*	C.102 (1962)	C.102 (1962) C.183 (2009)	C.102 (1962) C.128 (1969)	C.102 (1962) C.128 (1969)
Norway	C.102 (1954) C.130 (1972)	C.102 (1954) C.130 (1972)	C.102 (1954) C.168 (1990)	C.102 (1954) C.128 (1968)	C.102 (1954)	C.102 (1954)		C.128 (1968)	C.128 (1968)
Poland	C.102 (2003)			C.102 (2003)		C.102 (2003)	C.102 (2003)		C.102 (2003)
Portugal	C.102 (1994)	C.102 (1994)	C.102 (1994)	C.102 (1994)	C.102 (1994)	C.102 (1994)	C.102 (1994) C.183 (2012)	C.102 (1994)	C.102 (1994)
Romania	C.102 (2009)	C.102 (2009)	C.168 (1992)	C.102 (2009)		C.102 (2009)	C.102 (2009) C.183 (2002)		
Serbia	C.102 (2000)	C.102 (2000)	C.102 (2000)	C.102 (2000)	C.102 (2000) C.121 (2000)		C.102 (2000) C.183 (2010)		C.102 (2000)
Slovakia	C.102 (1993) C.130 (1993)	C.102 (1993) C.130 (1993)		C.102 (1993) C.128 (1993)		C.102 (1993)	C.102 (1993) C.183 (2000)	C.102 (1993)	C.102 (1993)

Table B.1 Ratification of ILO social security Conventions, by region

Country	Branch								
	Medical care C.102 C.130	Sickness C.102 C.130	Unemployment C.102 C.168	Old age C.102 C.128	Employment injury C.102 C.121	Family C.102	Maternity C.102 C.183	Invalidity C.102 C.128	Survivors C.102 C.128
Slovenia	C.102 (1992)	C.102 (1992)	C.102 (1992)	C.102 (1992)	C.102 (1992) C.121 (1992)		C.102 (1992) C.183 (2010)		C.102 (1992)
Spain	C.102 (1988)	C.102 (1988)	C.102 (1988)		C.102 (1988)				
Sweden	C.102 (1953) C.130 (1970)	C.102 (1953) C.130 (1970)	C.102 (1953) C.168 (1990)	C.128 (1968)	C.102 (1953) C.121 (1969)	C.102 (1953)	C.102 (1953)	C.128 (1968)	C.128 (1968)
Switzerland			C.168 (1990)	C.102 (1977) C.128 (1977)	C.102 (1977)	C.102 (1977)		C.102 (1977) C.128 (1977)	C.102 (1977) C.128 (1977)
The Former Yugoslav Rep. of Macedonia	C.102 (1991)	C.102 (1991)	C.102 (1991)	C.102 (1991)	C.102 (1991) C.121 (1991)		C.102 (1991) C.183 (2012)		C.102 (1991)
Turkey	C.102 (1975)	C.102 (1975)		C.102 (1975)	C.102 (1975)		C.102 (1975)	C.102 (1975)	C.102 (1975)
United Kingdom	C.102 (1954)	C.102 (1954)	C.102 (1954)	C.102 (1954)		C.102 (1954)			C.102 (1954)

* Has accepted the text of the List of Occupational Diseases (Schedule I) amended by the ILC at its 66th Session (1980).

Sources: ILO (International Labour Office): ILO International labour standards and national legislation database (NORMLEX) (incorporates the former ILOLEX and NATLEX databases). Available at: http://www.ilo.org/dyn/normlex/en/ [6 June 2014].

Table B.2 Overview of national social security systems

Country	Number of policy areas covered by at least one programne		Existence of programme(s) anchored in national legislation							
	Number of policy areas (branches) covered by at least one programme	Number of social security policy areas covered by at least one programme	Sickness (cash)	Maternity (cash)[1]	Old age[2]	Employment injury[3]	Invalidity	Survivors	Family allowances	Unemployment[4]
Africa										
Algeria	8	Comprehensive scope of legal coverage | 8	●	●	●	●	●	●	●	●
Angola	...	...	...	●	●	●	●	●	...	...
Benin	6	Limited scope of legal coverage | 5 to 6	▲	●	●	●	●	●	●	None
Botswana	4	Very limited scope of legal coverage | 1 to 4	▲	▲	●	●	None	●	●	▲
Burkina Faso	6	Limited scope of legal coverage | 5 to 6	▲	●	●	●	●	●	●	None
Burundi	6	Limited scope of legal coverage | 5 to 6	●	▲	●	●	●	●	●	None
Cameroon	6	Limited scope of legal coverage | 5 to 6	▲	●	●	●	●	●	●	▲
Cabo Verde	7	Semi-comprehensive scope | 7	●	●	●	●	●	●	●	None
Central African Republic	6	Limited scope of legal coverage | 5 to 6	▲	●	●	●	●	●	●	None
Chad	6	Limited scope of legal coverage | 5 to 6	▲	●	●	●	●	●	●	None
Congo	6	Limited scope of legal coverage | 5 to 6	▲	●	●	●	●	●	●	None
Congo, Democratic Republic of	6	Limited scope of legal coverage | 5 to 6	▲	●	●	●	●	●	●	None
Côte d'Ivoire	6	Limited scope of legal coverage | 5 to 6	△	●	●	●	●	●	●	▲
Djibouti	6	Limited scope of legal coverage | 5 to 6	●	●	●	●	None	●	●	None
Egypt	7	Semi-comprehensive scope | 7	●	●	●	●	●	●	None	●
Equatorial Guinea	7	Semi-comprehensive scope | 7	●	●	●	●	●	●	●	None
Eritrea	...	...	...	▲	...	...	...	...	...	None
Ethiopia	4	Very limited scope of legal coverage | 1 to 4	▲	▲	●	●	●	●	None	▲
Gabon	6	Limited scope of legal coverage | 5 to 6	▲	●	●	●	●	●	●	▲
Gambia	4	Very limited scope of legal coverage | 1 to 4	None	▲	●	●	●	●	None	None
Ghana	4	Very limited scope of legal coverage | 1 to 4	△	▲	●	●	●	●	None	None
Guinea	7	Semi-comprehensive scope | 7	●	●	●	●	●	●	●	None
Guinea-Bissau	...	...	...	▲	●	●	●	●	...	None
Kenya	4	Very limited scope of legal coverage | 1 to 4	▲	▲	●	●	●	●	None	None

Table B.2 Overview of national social security systems

Country	Number of policy areas covered by at least one programne		Existence of programme(s) anchored in national legislation							
	Number of policy areas (branches) covered by at least one programme	Number of social security policy areas covered by at least one programme	Sickness (cash)	Maternity (cash)[1]	Old age[2]	Employment injury[3]	Invalidity	Survivors	Family allowances	Unemployment[4]
Lesotho	3	Very limited scope of legal coverage | 1 to 4	▲	▲	●	●	●	●	...	▲
Liberia	4	Very limited scope of legal coverage | 1 to 4	None	None	●	●	●	●	None	None
Libya	6	Limited scope of legal coverage | 5 to 6	●	●	●	●	●	●	None	▲
Madagascar	6	Limited scope of legal coverage | 5 to 6	▲	●	●	●	●	●	●	None
Malawi	1	Very limited scope of legal coverage | 1 to 4	△	▲	●	●	None	None	None	None
Mali	6	Limited scope of legal coverage | 5 to 6	▲	●	●	●	●	●	●	None
Mauritania	6	Limited scope of legal coverage | 5 to 6	△	●	●	●	●	●	●	None
Mauritius	6	Limited scope of legal coverage | 5 to 6	▲	▲	●	●	●	●	●	⊘
Morocco	7	Semi-comprehensive scope | 7	●	●	●	●	●	●	●	▲
Mozambique	6	Limited scope of legal coverage | 5 to 6	●	●	●	...	●	●	●	None
Namibia	7	Semi-comprehensive scope | 7	●	●	●	●	●	●	●	▲
Niger	6	Limited scope of legal coverage | 5 to 6	▲	●	●	●	●	●	●	None
Nigeria	4	Very limited scope of legal coverage | 1 to 4	△	▲	●	●	●	●	None	▲
Réunion	...	...	...	...	...	...	...	...	...	...
Rwanda	4	Very limited scope of legal coverage | 1 to 4	▲	▲	●	●	●	●	None	▲
Sao Tome and Principe	6	Limited scope of legal coverage | 5 to 6	●	●	●	●	●	●	None	None
Senegal	5	Limited scope of legal coverage | 5 to 6	△	●	●	●	None	●	●	None
Seychelles	7	Semi-comprehensive scope | 7	●	●	●	●	●	●	None	●
Sierra Leone	4	Very limited scope of legal coverage | 1 to 4	None	None	●	●	●	●	None	None
Somalia	...	...	...	▲	...	...	...	...	None	None
South Africa	8	Comprehensive scope of legal coverage | 8	●	●	●	●	●	●	●	●
South Sudan	...	...	...	...	...	...	...	...	...	None
Sudan	4	Very limited scope of legal coverage | 1 to 4	None	▲	●	●	●	●	None	None
Swaziland	4	Very limited scope of legal coverage | 1 to 4	None	△	●	●	●	●	None	None
Tanzania, United Republic of	5	Limited scope of legal coverage | 5 to 6	△	●	●	●	●	●	None	▲

Table B.2 Overview of national social security systems

Country	Number of policy areas covered by at least one programne		Existence of programme(s) anchored in national legislation							
	Number of policy areas (branches) covered by at least one programme	Number of social security policy areas covered by at least one programme	Sickness (cash)	Maternity (cash)[1]	Old age[2]	Employment injury[3]	Invalidity	Survivors	Family allowances	Unemployment[4]
Togo	6	Limited scope of legal coverage | 5 to 6	▲	●	●	●	●	●	●	None
Tunisia	8	Comprehensive scope of legal coverage | 8	●	●	●	●	●	●	●	●
Uganda	4	Very limited scope of legal coverage | 1 to 4	△	▲	●	●	●	●	None	▲
Zambia	4	Very limited scope of legal coverage | 1 to 4	△	None	●	●	●	●	None	None
Zimbabwe	4	Very limited scope of legal coverage | 1 to 4	None	▲	●	●	●	●	None	None
Asia										
Afghanistan	...	...	...	▲	...	...	...	...	...	None
Armenia	8	Comprehensive scope of legal coverage | 8	●	●	●	●	●	●	●	●
Azerbaijan	8	Comprehensive scope of legal coverage | 8	●	●	●	●	●	●	●	●
Bahrain	5	Limited statutory provision | 5 to 6	None	▲	●	●	●	●	None	●
Bangladesh	4	Very limited scope of legal coverage | 1 to 4	●	●	●	●	None	None	None	▲
Bhutan	...	...	...	...	●	●	●	●	...	None
Brunei Darussalam	4	Very limited scope of legal coverage | 1 to 4	△	▲	●	●	●	●	None	None
Cambodia	...	...	...	▲	...	...	...	...	...	▲
China	8	Comprehensive scope of legal coverage | 8	●	●	●	●	●	●	●	●
Georgia	7	Semi-comprehensive scope | 7	●	●	●	●	●	●	●	▲
Hong Kong, China	8	Comprehensive scope of legal coverage | 8	●	●	●	●	●	●	●	●
India	7	Semi-comprehensive scope | 7	●	●	●	●	●	●	None	●
Indonesia	4	Very limited scope of legal coverage | 1 to 4	△	▲	●	●	●	●	None	▲
Iran, Islamic Rep. of	8	Comprehensive scope of legal coverage | 8	●	●	●	●	●	●	●	●
Iraq	...	...	...	▲	...	...	...	...	...	None
Israel	8	Comprehensive scope of legal coverage | 8	●	●	●	●	●	●	●	●
Japan	8	Comprehensive scope of legal coverage | 8	●	●	●	●	●	●	●	●
Jordan	6	Limited scope of legal coverage | 5 to 6	△	●	●	●	●	●	None	●
Kazakhstan	8	Comprehensive scope of legal coverage | 8	●	●	●	●	●	●	●	●

Table B.2 Overview of national social security systems

Country	Number of policy areas covered by at least one programme		Existence of programme(s) anchored in national legislation							
	Number of policy areas (branches) covered by at least one programme	Number of social security policy areas covered by at least one programme	Sickness (cash)	Maternity (cash)[1]	Old age[2]	Employment injury[3]	Invalidity	Survivors	Family allowances	Unemploy-ment[4]
Korea, Dem. People's Rep. of	...	...	...	...	...	...	...	...	...	None
Korea, Republic of	5	Limited scope of legal coverage | 5 to 6	△	▲	●	●	●	●	None	●
Kuwait	4	Very limited scope of legal coverage | 1 to 4	🗐	▲	●	●	●	●	None	None
Kyrgyzstan	8	Comprehensive scope of legal coverage | 8	●	●	●	●	●	●	●	●
Lao People's Dem. Rep.	6	Limited scope of legal coverage | 5 to 6	●	●	●	●	●	●	None	None
Lebanon	6	Limited scope of legal coverage | 5 to 6	△	●	●	●	●	●	●	None
Macau, China	...	...	...	...	...	...	...	...	...	...
Malaysia	4	Very limited scope of legal coverage | 1 to 4	△	▲	●	●	●	●	None	▲
Maldives	...	...	△	...	●	...	●	●	...	None
Mongolia	8	Comprehensive scope of legal coverage | 8	●	●	●	●	●	●	●	●
Myanmar[5]	3	Very limited scope of legal coverage | 1 to 4	●	●	▲	●	▲	▲	Not yet	Not yet
Nepal	4	Very limited scope of legal coverage | 1 to 4	▲	▲	●	●	●	●	None	▲
Occupied Palestinian Territory	...	...	...	●	...	...	...	...	...	None
Oman	4	Very limited scope of legal coverage | 1 to 4	None	▲	●	●	●	●	None	None
Pakistan	6	Limited scope of legal coverage | 5 to 6	●	●	●	●	●	●	None	▲
Philippines	6	Limited scope of legal coverage | 5 to 6	●	●	●	●	●	●	None	▲
Qatar	...	Very limited scope of legal coverage | 1 to 4	...	▲	●	...	●	●	None	None
Saudi Arabia	5	Limited scope of legal coverage | 5 to 6	▲	▲	●	●	●	●	None	●
Singapore	7	Semi-comprehensive scope | 7	●	●	●	●	●	●	●	None
Sri Lanka	5	Limited scope of legal coverage | 5 to 6	△	▲	●	●	●	●	●	▲
Syrian Arab Republic	4	Very limited scope of legal coverage | 1 to 4	None	▲	●	●	●	●	None	▲
Taiwan, China	7	Semi-comprehensive scope | 7	●	●	●	●	●	●	None	●
Tajikistan	6	Limited scope of legal coverage | 5 to 6	●	●	●	...	●	●	...	●
Thailand	8	Comprehensive scope of legal coverage | 8	●	●	●	●	●	●	●	●
Timor-Leste	...	...	...	▲	●	...	...	...	None	None

Table B.2 Overview of national social security systems

Country	Number of policy areas covered by at least one programne		Existence of programme(s) anchored in national legislation							
	Number of policy areas (branches) covered by at least one programme	Number of social security policy areas covered by at least one programme	Sickness (cash)	Maternity (cash)[1]	Old age[2]	Employment injury[3]	Invalidity	Survivors	Family allowances	Unemployment[4]
Turkmenistan	8	Comprehensive scope of legal coverage | 8	●	●	●	●	●	●	●	●
United Arab Emirates	…	…	…	▲	…	…	…	…	…	▲
Uzbekistan	8	Comprehensive scope of legal coverage | 8	●	●	●	●	●	●	●	●
Viet Nam	7	Semi-comprehensive scope | 7	●	●	●	●	●	●	None	●
Yemen	5	Limited scope of legal coverage | 5 to 6	●	▲	●	●	●	●	None	▲
Europe										
Albania	8	Comprehensive scope of legal coverage | 8	●	●	●	●	●	●	●	●
Andorra	8	Comprehensive scope of legal coverage | 8	●	●	●	●	●	●	●	●
Austria	8	Comprehensive scope of legal coverage | 8	●	●	●	●	●	●	●	●
Belarus	8	Comprehensive scope of legal coverage | 8	●	●	●	●	●	●	●	●
Belgium	8	Comprehensive scope of legal coverage | 8	●	●	●	●	●	●	●	●
Bosnia and Herzegovina	8	Comprehensive scope of legal coverage | 8	●	●	●	●	●	●	●	●
Bulgaria	8	Comprehensive scope of legal coverage | 8	●	●	●	●	●	●	●	●
Croatia	8	Comprehensive scope of legal coverage | 8	●	●	●	●	●	●	●	●
Cyprus	8	Comprehensive scope of legal coverage | 8	●	●	●	●	●	●	●	●
Czech Republic	8	Comprehensive scope of legal coverage | 8	●	●	●	●	●	●	●	●
Denmark	8	Comprehensive scope of legal coverage | 8	●	●	●	●	●	●	●	●
Estonia	8	Comprehensive scope of legal coverage | 8	●	●	●	●	●	●	●	●
Finland	8	Comprehensive scope of legal coverage | 8	●	●	●	●	●	●	●	●
France	8	Comprehensive scope of legal coverage | 8	●	●	●	●	●	●	●	●
Germany	8	Comprehensive scope of legal coverage | 8	●	●	●	●	●	●	●	●
Greece	8	Comprehensive scope of legal coverage | 8	●	●	●	●	●	●	●	●
Guernsey	8	Comprehensive scope of legal coverage | 8	●	●	●	●	●	●	●	●
Hungary	8	Comprehensive scope of legal coverage | 8	●	●	●	●	●	●	●	●
Iceland	8	Comprehensive scope of legal coverage | 8	●	●	●	●	●	●	●	●
Ireland	8	Comprehensive scope of legal coverage | 8	●	●	●	●	●	●	●	●

Table B.2 Overview of national social security systems

Country	Number of policy areas covered by at least one programne		Existence of programme(s) anchored in national legislation							
	Number of policy areas (branches) covered by at least one programme	Number of social security policy areas covered by at least one programme	Sickness (cash)	Maternity (cash)[1]	Old age[2]	Employment injury[3]	Invalidity	Survivors	Family allowances	Unemploy-ment[4]
Isle of Man	8	Comprehensive scope of legal coverage | 8	●	●	●	●	●	●	●	●
Italy	8	Comprehensive scope of legal coverage | 8	●	●	●	●	●	●	●	●
Jersey	8	Comprehensive scope of legal coverage | 8	●	●	●	●	●	●	●	●
Kosovo	8	Comprehensive scope of legal coverage | 8	●	●	●	●	●	●	●	●
Latvia	8	Comprehensive scope of legal coverage | 8	●	●	●	●	●	●	●	●
Liechtenstein	8	Comprehensive scope of legal coverage | 8	●	●	●	●	●	●	●	●
Lithuania	8	Comprehensive scope of legal coverage | 8	●	●	●	●	●	●	●	●
Luxembourg	8	Comprehensive scope of legal coverage | 8	●	●	●	●	●	●	●	●
Malta	8	Comprehensive scope of legal coverage | 8	●	●	●	●	●	●	●	●
Moldova, Republic of	8	Comprehensive scope of legal coverage | 8	●	●	●	●	●	●	●	●
Monaco	8	Comprehensive scope of legal coverage | 8	●	●	●	●	●	●	●	●
Montenegro	8	Comprehensive scope of legal coverage | 8	●	●	●	●	●	●	●	●
Netherlands	8	Comprehensive scope of legal coverage | 8	●	●	●	●	●	●	●	●
Norway	8	Comprehensive scope of legal coverage | 8	●	●	●	●	●	●	●	●
Poland	8	Comprehensive scope of legal coverage | 8	●	●	●	●	●	●	●	●
Portugal	8	Comprehensive scope of legal coverage | 8	●	●	●	●	●	●	●	●
Romania	8	Comprehensive scope of legal coverage | 8	●	●	●	●	●	●	●	●
Russian Federation	8	Comprehensive scope of legal coverage | 8	●	●	●	●	●	●	●	●
San Marino	8	Comprehensive scope of legal coverage | 8	●	●	●	●	●	●	●	●
Serbia	8	Comprehensive scope of legal coverage | 8	●	●	●	●	●	●	●	●
Slovakia	8	Comprehensive scope of legal coverage | 8	●	●	●	●	●	●	●	●
Slovenia	8	Comprehensive scope of legal coverage | 8	●	●	●	●	●	●	●	●
Spain	8	Comprehensive scope of legal coverage | 8	●	●	●	●	●	●	●	●
Sweden	8	Comprehensive scope of legal coverage | 8	●	●	●	●	●	●	●	●
Switzerland	8	Comprehensive scope of legal coverage | 8	●	●	●	●	●	●	●	●

Table B.2 Overview of national social security systems

Country	Number of policy areas covered by at least one programne		Existence of programme(s) anchored in national legislation							
	Number of policy areas (branches) covered by at least one programme	Number of social security policy areas covered by at least one programme	Sickness (cash)	Maternity (cash)[1]	Old age[2]	Employment injury[3]	Invalidity	Survivors	Family allowances	Unemployment[4]
The Former Yugoslav Republic of Macedonia	8	Comprehensive scope of legal coverage | 8	●	●	●	●	●	●	●	●
Turkey	7	Semi-comprehensive scope | 7	●	●	●	●	●	●	None	●
Ukraine	8	Comprehensive scope of legal coverage | 8	●	●	●	●	●	●	●	●
United Kingdom	8	Comprehensive scope of legal coverage | 8	●	●	●	●	●	●	●	●
Latin America and the Caribbean										
Antigua and Barbuda	5	Limited scope of legal coverage | 5 to 6	●	●	●	None	●	●	None	None
Argentina	8	Comprehensive scope of legal coverage | 8	●	●	●	●	●	●	●	●
Bahamas	6	Limited scope of legal coverage | 5 to 6	●	●	●	●	●	●	None	None
Barbados	7	Semi-comprehensive scope | 7	●	●	●	●	●	●	None	●
Belize	6	Limited scope of legal coverage | 5 to 6	●	●	●	●	●	●	None	None
Bermuda	4	Very limited scope of legal coverage | 1 to 4	▲	▲	●	●	●	●	None	None
Bolivia, Plurinational State of	7	Semi-comprehensive scope | 7	●	●	●	●	●	●	●	▲
Brazil	8	Comprehensive scope of legal coverage | 8	●	●	●	●	●	●	●	●
British Virgin Islands	6	Limited scope of legal coverage | 5 to 6	●	●	●	●	●	●	●	None
Chile	8	Comprehensive scope of legal coverage | 8	●	●	●	●	●	●	●	●
Colombia	8	Comprehensive scope of legal coverage | 8	●	●	●	●	●	●	●	●
Costa Rica	7	Semi-comprehensive scope | 7	●	●	●	●	●	●	●	▲
Cuba	6	Limited scope of legal coverage | 5 to 6	●	●	●	●	●	●	None[6]	None
Dominica	6	Limited scope of legal coverage | 5 to 6	●	●	●	●	●	●	None[7]	None
Dominican Republic	7	Semi-comprehensive scope | 7	●	●	●	●	●	●	●	None
Ecuador	7	Semi-comprehensive scope | 7	●	●	●	●	●	●	None[8]	●
El Salvador	6	Limited scope of legal coverage | 5 to 6	●	●	●	●	●	●	None	None
Grenada	6	Limited scope of legal coverage | 5 to 6	●	●	●	●	●	●	None	None
Guadeloupe	...	...	●	●	●	●	●	●	...	...
Guatemala	6	Limited scope of legal coverage | 5 to 6	●	●	●	●	●	●	None	None
Guyana	6	Limited scope of legal coverage | 5 to 6	●	●	●	●	●	●	None	None

Table B.2 Overview of national social security systems

Country	Number of policy areas covered by at least one programne		Existence of programme(s) anchored in national legislation							
	Number of policy areas (branches) covered by at least one programme	Number of social security policy areas covered by at least one programme	Sickness (cash)	Maternity (cash)[1]	Old age[2]	Employment injury[3]	Invalidity	Survivors	Family allowances	Unemployment[4]
French Guiana	...	...	...	...	●	●	●	●	...	...
Haiti	4	Very limited scope of legal coverage | 1 to 4	None	▲	●	●	●	●	None	None
Honduras	6	Limited scope of legal coverage | 5 to 6	●	●	●	●	●	●	None	None
Jamaica	6	Limited scope of legal coverage | 5 to 6	▲	●	●	●	●	●	●	None
Martinique	...	...	...	●	●	●	●	●	●	...
Mexico	7	Semi-comprehensive scope | 7	●	●	●	●	●	●	●	▲
Netherlands Antilles	...	...	●	●	●	●	●	●	●	...
Nicaragua	7	Semi-comprehensive scope | 7	●	●	●	●	●	●	●	None
Panama	6	Limited scope of legal coverage | 5 to 6	●	●	●	●	●	●	None	▲
Paraguay	6	Limited scope of legal coverage | 5 to 6	●	●	●	●	●	●	▲	None
Peru	6	Limited scope of legal coverage | 5 to 6	●	●	●	●	●	●	None	▲
Puerto Rico	...	...	●	●	...	●	●	●	...	...
Saint Kitts and Nevis	6	Limited scope of legal coverage | 5 to 6	●	●	●	●	●	●	None	None
Saint Lucia	6	Limited scope of legal coverage | 5 to 6	●	●	●	●	●	●	None	None
Saint Vincent and the Grenadines	6	Limited scope of legal coverage | 5 to 6	●	●	●	●	●	●	None	None
Suriname	...	...	...	...	...	...	...	...	...	None
Trinidad and Tobago	7	Semi-comprehensive scope | 7	●	●	●	●	●	●	●	None
Uruguay	8	Comprehensive scope of legal coverage | 8	●	●	●	●	●	●	●	●
Venezuela, Bolivarian Rep. of	7	Semi-comprehensive scope | 7	●	●	●	●	●	●	None	●
North America										
Canada	8	Comprehensive scope of legal coverage | 8	●	●	●	●	●	●	●	●
United States	8	Comprehensive scope of legal coverage | 8	●	●	●	●	●	●	●	●

Table B.2 Overview of national social security systems

Country	Number of policy areas covered by at least one programne		Existence of programme(s) anchored in national legislation							
	Number of policy areas (branches) covered by at least one programme	Number of social security policy areas covered by at least one programme	Sickness (cash)	Maternity (cash)[1]	Old age[2]	Employment injury[3]	Invalidity	Survivors	Family allowances	Unemploy-ment[4]
Oceania										
Australia	8	Comprehensive scope of legal coverage | 8	●	●	●	●	●	●	●	●
Fiji	5	Limited scope of legal coverage | 5 to 6	None	▲	●	●	●	●	●	None
Kiribati	4	Very limited scope of legal coverage | 1 to 4	None	▲	●	●	●	●	None	None
Marshall Islands	3	Very limited scope of legal coverage | 1 to 4	△	△	●	None	●	●	None	None
Micronesia, Fed. States	3	Very limited scope of legal coverage | 1 to 4	None	None	●	None	●	●	None	None
Nauru	...	...	...	...	...	...	...	...	...	None
New Zealand	8	Comprehensive scope of legal coverage | 8	●	●	●	●	●	●	●	●
Niue	...	...	...	...	...	...	...	...	...	None
Palau Islands	3	Very limited scope of legal coverage | 1 to 4	None	None	●	None	●	●	None	None
Papua New Guinea	4	Very limited scope of legal coverage | 1 to 4	▲	None	●	●	●	●	None	None
Samoa	4	Very limited scope of legal coverage | 1 to 4	...	...	●	●	●	●	None	None
Solomon Islands	4	Limited scope of legal coverage | 5 to 6	None	None	●	●	●	●	None	▲
Tonga	...	...	...	...	●	●	●	●	...	None
Tuvalu	...	...	...	...	●	●	●	●	...	▲
Vanuatu	3	Very limited scope of legal coverage | 1 to 4	▲	▲	●	None	●	●	None	▲

Main source

SSA (Social Security Administration of the United States); ISSA (International Social Security Association). Social security programs throughout the world (Washington, DC and Geneva): The Americas, 2013; Europe, 2012; Asia and the Pacific, 2012; Africa, 2013. Available at: http://www.ssa.gov/policy/docs/progdesc/ssptw/ [8 June 2014].

Other sources

Council of Europe: Mutual Information System on Social Protection of the Council of Europe (MISSCEO) (Strasbourg). Available at: http://www.coe.int/t/dg3/socialpolicies/socialsecurity/missceo/missceo_EN.asp [8 June 2014].
European Commission: Mutual Information System on Social Protection (MISSOC). Available at: http://www.missoc.org/MISSOC/MISSOCII/MISSOCII/index.htm [8 June 2014].
ILO (International Labour Office). ILO International labour standards and national legislation database (NORMLEX) (incorporates the former ILOLEX and NATLEX databases).
Available at: http://www.ilo.org/dyn/normlex/en/ [8 June 2014].
—. 2010. Profile of social security system in Kosovo (Budapest, ILO DWT and Country Office for Central and Eastern Europe).
National legislation.

Notes

…: Not available.

Symbols

● At least one programme anchored in national legislation.
● Legislation not yet implemented.
▲ Limited provision (e.g. labour code only).
△ Only benefit in kind (e.g. medical benefit).

1 Additional details in table B.5 Maternity: Key features of main social security programmes (cash benefits) (http://www.social-protection.org/gimi/gess/RessourceDownload.action?ressource.ressourceId=37580).

2 Additional details in table B.6 Old age pensions: Key features of main social security programmes (http://www.social-protection.org/gimi/gess/RessourceDownload.action?ressource.ressourceId=37137).

3 Additional details in table B.4 Employment injury: Key features of main social security programmes (cash benefits) (http://www.social-protection.org/gimi/gess/RessourceDownload.action?ressource.ressourceId=41917)

4 Additional details in table B.3 Unemployment: indicators of effective coverage (http://www.social-protection.org/gimi/gess/RessourceDownload.action?ressource.ressourceId=37697)

5 Myanmar enacted its social security law in 2012. The laws includes provisions for most social security branches including old age, survivors, disability, family benefits and unemployment insurance benefit (section 37), but the country is at the stage of drafting the regulations and provisions are not yet being implemented.

6 Cuba. Family/child benefits: Dependants of young workers conscripted into military service are eligible for assistance from social security. Cash benefits are available for families whose head of household is unemployed due to health, disability or other justifiable causes, and has insufficient income for food and medicine or basic household needs.

7 Dominica. Family/child benefits: Benefits are paid to unemployed single mothers with unmarried children younger than age 18 (age 21 if a full-time student, no limit if disabled) who lack sufficient resources to meet basic needs. (Social assistance benefits are provided under the Old Age, Disability, and Survivors programme.)

8 Ecuador. Family/child benefits: No statutory benefits are provided. Mothers assessed as needy with at least one child (younger than age 18) and low-income families receive a monthly allowance under the Bono de Desarrollo Humano programme.

Definitions

The scope of coverage is measured by the number of social security policy areas (branches) provided for by law. This indicator can take the value 0 to 8 according to the total number of social security policy areas (or branches) with a programme anchored in national legislation.
The eight following branches are taken into consideration: sickness, maternity, old age, survivors, invalidity, child/family allowances, employment injury and unemployment.

The number of branches covered by at least one programme provides an overview of the scope of legal social security provision.

Table B.3 Unemployment: Indicators of effective coverage. Unemployed who actually receive benefits (percentages)

Major area, region or country	Percentage of unemployed receiving unemployment benefits																					Unemployment benefit programme
	2000		2005		2007		2008		2009		2010		2011		Latest available year							
	Contributory and non-contributory schemes	Real year	Contributory and non-contributory schemes	Real year	Contributory and non-contributory schemes	Real year	Contributory and non-contributory schemes	Real year	Contributory and non-contributory schemes	Real year	Contributory and non-contributory schemes	Real year	Contributory and non-contributory schemes	Real year	Contributory schemes	Non-contributory schemes	Contributory and non-contributory schemes	Male	Female	Latest Year	Existence of unemployment programme anchored in legislation and type of programme
Regional estimates (weighted by the labour force)																						
Africa	0.7		0.8		0.8		0.5		0.6		0.8		0.7		0.9	0.0	1.0				
Middle East	2.9		2.0		2.1		2.3		2.7		2.6		2.8		2.2	0.0	2.2				
Latin America and the Caribbean	2.7		2.6		3.4		3.2		4.0		4.3		2.1		4.6	0.0	4.6				
Asia and the Pacific	6.4		10.4		9.2		9.2		8.2		6.6		6.4		6.8	0.4	7.2				
... *without China*	3.9		6.3		6.7						6.7		7.8		5.2	0.7	5.9				
Central and Eastern Europe	19.1		29.1		27.7		27.0		30.0		25.1		21.9		21.1	0.5	21.6				
North America	38.1		36.0		36.8		37.7		41.3		32.3		28.8		28.0	0.0	28.0				
Western Europe	61.3		68.9		66.0		64.5		69.3		67.4		64.2		44.6	19.2	63.8				
World	**11.2**		**14.6**		**13.9**		**13.8**		**13.8**		**11.6**		**11.3**		**10.2**	**1.5**	**11.7**				
... *without China*	11.6		12.8		12.8		13.4		13.8		12.5		12.1		10.6	2.0	12.6				
Africa																					
Algeria [1,c]	7.3	2000	8.8	2003	...	...	...	...	...	...	...	...	...	...	8.8	0.0	8.8	...	...	2003	Social insurance
Angola	n.a.	...	n.a.	...	n.a.	...	n.a.	...	n.a.	...	n.a.	...	n.a.	...	n.a.	n.a.	n.a.	n.a.	n.a.	2013	...
Benin	n.a.	...	n.a.	...	n.a.	...	n.a.	...	n.a.	...	n.a.	...	n.a.	...	n.a.	n.a.	n.a.	n.a.	n.a.	2013	No programme anchored in legislation
Botswana [2]	n.a.	...	n.a.	...	n.a.	...	n.a.	...	n.a.	...	n.a.	...	n.a.	...	n.a.	n.a.	n.a.	n.a.	n.a.	2013	Severance payment [a]
Burkina Faso	n.a.	...	n.a.	...	n.a.	...	n.a.	...	n.a.	...	n.a.	...	n.a.	...	n.a.	n.a.	n.a.	n.a.	n.a.	2013	No programme anchored in legislation
Burundi	n.a.	...	n.a.	...	n.a.	...	n.a.	...	n.a.	...	n.a.	...	n.a.	...	n.a.	n.a.	n.a.	n.a.	n.a.	2013	No programme anchored in legislation
Cameroon [2,3]	n.a.	...	n.a.	...	n.a.	...	n.a.	...	n.a.	...	n.a.	...	n.a.	...	n.a.	n.a.	n.a.	n.a.	n.a.	2013	Severance payment [a]
Cabo Verde	n.a.	...	n.a.	...	n.a.	...	n.a.	...	n.a.	...	n.a.	...	n.a.	...	n.a.	n.a.	n.a.	n.a.	n.a.	2013	No programme anchored in legislation
Central African Republic	n.a.	...	n.a.	...	n.a.	...	n.a.	...	n.a.	...	n.a.	...	n.a.	...	n.a.	n.a.	n.a.	n.a.	n.a.	2013	No programme anchored in legislation
Chad	n.a.	...	n.a.	...	n.a.	...	n.a.	...	n.a.	...	n.a.	...	n.a.	...	n.a.	n.a.	n.a.	n.a.	n.a.	2013	No programme anchored in legislation

Table B.3 Unemployment: Indicators of effective coverage. Unemployed who actually receive benefits (percentages)

Major area, region or country	Percentage of unemployed receiving unemployment benefits																				Unemployment benefit programme
	2000		2005		2007		2008		2009		2010		2011		Latest available year						
	Contributory and non-contributory schemes	Real year	Contributory and non-contributory schemes	Real year	Contributory and non-contributory schemes	Real year	Contributory and non-contributory schemes	Real year	Contributory and non-contributory schemes	Real year	Contributory and non-contributory schemes	Real year	Contributory and non-contributory schemes	Real year	Contributory schemes	Non-contributory schemes	Contributory and non-contributory schemes	Male	Female	Latest Year	Existence of unemployment programme anchored in legislation and type of programme
Comoros [2,4]	n.a.	...	n.a.	...	n.a.	...	n.a.	...	n.a.	...	n.a.	...	n.a.	...	n.a.	n.a.	n.a.	n.a.	n.a.	2013	No programme anchored in legislation. Severance payment without a decree adopted.
Congo	n.a.	...	n.a.	...	n.a.	...	n.a.	...	n.a.	...	n.a.	...	n.a.	...	n.a.	n.a.	n.a.	n.a.	n.a.	2013	No programme anchored in legislation
Congo, Democratic Republic of	n.a.	...	n.a.	...	n.a.	...	n.a.	...	n.a.	...	n.a.	...	n.a.	...	n.a.	n.a.	n.a.	n.a.	n.a.	2013	No programme anchored in legislation
Côte d'Ivoire [2,5]	n.a.	...	n.a.	...	n.a.	...	n.a.	...	n.a.	...	n.a.	...	n.a.	...	n.a.	n.a.	n.a.	n.a.	n.a.	2013	Severance payment[a]
Djibouti	n.a.	...	n.a.	...	n.a.	...	n.a.	...	n.a.	...	n.a.	...	n.a.	...	n.a.	n.a.	n.a.	n.a.	n.a.	2013	No programme anchored in legislation
Egypt	...	...	...	...	...	...	...	...	...	...	...	...	...	...	...	...	...	...	...		Social insurance
Equatorial Guinea	n.a.	...	n.a.	...	n.a.	...	n.a.	...	n.a.	...	n.a.	...	n.a.	...	n.a.	n.a.	n.a.	n.a.	n.a.	2013	No programme anchored in legislation
Eritrea	n.a.	...	n.a.	...	n.a.	...	n.a.	...	n.a.	...	n.a.	...	n.a.	...	n.a.	n.a.	n.a.	n.a.	n.a.	2013	No programme anchored in legislation
Ethiopia [2,6]	n.a.	...	n.a.	...	n.a.	...	n.a.	...	n.a.	...	n.a.	...	n.a.	...	n.a.	n.a.	n.a.	n.a.	n.a.	2013	Severance payment[a]
Gabon [2,7]	n.a.	...	n.a.	...	n.a.	...	n.a.	...	n.a.	...	n.a.	...	n.a.	...	n.a.	n.a.	n.a.	n.a.	n.a.	2013	Severance payment[a]
Gambia	n.a.	...	n.a.	...	n.a.	...	n.a.	...	n.a.	...	n.a.	...	n.a.	...	n.a.	n.a.	n.a.	n.a.	n.a.	2013	No programme anchored in legislation
Ghana	n.a.	...	n.a.	...	n.a.	...	n.a.	...	n.a.	...	n.a.	...	n.a.	...	n.a.	n.a.	n.a.	n.a.	n.a.	2013	No programme anchored in legislation
Guinea	n.a.	...	n.a.	...	n.a.	...	n.a.	...	n.a.	...	n.a.	...	n.a.	...	n.a.	n.a.	n.a.	n.a.	n.a.	2013	No programme anchored in legislation
Guinea-Bissau	n.a.	...	n.a.	...	n.a.	...	n.a.	...	n.a.	...	n.a.	...	n.a.	...	n.a.	n.a.	n.a.	n.a.	n.a.	2013	No programme anchored in legislation
Kenya	n.a.	...	n.a.	...	n.a.	...	n.a.	...	n.a.	...	n.a.	...	n.a.	...	n.a.	n.a.	n.a.	n.a.	n.a.	2013	No programme anchored in legislation
Lesotho [2,8]	n.a.	...	n.a.	...	n.a.	...	n.a.	...	n.a.	...	n.a.	...	n.a.	...	n.a.	n.a.	n.a.	n.a.	n.a.	2013	Severance payment[a]
Liberia	n.a.	...	n.a.	...	n.a.	...	n.a.	...	n.a.	...	n.a.	...	n.a.	...	n.a.	n.a.	n.a.	n.a.	n.a.	2013	No programme anchored in legislation
Libya [2,9]	n.a.	...	n.a.	...	n.a.	...	n.a.	...	n.a.	...	n.a.	...	n.a.	...	n.a.	n.a.	n.a.	n.a.	n.a.	2013	Severance payment[a]
Madagascar	n.a.	...	n.a.	...	n.a.	...	n.a.	...	n.a.	...	n.a.	...	n.a.	...	n.a.	n.a.	n.a.	n.a.	n.a.	2013	No programme anchored in legislation
Malawi	n.a.	...	n.a.	...	n.a.	...	n.a.	...	n.a.	...	n.a.	...	n.a.	...	n.a.	n.a.	n.a.	n.a.	n.a.	2013	No programme anchored in legislation
Mali	n.a.	...	n.a.	...	n.a.	...	n.a.	...	n.a.	...	n.a.	...	n.a.	...	n.a.	n.a.	n.a.	n.a.	n.a.	2013	No programme anchored in legislation
Mauritania	n.a.	...	n.a.	...	n.a.	...	n.a.	...	n.a.	...	n.a.	...	n.a.	...	n.a.	n.a.	n.a.	n.a.	n.a.	2013	No programme anchored in legislation
Mauritius [1,c]	0.5	2001	0.9	2005	0.9	2007	0.9	2008	0.9	2009	1.1	2010	1.2	2011	0.0	1.2	1.2	...	...	2011	Social assistance and social insurance

Table B.3 Unemployment: Indicators of effective coverage. Unemployed who actually receive benefits (percentages)

Major area, region or country	Percentage of unemployed receiving unemployment benefits																				Unemployment benefit programme
	2000		2005		2007		2008		2009		2010		2011		Latest available year						
	Contributory and non-contributory schemes	Real year	Contributory and non-contributory schemes	Real year	Contributory and non-contributory schemes	Real year	Contributory and non-contributory schemes	Real year	Contributory and non-contributory schemes	Real year	Contributory and non-contributory schemes	Real year	Contributory and non-contributory schemes	Real year	Contributory schemes	Non-contributory schemes	Contributory and non-contributory schemes	Male	Female	Latest Year	Existence of unemployment programme anchored in legislation and type of programme
Morocco [2.10]	n.a.	...	n.a.	...	n.a.	...	n.a.	...	n.a.	...	n.a.	...	n.a.	...	n.a.	n.a.	n.a.	n.a.	n.a.	2013	Severance payment[a]
Mozambique	n.a.	...	n.a.	...	n.a.	...	n.a.	...	n.a.	...	n.a.	...	n.a.	...	n.a.	n.a.	n.a.	n.a.	n.a.	2013	No programme anchored in legislation
Namibia [2.11]	n.a.	...	n.a.	...	n.a.	...	n.a.	...	n.a.	...	n.a.	...	n.a.	...	n.a.	n.a.	n.a.	n.a.	n.a.	2013	Severance payment[a]
Niger	n.a.	...	n.a.	...	n.a.	...	n.a.	...	n.a.	...	n.a.	...	n.a.	...	n.a.	n.a.	n.a.	n.a.	n.a.	2013	No programme anchored in legislation
Nigeria [12]	n.a.	...	n.a.	...	n.a.	...	n.a.	...	n.a.	...	n.a.	...	n.a.	...	n.a.	n.a.	n.a.	n.a.	n.a.	2013	Withdraw from provident fund
Rwanda [2.13]	n.a.	...	n.a.	...	n.a.	...	n.a.	...	n.a.	...	n.a.	...	n.a.	...	n.a.	n.a.	n.a.	n.a.	n.a.	2013	Severance payment[a]
Sao Tome and Principe	n.a.	...	n.a.	...	n.a.	...	n.a.	...	n.a.	...	n.a.	...	n.a.	...	n.a.	n.a.	n.a.	n.a.	n.a.	2013	No programme anchored in legislation
Senegal	n.a.	...	n.a.	...	n.a.	...	n.a.	...	n.a.	...	n.a.	...	n.a.	...	n.a.	n.a.	n.a.	n.a.	n.a.	2013	No programme anchored in legislation
Seychelles [14]	...	...	18.0	2005	...	...	...	...	...	...	...	...	...	...	0.0	18.0	18.0	...	...	2005	Social assistance [5]
Sierra Leone	n.a.	...	n.a.	...	n.a.	...	n.a.	...	n.a.	...	n.a.	...	n.a.	...	n.a.	n.a.	n.a.	n.a.	n.a.	2013	No programme anchored in legislation
Somalia	n.a.	...	n.a.	...	n.a.	...	n.a.	...	n.a.	...	n.a.	...	n.a.	...	n.a.	n.a.	n.a.	n.a.	n.a.	2013	No programme anchored in legislation
South Africa [1,c]	10.0	2004	11.0	2005	10.9	2007	9.7	2008	11.3	2009	14.5	2010	12.8	2011	13.5	0.0	13.5	...	...	2012	Social insurance
South Sudan	n.a.	...	n.a.	...	n.a.	...	n.a.	...	n.a.	...	n.a.	...	n.a.	...	n.a.	n.a.	n.a.	n.a.	n.a.	2013	No programme anchored in legislation
Sudan	n.a.	...	n.a.	...	n.a.	...	n.a.	...	n.a.	...	n.a.	...	n.a.	...	n.a.	n.a.	n.a.	n.a.	n.a.	2013	No programme anchored in legislation
Swaziland	n.a.	...	n.a.	...	n.a.	...	n.a.	...	n.a.	...	n.a.	...	n.a.	...	n.a.	n.a.	n.a.	n.a.	n.a.	2013	No programme anchored in legislation
Tanzania, United Republic of [2, 15]	n.a.	...	n.a.	...	n.a.	...	n.a.	...	n.a.	...	n.a.	...	n.a.	...	n.a.	n.a.	n.a.	n.a.	n.a.	2013	Severance payment[a]
Togo	n.a.	...	n.a.	...	n.a.	...	n.a.	...	n.a.	...	n.a.	...	n.a.	...	n.a.	n.a.	n.a.	n.a.	n.a.	2013	No programme anchored in legislation
Tunisia [1,c]	...	...	...	...	...	...	...	...	...	...	3.0	2008	...	...	0.0	3.0	3.0	...	...	2008	Social assistance
Uganda [2.16]	n.a.	...	n.a.	...	n.a.	...	n.a.	...	n.a.	...	n.a.	...	n.a.	...	n.a.	n.a.	n.a.	n.a.	n.a.	2013	Severance payment[a]
Zambia	n.a.	...	n.a.	...	n.a.	...	n.a.	...	n.a.	...	n.a.	...	n.a.	...	n.a.	n.a.	n.a.	n.a.	n.a.	2013	No programme anchored in legislation
Zimbabwe	n.a.	...	n.a.	...	n.a.	...	n.a.	...	n.a.	...	n.a.	...	n.a.	...	n.a.	n.a.	n.a.	n.a.	n.a.	2013	No programme anchored in legislation

Table B.3 Unemployment: Indicators of effective coverage. Unemployed who actually receive benefits (percentages)

Major area, region or country	Percentage of unemployed receiving unemployment benefits																				Unemployment benefit programme
	2000		2005		2007		2008		2009		2010		2011		Latest available year						
	Contributory and non-contributory schemes	Real year	Contributory and non-contributory schemes	Real year	Contributory and non-contributory schemes	Real year	Contributory and non-contributory schemes	Real year	Contributory and non-contributory schemes	Real year	Contributory and non-contributory schemes	Real year	Contributory and non-contributory schemes	Real year	Contributory schemes	Non-contributory schemes	Contributory and non-contributory schemes	Male	Female	Latest Year	Existence of unemployment programme anchored in legislation and type of programme
Asia																					
Afghanistan	n.a.	...	n.a.	...	n.a.	...	n.a.	...	n.a.	...	n.a.	...	n.a.	...	n.a.	n.a.	n.a.	n.a.	n.a.	2013	No programme anchored in legislation
Armenia [1,c]	12.0	2000	5.7	2005	20.1	2007	22.2	2008	30.5	2009	24.1	2010	20.8	2011	15.8	0.0	15.8	17.4	15.1	2012	Social insurance
Azerbaijan [1,c]	6.3	2000	3.7	2005	5.0	2007	4.7	2008	6.6	2009	6.6	2009	2.6	2011	2.5	0.0	2.5	2.9	2.1	2012	Social insurance
Bahrain [1,c]	n.a.	...	n.a.	...	...	...	...	...	7.9	2009	9.8	2010	...	...	9.8	0.0	9.8	...	...	2010	Social insurance and unemployment aid
Bangladesh [2,17]	n.a.	...	n.a.	...	n.a.	...	n.a.	...	n.a.	...	n.a.	...	n.a.	...	n.a.	n.a.	n.a.	n.a.	n.a.	2013	Severance payment[a]
Bhutan	n.a.	...	n.a.	...	n.a.	...	n.a.	...	n.a.	...	n.a.	...	n.a.	...	n.a.	n.a.	n.a.	n.a.	n.a.	2013	No programme anchored in legislation
Brunei Darussalam	n.a.	...	n.a.	...	n.a.	...	n.a.	...	n.a.	...	n.a.	...	n.a.	...	n.a.	n.a.	n.a.	n.a.	n.a.	2013	No programme anchored in legislation
Cambodia [2,18]	n.a.	...	n.a.	...	n.a.	...	n.a.	...	n.a.	...	n.a.	...	n.a.	...	n.a.	n.a.	n.a.	n.a.	n.a.	2013	Severance payment[a]
China [1,c]	9.9	2000	20.0	2005	17.1	2007	14.8	2008	14.0	2009	9.2	2010	9.1	2011	9.1	0.0	9.1	...	...	2011	Local government-administered social insurance programmes
Georgia [2,19]	2.4	2000	4.0	2005	n.a.	...	n.a.	...	n.a.	...	n.a.	...	n.a.	...	n.a.	n.a.	n.a.	n.a.	n.a.	2011	Severance payment[a]
Hong Kong (China), Special Administrative Region [1,c]	14.1	2000	21.0	2005	22.6	2007	24.4	2008	16.9	2009	n.a.	...	...	...	0.0	16.9	16.9	...	...	2009	Social assistance
India [20]	n.a.	...	n.a.	...	n.a.	...	3.0	2008	n.a.	...	n.a.	...	n.a.	...	3.0	0.0	3.0	...	...	2008	Social insurance and social assistance (public employment guarantee scheme)
Indonesia [2,21]	n.a.	...	n.a.	...	n.a.	...	n.a.	...	n.a.	...	n.a.	...	n.a.	...	n.a.	n.a.	n.a.	n.a.	n.a.	2013	Severance payment[a]
Iran, Islamic Rep. of	...	...	...	...	...	...	...	...	...	...	...	...	...	...	...	...	...	...	...		Social insurance
Iraq	n.a.	...	n.a.	...	n.a.	...	n.a.	...	n.a.	...	n.a.	...	n.a.	...	n.a.	n.a.	n.a.	n.a.	n.a.	2013	No programme anchored in legislation
Israel [1,c]	43.3	2000	29.1	2005	29.7	2007	33.1	2008	38.2	2009	36.3	2010	40.0	2011	29.4	0.0	29.4	...	...	2012	Social insurance
Japan [1,c]	32.5	2001	21.4	2005	22.1	2007	22.9	2008	25.4	2009	19.6	2010	21.5	2011	21.5	0.0	21.5	...	...	2011	Social insurance
Jordan [22]	n.a.	...	n.a.	...	n.a.	...	n.a.	...	n.a.	...	n.a.	...	n.a.	...	n.a.	n.a.	n.a.	n.a.	n.a.	2013	Saving accounts / social insurance
Kazakhstan [1,c]	0.5	2000	0.7	2005	0.9	2007	0.8	2008	1.0	2009	0.5	2010	0.4	2011	0.4	0.0	0.4	...	...	2011	Social insurance
Korea, Dem. People's Rep. of	n.a.	...	n.a.	...	n.a.	...	n.a.	...	n.a.	...	n.a.	...	n.a.	...	n.a.	n.a.	n.a.	n.a.	n.a.	2013	No programme anchored in legislation

Table B.3 Unemployment: Indicators of effective coverage. Unemployed who actually receive benefits (percentages)

Major area, region or country	Percentage of unemployed receiving unemployment benefits																			
	2000		2005		2007		2008		2009		2010		2011		Latest available year					Unemployment benefit programme
	Contributory and non-contributory schemes	Real year	Contributory and non-contributory schemes	Real year	Contributory and non-contributory schemes	Real year	Contributory and non-contributory schemes	Real year	Contributory and non-contributory schemes	Real year	Contributory and non-contributory schemes	Real year	Contributory and non-contributory schemes	Real year	Contributory schemes	Non-contributory schemes	Contributory and non-contributory schemes	Male	Female	Latest Year	Existence of unemployment programme anchored in legislation and type of programme
Korea, Republic of [1,c]	25.1	2004	27.5	2005	34.9	2007	39.4	2008	39.2	2009	36.0	2010	35.8	2011	45.5	0.0	45.5	...	...	2012	Social insurance
Kuwait	n.a.	...	n.a.	...	n.a.	...	n.a.	...	n.a.	...	n.a.	...	n.a.	...	n.a.	n.a.	n.a.	n.a.	n.a.	2013	No programme anchored in legislation
Kyrgyzstan [1,c]	8.2	2000	10.4	2005	3.3	2007	1.4	2008	1.4	2009	1.2	2010	1.2	2011	0.9	0.0	0.9	...	...	2012	Social insurance
Lao People's Dem. Rep.	n.a.	...	n.a.	...	n.a.	...	n.a.	...	n.a.	...	n.a.	...	n.a.	...	n.a.	n.a.	n.a.	n.a.	n.a.	2013	No programme anchored in legislation
Lebanon	n.a.	...	n.a.	...	n.a.	...	n.a.	...	n.a.	...	n.a.	...	n.a.	...	n.a.	n.a.	n.a.	n.a.	n.a.	2013	No programme anchored in legislation
Malaysia [2.23]	n.a.	...	n.a.	...	n.a.	...	n.a.	...	n.a.	...	n.a.	...	n.a.	...	n.a.	n.a.	n.a.	n.a.	n.a.	2013	Severance payment[a]
Maldives	n.a.	...	n.a.	...	n.a.	...	n.a.	...	n.a.	...	n.a.	...	n.a.	...	n.a.	n.a.	n.a.	n.a.	n.a.	2013	No programme anchored in legislation
Mongolia [1,c]	18.0	2003	16.9	2004	...	...	9.7	2008	9.0	2009	10.0	2010	...	...	10.0	0.0	10.0	...	...	2010	Social insurance
Myanmar [24]	n.a.	...	n.a.	...	n.a.	...	n.a.	...	n.a.	...	n.a.	...	n.a.	...	n.a.	n.a.	n.a.	n.a.	n.a.	2013	Unemployment insurance as part of social security law (August 2012, not yet implemented)
Nepal [2.25]	n.a.	...	n.a.	...	n.a.	...	n.a.	...	n.a.	...	n.a.	...	n.a.	...	n.a.	n.a.	n.a.	n.a.	n.a.	2013	Severance payment[a]
Occupied Palestinian Territory	n.a.	...	n.a.	...	n.a.	...	n.a.	...	n.a.	...	n.a.	...	n.a.	...	n.a.	n.a.	n.a.	n.a.	n.a.	2013	No programme anchored in legislation
Oman	n.a.	...	n.a.	...	n.a.	...	n.a.	...	n.a.	...	n.a.	...	n.a.	...	n.a.	n.a.	n.a.	n.a.	n.a.	2013	No programme anchored in legislation
Pakistan [2.26]	n.a.	...	n.a.	...	n.a.	...	n.a.	...	n.a.	...	n.a.	...	n.a.	...	n.a.	n.a.	n.a.	n.a.	n.a.	2013	Severance payment[a]
Philippines [2.27]	n.a.	...	n.a.	...	n.a.	...	n.a.	...	n.a.	...	n.a.	...	n.a.	...	n.a.	n.a.	n.a.	n.a.	n.a.	2013	Severance payment[a]
Qatar	n.a.	...	n.a.	...	n.a.	...	n.a.	...	n.a.	...	n.a.	...	n.a.	...	...	...	...	...	...		No programme anchored in legislation
Saudi Arabia	n.a.	...	n.a.	...	n.a.	...	n.a.	...	n.a.	...	n.a.	...	n.a.	...	...	...	...	...	...	2013	Social assistance
Singapore	n.a.	...	n.a.	...	n.a.	...	n.a.	...	n.a.	...	n.a.	...	n.a.	...	n.a.	n.a.	n.a.	n.a.	n.a.	2013	No programme anchored in legislation
Sri Lanka [2.28]	n.a.	...	n.a.	...	n.a.	...	n.a.	...	n.a.	...	n.a.	...	n.a.	...	n.a.	n.a.	n.a.	n.a.	n.a.	2013	Severance payment[a]
Syrian Arab Republic [2.29]	n.a.	...	n.a.	...	n.a.	...	n.a.	...	n.a.	...	n.a.	...	n.a.	...	n.a.	n.a.	n.a.	n.a.	n.a.	2013	Severance payment[a]
Taiwan, China [1,c]	...	...	32.5	2005	16.4	2007	23.7	2008	32.7	2009	14.6	2010	13.0	2011	15.8	0.0	15.8	12.4	20.7	2012	Social insurance
Tajikistan [1,c]	n.a.	...	5.1	2005	5.0	2007	5.2	2008	3.8	2009	5.3	2010	8.5	2011	9.2	0.0	9.2	...	...	2012	Social insurance
Thailand [1,c]	n.a.	2000	4.2	2005	11.1	2007	13.8	2008	24.3	2009	22.4	2010	37.1	2011	28.5	0.0	28.5	...	...	2012	Social insurance
Timor-Leste	n.a.	...	n.a.	...	n.a.	...	n.a.	...	n.a.	...	n.a.	...	n.a.	...	n.a.	n.a.	n.a.	n.a.	n.a.	2013	No programme anchored in legislation

Table B.3 Unemployment: Indicators of effective coverage. Unemployed who actually receive benefits (percentages)

Major area, region or country	Percentage of unemployed receiving unemployment benefits																				Unemployment benefit programme
	2000		2005		2007		2008		2009		2010		2011		Latest available year						
	Contributory and non-contributory schemes	Real year	Contributory and non-contributory schemes	Real year	Contributory and non-contributory schemes	Real year	Contributory and non-contributory schemes	Real year	Contributory and non-contributory schemes	Real year	Contributory and non-contributory schemes	Real year	Contributory and non-contributory schemes	Real year	Contributory schemes	Non-contributory schemes	Contributory and non-contributory schemes	Male	Female	Latest Year	Existence of unemployment programme anchored in legislation and type of programme
Turkmenistan	...	...	...	...	...	...	...	...	...	...	...	...	...	...	...	...	...	...	...		Social insurance
United Arab Emirates [2,30]	n.a.	...	n.a.	...	n.a.	...	n.a.	...	n.a.	...	n.a.	...	n.a.	...	n.a.	n.a.	n.a.	...	...	2013	Severance payment[a]
Uzbekistan [1,c]	57.1	2000	56.7	2005	61.1	2007	39.5	2008	n.a.	...	n.a.	...	...	...	39.5	0.0	39.5	...	...	2008	Social insurance
Viet Nam [1,c]	n.a.	2000	n.a.	2005	n.a.	2007	n.a.	2008	0.7	2009	10.8	2010	9.5	2011	8.4	0.0	8.4	...	...	2012	Social insurance
Yemen [2,31]	n.a.	...	n.a.	...	n.a.	...	n.a.	...	n.a.	...	n.a.	...	n.a.	...	n.a.	n.a.	n.a.	n.a.	n.a.	2013	Severance payment[a]
Europe																		...	...		
Albania [1,c]	10.2	2000	6.7	2005	7.8	2007	6.7	2008	6.3	2009	6.4	2010	6.0	2011	6.9	0.0	6.9	...	...	2012	Social insurance
Andorra [1,c]	...	...	...	...	...	...	...	...	...	...	8.3	2010	10.0	2011	0.0	11.1	11.1	...	...	2013	General social assistance
Austria [1,c]	94.1	2000	89.4	2005	89.8	2007	90.4	2008	91.3	2009	91.4	2010	90.5	2011	50.7	39.8	90.5	93.8	86.2	2011	Social insurance and social assistance
Belarus [1,c]	39.0	2000	55.7	2005	54.0	2007	46.6	2008	49.4	2009	44.0	2010	46.1	2011	46.1	0.0	46.1	29.1	57.4	2011	Social insurance
Belgium [1,c]	81.3	2000	84.0	2005	86.1	2007	85.7	2008	83.6	2009	82.8	2010	83.1	2011	80.2	0.0	80.2	80.2	80.3	2012	Social insurance and social assistance
Bosnia and Herzegovina [1,c]	1.2	2001	1.6	2005	1.6	2007	1.6	2008	2.4	2009	2.6	2010	2.0	2011	2.0	0.0	2.0	...	...	2011	Social insurance
Bulgaria [1,c]	21.1	2003	23.4	2005	27.1	2007	44.8	2008	45.6	2009	30.8	2010	28.4	2011	25.6	0.0	25.6	...	...	2013	Social insurance
Croatia [1,32,c]	17.7	2000	23.6	2005	22.5	2007	24.2	2008	26.2	2009	25.9	2010	24.4	2011	20.0	0.0	20.0	21.0	19.2	2013	Social insurance and social assistance
Cyprus [1,c]	...	2000	68.1	2005	81.5	2007	81.2	2008	79.1	2009	78.7	2010	...	...	78.7	0.0	78.7	...	...	2010	Social insurance
Czech Republic [1,c]	...	2000	27.6	2005	31.5	2007	42.7	2008	40.4	2009	30.8	2010	25.8	2011	21.2	0.0	21.2	...	...	2013	Social insurance
Denmark [1,c]	99.9	2000	98.9	2005	77.8	2007	72.0	2008	78.6	2009	70.9	2010	68.3	2011	59.5	17.7	77.2	78.4	75.9	2013	Subsidized voluntary insurance and social assistance;
Estonia [1,c]	17.3	2000	28.9	2005	25.9	2007	31.6	2008	45.1	2009	35.2	2010	25.7	2011	14.4	13.2	27.6	22.2	33.5	2012	Social insurance and social assistance
Finland [1,c]	63.7	2002	63.6	2005	58.8	2007	57.5	2008	47.9	2009	52.1	2010	57.8	2011	10.1	49.0	59.1	57.9	60.8	2012	Subsidized voluntary insurance and social assistance;
France [1,c]	57.4	2000	67.0	2005	67.4	2007	67.2	2008	66.0	2009	62.3	2010	59.8	2011	46.3	9.9	56.2	...	...	2013	Social insurance and social assistance
Germany [1,c]	81.2	2000	92.1	2004	80.6	2007	86.1	2008	86.4	2009	87.6	2010	86.3	2011	29.3	58.7	88.0	86.3	89.9	2012	Social insurance and social assistance
Greece [1,c]	52.9	2000	44.3	2002	53.9	2007	58.0	2008	57.7	2009	40.3	2010	29.5	2011	16.4	0.0	16.4	...	...	2014	Social insurance and social assistance
Hungary [1,c]	45.1	2003	42.6	2005	42.6	2007	41.3	2008	48.0	2009	39.5	2010	35.7	2011	13.1	18.3	31.4	...	...	2012	Social insurance and social assistance

Table B.3 Unemployment: Indicators of effective coverage. Unemployed who actually receive benefits (percentages)

Major area, region or country	Percentage of unemployed receiving unemployment benefits																				Unemployment benefit programme
	2000		2005		2007		2008		2009		2010		2011		Latest available year						
	Contributory and non-contributory schemes	Real year	Contributory and non-contributory schemes	Real year	Contributory and non-contributory schemes	Real year	Contributory and non-contributory schemes	Real year	Contributory and non-contributory schemes	Real year	Contributory and non-contributory schemes	Real year	Contributory and non-contributory schemes	Real year	Contributory schemes	Non-contributory schemes	Contributory and non-contributory schemes	Male	Female	Latest Year	Existence of unemployment programme anchored in legislation and type of programme
Iceland [1,32,c]	50.4	2000	72.6	2005	39.1	2007	49.8	2008	17.7	2009	21.6	2010	28.6	2011	28.6	0.0	28.6	18.3	43.0	2011	Social insurance
Ireland [1,32,c]	74.7	2000	81.5	2005	85.9	2007	n.a.	...	91.3	2009	87.2	2010	85.4	2011	21.6	63.8	85.4	...	...	2011	Social insurance and social assistance
Isles of Man [1,c]	33.2	2001	60.3	2006	42.3	2007	42.8	2008	62.4	2009	56.4	2010	56.6	2011	10.0	46.6	56.6	...	...	2011	Social insurance and social assistance
Italy [1,c]	22.6	2000	35.4	2005	42.5	2007	43.9	2008	61.3	2009	56.2	2010	55.8	2011	55.8	0.0	55.8	...	...	2011	Social insurance
Latvia [1,c]	26.2	2001	37.1	2005	47.0	2007	34.8	2008	33.4	2009	27.9	2010	20.8	2011	19.5	0.0	19.5	...	...	2012	Social insurance
Liechtenstein [1,c]	63.0	2000	71.8	2005	66.9	2007	64.6	2008	66.8	2009	78.9	2010	67.2	2011	67.2	0.0	67.2	65.5	68.8	2011	Social insurance
Lithuania [1,c]	...		11.6	2005	26.1	2007	24.8	2008	31.4	2009	20.1	2010	15.6	2011	21.5	0.0	21.5	...	...	2012	Social insurance
Luxembourg [1,c]	42.3	2000	55.1	2005	52.5	2007	51.3	2008	53.4	2009	50.5	2010	50.9	2011	43.8	0.0	43.8	...	...	2012	Social insurance
Macedonia, The Former Yugoslav Rep. of [1,c]	9.9	2003	10.7	2004	7.8	2007	7.7	2008	8.2	2009	...	...	...	...	8.2	0.0	8.2	...	...	2009	Social insurance
Malta [1,c]	89.2	2003	98.7	2005	96.3	2007	94.8	2008	94.2	2009	84.4	2010	86.9	2011	37.4	49.5	86.9	...	...	2011	Social insurance and social assistance
Moldova, Republic of [1,c]	22.8	2000	6.5	2005	10.6	2007	11.8	2008	14.0	2009	11.1	2010	8.5	2011	11.4	0.0	11.4	...	...	2012	Social insurance
Montenegro [1,c]	...		...	...	...	...	32.9	2008	43.9	2009	41.6	2010	40.9	2011	35.6	0.0	35.6	...	...	2012	Social insurance
Netherlands [33]	66.7	2002	69.3	2005	65.1	2007	59.7	2008	60.1	2009	65.1	2010	64.8	2011	59.8	2.1	61.9	62.4	61.4	2012	Social insurance and social assistance
Norway [1,c]	...		58.1	2006	50.9	2007	42.1	2008	74.6	2009	73.4	2010	69.5	2011	61.8	0.0	61.8	...	...	2012	Universal and social insurance
Poland [1,c]	20.3	2000	13.5	2005	14.3	2007	18.4	2008	20.1	2009	16.7	2010	16.5	2011	16.8	0.0	16.8	...	...	2012	Social insurance
Portugal [1,c]	64.6	2003	67.3	2005	60.8	2007	59.5	2008	61.9	2009	57.2	2010	41.9	2011	34.6	7.5	42.1	...	...	2012	Social insurance and social assistance
Romania [1,c]	45.2	2001	38.0	2005	33.2	2007	30.0	2008	52.3	2009	55.4	2010	26.8	2011	35.6	0.0	35.6	32.8	39.2	2012	Social insurance
Russian Federation [1,32,c]	11.8	2000	29.8	2005	28.4	2007	26.2	2008	29.4	2009	24.1	2010	21.3	2011	20.6	0.0	20.6	...	...	2012	Social insurance and social assistance
Serbia [1,c]	11.1	2000	10.4	2005	7.7	2007	9.6	2008	11.6	2009	10.2	2010	8.5	2011	8.8	0.0	8.8	9.9	7.8	2012	Social insurance
Slovakia [1,c]	23.1	2000	9.1	2005	7.6	2007	9.1	2008	15.8	2009	11.1	2010	11.5	2011	11.2	0.0	11.2	...	...	2012	Social insurance
Slovenia [1,c]	21.7	2000	19.2	2005	20.0	2007	26.4	2008	36.1	2009	34.4	2010	32.8	2011	30.8	0.0	30.8	...	...	2012	Social insurance
Spain [1,c]	41.4	2000	65.1	2005	73.9	2007	67.4	2008	62.3	2009	63.0	2010	53.2	2011	23.9	23.0	46.9	49.2	44.4	2012	Social insurance and social assistance
Sweden [1,c]	...	...	86.2	2005	64.8	2007	44.5	2008	39.2	2009	33.9	2010	28.4	2011	28.0	0.0	28.0	25.7	30.7	2012	Subsidized voluntary insurance and social assistance;

Table B.3 Unemployment: Indicators of effective coverage. Unemployed who actually receive benefits (percentages)

Major area, region or country	Percentage of unemployed receiving unemployment benefits																				Unemployment benefit programme
	2000		2005		2007		2008		2009		2010		2011		Latest available year						
	Contributory and non-contributory schemes	Real year	Contributory and non-contributory schemes	Real year	Contributory and non-contributory schemes	Real year	Contributory and non-contributory schemes	Real year	Contributory and non-contributory schemes	Real year	Contributory and non-contributory schemes	Real year	Contributory and non-contributory schemes	Real year	Contributory schemes	Non-contributory schemes	Contributory and non-contributory schemes	Male	Female	Latest Year	Existence of unemployment programme anchored in legislation and type of programme
Switzerland [1,c]	79.2	2000	82.4	2005	71.4	2007	68.3	2008	72.2	2009	74.8	2010	64.7	2011	61.9	0.0	61.9	63.8	59.9	2012	Mandatory insurance
Turkey [1,c]	8.7	2004	5.4	2005	4.3	2007	5.1	2008	7.9	2009	6.3	2010	6.5	2011	7.7	0.0	7.7	...	...	2012	Social insurance
Ukraine [1,32,c]	23.6	2000	40.3	2005	34.4	2007	31.3	2008	26.2	2009	18.7	2010	21.3	2011	20.9	0.0	20.9	...	...	2012	Social insurance and social assistance
United Kingdom [1,c]	68.2	2000	61.0	2005	53.8	2007	52.0	2008	65.0	2009	61.6	2010	60.8	2011	62.6	0.0	62.6	72.8	49.1	2012	Social insurance and social assistance
Latin America and the Caribbean																					
Antigua and Barbuda	n.a.	...	n.a.	...	n.a.	...	n.a.	...	n.a.	...	n.a.	...	n.a.	...	n.a.	n.a.	n.a.	n.a.	n.a.	2013	No statutory provision
Argentina [1,c]	4.1	2001	2.3	2005	4.3	2007	5.6	2008	5.7	2009	5.7	2010	4.9	2011	4.9	0.0	4.9	...	...	2011	Social insurance
Aruba [1,c]	n.a.	...	15.7	2003	...	...	...	...	...	...	...	...	...	...	15.7	...	15.7	...	...	2003	Social insurance
Bahamas [1,c]	n.a.	...	n.a.	...	n.a.	...	n.a.	...	...	...	21.7	2010	18.8	2011	25.7	0.0	25.7	...	...	2012	Social insurance
Barbados [1,c]	79.2	2000	...	...	...	...	...	...	...	...	...	...	...	...	77.7	0.0	77.7	...	...	2003	Social insurance
Belize	n.a.	...	n.a.	...	n.a.	...	n.a.	...	n.a.	...	n.a.	...	n.a.	...	n.a.	n.a.	n.a.	n.a.	n.a.	2013	No statutory provision
Bolivia, Plurinational State of [2,34]	n.a.	...	n.a.	...	n.a.	...	n.a.	...	n.a.	...	n.a.	...	n.a.	...	n.a.	n.a.	n.a.	n.a.	n.a.	2013	Severance paymenta
Brazil [1,c]	...	...	5.1	2005	6.2	2007	8.0	2008	7.2	2009	7.8	2010	...	...	7.8	0.0	7.8	...	...	2010	Social insurance and social assistance
British Virgin Islands	n.a.	...	n.a.	...	n.a.	...	n.a.	...	n.a.	...	n.a.	...	n.a.	...	n.a.	n.a.	n.a.	n.a.	n.a.	2013	No programme anchored in legislation
Chile [1,c]	5.7	2004	9.7	2005	19.6	2007	19.5	2008	20.7	2009	21.1	2010	23.7	2011	29.9	0.0	29.9	38.1	21.4	2013	Mandatory private account and employment-related benefit
Colombia [35]	n.a.	...	n.a.	...	n.a.	...	n.a.	...	n.a.	...	n.a.	...	n.a.	...	n.a.	n.a.	n.a.	n.a.	n.a.	2013	Social insurance and individual account system
Costa Rica [2,36]	n.a.	...	n.a.	...	n.a.	...	n.a.	...	n.a.	...	n.a.	...	n.a.	...	n.a.	n.a.	n.a.	n.a.	n.a.	2013	Severance payment[a]
Cuba	n.a.	...	n.a.	...	n.a.	...	n.a.	...	n.a.	...	n.a.	...	n.a.	...	n.a.	n.a.	n.a.	n.a.	n.a.	2013	No programme anchored in legislation
Dominica	n.a.	...	n.a.	...	n.a.	...	n.a.	...	n.a.	...	n.a.	...	n.a.	...	n.a.	n.a.	n.a.	n.a.	n.a.	2013	No programme anchored in legislation
Dominican Republic	n.a.	...	n.a.	...	n.a.	...	n.a.	...	n.a.	...	n.a.	...	n.a.	...	n.a.	n.a.	n.a.	n.a.	n.a.	2013	No programme anchored in legislation
Ecuador [1,c]	6.7	2000	4.2	2005	...	...	...	...	...	...	...	...	...	...	4.2	0.0	4.2	...	...	2005	Mandatory individual account (no periodic benefit)
El Salvador	n.a.	...	n.a.	...	n.a.	...	n.a.	...	n.a.	...	n.a.	...	n.a.	...	n.a.	n.a.	n.a.	n.a.	n.a.	2013	No programme anchored in legislation

Table B.3 Unemployment: Indicators of effective coverage. Unemployed who actually receive benefits (percentages)

Major area, region or country	Percentage of unemployed receiving unemployment benefits																				
	2000		2005		2007		2008		2009		2010		2011		Latest available year						Unemployment benefit programme
	Contributory and non-contributory schemes	Real year	Contributory and non-contributory schemes	Real year	Contributory and non-contributory schemes	Real year	Contributory and non-contributory schemes	Real year	Contributory and non-contributory schemes	Real year	Contributory and non-contributory schemes	Real year	Contributory and non-contributory schemes	Real year	Contributory schemes	Non-contributory schemes	Contributory and non-contributory schemes	Male	Female	Latest Year	Existence of unemployment programme anchored in legislation and type of programme
Grenada	n.a.	...	n.a.	...	n.a.	...	n.a.	...	n.a.	...	n.a.	...	n.a.	...	n.a.	n.a.	n.a.	n.a.	n.a.	2013	No programme anchored in legislation
Guatemala	n.a.	...	n.a.	...	n.a.	...	n.a.	...	n.a.	...	n.a.	...	n.a.	...	n.a.	n.a.	n.a.	n.a.	n.a.	2013	No programme anchored in legislation
Guyana	n.a.	...	n.a.	...	n.a.	...	n.a.	...	n.a.	...	n.a.	...	n.a.	...	n.a.	n.a.	n.a.	n.a.	n.a.	2013	No programme anchored in legislation
Haiti	n.a.	...	n.a.	...	n.a.	...	n.a.	...	n.a.	...	n.a.	...	n.a.	...	n.a.	n.a.	n.a.	n.a.	n.a.	2013	No programme anchored in legislation
Honduras	n.a.	...	n.a.	...	n.a.	...	n.a.	...	n.a.	...	n.a.	...	n.a.	...	n.a.	n.a.	n.a.	n.a.	n.a.	2013	No programme anchored in legislation
Jamaica	n.a.	...	n.a.	...	n.a.	...	n.a.	...	n.a.	...	n.a.	...	n.a.	...	n.a.	n.a.	n.a.	n.a.	n.a.	2013	No programme anchored in legislation
Mexico [2.37]	n.a.	...	n.a.	...	n.a.	...	n.a.	...	n.a.	...	n.a.	...	n.a.	...	n.a.	n.a.	n.a.	n.a.	n.a.	2013	Severance payment (no statutory). Possible withdraw from social security institute.
Nicaragua	n.a.	...	n.a.	...	n.a.	...	n.a.	...	n.a.	...	n.a.	...	n.a.	...	n.a.	n.a.	n.a.	n.a.	n.a.	2013	No programme anchored in legislation
Panama [2.38]	n.a.	...	n.a.	...	n.a.	...	n.a.	...	n.a.	...	n.a.	...	n.a.	...	n.a.	n.a.	n.a.	n.a.	n.a.	2013	Severance payment [a]
Paraguay	n.a.	...	n.a.	...	n.a.	...	n.a.	...	n.a.	...	n.a.	...	n.a.	...	n.a.	n.a.	n.a.	n.a.	n.a.	2013	No programme anchored in legislation
Peru [2.39]	n.a.	...	n.a.	...	n.a.	...	n.a.	...	n.a.	...	n.a.	...	n.a.	...	n.a.	n.a.	n.a.	n.a.	n.a.	2013	Severance payment [a]
Saint Kitts and Nevis	n.a.	...	n.a.	...	n.a.	...	n.a.	...	n.a.	...	n.a.	...	n.a.	...	n.a.	n.a.	n.a.	n.a.	n.a.	2013	No programme anchored in legislation
Saint Lucia	n.a.	...	n.a.	...	n.a.	...	n.a.	...	n.a.	...	n.a.	...	n.a.	...	n.a.	n.a.	n.a.	n.a.	n.a.	2013	No programme anchored in legislation
Saint Vincent and the Grenadines	n.a.	...	n.a.	...	n.a.	...	n.a.	...	n.a.	...	n.a.	...	n.a.	...	n.a.	n.a.	n.a.	n.a.	n.a.	2013	No programme anchored in legislation
Suriname	n.a.	...	n.a.	...	n.a.	...	n.a.	...	n.a.	...	n.a.	...	n.a.	...	n.a.	n.a.	n.a.	n.a.	n.a.	2013	No programme anchored in legislation
Trinidad and Tobago	n.a.	...	n.a.	...	n.a.	...	n.a.	...	n.a.	...	n.a.	...	n.a.	...	n.a.	n.a.	n.a.	n.a.	n.a.	2013	No programme anchored in legislation
Uruguay [1, c]	15.6	2000	9.3	2005	12.5	2007	16.1	2008	21.3	2009	22.4	2010	25.4	2011	27.9	0.0	27.9	...	...	2012	Social insurance
Venezuela, Bolivarian Rep. of	...		...												...	...	...	...	...		Social insurance
North America																					
Canada [1, c]	46.1	2000	44.2	2005	44.5	2007	43.6	2008	48.4	2009	46.1	2010	41.8	2011	40.5	0.0	40.5	43.6	36.2	2013	Social insurance
United States [1, c]	37.1	2000	35.0	2005	35.9	2007	37.0	2008	40.4	2009	30.6	2010	27.2	2011	26.5	0.0	26.5	...	...	2012	Social insurance

Table B.3 Unemployment: Indicators of effective coverage. Unemployed who actually receive benefits (percentages)

Major area, region or country	Percentage of unemployed receiving unemployment benefits																				Unemployment benefit programme
	2000		2005		2007		2008		2009		2010		2011		Latest available year						
	Contributory and non-contributory schemes	Real year	Contributory and non-contributory schemes	Real year	Contributory and non-contributory schemes	Real year	Contributory and non-contributory schemes	Real year	Contributory and non-contributory schemes	Real year	Contributory and non-contributory schemes	Real year	Contributory and non-contributory schemes	Real year	Contributory schemes	Non-contributory schemes	Contributory and non-contributory schemes	Male	Female	Latest Year	Existence of unemployment programme anchored in legislation and type of programme
Oceania																					
Australia [1,c]	73.4	2000	70.4	2005	62.4	2007	65.8	2008	58.2	2009	51.3	2010	51.4	2011	0.0	52.7	52.7	60.0	44.4	2012	Social assistance
Fiji	n.a.	...	n.a.	...	n.a.	...	n.a.	...	n.a.	...	n.a.	...	n.a.	...	n.a.	n.a.	n.a.	n.a.	n.a.	2013	No programme anchored in legislation
Kiribati	n.a.	...	n.a.	...	n.a.	...	n.a.	...	n.a.	...	n.a.	...	n.a.	...	n.a.	n.a.	n.a.	n.a.	n.a.	2013	No programme anchored in legislation
Marshall Islands	n.a.	...	n.a.	...	n.a.	...	n.a.	...	n.a.	...	n.a.	...	n.a.	...	n.a.	n.a.	n.a.	n.a.	n.a.	2013	No programme anchored in legislation
Micronesia (Fed. States)	n.a.	...	n.a.	...	n.a.	...	n.a.	...	n.a.	...	n.a.	...	n.a.	...	n.a.	n.a.	n.a.	n.a.	n.a.	2013	No programme anchored in legislation
Nauru	n.a.	...	n.a.	...	n.a.	...	n.a.	...	n.a.	...	n.a.	...	n.a.	...	n.a.	n.a.	n.a.	n.a.	n.a.	2013	No programme anchored in legislation
New Caledonia [1,c]	17.4	2002	15.8	2005	18.1	2007	20.3	2008	24.4	2009	23.0	2010	24.5	2011	28.4	0.0	28.4	...	...	2012	Social insurance
New Zealand [1,c]	...	...	...	...	28.0	2007	18.6	2008	35.8	2009	41.8	2010	37.5	2011	0.0	32.9	32.9	45.8	20.6	2013	Social assistance
Niue	n.a.	...	n.a.	...	n.a.	...	n.a.	...	n.a.	...	n.a.	...	n.a.	...	n.a.	n.a.	n.a.	n.a.	n.a.	2013	No programme anchored in legislation
Palau Islands	n.a.	...	n.a.	...	n.a.	...	n.a.	...	n.a.	...	n.a.	...	n.a.	...	n.a.	n.a.	n.a.	n.a.	n.a.	2013	No programme anchored in legislation
Papua New Guinea	n.a.	...	n.a.	...	n.a.	...	n.a.	...	n.a.	...	n.a.	...	n.a.	...	n.a.	n.a.	n.a.	n.a.	n.a.	2013	No programme anchored in legislation
Samoa	n.a.	...	n.a.	...	n.a.	...	n.a.	...	n.a.	...	n.a.	...	n.a.	...	n.a.	n.a.	n.a.	n.a.	n.a.	2013	No programme anchored in legislation
Solomon Islands	n.a.	...	n.a.	...	n.a.	...	n.a.	...	n.a.	...	n.a.	...	n.a.	...	n.a.	n.a.	n.a.	n.a.	n.a.	2013	Withdraw from provident fund
Tonga	n.a.	...	n.a.	...	n.a.	...	n.a.	...	n.a.	...	n.a.	...	n.a.	...	n.a.	n.a.	n.a.	n.a.	n.a.	2013	No programme anchored in legislation
Tuvalu	n.a.	...	n.a.	...	n.a.	...	n.a.	...	n.a.	...	n.a.	...	n.a.	...	n.a.	n.a.	n.a.	n.a.	n.a.	2013	Severance payment [a]
Vanuatu [40]	n.a.	...	n.a.	...	n.a.	...	n.a.	...	n.a.	...	n.a.	...	n.a.	...	n.a.	n.a.	n.a.	n.a.	n.a.	2013	Severance payment [a]

Notes

n.a: Not applicable.

...: Not available.

[a] Severance payment: in the national law (e.g. labour code) and directly paid by employers but no unemployment benefit programme anchored in national legislation.

[b] Unemployed beneficiaries of general social assistance schemes are not included due to unavailability of data. Including them would increase coverage rates but only in countries where such schemes exist on a larger scale (high-income and some middle-income countries).

[c] Detailed sources and notes by country available at: http://www.social-protection.org/gimi/gess/RessourceDownload.action?ressource.ressourceId=37697

Main source
ILO (International Labour Office). ILO Social Security Inquiry. Available at: www.ilo.org/dyn/ilossi/ssimain.home [6 June 2014].

Other sources (Existence of unemployment programme anchored in legislation and type of programme)
Council of Europe: Mutual Information System on Social Protection of the Council of Europe (MISSCEO) (Strasbourg). Available at: http://www.coe.int/t/dg3/socialpolicies/socialsecurity/missceo/missceo_EN.asp [6 June 2014].
European Commission: Mutual Information System on Social Protection (MISSOC). Available at: http://www.missoc.org/MISSOC/MISSOCII/MISSOCII/index.htm [6 June 2014].
ILO (International Labour Office): ILO Employment protection legislation database (EPLex). Available at: http://www.ilo.org/dyn/eplex/termmain.home?p_lang=en [20 Apr. 2014]
—. ILO International labour standards and national legislation database (NORMLEX) (incorporates the former ILOLEX and NATLEX databases). Available at: http://www.ilo.org/dyn/normlex/en/ [6 June 2014].
National legislation (detailed sources and notes by country available online, see link above, c)
SSA (Social Security Administration of the United States); ISSA (International Social Security Association). Social security programs throughout the world (Washington, DC and Geneva): The Americas, 2013; Europe, 2012; Asia and the Pacific, 2012; Africa, 2013. Available at: http://www.ssa.gov/policy/docs/progdesc/ssptw/ [6 June 2014].

1 Data repository: International Labour Office (ILO) ILO Social Security Inquiry. Available at: www.ilo.org/dyn/ilossi/ssimain.home.

2 In the absence of social security benefit in case of unemployment, workers covered by the labour law may be entitled to severance payment (as a lump-sum payment) on the basis usually of a minimum length of service and/or the reason for the termination of the employment relation, sometimes depending on professional categories, size of enterprise or other criteria. Severance payment is a lump sum. 31 countries without unemployment benefit programme anchored in legislation provide such labour protection (information available in the ILO Employment Protection Legislation database (EPLex) and in SSA and ISSA, Social security programs throughout the world, Washington, DC and Geneva).

3 Cameroon. No programme anchored in legislation. Arts 1 and 2 of the Order No. 016 of 26 May 1993: a worker is entitled to severance pay provided he has been employed for at least two years and he has not committed any serious misconduct. Severance pay corresponds to a percentage of the monthly overall wages per year of service and is set according to the length of service.

4 Comoros: No programme anchored in legislation. Article 48 of the Labour Code (former art. 50): severance pay and redundancy pay are to be defined by decree after consultation of the Advisory Council of Labour and Employment (former Supreme Labour Council) and must take into account, in particular, worker's tenure and professional categories. No decree has been adopted as of October 2012.

5 Côte d'Ivoire. No programme anchored in legislation. Art. 3 Decree No. 96-200: a worker is entitled to severance pay provided he has been employed continuously for a period of at least one year and he has not committed any serious misconduct. Severance pay corresponds to a percentage of the monthly overall wages for each year of service.

6 Ethiopia. No programme anchored in legislation. Art. 40 (1) &(2) LP: severance pay amounts to 30 times the average daily pay of the last week of service for the first year of service.

7 Gabon. No programme anchored in legislation. Arts 70 and 73 LC: a worker is entitled to severance pay provided he has been employed for at least two years and he has not committed any serious misconduct. Severance pay corresponds, as a minimum, to 20% of the monthly overall wages per year of service.

8 Lesotho. No programme anchored in legislation. Art. 79 LC: A worker is entitled to severance pay provided he has not been dismissed for misconduct and has completed more than one year of service. Severance pay shall amount to two weeks' wages for each year of service. However, the 1997 Labour Code Amendment Act provides for exemptions from statutory severance pay.

9 Libya: The 1980 Social Security Law requires employers to pay a severance benefit to laid-off employees equal to 100 per cent of earnings for up to six months.

10 Morocco. No programme anchored in legislation. According to art. 53 LC, severance pay is due after 6 months of service. It corresponds to a number of hours per year that varies according to the length of service.

11 Namibia. No programme anchored in legislation. An employer must pay severance pay to an employee who has completed 12 months of continuous service (sec. 35 LA), if the employee is dismissed, dies while employed or resigns after reaching the age of 65 years. The amount of severance pay must be equal to at least one week's remuneration for each year of continuous service with the employer (sec. 35 (3)).

12 Nigeria. The Pension Reform Act of 2004 provides enabling legislation for the National Social Insurance Trust Fund to introduce a social insurance programme for unemployment benefits. No scheme has been implemented to date. The Provident Fund Act of 1961 permits limited cash drawdown payments after one year of unemployment for insured persons who contributed under the previous provident fund system.

13 Rwanda. No programme anchored in legislation. According to art. 35 LL, upon dismissal, workers are entitled to severance pay ("dismissal compensation") provided that they have completed a period of at least twelve (12) consecutive months of work.

14 Seychelles. Under the 1980 Unemployment Fund Act, the social security fund provides subsistence income for unemployed persons. Data available refer to the unemployment relief scheme. National Bureau of Statistics: Seychelles in figures, 2008 and 2012 (available at: http://www.nbs.gov.sc/wp-content/uploads/2011/08/Seychelles-In-Figures-2011-Edition1.pdf, accessed May 2014).

15 Tanzania, United Republic of. No programme anchored in legislation. Severance pay is defined in the ELRA as an amount equal to seven days basic wage for each completed year of continuous service with that employer up to a maximum of ten years (art. 42(1) ELRA). An employer is required to pay severance on termination of employment if the employee has completed 12 months of continuous service with an employer and the employer terminates the employment (art. 42(2) ELRA).

16 Uganda. No programme anchored in legislation. The amount of severance pay is subject to negotiation between the employer and the workers or the trade union that represents them (art. 89 EA). The law also lists circumstances where severance pay is not due (i.e summary dismissal) (art. 88 EA). It seems that, in the event of ordinary fair dismissal (including collective dismissals for economic reasons), the dismissed employee is not entitled to severance pay.

17 Bangladesh. No programme anchored in legislation. The 2008 labour law requires employers to provide a termination benefit, a retrenchment and lay-off benefit, and a benefit for discharge from service on the grounds of ill health to workers in shops and commercial and industrial establishments. Monthly paid permanent employees receive half the average basic wage for 120 days (plus a lump-sum payment of one month's salary for each year of service); casual workers for 60 days (plus a lump-sum payment of 14 days' wages for each year of service); and temporary workers for 30 days.

18 Cambodia. No programme anchored in legislation. Art. 89 LC: if the worker is dismissed for a reason other than serious misconduct, the employer must pay an indemnity for dismissal. The amount of the indemnity depends upon the employee's length of continuous service. This only applies to contracts of an unspecified duration. Art. 73 LC provides that at the expiration of a fixed-term contract (the end of the term or completion of the task), the employer must pay the employee severance pay which may be fixed by collective agreement but should not in any case be less than 5% of the total wages paid during the length of the contract.

19 Georgia. For years 2000 and 2005: Interstate Statistical Committee of the Commonwealth of independent States (CIS) (available at: http://www.cisstat.com/0base/index-en.htm, accessed May 2014). From 2006: the 2006 (labour code) regulates severance pay for employed persons. In the case of termination by the employer, the employer pays one month of average monthly earnings (unless otherwise stated in the employment contract).

20 India. Numerator: ILO Social security inquiry. "Unemployment allowance" was added in 2005 to the existing Employees' State Insurance Corporation scheme, which covers sickness and maternity, and covers 24% of all formal-sector workers, or 2% of the entire workforce. Does not include beneficiaries from the National Rural Employment Guarantee Scheme. The target group for this programme is broader than unemployed.

21 Indonesia. No programme anchored in legislation. Under art. 156 of the Manpower Act, termination of the employment relationship gives rise to termination payments that include severance pay and /or long service pay. The amounts provided here correspond to severance pay: one month's wages for each year of service, up to a maximum of nine months' pay. The extent of the termination package depends on the

circumstances of termination. In the event of termination on the grounds of grave wrongdoing, or absence for five consecutive workdays without explanation, the worker is not entitled to any severance pay or long service pay (art. 160 MA). However, if a worker is terminated on the grounds of violation of the terms of employment, he will be nonetheless entitled to severance pay and reward pay (arts 158 (1) and 168 (1) MA).

[22] Jordan. The recent social security reform includes unemployment Insurance but statistics are not yet available.

[23] Malaysia. No programme anchored in legislation. The Employment (Termination and Lay-off Benefits) Regulations 1980 provide for statutory severance pay in the event of termination: ten days' wages for each completed year of service of less than two years; 15 days' wages for each year of two to five years' service; 20 days' wages for each year of service exceeding five years. These regulations apply to employees with more than one year's service (sec. 3(1)) and do not apply to dismissals for misconduct, after due inquiry (sec. 4).

[24] Myanmar. Myanmar enacted its social security law in 2012. The law includes unemployment insurance benefit (sec. 37), but the country is at the stage of drafting the regulations and provisions are not yet being implemented.

[25] Nepal. No programme anchored in legislation. The 1992 Labour Act requires employers to pay lump-sum severance benefits to laid-off employees equal to one month of wages for each year of service in all establishments employing ten or more workers. The 1993 Labour Rules require employers in establishments with ten or more workers to pay a cash benefit to workers with at least three years of employment when they retire or resign, as follows: 50% of monthly wages for each of the first seven years of service, 66% of monthly wages for each year between seven and 15 years, and 100% of monthly wages for each year of service exceeding 15 years. The employee may choose between a cash benefit and a lump sum.

[26] Pakistan. No programme anchored in legislation. The labour code requires employers with 20 employees or more to pay a severance payment equal to the last 30 days of wages for each year of employment.

[27] Philippines. No programme anchored in legislation.

[28] Sri Lanka. No programme anchored in legislation. Under the Payment of Gratuity Act (PGA), upon any termination of employment, every employer who employs 15 or more shall pay to any monthly paid employee who has worked for at least five years a gratuity payment which amounts to half a month's salary for each completed year of service, or 14 days' wages per year of service for non-monthly paid workers. This indemnity is payable regardless of the reason for termination (resignation, dismissal, retirement, death of the worker, by operation of law, or otherwise). See secs 5(1) and 6 PGA.

[29] Syrian Arab Republic. No programme anchored in legislation. Termination by notice does not automatically entail severance pay. Under the LL, workers are entitled to severance pay only when the contract terminates in specified circumstances (art. 62 LL): (1) Whenever both parties agree in writing to terminate the contract. (2) Whenever workers reach the age of 60, except in the case of a fixed-term contract exceeding such date. In this case, the contract shall expire on expiry date thereof. In any case, the Social Security Law shall be observed in respect of pension eligibility age and the right of workers to continue working until completion of the qualifying service or until the age of 65, whereupon the contract shall automatically expire. (3) Upon the death of the worker. (4) In the event of total disability, for any reason whatsoever. (5) Whenever the worker contracts a disease requiring work interruption for no less than 180 consecutive days, or intermittent periods exceeding, in total, 200 days per one single contractual year. (6) In case of force majeur. In these specified circumstances, employers shall pay workers who are not covered by the Social Security Law a severance pay at the rate of one month's wages for each year of service. Workers shall further be entitled to receive severance pay for any fraction of a year on a pro rata basis (art. 63 (a) LL).

[30] United Arab Emirates. No programme anchored in legislation. According to art. 132 FLLR, a worker who has completed one year or more of continuous service is entitled to severance pay (also referred to as "end of service gratuity") at the end of his employment (21 days' wages for each year of the first five years of service and 30 days' wages for each additional year, provided that the total amount does not exceed two years' wages). A worker shall be entitled to severance pay for any fraction of a year during which he actually served, provided that he has completed one year of continuous service (art. 133 FLLR).

[31] Yemen. No programme anchored in legislation. According to art. 120(2) LC, at end of their service, where employees are not entitled to a monthly pension or a lump-sum payment pursuant to the Social Insurance Act or other regulations, they shall be entitled to receive severance pay equivalent to at least one month's wages for each year of service (calculated on the basis of the last wage received by the employee).

[32] Unemployment assistance schemes exist but no data are available. Accordingly, coverage is underestimated for Croatia; Ireland (Jobseeker's Allowance); Russian Federation; Ukraine

[33] Netherlands. Numerator: Statline: Number of benefits. Available at: http://statline.cbs.nl/StatWeb/selection/default.aspx?DM=SLEN&PA=37789ENG&LA=EN&VW=T, accessed May 2014). Note: social assistance benefits include IOAW benefit. The number of benefits paid to older and partially disabled employees (IOAW) younger than 65 years in the following categories: (a) unemployed persons who have reached the maximum period of unemployment benefit and who were aged 50–57.5 years when they lost their jobs; (b) unemployed persons who lost their jobs after the age of 57.5 years and who are entitled only to short-term unemployment benefit; (c) unemployed persons who are incapable of work and are entitled to partial disability (WAO) benefit (less than 80%), and who have reached the maximum period of unemployment benefit; (d) young disabled recipients of partial Wajong benefits (less than 80%). Denominator: Statline. Central Bureau of Statistics (available at: http://statline.cbs.nl/StatWeb/dome/?LA=EN, accessed May 2014).

[34] Bolivia (Plurinational State of). No programme anchored in legislation. The labour law requires employers to grant severance pay to dismissed employees. Dismissed workers are covered for medical and maternity benefits for two months after employment ceases.

[35] Colombia. Mandatory individual severance account system.

[36] Costa Rica. No programme anchored in legislation. The labour law requires employers to contribute 1.5% of payroll to finance a mandatory severance pay scheme.

[37] Mexico. There is no unemployment insurance in Mexico, but there are programmes to support unemployed persons, such as the Programa de Apoyo al Empleo (PAE) and the Programa de Empleo Temporal (PET). The PAE consists of a set of active labour market policies implemented by the Ministry of Labor and Social (STPS), through the General Coordination of Employment (CGE), which designs, coordinates, oversees and funds the programme, which is operated by the National Employment Service (SNE) in the states. The beneficiaries of the PET represented 11.1% of jobseekers in 2008 and 16.7% in 2009.

[38] Panama. No programme anchored in legislation. Under the 1972 Labor Code, employers are required to provide workers with a severance payment at the end of the labor contract.

[39] Peru. No programme anchored in legislation. The labour code requires private-sector employers to provide a severance payment to employees at the end of the labour contract.

[40] Vanuatu. No programme anchored in legislation. The 1983 Employment Act requires employers to provide one month of severance pay for each year of employment. Employees are eligible after 12 months of work.

Table B.4 Employment injury: Key features of main social security programmes

Major area, region or country	Type of programme[a]	Contribution rates (%)[b]				Estimate of legal employment injury coverage[c] as % of the labour force	
		Employee	Employer	Self-employed	Financing from Government	Mandatory coverage	Voluntary coverage
Africa							
Algeria	Social insurance	No contribution	1.25	Not covered	No contribution	53.8	0.0
Angola	Social insurance					...	...
Benin	Social insurance	No contribution	2.5 (between 1 and 4% of gross payroll according to assessed risk)	Not covered	No contribution	5.2	0.0
Botswana	Employer-liability (normally involving insurance with private)	No contribution	Whole cost	Not covered	No contribution	43.1	0.0
Burkina Faso	Social insurance	No contribution	3.5	Not covered	No contribution	5.5	0.0
Burundi	Social insurance	No contribution	3	Not covered	No contribution	4.9	0.0
Cameroon	Social insurance	No contribution	3.4 (1.75 to 5% of gross payroll according to assessed risk)	Not covered (voluntary coverage not yet implemented)	No contribution	12.4	0.0
Cabo Verde	Social insurance	No contribution	Between 2 and 6% depending on worker's status. Fixed amount for household workers	6	No contribution	56.6	0.0
Central African Republic	Social insurance	No contribution	3	Not covered	No contribution	13.9	0.0
Chad	Social insurance	No contribution	4	Not covered	No contribution	4.7	0.0
Congo	Social insurance	No contribution	2.25	Not covered	No contribution	14.2	0.0
Congo, Democratic Republic of	Social insurance	No contribution	1.5	Not covered	No contribution	26.2	0.0
Côte d'Ivoire	Social insurance	No contribution	3.5 (2 to 5% of gross payroll according to assessed risk)	Voluntary basis	No contribution	14.7	46.2
Djibouti	Social insurance	No contribution	6.2	7	No contribution	...	...
Egypt	Social insurance	No contribution	3	Not covered	No contribution	51.1	0.0
Equatorial Guinea	Social insurance	Global contribution, under old-age (4.5%)	Global contribution, under old age (21.5%)	Not covered	Global contribution, under old age (included in 25% annual social security receipts)	14.5	0.0

Table B.4 Employment injury: Key features of main social security programmes

Major area, region or country	Type of programme[a]	Contribution rates (%)[b]				Estimate of legal employment injury coverage[c] as % of the labour force	
		Employee	Employer	Self-employed	Financing from Government	Mandatory coverage	Voluntary coverage
Ethiopia	Social insurance	Global contribution, under old age (included in 7% of basic salary)	Global contribution, under old age (11% civilian and 25% military)	Not covered	No contribution	17.4	0.0
Gabon	Social insurance	No contribution	3	Special system	No contribution	45.0	45.0
Gambia	Employer-liability	No contribution	1	Not covered	No contribution	23.4	0.0
Ghana	Employer-liability (normally involving insurance with private)	No contribution	Whole cost	Not covered	No contribution	16.6	0.0
Guinea	Social insurance	No contribution	4	Not covered	No contribution	14.5	0.0
Kenya	Employer-liability (normally involving insurance with private)	No contribution	Whole cost	Not covered	No contribution	9.3	0.0
Lesotho	Social insurance	No contribution	Percentage of monthly earnings (variable according to terms of agreement, industry or ministerial directive	Not covered	No contribution	...	...
Liberia	Social insurance	No contribution	1.75	1.75	No contribution	80.5	0.0
Libya	Social insurance; employer-liability	Global contribution, under old age	Global contribution, under old age for cash benefits and under sickness for medical benefits	Global contribution, under old age for cash benefits and under sickness for medical benefits	Cash benefits: under old age, disability, survivors. Medical benefits: under sickness	...	...
Madagascar	Social insurance	No contribution	1.25	Not covered	No contribution	9.3	0.0
Malawi	Employer-liability (normally involving insurance with private)	No contribution	Whole cost	Not covered	No contribution	6.9	0.0
Mali	Social insurance	No contribution	2.5% (1 to 4% depending to assessed risk)	2.5% (1 to 4% depending on assessed risk). Voluntary basis	No contribution	9.1	48.1
Mauritania	Social insurance	No contribution	3	Not covered	No contribution	8.6	0.0
Mauritius	Social insurance	No contribution	Global contribution, under old age (6% to 10.5% of payroll)	Not covered	No contribution	68.2	0.0

Table B.4 Employment injury: Key features of main social security programmes

Major area, region or country	Type of programme[a]	Contribution rates (%)[b]				Estimate of legal employment injury coverage[c] as % of the labour force	
		Employee	Employer	Self-employed	Financing from Government	Mandatory coverage	Voluntary coverage
Morocco	Employer-liability (involving insurance with private)	No contribution	Whole cost	Not covered	No contribution	39.0	0.0
Namibia	Social insurance	No contribution	Whole cost	Not covered	No contribution	47.1	0.0
Niger	Social insurance	No contribution	2	1.75	No contribution	90.9	0.0
Nigeria	Social insurance	No contribution	1	Financing mechanisms still undetermined	No contribution	32.8	0.0
Rwanda	Social insurance	No contribution	2	Not covered	No contribution	4.5	0.0
Sao Tome and Principe	Social insurance	Global contribution, under old age (4% of gross earnings)	Global contribution, under old age (6% of gross payroll)	Not covered	No contribution	28.9	0.0
Senegal	Social insurance	No contribution	1%, 3%, or 5% depending on assessed degree of risk	1%, 3% or 5% depending on assessed degree of risk	No contribution	27.3	34.0
Seychelles	Social insurance	No contribution	No contribution	Not covered	Total cost is financed from earmarked income tax	69.1	0.0
Sierra Leone	Employer-liability (normally involving insurance with private)	No contribution	Whole cost	Not covered	An approved annual contribution	6.1	0.0
South Africa	Employer-liability (involving insurance with private)	No contribution	Whole cost	Not covered	No contribution	67.5	0.0
Sudan	Social insurance	No contribution	2	Global contribution, under old age (25% of declared monthly income)	No contribution	62.1	0.0
Swaziland	Employer-liability (involving insurance with private)	No contribution	Whole cost	Not covered	No contribution	62.6	0.0
Tanzania, United Republic of	Social insurance	Global contribution, under old age (10% to 20% – if voluntary – of gross earnings)	Global contribution, under old age (10% of gross payroll)	Global contribution, under old age (20% of declared income)	No contribution	8.8	68.0
Togo	Social insurance	No contribution	2	2	No contribution	84.2	0.0
Tunisia	Social insurance	No contribution	0.4% to 4.0% of gross payroll, depending on the assessed degree of risk	Voluntary contributions	No contribution	42.0	15.3
Uganda	Employer-liability (involving insurance with private)	No contribution	Whole cost	Not covered	No contribution	16.0	0.0

Table B.4 Employment injury: Key features of main social security programmes

Major area, region or country	Type of programme[a]	Contribution rates (%)[b]				Estimate of legal employment injury coverage[c] as % of the labour force	
		Employee	Employer	Self-employed	Financing from Government	Mandatory coverage	Voluntary coverage
Zambia	Employer-liability (involving insurance with private)	No contribution	Varies according to the assessed degree of risk	Not covered	No contribution	11.9	0.0
Zimbabwe	Employer-liability	No contribution	Whole cost	Not covered	No contribution	25.4	0.0
Asia							
Armenia	Social insurance	Global contribution, under old age (3% of net monthly earnings) for cash benefits	Global contribution, under old age (fixed amount depending on employee monthly income range) for cash benefits	Not covered	Cash benefits: subsidies as needed. Medical benefits: total cost is paid by central and local governments	59.3	0.0
Azerbaijan	Employer-liability involving compulsory insurance	No contribution	Whole cost	Whole cost. Voluntary basis	Whole cost of the funeral grant	39.7	0.0
Bahrain	Social insurance	No contribution	3% of the employee's monthly earnings	Not covered	No contribution	84.6	0.0
Bangladesh	Employer-liability	No contribution	Whole cost	Not covered	No contribution	12.5	0.0
Bhutan	Social insurance	No contribution	Whole cost	Not covered	No contribution	...	...
Brunei Darussalam	Employer-liability	No contribution	Provides benefits directly to employees	Not covered	No contribution	88.0	0.0
China	Social insurance; employer-liability	No contribution	1% of total payroll (on average) for social insurance; whole costs for employer-liability	Contribute as employer for employees	Subsidies as needed	24.2	0.0
Georgia	Employer-liability; social assistance	No contribution for employer liability; under old age, disability and survivors for social assistance	Whole cost for cash and medical benefits for employer-liability; no contribution for social assistance	Not covered for employer-liability; under old-age, disability and survivors for social assistance	Employer liability: whole cost for cash and medical benefits. Social assistance: under old age, disability and survivors	23.3	0.0
Hong Kong (China), Special Administrative Region	Employer-liability involving compulsory insurance	No contribution	Whole cost	Not covered	No contribution	85.6	0.0
India	Social insurance	Global contribution, under sickness	Global contribution, under sickness	Not covered	Global contribution, under sickness	7.9	0.0
Indonesia	Social insurance	No contribution	Whole cost	1% of monthly declared earnings. Voluntary basis	No contribution	28.7	44.3

Table B.4 Employment injury: Key features of main social security programmes

Major area, region or country	Type of programme[a]	Contribution rates (%)[b]				Estimate of legal employment injury coverage[c] as % of the labour force	
		Employee	Employer	Self-employed	Financing from Government	Mandatory coverage	Voluntary coverage
Iran, Islamic Rep. of	Social insurance	Global contribution, under old age	Global contribution, under old age	Not covered	Global contribution, under old age	38.7	0.0
Israel	Social insurance	No contribution	0.37% to 0.90% of earnings above 60% of the national average wage	0.39 to 0.68% of earnings above 60% of the national average wage	0.03% of payroll and earnings	74.1	0.0
Japan	Social insurance	No contribution	0.25% to 8.9% of payroll, according to a three-year accident rate	0.25% to 8.9% of declared earnings	No contribution	85.0	0.0
Jordan	Social insurance	No contribution	At least 2% of monthly payroll	Not covered	Any deficit	44.6	0.0
Kazakhstan	Employer-liability involving compulsory insurance; social assistance	No contribution	Total cost of insurance premiums (from 0.04% to 9.9% of payroll) or directly provides benefits to the insured	Cost of certain benefits	Cost of permanent disability and survivor benefits	56.1	0.0
Korea, Republic of	Social insurance	No contribution	0.6% to 35.4% of annual payroll, according to the assessed degree of risk	0.6% to 35.4% of declared earnings or payroll. Voluntary basis	No contribution	85.2	0.0
Kuwait	Social insurance | No specific program for employment injury	Global contribution, under old age	Global contribution, under old age	...	Whole cost for cash benefits. Permanent disability under long-term benefits	95.1	2.6
Kyrgyzstan	Social insurance (cash benefits); universal (medical benefits)	Global contribution, under old age for cash benefits	Global contribution, under old-age (cash benefits)	None (medical benefits)	Whole cost for medical benefits; permanent disability under long-term benefits	44.0	0.0
Lao People's Dem. Rep.	Social insurance (employer liability for non covered employees)	No contribution	Global contribution, under old age (5% of monthly payroll)	Not covered	Administrative costs for the social security administration	6.7	0.0
Lebanon	Employer-liability involving compulsory insurance	No contribution	Whole cost	Not covered	No contribution	47.8	0.0
Malaysia	Social insurance	No contribution	1.25% of monthly payroll, according to 34 wage classes	Not covered	No contribution	36.2	0.0
Myanmar	Social insurance	No contribution; under sickness for the funeral grant	1% of monthly payroll; under sickness for the funeral grant	Not covered	No contribution	...	...
Nepal	Employer-liability involving compulsory insurance	No contribution	Whole cost	Not covered	No contribution	3.8	0.0

Table B.4 Employment injury: Key features of main social security programmes

Major area, region or country	Type of programme[a]	Contribution rates (%)[b]				Estimate of legal employment injury coverage[c] as % of the labour force	
		Employee	Employer	Self-employed	Financing from Government	Mandatory coverage	Voluntary coverage
Oman	Social insurance	No contribution	1% of payroll	Not covered	No contribution	40.2	0.0
Pakistan	Social insurance; employer-liability	No contribution	Global contribution, under sickness (6% of monthly payroll)	Not covered	No contribution	28.6	0.0
Philippines	Social insurance	No contribution	0.2% for monthly earnnings of at least 15 000 pesos	Not covered	Any deficit	45.8	0.0
Saudi Arabia	Social insurance	No contribution	2% of payroll	Not covered	Discretionary | Irregular contribution	77.4	0.0
Singapore	Employer-liability involving compulsory insurance	No contribution	Whole cost	Not covered	No contribution	72.6	0.0
Sri Lanka	Employer-liability	No contribution	Whole cost or (1 to 7.5% of gross payroll according to assessed risk)	Not covered	Whole cost of medical benefits	42.3	0.0
Syrian Arab Republic	Social insurance	No contribution	3% of payroll	Not covered	No contribution	47.8	0.0
Taiwan, China	Social insurance	No contribution	Cash: 0.21% on average: 0.02% to 2.94% of monthly payroll according to assessed risk. Medical benefits: under sickness and maternity	Not covered with exceptions	Cash: cost of administration. Medical benefits: under sickness and maternity	74.1	0.0
Thailand	Employer-liability involving compulsory insurance	No contribution	0.2% to 1% of annual payroll according to assessed risk	Not covered	No contribution	26.2	0.0
Turkmenistan	Social insurance (cash benefits); universal (medical benefits)	Cash: contribution older old age, disability, survivor Medical benefits: no contribution	Cash: global contribution, under old age (20% of payroll) Medical benefits: no contribution	Not covered	Cash: global contribution, under old age, disability, survivors. Medical benefits: total cost. Medical benefits: no contribution	52.6	0.0
Uzbekistan	Social insurance (cash benefits); universal (medical benefits)	Global contribution, under old age (5.5% of wages)	Global contribution, under old age (25% of payroll)	Not covered	Subsidies for work injury benefits. Total cost of medical benefits	44.1	0.0
Viet Nam	Social insurance	No contribution	1% of monthly payroll	Not covered	No contribution	30.4	0.0
Yemen	Social insurance	No contribution	4% of total payroll	Not covered	No contribution, contributes at 1% of payroll as an employer	37.7	0.0

Table B.4 Employment injury: Key features of main social security programmes

Major area, region or country	Type of programme[a]	Contribution rates (%)[b]				Estimate of legal employment injury coverage[c] as % of the labour force	
		Employee	Employer	Self-employed	Financing from Government	Mandatory coverage	Voluntary coverage
Europe							
Albania	Social insurance	No contribution	0.3	Not covered	No contribution	34.7	0.0
Austria	Social insurance	No contribution	1.4	1.9% of covered income or flat rate	Federal government contributes to farmers' accident insurance	77.4	0.0
Belarus	Social insurance	No contribution	Federal government contributes to farmers' accident insurance	Not covered	No contribution	70.9	0.0
Belgium	Social insurance	No contribution	0.32% of reference earnings for work injury; 1% of reference earnings for occupational disease	Not covered	No contribution	63.1	0.0
Bulgaria	Social insurance	No contribution	0.4% to 1.1% of payroll, according to the assessed degree of risk	0.4% to 1.1% of income, according to the assessed degree of risk. Voluntary basis	No contribution, contributes as an employer	66.2	8.6
Croatia	Social insurance	No contribution	0.5	0.5	No contribution	68.2	0.0
Czech Republic	Social insurance	No contribution	The premium depends on the type of activity performed	Not covered	Any deficit	66.2	0.0
Cyprus	Social insurance	Global contribution, under old age (6.8% of covered earnings)	Global contribution, under old age (6.8% of covered payroll)	Not covered	Global contribution, under old age (4.3% of covered payroll)	68.2	0.0
Denmark	Universal (medical benefits); direct provision (cash benefits)	No contribution	Whole cost for permanent disability. Under sickness and maternity for temporary disability	Voluntary contributions	Global contribution, under sickness	88.0	7.9
Estonia	Social insurance	No contribution	Global contribution, under sickness (13% of payroll)	Global contribution, under sickness (13% of declared earnings)	Any deficit	76.8	0.0
Finland	Employer-liability; mandatory private insurance	No contribution	0.3% to 8% of annual payroll, according to the profession's assessed degree of risk	Annual premium according to the assessed degree of risk for the profession. Voluntary basis	No contribution	66.5	9.4

Table B.4 Employment injury: Key features of main social security programmes

Major area, region or country	Type of programme[a]	Contribution rates (%)[b]				Estimate of legal employment injury coverage[c] as % of the labour force	
		Employee	Employer	Self-employed	Financing from Government	Mandatory coverage	Voluntary coverage
France	Social insurance	No contribution. Voluntarily insured persons pay variable contributions according to the assessed degree of risk	The total cost. Varies according to assessed degree of risk	Contribution to special schemes	No contribution	74.1	0.0
Germany	Social insurance	No contribution	1.32% on average	Not covered (with few exceptions)	A subsidy for agricultural accident insurance. Contributions for specific groups (students, specified voluntary activities)	63.0	0.0
Greece	Social insurance	Global contribution, under sickness (0.4% of covered monthly earnings for cash benefits and 2.15% for medical benefits)	Global contribution, under sickness + 1% payroll	Not covered	A guaranteed annual subsidy	46.9	0.0
Hungary	Social insurance	Global contribution, under old age (10% of covered monthly earnings)	Global contribution, under old age (27% of monthly payroll)	Global contribution, under old age (37% of declared monthly earnings)	Any deficit	78.3	0.0
Iceland	Social insurance; social assistance	No contribution	Global contribution, under old-age (part of 7.79% of gross earnings for the universal pension)	Global contribution, under oldage (part of 7.79% of gross earnings for the universal pension)	Partially finances through general taxation	95.1	0.3
Ireland	Social insurance	Global contribution, under old age (4% of covered weekly earnings)	Global contribution, under old-age (4.25% to 10.75% of gross wages according to weekly earnings)	Not covered	Any deficit (private-sector employees); the total cost (public-sector employees)	71.8	0.0
Italy	Social insurance	No contribution	3% on average (0.5% to 16% of payroll, according to the assessed degree of risk)	Variable contribution according to assessed degree of risk	No contribution	72.2	0.0
Latvia	Social insurance	No contribution	Global contribution, under old age	Not covered	Cost of state-guaranteed health care services (annual state budget). Contributes as an employer	69.2	0.0

Table B.4 Employment injury: Key features of main social security programmes

Major area, region or country	Type of programme[a]	Contribution rates (%)[b]				Estimate of legal employment injury coverage[c] as % of the labour force	
		Employee	Employer	Self-employed	Financing from Government	Mandatory coverage	Voluntary coverage
Liechtenstein	Social insurance	No contribution	Variable contribution according to assessed degree of risk	Variable contribution according to the extent of coverage required and the assessed degree of risk. Voluntary basis	No contribution	…	…
Lithuania	Social insurance	No contribution	0.18% to 0.9% of earnings, according to three employment categories	Not covered	No contribution	64.7	0.0
Luxembourg	Social insurance	No contribution	1.15% of covered income	1.15% of covered income	50% of the cost of administration	77.1	0.0
Malta	Social insurance	Global contribution, under old age (10% of covered wages)	Global contribution, under old age (10% of covered payroll)	Global contribution, under old age. Variable amount depending on net income	50% of the value of total contributions	73.5	0.0
Moldova, Republic of	Social insurance (cash benefits); universal (medical benefits)	No contribution	Global contribution, under old age (22–23% of payroll depending on sector)	Annual flat rate. Voluntary basis	No contribution	60.2	22.8
Monaco	Mandatory private insurance	No contribution	Whole cost	Not covered	No contribution	…	…
Netherlands	Social insurance	Global contribution, under sickness, old age, disability, survivors	Global contribution, under sickness, old age, disability, survivors	…	Global contribution, under sickness, old- age, disability, survivors	97.6	0.0
Norway	Social insurance; universal.	No contribution	Global contribution, under old age	0.4% of income. Voluntary basis	Any deficit	89.6	1.8
Poland	Social insurance	No contribution	From 0.67% to 3.33% of payroll, according to the assessed degree of risk and number of employees	1.67% of declared earnings	The cost of specialized procedures promoting good public health practices	100.0	0.0
Portugal	Employer-liability (work injury); social insurance (occupational diseases)	No contribution	Liability insurance (work injury) with a private carrier (premiums vary according to assessed degree of risk). 0.50% of payroll (occupational diseases)	Contributions for occupational diseases under old-age, disability, survivors	No contribution	77.3	0.0
Romania	Social insurance	No contribution. Voluntarily insured pay 1% of the average monthly income.	From 0.5% to 0.85% of average gross monthly income, according to the assessed degree of risk	1% of average monthly income. Voluntary basis	Subsidies	63.1	16.6

Table B.4 Employment injury: Key features of main social security programmes

Major area, region or country	Type of programme[a]	Contribution rates (%)[b]				Estimate of legal employment injury coverage[c] as % of the labour force	
		Employee	Employer	Self-employed	Financing from Government	Mandatory coverage	Voluntary coverage
Russian Federation	Social insurance	No contribution	From 0.2% to 8.5% of payroll according to 32 classes of professional risk related to 22 industry categories	Not covered	No contribution	74.4	0.0
San Marino	Social insurance	Global contribution, under old age	Global contribution, under old age	Global contribution, under old age	Global contribution, under old age	96.9	0.0
Serbia	Social insurance	Provided under old age, disability and survivors and sickness	Provided under old age, disability and survivors and sickness	...	Provided under old age, disability and survivors, and sickness	66.2	0.0
Slovakia	Social insurance	No contribution	0.8% of gross payroll	Not covered	Any deficit and the cost of spa treatment	66.4	0.0
Slovenia	Social insurance	Under sickness for temporary disability; under old age, disability and survivors for permanent disability	0.53% of gross earnings for temporary disability; under old age, disability and survivors for permanent disability	0.53% of payroll for temporary disability; under old age, disability and survivors for permanent disability	Any deficit caused by a decline in contribution rates for permanent disability benefits	80.2	0.0
Spain	Social insurance	No contribution	1.98% (0.81 to 16.2% according to assessed degree of risk)	Voluntary contributions depending on the level of coverage chosen	No contribution	48.3	22.2
Sweden	Social insurance	No contribution	0.68% of payroll	0.68% of declared earnings	No contribution	84.8	0.0
Switzerland	Mandatory private insurance	No contribution	Whole cost	Voluntary contributions	No contribution	66.7	11.1
Turkey	Social insurance	No contribution	Provided under sickness (included in 1% to 6.5% monthly earnings, according to degree of risk)	Provided under sickness (included in 1% to 6.5% monthly earnings, according to degree of risk)	The cost of contributions for apprentices and students in technical schools. Contributes as an employer	68.4	0.0
Ukraine	Social insurance (cash benefits); universal (medical benefits)	None for cash benefits; included uuder sickness for medical benefits	Global contribution, under old-age	...	None for cash benefits; included under sickness for medical benefits	64.1	0.0
United Kingdom	Social insurance; social assistance	Global contribution, under old age	Global contribution, under old age	Not covered	Global contribution, under old age	68.0	0.0

Table B.4 Employment injury: Key features of main social security programmes

Major area, region or country	Type of programme[a]	Contribution rates (%)[b]				Estimate of legal employment injury coverage[c] as % of the labour force	
		Employee	Employer	Self-employed	Financing from Government	Mandatory coverage	Voluntary coverage
Latin America and the Caribbean							
Argentina	Employer-liability	No contribution	Whole cost	Not covered	No contribution	44.9	0.0
Bahamas	Social insurance	No contribution	Whole cost	2	No contribution	82.6	0.0
Barbados	Social insurance	Global contribution, under old age (5.93 to 13.5% of covered earnings)	Global contribution, under old age (5.93 to 6.75% of covered payroll)	Not covered	No contribution	65.6	0.0
Belize	Social insurance	Contributions under old age, disability, survivors	Contributions under old age, disability, survivors	Contributions under old age, disability, survivors	Contributes as an employer	80.6	0.0
Bermuda	Employer-liability (normally involving insurance with private)	No contribution	Whole cost	Not covered	No contribution	32.2	0.0
Bolivia, Plurinational State of	Social insurance; mandatory private insurance	Under sickness and maternity for temporary disability benefits and medical benefits	Under sickness and maternity for temporary disability and medical benefits; under old age, disability, survivors for permanent disability	Temporary disability and medical benefits: under sickness. Permanent disability: under old age, disability, survivors. Voluntary basis.	Contributes as an employer	16.0	18.4
Brazil	Social insurance	No contribution	1% to 3% of gross payroll according to the assessed degree of risk; 0.1% of gross payroll for employers of rural workers	Not covered	No contribution	56.5	0.0
British Virgin Islands	Social insurance	No contribution	0.5% of covered monthly payroll	0.5% of declared monthly earnings	No contribution	98.4	0.0
Chile	Social insurance	No contribution	0.95% plus up to 3.4% of covered payroll according to assessed risk	0.95% declared income + up to 3.4% declared earnings depending on the occupation.	No contribution; contributes as an employer	76.0	0.0
Colombia	Social insurance	No contribution	0.348% to 8.7% of covered payroll according to assessed risk	0.348% to 8.7% of declared covered earnings according to assessed risk. Voluntary basis.	Global contribution | Contributes as an employer	44.5	40.5
Costa Rica	Employer-liability involving compulsory and voluntary insurance with a public carrier	No contribution	Whole cost	Not covered	No contribution	60.1	0.0

Table B.4 Employment injury: Key features of main social security programmes

Major area, region or country	Type of programme[a]	Contribution rates (%)[b]				Estimate of legal employment injury coverage[c] as % of the labour force	
		Employee	Employer	Self-employed	Financing from Government	Mandatory coverage	Voluntary coverage
Cuba	Social insurance (cash); universal (medical care)	Global contribution, under old age	Global contribution, under old age	Global contribution, under old age	Global contribution, under old age	94.4	0.0
Dominica	Employer-liability	No contribution	1% of employee's gross earnings	Not covered	No contribution; contributes as an employer	60.8	0.0
Dominican Republic	Social insurance	No contribution	1.2% of payroll on average, according to assessed risk	Not covered	No contribution; contributes as an employer	…	…
Ecuador	Social insurance	No contribution. 0.55% of gross earnings for voluntary contributors	0.55% of gross declared earnings	0.55% of gross declared earnings	40% of the cost of work injury pensions	49.0	30.1
El Salvador	Social insurance	Global contribution, under sickness	Global contribution, under sickness	Global contribution, under sickness	Global contribution, under sickness	26.8	0.0
Grenada	Social insurance	No contribution	Old age, disability, survivors (included in 4%)	Global contribution, under old age, disability and survivors	No contribution; contributes as an employer	60.7	0.0
Guatemala	Social insurance	1% of gross earnings	3% of gross payroll	Not covered	1.5% of gross payroll	65.6	0.0
Guyana	Social insurance	Global contribution, under old age	Global contribution, under old age	Not covered	No contribution; contributes as an employer	56.6	0.0
Haiti	Social insurance	No contribution	2% to 6% of payroll depending on sector	Not covered	No contribution; contributes 2% of payroll as an employer	15.7	0.0
Honduras	Social insurance	No contribution	0.2% of payroll	Not covered	No contribution	16.3	0.0
Jamaica	Social insurance	No contribution	Global contribution, under old age	Not covered	No contribution; contributes as an employer	52.0	0.0
Mexico	Social insurance	No contribution	0.5% to 15% of payroll depending of assessed degree of risk	Variable contributions. Voluntary basis.	No contribution	49.3	8.9
Nicaragua	Social insurance	No contribution	1.5% of covered payroll (+1.5% of covered payroll for war victims' pensions)	Not covered	No contribution; contributes as an employer	44.9	0.0
Panama	Employer-liability involving compulsory insurance with a public carrier	No contribution	Whole cost, varies with the assessed degree of risk	Not covered	No contribution	59.6	0.0
Paraguay	Social insurance	Global contribution, under old age	Global contribution, under old age	Not covered	Global contribution, under old-age	32.1	0.0

Table B.4 Employment injury: Key features of main social security programmes

Major area, region or country	Type of programme[a]	Contribution rates (%)[b]				Estimate of legal employment injury coverage[c] as % of the labour force	
		Employee	Employer	Self-employed	Financing from Government	Mandatory coverage	Voluntary coverage
Peru	Social insurance	No contribution	0.63% to 1.84% of covered payroll depending of assessed degree of risk and the reported accident rate	Flat-rate contribution from 10 to 30 nuevos soles	No contribution; contributes as an employer	39.5	0.0
Saint Kitts and Nevis	Social insurance	No contribution	1% of covered payroll	Not covered	No contribution; contributes as an employer	80.6	0.0
Saint Lucia	Social insurance	Global contribution, under old age (5% of covered monthly earnings)	Global contribution, under old age (5% of covered monthly payroll)	Not covered	No contribution; contributes as an employer	49.5	0.0
Saint Vincent and the Grenadines	Social insurance	No contribution	0.5% of payroll	Not covered	No contribution; contributes as an employer	59.4	0.0
Trinidad and Tobago	Social insurance; Employer liability	0.185% of covered earnings or one-third of the overall contribution rate	0.37% of payroll or two-thirds of the overall contribution rate	Not covered	No contribution; contributes as an employer	65.5	0.0
Uruguay	Mandatory insurance through a public carrier	No contribution	Whole cost	Not covered	No contribution	54.6	0.0
Venezuela, Bolivarian Rep. of	Social insurance	No contribution	0.75% to 10% of covered payroll depending of assessed degree of risk	Not covered	At least 1.5% of total covered earnings to cover the cost of administration	57.9	0.0
North America							
Canada	Social insurance	No contribution	Whole cost	Not covered	No contribution	69.1	0.0
United States	Compulsory (elective for employers in one state) insurance through a public or private carrier (according to the state) or self-insurance	Nominal contributions in a few states	Whole cost or most of the costs, 1.3% of payroll on average in 2009	Not covered	No contribution; contributes as an employer	84.8	
Oceania							
Australia	Employer-liability involving compulsory insurance	No contribution	Whole cost	Total cost of self-insurance. Voluntary basis	No contribution; contributes as an employer	72.0	9.4
Fiji	Employer liability	No contribution	Whole cost: provides benefits directly to employees	Not covered	No contribution	40.1	0.0
Kiribati	Employer-liability involving compulsory insurance	No contribution	Whole cost	Not covered	No contribution	32.8	0.0

Table B.4 Employment injury: Key features of main social security programmes

Major area, region or country	Type of programme[a]	Contribution rates (%)[b]				Estimate of legal employment injury coverage[c] as % of the labour force	
		Employee	Employer	Self-employed	Financing from Government	Mandatory coverage	Voluntary coverage
New Zealand	Universal; employer-liability	No contribution for work injury; contribution rates set each year for non-work injury	Contribution rates set each year	Contribution rates set each year	Contributes as an employer	100.0	0.0
Palau Islands	Employer liability	No contribution	Whole cost	Not covered	No contribution	...	...
Papua New Guinea	Employer-liability involving compulsory insurance	No contribution	Whole cost	Not covered	No contribution	6.4	0.0
Samoa	Employer-liability involving compulsory insurance	No contribution for work-related injuries; 1% of earnings for non-work-related injuries	1% payroll for work-related injuries	Not covered	No contribution	53.5	0.0
Solomon Islands	Employer-liability involving compulsory insurance	No contribution	Whole cost	Not covered	No contribution	14.5	0.0

Notes

n.a.: Not applicable.

...: Not available.

[a] Definitions regarding the type of programme are available in the electronic version of this table (http://www.social-protection.org/gimi/gess/RessourceDownload.action?ressource.ressourceId=41917) and in the glossary (Annex I).

[b] Contribution rates: where there are several contribution rates, the average or most common rate is indicated or a reference to a specific note.

[c] Global estimates of legal coverage (for definition, see Annex II) are weighted by total population 2012 (UN World Population Prospects, 2012 Revision),

Main source

SSA (Social Security Administration of the United States); ISSA (International Social Security Association). Social security programs throughout the world (Washington, DC and Geneva): The Americas, 2013; Europe, 2012; Asia and the Pacific, 2012; Africa, 2013. Available at: http://www.ssa.gov/policy/docs/progdesc/ssptw/ [6 June 2014].

Other sources

ILO (International Labour Office): ILO National Legislation on Labour and Social Rights database (NATLEX) available at: http://www.ilo.org/dyn/natlex/natlex_browse.home [6 June 2014].

—. ILO database of labour statistics (ILOSTAT). Available at: http://www.ilo.org/ilostat/ [6 June 2014].

—. ILO Key Indicators of the Labour Market (KILM), 8th edition. Available at: http://www.ilo.org/empelm/what/WCMS_114240/lang--en/index.htm [5 June 2014].

National statistical offices. Data sets and reports from national labour force surveys or other household or establishment surveys (link to national statistical offices websites available at: http://laborsta.ilo.org/links_content_E.html#m2 [6 June 2014].

Table B.5 Maternity: Key features of main social security programmes (cash benefits)

Country or area	Date of the first law (or Labour Act*)	Provider of maternity benefits, type of programme and financing sources			Coverage of self-employed	Length of maternity leave			Percentage of wages paid in covered period (%)	
		Provider of maternity benefits	Type of programme	Sources of financing		Period (no. and unit)		No. of weeks	%	Note
Africa										
Algeria	1949	Social security	Social insurance	Employer & employee	No	14	weeks	14	100	
Angola	...	Social security (the employer advances the payment and is reimbursed by social insurance)	Social insurance	Employer & employee	...	13	weeks	13	100	
Benin	1952	Social security (50%); Employer (50%)	Social insurance	Employer	No	14	weeks	14	100	
Botswana [1]	1994*	Employer (no statutory social security benefits)	Employer liability	Employer	No	12	weeks	12	50	
Burkina Faso [2]	1952	Social insurance (if necessary, the employer adds up to the full wage)	Social insurance	Employer	No	14	weeks	14	100	
Burundi [3]	1993*	Employer (50%); Social security (50%)	Employer liability	Employer	No	12	weeks	12	100	
Cameroon	1956	National Social Insurance Fund	Social insurance	Employer	No	14	weeks	14	100	
Cabo Verde	1976	Social security	Social insurance	Employer & employee	Yes, with exceptions	60	days	8.5	90	4
Central African Republic	1952	Social security	Social insurance	Employer	No	14	weeks	14	50	
Chad	1952	Social security	Social insurance	Employer & Government	No	14	weeks	14	100	
Comoros	...	Employer (no statutory social security benefits)	Employer liability	Employer	No	14	weeks	14	100	
Congo	1952	Social security (50%); Employer (50%)	Social insurance	Employer	No	15	weeks	15	100	
Congo, Democratic Republic of [5]	...	Employer (no statutory social security benefits)	Employer liability	Employer	No	14	weeks	14	67	
Côte d'Ivoire	1955	National social insurance fund	Social insurance	Employer	Yes, voluntary basis	14	weeks	14	100	
Djibouti	...	Social Protection Body (50%); Employer (50%)	...	...	...	14	weeks	14	100	
Egypt	1959, 1964	Social insurance (75%); Employer (25%)	Social insurance	Employer & employee	No	90	days	13	100	
Equatorial Guinea	1947	Social security	Social insurance	Employer, employee & government	No	12	weeks	12	75	
Eritrea	...	Employer (no statutory social security benefits)	Employer liability	Employer	No	60	days	8.5	...	6

Table B.5 Maternity: Key features of main social security programmes (cash benefits)

Country or area	Date of the first law (or Labour Act*)	Provider of maternity benefits, type of programme and financing sources			Coverage of self-employed	Length of maternity leave			Percentage of wages paid in covered period (%)	
		Provider of maternity benefits	Type of programme	Sources of financing		Period (no. and unit)		No. of weeks	%	Note
Ethiopia [7]	2002*	Employer (for up to 45 days)	Employer liability	Employer	No	90	days	13	100	
Gabon	1952, 1975	National Social Security Fund	Social insurance	Employer	Yes	14	weeks	14	100	
Gambia	...	Employer (no statutory social security benefits)	Employer liability	Employer	No	12	weeks	12	100	
Ghana	...	Employer (no statutory social security benefits)	Employer liability	Employer	No	12	weeks	12	100	
Guinea	1960	Social security (50%); Employer (50%)	Social insurance	Employer & employee	No	14	weeks	14	100	
Guinea-Bissau [8]	...	Social security; Employer	Social insurance and employer	Employer	No	60	days	8.5	100	
Kenya [9]	1966*	Employer (no statutory social security benefits)	Employer liability	Employer	No	3	months	13	100	
Lesotho	...	Employer (no statutory social security benefits)	Employer liability	Employer	No	12	weeks	12	100	10
Liberia	...	Employer	Employer liability	Employer	No	90	days	13	100	
Libya	1957	Employer, Social security for self-employed women	Employer, social insurance (self-employed)	Employer, employee & Government	Yes	14	weeks	14	50, 100	11
Madagascar	1952	Social insurance (50%); Employer (50%)	Social insurance	Employer	No	14	weeks	14	100	
Malawi	...	Employer (no statutory social security benefits)	Employer liability	No statutory provision or employer liability	No	8 [12]	weeks	8	100	
Mali	1952	Social security	Social insurance	Employer & employee	Yes, voluntary basis	14	weeks	14	100	
Mauritania	1952	National Social Security Fund	Social insurance	Employer	No	14	weeks	14	100	
Mauritius [13]	2008*	Employer (no statutory social security benefits)	Employer liability	Employer	No	12	weeks	12	100	
Morocco	1959	Social security	Social insurance	Employer & employee	No	14	weeks	14	100	
Mozambique	...	Social security	Social insurance	...	...	60	days	8.5	100	
Namibia	1994	Social security; Employer (topped up)	Social insurance	...	...	12	weeks	12	100	
Niger [14]	1952	Social insurance (50%); Employer (50%)	Social insurance	Employer	No	14	weeks	14	50	
Nigeria [15]	...	Employer (no statutory social security benefits)	Employer liability	Employer	No	12	weeks	12	50	

Table B.5 Maternity: Key features of main social security programmes (cash benefits)

Country or area	Date of the first law (or Labour Act*)	Provider of maternity benefits, type of programme and financing sources			Coverage of self-employed	Length of maternity leave			Percentage of wages paid in covered period (%)	
		Provider of maternity benefits	Type of programme	Sources of financing		Period (no. and unit)		No. of weeks	%	Note
Rwanda [16]	...	Employer (if women not covered by social security)	Employer liability	Employer	No	12	weeks	12	100, 20	17
Sao Tome and Principe	1979	Social security (Employer if women not covered by social security)	Social insurance	Employer, employee & Government	No	60	days	8.5	100	
Senegal	1952	Social security	Social insurance	Employer & employee	No	14	weeks	14	100	
Seychelles	1979	Social Security Fund	Social insurance	Employer & employee	Yes	14 [12]	weeks	14 [12]	...	18
Sierra Leone	...	Employer (no statutory social security benefits)	Employer liability	Employer	No	12	weeks	12	100	
Somalia	...	Employer (no statutory social security benefits)	Employer liability	Employer	No	14	weeks	14	50	
South Africa	1937	Unemployment Insurance Fund	Social insurance	Employer, employee & Government	No	4	months	17	60	19
Sudan	...	Employer (no statutory social security benefits)	Employer liability	Employer	No	8	weeks	8	100	
Swaziland	n.a.	No statutory benefit	Employer liability	Employer	No	12 [2]	weeks	12 [2]	100	20
Tanzania, United Republic of	1997	Social insurance system	Social insurance	Employer, employee & Government	Yes	12	weeks	12	100	
Togo	1956	Social security (50%); Employer (50%)	Social insurance	Employer (and self-employed)	Yes	14	weeks	14	100	
Tunisia	1960	National Social Security Fund	Social insurance	Employer & employee	Yes	1, 2 [21]	month(s)	4.3	67, 50, 100	22
Uganda	...	Employer (no statutory social security benefits)	Employer liability	Employer	No	60	working days	10	100	
Zambia	1973*	Employer (no statutory social security benefits)	Employer liability	Employer	No	12	weeks	12	100	
Zimbabwe [23]	...	Employer (no statutory social security benefits)	Employer liability	Employer	No	98	days	14	100	
Asia										
Afghanistan	...	Employer (no statutory social security benefits)	Employer liability	Employer	No	90	days	13	100	
Armenia	1912	Social insurance	Social insurance	Employer, employee & Government	Yes	140	days	20	100	
Azerbaijan	1912	Social security	Social insurance	Employer & employee	Yes	126	calendar days	18	100	

Table B.5 Maternity: Key features of main social security programmes (cash benefits)

Country or area	Date of the first law (or Labour Act*)	Provider of maternity benefits, type of programme and financing sources			Coverage of self-employed	Length of maternity leave			Percentage of wages paid in covered period (%)	
		Provider of maternity benefits	Type of programme	Sources of financing		Period (no. and unit)		No. of weeks	%	Note
Bahrain	...	Employer	Employer liability	...	...	60 [45] [24]	days	8.5 [6.4]	100	
Bangladesh	1939	Employer; Government[25]	Employer liability, social assistance	Employer, Government	Yes, by social assistance	16	weeks	16	100	
Brunei Darussalam	...	Employer (no statutory social security benefits)	Employer liability	Employer	No	9 [8] [26]	weeks	9 [8]	100	26
Cambodia	...	Employer (no statutory social security benefits)	Employer liability	Employer	No	90	days	13	50	
China	1951	Social insurance	Social insurance & mandatory private insurance or mandatory individual account	Employer & Government	Yes, voluntary basis	98 [27]	days	14	100	27
Georgia	1955	Employees and self-employes; subsidized by Government	Social insurance	Government	Yes	18	weeks	18	100	
Hong Kong (China), Special Administrative Region	1968	Employer	Mixed: employer liability & social assistance	Employer and Government	Yes, by social assistance	10	weeks	10	80	
India	1948	Social security; Government	Mixed: social insurance and social assistance	Employer, employee & Government	Yes, by social assistance	12	weeks	12	100	
Indonesia	...	Employer (no statutory social security benefits)	Employer liability	Employer	No	3	months	13	100	
Iran, Islamic Republic of	1949	Social security	Social insurance	Employer, employee & Government	No	90	days	13	67	
Iraq	...	Employer (no statutory social security benefits)	Employer liability	Employer	No	62	days	9	100	
Israel	1953	Social security	Social insurance	Employer, employee & Government	Yes	12-14	weeks	14	100	28
Japan	1922	One-eighth National Treasury, seven-eighths Employment Insurance Fund	Social insurance	Employer, employee & Government[29]	Yes	14	weeks	14	67	30
Jordan	2010	Social Security	Social insurance	Employer & Government	No	10	weeks	10	100	
Kazakhstan	1999	Employer	Social insurance	Employer	No	126	calendar days	18	100	

Table B.5 Maternity: Key features of main social security programmes (cash benefits)

Country or area	Date of the first law (or Labour Act*)	Provider of maternity benefits, type of programme and financing sources			Coverage of self-employed	Length of maternity leave			Percentage of wages paid in covered period (%)	
		Provider of maternity benefits	Type of programme	Sources of financing		Period (no. and unit)		No. of weeks	%	Note
Korea, Republic of	1963	Employer (67%); Employment Insurance Fund (no cash benefit provided) (33%)	Social insurance	Employer; employment insurance fund	...	90	days	13	100	31
Kuwait	...	Employer (no statutory social security benefits)	Employer liability	Employer	No	70	days	10	100	
Kyrgyzstan	1922	Social security (Employer covers the first 10 working days)	Social insurance	Employer & employee	No	126	calendar days	18	...	32
Lao People's Democratic Republic	1999	Social security or employer	Social insurance	Employer, employee & Government	No	90	days	13	100	33
Lebanon	...	Employer (no statutory social security benefits)	Employer liability	Employer	No	7	weeks	7	100	34
Malaysia [35]	2012*	Employer (no statutory social security benefits)	Employer liability	Employer	No	60	days	8.5	100	
Mongolia	1994	Social Insurance Fund	Social insurance	...	...	120	days	17	70	
Myanmar	1954	Social security	Social insurance	Employer, employee & government	No	12	weeks	12	67	
Nepal [36]	1983*	Employer (no statutory social security benefits)	Employer liability	Employer	No	52, 60	days	7.4, 8.5	100	
Occupied Palestinian Territory	...	Employer (no statutory social security benefits)	Employer liability	Employer	No	70	days	10	100	
Oman	n.a.	Employer[37]	Employer liability	Employer	No	50	days	7	100	
Pakistan	1965	Employer	Social insurance	Employer	No	12	weeks	12	100	
Philippines	1977	Social security or employer	Social insurance	Employer, employee & Government	Yes	60 [38]	days	8.5	100	
Qatar	...	Employer (no statutory social security benefits)	Employer liability	Employer	No	50	days	7	100	
Saudi Arabia	1969*	Employer (no statutory social security benefits)	Employer liability	Employer	No	10	weeks	10	50, 100	39
Singapore	1968	Employer and Government	Employer liability	Employer & Government	No	16	weeks	16	100	40
Sri Lanka [41]	...	Employer (no statutory social security benefits)	Employer liability	Employer	No	12	weeks	12	86, 100	42

Table B.5 Maternity: Key features of main social security programmes (cash benefits)

Country or area	Date of the first law (or Labour Act*)	Provider of maternity benefits, type of programme and financing sources			Coverage of self-employed	Length of maternity leave			Percentage of wages paid in covered period (%)	
		Provider of maternity benefits	Type of programme	Sources of financing		Period (no. and unit)		No. of weeks	%	Note
Syrian Arab Republic	...	Employer (no statutory social security benefits)	Employer liability	Employer	No	120, 90, 75 [43]	days	17	100	
Taiwan, China	1950	Social security	Social insurance	Employer, employee & Government	Yes, with exceptions		lump sum	Lump sum	One lump sum	
Tajikistan	1997	Social security	Social insurance	Employer & Government	Yes	140	calendar days	20	100	
Thailand	1990	Employer (67%); Social insurance system (33%)	Social insurance	Employer, employee & Government	Yes, voluntary basis	90	days	13	100, 50	44
Timor Leste	2002	Employer	Employer liability	Employer	No	12	weeks	12	67	
Turkmenistan	1994	Social security	Social insurance	Employer, employee & Government	Yes	112	days	16	100	45
United Arab Emirates	...	Employer (no statutory social security benefits)	Employer liability	Employer	No	45	days	6.4	100, 50	46
Uzbekistan	1955	State social insurance scheme	Social insurance	Employer, employee & Government	No	126	calendar days	18	100	47
Viet Nam	1961	Social insurance fund	Social insurance	Employer & employee	Yes, voluntary basis	6	months	26	100	
Yemen	...	Employer (no statutory social security benefits)	Employer liability	Employer	No	60	days	8.5	100	
Europe										
Albania	1947	Social insurance system	Social insurance	Employer & employee	Yes	365	calendar days	52	80, 50	48
Andorra	1966	Social insurance system	Social insurance	Employer & employee	Yes	16	weeks	16	100	
Austria	1955	Statutory health insurance, family burden equalization fund, or employer	Social insurance	Employer, employee & Government	Yes	16	weeks	16	100	
Belarus	1955	State social insurance	Social insurance	Employer & Government	No	126	calendar days	18	100	49
Belgium	1894	Social security	Social insurance	Employer, employee & Government	Yes	15	weeks	15	82, 75	50
Bosnia and Herzegovina	...	Social insurance; Government	Social insurance	Employer & Government	...	1	year	52	50-100	51
Bulgaria	1918	State public insurance (the General Sickness and Maternity Fund)	Social insurance	Employer, employee & Government	Yes, voluntary basis	227 [52]	days	32	90	

Table B.5 Maternity: Key features of main social security programmes (cash benefits)

Country or area	Date of the first law (or Labour Act*)	Provider of maternity benefits, type of programme and financing sources			Coverage of self-employed	Length of maternity leave			Percentage of wages paid in covered period (%)	
		Provider of maternity benefits	Type of programme	Sources of financing		Period (no. and unit)		No. of weeks	%	Note
Channel Islands, Guernsey	1971	Social insurance and social assistance	Social insurance and social assistance	Employer, employee & Government	Yes	18	weeks	18	...	53
Channel Islands, Jersey	1951	Social insurance	Social insurance	Employer, employee	Yes	18	weeks	18	...	53
Croatia	1954	Health insurance fund (until the child reaches the age of 6 months), and the rest is paid from the State budget	Mixed: social insurance and social assistance	Employer, Government	Yes	1+ [54]	year	58	100	55
Cyprus	1957	Social security	Social insurance	Employer, employee & Government	Yes	18	weeks	18	75	
Czech Republic	2006	Social security	Social insurance	Employer, employee & Government	Yes	28	weeks	28	70	
Denmark [56]	1892	Employer; Government	Employment related system	Employer & Government	Yes	18	weeks	18	100	
Estonia	1924	Social security	Social insurance	Employer (and self-employed)	Yes	140	calendar days	20	100	
Finland	1963	Social insurance system	Social insurance	Employer, employee & Government	Yes	105	working days	18	70	57
France	1928	Social security and health insurance funds	Social insurance	Employer, employee & Government	Yes	16	weeks	16	100	58
Germany	1924	Statutory health insurance scheme; Employer	Social insurance	Employer, employee & Government	Yes, voluntary basis	14	weeks	14	100	58
Greece	1922	Social security; Government	Social insurance	Employer, employee & Government	Yes, certain urban self-employed	17	weeks	17	100	45,59
Hungary	1891	Health insurance	Social insurance	Employer, employee & Government	Yes	24	weeks	24	70	
Iceland	1975	Social Insurance Fund	Mixed: social insurance and social assistance	Employer & Government	Yes	3	months	13	80	
Ireland	1911	Social insurance	Social insurance	Employer, employee & Government	Yes	26 + 16 [60]	weeks	42 [26]	80	61
Isle of Man	1951	Social security and social assistance system	Social insurance; social assistance	Employer, employee & Government (social assistance)	...	26	weeks	26	90	62

Table B.5 Maternity: Key features of main social security programmes (cash benefits)

Country or area	Date of the first law (or Labour Act*)	Provider of maternity benefits, type of programme and financing sources			Coverage of self-employed	Length of maternity leave			Percentage of wages paid in covered period (%)	
		Provider of maternity benefits	Type of programme	Sources of financing		Period (no. and unit)		No. of weeks	%	Note
Italy	1912	Social insurance	Social insurance	Employer & Government	Yes	5	months	22	80	
Latvia	1924	State social insurance	Social insurance	Employee, employer	Yes	112	calendar days	16	80	
Liechtenstein	1910	Social insurance	Social insurance	Employer, employee & Government	Yes, voluntary basis	20	weeks	20	80	
Lithuania	1925	Social Insurance	Social insurance	Employer & Government	Yes	126	calendar days	18	100	
Luxembourg	1901	Social security	Social insurance	Employer, employee & Government	Yes	16	weeks	16	100	
Macedonia, The former Yugoslav Rep. of	...	Health insurance fund	Social insurance	...	...	9	months	39	100	
Malta	1981	Employer; social security	Employer, social insurance and social assistance	Employer, employee & Government	Yes	18 [63]	weeks	18	100	63
Moldova, Republic of	1993	Social security	Social insurance	Employer, employee & government	Yes	126	calendar days	18	100	
Monaco	1944	Social insurance	Social insurance	Employer	Yes	16	weeks	16	90	58
Montenegro	...	Social insurance	Social insurance	Employer, employee & Government	...	52	weeks	52	100	
Netherlands	1931	Social security	Social insurance	Employer & employee	Yes	16	weeks	16	100	58
Norway	1909	Social insurance	Social insurance	Employer, employee & Government	Yes	35 (or 45) weeks	weeks	35, 45	80, 100	64
Poland	1920	Social insurance fund	Social insurance	Employee and self-employed	Yes, voluntary basis	26	weeks	26	100	
Portugal	1935	Social insurance	Social insurance and social assistance	Employer, employee & Government	Yes	120-150	days	17, 21	100-80	65
Romania	1930	State health insurance fund	Social insurance	Employer (and self-employed)	Yes	126	calendar days	18	85	
Russian Federation	1912	Social insurance fund	Social insurance	Employer	No	140	calendar days	20	100	45,58
San Marino	1977	Social security	Social insurance	Employer (and self-employed)	Yes	5	months	22	100	
Serbia	1922	Social insurance	Social insurance	Employer & employee	Yes	140 [66]	days	20	100	67

Table B.5 Maternity: Key features of main social security programmes (cash benefits)

Country or area	Date of the first law (or Labour Act*)	Provider of maternity benefits, type of programme and financing sources			Coverage of self-employed	Length of maternity leave				Percentage of wages paid in covered period (%)	
		Provider of maternity benefits	Type of programme	Sources of financing		Period (no. and unit)			No. of weeks	%	Note
Slovakia	1888	Social insurance (part of sickness insurance)	Social insurance	Employer, employee & Government	Yes	28		weeks	34	65	
Slovenia	1949	Social security	Social insurance	Employer, employee & Government	Yes	105		calendar days	15	100	68
Spain	1929	Social security	Social insurance	Employer, employee & Government	Yes, with exceptions	16		weeks	16	100	
Sweden	1891	Social insurance	Social insurance	Employer (and self-employed)	Yes	14	69	weeks	14	80	58.70
Switzerland	1911	Social security and mandatory private insurance	Social insurance	Employer & employee	Yes	14	71	weeks	14	80	58.72
Turkey	1945	Social security	Social insurance	Employer (and self-employed)	Yes	16		weeks	16	67	73
Ukraine	1912	Social security	Social insurance and social assistance	Employer, employee & Government	Yes, if in insured employment	126		days	18	100	
United Kingdom	1911	Social security; Government (92% refunded by public funds)[74]	Mixed: social insurance and social assistance	Employer, employee and Government	Yes	52 [39]	75	weeks	52 [39]	90	76
Latin America and the Caribbean											
Antigua and Barbuda	1972	Social insurance (60%); employer (40% for 6 weeks)	Social insurance; employer	Employer & employee	Yes	13		weeks	13	100, 60	77
Argentina	1934	Family allowance funds (financed through state and employer contributions)	Social insurance and social assistance	Employer & Government	Yes, social assistance	90		days	13	100	78
Bahamas	1972	National insurance board (two-thirds) and employer (one-third)	Social insurance	Employer & employee	Yes	12		weeks	12	100	
Barbados	1966	National insurance system	Social insurance	Employer, employee & Government	Yes	12		weeks	12	100	
Belize	1979	Social security or employer (for women who are not entitled to receive benefits from social security)	Social insurance	Employer & employee	Yes	14		weeks	14	100	
Bermuda	2000*	Employer (no statutory social security benefits)	Employer liability	Employer	No	12		weeks	12	100	79

Table B.5 Maternity: Key features of main social security programmes (cash benefits)

Country or area	Date of the first law (or Labour Act*)	Provider of maternity benefits, type of programme and financing sources			Coverage of self-employed	Length of maternity leave			Percentage of wages paid in covered period (%)	
		Provider of maternity benefits	Type of programme	Sources of financing		Period (no. and unit)		No. of weeks	%	Note
Bolivia, Plurinational State of)	1949	Social insurance	Social insurance	Employer (and self-employed)	Yes, voluntary basis	90 [80]	weeks	13	95	81
Brazil	1923	Social insurance	Social insurance	Employer & employee	Yes	120 [82]	days	17	100	
British Virgin Islands	1979	Social security	Social insurance	Employer & employee	Yes	13	weeks	13	67	83
Chile	1924	Social security	Social insurance & mandatory private insurance	Employer, employee & Government	Yes	18	weeks	18	100	58
Colombia	1938	Social security	Social insurance	Employer, employee & Government	Yes	14	weeks	14	100	
Costa Rica	1941	Social security (50%); employer (50%)	Social insurance	Employer, employee & Government	Yes	4	months	17	100	84
Cuba	1934	Social security	Social insurance	Employer, employee & Government	Yes	18	weeks	18	100	
Dominica	1975	Social security	Social insurance	Employer, employee & Government	Yes	12	weeks	12	60	83
Dominican Republic	1947	Social security (50%); employer (50%)	Social insurance	Employer, employee & Government	Not yet implemented	12	weeks	12	100	85
Ecuador	1935	Social security (75%); employer (25%)	Social insurance	Employer & Government	Yes	12	weeks	12	100	
El Salvador	1949	Social insurance institute	Social insurance	Employer, employee & Government	Yes	12	weeks	12	75	
Grenada	1980	Social security (65% for 3 months); employer (35% for 2 months)	Social insurance	Employer, employee & Government	Yes	3	months	13	100, 65	86
Guatemala	1952	Social security (two-thirds), employer (one-third)	Social insurance	Employer, employee & Government	No	84	days	12	100	85
Guyana	1969	Social security	Social insurance	Employer & employee	Yes	13	weeks	13	70	83
Haiti	1999	Office of Workers' Compensation Insurance, Maternity and Sickness	Social insurance	...	...	12 [6]	weeks	12 [6]	100	87
Honduras	1959	Social security (two-thirds), employer (one-third)	Social insurance	Employer, employee & Government	Yes	84 [88]	days	12	100	85
Jamaica	1965	Employer or social security for domestic workers	Social insurance	Employer, employee & Government	No	12 [8]	weeks	12 [8]	100	89

Table B.5 Maternity: Key features of main social security programmes (cash benefits)

Country or area	Date of the first law (or Labour Act*)	Provider of maternity benefits, type of programme and financing sources			Coverage of self-employed	Length of maternity leave			Percentage of wages paid in covered period (%)	
		Provider of maternity benefits	Type of programme	Sources of financing		Period (no. and unit)		No. of weeks	%	Note
Mexico	1943	Social security	Social insurance	Employer, employee & Government	Yes, Mexico city	12	weeks	12	100	
Nicaragua	1956	Social security (60%); employer (40%)	Social insurance	Employer, employee & Government	Yes, voluntary basis	12	weeks	12	100	85
Panama	1941	Social insurance fund; employer[90]	Social insurance	Employer, employee & Government	Yes, voluntary basis	14	weeks	14	100	85
Paraguay	1943	Social security	Social insurance	Employer, employee & Government	Yes, voluntary basis	12 [9]	weeks	12 [9]	50	91
Peru	1936	Social security system	Social insurance & mandatory private insurance	Employer (and self-employed)	Yes	90	days	13	100	
Puerto Rico	...	Employer (no statutory social security benefits)	Employer liability	Employer	No	8	weeks	8	100	
Saint Kitts and Nevis	1977	Social security	Social insurance	Employer & employee	Yes	13	weeks	13	65	
Saint Lucia	1978	Social security	Social insurance	Employer, employee & Government	Yes	3	months	13	65	
Saint Vincent and the Grenadines	1986	Social security	Social insurance	Employer, employee & Government	Yes	13	weeks	13	65	
Trinidad and Tobago	1939	Employer and national insurance board	Mixed: social insurance and social assistance	Employer & employee	No	13	weeks	13	100, 50	92
Uruguay	1958	Social security system	Social insurance	Government	Ye	12	weeks	12	100	93
Venezuela, Bolivarian Republic of	1940	Social security	Social insurance	Employer, employee & Government	No	26 [94]	weeks	26	100	
North America										
Canada	1996, 2006	Federal and state; employment insurance	Social insurance	Employer & employee	Yes, for some on a voluntary basis	17 [95]	weeks	17	55	58.96
United States	...	No federal programme	Unpaid	...	No	12 [0]	weeks	12 [0]	...	97

Table B.5 Maternity: Key features of main social security programmes (cash benefits)

Country or area	Date of the first law (or Labour Act*)	Provider of maternity benefits, type of programme and financing sources			Coverage of self-employed	Length of maternity leave			Percentage of wages paid in covered period (%)	
		Provider of maternity benefits	Type of programme	Sources of financing		Period (no. and unit)		No. of weeks	%	Note
Oceania										
Australia	2010	Social assistance system financed by the State	Universal	Government	Yes	18 (+34) [98]	weeks	18	…	98
Fiji	…	Employer (no statutory social security benefits)	Employer liability	Employer	No	84	days	12	100	99
Kiribati [100]	…	Employer (no statutory social security benefits)	Employer liability	Employer	No	12	weeks	12	25	
Marshall Islands	…	No statutory provision	No benefit	…	No			0	…	
New Zealand	1938	State funds (universal and social assistance system)	Universal and social assistance	Government	Yes, if single women	14	weeks	14	100	58
Papua New Guinea [101]	1981*	No social security benefit	Unpaid	No statutory provision or employer liability	No	6+ [0]	weeks	6 [0]	…	102
Solomon Islands [103]	n.a.	Employer (no statutory social security benefits)	Employer liability	Employer	No	12	weeks	12	25	
Vanuatu [104]	1983*	Employer (no statutory social security benefits)	Employer liability	Employer	No	12	weeks	12	66	

Main source

United Nations Statistics Division, UN Data, Maternity leave benefits (New York). Available at: http://data.un.org/Default.aspx [8 June 2014], based on ILO (International Labour Office): Working Conditions Laws database. Available at: http://www.ilo.org/dyn/travail/travmain.home [8 June 2014].

Other sources

SSA (Social Security Administration of the United States); ISSA (International Social Security Association). Social security programs throughout the world (Washington, DC and Geneva): The Americas, 2013; Europe, 2012; Asia and the Pacific, 2012; Africa, 2013. Available at: http://www.ssa.gov/policy/docs/progdesc/ssptw/ [8 June 2014].

Notes

n.a.: Not applicable.

…: Not available.

* Labour Act (or labour code) which places the obligation within the employer's liability.

1 Botswana. No statutory benefits are provided. The amended 2010 Employment Order requires employers in designated areas to pay maternity benefits to female employees. The maternity benefit is at least 50% of the basic pay and other benefits she would otherwise be entitled to receive, and is paid for six weeks before and six weeks after the expected date of childbirth; may be extended by two weeks if there are complications arising from pregnancy or childbirth.

2 Burkina Faso. The benefit provided by the Social Security Fund is equivalent to the percentage of the woman's previous earnings on which social security contributions have been paid. The employer is mandated to cover the difference between this amount and the woman's earnings gained just before maternity leave.

3 Burundi. The labour code (1993) requires employers to pay 50% of wages for maternity leave of up to 12 weeks (14 weeks in the event of complications arising from pregnancy or childbirth), including at least 6 weeks after childbirth, if the woman has at least 6 months of service during the year before the expected date of birth.
The 1984 provision established a medical assistance programme to provide medical, surgical, maternity, hospitalization, dental and pharmaceutical services to the low-income population.

4 Cabo Verde. The employer pays the difference between 90% of the worker's "normal" salary and cash benefits paid by social security. If none is paid, then the employer must pay the full amount of the benefits during the maternity leave period.

5 Congo, Democratic Republic. No statutory social security benefits are provided. The labour code requires employers to provide 14 weeks of paid maternity leave, and to provide medical care for workers and their dependants.

6 Eritrea. Paid, amount not specified or unidentified.

[7] Ethiopia. No statutory social security benefits are provided. The public service amendment proclamation (2002) and the labour proclamation (2003) require employers to provide paid maternity leave for up to 45 days after childbirth; thereafter, sick leave may be paid if there are complications arising from childbirth.

[8] Guinea Bissau. The employer is mandated to pay the difference between social security benefits and previous earnings.

[9] Kenya. No statutory social security benefits are provided. The 1976 Employment Act requires employers to pay 100% of earnings for up to two months of maternity leave. Employers also provide some obstetric benefits. Accredited government and certain private and faith-based hospitals provide comprehensive maternity care to members of the National Health Insurance Fund and their dependants.

[10] Lesotho. According to art. 134 of the labour code (Order No. 24 of 1992, as amended in 2006), there is no legal obligation for employers to pay wages during maternity leave. However, the Labour Code Wages (Amendment) Order 2011 (LN No. 147 of 2011) sets out that workers in the textile, clothing, leather clothing and leather manufacturing industries are entitled to two weeks' paid maternity leave, and workers in the private security sector to six weeks' paid maternity leave and six weeks' unpaid maternity leave. Any other employee in neither of these named sectors shall be entitled to receive six weeks' paid maternity leave before confinement and six weeks' paid maternity leave after confinement.

[11] Libya. Maternity leave cash benefits are 50% of wages for employees, and 100% of presumptive income for self-employed women, paid by social insurance for 13 weeks (three months).

[12] Malawi. Every three years.

[13] Mauritius. No statutory social security benefits are provided. The 2008 Employment Rights Act requires employers to provide 12 weeks of paid maternity leave (at least six weeks after the expected date of childbirth) or five days of paid paternity leave to employees who have been in their continuous employment for at least 12 months. Government clinics and hospitals provide free medical services. Some mother and child health services and financial assistance to needy persons are provided.

[14] Niger. A woman who has worked for at least two years at the same company shall receive from the employer the totality of her salary, minus any amount already provided by social security or any other fund replacing this service.

[15] Nigeria. No statutory social security cash benefits for maternity are provided. The labour code requires employers to give employees up to 12 days of paid sick leave a year and paid maternity leave at 50% of wages for six weeks before and six weeks after the expected date of childbirth.

[16] Rwanda. No statutory social security benefits are provided yet. The employer remains liable for the payment of maternity benefits until the maternity insurance fund is implemented. The labour code requires employers to pay 66.7% of wages for maternity benefits for up to 12 weeks.

[17] Rwanda. Level of benefit: 100 per cent of salary during the first six weeks of maternity leave; during the last six weeks of maternity leave, 20 per cent of salary.

[18] Seychelles. A flat monthly rate is paid for 12 weeks.

[19] South Africa. Up to a maximum amount of 60% depending on level of income of the contributor. Benefits are paid for a maximum of 17.32 weeks.

[20] Swaziland. No statutory social security benefits are provided. 100% of previous earnings for two weeks.

[21] Tunisia. Duration: Civil servants are entitled to two months of maternity leave.

[22] Tunisia. Level of benefit: for women covered by the labour code the amount is two-thirds (66.7%) of the average daily wage. For women working in agriculture, it amounts to 50% of the flat-rate daily wage calculated on the basis of the guaranteed minimum wage in agriculture. For civil servants, the full salary is paid during maternity leave.

[23] Zimbabwe. No statutory cash benefits are provided. The Labor Relations Act requires employers to provide a maternity benefit. The maternity benefit is 100% of wages and is paid for at least 21 days before and 77 days after the expected date of childbirth. A health care programme provides free primary health care for low-paid workers. Government and mission hospitals serve rural areas; government and private hospitals and doctors serve urban areas.

[24] Bahrain. 45 days paid at 100% per cent. 15 remaining days are unpaid.

[25] Bangladesh. The Government of Bangladesh launched the maternity allowance programme to ensure safe motherhood in 2008 under the Ministry of Women's and Children's Affairs, targeting vulnerable and rural poor pregnant mothers. Each selected beneficiary receives 300 taka (BDT) per month for a period of two years, increased to BDT350 per month in 2010 for the same period.

[26] Bahrain. The duration of paid maternity leave benefits is eight weeks.

[27] China. Duration of maternity leave: On 28 April 2012, China's State Council published the Special Provisions on Labour Protection of Female Employees. The aim is to improve Chinese labour practices to enhance the protection of female employees' well-being in the workplace. According to the Special Provisions, female employees are now entitled to 98 days of maternity leave for childbirth, an increase of eight days from the previous duration.
Level of benefit: The social insurance programme applies to urban areas and the maternity insurance programme covers all employees in urban enterprises, including all state-owned enterprises, regardless of their location. Since July 2011, the country's first national law on social insurance has been gradually unifying existing regional and local social security schemes, which include pooling arrangements.

[28] Israel: Employment law allows 12 weeks of maternity leave, but maternity allowance can be paid up to 14 weeks. To be entitled to a full maternity allowance (14 weeks), the woman worker must have contributed for ten out of the previous 14 months or for 15 out of the previous 22 months before the day the woman discontinued work during pregnancy. In the event the woman worker contributed six out of the previous 14 months she will be entitled to a partial maternity allowance (seven weeks). Benefit amount: Up to ceiling. A female worker who has given birth to three or more children in one birth is entitled to a childbirth allowance in addition to the the maternity allowance from the birth and up to 20 months after this date.

[29] Japan. Social insurance and public funds for one-eighth of the total cost.

[30] Japan. Upon return to work after child-care leave, the mother will receive a further 10% of her pre-leave wage, for the duration of the leave taken, as a re-engagement benefit for workers returning from child-care leave. The legal amount has changed in recent years and the currently available allowance (2011) is paid at appoximately 66.67% of the average daily basic wage, according to wage class, for a period of 42 days before birth and 56 days after the expected date of childbirth.

[31] Korea, Republic. For employees of enterprises meeting the criteria of the Employment Insurance Act, the Employment Insurance Fund pays the whole maternity leave period. If the enterprise does not meet these criteria, then the employer pays the first 60 days of maternity leave.

[32] Kyrgyzstan. Seven times the minimum wage level.

[33] Lao People's Democratic Republic. Under the Social Security Decree, a woman is entitled to childbirth benefits equal to 70% of insured earnings for a maximum period of three months.

[34] Lebanon. Cash benefits will be statutorily provided by the Social Security Act (art. 26), for a duration of ten weeks paid at two-thirds of previous earnings. However, this social security system has not been implemented yet. The entitlements set out in the labour code are still valid.

[35] Malaysia. Under the Employment Act of 2012, which amended the Employment Act of 1995, employers are required to provide 60 days of paid maternity leave to all female employees.

[36] Nepal. No statutory social security cash benefits are provided. The 1992 Labour Act requires employers to pay 100% of wages for maternity leave of up to 52 days before or after each childbirth for up to two births. The 1992 Civil Servant Act provides maternity leave to employed women for up to 60 days before or after childbirth, for up to two births. Additional maternity leave without pay is possible for up to six months.

[37] Oman. According to Article 83 of the Omani Labour Law (2012), a female employee shall have the right to a special 50-day maternity leave covering the periods before and after delivery with full salary for not more than three times during her service with the employer.

[38] Philippines. 60 days for government employees.

[39] Saudi Arabia. 50% if the employee has one to three years in service before the beginning of maternity leave; 100% with three years or more.

[40] Singapore. The first eight weeks paid by employer, the second eight weeks funded by the Government up to a ceiling. For the third and subsequent births, the full 16 weeks will be funded by the Government up to a ceiling.

[41] Sri Lanka. No statutory social security maternity benefits are provided. Plantations have their own dispensaries and maternity wards and must provide medical care for their employees. The Maternity Benefits Ordinance Act and the Shops and Offices Employees Act require employers to provide maternity

leave. The duration of maternity leave is six weeks for the third and each subsequent child. The amount of maternity leave benefits is six-sevenths of previous earnings for employees covered by the Maternity Benefits Ordinance Act; 100% for those covered by the Shops and Offices Employees Act.

[42] Sri Lanka. Level of benefit: Six-sevenths (86%) of wages for workers paid at a time-rate or piece-rate. Employees covered by the Shops and Offices Employees Act receive 100% of remuneration.

[43] Syrian Arab Republic. 120 days for the first childbirth, 90 days for the second childbirth and 75 days for the third childbirth.

[44] Thailand. 100% for first 45 days (employer); 50% for the last 45 days (social insurance). Under the Labour Protection Act, an employer is required to pay an employee for up to 45 days of maternity leave. A new voluntary social security system for informal sector workers was initiated in 2011. The scheme is based on contributions from workers and Government to finance old-age, disability, survivors, sickness, and maternity benefits.

[45] Turkmenistan. In addition, a birth grant is paid as a lump sum.

[46] United Arab Emirates. 100% after one continuous year of employment, 50% per cent for employment less than one year.

[47] Uzbekistan. A lump sum paid for each child.

[48] Albania. 80% for the period prior to birth and for 150 days after birth, and 50% for the rest of the leave period.

[49] Belarus. Not less than 50% per cent of the minimum per capita subsistence wage (1 February to 30 April 2009: 117,190 rubles).

[50] Belgium. 82% for the first 30 days and 75% for the remaining period (up to a ceiling). For unemployed women, 60% of the gross salary prior to being unemployed, up to a ceiling, and a complementary indemnity of 19.5% for the first 30 days and of 15% for the remaining period.

[51] Bosnia and Herzegovina. The replacement rate varies depending upon the various cantonal regulations: 50–80% (Federation of Bosnia and Herzegovina); 100% (Republic of Srpska).The employer is reimbursed for initial payment.

[52] Bulgaria. The duration of maternity leave is calculated by adding the 45 days of compulsory leave to the 182 days (6 months) of post-natal leave.

[53] Channel Islands, Guernsey and Jersey. Flat rate for the normal duration of maternity leave. In addition, a lump sum maternity grant is paid.

[54] Croatia. 45 days before delivery and 1 year after.

[55] Croatia. Level of benefit: 100% until the child reaches the age of six months, then at a flat rate determined by the Act on the Execution of the State Budget for the remaining period.

[56] Denmark: about 75% of the workforce is covered by collective agreements, mandating employers to top up the state benefits, which represents on average around 50 per cent of previous earnings (daily cash benefits in relation to previous earnings up to a ceiling). In this framework, workers receive compensation during leave from their employer up to their full previous earnings.

[57] Finland. 70% up to a ceiling, plus 40% of the additional amount up to a ceiling, plus 25% of additional amount.

[58] Up to a ceiling.

[59] Greece: The minimum benefit is 66.7% of the insured's earnings. The insured may also receive a maternity supplement of up to 33.3% of earnings.

[60] Ireland. Duration: plus 16 weeks unpaid maternity leave after confinement.

[61] Ireland. Level of benefit: subject to a minimum and maximum amount.

[62] Isle of Man. Maternity allowance is paid for a period of up to 39 weeks at 90% of earnings, up to a ceiling.

[63] Malta. Duration of benefit: Paid maternity leave increased to 16 weeks (from 14) in 2012 and to 18 weeks in 2013. Level of benefit: 100% for 14 weeks. The Employment and Industrial Relations Act (Cap 452 of the Laws of Malta) requires employers to provide 100% of previous earnings for 14 weeks of maternity leave. Since January 2013, the Protection of Maternity (Employment) Regulations, No. 452.91, 2004, as amended in 2012, entitles women employees to four additional unpaid weeks of maternity leave. Upon the expiry of the 18th week of leave, the employee can claim a four-week flat-rate "maternity leave benefit" (c.€160 per week), which is provided by social insurance in one lump-sum. If for any reason a woman does not avail herself of part of the maternity leave paid by the employer, she will be entitled to a "Maternity Benefit" for the weeks maternity leave was not availed of (c.€90 per week for a maximum of 14 weeks paid by the Government).

[64] Norway. System of paid parental leave (with no distinction between maternity and paternity leave) of 57 weeks or 47 weeks altogether (paid respectively at 80% or 100% of previous earnings). For the purpose of determining the length of maternity leave, the 12 weeks of paid leave exclusively reserved for the father have been left out of consideration. The mother may use the remainder of 45 or 35 weeks, of which 9 weeks are exclusively reserved for her, three before birth and six after. The beneficiary may decide whether to receive 100% of benefits for a shorter period (35 weeks) or 80% of benefits for a longer period (45 weeks).

[65] Portugal. 100% of the average daily wages (if the parents opted for a leave period of 120 days) or 80% (if the parents opted for a 150-day leave period).

[66] Serbia. Duration: an employed woman is entitled to leave for pregnancy and childbirth, as well as leave for child care, for a total duration of 365 days. She may start her maternity leave pursuant the advice of a competent medical authority 45 days before the delivery term at the earliest and 28 days at the latest. Maternity leave shall last until three months after childbirth.

[67] Serbia. Level of benefit: 100% of earnings are paid for the first six months; 60% from the sixth to the ninth month; and 30% for the last three months.

[68] Slovenia. Parental allowance is cash aid to parents which is provided when they are not entitled to parental benefits after the birth of a child. The right to parental allowance shall be granted for 365 days, including payment to the mother for 77 days after the birth of the child provided the mother and the child have permanent residence in the Republic of Slovenia and are citizens of the Republic of Slovenia.

[69] Sweden. Duration: 480 days shared between both parents. 60 of these days are reserved for each parent while the rest are freely transferable between both parents. In cases of sole custody, all 480 days accrue to the custodial parent.

[70] Sweden. Level of benefit: 480 calendar days paid parental leave: 80% for 390 days; flat rate for remaining 90 days.

[71] Switzerland. Some cantons provide longer leaves. In the Canton of Geneva paid leave is 16 weeks. Employees of the Swiss Confederation are entitled to 98 days (or 14 weeks) if the woman has completed a year of service.

[72] Switzerland. Level of benefit: Employees of the Confederation are entitled to 4 month paid maternity at 100%.

[73] Turkey. 12 weeks' coverage.

[74] United Kingdom. The employer administers the payment. Employers in medium and large companies can be reimbursed for 92% per cent of the costs by the State (general revenues). Small employers can claim back 103% through reductions of national insurance contributions paid by employers to the Government's tax authorities.

[75] United Kingdom. Duration: Consisting of 26 weeks of ordinary maternity leave and 26 weeks of additional maternity leave.

[76] United Kingdom. Level of benefit: Statutory maternity leave is paid for a continuous period of up to 39 weeks. 90% for the first six weeks and a flat rate for the remaining weeks.

[77] Antigua and Barbuda. Social Insurance (60% for 13 weeks) and employer (40 per cent for the first six weeks).

[78] Argentina. In addition, a means-tested birth grant is paid in lump sum.

[79] Bermuda. No statutory social security benefits are provided. Under the 2000 Employment Act, employers are required to provide paid and unpaid maternity leave.

[80] Bolivia (Plurinational State of). Duration: Domestic workers are entitled to 90 days.

[81] Bolivia (Plurinational State of). Level of benefit: 100% of minimum wage plus 70% of the difference between minimum wage and regular earnings.

[82] Brazil. Duration: optional leave paid by the employer can be provided for 60 additional days.

[83] British Virgin Islands; Dominica; Guyana. In addition, a maternity grant is paid in lump sum.

[84] Costa Rica. The amount of maternity benefits is paid as follows; 50% of the salary from three to six months of contributions to the Social Security Fund, 75% from six to nine months, and 100% for nine months or more.

[85] Dominican Republic, Guatemala, Honduras, Nicaragua, Panama. If the worker is not entitled to social security benefits, the employer shall cover the full cost of benefit.

[86] Grenada. 100% for two months and 65% for the last month.

[87] Haiti. 100% for six weeks.

[88] Honduras. Duration: The Labour Code (31 March 2003) provides ten weeks' maternity leave, while according to the General Regulation of Social Security Act (15 February 2005) maternity benefits are paid for 84 days by social insurance up to 66% of previous earnings. Beneficiaries of the maternity benefits should abstain from work (Art. 69).

[89] Jamaica. 100% paid for eight weeks. Domestic workers are paid the national minimum weekly wage for eight weeks.

[90] Panama. Employer makes up the difference between social security or mandatory individual account payments and wages.

[91] Paraguay. 50% is paid for 9 weeks' coverage.

[92] Trinidad and Tobago. The Maternity Protection Act entitles an employee to 100% pay for one month and 50% for two months by employer; social insurance system pays a sum depending on earnings. When the sum of the amount paid under the Maternity Protection Act and social insurance is less than full pay, the employer shall pay the difference to the employee.

[93] Uruguay. For private sector employees. Special system for civil servants.

[94] The Bolivarian Republic of Venezuela's new Labour Law for Workers came into effect on 7 May 2013. Under the law, the country now has the world's third-longest maternity leave scheme. Mothers are entitled to six weeks pre-natal leave, and 20 post-natal. Fathers are also entitled to two weeks' paternal leave.

[95] Canada. Duration of maternity leave depends on the province. For Federal and Ontario, maternity leave is 17 weeks, while in Quebec, it is 18.

[96] Canada. Level of benefit: federal and state. A claimant whose family income is below $25,921 and who is receiving the Child Tax Benefit is entitled to a family supplement, thereby increasing the benefit rate. An employee may continue working while receiving parental benefits; there is no financial penalty as long as weekly employment earnings are no more than $50 or 25% of the weekly benefits, whichever is higher.

[97] United States. There is no national programme. Cash benefits may be provided at the state level. Provisions for paid maternity leave benefits exist in five states (New York, New Jersey, California, Hawaii and Rhode Island). For instance, California provides 6 weeks paid at 55% of previous earnings.

[98] Australia. Duration: a single parental leave system provides 52 weeks, which may be shared between the parents. The mother may take six weeks of pre-natal leave. Level of benefit: 18 weeks paid at the federal minimum wage level.

[99] Fiji. From the fourth birth, the woman will be entitled to only half the normal remuneration.

[100] Kiribati. No statutory benefits are provided for maternity. Government employees are entitled to maternity leave at full pay for six weeks before and six weeks after childbirth for up to two children.

[101] Papua New Guinea. The 1981 Employment Act requires employers to provide sick leave and maternity leave to employees. A female employee is entitled to take maternity leave for a period necessary for hospitalization before confinement and six weeks after confinement.

[102] Maternity leave is unpaid. However, annual leave or sick leave credits, paid by the employer, may be used for maternity leave.

[103] Solomon Islands. No statutory sickness and maternity benefits are provided. The Labor Act requires employers to provide up to 12 weeks of maternity leave to female employees (including up to at least six weeks after childbirth).

[104] Vanuatu. No statutory social security benefits are provided for maternity. The 1983 Employment Act requires employers to provide 66% of wages for mandatory maternity leave for six weeks before and six weeks after childbirth if the employee has been in continuous employment with the employer for at least six months. Employers are required to allow a mother to interrupt work twice a day for an hour to feed a nursing child until the child reaches age 2.

Table B.6 Old-age pensions: Key features of main social security programmes

Major area, region or country	Note	Date of first law	Type of programme [a]	Statutory pensionable age [a]		Contribution rates: Old-age. disability. survivors [a]			Estimate of legal coverage[a] for old age as a percentage of the working-age population							
									Total (mandatory and voluntary; contributory and non-contributory)		Contributory mandatory		Contributory voluntary		Non-contributory	
				Men	Women	Insured person	Employer	Financing from Government	Total	Women	Total	Women	Total	Women	Total	Women
Africa																
Algeria		1949	Social insurance	60	55	7	10.25	Subsidized minimum pension	36.0	10.5	36.0	10.5	0.0	0.0	...	...
			Non-contributory pension	...	...	n.a.	n.a.	Total cost								
Benin		1970	Social insurance	60	60	3.6	6.4	No contribution	4.3	2.3	4.3	2.3	0.0	0.0	0.0	0.0
Botswana	1	1996	Universal non-contributory pension	65	65	n.a.	n.a.	Total cost	100.0	100.0	13.3	11.4	0.0	0.0	100.0	100.0
Burkina Faso		1960	Social insurance	56	56	5.5	5.5	No contribution	45.2	18.3	5.8	2.8	39.4	15.5	0.0	0.0
Burundi		1956	Social insurance	60	60	4	6	No contribution	4.4	0.9	4.4	0.9	0.0	0.0	0.0	0.0
Cameroon		1969	Social insurance	60	60	2.8	4.2	No contribution	13.6	6.2	13.6	6.2	0.0	0.0	0.0	0.0
Cabo Verde		1957	Social insurance	65	60	3	7	No contribution	43.5	35.7	43.5	35.7	0.0	0.0	...	...
		2006	Means-tested non-contributory pension	60	60	n.a.	n.a.	Total cost								
Central African Republic		1963	Social insurance	60	60	3	4	No contribution	54.1	60.3	14.7	13.4	39.4	21.5	0.0	0.0
Chad		1977	Social insurance	60	60	3.5	5	No contribution	3.6	0.5	3.6	0.5	0.0	0.0	0.0	0.0
Congo		1962	Social insurance	60	60	4	8	Provides annual subsidies if needed	10.2	5.9	10.2	5.9	0.0	0.0	0.0	0.0
Congo, Democratic Republic of		1956	Social insurance	65	60	3.5	3.5	An annual subsidy. up to a maximum	39.1	27.2	39.1	27.2	0.0	0.0	0.0	0.0
Côte d'Ivoire		1960	Social insurance	60	60	3.2	4.8	No contribution	10.0	4.9	10.0	4.9	0.0	0.0	0.0	0.0
Djibouti		1976	Social insurance	60	60	4	4	No contribution	14.1	6.8	14.1	6.8	0.0	0.0	0.0	0.0
Egypt		1950	Social insurance	60	60	13	17	1% of covered monthly payroll plus the cost of any deficit	39.3	13.1	39.3	13.1	0.0	0.0	0.0	0.0
Equatorial Guinea		1947	Social insurance	60	60	4.5	21.5	At least 25% of annual social security receipts	13.0	2.4	13.0	2.4	0.0	0.0	0.0	0.0

Table B.6 Old-age pensions: Key features of main social security programmes

Major area, region or country	Note	Date of first law	Type of programme [a]	Statutory pensionable age [a]		Contribution rates: Old-age, disability, survivors [a]			Estimate of legal coverage[a] for old age as a percentage of the working-age population							
									Total (mandatory and voluntary; contributory and non-contributory)		Contributory mandatory		Contributory voluntary		Non-contributory	
				Men	Women	Insured person	Employer	Financing from Government	Total	Women	Total	Women	Total	Women	Total	Women
Ethiopia		1963	Social insurance	60	60	7	11	No contribution	40.3	23.3	6.4	4.7	33.8	18.7	0.0	0.0
Gabon		1963	Social insurance	55	55	2.5	5	No contribution	11.6	9.5	11.6	9.5	0.0	0.0	0.0	0.0
Gambia		1987	Social insurance	60	60	none	19	No contribution	4.0	2.5	4.0	2.5	0.0	0.0	0.0	0.0
		1981	Provident Fund	60	60	5	10	No contribution								
Ghana		1965	Social insurance and mandatory occupational (lump sum benefit)	60	60	5.5	13	No contribution	51.0	45.0	11.7	5.8	39.4	39.2	0.0	0.0
Guinea		1958	Social insurance	55-65 (depending on profession)	55-65 (depending on profession)	2.5	10	No contribution	10.6	7.0	10.6	7.0	0.0	0.0	0.0	0.0
Kenya		1965	Provident fund	60	60	5	5	No contribution	45.9	26.8	45.9	26.8	0.0	0.0	...	...
		2006	Means-tested non-contributory pension	65	65	n.a.	n.a.	Total cost								
Lesotho		2004	Pensions-tested non-contributory pension	70	70	n.a.	n.a.	Total cost	100.0	100.0					100.0	100.0
Liberia		1972	Social insurance	60	60	3	4.75	No contribution	50.2	50.4	9.1	4.4	33.0	36.0	...	...
			Means-tested non-contributory pension	...	...	n.a.	n.a.	Total cost								
Libya		1957	Social insurance	65	60	3.75	10.5	0.75% of covered earnings; annual subsidies and the cost of income-tested benefits	52.7	22.6	52.7	22.6	0.0	0.0	0.0	0.0
Madagascar		1969	Social insurance	60	55	1	9.5	No contribution	11.4	8.9	11.4	8.9	0.0	0.0	0.0	0.0
Malawi	2	2011	Mandatory individual accounts (not yet implemented)	...	...	...	...	...	10.8	8.9	10.8	8.9	0.0	0.0	0.0	0.0
Mali		1961	Social insurance	58	58	3.6	5.4	No contribution	38.3	29.4	6.1	3.7	32.2	25.7	32.2	25.7
Mauritania		1965	Social insurance	60	55	3	6	No contribution	4.7	1.3	4.7	1.3	0.0	0.0	0.0	0.0
Mauritius		1950	Social insurance	62.25	62.25	3	6	Any deficit	100.0	100.0	43.9	31.0	9.6	4.3	100.0	100.0
		1950	Universal	60	60	n.a.	n.a.	Total cost								

Table B.6 Old-age pensions: Key features of main social security programmes

Major area, region or country	Note	Date of first law	Type of programme [a]	Statutory pensionable age [a]		Contribution rates: Old-age. disability. survivors [a]			Estimate of legal coverage[a] for old age as a percentage of the working-age population							
									Total (mandatory and voluntary; contributory and non-contributory)		Contributory mandatory		Contributory voluntary		Non-contributory	
				Men	Women	Insured person	Employer	Financing from Government	Total	Women	Total	Women	Total	Women	Total	Women
Morocco		1959	Social insurance	60	60	3.96	7.93	No contribution	21.7	8.8	21.7	8.8	0.0	0.0	0.0	0.0
Mozambique		....	Social insurance			3	4	Finances public sector pensions	3.7	1.4	3.7	1.4	...	...	...	...
		2009	Means-tested non-contributory pension	60	55	n.a.	n.a.	Total cost	...	...						
Namibia		1956	Social insurance	60	60	0.9	0.9	Any deficit	100.0	100.0	8.3	7.5	0.0	0.0	100.0	100.0
		1992	Universal non-contributory pension	60	60	n.a.	n.a.	Total cost								
Niger		1967	Social insurance	60	60	5.25	5.25	No contribution	3.4	1.6	3.4	1.6	0.0	0.0	0.0	0.0
Nigeria		1961	Mandatory individual accounts	50	50	7.5	7.5	No contribution	3.7	1.9	3.7	1.9	0.0	0.0	0.0	0.0
Rwanda		1956	Social insurance	55	55	3	3	No contribution	44.0	42.9	3.9	2.2	40.1	40.7	0.0	0.0
Sao Tome and Principe		1979	Social insurance	62	57	4	6	Subsidies as needed	29.6	27.0	18.3	17.6	11.3	9.4	0.0	0.0
Senegal		1975	Social insurance	55	55	5.6	8.4	No contribution	11.9	6.6	11.9	6.6	0.0	0.0	0.0	0.0
Seychelles	3	1971	Social insurance	63	63	1.5	3	n.a	100.0	100.0	39.2	33.9	5.4	2.4	100.0	100.0
		1971	Universal non-contributory pension	63	63	n.a.	n.a.	Total cost from earmarked taxes								
Sierra Leone		2001	Social insurance	60	60	5	10	2.5 to 10%[4]	57.9	52.3	5.3	2.4	52.5	49.8	0.0	0.0
South Africa	1	1928	Means-tested non-contributory pension	60	60	n.a.	n.a.	Total cost	100.0	100.0	0.0	0.0	0.0	0.0	100.0	100.0
Sudan		1974	Social insurance	60	60	8	17	No contribution	33.8	18.3	33.8	18.3	0.0	0.0	0.0	0.0
Swaziland	1	1974	Provident Fund	50	50	5	5	No contribution	100.0	100.0	36.7	26.4	0.0	0.0		
		2005	Pensions-tested non-contributory pension	60	60	n.a.	n.a.	Total cost							63.3	73.6
Tanzania, United Republic of		1964	Social insurance	60	60	10	10	No contribution	69.6	58.0	69.6	58.0	0.0	0.0	0.0	0.0
Togo		1968	Social insurance	60	60	4	12.5	No contribution	57.7	57.1	57.7	57.1	0.0	0.0	0.0	0.0

Table B.6 Old-age pensions: Key features of main social security programmes

Major area, region or country	Note	Date of first law	Type of programme [a]	Statutory pensionable age [a]		Contribution rates: Old-age. disability. survivors [a]			Estimate of legal coverage[a] for old age as a percentage of the working-age population							
									Total (mandatory and voluntary; contributory and non-contributory)		Contributory mandatory		Contributory voluntary		Non-contributory	
				Men	Women	Insured person	Employer	Financing from Government	Total	Women	Total	Women	Total	Women	Total	Women
Tunisia		1960	Social insurance	60	60	4.74	7.76	Subsidized contributions for young graduates, persons with disabilities, and other categories of workers	44.6	23.1	44.6	23.1	0.0	0.0	0.0	0.0
Uganda		1967	Provident Fund	55	55	5	10	No contribution	12.5	6.0	12.5	6.0	0.0	0.0	0.0	0.0
Zambia		1966	Social insurance	55	55	5	5	No contribution	48.1	35.9	12.0	5.5	36.1	30.3	0.0	0.0
Zimbabwe		1993	Social insurance	60	60	3.5	3.5	No contribution	20.5	12.3	20.5	12.3	0.0	0.0	0.0	0.0
Asia																
Armenia		1956	Social insurance, individual account system not yet implemented	63	63	3	Flat rate plus 15% of the employee's monthly income from 20.000 drams to 100.000 drams. plus 5% of income greater than 100.000 drams.	Subsidies as needed	100.0	100.0	45.1	56.6	0.0	0.0	59.4	44.4
			Pensions-tested non-contributory pension	65	65	n.a.	n.a.	Total cost								
Azerbaijan		1956	Social insurance and notional defined contribution (NDC)	63	58.5	3	22	Provides subsidies for social insurance	100.0	100.0	65.8	63.8	0.0	0.0	34.2	36.2
			Pensions-tested non-contributory pension	67	62 (57)[5]	n.a.	n.a.	Total cost								
Bahrain		1976	Social insurance	60	55	6	9	No contribution	63.3	31.8	61.0	31.2	2.3	0.6	0.0	0.0
Bangladesh		1998	Means-tested non-contributory pension	65	62	n.a.	n.a.	Total cost	2.2	0.8	2.2	0.8	0.0	0.0	0.0	0.0
Brunei Darussalam		1955	Provident fund, supplementary individual account scheme	55	55	8.5	8.5	Any deficit and supplements	100.0	100.0	59.4	41.6	2.9	1.4	40.6	58.4

Table B.6 Old-age pensions: Key features of main social security programmes

Major area, region or country	Note	Date of first law	Type of programme [a]	Statutory pensionable age [a]		Contribution rates: Old-age. disability. survivors [a]			Estimate of legal coverage[a] for old age as a percentage of the working-age population							
									Total (mandatory and voluntary; contributory and non-contributory)		Contributory mandatory		Contributory voluntary		Non-contributory	
				Men	Women	Insured person	Employer	Financing from Government	Total	Women	Total	Women	Total	Women	Total	Women
		1984	Universal non-contributory pension	65	65	n.a.	n.a.	Total cost								
China	1, 6	1951	Budget-funded pension scheme for civil servants and employees of public cultural, educational and scientific institutions	60	55	n.a.	n.a.	Total cost	6.8	...	0	...	0	...	6.8	...
			The Basic pension scheme for urban workers	60	55 (cadres)/ 50 (workers)	8	20	Subsidies as needed	29.8	...	22.3	...	7.5	...	0	...
			The voluntary rural and nonsalaried urban pensions						63.4	...	0	...	63.4	...	[7]	...
		2009	The voluntary rural pension scheme non-contributory government budget financed basic pension	60	60	n.a.	n.a.	Total cost for non-contributory pension (at least CNY55 a month per insured person)								
			Individual account pension[8]	60	60	CNY 100–500	n.a.	Local governments contribute at least CNY30 a year per insured person to the individual account								
		2011	The voluntary non-salaried urban pension scheme non-contributory government budget financed basic pension	60	60	n.a.	n.a.	Total cost for non-contributory pension (at least CNY55 a month per insured person)								
			Individual account pension [8]	60	60	CNY 100–1 000	n.a.	Government contributes at least CNY30 a year per insured person to the individual account								
			Total						100.0	...	22.3		70.9	...	6.8	...

Table B.6 Old-age pensions: Key features of main social security programmes

Major area, region or country	Note	Date of first law	Type of programme [a]	Statutory pensionable age [a]		Contribution rates: Old-age. disability. survivors [a]			Estimate of legal coverage[a] for old age as a percentage of the working-age population							
									Total (mandatory and voluntary; contributory and non-contributory)		Contributory mandatory		Contributory voluntary		Non-contributory	
				Men	Women	Insured person	Employer	Financing from Government	Total	Women	Total	Women	Total	Women	Total	Women
Hong Kong (China), Special Administrative Region		1995	Private provident funds	65	65	5	5	No contribution	100.0	100.0	65.9	58.4	0.0	0.0	34.1	41.6
		1971	Universal non-contributory pension (Fruit Money)	70	70	n.a.	n.a.	Total cost								
		2013	Means-tested non-contributory pension	65	65	n.a.	n.a.	Total cost								
India		1952	Provident Fund complemented with social insurance (Pension Scheme)	55	55	12	17.61	1.17% of the insured's basic wages	12.5	4.6	1.9	0.8	10.6	3.8	...	...
			Gratuity schemes for industrial workers (lump sum benefit)			No contribution	4	No contribution								
		1995	Means-tested non-contributory pension	60	60	n.a.	n.a.	Total cost								
Indonesia		1977	Provident fund with a small social insurance component	55	55	2	4	No contribution	42.9	24.2	10.5	7.3	32.4	16.9	0.0	0.0
Iran, Islamic Rep. of		1953	Social insurance	60	55	7	20	3% of payroll, including voluntarily insured persons; 13.5% of payroll for commercial drivers. The Government pays the employer's contributions for up to five employees per company for certain strategic industries	34.5	8.8	34.5	8.8	0.0	0.0	0.0	0.0
Israel	9	1953	Social insurance	70	67.33	0.34-3.85	1.3-2.04	0.25% of insured persons' earnings	100.0	100.0	61.5	56.6	0.0	0.0	38.5	43.4
			Means-tested non-contributory pension	65-67	60-64	n.a.	n.a.	Total cost								

Table B.6 Old-age pensions: Key features of main social security programmes

Major area, region or country	Note	Date of first law	Type of programme [a]	Statutory pensionable age [a]		Contribution rates: Old-age. disability. survivors [a]			Estimate of legal coverage[a] for old age as a percentage of the working-age population							
									Total (mandatory and voluntary; contributory and non-contributory)		Contributory mandatory		Contributory voluntary		Non-contributory	
				Men	Women	Insured person	Employer	Financing from Government	Total	Women	Total	Women	Total	Women	Total	Women
Japan	10	1941	Social insurance: flat rate benefit and earning related benefit	65	65	8.34	8.34	50% of the cost of benefits for the National pension programme and 100% of administrative costs for both national pension and employees' pension insurance financed by the national tax	100.0	100.0	100.0	100.0	0.0	0.0	0.0	0.0
Jordan		1978	Social insurance	60	55	5.5	9	Discretionary/irregular contribution	41.7	12.7	33.3	12.0	8.4	0.7	0.0	0.0
Kazakhstan		1991	Social insurance: defined contribution (DC) based on individual accounts	63	58	10	11	Cost of State basic pension. Old-age solidarity pension: Subsidies as needed	100.0	100.0	73.3	69.2	0.0	0.0	26.7	30.8
		1991	Pensions-tested non-contributory pension	63	58	n.a.	n.a.	Total cost								
Korea, Republic of		1973	Social insurance	60	60	4.5	4.5	Part of administration costs of social insurance and contributions certain groups	58.2	45.8	58.2	45.8	0.0	0.0	...	...
		2007	Means-tested non-contributory pension	65	65	n.a.	n.a.	Total cost								
Kuwait		1976	Social insurance	50	50	5	10	10% to 32.5%[11]	68.2	45.0	66.4	44.8	1.8	0.2	0.0	0.0
Kyrgyzstan		1922	Social insurance: NDC	63	58	10	17.25	No contribution	100.0	100.0	56.1	43.5	0.0	0.0	43.9	56.5
			Pensions-tested non-contributory pension	63	58	n.a.	n.a.	Total cost								
Lao People's Dem. Rep.		1999	Social insurance	60	60	4.5	5	Administrative costs for the Social Security Organization	9.5	6.4	9.5	6.4	0.0	0.0	0.0	0.0
Lebanon		1963	Social insurance: lump-sum benefits only	64	64	No contribution	8.5	No contribution	0.0	0.0	0.0	0.0	0.0	0.0	0.0	0.0

Table B.6 Old-age pensions: Key features of main social security programmes

Major area, region or country	Note	Date of first law	Type of programme [a]	Statutory pensionable age [a]		Contribution rates: Old-age. disability. survivors [a]			Estimate of legal coverage[a] for old age as a percentage of the working-age population							
									Total (mandatory and voluntary; contributory and non-contributory)		Contributory mandatory		Contributory voluntary		Non-contributory	
				Men	Women	Insured person	Employer	Financing from Government	Total	Women	Total	Women	Total	Women	Total	Women
Malaysia		1951	Social insurance	55	55	0.5	0.5	No contribution	45.0	34.4	45.0	34.4	0.0	0.0	0.0	0.0
			Provident Fund	55	55	11	13	For self-employed persons only, 5% of contributions up to 60 ringgits a year								
Mongolia			Social insurance: NDC (for those born after 1960)	60	55	5.5	13.5	n.a.	100.0	100.0	23.2	24.0	18.6	9.7	58.2	66.3
			Means-tested non-contributory pension	60	55	n.a.	n.a.	Total cost								
Nepal		1962	Provident Fund	58	58	10	10		29.1	29.6	2.0	0.8	0.0	0.0	27.1	28.8
		1995	Pensions-tested non-contributory pension	70 (60 in some areas)	70 (60 in some areas)	n.a.	n.a.	Total cost								
Oman		1991	Social insurance	60	55	6.5	9.5	4% of monthly salary	26.3	0.0	26.3	0.0	0.0	0.0	0.0	0.0
Pakistan		1976	Social insurance	60	55	1	5	No contribution	17.5	4.4	17.5	4.4	0.0	0.0	0.0	0.0
Philippines		1954	Social insurance	60	60	3.33	7.07	Any deficit	53.2	39.0	53.2	39.0	0.0	0.0	...	...
		2011	Means-tested non-contributory pension	77	77	n.a.	n.a.	Total cost								
Qatar		2002	Social insurance	60	55	5	10	Covers administrative costs and any deficit	...	...	...	...	...	...	...	...
Saudi Arabia		1969	Social insurance	60	55	9	9	Any operating deficit	18.8	6.3	18.8	6.3	0.0	0.0	0.0	0.0
Singapore		1953	Provident Fund	55	55	20	16	No contribution	53.5	47.9	53.5	47.9	0.0	0.0	0.0	0.0
Sri Lanka		1958	Provident Fund	55	50	8	12	No contribution	31.5	20.6	31.5	20.6	0.0	0.0	0.0	0.0
Syrian Arab Republic		1959	Social insurance	60	55	7	14	No contribution	23.8	7.9	23.8	7.9	0.0	0.0	0.0	0.0
Taiwan, China		1950	Social insurance and mandatory individual account system	60	60	5.7	11.25	Various contribution rates[12]	100.0	100.0	41.7	36.0	58.3	64.0	...	...
		2008	Means-tested non-contributory pension	65	65	n.a.	n.a.	Total cost								

Table B.6 Old-age pensions: Key features of main social security programmes

Major area, region or country	Note	Date of first law	Type of programme [a]	Statutory pensionable age [a]		Contribution rates: Old-age. disability. survivors [a]			Estimate of legal coverage[a] for old age as a percentage of the working-age population							
									Total (mandatory and voluntary; contributory and non-contributory)		Contributory mandatory		Contributory voluntary		Non-contributory	
				Men	Women	Insured person	Employer	Financing from Government	Total	Women	Total	Women	Total	Women	Total	Women
Tajikistan		1993	Social insurance. NDC system scheduled to be introduced in 2013	63	58	1	25	Subsidies as needed	...	...	...	...	...	...	...	...
			Pensions-tested non-contributory pension	65	60	n.a.	n.a.	Provides partial subsidies; local authorities may provide supplementary benefits from their own budgets								
Thailand		1990	New social insurance system[13]	55	55	3	3	1% and THB30 or THB50[14]	100.0	100.0	35.9	29.4	25.9	19.3	38.2	51.3
		1993	Pensions-tested non-contributory pension	60	60	n.a.	n.a.	Total cost								
Timor-Leste		2008	Pension-tested non-contributory pension	60	60	n.a.	n.a.	Total cost	100.0	100.0	0.0	0.0	0.0	0.0	100.0	100.0
Turkmenistan		1956	Social insurance (NDC to be introduced in 2013)	62	57	No contribution	20	Subsidies as needed	100.0	100.0	36.9	34.2	0.0	0.0	63.1	65.8
			Pensions-tested non-contributory pension	62	57	n.a.	n.a.	Total cost								
Uzbekistan		1956	Mandatory individual account, social insurance.	60	55	6.5	25	Subsidies as needed	62.3	56.0	62.3	56.0	0.0	0.0	37.7	44.0
			Means-tested non-contributory pension	60	55	n.a.	n.a.	Total cost								
Viet Nam		1961	Social insurance	60	55	7	13 (14 from 2014)	Subsidies as needed[15]	65.6	59.0	26.4	20.9	39.2	38.1	...	...
		2004	Means-tested non-contributory pension/ Pension tested above 80	60	60	n.a.	n.a.	Total cost								
Yemen		1980	Social insurance	60	55	6	9	No contribution	18.9	2.2	18.9	2.2	0.0	0.0	0.0	0.0

Table B.6 Old-age pensions: Key features of main social security programmes

Major area, region or country	Note	Date of first law	Type of programme [a]	Statutory pensionable age [a]		Contribution rates: Old-age. disability. survivors [a]			Estimate of legal coverage[a] for old age as a percentage of the working-age population							
									Total (mandatory and voluntary; contributory and non-contributory)		Contributory mandatory		Contributory voluntary		Non-contributory	
				Men	Women	Insured person	Employer	Financing from Government	Total	Women	Total	Women	Total	Women	Total	Women
Europe																
Albania		1947	Social insurance	65	60	8.8	12.8	Any deficit; pays contributions for persons in compulsory military service; covers the costs of the special state pensions for certain persons	38.5	23.6	38.5	23.6	0.0	0.0	0.0	0.0
Andorra		1966	Social insurance	65	65	2.5-7.5	14.5	No contribution	...	...	...	...	...	...	...	...
Austria		1906	Social insurance	65	60	10.25	12.55	A subsidy and the cost of the care benefit and income-tested allowance	70.7	65.1	70.7	65.1	0.0	0.0	0.0	0.0
Belarus		1956	Social insurance	60	55	1	28	The cost of social and military personnel pensions and subsidies pensions and subsidies	100.0	100.0	51.1	50.8	0.0	0.0	48.9	49.2
Belgium		1900	Social insurance	65	65	7.5	8.86	Annual subsidies	61.4	55.5	61.4	55.5	0.0	0.0	...	...
		2001	Means-tested non-contributory pension	65	65	n.a.	n.a.	Total cost								
Bosnia and Herzegovina			Social insurance	65	65	17	7	....	...	...	...	...	...	...	...	...
Bulgaria		1924	Social insurance, mandatory individual account	63.33	60.33	7.9	9.9	Any deficit	59.0	55.6	59.0	55.6	0.0	0.0	...	...
			Means-tested non-contributory pension	70	70	n.a.	n.a.	Total cost								
Croatia		1922	Social insurance and mandatory individual account	65	60.25	25	No contribution	Pays contribution for categories of state employees	52.8	47.0	52.8	47.0	0.0	0.0	0.0	0.0
Cyprus		1957	Social insurance	65	65	6.8	6.8	4.3% of payroll (3.8% for voluntary insured)	100.0	100.0	68.7	61.6	0.0	0.0	31.3	38.4
		1995	Pensions-tested non-contributory pension	65	65	n.a.	n.a.	Total cost								

Table B.6 Old-age pensions: Key features of main social security programmes

Major area, region or country	Note	Date of first law	Type of programme [a]	Statutory pensionable age [a]		Contribution rates: Old-age. disability. survivors [a]			Estimate of legal coverage[a] for old age as a percentage of the working-age population							
									Total (mandatory and voluntary; contributory and non-contributory)		Contributory mandatory		Contributory voluntary		Non-contributory	
				Men	Women	Insured person	Employer	Financing from Government	Total	Women	Total	Women	Total	Women	Total	Women
Czech Republic		1906	Social insurance	62.2	61.33	6.5	21.5	Any deficit	70.3	61.5	65.0	56.3	5.3	5.3	0.0	0.0
Denmark		1891	Social insurance	65	65	A set amount	A set amount	No contribution	100.0	100.0	67.0	67.3	6.1	3.5	100.0	100.0
		1891	Universal	65	65	n.a.	n.a.	Total cost								
Estonia		1924	Social insurance and mandatory individual account	63	61	2	20	Pension supplements and allowances for some categories of insured persons; and the cost of funeral grants	100.0	100.0	61.0	60.5	0.0	0.0	39.0	39.5
			Pensions-tested non-contributory pension	63	63	n.a.	n.a.	Total cost								
Finland		1937	Mandatory occupational pension	65	65	5.15	17.65	No contribution	100.0	100.0	59.5	61.2	0.0	0.0	40.5	38.8
		1937	Means-tested non-contributory pension	65	65	n.a.	n.a.	Total cost[16]								
France		1910	Social insurance	60	60	6.75	9.9	Variable subsidies	100.0	100.0	63.8	59.7	0.0	0.0	36.2	40.3
		2004	Means-tested non-contributory pension	65	65	n.a.	n.a.	Total cost								
Germany		1889	Social insurance	65.08	65.08	9.8	9.8	Finances grants for certain benefits not covered by contributions	76.6	70.8	76.6	70.8	0.0	0.0	0.0	0.0
Greece		1934	Social insurance	65	65	6.67	13.33	A guaranteed annual subsidy	56.3	43.9	56.3	43.9	0.0	0.0	...	...
		1996	Means-tested non-contributory pension	60	60	n.a.	n.a.	Total cost								
Guernsey		1925	Social insurance	65	65	6	6.5	15% of total contributions	...	....	...	...	...	...	...	...
		1984	Means-tested non-contributory pension	60	60			Total cost								
Hungary		1928	Social insurance & mandatory individual account (voluntary)[17]	62.5	62.5	10	27	Any deficit	62.4	56.7	62.4	56.7	0.0	0.0	...	...
		1993	Means-tested non-contributory pension	62.5	62.5	n.a.	n.a.	Total cost								

Table B.6 Old-age pensions: Key features of main social security programmes

Major area, region or country	Note	Date of first law	Type of programme [a]	Statutory pensionable age [a]		Contribution rates: Old-age. disability. survivors [a]			Estimate of legal coverage[a] for old age as a percentage of the working-age population							
									Total (mandatory and voluntary; contributory and non-contributory)		Contributory mandatory		Contributory voluntary		Non-contributory	
				Men	Women	Insured person	Employer	Financing from Government	Total	Women	Total	Women	Total	Women	Total	Women
Iceland		1909	Mandatory occupational pension	67	67	4	7.79	No contribution	100.0	100.0	77.7	75.8	0.0	0.0	22.3	24.2
			Means-tested non-contributory pension	67	67	n.a.	n.a.	Any deficit								
Ireland		1908	Social insurance	65	65	4	4.25	Any deficit	59.7	55.7	47.3	42.1	0.0	0.0	12.4	13.6
			Means-tested non-contributory pension	66 (rising gradually to 67 by 2021. 68 by 2028)	66 (rising gradually to 67 by 2021. 68 by 2028)	n.a.	n.a.	Total cost								
Isle of Man		1948	Social insurance	65	60	11	12.8	No contribution	...	...	...	....	...	...	...	...
			Pensions-tested non-contributory pension	80	80	n.a.	n.a.	The total cost of means-tested allowances and other non-contributory benefits								
Italy		1919	Social insurance -phasing out	66	62	9.19	23.81	Any deficit	56.0	45.1	56.0	45.1	0.0	0.0	...	...
		1996	NDC	66	62 (gradually increasing to 66)	9.19	23.81	Any deficit								
			Means-tested non-contributory pension	65	65	n.a.	n.a.	Total cost								
Jersey						5.2	5.3		...	...	....	...	....	...	...	...
Kosovo[b]		2002	Universal non-contributory pension	65	65	n.a.	n.a.	Total cost	...	...	....	...	....	...	...	...
Latvia		1922	Social insurance: NDC[18]	62	62	11	24.09	Contributes for persons residing in Latvia caring for a child younger than 18 months and receiving child-care benefits, unemployed persons with disabilities, and certain social insurance beneficiaries	100.0	100.0	59.3	59.4	40.7	40.6	...	...
			Pensions-tested non-contributory pension	67	67	n.a.	n.a.	Total cost								

Table B.6 Old-age pensions: Key features of main social security programmes

Major area, region or country	Note	Date of first law	Type of programme [a]	Statutory pensionable age [a]		Contribution rates: Old-age, disability, survivors [a]			Estimate of legal coverage[a] for old age as a percentage of the working-age population							
									Total (mandatory and voluntary; contributory and non-contributory)		Contributory mandatory		Contributory voluntary		Non-contributory	
				Men	Women	Insured person	Employer	Financing from Government	Total	Women	Total	Women	Total	Women	Total	Women
Liechtenstein		1952	Social insurance and mandatory occupational pension	64	64	10.55	12.75	Contributes 50 million francs annually, adjusted according to changes in prices for social insurance	...	...	...	...	...	...	...	...
Lithuania		1922	Social insurance	62.5	60	3	23.3	Any deficit	100.0	100.0	57.8	58.7	0.0	0.0	42.2	41.3
		1994	Pensions-tested non-contributory pension	62.5	60	n.a.	n.a.	Total cost								
Luxembourg		1911	Social insurance	65	65	8	8	8	63.6	60.3	68.2	60.3	0.0	0.0	0.0	0.0
Malta		1956	Social insurance	61	60	10	10	50% of the value of total contributions	56.1	39.2	56.1	39.2	0.0	0.0	...	...
			Means-tested non-contributory pension	60	60	n.a.	n.a.	Total cost								
Moldova, Republic of		1956	Social insurance	62	57	6	23	50% of pensions for civil servants, and judges and prosecutors	100.0	100.0	43.1	41.3	0.0	0.0	56.9	58.7
			Pensions-tested non-contributory pension	62	57	n.a.	n.a.	Total cost								
Monaco		1944	Social insurance	65	65	6.15	6.15	No contribution	...	...	...	...	....	...	....	...
Netherlands		1901	Social insurance	65	65	19	5.7	A subsidy to increase all benefits up to the applicable social minimum; the cost of pensions for persons with a disability since childhood	100.0	100.0	100.0	100.0	0.0	0.0	0.0	0.0
Norway		1936	Social insurance: (old system) and NDC[19]	67	67	7.8	14.1	Any deficit.	100.0	100.0	75.2	73.1	0.0	0.0	24.8	26.9
			Pensions-tested non-contributory pension	62 (flexible)	62 (flexible)	n.a.	n.a.	Total cost								
Poland		1927	Social insurance: NDC	65	60	11.26	14.26	Total cost of the guaranteed minimum pension; pays pension contributions for certain groups[20]	63.1	59.0	65.6	59.0	0.0	0.0	0.0	0.0

Table B.6 Old-age pensions: Key features of main social security programmes

Major area, region or country	Note	Date of first law	Type of programme [a]	Statutory pensionable age [a]		Contribution rates: Old-age. disability. survivors [a]			Estimate of legal coverage[a] for old age as a percentage of the working-age population							
									Total (mandatory and voluntary; contributory and non-contributory)		Contributory mandatory		Contributory voluntary		Non-contributory	
				Men	Women	Insured person	Employer	Financing from Government	Total	Women	Total	Women	Total	Women	Total	Women
Portugal		1935	Social insurance	65	65	11	23.25	No contribution	100.0	100.0	59.3	55.9	5.7	4.5	35.0	39.5
			Means-tested non-contributory pension	65	65	n.a.	n.a.	Total cost								
Romania		1912	Social insurance and individual account	64.25	59.25	10.5	31.3	Any deficit	65.9	55.4	63.0	55.4	0.0	0.0	0.0	0.0
Russian Federation		1922	Social insurance: NDC	60	55	0	22	No contribution	100.0	100.0	66.2	62.7	0.0	0.0	33.8	37.3
		2002	Pensions-tested non-contributory pension	65	60	n.a.	n.a.	The total cost of social pensions. Regional and local governments may finance supplementary benefits out of their own budgets								
San Marino		1955	Social insurance and mandatory individual accounts[21]	65	65	4.2	16.1	10% of total contributions (higher contributions are made for agricultural workers) or up to 25% to cover any deficit	68.9	59.5	65.7	57.5	0.0	0.0	0.0	0.0
Serbia		1922	Social insurance	65	60	11	11	Guarantees cash benefits; covers any deficit; contributes as an employer. Finances medical benefits and work injury and occupational disease benefits for pensioners	52.0	40.8	52.0	40.8	0.0	0.0	0.0	0.0
Slovakia		1906	Social insurance and individual account[22]	62	59.75	7	20	Any deficit; contributes for certain groups[23]	58.8	52.3	58.8	52.3	0.0	0.0	0.0	0.0
Slovenia		1922	Social insurance	63	61	15.5	8.85	Covers the cost for war veterans and certain groups of insured persons; any deficit[24]	69.2	67.4	71.5	67.4	0.0	0.0	...	...
		1999	Means-tested non-contributory pension	68	68	n.a.	n.a.	Total cost								

Table B.6 Old-age pensions: Key features of main social security programmes

Major area, region or country	Note	Date of first law	Type of programme [a]	Statutory pensionable age [a]		Contribution rates: Old-age. disability. survivors [a]			Estimate of legal coverage[a] for old age as a percentage of the working-age population							
									Total (mandatory and voluntary; contributory and non-contributory)		Contributory mandatory		Contributory voluntary		Non-contributory	
				Men	Women	Insured person	Employer	Financing from Government	Total	Women	Total	Women	Total	Women	Total	Women
Spain		1919	Social insurance[25]	65	65	4.7	23.6	An annual subsidy	58.6	52.3	58.6	52.3	0.0	0.0	...	...
		1994	Means-tested non-contributory pension	65	65	n.a.	n.a.	Total cost								
Sweden		1913	Social insurance, NDC and mandatory individual account	65	65	7	10.21	The total cost of the guarantee pension and guaranteed disability pension (sickness compensation). The government pays earnings-related contributions for central government civil servants	100.0	100.0	69.0	68.1	0.0	0.0	31.0	31.9
			Pensions-tested non-contributory pension	65	65	n.a.	n.a.	Total cost								
Switzerland		1946	Social insurance and mandatory occupational pension	65	64	11.9	11.9	Base pension: Annual federal subsidies cover 19.55% of the cost of old-age and survivors benefits and 37.7% of the cost of disability benefits	100.0	100.0	100.0	100.0	0.0	0.0	0.0	0.0
			Pensions-tested non-contributory pension	65	64	n.a.	n.a.	Provided by the cantons							...	...
Turkey		1949	Social insurance[26]	60	58	9	11	25% of total contributions collected by the Social Security Institution	40.1	17.2	40.1	17.2	0.0	0.0	0.0	0.0
Ukraine		1922	Social insurance	60	55.5	2	33.2	Subsidies as needed for central and local governments	100.0	100.0	64.9	60.1	0.0	0.0	35.1	39.9
			Means-tested non-contributory pension	63	58	n.a.	n.a.	The cost of state social benefits								

Table B.6 Old-age pensions: Key features of main social security programmes

Major area, region or country	Note	Date of first law	Type of programme [a]	Statutory pensionable age [a]		Contribution rates: Old-age. disability. survivors [a]			Estimate of legal coverage[a] for old age as a percentage of the working-age population							
									Total (mandatory and voluntary; contributory and non-contributory)		Contributory mandatory		Contributory voluntary		Non-contributory	
				Men	Women	Insured person	Employer	Financing from Government	Total	Women	Total	Women	Total	Women	Total	Women
United Kingdom		1908	Social insurance	65	61	9.95	11.9	Treasury grant to contributory programmes for any deficit	100.0	100.0	69.1	64.2	0.0	0.0	30.9	35.8
			Means-tested non-contributory pension	60	60	n.a.	n.a.	The total cost of means-tested old-age pension and other non-contributory benefits								
Latin America and the Caribbean																
Antigua and Barbuda		1972	Social insurance	60	60	3	5	No contribution	59.8	56.9	59.8	56.9	0.0	0.0	...	...
		1993	Means-tested non-contributory pension	77	77	n.a.	n.a.	Total cost								
Argentina		1904	Social insurance[27]	65	60	11	10.17-12.71	Contributes for social insurance through general revenue, investment income, and certain taxes earmarked to fund social insurance pensions	100.0	100.0	40.3	34.1	0.0	0.0	59.7	65.9
		1994	Means-tested non-contributory pension	70	70	n.a.	n.a.	Total cost								
Aruba		1960	Universal non-contributory pension	60	60	na.	n.a.	Total cost	100.0	100.0	...	...	...	...	100.0	100.0
Bahamas		1956	Social insurance	65	65	3.9	5.9	No contribution	100.0	100.0	76.2	72.2	0.0	0.0	23.8	27.8
			Pensions-tested non-contributory pension	65	65	n.a.	n.a.	Total cost								
Barbados		1966	Social insurance	66	66	5.93-13.5	5.93-6.75	No contribution	100.0	100.0	62.5	57.3	0.0	0.0	37.5	42.7
		1937	Pensions-tested non-contributory pension	66	66	n.a.	n.a.	Total cost								

Table B.6 Old-age pensions: Key features of main social security programmes

Major area, region or country	Note	Date of first law	Type of programme [a]	Statutory pensionable age [a]		Contribution rates: Old-age, disability, survivors [a]			Estimate of legal coverage[a] for old age as a percentage of the working-age population							
									Total (mandatory and voluntary; contributory and non-contributory)		Contributory mandatory		Contributory voluntary		Non-contributory	
				Men	Women	Insured person	Employer	Financing from Government	Total	Women	Total	Women	Total	Women	Total	Women
Belize		1979	Social insurance	65	65	Contribution rates according to wage classes	Contribution rates according to wage classes	No contribution	100.0	100.0	52.8	35.3	0.0	0.0	47.2	64.7
		2003	Means-tested non-contributory pension	67	65	n.a.	n.a.	The total cost of non-contributory pension is met by the Social Security Board								
Bermuda		1967	Social insurance	65	65	Flat rate	Flat rate	No contribution	…	…	…	…	…	…	…	…
		1998	Mandatory occupational pension	65	65	5	5	No contribution								
			Pensions-tested non-contributory pension	65	65	n.a.	n.a.	Total cost								
Bolivia (Plurinational State of)		1949	Mandatory individual account with solidarity pensions[28]	58	58 (minus one per child. for a maximum of three children)	12.71	2 or 3	Finances the value of accrued rights under the social insurance system and the funeral grant. There is solidarity in the system through the Basic Pension Account (financing the additional cost of the minimum pension)	100.0	100.0	24.7	13.9	28.4	21.9	46.9	64.2
		1996	Universal non-contributory pension	60	60	n.a.	n.a.	Total cost: special earmarked sources in the budget (carbohydrate taxes)								
Brazil		1923	Social insurance	65	60	8 to 11	20	Earmarked taxes finance administrative costs and any deficit of social insurance	77.0	67.8	71.3	59.7	3.3	4.3	2.5	3.8
		1974 (first form)	Means-tested non-contributory pension	65	65	n.a.	n.a.	Total cost								
British Virgin Islands		1979	Social insurance	65	65	3.25	3.25	No contribution	79.6	71.1	79.6	71.1	0.0	0.0	0.0	0.0

Table B.6 Old-age pensions: Key features of main social security programmes

Major area, region or country	Note	Date of first law	Type of programme [a]	Statutory pensionable age [a]		Contribution rates: Old-age. disability. survivors [a]			Estimate of legal coverage[a] for old age as a percentage of the working-age population							
									Total (mandatory and voluntary; contributory and non-contributory)		Contributory mandatory		Contributory voluntary		Non-contributory	
				Men	Women	Insured person	Employer	Financing from Government	Total	Women	Total	Women	Total	Women	Total	Women
Chile		1924	Social insurance	65	60	18.84	No contribution	Special subsidies as needed	100.0	100.0	56.7	42.2	0.0	0.0	43.3	57.8
		1980	Mandatory individual account	65	60	10	No contribution	Finances the minimum benefit, old-age and disability social security solidarity benefits, and the value of accrued rights under the social insurance system								
		2008	Means-tested and pension tested non-contributory pension and death allowance	65	65	n.a.	n.a.	Total cost, with earmarked sources								
Colombia		1946	Social insurance and individual account	60	55	4	12	Partially finances the Solidarity and Guarantee Fund	60.0	46.4	60.0	46.4	0.0	0.0	...	...
		2003	Means-tested non-contributory pension	57	52	n.a.	n.a.	Mainly funded from state budget with dedicated contribution of high earners								
Costa Rica	29	1941	Social insurance and individual account	65	65	3.67	8.17	0.41% of the gross income of all workers and self-employed persons for social insurance	61.1	44.2	61.1	44.2	0.0	0.0	0.0	0.0
		1974	Means-tested non-contributory pension	65	65	n.a.	n.a.	20% of the total income of the Social Development and Family Allowances Fund and earmarked taxes (tobacco and alcohol)								
Cuba		1963	Social insurance	65	60	1 to 5	12.5- 14.5	Any deficit	100.0	100.0	53.7	46.6	0.0	0.0	46.3	53.4
			Means-tested non-contributory pension	65	60	n.a.	n.a.	n.a.								
Dominica		1970	Social insurance	60	60	4	6.75	No contribution	50.2	39.8	50.2	39.8	0.0	0.0	0.0	0.0

Table B.6 Old-age pensions: Key features of main social security programmes

Major area, region or country	Note	Date of first law	Type of programme [a]	Statutory pensionable age [a]		Contribution rates: Old-age. disability. survivors [a]			Estimate of legal coverage[a] for old age as a percentage of the working-age population							
									Total (mandatory and voluntary; contributory and non-contributory)		Contributory mandatory		Contributory voluntary		Non-contributory	
				Men	Women	Insured person	Employer	Financing from Government	Total	Women	Total	Women	Total	Women	Total	Women
Dominican Republic		1947	Mandatory individual accounts	60	60	2.87	7.1	Finances the the guaranteed minimum pension and other subsidies as needed	...	...	...	...	...	...	...	...
			Means-tested non-contributory pension	60	60	n.a.	n.a.	Total cost								
Ecuador		1928	Social insurance	60	60	6.64- 8.64	1 to 3.1	40% of the cost of old-age, disability, and survivor social insurance pensions	60.2	44.0	62.0	44.0	0.0	0.0	...	...
		2003	Means-tested non-contributory pension	65	65	n.a.	n.a.									
El Salvador		1953	Social insurance and mandatory individual account	60	55	6.25	4.05	Finances the guaranteed minimum pension of mandatory individual account and special subsidies as needed to finance social insurance. Finances the value of accrued rights under the social insurance system	55.1	43.6	55.1	43.6	0.0	0.0	0.0	0.0
		2009	Means-tested and geographically targeted non-contributory pension	70	70	n.a.	n.a.	Total cost from general revenue								
Grenada		1969	Social insurance	60	60	4	5	No contribution	51.9	41.8	51.9	41.8	0.0	0.0	0.0	0.0
Guatemala		1977	Social insurance	60	60	1.83	3.67	25% of total contributions paid (not yet implemented)	55.4	38.4	51.1	0.0	22.8	0.0	0.0	0.0
Guyana		1944	Social insurance	60	60	5.2	7.8	Provides loans to cover any deficit	100.0	100.0	47.6	27.5	0.0	0.0	100.0	100.0
		2003	Universal non-contributory pension	65	65	n.a.	n.a.	Total cost								
Haiti		1965	Social insurance	55	55	6	6	Subsidies as needed	10.5	10.3	10.5	10.3	0.0	0.0	0.0	0.0
Honduras		1959	Social insurance	65	60	1	2	0.5% of covered payroll	55.3	37.4	30.0	18.4	25.3	19.0	0.0	0.0

Table B.6 Old-age pensions: Key features of main social security programmes

Major area, region or country	Note	Date of first law	Type of programme [a]	Statutory pensionable age [a]		Contribution rates: Old-age. disability. survivors [a]			Estimate of legal coverage[a] for old age as a percentage of the working-age population							
									Total (mandatory and voluntary; contributory and non-contributory)		Contributory mandatory		Contributory voluntary		Non-contributory	
				Men	Women	Insured person	Employer	Financing from Government	Total	Women	Total	Women	Total	Women	Total	Women
Jamaica		1965	Social insurance	65	60	2.5	2.5	No contribution	68.1	57.9	68.1	57.9	0.0	0.0	...	...
			Means-tested non-contributory pension	60	60	n.a.	n.a.	Total cost								
Mexico		1943	Social insurance and mandatory individual account	65	65	1.75	6.9	0.225% of covered earnings and a contribution from Government finances the guaranteed minimum pension[30]	53.7	37.5	37.8	26.8	16.0	10.7	0.0	0.0
			Pensions-tested non-contributory pension	65	65	n.a.	n.a.	Total cost	100.0	100.0					46.3	62.5
Nicaragua		1956	Social insurance	60	60	4	7	No contribution	55.9	41.9	55.9	0.0	23.9	0.0	0.0	0.0
Panama		1941	Social insurance and individual account	62	57	9.25	4.25	A deposit of 140 million balboas a year to a reserve fund for old-age, disability, and survivors' social insurance benefits yearly until 2060	65.6	47.3	56.3	41.8	9.3	5.5	0.0	0.0
Paraguay		1943	Social insurance	60	60	9	14	1.5% of gross earnings	38.2	47.4	38.2	47.4	0.0	0.0	0.0	0.0
Peru		1936	Social insurance and individual account[31]	65	65	13	13	Cost of minimum pension and subsidies as needed for social insurance	67.0	61.2	67.0	...	27.0	...	0.0	0.0
		2011	Means-tested non-contributory pension	65	65	n.a.	n.a.	Total cost								
Saint Kitts and Nevis		1968	Social insurance	62	62	5	5	No contribution	56.9	35.1	56.9	35.1	0.0	0.0	...	...
		1998	Means-tested non-contributory pension	62	62	n.a.	n.a.	Total cost								
Saint Lucia		1970	Social insurance	63	63	5	5	No contribution	65.7	56.6	65.7	56.6	0.0	0.0	0.0	0.0
Saint Vincent and the Grenadines		1970	Social insurance	60	60	3.5	4.5	No contribution	56.8	46.2	56.8	46.2	0.0	0.0	...	...
		2010	Means-tested non-contributory pension	65	65	n.a.	n.a.	Total cost								

Table B.6 Old-age pensions: Key features of main social security programmes

Major area, region or country	Note	Date of first law	Type of programme [a]	Statutory pensionable age [a]		Contribution rates: Old-age. disability. survivors [a]			Estimate of legal coverage[a] for old age as a percentage of the working-age population							
									Total (mandatory and voluntary; contributory and non-contributory)		Contributory mandatory		Contributory voluntary		Non-contributory	
				Men	Women	Insured person	Employer	Financing from Government	Total	Women	Total	Women	Total	Women	Total	Women
Trinidad and Tobago		1939	Social insurance	60	60	3.2	6.4	No contribution	46.4	40.4	46.4	40.4	0.0	0.0	0.0	0.0
		2010	Means-tested non-contributory pension	65	65	n.a.	n.a.	Total cost								
Uruguay		1995	Social insurance and individual account[32]	60	60	15	No contribution	No contribution	71.8	61.3	53.8	42.9	17.9	18.4	0.0	0.0
		1829	Social insurance			15	7.5	Finances pension deficits								
		1919	Means-tested non-contributory pension	70	70	n.a.	n.a.	Total cost								
Venezuela, Bolivarian Rep. of		1940	Social insurance	60	55	4	9	A least 1.5% of total covered earnings to cover the cost of administration	64.7	50.0	42.8	33.4	21.9	0.0	...	...
		2010	Means-tested non-contributory pension	60	55	n.a.	n.a.	Total cost								
North America																
Canada		1967	Social insurance	65	65	4.95	4.95	Co-contribution, matches C$0.50 for each C$1 of the insured's voluntary contributions up to C$500 a year for annual after-tax incomes up to C$31,920	100.0	100.0	73.6	70.0	0.0	0.0	26.4	30.0
		1927	Universal non-contributory pension (with tax recovery from high earners)	65	65	n.a.	n.a.	Total cost								
United States		1935	Social insurance	66	66	6.2	6.2	No contribution	73.8	69.7	72.4	68.0	0.0	0.0	...	...
		1935	Means-tested non-contributory pension	65	65	n.a.	n.a.	Total cost								

Table B.6 Old-age pensions: Key features of main social security programmes

Major area, region or country	Note	Date of first law	Type of programme [a]	Statutory pensionable age [a]		Contribution rates: Old-age. disability. survivors [a]			Estimate of legal coverage[a] for old age as a percentage of the working-age population							
									Total (mandatory and voluntary; contributory and non-contributory)		Contributory mandatory		Contributory voluntary		Non-contributory	
				Men	Women	Insured person	Employer	Financing from Government	Total	Women	Total	Women	Total	Women	Total	Women
Oceania																
Australia		1908	Mandatory occupational pension system	65	64.5	Voluntary contribution	9		100.0	100.0	65.1	61.0	0.0	0.0	34.9	39.0
			Means-tested non-contributory pension	65	64.5	n.a.	n.a.	The total cost from general revenue[33]								
Fiji		1966	Provident fund	55	55	8	8 to 30		58.6	38.4	34.3	21.8	24.3	16.7	…	…
		2000	Pensions-tested non-contributory pension	65	65	n.a.	n.a.	Total cost								
Kiribati		1976	Provident fund	50	50	7.5	7.5	No contribution	100.0	100.0	20.8	15.4	0.0	0.0	100.0	100.0
			Universal non-contributory pension	60	60	n.a.	n.a.	Total cost								
Marshall Islands		1967	Social insurance	60	60	7	7	No contribution	55.0	33.3	55.0	33.3	0.0	0.0	0.0	0.0
Micronesia (Fed. States of)		1968	Social insurance	65	65	7.5	7.5 34	No contribution								
New Zealand		1898	Universal non-contributory pension with means-tested top-up	65	65	n.a.	n.a.	Total cost	100.0	100.0	0.0	0.0	0.0	0.0	100.0	100.0
Palau Islands		1967	Social insurance	60	60	6	6	No contribution								
Papua New Guinea		1980	Provident fund	55	55	6	8.4	No contribution	15.5	15.7	6.2	6.3	9.3	9.4	0.0	0.0
Samoa		1972	Provident fund with annuity option	55	55	5	5	No contribution	100.0	100.0	23.5	17.9	2.3	1.6	74.2	80.5
			Universal	65	65	n.a.	n.a.	Total cost								
Solomon Islands		1973	Provident fund	50	50	5	7.5	No contribution	10.1	5.5	10.1	5.5	0.0	0.0	0.0	0.0
Vanuatu		1986	Provident fund	55	55	4	4	No contribution	61.7	53.3	17.9	13.3	43.8	40.0	0.0	0.0

Main source

SSA (Social Security Administration of the United States); ISSA (International Social Security Association). Social security programs throughout the world (Washington, DC and Geneva): The Americas, 2013; Europe, 2012; Asia and the Pacific, 2012; Africa, 2013.
Available at: http://www.ssa.gov/policy/docs/progdesc/ssptw/ [8 June 2014].

Other sources

HelpAge International: HelpAge's social pensions database. Available at: http://www.pension-watch.net/about-social-pensions/about-social-pensions/social-pensions-database/ [6 June 2014].
FIAP (International Federation of Pension Funds Administrators). 2011. Non-contributory Pension Systems in FIAP countries (Santiago). Available at: http://www.fiap.cl/prontus_fiap/site/edic/base/port/inicio.html [8 June 2014]
ILO (International Labour Office): ILO database of labour statistics (ILOSTAT). Available at: http://www.ilo.org/ilostat/ [8 June 2014].
—. ILO Key Indicators of the Labour Market (KILM), 8th edition. Available at: http://www.ilo.org/empelm/what/WCMS_114240/lang--en/index.htm [8 June 2014].
National statistical offices. Data sets and reports from national labour force surveys or other household or establishment surveys (link to national statistical offices websites available at: http://laborsta.ilo.org/links_content_E.html#m2 [8 June 2014]

Notes

n.a.: Not applicable.

...: Not available.

[a] Detailed notes and definition available at: http://www.social-protection.org/gimi/gess/RessourceDownload.action?ressource.ressourceId=37137

[b] As defined in United Nations Security Council resolution 1244 of 1999.

This table is complementary to table B.7. Non-contributory pension schemes: Main features and indicators (available at: http://www.social-protection.org/gimi/gess/RessourceDownload.action?ressource.ressourceId=43197).

[1] Beneficiaries from the contributory pension can cumulate the basic benefits from the non-contributory pension and the top-up benefit from the contributory pension. Percentages indicated as an estimate of legal coverage correspond to the legal coverage from the non-contributory pension.

[2] Malawi. In March 2011, a pension law established a mandatory old-age pension system based on individual accounts for private-sector workers earning above a minimum salary threshold. The law has yet to be implemented.

[2] Seychelles. Social security fund: the Government contributes as an employer and guarantees the pension benefits. Makes contributions out of the general budget. Seychelles pension fund: 1% of monthly earnings for each insured person.

[4] Sierra Leone. 2.5% of monthly income; 10% for civil servants and teachers; 12% for military and police personnel.

[5] Azerbaijan. 57 years old for a woman with three children or with a disabled child under 8.

[6] China: (1) Basic pension insurance: Central and local governments provide subsidies as needed.
(2) Pension schemes for rural and non salaried urban residents:
– The basic pension of 55 yuan (CNY) (US$8.83 or PPP$35.17) per month is payable to older people aged 60 and over whose children participate in the scheme – "family-binding" eligibility criteria.
– Mandatory individual account: Central and local governments provide subsidies as needed. Rural residents who are aged 16 and over, not in education and not enrolled in an urban pension scheme are eligible for an individual pension account. Participation is voluntary.
* Individual contributions range from CNY100 to CNY500 annually (equivalent to between US$1.28 and US$6.24 per month). Local governments are to provide a partial matched contribution of at least CNY30 (US$4.81 or PPP$19.50) per year regardless of individual contribution.
* Participants aged 45 and over are encouraged to contribute higher amounts to meet the shortfall in contributions over their working lives.
* Pensioners who have contributed for 15 years will be eligible for a basic flat-rate pension calculated by dividing accumulated contributions at 60 years by 139.

[7] China. Estimates of legal coverage: legal coverage in rural areas: in June 2011, the Chinese Government decided to accelerate the pace of extension to cover 60% of the rural areas by the end of 2011, and all rural areas by the end of 2012. By law, 100% coverage is provided (on a voluntary basis) in rural areas.
The same applied to the voluntary non-salaried urban pension scheme. On 1 June 2011 the Chinese Premier announced a new pilot pension insurance programme for non-employed urban residents, to be implemented as of 1 July 2011. Modelled on the new type of rural pension scheme, it was expected to cover 60% of China by the end of that year and to benefit all uninsured urban residents (around 50 million) by the end of 2012, in parallel with the new voluntary Rural Pension Scheme. The scheme covers, by law, all urban residents aged 16 and over (excluding school students) who are not engaged in employment and hence do not qualify for enrolment under the basic pension scheme for urban employees. All such residents can join the urban resident pension insurance programme on a voluntary basis at the place where their households have been registered. Enrolled residents can elect one of the ten scales ranging from CNY100 to CNY1 000 as an annual contribution to their individual accounts, for which the Government will provide a subsidy of no less than CNY30 to each person every year. The scales may differ in different regions.

[8] China. Individual accounts (under contributory) also corresponds to legal coverage for the non-contributory component of rural and urban non-salaried pension schemes.

[9] Israel: Through a contribution of 0.25% of insured persons' earnings (old-age and survivor pensions), 0.10% of insured persons' earnings (disability benefits), and 0.02% of insured and self-employed persons' earnings (long-term care), the Government subsidizes the following: 17.1% of total insured person and employer contributions; the total cost of special old-age and survivor benefits and long-term care benefits for new immigrants; and the total cost of social assistance income support programmes and the mobility allowance.

[10] Japan: The social insurance system consists of a flat-rate benefit under the national pension program (NP) and an earnings-related benefit under the employees' pension insurance program (EPI). Employers with more than 1 000 employees may contract out a portion of the EPI if they provide more generous benefits.

[11] Kuwait: Basic system: Government: 10% of covered earnings (public employees), 32.5% of payroll (military personnel), and 25% of monthly income minus the self-employed person's contributions (self-employed persons).

[12] Taiwan (China): National pension programme: 2.8% of the monthly minimum wage. For disabled and low-income insured persons, 7%, 4.9% or 3.85% of the monthly minimum wage, depending on the degree of disability or total family income. The monthly minimum wage is 18,780 Taiwan new dollars (TWD).
Labour insurance programme (social insurance): 0.75% of employee earnings (0.8% in 2013, gradually rising to 1.2% by 2030); 3% of income for self-employed persons (3.2% in 2013, gradually rising to 4.8% by 2030); the cost of administration. The maximum monthly earnings used to calculate contributions are TWD$43,900. (The monthly earnings used to calculate contributions are adjusted according to changes in the minimum wage.)
The Government's contributions also finance cash sickness and maternity benefits.
Labour pension fund (individual account): None.

[13] Thailand: A new voluntary social security system for informal sector workers was initiated in 2011. The scheme is based on contributions from workers and Government to finance old-age, disability, survivors', sickness and maternity benefits.

[14] Thailand: Formal-sector system: 1% of gross monthly earnings (old-age benefits).
The Government's contributions also finance family benefits. Disability and survivor benefits are financed under sickness and maternity.
The minimum monthly earnings used to calculate contributions are 1 650 baht (THB).
The maximum monthly earnings used to calculate contributions are THB15 000.
Informal-sector system: THB30 a month (sickness, disability, and survivor benefits) or THB50 a month (old-age, sickness, disability, and survivor benefits).

[15] Viet Nam. Subsidies as necessary and the total cost of old-age pensions for workers who retired before 1995; contributions for those employed in the public sector before January 1995.

[16] Finland. Universal pension: total cost of universal pensions, housing allowances, disability allowances, pensioner care allowances and war veterans' benefits.
Earnings-related pension: The total cost of covered study periods for students and unpaid periods of child care for persons caring for a child younger than age 3.

[17] Hungary: A 2010 amendment to the social security law terminated the diversion of contributions to second-pillar individual accounts and automatically transferred account balances to the social insurance programme (unless an account holder opted out). Since 2009, participation in the individual account programme is voluntary.

[18] Latvia: Municipalities provide social assistance benefits (means-tested and conditional) to the needy.

[19] Norway: A new pension system introduced in 2011 replaces the universal pension with a guaranteed minimum benefit and the earnings-related pension with an NDC scheme. The new system covers persons born since 1963. Persons born before 1954 remain under the old system. A transitional (mixed) system, a combination of the old and new systems, covers persons born between 1954 and 1962.

[20] Poland: The total cost of the guaranteed minimum pension; pays pension contributions for insured persons taking child-care leave or receiving maternity allowances, for persons receiving unemployment benefits and for unemployed graduates.

[21] San Marino: A system of mandatory individual accounts was introduced in 2012 as a supplement to the social insurance system. Both the insured person and the employer are required to contribute.

[22] Slovakia: Since 1 April 2012, individual accounts are mandatory for new entrants to the labour force. They may opt out of the system within two years.

[23] Slovakia: Finances any deficit; contributes for persons caring for children up to age 6 (age 18 with serious chronic health conditions), for maternity benefit recipients, and disability benefit recipients (until retirement age or until the early retirement pension is paid).

[24] Slovenia: Covers the cost for certain groups of insured persons, including war veterans, police personnel and former military personnel; pays employer contributions for farmers; covers any deficit in the event of an unforeseen decline in contributions; finances social assistance benefits; contributes as an employer.

[25] Spain: Non-contributory pensions and in-kind complementary benefits are provided for elderly persons and persons with disabilities.

[26] Turkey: In May 2006, the separate systems for public and private-sector employees and the self-employed were merged into one under the newly created Social Security Institution.

[27] Argentina: From 1994 until the end of 2008, there was a mixed system where all insured workers were in the first-pillar public pay-as-you-go (PAYG) system; for the second pillar, workers chose between contributing to an individual account and to the PAYG defined benefit system. A 2008 law closed the second-pillar individual accounts and transferred all workers and their account balances to the new one-pillar PAYG system.

[28] Bolivia: In 1997, all active members of the social insurance system transferred to a system of privately managed mandatory individual accounts.

[29] Costa Rica: The minimum monthly pension is 113,181 colones; if the calculated pension amount is lower, a lump sum is paid.

[30] Mexico: social insurance old-age benefits, 0.225% of covered earnings plus an average flat-rate amount of 3.55 pesos (depending on the salary range) for each day the insured contributes; for disability and survivor benefits, 0.125% of covered earnings; finances the guaranteed minimum pension.

[31] Peru: When public- and private-sector employees enter the workforce, they may choose between the individual account system (SPP) and the public social insurance system (SNP). Insured persons who do not make a choice become SPP members. SNP members may switch to the SPP but may not switch back, except under certain circumstances.

[32] Uruguay: The mixed social insurance and individual account system is mandatory for employed and self-employed persons born after 1 April 1956, with monthly earnings greater than 24,709 pesos (UYU) and voluntary for those with monthly earnings of UYU24,709 or less. All others are covered only by the social insurance system.

[33] Australia: Social security: the total cost from general revenue. Mandatory occupational pension (superannuation): matches voluntary contributions by the insured, up to 1 000 Australian dollars (AUD) a year for those with annual incomes up to AUD31 920 (co-contribution gradually decreases to 0 for annual incomes between AUD31 920 and AUD61 920). Contributions are calculated based on after-tax income and are not tax deductible.

[34] Micronesia: Contribution from employer is 7.5% of twice the salary of the highest-paid employee per quarter (January 2013).

Table B.7 Non-contributory pension schemes: Main features and indicators

Country	Notes	Year introduced	Name of scheme	Legal requirements and characteristics of the schemes: Age of eligibility	Citizenship	Residency	Income test	Asset test	Pension-tested	Level of benefit (monthly): National currency	US$	PPP	Year	% of average wage	Coverage (number, %): Number of recipients (unit)	Population 60 and over (%)	Population 65 and over (%)	Population above eligible age (%)	Year	Cost: Cost (% of GDP)	Year
Algeria		1994	Allocation forfaitaire de solidarité	...	...	...	...		...	3000	41.2	70.9	2009	11.8	292 664	12.5	18.4	...	2009	0.13	2009
Antigua and Barbuda		1993	Old-Age Assistance Programme	77	...	...	●	...	●	255	94.4	125.4	2012	...	152	1.8	2.4	7.3	2011	...	
Argentina		1948	Pensiones Graciables y Asistenciales	70	●	●	●	●	●	1020	246.5	393.1	2011	40.4	143 650	2.3	3.2	4.7	2012	0.50	2012
Aruba		1960	Pensioen di biehes AOV	60	●	●	○	○	○	1057			2013		14 000	79.3	100.0	79.3	2013	...	
Armenia		...	Old-Age Social Pension	65	...	...	○	○	●	10500	28.2	49.6	2011	9.1	48 000	11.6	14.2	14.2	2007	...	
Australia		1900	Age Pension	65 (m) 64.5 (w)	○	●	●	●	●	1654	1590.2	1067.1	2013	37.4	2 116 798	51.6	72.4	72.4	2009	2.24	2009
Austria		1978	Ausgleichszulage (Austrian Compensatory Supplement)	65 (m) 60 (w)	...	...	●	...	●	837.63	1110.7	959.5	2013	25.6	103 431	5.3	6.8	5.9	2011	...	
Azerbaijan		2006	Social Allowance (Old-Age)	67 (m) 62 (w)	...	...	○	○	●	45	54.9	91.3	2008	12.4	231 000	30.1	43.6	40.9	2012	...	
Bahamas		1972	Old-Age Non-Contributory Pension (OANCP)	65	○	●	●	●	●	268	268.0	362.7	2012	...	2 024	4.8	7.3	7.3	2012	0.08	2012
Bangladesh		1998	Old-Age Allowance and Allowance for Widow, Deserted and Destitute Women	65 (m) 62 (w)	...	...	●	●	●	300	3.8	8.8	2013	5.5	2 475 000	23.6	34.6	39.2	2011	0.17	2011
Barbados		1937	Non-contributory Old-Age Pension	66	●	●	●	...	●	579.6	289.8	477.4	2012	...	10 403	23.9	35.1	36.9	2011	0.67	2011
Belarus		...	Social old-age pension (social assistance)	65 (m) 60 (w)	...	●	○	○	●	133115	44.7	105.8	2010	6.9	51 900	2.9	4.0	3.2	2011	...	
Belgium		2001	IGO/GRAPA (Income Guarantee for the Elderly)	65	●	●	●	...	●	1011.7	1341.5	1115.4	2013	35.7	93 620	3.6	4.8	4.8	2012	0.12	2012
Belize		2003	Non-Contributory Pension Programme (NCP)	67 (m) 65 (w)	○	●	●	...	●	100	50.0	95.7	2010	...	4 297	22.2	32.6	35.4	2013	0.18	2013
Bermuda		1967	Non-contributory old-age pension	65	●	●	○	○	●	449.22			2011	...	...	...	...	...		...	
Bolivia, Plurinational State of		1996	Renta Dignidad or Renta Universal de Vejez (previously Bonosol)	60	●	●	○	...	○	200	29.2	58.5	2012	21.3	788 969	100.0	100.0	100.0	2013	1.06	2013
Botswana		1996	Old-Age Pension (OAP)	65	●	●	○	...	○	220	27.0	59.1	2013	5.0	91 446	87.5	100.0	100.0	2010	0.33	2010
Brazil		1974	Beneficio de Prestacao Continuada (BPC/ Continuous Cash Benefit)	65	...	...	●	...	●	622	318.3	329.3	2012	39.9	5 851 554	28.3	41.8	41.8	2011	0.30	2010

Table B.7 Non-contributory pension schemes: Main features and indicators

Country	Notes	Year introduced	Name of scheme	Legal requirements and characteristics of the schemes: Age of eligibility	Citizenship	Residency	Income test	Asset test	Pension-tested	Level of benefit (monthly): National currency	US$	PPP	Year	% of average wage	Coverage (number, %): Number of recipients (unit)	Population 60 and over (%)	Population 65 and over (%)	Population above eligible age (%)	Year	Cost: Cost (% of GDP)	Year
Brazil		1971	Previdencia Rural (Rural Pension)	65 (m) 60 (w)	...	...	...	...	●	622	318.3	329.3	2012	39.9	1660446	8.0	11.9	9.5	2009	1.30	2009
Brunei Darussalam		1984	Old-Age pension	60	●	●	○	○	○	250	198.8	250.8	2011	...	21888	81.7	100.0	81.7	2011	0.40	2011
Bulgaria		...	Pensions not Related to Labour Activity Fund	70	...	●	●	...	●	101	76.0	145.3	2008	14.3	4917	0.3	0.4	0.5	2011	0.03	2011
Canada		1951	Pension de la Sécurité Vieillesse (S.V.) (Old-Age Security Pension) and Guaranteed Income Supplement	65	○	●	●	...	●	1283.1	1284.1	1038.9	2012	33.8	4764820	67.9	95.6	95.6	2011	1.58	2011
Cabo Verde		2006	Pensao Social Minima (Minimum Social Pension)	60	...	...	●	...	●	5000	63.1	70.0	2009	...	12317	37.5	43.1	37.5	2011	0.40	2011
Chile		2008	Pensión Básica Solidaria de Vejez (PBS-Vejez)	65	○	●	●	●	●	78449	161.3	190.6	2012	21.0	400134	16.0	22.8	22.8	2013	0.90	2013
Colombia		2003	Programa de Protección Social al Adulto Mayor (PPSAM) (Social Protection Programme for Older People) (Regional scheme)	57 (m) 52 (w)	●	●	●	●	●	532500	297.5	400.9	2012	52.7	486211	11.6	17.9	7.7	2011	0.02	2011
Cook Islands		1966	Old-Age Pension	60	○	●	○	○	○	400			2010	...	...	...	...	...		...	
Costa Rica		1974	Programa Regimen No Contributivo	65	●	●	●	●	●	115331	229.3	297.7	2012	24.6	83438	19.7	28.6	28.6	2009	0.21	2009
Cuba		...	...	65 (m) 60 (w)	...	...	●	...	●	...			2012	...	71000	3.7	5.1	4.3	2010	...	
Cyprus		1995	Social Pension Scheme	65	○	●	○	○	●	316	439.7	413.6	2011	15.8	15537	8.1	11.5	11.5	2012	0.33	2012
Denmark		1891	Folkepension (national pension – Universal basic pension)	65	○	●	●	...	●	5713	986.3	652.4	2012	15.6	988047	73.9	100.0	100.0	2012	...	
Dominican Republic		...	Programa Nonagenarios (Nonagenarians Programme)	60	...	...	●	...	○	4086	104.0	172.3	2012	37.1	...	...	...	...		...	
Ecuador		2003	Pension para Adultos Mayores (Pension for Older People/ Bono de Desarrollo Humano)	65	...	●	●	...	●	50	50.0	86.2	2013	10.5	583817	39.2	57.0	57.0	2013	0.31	2013
El Salvador		2009	Pension Basica Universal (Universal basic pension)	70	●	●	●	...	●	50	50.0	96.2	2013	18.4	26850	4.3	5.9	8.6	2013	0.04	2013
Estonia		...	National Pension	63	○	●	...	...	●	140.81	186.7	230.1	2013	16.8	6436	2.1	2.8	2.2	2013	...	
Fiji		...	Universal scheme to be launched	70	...	...	○	○	●	...			2013	...	6654	9.8	15.8	28.9	2013	...	
Finland		1937	Kansanelake (Old-Age Pension)	65	○	●	○	○	●	608.63	807.0	607.4	2013	19.6	482687	36.3	52.5	52.5	2010	0.00	2010

Table B.7 Non-contributory pension schemes: Main features and indicators

Country	Notes	Year introduced	Name of scheme	Legal requirements and characteristics of the schemes						Level of benefit (monthly)					Coverage (number, %)					Cost	
				Age of eligibility	Citizenship	Residency	Income test	Asset test	Pension-tested	National currency	US$	PPP	Year	% of average wage	Number of recipients (unit)	Population 60 and over (%)	Population 65 and over (%)	Population above eligible age (%)	Year	Cost (% of GDP)	Year
France		2004	ASPA (allocation de solidarité aux personnes âgées)	65	●	●	●	...	●	786.26	1042.6	865.0	2013	30.0	512727	3.8	5.0	5.0	2010	0.25	2007
Georgia		2006	Old-Age Pension	65 (m) 60 (w)	...	...	●	...	●	100	56.1	100.0	2011	14.5	654931	78.5	100.0	67.1	2010	3.70	2010
Greece		1982	Pension to uninsured elderly	60	○	●	●	...	●	230	320.0	317.2	2011	13.8	416183	15.5	20.0	15.5	2008	0.14	2008
Guatemala		2005	Programa de aporte económico del Adulto Mayor (Economic contribution programme for older people)	65	●	○	●	●	●	400	51.1	79.1	2012	20.3	103125	11.2	16.3	16.3	2010	...	
Guernsey		1984	Supplementary benefits	60	...	...	●	...	●	1764			2012	...	...	...	...	...		...	
Guyana		1944	Old-Age Pension	65	●	●	○	○	○	10000	48.5	106.0	(2012)	...	42000	100.0	100.0	100.0	2012	0.58	2012
Hong Kong (China), Special Administrative Region		2013	Old-Age Living Allowance (Fruit Money)	70	○	●	○	○	○	1135	146.3	199.7	2013	8.9	396847	27.4	39.3	56.2	2013	...	
Hong Kong (China), Special Administrative Region		1973	Old-Age Allowance	65	○	●	●	●	●	2200	283.6	387.1	2013	17.3	194491	13.4	19.3	19.3	2013	...	
Hungary		1993	Időskorúak járadéka (Allowance to the elderly)	62,5	○	●	●	○	●	27075	122.4	184.3	2013	12.7	5802	0.3	0.3	0.3	2010	...	
Iceland		1937	lífeyristryggingar almannatrygginga (National Basic Pension) and pension supplement	67	○	●	●	○	●	141514	1152.7	1036.3	2013	38.8	26293	47.2	66.3	78.2	2011	...	
India		1995	Indira Gandhi National Old-Age Pension Scheme	60	...	...	●	...	●	200	4.2	10.0	2011	3.2	19200000	19.1	29.8	19.1	2012	0.05	2012
Indonesia		2006	Program Jaminan Sosial Lanjut Usia (Elderly Social Security Programme) (Pilot)	60	...	●	●	●	●	300000	32.0	43.8	2012	23.2	13250	0.1	0.1	0.1	2010	0.00	2010
Ireland		...	State Pension (non-contributory)	66	○	●	●	●	●	919.8	1219.6	1051.2	2013	30.7	97179	13.5	19.2	13.5	2010	0.63	2010
Israel		...	Income support benefit: Special old-age benefit	65-67 (m) 60-64 (w)	○	●	●	...	●	1502	389.9	392.5	2013	17.5	701288	60.7	86.3	70.6	2012	...	
Italy		1996	Pensione Sociale (Social Pension)	65	○	●	●	●	●	481	618.7	556.7	2012	22.2	859985	5.3	6.9	6.9	2011	...	
Jamaica		2002	The Programme for Advancement through Health and Education (PATH)	60	...	...	●	●	●	1500	15.0	26.2	2013	2.0	51846	17.9	24.1	17.9	2010	0.04	2010

Table B.7 Non-contributory pension schemes: Main features and indicators

Country	Notes	Year introduced	Name of scheme	Legal requirements and characteristics of the schemes: Age of eligibility	Citizenship	Residency	Income test	Asset test	Pension-tested	Level of benefit (monthly): National currency	US$	PPP	Year	% of average wage	Coverage (number, %): Number of recipients (unit)	Population 60 and over (%)	Population 65 and over (%)	Population above eligible age (%)	Year	Cost: Cost (% of GDP)	Year
Japan		...	Public Assistance	65	...	...	●	...	...	80818	1012.9	777.6	2011	25.0	...	...	...	...		...	
Kazakhstan		...	State social benefit	63 (m) 58 (w)	...	...	○	○	●	9330	62.1	67.2	2013	10.4	...	...	...	...		...	
Kenya		2006	Older Persons Cash Transfer – Pilot	65	...	●	●	...	●	2000	23.7	43.6	2012	6.1	33000	1.9	3.0	3.0	2011	0.02	2011
Kenya		2008	Hunger Safety Net Programme – Pilot	55	...	●	○	○	○	1075	12.7	23.4	2012	3.3	...	...	...	...		...	
Kiribati		2003	Elderly pension	60	...	...	○	○	○	40	41.4	158.1	2012	...	1974	40.4	61.9	40.4	2004	0.65	2004
Korea, Republic of		2007	Basic Senior Pension	65	...	...	●	○	●	94600	84.0	118.8	2012	3.3	3609794	49.7	70.0	70.0	2009	0.32	2009
Kosovo	b	2002	Old-age "basic pension"	65	○	●	○	○	○	40	58.9	113.0	2008	...	107145	63.1	91.7	91.7	2013	3.39	2013
Kyrgyzstan		...	Social assistance allowance (old age)	63 (m) 58 (w)	...	...	○	○	●	530	14.5	32.5	2008	5.7	...	...	...	...		...	
Latvia		...	State social security benefit	67	●	●	○	○	●	45	82.3	106.9	2012	9.7	1077	0.2	0.3	0.3	2011	...	
Lesotho		2004	Old-Age Pension	70	...	●	○	○	●	450	54.8	90.0	2012	41.4	80000	62.9	93.1	138.4	2010	1.98	2010
Liberia		...	...	...	...	...	...	...	...					...	...	...	...	...		...	
Lithuania		...	Old-age social assistance pension	62.5 (m) 62 (w)	...	...	○	○	●	360	134.0	204.5	2012	17.6	...	...	...	...		...	
Malaysia		1982	Bantuan Orang Tua (Elderly Assistance Scheme)	60	...	...	●	...	●	300	94.4	158.7	2013	12.7	120496	5.5	8.8	5.5	2010	0.06	2010
Maldives		2009	Old-age Basic Pension	65	●	●	○	○	●	2000	129.9	175.9	2013	48.3	15252	67.9	90.6	90.6	2012	...	
Malta		1956	Old-age non-contributory pension	60	○	●	●	...	●	417.94	537.6	687.4	2012	33.3	4830	5.5	8.1	5.5	2009	...	
Mauritius		1950	Basic Retirement Pension	60	●	●	○	○	○	3146	109.6	185.3	2011	15.7	160947	98.4	100.0	98.4	2012	1.70	2012
Mexico		2007	Pension Para Adultos Mayores (Pension for Older People)	65	○	●	○	○	○	525	42.0	58.4	2013	9.1	1511684	15.4	22.2	33.6	2009	0.11	2009
Moldova, Republic of		1999	State Social Allocation for Older Persons	62(m) 57(w)	●	...	○	○	●	50	4.1	6.5	2013	1.6	3232	0.6	0.8	0.5	2009	0.21	2009
Mongolia		...	Social welfare pension	60 (m) 55 (w)	...	...	●	●	●	34500	25.6	45.0	2010	8.1	60658	37.4	56.9	29.0	2012	...	
Mozambique		1990	Programa Subsidio de Alimentos (PSA)	60 (m) 55 (w)	...	...	●	...	●	130	4.6	8.3	2011	20.6	...	...	...	...		...	
Namibia		1949	Old-Age Pension (OAP)	60	...	...	○	○	○	550	56.7	82.0	2013	...	131921	100.0	100.0	100.0	2008	1.36	2008

Table B.7 Non-contributory pension schemes: Main features and indicators

Country	Notes	Year introduced	Name of scheme	Legal requirements and characteristics of the schemes: Age of eligibility	Citizenship	Residency	Income test	Asset test	Pension-tested	Level of benefit (monthly): National currency	US$	PPP	Year	% of average wage	Coverage (number, %): Number of recipients (unit)	Population 60 and over (%)	Population 65 and over (%)	Population above eligible age (%)	Year	Cost: Cost (% of GDP)	Year
Nepal		1995	Old-Age Allowance	70	●	...	○	○	●	500	7.0	13.6	2011	9.8	640 119	32.3	48.4	84.3	2010	0.35	2010
Netherlands		1957	AOW Pension	65	○	●	○	○	○	1025.14	1359.3	1182.4	2013	45.7	3 076 200	80.0	100.0	100.0	2012	...	
New Zealand		1898	Superannuation	65	●	●	○	○	○	1549	1256.0	943.4	2013	39.8	571 239	69.5	97.6	97.6	2011	0.02	2011
Nigeria		2011	Ekiti State Social Security Scheme for Elderly (Ekiti State only)	65	○	●	●	...	●	5000	32.1	52.6	2013	13.2	20 000	0.3	0.4	0.4	2012	...	
Niue		...	...	60	...	...	○	○	○	483			2013	...	...	...	...	...		...	
Norway		1937	Grunnpensjon (Basic Pension)	62 (Flexible)	○	●	●	...	●	6844	1176.4	110.9	2012	18.0	760 025	71.1	98.1	82.5	2012	...	
Panama		2009	100 a los 70	70	●	●	○	○	●	100	100.0	151.5	2013	14.2	86 392	22.5	32.2	48.4	2012	...	
Paraguay		2009	Pensión alimentaria para adultos mayores en situación de pobreza	65	○	●	○	○	○	414558	97.7	146.7	2013	29.6	91 592	17.9	26.8	26.8	2013	0.12	2013
Peru		2011	Pension 65	65	...	...	●	...	●	125	46.0	75.4	2013	11.4	290 298	11.3	15.9	15.9	2013	...	
Philippines		2011	Social Pension Scheme	77	○	●	●	...	●	500	11.5	19.9	2011	6.0	148 768	2.5	4.0	18.7	2012	0.34	2012
Poland		...	Targeted pension	65 (m) 60 (w)	...	...	●	...	●	419.2	128.7	208.2	2012	12.3	49 205	0.6	0.9	1.0	2011	...	
Portugal		1980	Pensao Social de Velhice (Old-Age Social Pension)	65	●	●	●	...	●	...	...	...	...	...	...	...	...	...		...	
Russian Federation		...	State social pension	65 (m) 60 (w)	...	...	...	...	●	3172	102.9	126.0	2012	13.4	...	...	...	...		...	
Saint Kitts and Nevis		1998	Old-age social assistance pension	62+	○	●	●	...	●	250	92.6	116.2	2012	...	475	8.0	12.0	8.3	2011	...	...
Saint Vincent and the Grenadines		2010	The Non-Contributory Assistance Age Pension (NAAP)	65	...	...	●	...	●	220	81.5	147.6	2012	...	5 800	53.3	77.0	77.0	2012	...	
Samoa		1990	Senior Citizens Benefit	65	●	●	○	○	○	130	57.0	93.3	2012	...	8 700	65.2	92.6	92.6	2010	1.30	2010
Seychelles		1987	Old-age pension (social security fund)	63	○	●	○	○	○	2400	198.8	418.3	2010	...	6 951	71.2	99.0	88.6	2011	...	
Slovenia		1999	State pension	68	○	●	●	...	●	181.36	240.6	287.4	2010	11.9	17 085	3.7	4.9	5.9	2011	0.10	2011
South Africa		1927	Old-Age Grant	60	●	●	●	●	●	1270	130.9	220.4	2013	10.1	2 789 076	64.9	100.0	64.9	2011	1.14	2011

Table B.7 Non-contributory pension schemes: Main features and indicators

Country			Name of scheme	Legal requirements and characteristics of the schemes						Level of benefit (monthly)					Coverage (number, %)					Cost	
	Notes	Year introduced		Age of eligibility	Citizenship	Residency	Income test	Asset test	Pension-tested	National currency	US$	PPP	Year	% of average wage	Number of recipients (unit)	Population 60 and over (%)	Population 65 and over (%)	Population above eligible age (%)	Year	Cost (% of GDP)	Year
Spain		1994	Non Contributory Pension for retirement (Pensión no Contributiva de Jubilación)	65	○	●	●	...	●	342.37	440.4	461.4	2012	18.1	258 873	2.4	3.2	3.2	2012	0.11	2012
Suriname		1973	State Old-Age Pension (Algemene Oudedags Voorzieningsfonds (AOV))	60	●	●	○	○	○	525	159.1	226.1	2013	...	44 739	100.0	100.0	100.0	2003	1.90	2003
Swaziland		2005	Old-Age Grant	60	...	...	○	○	●	100	11.6	19.0	2013	...	55 000	86.0	133.9	86.0	2011	0.60	2011
Sweden		1939	Guarantee Pension	65	○	●	○	○	●	7810	1152.8	847.6	2012	26.9	818 915	34.4	46.7	46.7	2011	0.52	2011
Switzerland		...	Targeted pension	65 (m) 60 (w)	●	...	...	...	●	1512	1612.5	916.9	(2012)	21.5	...	...	...	...		...	
Taiwan, China		2008	National Pension System	65	●	●	○	○	●	3500	118.2	222.9	2012	7.7	...	...	...	...		...	
Tajikistan		...	Old-age pension	65 (m) 60 (w)	...	...	●	...	●	40	8.4	19.4	2012	11.3	85 156	23.5	33.8	27.6	2010	...	
Thailand		1993	Bia Yung Cheep, Old-Age Allowance (THA)	60	●	...	●	...	●	600	20.0	33.7	2013	6.0	6 123 370	68.6	100.0	68.6	2011	0.33	2011
Timor-Leste		2008	Support allowance for the elderly	60	●	●	○	○	●	20	20.0	101.0	2009	11.5	63 614	121.9	197.4	121.9	2009	3.26	2009
Trinidad and Tobago		1939	Senior Citizens' Pension	65	○	●	●	...	●	3000	475.3	607.9	2006	...	79 942	45.3	68.1	68.1	2012	...	
Turkey		1976	Means-tested Old-Age Pension	65	...	...	●	...	●	109.65	65.5	90.2	2011	7.3	...	...	...	...		...	
Turkmenistan		...	Social Allowance	62 (m) 57 (w)	...	...	○	○	●	105	36.8	50.8	2012	12.4	...	...	...	...		...	
Tuvalu		...			...	...	●	...	●	...	...	...	...	...	...	...	...	...		...	
Uganda		2011	Senior Citizens Grant (Pilot in 14 districts)	65	...	●	●	...	●	24000	9.6	22.9	2012	6.2	28 000	2.1	3.3	3.3	2012	...	
Ukraine		...	Social pension + social pension supplement	63 (m) 58 (w)	...	...	●	...	●	838	105.6	234.9	2010	31.8	213 000	2.3	3.0	2.2	2011	...	
United Kingdom		1909	Pension credit (Guarantee Credit)	60	○	●	●	●	●	610.68	941.2	899.4	2013	28.7	2 930 960	20.0	26.5	20.0	2013	0.47	2013
United States of America		1935	Old-age supplemental income benefit	65	●	●	●	...	●	674	674.0	674.0	2011	19.6	2 065 239	3.4	4.8	4.8	2012	...	
Uruguay		1919	Pensión por Vejez (Programa de Pensiones No-Contributivas)	70	●	●	●	●	●	5415	266.6	286.4	2012	32.6	32 789	5.2	6.9	9.6	2012	0.62	2012

Table B.7 Non-contributory pension schemes: Main features and indicators

Country	Notes	Year introduced	Name of scheme	Legal requirements and characteristics of the schemes						Level of benefit (monthly)					Coverage (number, %)					Cost	
				Age of eligibility	Citizenship	Residency	Income test	Asset test	Pension-tested	National currency	US$	PPP	Year	% of average wage	Number of recipients (unit)	Population 60 and over (%)	Population 65 and over (%)	Population above eligible age (%)	Year	Cost (% of GDP)	Year
Uzbekistan		...	Social pension	60 (m) 55 (w)	...	...	●	...	●	95520	50.5	102.6	2012	...	5700	0.3	0.5	0.3	2011	...	...
Venezuela, Bolivarian Republic of		2011/12	Gran Mision Amor Mayor	60 (m) 55 (w)	●	●	○	○	●	...				...	675000	24.6	37.7	20.2	2012	...	...
Viet Nam [80 years old and over]		2004	Social assistance benefit (clause 3)	80	...	...	○	...	●	180000	9.4	24.2	2010	7.1	139338	1.7	2.4	8.4	2011	0.01	2011
Viet Nam [60–79 years old]		2005	Social assistance benefit (clause 2)	60	...	...	●	...	●	120000	6.3	16.1	2010	4.8	808773	9.9	13.8	12.5	2011	0.04	2011
Zambia		2007	Social Cash Transfer Programme, Katete (Pilot)	60	...	...	○	○	○	60000	10.8	13.3	2010	...	4500	0.9	1.3	0.9	2009	...	

Main source
HelpAge International: HelpAge's social pensions database. Available at: http://www.pension-watch.net/about-social-pensions/about-social-pensions/social-pensions-database/ [6 June 2014].

Other sources
Qualitative information
SSA (Social Security Administration of the United States); ISSA (International Social Security Association). Social security programs throughout the world (Washington, DC and Geneva): The Americas, 2013; Europe, 2012; Asia and the Pacific, 2012; Africa, 2013. Available at: http://www.ssa.gov/policy/docs/progdesc/ssptw/ [6 June 2014].
Quantitative information
ILO (International Labour Office). ILO Social Security Inquiry. Available at: www.ilo.org/dyn/ilossi/ssimain.home [6 June 2014].
National sources (see below). Detailed links to national sources available at: http://www.social-protection.org/gimi/gess/RessourceDownload.action?ressource.ressourceId=43197

Additional sources for data used as denominators
ILO (International Labour Office): The ILO Global Wage Database. Available at: http://www.ilo.org/travail/info/db/lang--en/index.htm [6 June 2014].
United Nations: World Population Prospects, 2012 Revision. Available at: http://esa.un.org/wpp/index.htm [6 June 2014]

Notes
...: not available
[a] Exceeds 100%.
Year introduced: the first scheme that is the legal predecessor of any current scheme is indicated. Most schemes have been reformed since and the current legislation is rarely that of the founding year.
Legal requirements: categories of criteria applicants have to fulfil, e.g. holding citizenship of the country in question, having a legal residence, having income below a set level or passing an income test, having assets below a set level, not receiving any other pension or receiving only a low pension. Other criteria includes all other legal requirements. Geographical targeting means that the pension is available only in specific areas in the country. Non-working means that the potential beneficiary cannot either be formally employed or practise any gainful activity. Not in state institution means that elderly who are at home are excluded in the given country. It is also in this column that it is indicated if the programme is comprehensive, offering other services such as elderly care or discounts in utilities (the two most common). Special amount indicates whether there is a differentiated amount depending on civil status or age or any other criterion.
[b] As defined in United Nations Security Council resolution 1244 of 1999.

Symbols
● Yes
○ No

Table B.8 Old-age effective coverage: Active contributors (latest available year)

Major area, region or country	Active contributors to a pension scheme in the working-age population 15–64 (%)					Active contributors to a pension scheme in the labour force 15+ (%)				
	Total	Male	Female	Year	Age	Total	Male	Female	Age	Year
Regional estimates (weighted by working-age population)										
Africa	10.5	...	...			18.4	...	...		
Sub-Saharan Africa	5.9					8.4				
North Africa	23.9					47.4				
Middle East	18.6	...	...			37.1	...	...		
Latin America and the Caribbean	27.9	33.6	22.3			38.0	38.5	37.4		
Asia and the Pacific	26.5	...	...			34.0	...	...		
Central and Eastern Europe	48.9	...	...			69.7	...	...		
North America	77.5	...	...			98.5	...	...		
Western Europe	66.7	...	...			89.2	...	...		
World	30.9	...	...			41.4	...	...		
Developing economies	22.0	...	...			29.5	...	...		
Transition economies	45.7	...	...			63.8	...	...		
Developed economies	71.5	...	...			92.9	...	...		
Africa										
Algeria	40.3	...	...	2011	15–64	86.6	...	...	15+	2011
Angola	0.6	...	...	2012	15–64	0.8	...	...	15+	2012
Benin	5.2	...	...	2009	15–64	6.8	...	...	15+	2009
Botswana	12.5	...	...	2009	15–64	15.5	...	...	15+	2009
Burkina Faso	3.2	4.9	1.7	2009	15–64	3.7	5.2	2.0	15+	2009
Burundi	4.5	8.2	1.0	2011	15–64	5.2	9.6	1.1	15+	2011
Cameroon	5.2	8.7	1.7	2011	15–64	6.9	10.6	2.5	15+	2011
Cabo Verde	20.7	23.6	17.7	2010	15–64	28.4	26.4	31.6	15+	2010
Central African Republic	1.3	...	...	2003	15–64	1.5	...	...	15+	2003
Chad	1.5	...	...	2005	15–64	2.0	...	...	15+	2005
Congo	6.9	9.5	4.2	2012	15–64	9.1	12.3	5.8	15+	2012
Congo, Democratic Republic of	10.5	...	...	2009	15–64	14.0	...	...	15+	2010
Côte d'Ivoire	6.3	...	...	2010	15–64	8.8	...	...	15+	2010
Djibouti	6.6	...	...	2003	15–64	12.6	...	...	15+	2003
Egypt	29.0	45.1	12.7	2009	15–64	55.3	56.9	50.3	15+	2009
Gabon	56.6	89.1	23.6	2010	15–64	87.3	...	...	15+	2010
Gambia	2.3	...	...	2006	15–64	2.9	...	...	15+	2006
Ghana	6.7	9.4	3.9	2011	15–64	9.0	12.5	5.5	15+	2011
Guinea	11.1	...	...	2006	15–64	14.7	...	...	15+	2006
Guinea-Bissau	0.5	...	...	2010	15–64	0.6	...	...	15+	2010
Kenya	11.3	...	...	2009	15–64	16.3	...	...	15+	2009
Lesotho	3.1	...	...	2005	15–64	4.2	...	...	15+	2005
Libya	11.2	18.5	3.5	2008	15–64	19.6	22.9	10.9	15+	2008
Madagascar	5.7	...	...	2011	15–64	6.2	...	...	15+	2011
Malawi	0.0	0.0	0.0	2011	15–64	0.0	...	...	15+	2011
Mali	4.4	...	...	2010	15–64	7.9	...	...	15+	2010
Mauritania	9.4	...	...	2005	15–64	17.2	...	...	15+	2005
Mauritius	39.7	...	...	2010	15–64	60.9	...	...	15+	2010

Table B.8 Old-age effective coverage: Active contributors (latest available year)

Major area, region or country	Active contributors to a pension scheme in the working-age population 15–64 (%)					Active contributors to a pension scheme in the labour force 15+ (%)				
	Total	Male	Female	Year	Age	Total	Male	Female	Age	Year
Morocco	15.6	...	...	2011	15–64	30.2	...	...	15+	2011
Mozambique	3.8	...	...	2008	15–64	4.2	...	...	15+	2008
Namibia	5.6	...	...	2008	15–64	8.2	...	...	15+	2008
Niger	1.3	1.9	0.7	2006	15–64	1.9	2.0	1.6	15+	2006
Nigeria	5.3	7.6	3.1	2010	15–64	9.0	11.3	6.0	15+	2010
Rwanda	3.8	5.7	2.0	2009	15–64	4.3	6.5	2.2	15+	2009
Sao Tome and Principe	10.4	...	...	2010	15–64	16.4	...	...	15+	2010
Senegal	5.0	...	...	2008	15–64	6.2	...	...	15+	2008
Sierra Leone	4.6	...	...	2007	15–64	6.6	...	...	15+	2007
South Africa	3.5	...	...	2010	15–64	6.3	...	...	15+	2010
Sudan	2.8	...	...	2008	15–64	4.9	...	...	15+	2008
Swaziland	15.2	...	...	2010	15–64	25.5	...	...	15+	2010
Tanzania, United Republic of	3.1	4.2	1.9	2007	15–64	3.3	4.5	2.1	15+	2007
Togo	3.1	...	...	2009	15–64	3.7	...	...	15+	2009
Tunisia	41.4	...	...	2011	15–64	79.0	...	...	15+	2011
Uganda	3.8	3.4	4.2	2007	15–64	4.6	4.1	5.1	15+	2007
Zambia	8.8	12.1	5.5	2010	15–64	10.5	13.4	7.0	15+	2010
Zimbabwe	17.0	...	...	2009	15–64	18.3	...	...	15+	2009
Asia, Oceania and the Middle East										
Afghanistan	2.2	...	...	2006	15–64	4.4	...	...	15+	2006
Armenia	22.4	...	...	2009	15–64	31.7	...	...	15+	2009
Australia	69.6	74.5	64.6	2008	15–64	88.8	87.1	90.9	15+	2008
Azerbaijan	22.5	...	...	2007	15–64	33.3	...	...	15+	2007
Bahrain	10.5	12.4	7.3	2007	15–64	15.1	14.1	19.0	15+	2007
Bangladesh	0.0	0.0	0.0	2011	15–64	0.0	...	...	15+	2011
Bhutan	9.1	12.1	6.1	2012	15–64	12.1	14.8	8.6	15+	2012
Cambodia	0.0	0.0	0.0	2010	15–64	0.0	0.0	0.0	15+	2010
China	46.4	...	...	2011	15–64	56.1	...	...	15+	2011
Fiji	64.2	...	...	2011	15–64	99.0	...	...	15+	2011
Georgia	22.7	...	...	2008	15–64	29.5	...	...	15+	2008
Hong Kong (China), Special Administrative Region	52.3	...	...	2011	15–64	75.7	...	...	15+	2011
India	7.4	...	...	2010	15–64	12.4	...	...	15+	2010
Indonesia	6.0	...	...	2011	15–64	8.6	...	...	15+	2011
Iran, Islamic Rep. of	18.7	...	...	2010	15–64	39.3	...	...	15+	2010
Iraq	19.8	...	...	2009	15–64	45.2	...	...	15+	2009
Israel	69.8	...	...	2011	15–64	100.0	100.0	100.0	15+	2011
Japan	84.9	...	...	2010	15–64	100.0	100.0	100.0	15+	2010
Jordan	22.6	33.0	11.5	2010	15–64	51.5	47.4	70.1	15+	2010
Kazakhstan	73.8	...	...	2011	15–64	94.1	...	...	15+	2011
Korea, Republic of	53.7	...	...	2009	15–64	77.8	...	...	15+	2009
Kuwait	12.9	...	...	2010	15–64	18.4	...	...	15+	2010
Kyrgyzstan	30.0	...	...	2008	15–64	42.4	...	...	15+	2008
Lao People's Dem. Rep.	1.3	...	...	2010	15–64	1.6	...	...	15+	2010
Lebanon	0.0	...	...	2012	15–64	0.0	...	...	15+	2012
Malaysia	28.1	32.4	23.6	2010	15–64	43.2	39.3	50.2	15+	2010

Table B.8 Old-age effective coverage: Active contributors (latest available year)

Major area, region or country	Active contributors to a pension scheme in the working-age population 15–64 (%)					Active contributors to a pension scheme in the labour force 15+ (%)				
	Total	Male	Female	Year	Age	Total	Male	Female	Age	Year
Maldives	19.9	...	...	2010	15–64	28.1	...	...	15+	2010
Mongolia	39.6	...	...	2011	15–64	62.6	...	...	15+	2011
Nepal	2.5	4.1	1.0	2011	15–64	2.8	4.4	1.1	15+	2011
Occupied Palestinian Territory	5.2	...	...	2010	15–64	12.0	...	...	15+	2010
Oman	8.7	11.3	4.4	2011	15–64	13.7	13.4	15.4	15+	2011
Pakistan	3.1	...	...	2009	15–64	5.4	...	...	15+	2009
Papua New Guinea	3.0	...	...	2010	15–64	4.0	...	...	15+	2010
Philippines	17.5	...	...	2011	15–64	25.6	...	...	15+	2011
Qatar	3.3	...	...	2008	15–64	3.9	...	...	15+	2008
Samoa	22.8	...	...	2011	15–64	34.4	...	...	15+	2011
Saudi Arabia	26.2	43.8	2.1	2010	15–64	50.1	56.8	11.5	15+	2010
Singapore	0.0	0.0	0.0	2011	15–64	0.0	...	...	15+	2011
Solomon Islands	46.9	66.5	26.1	2008	15–64	66.6	79.4	46.3	15+	2008
Sri Lanka	7.1	...	...	2010	15–64	11.5	...	...	15+	2010
Syrian Arab Republic	13.4	...	...	2008	15–64	28.4	...	...	15+	2008
Taiwan, China	56.6	55.4	57.8	2011	15–64	86.8	75.8	99.9	15+	2011
Thailand	21.4	...	...	2012	15–64	27.7	...	...	15+	2012
Timor-Leste	0.0	0.0	0.0	2011	15–64	0.0	...	...	15+	2011
Tonga	6.5	...	...	2012	15–64	9.8	...	...	15+	2012
Vanuatu	16.9	16.4	17.5	2011	15–64	22.6	19.4	26.9	15+	2011
Viet Nam	17.3	17.7	16.8	2010	15–64	20.7	20.4	21.0	15+	2010
Yemen	2.6	4.8	0.5	2011	15–64	5.2	6.4	1.8	15+	2011
Europe										
Albania	29.8	...	...	2006	15–64	43.3	...	...	15+	2006
Austria	66.5	...	...	2010	15–64	87.1	...	...	15+	2010
Belarus	44.0	29.1	57.4	2010	15–64	66.6	41.6	91.9	15+	2010
Belgium	64.5	...	...	2010	15–64	94.4	...	...	15+	2010
Bosnia and Herzegovina	24.4	...	...	2008	15–64	44.6	0.0	0.0	15+	2008
Bulgaria	54.4	57.2	51.6	2009	15–64	79.2	77.2	81.5	15+	2009
Croatia	50.8	54.9	46.8	2010	15–64	77.3	77.0	77.6	15+	2010
Cyprus	58.1	59.0	57.1	2010	15–64	77.5	72.3	84.3	15+	2010
Czech Republic	67.7	...	...	2010	15–64	95.7	...	...	15+	2010
Denmark	78.1	...	...	2010	15–64	96.6	...	...	15+	2010
Estonia	63.6	...	...	2010	15–64	82.3	...	...	15+	2010
Finland	64.5	...	...	2010	15–64	85.0	...	...	15+	2010
France	66.2	...	...	2010	16-64	93.3	...	...	15+	2010
Germany	59.9	61.1	58.7	2010	16-64	76.8	72.7	81.8	15+	2010
Greece	64.3	72.7	55.8	2010	15–64	92.3	90.4	95.1	15+	2010
Hungary	71.0	70.9	71.1	2009	15–64	100.0	100.0	100.0	15+	2009
Iceland	...	...	...	...	...	...	...	...	...	...
Ireland	77.6	...	...	2010	15–64	100.0	100.0	100.0	15+	2010
Italy	58.2	...	...	2010	15–64	91.9	...	...	15+	2010
Latvia	56.6	...	...	2010	15–64	74.9	...	...	15+	2010
Lithuania	54.5	...	...	2010	15–64	76.0	...	...	15+	2010
Luxembourg	100.0	100.0	100.0	2010	15–64	100.0	100.0	100.0	15+	2010
Malta	53.5	...	...	2010	15–64	87.2	...	...	15+	2010

Table B.8 Old-age effective coverage: Active contributors (latest available year)

Major area, region or country	Active contributors to a pension scheme in the working-age population 15–64 (%)					Active contributors to a pension scheme in the labour force 15+ (%)				
	Total	Male	Female	Year	Age	Total	Male	Female	Age	Year
Moldova, Republic of	33.6	33.5	33.7	2011	15–64	70.1	66.5	73.8	15+	2011
Montenegro	36.8	...	...	2007	15–64	80.4	...	...	15+	2007
Netherlands	100.0	100.0	100.0	2010	15–64	100.0	100.0	100.0	15+	2010
Norway	77.1	...	...	2010	15–64	95.9	...	...	15+	2010
Poland	59.1	...	...	2010	15–64	88.8	...	...	15+	2010
Portugal	58.6	...	...	2010	15–64	74.5	...	...	15+	2010
Romania	37.2	...	...	2010	16-64	54.7	...	...	15+	2010
Russian Federation	48.7	...	...	2009	15–64	65.9	...	...	15+	2009
Serbia	29.7	...	...	2010	15–64	61.1	...	...	15+	2010
Slovakia	53.2	...	...	2010	15–64	77.1	...	...	15+	2010
Slovenia	61.7	67.9	55.4	2011	15–64	84.4	88.0	80.3	15+	2011
Spain	66.0	72.4	59.4	2010	15–64	89.0	88.0	89.3	15+	2010
Sweden	92.8	...	...	2010	15–64	100.0	100.0	100.0	15+	2010
The Former Yugoslav Rep. of Macedonia	52.3	...	...	2011	15–64	80.0	...	...	15+	2011
Turkey	27.8	44.1	11.7	2011	15–64	52.1	58.4	37.1	15+	2011
Ukraine	43.4	...	...	2007	15–64	60.6	...	...	15+	2007
United Kingdom	71.4	...	...	2005	15–64	92.9	...	...	15+	2005
Latin America and the Caribbean										
Antigua and Barbuda	71.8	...	...	2007	15–64	78.3	...	...	15+	2007
Argentina	35.7	45.7	25.8	2011	15–64	50.4	53.8	45.5	15+	2011
Aruba	64.1	72.9	56.3	2006	15–64	88.2	89.4	86.7	15+	2006
Bahamas	66.7	...	...	2011	15–64	81.9	...	...	15+	2011
Barbados	65.1	...	...	2009	15–64	79.6	...	...	15+	2009
Belize	44.2	58.0	30.6	2011	15–64	64.0	66.8	59.4	15+	2011
Bolivia (Plurinational State of)	22.2	28.6	15.8	2010	15–64	28.5	33.0	22.8	15+	2010
Brazil	31.4	36.8	26.2	2010	15–64	40.7	41.5	39.6	15+	2010
Chile	40.4	48.8	32.0	2012	15–64	58.5	58.7	58.2	15+	2012
Colombia	23.6	25.7	22.5	2009	15–64	32.7	30.0	37.8	15+	2009
Costa Rica	40.6	53.4	27.2	2011	15–64	58.8	62.2	53.0	15+	2011
Dominica	52.9	49.9	56.1	2011	15–64	...	...	...	n.a.	n.a.
Dominican Republic	20.0	22.5	17.5	2012	15–64	28.0	26.1	30.9	15+	2012
Ecuador	14.7	18.1	11.5	2009	15–64	20.2	20.4	20.0	15+	2009
El Salvador	19.8	24.0	16.3	2009	15–64	30.7	29.4	32.4	15+	2009
Grenada	58.7	...	...	2010	15–64	...	...	...	n.a.	2010
Guatemala	14.2	18.3	10.5	2010	15–64	19.5	19.3	19.8	15+	2010
Guyana	29.7	0.0	0.0	2009	15–64	45.7	0.0	0.0	15+	2009
Honduras	11.1	12.8	9.6	2009	15–64	16.8	14.4	21.1	15+	2009
Jamaica	12.5	...	...	2004	15–64	16.7	...	...	15+	2004
Mexico	25.1	32.1	18.3	2010	15–64	37.0	36.6	37.7	15+	2010
Nicaragua	14.4	16.6	12.4	2010	15–64	17.5	17.6	17.3	15+	2010
Panama	46.5	57.5	35.3	2009	15–64	64.0	63.4	65.1	15+	2009
Paraguay	13.5	15.9	11.1	2011	15–64	18.9	18.5	19.5	15+	2011
Peru	24.8	32.4	17.6	2010	15–64	29.2	36.9	20.4	15+	2010
Saint Kitts and Nevis	77.9	76.6	79.3	2010	15–64	...	...	...	n.a.	n.a.
Saint Lucia	43.1	44.1	42.3	2008	15–64	56.5	53.1	60.3	15+	2008
Saint Vincent and the Grenadines	49.5	...	...	2007	15–64	67.3	...	...	15+	2007

Table B.8 Old-age effective coverage: Active contributors (latest available year)

Major area, region or country	Active contributors to a pension scheme in the working-age population 15–64 (%)					Active contributors to a pension scheme in the labour force 15+ (%)				
	Total	Male	Female	Year	Age	Total	Male	Female	Age	Year
Trinidad and Tobago	49.7	...	...	2010	15–64	68.8	...	...	15+	2010
Uruguay	65.3	72.7	58.1	2011	15–64	81.8	81.0	82.9	15+	2011
Venezuela, Bolivarian Rep. of	24.1	27.4	20.8	2009	15–64	33.9	31.8	37.3	15+	2009
North America										
Canada	68.4	69.9	66.8	2009	15–64	85.4	82.9	88.3	15+	2009
United States	78.5	81.1	76.0	2010	15–64	100.0	100.0	100.0	15+	2010

Main source

ILO (International Labour Office): ILO Social Security Inquiry; Indicator: old-age contributor ratio: % working age. Available at: http://www.ilo.org/dyn/ilossi/ssiindic.viewMultiIndic3?p_lang=en&p_indicator_code=CP-1b%20OA [6 June 2014].

Other sources

ADB (Asian Development Bank): Social Protection Index database. Available at: http://spi.adb.org/spidmz/index.jsp [6 June 2014]

CISSTAT (Interstate Statistical Committee of the Commonwealth of Independent States): WEB Database Statistics of the CIS. Available at: http://www.cisstat.org/0base/index-en.htm [6 June 2014].

European Commission. 2012c. The 2012 ageing report: Economic and budgetary projections for the 27 EU Member States (2010–2060) (Brussels). Available at: http://ec.europa.eu/economy_finance/publications/european_economy/2012/2012-ageing-report_en.htm [16 Apr. 2014].

Hirose, K. (ed.). 2011. Pension reform in Central and Eastern Europe in times of crisis, austerity and beyond (Budapest, ILO Regional Office for Central and Eastern Europe).

World Bank pensions data. Available at: http://web.worldbank.org/WBSITE/EXTERNAL/TOPICS/EXTSOCIALPROTECTION/EXTPENSIONS/0,,contentMDK:23231994~menuPK:8874064~pagePK:148956~piPK:216618~theSitePK:396253,00.html [20 Apr. 2014].

National sources (see below).

Notes

n.a.: Not applicable

...: Not available

Additional notes by country

Africa

Algeria. Including old age 'reversion pension' but excluding anticipated pension. Office national de la statistique (available at: http://www.ons.dz/IMG/pdf/AQC_R_2011_ED_2012_-_Francais.pdf, accessed May 2014).

Burundi. Includes old age, survivors pensions for people aged 60 and over.

Cabo Verde. For the contributory pension provided by CNPS, the statutory pensionable age is 65 and over for men and 60 and over for women. As the non-contributory pension targets people aged 60 and over (either men or women), the population of reference for the denominator has been set at age 60.

Côte d'Ivoire. Data from the CNPS (Caisse Nationale de Prévoyance Sociale) and CGRAE (Caisse Générale de Retraite des Agents de l'Etat).

Madagascar. Data refer to the Caisse Nationale de la Prévoyance Sociale (CNaPS) and two occupational schemes for civil servants: the Caisse de Retraites Civiles et Militaires (CRCM), which covers civil servants, government workers and the military; and the Caisse de Prévoyance et de Retraites (CPR), which covers auxiliary agents employed by the Government, who have not yet been granted full government employee status.

Malawi. There is no national social insurance scheme in Malawi. The Government Public Pension Scheme is a non-contributory, defined benefit, PAYG system. There are around 600 private pension funds in Malawi not included here.

Asia, Oceania and the Middle East

Bangladesh. The Government of Bangladesh provides its own employees with a non-contributory, defined benefit pension with survivor benefits, funded through tax revenues. Civil servants are eligible to receive a pension at the age of 57.

China. The indicator for China includes contributors to the new rural social pension plan introduced nationwide in 2009. This new pension has two components: a basic pension component financed by local and central Government and a personal account component based on contributions from enrolled individuals. In relatively poor regions the central Government pays approximately 80% of the cost of the basic pension component and the local Government bears the rest. The first basic pension component justifies inclusion in this indicator, focusing on periodic cash benefits for the elderly to ensure basic income security.

Iran, Islamic Rep. of. Corresponds to total number of insured as principal contributors and refers to the social security organization and State retirement fund.

Lebanon. There is currently no income security for the elderly through regular old-age pension benefits, only a lump sum.

Sri Lanka. Number of contributors under the widows and orphans and widowers and orphans pensions, 2003–09, which is in Sri Lanka the only mandatory contributory scheme providing pensions, i.e. monthly cash periodic benefits. This indicator refers to contributory mandatory schemes providing pensions for people above statutory retirement age (i.e. it excludes PSPS, which is a non-contributory scheme; EPF and ETF, providing lump sums; and the three voluntary social security schemes, Farmers' Pension and Social Security Benefit Scheme, Fishermen's Pension and Social Security Benefit Scheme, and Social Pension and Social Security Benefit Scheme (initially for self-employed only), which are voluntary and provide either lump-sum or periodic benefits.

Tonga. In September 2010, the National Retirement Benefits Scheme (NRBS) Bill 2010 was passed by the Legislative Assembly, providing a similar mandatory superannuation plan for the private sector and other organizations. No statistics available yet (see: http://www.nrbf.to/, accessed May 2014).

Vanuatu. Active member refers to a person who has at least one contribution paid on that member's behalf for the current or any of the preceding three months (see: http://www.vnpf.com.vu/p/vnpf-index.html, accessed May 2014).

Latin America and the Caribbean

Uruguay. According to household survey data, where the question is put to employed persons, the proportions were lower in 2011 (52.6% of people of working age and 67.6% of the labour force). See Insituto Nacional de Estadística: Encuesta continua de hogares 2011 (available at: http://www.ine.gub.uy/microdatos/microdatosnew2008.asp#ech, accessed May 2014).

Table B.9 Old-age effective coverage: Old-age pension beneficiaries. Proportion of older women and men (above statutory pensionable age) receiving an old-age pension, latest available year

Major area, region or country	Proportion by sex (%)		
	Total	Male	Female
Regional estimates (weighted by total population)			
Africa	21.5	...	...
Middle East	29.5	...	...
Latin America and the Caribbean	56.1	62.3	52.4
Asia and the Pacific	47.0	...	...
Central and Eastern Europe	94.3	97.2	93.8
North America	93.0	...	...
Western Europe	92.4	99.2	86.5
World	51.5	...	...
Developing economies	44.3	...	...
Least developed countries[1]	16.8	...	...
Low- and medium-income countries[2]	24.6	...	...
Emerging economies[3]	71.5	...	...
Developed economies	89.1	...	...

Major area, region or country	Proportion by sex (%)			Proportion by type of programme (contributory or not). (%)			Year	Statutory pensionable age (basis for reference population)
	Total	Male	Female	No distinction available	Contributory	Non-contributory[1]		
Africa								
Algeria	63.6	...	...	...	51.1	12.5	2010	60+ Men 55+ Women
Angola	14.5	...	...	...	14.5	...	2012	60+
Benin	9.7	...	...	...	9.7	...	2009	60+
Botswana	100.0	100.0	100.0	...	...	100.0	2010	65+
Burkina Faso	3.2	7.1	0.5	...	3.2	...	2009	55+
Burundi	4.0	6.8	2.0	...	4.0	...	2011	60+
Cameroon	12.5	20.2	5.9	...	12.5	...	2011	60+
Cabo Verde	55.7	59.8	52.8	...	18.2	37.5	2009	60+
Chad	1.6	...	...	...	1.6	...	2008	55+
Congo	22.1	42.4	4.7	...	22.1	...	2011	60+
Congo, Democratic Republic of	15.0	...	...	...	15.0	...	2009	65+ Men 60+ Women
Côte d'Ivoire	7.7	...	...	...	7.7	...	2010	55+ as common denominator (Eligibility: 65+ for non contributory pension except 60 in specific region)
Djibouti	12.0	...	...	...	12.0	...	2002	60+
Egypt	32.7	61.7	8.0	32.7	...	...	2008	60+
Ethiopia	9.0	...	...	...	9.0	...	2006	60+
Gabon	38.8	...	...	...	38.8	...	2010	55+

Table B.9 Old-age effective coverage: Old-age pension beneficiaries. Proportion of older women and men (above statutory pensionable age) receiving an old-age pension, latest available year

Major area, region or country	Proportion by sex (%)			Proportion by type of programme (contributory or not). (%)			Year	Statutory pensionable age (basis for reference population)
	Total	Male	Female	No distinction available	Contributory	Non-contributory[1]		
Gambia	10.8	...	...	...	10.8	...	2006	60+
Ghana	7.6	...	...	...	7.6	...	2011	60+
Guinea	8.8	...	...	...	8.8	...	2008	55+
Guinea-Bissau	6.2	...	...	...	6.2	...	2008	60+
Kenya	7.9	...	...	...	6.6	1.4	2010	55+
Lesotho	100.0	100.0	100.0	...	...	100.0	2010	70+
Libya	43.3	...	...	...	43.3	...	2006	65+ Men 60+ Women
Madagascar	4.6	...	...	...	4.6	...	2011	60+
Malawi	4.1	...	...	...	4.1	...	2010	60+
Mali	5.7	8.5	3.7	...	5.7	...	2010	58+
Mauritania	9.3	...	...	...	9.3	...	2002	60+ Men 55+ Women
Mauritius	100.0	100.0	100.0	...	...	100.0	2010	60+
Morocco	39.8	...	...	...	39.8	...	2009	60+
Mozambique	17.3	20.0	15.9	...	1.7	15.6	2011	60+ Men 55+ Women
Namibia	98.4	...	...	...	...	98.4	2011	60+
Niger	6.1	...	...	...	6.1	...	2007	60+
Nigeria	...	...	...	...	...	0.4	n.a.	
Rwanda	4.7	...	...	...	4.7	...	2004	55+
Sao Tome and Principe	41.8	...	...	...	41.8	...	2010	62 + Men 57 + Women
Senegal	23.5	...	...	...	23.5	...	2010	55+
Seychelles	100.0	100.0	100.0	...	11.4	88.6	2011	63+
Sierra Leone	0.9	...	...	...	0.9	...	2007	60+
South Africa	92.6	...	...	...	27.7	64.9	2012	60+
Sudan	4.6	...	...	...	4.6	...	2010	60+
Swaziland	86.0	...	...	...	...	86.0	2011	60+
Tanzania, United Republic of	3.2	...	...	...	3.2	...	2008	60+
Togo	10.9	...	...	...	10.9	...	2009	60+
Tunisia	68.8	...	...	...	68.8	...	2006	60+
Uganda	6.6	...	...	...	4.5	2.1	2012	55+
Zambia	7.7	...	...	...	6.9	0.8	2008	55+
Zimbabwe	6.2	...	...	...	6.2	...	2006	60+
Middle East, Asia and the Pacific								
Afghanistan	10.7	...	...	...	...	...	2010	60+ Men 55+ Women
Armenia	80.0	...	...		64.6	15.4	2011	63 Men 62.5 Women
Australia	83.0	77.5	87.6	...	...	70.7	2010	65+ Men 64+ Women
Azerbaijan	81.7	82.6	79.0	...	40.8	40.9	2012	62.5 Men 57.5 Women
Bahrain	40.1	...	...	...	...	...	2011	60+ Men 55+ Women

Table B.9 Old-age effective coverage: Old-age pension beneficiaries. Proportion of older women and men (above statutory pensionable age) receiving an old-age pension, latest available year

Major area, region or country	Proportion by sex (%)			Proportion by type of programme (contributory or not). (%)			Year	Statutory pensionable age (basis for reference population)
	Total	Male	Female	No distinction available	Contributory	Non-contributory[1]		
Bangladesh	39.5	...	...	...	4.9	34.6	2011	65+ (62+ for OA allowances for women)
Bhutan	3.2	...	...	...	3.2	...	2012	60+
Brunei Darussalam	81.7	...	...	...	...	81.7	2011	60+
Cambodia	5.0	...	...	...	...	...	2010	55+
China	74.4	...	...	...	32.2	42.1	2011	60+ Men 55+ Women
Fiji	10.6	...	...	...	...	...	2010	55+
Georgia	89.8	...	...	...	...	...	2011	65 + Men 60+ Women
Hong Kong (China), Special Administrative Region	72.9	...	...	...	...	72.9	2009	65+
India	24.1	...	...	...	9.9	14.2	2011	58+
Indonesia	8.1	...	...	...	...	...	2010	55+
Iran, Islamic Rep. of	26.4	...	...	...	...	...	2010	60+ Men 55+ Women
Iraq	56.0	...	...	...	...	...	2007	55/60+
Israel	73.6	...	...	...	...	...	2011	67 + Men 62+ Women
Japan	80.3	...	...	...	...	...	2008	65+
Jordan	42.2	82.3	11.8	...	42.2	...	2010	60+ Men 55+ Women
Kazakhstan	95.9	...	...	...	...	...	2011	63+ Men 58+ Women
Korea, Republic of	77.6	...	...	...	...	...	2010	60+
Kuwait	27.3	...	...	...	...	...	2008	50+
Kyrgyzstan	100.0	100.0	100.0	...	...	...	2011	63+ Men 58+ Women
Lao People's Dem. Rep.	5.6	...	...	...	...	...	2010	60+
Lebanon	0.0	...	...	...	0.0	0.0	2013	64+
Malaysia	19.8	...	...	...	16.2	3.6	2010	55+
Maldives	99.7	...	...	...	9.1	90.6	2012	65+
Marshall Islands	64.2	...	...	...	64.2	...	2010	60+
Mongolia	100.0	100.0	100.0	...	62.6	37.4	2011	60+
Nauru	56.5	...	...	...	15.5	41.0	2010	55+
Nepal	62.5	...	...	...	9.2	53.3	2010	58+
New Zealand	98.0	99.8	96.5	...	...	98.0	2012	65+
Occupied Palestinian Territory	8.0	...	...	...	...	...	2009	65+
Oman	24.7	...	...	...	...	...	2010	60+ Men 55+ Women
Pakistan	2.3	...	...	...	...	...	2010	60+ Men 55+ Women
Palau	48.0	...	...	...	...	...	2010	60+
Papua New Guinea	0.9	...	...	...	...	...	2010	55+
Philippines	28.5	...	...	...	24.3	4.2	2011	60+

Table B.9 Old-age effective coverage: Old-age pension beneficiaries. Proportion of older women and men (above statutory pensionable age) receiving an old-age pension, latest available year

Major area, region or country	Proportion by sex (%)			Proportion by type of programme (contributory or not). (%)			Year	Statutory pensionable age (basis for reference population)
	Total	Male	Female	No distinction available	Contributory	Non-contributory[1]		
Qatar	7.9	...	...	...	...	...	2007	60+
Samoa	49.5	...	...	...	3.7	45.8	2011	55+
Singapore	0.0	...	...	...	0.0	0.0	2011	55+
Solomon Islands	13.1	...	...	...	...	...	2010	50+
Sri Lanka	17.1	...	...	...	...	...	2010	55+ Men 50+ Women
Syrian Arab Republic	16.7	...	...	...	...	...	2006	60+ Men 55+ Women
Tajikistan	80.2	95.6	72.1	...	61.4	18.8	2011	60+ Men 55+ Women
Thailand	81.7	77.9	84.6	...	13.1	68.6	2010	60+
Timor-Leste	100.0	100.0	100.0	...	0.0	100.0	2011	60+
Tonga	1.0	...	...	...	...	...	2012	55+
Tuvalu	19.5	...	...	...	...	...	2005	55+
Uzbekistan	98.1	...	...	...	97.8	0.3	2010	60+ Men 55+ Women
Vanuatu	3.5	...	...	...	...	...	2011	55+
Viet Nam	34.5	...	...	...	25.8	8.7	2010	60+ Men 55+ Women
Yemen	8.5	...	...	...	...	...	2011	60+ Men 55+ Women
Europe								
Albania	77.0	100.0	60.8	...	...	...	2011	65+ Men 60+ Women
Austria	100.0	77.5	93.7	...	94.0	6.0	2010	65+ Men 60+ Women
Belarus	93.6	...	...	...	91.1	2.5	2011	60+ Men 55+ Women
Belgium	84.6	100.0	67.8	...	79.5	5.1	2010	65+
Bosnia and Herzegovina	29.6	...	...	...	29.6	...	2009	65+
Bulgaria	96.9	99.4	95.5	...	96.5	0.4	2010	63 + Men 60+ Women
Croatia	57.6	85.1	44.2	...	...	...	2010	65 + Men 60+ Women
Cyprus	85.2	100.0	57.2	...	72.3	12.9	2010	65+
Czech Republic	100.0	100.0	100.0	...	...	0.0	2010	62.2 + Men 60.7 Women
Denmark	100.0	100.0	100.0	...	...	100.0	2011	65+
Estonia	98.0	98.5	97.5	...	96.0	2.0	2011	63 + Men 61+ Women
Finland	100.0	100.0	100.0	...	47.5	52.5	2010	65+
France	100.0	100.0	100.0	...	95.0	5.0	2010	60+
Germany	100.0	100.0	100.0	...	...	...	2010	65+
Greece	77.4	100.0	54.6	...	60.4	17.0	2010	65 + Men 60+ Women
Hungary	91.4	97.7	87.6	...	91.1	0.3	2010	62+
Iceland	100.0	100.0	100.0	...	17.2	82.8	2010	67+

Table B.9 Old-age effective coverage: Old-age pension beneficiaries. Proportion of older women and men (above statutory pensionable age) receiving an old-age pension, latest available year

Major area, region or country	Proportion by sex (%)			Proportion by type of programme (contributory or not). (%)			Year	Statutory pensionable age (basis for reference population)
	Total	Male	Female	No distinction available	Contributory	Non-contributory[1]		
Ireland	90.5	100.0	66.3	...	71.3	19.2	2010	65+
Italy	81.1	100.0	69.2	...	75.1	6.0	2010	65 + Men 60+ Women
Latvia	100.0	100.0	100.0	...	99.8	0.2	2010	62+
Lithuania	100.0	100.0	100.0	...	96.0	4.0	2010	62.5 + Men 60+ Women
Luxembourg	90.0	100.0	56.4	...	...	...	2010	65+
Malta	60.5	97.5	32.0	...	55.3	5.2	2010	61 + Men 60+ Women
Moldova, Republic of	72.8	63.7	77.0	...	...	...	2011	62+ Men 57 + Women
Montenegro	52.3	...	...	...	...	...	2011	65 + Men 60+ Women
Netherlands	100.0	100.0	100.0	...	...	...	2010	65+
Norway	100.0	100.0	100.0	...	...	...	2010	67+
Poland	96.5	100.0	94.9	...	93.9	2.6	2009	65 + Men 60+ Women
Portugal	100.0	100.0	100.0	...	...	...	2010	65+
Romania	98.0	100.0	88.0	...	...	...	2010	63.75 + Men 58.75+ Women
Russian Federation	100.0	100.0	100.0	...	...	...	2011	60+ Men 55+ Women
Serbia	46.1	48.4	44.8	...	...	...	2010	64+ Men 59+ Women
Slovakia	100.0	100.0	100.0	...	99.5	0.5	2010	62+
Slovenia	95.1	100.0	85.9	...	91.1	4.0	2010	63+ Men 61+ Women
Spain	68.2	97.4	46.6	...	64.9	3.3	2010	65+
Sweden	100.0	100.0	100.0	...	52.0	48.0	2010	65+
Switzerland	100.0	100.0	100.0	...	...	...	2010	65+ Men 64+ Women
The Former Yugoslav Republic of Macedonia	52.2	...	...	...	...	...	2011	64+ Men 62+ Women
Turkey	88.1	...	...	...	...	...	2010	60 + Men 58+ Women
Ukraine	95.0	...	...	...	93.0	2.0	2011	60 + Men 55.5+ Women
United Kingdom	99.5	100.0	99.2	...	75.5	24.0	2010	65 + Men 60+ Women
Latin America and the Caribbean								
Antigua and Barbuda	69.7	...	...	...	68.0	1.7	2010	60+
Argentina	90.7	86.8	93.3	...	63.6	27.1	2010	65+
Aruba	79.3	...	...	...	...	79.3	2013	60+
Bahamas	84.2	...	...	...	75.3	8.9	2011	65+
Barbados	68.3	...	...	...	33.2	35.1	2011	65+
Belize	64.6	...	...	...	32.0	32.6	2011	65+
Bolivia, Plurinational State of	100.0	100.0	100.0	...	...	100.0	2013	60+ (eligible age for Renta Dignidad)

Table B.9 Old-age effective coverage: Old-age pension beneficiaries. Proportion of older women and men (above statutory pensionable age) receiving an old-age pension, latest available year

Major area, region or country	Proportion by sex (%)			Proportion by type of programme (contributory or not). (%)			Year	Statutory pensionable age (basis for reference population)
	Total	Male	Female	No distinction available	Contributory	Non-contributory[1]		
Brazil	86.3	90.6	83.0	...	50.0	36.3	2009	65+ Men 60+ Women
Chile	74.5	76.4	73.4	...	29.5	45.0	2012	65+ Men 60+ Women
Colombia	23.0	28.3	18.4	...	13.9	9.1	2009	60+ Men 55+ Women.
Costa Rica	55.8	65.4	48.8	...	30.2	25.6	2010	65+ Men 62+ Women
Dominica	38.5	...	...	...	38.5	...	2011	60+
Dominican Republic	11.1	16.5	6.2	11.1	...	...	2009	65+ Men 60+ Women
Ecuador	53.0	55.5	50.8	...	16.0	37.0	2011	60+
El Salvador	18.1	31.6	10.3	...	15.9	2.2	2009	60+ Men 55+ Women
Grenada	34.0	...	...	...	34.0	...	2010	60+
Guatemala	14.1	18.2	10.3	...	12.5	1.6	2006	60+
Guyana	100.0	100.0	100.0	...	4.6	100.0	2012	60+ (65+ for non-L2 65contributory pension)
Haiti	1.0	...	...	...	...	...	2001	60+
Honduras	8.4	13.8	5.8	...	8.4	...	2009	65+ Men 60+ Women
Jamaica	55.5	...	...	...	36.1	19.4	2010	65+ Men 60+ Women
Mexico	25.2	34.6	17.2	...	3.0	22.2	2009	65+
Nicaragua	23.7	42.3	16.2	...	23.7	...	2011	60+
Panama	37.3	49.4	28.9	37.7	...	...	2008	62+ Men 57 + Women
Paraguay	22.2	24.9	20.0	...	4.3	17.9	2013	60+
Peru	33.2	41.4	26.1	...	21.9	11.3	2013	60+
Saint Kitts and Nevis	44.7	51.6	39.7	...	36.4	8.3	2010	62+
Saint Lucia	26.5	10.3	8.3	...	26.5	...	2008	62+
Saint Vincent and the Grenadines	76.6	...	...	...	23.3	53.3	2012	60+
Trinidad and Tobago	98.7	...	...	...	50.7	47.7	2009	60+
Uruguay	76.5	74.6	77.7	...	66.9	9.6	2011	60+
Venezuela, Bolivarian Rep. of	59.4	70.0	50.2	...	39.2	20.2	2012	60+ Men 55+ Women
North America								
Canada	97.7	...	...	...	2.1	95.6	2011	65+
United States	92.5	94.8	90.8	...	87.6	4.9	2011	65+

Notes

[1] Differences from proportions indicated in table B.7 may result from: differences in reference years; differences in population of reference between the non-contributory pension and the statutory pensionable age considered here as the main criterion to define the population of reference applied to all pensions.

Main source

ILO (International Labour Office): ILO Social Security Inquiry; Indicator: old-age pensioners recipient ratio above retirement age. Available at: http://www.ilo.org/dyn/ilossi/ssiindic.viewMultiIndic3?p_lang=en&p_indicator_code=CR-1f%20OA [6 June 2014].

Other sources

ADB (Asian Development Bank): Social Protection Index database. Available at: http://spi.adb.org/spidmz/index.jsp [6 June 2014]

Barrientos, A; Nino-Zarazúa, M.; Maitrot, M. 2010. *Social Assistance in Developing Countries database (version 5.0)* (Manchester and London, Brooks World Poverty Institute and Overseas Development Institute). Available at: http://www.chronicpoverty.org/publications/details/social-assistance-in-developing-countries-database [6 June 2014].

CISSTAT (Interstate Statistical Committee of the Commonwealth of Independent States): WEB Database Statistics of the CIS. Available at: http://www.cisstat.org/0base/index-en.htm [6 June 2014].

Eurostat. Pensions beneficiaries database: Number of pension beneficiaries by country and type of pension. Are included for the purpose of this indicator old-age pension beneficiaries excluding beneficiaries from anticipated old-age pension. Available at: http://appsso.eurostat.ec.europa.eu/nui/show.do?dataset=spr_pns_ben&lang=en [6 May 2014].

HelpAge International: HelpAge's social pensions database. Available at: http://www.pension-watch.net/about-social-pensions/about-social-pensions/social-pensions-database/ [6 June 2014].

Hirose, K. (ed.). 2011. *Pension reform in Central and Eastern Europe in times of crisis, austerity and beyond* (Budapest, ILO Regional Office for Central and Eastern Europe).

World Bank pensions data. Available at: http://web.worldbank.org/WBSITE/EXTERNAL/TOPICS/EXTSOCIALPROTECTION/EXTPENSIONS/0,,contentMDK:23231994~menuPK:8874064~pagePK:148956~piPK:216618~theSitePK:396253,00.html [20 Apr. 2014].

National sources (see below).

Additional notes by country

Africa

Algeria. Including old-age reversion pension but excluding anticipated pension. Non-contributory pension (data for 2009): *Evolution de la catégorie des personnes âgées bénéficiaires de l'AFS (périodes: 2004-2009).* Reference population: eligible age 60 years.

Angola. Total number of pensioners. There is no general social assistance programme aimed at the elderly.

Burundi. Includes old age, survivors and ascendent pensions for people aged 60 and over.

Cameroon. Data for the public pension schemes are estimated based on data available for previous years.

Cabo Verde. Regarding the contributory pension provided by CNPS, the statutory retirement age is 65 and over for men and 60 and over for women. However, as the age of eligibility for the non-contributory pension is 60 for both men and women, the reference population for the denominator has been set at 60. Survey data (provided in this Statistical Annex) provide lower numbers than administrative sources.

Congo. Includes disability and survivors' pensioners above statutory pensionable age of 60.

Côte d'Ivoire. Data from the CNPS (Caisse Nationale de Prévoyance Sociale) and CGRAE (Caisse Générale de Retraite des Agents de l'Etat).

Gabon. The number refers to all pensions, resulting in a possible overestimation of old-age pensioners.

Middle East, Asia and the Pacific

Azerbaijan. Eligible age for non-contributory pension: 67 years old and over for men and 62 for women. For the calculation of the coverage, the lower eligible age (statutory pensionable age) is taken for consistency reasons.

China. The indicator for China includes old-age pension recipients from the new rural social pension plan introduced nationwide in 2009. This new pension has two components: a basic pension component financed by local and central Government, and a personal account component based on contributions from enrolled individuals. In relatively poor regions the central Government pays approximately 80% of the cost of the basic pension component and the local Government bears the rest. The first basic pension component justifies inclusion in this indicator, focusing on periodic cash benefits for elderly to ensure basic income security.

Iran, Islamic Rep. of. Refers to the social security organization and State retirement fund.

Lebanon. There is currently no income security for elderly through regular old-age pension benefits, only a lump sum.

Malaysia. Includes government pension scheme, which is the only one providing cash periodic benefits, and a social assistance programme targeting poor elderly with no family support.

New Zealand. Percentage by sex estimated based on distribution from 2011.

Philippines. The old-age grant, launched in 2011, and the retirement programme for veterans, are considered non-contributory schemes.

Samoa. The Samoa National Provident Fund provides the option for a retirement pension or full withdrawal. Since the majority of SNPF members take the option of full withdrawal, there were only 445 pensioners and 276 beneficiaries (i.e. 3.7% of persons age 55 and over) in 2011.

Sri Lanka. This indicator refers to contributory mandatory schemes providing pensions for people above statutory retirement age (i.e. it excludes PSPS, which is a non-contributory schemes; EPF and ETF, providing lump sums; and the three voluntary social security schemes, Farmers' Pension and Social Security Benefit Scheme, Fishermen's Pension and Social Security Benefit Scheme, and Social Pension and Social Security Benefit Scheme (initially for self-employed only), which are voluntary and provide either lump-sum or periodic benefits (available at: http://www.statistics.gov.lk/abstract2010/Pages/index.htm, accessed December 2013).

Thailand. These proportions refer only to beneficiaries of the old-age or disability social pensions. As a result the reference taken is not the statutory pensionable age of 55 but the age of eligibility for the old-age social pension (60 and over).

Tonga. Only a minority of members opt for a regular pension once reaching pensionable age. In September 2010, the National Retirement Benefits Scheme (NRBS) Bill 2010 was passed by the Legislative Assembly, Providing a similar mandatory superannuation plan for the private sector and other organizations. No statistics available yet.

Vanuatu. Mainly withdrawals.

Europe

Albania. Includes old-age pensions including war veteran, special merit and supplementary pensions. Ratio above statutory retirement age.

Latin America and the Caribbean

Brazil. Age range used for the indicators: 65 and over for both men and woment despite a statutory retirement age of 60 for women.

Colombia. Age range used for the indicator: 65 and over.

Costa Rica. The normal retirement age is 65 years with at least 300 months of contributions. Age 65 years is used as a basis to define the reference population for this indicator.

Dominican Republic. Age range used for the indicator: 65 and over.

Nicaragua. The normal retirement age of 60 years is used as a basis to define the reference population for this indicator.

Panama. The normal retirement age of 62 (men) or 57 (women) is used as a basis to define the reference population for this indicator.

Uruguay. Proportion calculated for people aged 60 and over. For people aged 65 and over, this proportion reaches 85.9%,

North America

United States. Retirement (includes OASI), all beneficiaries aged 65 and over. Includes beneficiaries in foreign countries.

Concepts, definitions and interpretation guidelines available at: http://www.social-protection.org/gimi/gess/RessourceDownload.action?ressource.ressourceId=37897

Table B.10 Total (public and private) health-care expenditure not financed by private households' out-of-pocket payments (percentage)

Major area, region or country	2011	2010	2009	2008	2007	2006	2005	2000	1995
Africa									
Northern Africa									
Algeria	81.8	80.9	80.3	80.6	78.5	75.7	73.6	74.2	76.1
Egypt	41.8	40.6	42.9	43.5	42.5	44.9	40.5	42.0	52.0
Libya	68.8	70.0	68.8	67.6	66.4	65.1	65.4	50.8	49.6
Morocco	42.0	42.8	43.7	43.0	42.7	42.0	40.2	45.9	47.3
Sudan	30.0	30.5	32.4	35.9	36.7	37.7	40.0	33.6	19.4
Tunisia	60.5	59.8	60.7	60.1	58.6	59.2	59.2	63.9	59.6
Sub-Saharan Africa									
Angola	72.7	72.4	83.4	80.3	73.1	77.3	66.9	73.7	78.1
Benin	57.4	55.5	57.5	55.3	53.8	52.8	52.3	44.3	45.1
Botswana	95.4	95.5	95.4	96.1	97.0	95.8	95.3	86.1	82.2
Burkina Faso	63.4	67.1	62.6	61.9	62.8	60.6	61.9	43.1	42.3
Burundi	57.9	59.5	57.8	58.7	62.3	53.3	52.0	48.4	49.5
Cameroon	34.9	33.5	30.0	24.4	26.7	27.2	27.8	25.3	28.1
Cabo Verde	76.6	77.3	77.8	77.9	78.4	78.6	76.4	74.5	81.6
Central African Republic	55.7	54.9	51.6	60.2	57.5	53.0	53.8	53.7	46.2
Chad	29.5	27.5	22.4	24.2	25.8	34.4	43.1	44.7	37.0
Comoros	57.8	57.2	42.6	57.4	55.0	53.4	50.5	42.1	61.7
Congo	68.7	62.8	51.9	60.2	61.5	63.4	59.7	58.0	59.9
Congo, Democratic Republic of	60.3	55.9	62.5	60.8	49.7	45.5	43.5	26.4	31.5
Côte d'Ivoire	35.7	31.2	32.7	30.6	29.0	20.7	21.5	27.7	23.8
Djibouti	68.4	68.8	69.0	68.3	69.5	67.1	68.8	68.3	60.7
Equatorial Guinea	68.4	59.4	67.6	59.3	74.4	72.0	64.0	51.2	57.0
Eritrea	48.8	45.2	44.6	56.9	45.3	45.6	38.8	39.1	47.9
Ethiopia	65.8	64.1	62.9	61.5	65.2	63.9	68.5	63.2	50.7
Gabon	53.4	51.8	46.6	43.7	43.9	42.7	42.3	42.0	37.9
Gambia	80.5	80.0	79.7	76.5	76.8	80.3	79.0	64.6	63.5
Ghana	68.6	71.8	71.0	71.6	74.7	71.3	78.6	67.0	73.0
Guinea	31.9	37.4	28.1	22.6	18.6	17.7	18.4	19.8	20.9
Guinea-Bissau	58.7	60.4	57.9	52.6	55.3	52.1	53.9	51.0	55.8
Kenya	54.1	54.2	56.3	53.7	55.9	56.9	55.4	56.8	57.9
Lesotho	84.4	82.4	80.3	78.2	76.6	71.5	67.3	64.6	57.9
Liberia	78.9	75.4	76.9	65.0	62.0	57.1	58.3	62.0	...
Madagascar	74.8	71.6	73.2	75.1	77.1	78.5	79.4	82.3	75.3
Malawi	85.5	85.3	86.3	86.8	83.6	91.2	91.2	78.1	70.6
Mali	45.7	43.8	46.4	46.9	48.6	48.5	48.3	33.5	52.3
Mauritania	62.7	67.8	64.8	54.2	60.2	64.3	64.8	68.4	61.3
Mauritius	47.0	50.0	45.1	41.3	43.5	49.9	56.0	64.2	66.4
Mozambique	90.4	87.8	89.0	93.8	91.9	89.7	89.8	87.8	86.9
Namibia	90.6	90.7	91.1	91.9	91.5	96.8	96.3	94.4	93.7
Niger	62.4	57.3	58.0	58.5	53.9	56.3	52.4	55.3	51.6
Nigeria	39.6	34.6	34.3	40.0	36.5	35.9	32.1	38.3	28.8
Rwanda	78.9	77.7	77.0	76.4	76.4	77.8	83.6	75.2	73.7
Sao Tome and Principe	43.1	43.2	47.5	37.3	45.3	47.4	65.4	56.7	54.5

Table B.10 Total (public and private) health-care expenditure not financed by private households' out-of-pocket payments (percentage)

Major area, region or country	2011	2010	2009	2008	2007	2006	2005	2000	1995
Senegal	67.1	66.1	65.3	63.8	65.2	66.7	65.9	42.1	35.8
Seychelles	94.6	94.5	95.0	94.8	94.4	94.7	93.4	82.9	85.3
Sierra Leone	23.4	22.6	27.9	14.5	15.0	20.8	26.0	25.3	19.5
Somalia	...	...	...	...	...	...	...	44.8	43.5
South Africa	92.8	92.6	92.2	91.5	90.6	81.9	81.6	87.0	86.0
South Sudan	44.6	34.8	29.5	32.4	...	...	...	...	...
Swaziland	86.6	85.7	85.9	86.7	86.4	86.0	86.3	81.5	86.5
Tanzania, United Republic of	67.5	68.1	85.4	84.5	85.1	77.7	62.7	52.7	52.2
Togo	59.6	54.3	54.0	47.0	43.5	45.1	39.9	36.9	43.0
Uganda	52.2	50.1	48.7	46.8	46.7	48.3	51.2	58.5	49.6
Zambia	74.7	73.3	69.8	68.2	67.3	73.6	72.6	60.8	65.0
Zimbabwe	...	...	...	...	...	...	...	77.4	83.5
Asia and the Middle East									
Asia									
Afghanistan	20.6	27.2	27.1	24.6	16.2	17.7	14.6	...	...
Armenia	42.6	44.9	47.5	48.2	45.1	42.3	33.4	22.9	34.1
Azerbaijan	29.9	30.8	31.5	28.3	27.4	21.6	17.6	36.7	33.6
Bangladesh	38.7	38.7	38.7	37.9	36.7	38.8	37.4	42.0	38.7
Bhutan	84.6	85.4	85.5	86.5	85.3	78.3	74.9	79.3	69.2
Brunei Darussalam	85.2	85.6	85.3	86.2	84.7	84.2	84.3	86.7	78.1
Cambodia	43.1	40.8	38.9	38.0	45.6	43.0	39.7	28.9	31.3
China	65.2	64.7	62.5	59.6	55.9	50.7	47.8	41.0	53.6
Georgia	35.1	30.9	33.5	35.8	29.2	27.8	23.2	17.5	5.2
India	40.2	38.2	37.3	35.8	33.9	31.8	29.7	32.0	32.4
Indonesia	50.1	51.6	51.6	51.6	51.5	48.3	46.1	53.5	53.4
Japan	83.6	83.8	84.0	84.2	83.9	83.0	84.6	84.6	86.0
Kazakhstan	58.5	59.6	59.7	59.0	52.8	59.0	62.5	51.5	64.5
Kiribati	98.7	98.8	...	...	...	...	...	...	...
Korea, Democratic People's Republic									
Korea, Republic of	67.1	67.9	67.6	65.8	65.3	64.3	62.1	58.5	48.1
Kyrgyzstan	65.6	61.3	60.8	57.7	54.9	51.9	44.0	50.2	60.8
Lao People's Democratic Republic	60.3	58.2	69.9	42.9	43.6	45.7	37.7	40.4	64.2
Malaysia	64.6	66.8	68.3	64.7	63.6	63.8	61.2	65.7	66.8
Maldives	50.9	71.9	80.1	79.1	73.5	72.1	70.0	76.7	84.9
Mongolia	60.3	60.0	59.0	60.8	58.9	55.9	53.3	88.1	88.4
Myanmar	19.0	18.5	17.8	14.9	15.7	18.4	9.4	13.8	19.0
Nepal	45.2	43.5	47.0	44.7	42.2	54.0	51.1	31.2	30.4
Pakistan	36.8	36.8	34.5	35.3	37.9	43.6	40.5	36.8	27.8
Philippines	44.1	46.4	45.5	42.6	44.8	47.7	50.8	59.5	50.0
Singapore	39.6	39.8	39.2	35.7	33.9	33.5	33.8	47.3	51.1
Sri Lanka	54.1	55.4	57.4	57.4	58.5	57.5	55.6	58.3	54.3
Taiwan, China									
Tajikistan	39.9	33.5	32.2	27.7	27.0	25.4	26.3	21.2	41.9
Thailand	86.5	86.1	84.9	85.5	85.5	82.6	72.8	66.3	57.4

Table B.10 Total (public and private) health-care expenditure not financed by private households' out-of-pocket payments (percentage)

Major area, region or country	2011	2010	2009	2008	2007	2006	2005	2000	1995
Timor-Leste	96.0	96.4	97.1	97.4	97.5	97.9	98.1	97.1	...
Turkey	83.9	83.8	84.0	82.6	78.2	78.0	77.2	72.4	70.3
Turkmenistan	60.8	60.4	55.9	51.1	65.8	70.5	68.4	81.8	60.5
Uzbekistan	56.1	53.9	52.0	51.0	46.9	49.2	52.0	45.7	55.9
Viet Nam	43.9	41.5	43.1	39.1	44.3	37.9	32.4	34.0	37.1
Middle East									
Bahrain	85.1	85.7	82.7	82.8	80.8	79.2	78.3	77.7	78.4
Iran, Islamic Republic of	41.5	42.0	40.6	46.4	48.3	49.7	45.1	43.8	46.4
Iraq	81.7	81.2	78.1	74.6	69.5	63.8	67.3	1.1	...
Israel	78.6	79.6	79.2	80.0	79.7	76.8	74.1	83.0	73.7
Jordan	75.3	75.2	77.4	68.1	64.1	60.0	59.2	61.0	75.6
Kuwait	83.9	82.2	86.8	80.3	80.7	82.8	81.7	77.6	83.0
Lebanon	43.5	44.6	55.3	57.3	54.7	56.4	60.6	47.6	44.7
Oman	88.6	88.4	87.7	86.5	88.0	88.4	89.4	88.3	89.9
Qatar	86.4	84.0	84.2	84.0	84.1	84.1	84.2	72.3	65.4
Saudi Arabia	81.7	80.0	78.4	79.8	82.8	84.2	83.5	81.5	65.8
Syrian Arab Republic	49.0	46.0	46.0	46.5	49.1	48.5	50.5	40.4	39.7
United Arab Emirates	83.8	82.9	84.6	75.0	70.4	70.2	69.9	83.9	85.1
Yemen	21.9	22.1	24.6	32.0	30.8	36.7	35.2	56.3	34.5
Europe									
Western Europe									
Andorra	80.4	80.4	77.9	77.7	77.7	78.5	77.8	73.4	73.3
Austria	83.7	84.1	84.1	84.0	83.5	83.4	83.2	84.9	84.9
Belgium	80.9	80.6	81.1	79.7	79.1	79.5	81.4	78.7	80.4
Cyprus	50.6	50.6	50.5	50.3	52.2	53.4	53.0	44.1	36.7
Denmark	86.8	86.8	86.8	86.5	86.1	86.2	86.0	85.3	83.7
Finland	80.8	80.8	81.5	80.9	80.7	80.9	81.5	77.7	77.3
France	92.5	92.6	92.6	92.4	93.0	93.4	93.4	92.9	92.4
Germany	87.6	88.1	88.2	87.9	87.6	87.5	87.8	89.6	90.0
Greece	70.2	71.9	72.8	69.2	68.0	64.8	62.7	62.2	54.1
Iceland	81.8	81.8	83.4	84.0	84.0	83.4	82.8	81.5	84.4
Ireland	85.5	84.8	87.7	85.6	86.1	85.6	85.9	91.8	89.3
Italy	80.1	80.4	80.3	80.3	79.9	80.1	79.5	75.5	73.4
Luxembourg	88.6	88.6	88.4	87.6	87.8	88.5	88.4	88.2	93.8
Malta	66.1	66.6	67.5	67.0	68.9	70.4	71.1	73.4	68.9
Monaco	93.0	93.0	93.0	93.0	93.0	93.0	93.0	93.0	93.0
Netherlands	94.9	94.9	94.7	93.8	94.0	94.4	92.9	91.0	90.4
Norway	86.4	86.3	85.4	85.2	85.0	84.6	84.3	83.3	82.2
Portugal	72.7	74.0	74.1	73.1	74.5	74.9	76.1	75.7	76.1
San Marino	85.3	85.3	84.0	85.7	86.1	86.0	86.4	89.4	89.9
Spain	79.9	80.3	80.9	79.8	79.6	78.9	77.9	76.4	76.5
Sweden	83.1	83.2	83.6	83.6	83.5	83.4	83.3	86.2	86.7
Switzerland	75.0	74.9	75.3	75.2	69.4	69.2	69.4	67.0	66.9
United Kingdom	90.8	91.1	90.9	90.8	89.9	90.1	90.2	88.6	89.1

Table B.10 Total (public and private) health-care expenditure not financed by private households' out-of-pocket payments (percentage)

Major area, region or country	2011	2010	2009	2008	2007	2006	2005	2000	1995
Central and Eastern Europe									
Albania	44.5	42.3	45.0	47.1	47.5	48.5	47.4	36.2	49.5
Belarus	73.3	80.2	73.1	72.5	76.4	77.8	80.1	86.0	81.4
Bosnia and Herzegovina	68.7	68.6	68.8	67.7	63.7	60.1	57.3	57.6	47.1
Bulgaria	56.8	57.1	56.6	59.6	59.4	58.2	62.1	60.9	74.0
Croatia	85.4	85.4	85.5	85.5	87.6	86.6	86.6	86.1	86.5
Czech Republic	84.9	85.1	85.6	84.3	86.8	88.7	89.3	90.3	90.9
Estonia	81.4	82.2	83.5	81.8	78.9	75.0	79.6	79.9	89.8
Hungary	73.8	73.8	74.7	74.3	74.6	75.8	75.0	73.7	84.0
Latvia	60.4	62.7	64.7	66.3	65.1	67.6	59.4	55.9	66.3
Lithuania	72.1	73.6	73.5	73.0	73.4	70.0	68.3	73.9	77.6
Moldova, Republic of	55.1	55.1	56.3	54.9	54.3	53.9	55.3	57.1	72.6
Montenegro	70.0	69.5	73.9	73.1	72.0	70.9	72.0	71.8	70.0
Poland	77.1	77.9	77.3	77.2	75.4	74.4	73.9	70.0	72.9
Romania	80.6	80.8	79.4	82.4	82.7	80.2	81.5	81.2	74.5
Russian Federation	64.6	63.7	72.8	72.7	70.3	70.0	68.7	70.0	83.1
Serbia	63.8	63.6	64.8	64.9	65.2	67.1	70.1	74.7	75.3
Slovakia	73.8	74.3	74.7	75.1	74.0	74.6	77.4	90.5	88.5
Slovenia	87.0	87.1	87.6	87.9	86.8	88.2	87.4	88.5	88.8
The Former Yugoslav Republic of Macedonia	61.7	62.2	65.2	67.3	64.5	65.2	62.0	57.8	58.7
Ukraine	58.5	59.5	58.0	60.6	65.3	63.7	62.5	55.9	64.2
Latin America and the Caribbean									
Antigua and Barbuda	71.8	74.1	71.5	72.7	72.7	72.1	70.8	73.1	70.8
Argentina	78.1	78.6	79.9	77.4	74.3	70.9	70.1	71.0	72.0
Bahamas	71.1	71.2	71.6	70.8	70.3	72.7	70.5	79.1	75.9
Barbados	71.0	71.8	66.6	72.2	71.0	71.4	71.3	73.6	75.7
Belize	76.6	76.4	76.1	74.3	72.8	70.8	68.1	61.3	69.9
Bolivia, Plurinational State of	74.2	73.7	73.2	73.2	76.8	78.8	73.7	67.4	72.2
Brazil	68.7	69.4	67.7	67.9	66.0	64.0	62.4	62.0	61.3
Chile	62.8	63.5	64.2	60.5	60.6	60.1	59.3	63.5	61.2
Colombia	83.0	82.8	80.7	75.5	71.7	76.1	78.2	87.8	61.9
Costa Rica	77.0	76.0	75.3	72.9	71.3	73.1	75.2	81.2	79.4
Cuba	94.7	95.2	95.8	95.4	94.9	92.3	92.0	90.8	90.2
Dominica	78.2	76.8	71.6	68.2	68.8	71.0	68.7	72.4	72.0
Dominican Republic	60.0	61.0	59.6	61.6	58.2	56.8	52.6	52.9	43.0
Ecuador	48.0	48.8	47.9	45.7	47.1	45.0	37.7	41.4	67.4
El Salvador	67.7	66.2	65.1	64.0	63.6	66.2	56.6	48.2	39.3
Grenada	49.3	46.3	50.3	46.3	48.6	51.1	49.1	52.0	43.5
Guatemala	46.6	47.1	48.5	46.8	45.6	44.8	46.0	46.5	40.8
Guyana	82.0	82.1	85.1	83.8	74.3	77.7	84.4	86.9	83.7
Haiti	95.2	76.1	63.3	56.1	58.9	58.4	42.5	49.6	54.5
Honduras	52.1	52.7	54.3	47.3	49.0	48.6	52.1	56.5	58.5
Jamaica	67.1	69.0	68.8	67.0	66.0	71.1	67.4	69.2	70.6
Mexico	53.5	52.9	52.2	50.8	49.1	48.7	48.3	49.1	43.8
Nicaragua	57.8	60.4	60.4	58.0	58.0	58.0	60.1	57.4	64.9

Table B.10 Total (public and private) health-care expenditure not financed by private households' out-of-pocket payments (percentage)

Major area, region or country	2011	2010	2009	2008	2007	2006	2005	2000	1995
Panama	72.9	75.0	78.6	74.2	70.3	73.7	75.4	74.1	73.1
Paraguay	43.9	39.9	48.5	48.9	46.4	48.4	46.1	47.9	42.1
Peru	62.5	62.9	64.2	67.4	64.6	64.1	67.8	66.4	61.7
Saint Kitts and Nevis	58.6	58.3	51.8	51.6	55.6	60.0	57.0	62.7	61.4
Saint Lucia	47.1	55.1	55.6	49.0	45.3	50.9	47.8	53.5	65.2
Saint Vincent and the Grenadines	81.7	82.0	84.4	84.0	82.1	82.0	80.9	82.3	84.8
Suriname	89.0	88.6	89.0	87.5	88.6	88.5	85.2	79.5	90.6
Trinidad and Tobago	60.8	64.5	56.8	58.3	58.5	62.1	61.0	50.8	54.3
Uruguay	86.9	86.3	85.7	87.8	86.4	85.4	84.1	85.8	86.9
Venezuela, Bolivarian Republic of	42.6	44.4	49.0	47.8	50.6	48.7	49.3	46.8	49.4
North America									
Canada	85.6	85.8	85.8	85.4	85.3	85.0	85.4	84.1	84.0
United States	88.7	88.2	88.0	87.5	87.3	87.2	86.8	85.5	85.4
Oceania									
Australia	80.2	81.3	81.4	81.9	82.0	81.3	81.4	80.2	83.9
Cook Islands	92.5	92.9	92.8	92.0	92.1	92.9	94.3	90.5	91.3
Fiji	79.0	80.4	78.2	84.5	84.6	86.3	88.2	90.2	87.6
Marshall Islands	87.4	87.9	88.3	88.2	87.6	87.6	87.0	90.9	87.1
Micronesia	91.0	91.6	90.9	90.6	93.3	92.8	93.6	93.9	95.2
Nauru	92.2	92.1	92.5	95.6	96.1	94.4	93.9	96.8	96.2
New Zealand	89.5	89.5	89.4	88.8	88.5	86.2	85.9	84.6	83.8
Niue	99.2	99.2	99.3	99.2	99.2	99.2	99.0	98.5	98.4
Palau	88.4	89.1	87.9	88.7	89.3	88.3	87.5	85.6	77.9
Papua New Guinea	88.3	86.2	84.6	88.0	87.8	86.4	86.9	89.8	93.6
Solomon Islands	97.0	96.5	96.9	95.9	96.2	96.1	96.6	96.8	96.0
Tonga	88.9	87.3	85.9	89.8	89.8	91.9	92.0	77.1	72.6
Tuvalu	...	...	...	...	...	...	...	...	...
Vanuatu	93.1	94.4	94.4	94.5	93.8	88.0	80.6	83.3	80.9
Western Samoa	92.8	92.1	90.9	91.2	91.0	90.6	87.2	81.0	75.4

Sources

This indicator is calculated using the national health accounts estimates available in: WHO (World Health Organization): National Health Accounts (Global Health Expenditure database). Available at: http://apps.who.int/nha/database [6 June 2014].

For further information on estimating out-of-pocket (OOP) expenditures, see http://www.who.int/entity/nha/methods/estimating_OOPs_ravi_final.pdf?ua=1

Notes

… not available.

Definitions

Out-of-pocket spending by private households (OOPs) is the direct outlay of households, including gratuities and payments in kind, made to health practitioners and suppliers of pharmaceuticals, therapeutic appliances and other goods and services, whose primary intent is to contribute to the restoration or to the enhancement of the health status of individuals or population groups. It includes household payments to public services, non-profit institutions and non-governmental organizations. It includes non-reimbursable cost-sharing, deductibles, co-payments and fee-for-service, but excludes payments made by companies that deliver medical and paramedical benefits, whether required by law or not, to their employees. It excludes payments for overseas treatment.

Total (public and private) health-care expenditure not financed by private households' out-of-pocket payments

The effective level of financial protection provided to the population by social health protection systems is measured here by a proxy indicator expressed as a percentage of total (public and private) health-care expenditure in the country not financed by private households through out-of-pocket payments. The proxy is more or less equivalent to the percentage of total (public and private) health-care expenditure in the country financed either by general Government or by pre-paid private insurance, by employers or NGOs.

Table B.11 The multiple dimensions of health coverage

Mayor area, region or country	Extent of coverage		Financial resources: Composition. level and trends (2011)										Human resources (and access indicators)		Live births attended by skilled health staff		Maternal mortality rate (2010)
					Trends in government expenditure on health (constant US$ per capita)			Trends in out-of-pocket expenditure (constant US$ per capita)									
	Estimate of health coverage as a percentage of total population[1,6]	Year	Percentage of health expenditure not financed by out of pocket[2,3,7]	Per capita health expenditure not financed by private households' out-of-pocket payments (US$)[3]	Government expenditure on health in constant US$ per capita (2007)[2]	Government expenditure on health in constant US$ per capita (2011)[2]	Trends in per capita government expenditure on health (constant US$ per capita | 2007–11; (% average annual change)[3]	Out-of- pocket expenditure in constant US$ per capita (2007)[2]	Out-of- pocket expenditure in constant US$ per capita (2011)[2]	Trends in per capita out-of-pocket expenditure on health (constant US$ per capita | 2007–11; % average annual change)[3]	Coverage gap due to financial resources deficit (benchmark: US$60 MDG target for 2015 in low income)[2,9,10]	Coverage gap due to financial resources deficit, % (benchmark: median in low vulnerability group US$239)[3,10]	Coverage gap due to health professional staff deficit (WHO benchmark: 23)[3,8,9]	Coverage gap due to health professional staff deficit: (benchmark relative: 41.1)[3,8,13]	% live births attended by skilled health staff[2,4]	Year	Maternal mortality rate (modelled estimate. per 10.000 live births)[5]
Africa	24.7		57.1	73.6	30.5	36.0		23.2	24.5		50.6	78.0	66.5	52.3	53.5		42.9
Latin America and the Caribbean	81.7		64.4	531.8	180.8	215.1		145.2	145.8		1.2	9.2	18.0	5.2	93.2		7.5
North America	85.6		88.4	7357.2	3120.8	3415.6		861.6	828.5		0.0	0.0	0.0	0.0	99.3		2.0
Western Europe	99.7		86.2	3918.0	2597.0	2747.0		472.6	480.3		0.0	0.0	0.0	0.0	98.9		0.7
Central and Eastern Europe	91.6		67.6	496.7	258.8	287.7		99.3	127.2		0.0	7.2	0.3	0.0	99.5		2.5
Asia and the Pacific	58.0		53.4	263.5	126.7	172.9		53.3	66.6		31.2	56.5	44.2	19.6	77.6		12.5
Middle East	72.9		57.2	357.5	173.7	183.6		89.5	86.8		10.4	31.4	40.6	12.0	90.2		5.2
World	61.1		59.2	851.4	422.0	479.7		125.8	133.9		26.7	47.4	38.4	20.0	78.8		14.8
Africa																	
Algeria	85.2	2005	81.8	183.9	86.2	109.4	6.1	24.0	24.7	0.8	0.0	23.1	0.0	32.5	95.2	2009	9.7
Angola	0.0	2005	72.7	135.4	52.8	57.5	2.2	21.7	25.5	4.1	0.0	43.4	32.0	62.0	49.4	2009	45.0
Benin	9.0	2009	57.4	21.1	13.5	14.5	1.9	12.3	11.6	-1.3	72.5	91.2	66.8	81.4	84.1	2012	35.0
Botswana	...	...	95.0	410.4	411.2	220.8	-14.4	14.8	16.2	2.2	0.0	0.0	0.0	32.0	99.1	2010	16.0
Burkina Faso	1.0	2010	63.4	23.6	16.1	13.3	-4.6	9.9	9.7	-0.6	57.4	90.1	75.3	86.2	67.1	2010	30.0
Burundi	28.4	2009	56.4	13.2	6.0	4.9	-4.9	6.0	5.9	-0.2	78.3	94.5	93.2	96.2	60.3	2010	80.0
Cameroon	2.0	2009	34.9	23.8	10.3	16.7	12.9	33.6	34.9	1.0	66.0	90.0	82.0	89.9	63.6	2011	69.0
Cabo Verde	65.0	...	76.6	121.1	92.7	88.3	-1.2	26.0	27.5	1.5	0.0	49.3	62.7	79.1	75.6	2009	7.9
Central African Republic	6.0	...	56.6	10.4	8.1	7.0	-3.3	6.4	6.1	-1.2	88.4	95.7	87.5	93.0	53.8	2010	89.0

Table B.11 The multiple dimensions of health coverage

Mayor area, region or country	Extent of coverage		Financial resources: Composition. level and trends (2011)										Human resources (and access indicators)		Live births attended by skilled health staff		Maternal mortality rate (2010)
					Trends in government expenditure on health (constant US$ per capita)			Trends in out–of–pocket expenditure (constant US$ per capita)									
	Estimate of health coverage as a percentage of total population[1,6]	Year	Percentage of health expenditure not financed by out of pocket[2,3,7]	Per capita health expenditure not financed by private households' out–of–pocket payments (US$)[3]	Government expenditure on health in constant US$ per capita (2007)[2]	Government expenditure on health in constant US$ per capita (2011)[2]	Trends in per capita government expenditure on health (constant US$ per capita | 2007–11; (% average annual change)[3]	Out-of- pocket expenditure in constant US$ per capita (2007)[2]	Out-of- pocket expenditure in constant US$ per capita (2011)[2]	Trends in per capita out-of-pocket expenditure on health (constant US$ per capita | 2007–11; % average annual change)[3]	Coverage gap due to financial resources deficit (benchmark: US$60 MDG target for 2015 in low income)[2,9,10]	Coverage gap due to financial resources deficit, % (benchmark: median in low vulnerability group US$239)[3,10]	Coverage gap due to health professional staff deficit (WHO benchmark: 23)[3,8,9]	Coverage gap due to health professional staff deficit: (benchmark relative: 41.1)[3,8,13]	% live births attended by skilled health staff[2,4]	Year	Maternal mortality rate (modelled estimate. per 10.000 live births)[5]
Chad	...	...	29.5	10.4	5.0	5.4	2.0	16.0	14.1	–3.1	85.8	95.7	92.1	95.6	16.6	2010	110.0
Comoros	5.0	...	57.8	24.6	16.2	17.0	1.3	13.2	12.4	–1.5	63.0	89.7	57.4	76.2	62.0	2000	28.0
Congo	...	...	68.5	59.8	26.4	33.0	5.8	16.7	15.3	–2.1	44.0	75.0	61.0	78.2	93.6	2012	56.0
Congo, Democratic Republic	10.0	2010	56.5	11.1	2.6	4.3	13.1	3.9	4.5	3.7	82.9	95.3	77.1	87.2	80.4	2010	54.0
Côte d'Ivoire	1.2	2008	35.7	28.4	11.5	15.2	7.2	36.8	36.8	–0.0	77.5	88.1	73.8	85.3	59.4	2012	40.0
Djibouti	30.0	2006	68.4	71.9	49.7	54.2	2.2	21.9	25.2	3.6	0.0	69.9	57.0	75.9	78.4	2006	20.0
Egypt	51.1	2008	41.8	57.1	28.3	30.6	2.0	39.4	44.0	2.8	20.4	76.1	0.0	0.0	78.9	2008	6.6
Equatorial Guinea	...	...	68.4	845.5	211.7	496.9	23.8	77.6	237.1	32.2	0.0	0.0	75.0	86.0	65.0	2000	24.0
Eritrea	5.0	2011	48.8	6.8	3.4	3.0	–3.4	4.1	3.1	–6.7	90.4	97.2	80.7	89.2	28.0	2002	24.0
Ethiopia	5.0	2011	66.2	11.0	5.3	6.8	6.6	3.2	4.1	5.9	83.3	95.4	88.8	93.7	10.0	2011	35.0
Gabon	57.6	2011	53.4	191.5	82.0	105.6	6.5	104.9	92.0	–3.2	0.0	19.9	0.0	0.0	87.0	2000	23.0
Gambia	99.9	2011	77.7	21.3	8.5	12.4	9.9	3.8	4.0	1.6	67.0	91.1	61.5	78.5	56.1	2010	36.0
Ghana	73.9	2010	70.9	53.2	20.1	18.1	–2.5	8.1	10.6	6.8	18.4	77.7	53.7	74.1	54.7	2008	35.0
Guinea	0.2	2010	32.6	9.7	3.6	...	...	16.4	...	...	95.5	95.9	94.9	97.2	46.1	2007	61.0
Guinea-Bissau	1.6	2011	58.7	21.8	5.9	...	...	11.8	...	...	73.7	90.9	69.5	83.0	44.0	2010	79.0
Kenya	39.4	2009	53.6	19.4	10.7	10.3	–1.0	11.1	11.8	1.5	64.7	91.9	59.2	77.2	43.8	2009	36.0
Lesotho	17.6	2009	82.1	115.9	39.7	75.9	17.5	14.1	15.2	2.0	0.0	51.5	74.3	85.6	61.5	2009	62.0
Liberia	...	...	82.3	45.2	5.5	11.8	21.1	7.7	8.4	2.2	68.7	81.1	89.3	94.0	46.3	2007	77.0
Libyan Arab Jamahiriya	100.0	2004	68.8	273.7	135.9	170.4	5.8	68.9	77.3	2.9	0.0	0.0	0.0	0.0	98.3	2007	5.8

Table B.11 The multiple dimensions of health coverage

Mayor area, region or country	Extent of coverage		Financial resources: Composition. level and trends (2011)										Human resources (and access indicators)		Live births attended by skilled health staff		Maternal mortality rate (2010)
					Trends in government expenditure on health (constant US$ per capita)			Trends in out-of-pocket expenditure (constant US$ per capita)									
	Estimate of health coverage as a percentage of total population[1,6]	Year	Percentage of health expenditure not financed by out of pocket[2,3,7]	Per capita health expenditure not financed by private households' out-of-pocket payments (US$)[3]	Government expenditure on health in constant US$ per capita (2007)[2]	Government expenditure on health in constant US$ per capita (2011)[2]	Trends in per capita government expenditure on health (constant US$ per capita | 2007–11; (% average annual change)[3]	Out-of- pocket expenditure in constant US$ per capita (2007)[2]	Out-of- pocket expenditure in constant US$ per capita (2011)[2]	Trends in per capita out-of-pocket expenditure on health (constant US$ per capita | 2007–11; % average annual change)[3]	Coverage gap due to financial resources deficit (benchmark: US$60 MDG target for 2015 in low income)[2,9,10]	Coverage gap due to financial resources deficit, % (benchmark: median in low vulnerability group US$239)[3,10]	Coverage gap due to health professional staff deficit (WHO benchmark: 23)[3,8,9]	Coverage gap due to health professional staff deficit: (benchmark relative: 41.1)[3,8,13]	% live births attended by skilled health staff[2,4]	Year	Maternal mortality rate (modelled estimate. per 10.000 live births)[5]
Madagascar	3.7	2009	74.8	14.2	8.1	7.1	-3.1	2.8	2.9	0.4	80.6	94.1	82.8	90.4	43.9	2009	24.0
Malawi	...	...	85.8	26.5	10.0	16.3	13.0	2.5	3.2	7.0	61.5	88.9	86.1	92.2	71.4	2010	46.0
Mali	1.9	2008	45.7	20.4	14.5	13.6	-1.5	15.4	16.3	1.4	75.0	91.5	76.6	86.9	49.0	2006	54.0
Mauritania	6.0	2009	62.7	36.2	16.5	19.1	3.7	11.3	11.8	0.9	60.1	84.9	68.5	82.4	57.1	2007	51.0
Mauritius	100.0	2010	47.0	239.5	101.5	153.4	10.9	158.8	202.2	6.2	0.0	0.0	0.0	0.0	99.5	2010	6.0
Morocco	42.3	2007	42.0	78.1	39.9	51.0	6.3	66.4	86.2	6.7	0.0	67.3	32.7	62.3	73.6	2011	10.0
Mozambique	4.0	2011	91.0	32.0	12.1	11.5	-1.4	1.7	2.7	12.6	69.8	86.6	86.8	92.6	54.3	2011	49.0
Namibia	28.0	2007	92.3	261.2	143.4	120.3	-4.3	22.4	24.0	1.7	0.0	0.0	0.0	29.7	81.4	2007	20.0
Niger	3.1	2003	62.4	12.6	7.1	7.0	-0.3	6.6	4.8	-7.7	82.4	94.7	93.9	96.6	17.7	2006	59.0
Nigeria	2.2	2008	39.6	31.5	20.5	19.9	-0.7	38.7	32.8	-4.0	57.1	86.8	27.8	59.6	34.4	2008	63.0
Rwanda	91.0	2010	78.6	49.3	13.8	23.1	13.7	6.9	8.5	5.3	27.4	79.4	71.4	84.0	69.0	2010	34.0
Sao Tome and Principe	2.1	2009	43.1	50.6	17.4	23.9	8.3	31.8	40.9	6.5	30.2	78.8	10.1	49.7	80.6	2009	7.0
Senegal	20.1	2007	67.3	45.1	25.7	28.6	2.7	16.1	16.2	0.1	36.0	81.2	81.0	89.4	65.1	2011	37.0
Seychelles	90.0	2011	94.6	414.7	407.9	464.9	3.3	24.7	27.5	2.7	0.0	0.0	0.0	0.0	99.0	2009	...
Sierra Leone	0.0	2008	25.1	17.2	5.5	9.5	14.5	40.4	47.1	3.9	85.2	92.8	91.6	95.3	60.8	2010	89.0
Somalia	20.0	2006	...	...	...	...	...	...	...	...	...	...	94.6	97.0	9.4	2006	100.0
South Africa	100.0	2010	92.8	639.6	195.4	245.2	5.8	41.1	37.1	-2.6	0.0	0.0	0.0	0.0	91.0	2003	30.0
South Sudan	...	...	...	...	...	...	...	...	...	...	...	...	...	...	...	...	...
Sudan	29.7	2009	30.9	32.0	16.5	15.9	-1.0	31.4	41.0	6.8	54.1	86.6	49.4	71.7	23.2	2006	73.0

Table B.11 The multiple dimensions of health coverage

Mayor area, region or country	Extent of coverage		Financial resources: Composition. level and trends (2011)										Human resources (and access indicators)		Live births attended by skilled health staff		Maternal mortality rate (2010)
					Trends in government expenditure on health (constant US$ per capita)			Trends in out-of-pocket expenditure (constant US$ per capita)									
	Estimate of health coverage as a percentage of total population[1,6]	Year	Percentage of health expenditure not financed by out of pocket[2,3,7]	Per capita health expenditure not financed by private households' out-of-pocket payments (US$)[3]	Government expenditure on health in constant US$ per capita (2007)[2]	Government expenditure on health in constant US$ per capita (2011)[2]	Trends in per capita government expenditure on health (constant US$ per capita | 2007–11; (% average annual change)[3]	Out-of- pocket expenditure in constant US$ per capita (2007)[2]	Out-of- pocket expenditure in constant US$ per capita (2011)[2]	Trends in per capita out-of-pocket expenditure on health (constant US$ per capita | 2007–11; % average annual change)[3]	Coverage gap due to financial resources deficit (benchmark: US$60 MDG target for 2015 in low income)[2,9,10]	Coverage gap due to financial resources deficit, % (benchmark: median in low vulnerability group US$239)[3,10]	Coverage gap due to health professional staff deficit (WHO benchmark: 23)[3,8,9]	Coverage gap due to health professional staff deficit: (benchmark relative: 41.1)[3,8,13]	% live births attended by skilled health staff[2,4]	Year	Maternal mortality rate (modelled estimate. per 10.000 live births)[5]
Swaziland	6.2	2006	86.9	230.2	114.2	135.5	4.4	23.0	26.4	3.5	0.0	3.7	0.0	0.0	82.0	2010	32.0
Tanzania, United Rep. of	13.0	2010	68.3	25.5	14.4	13.0	−2.6	3.4	11.0	34.6	55.4	89.3	91.1	95.0	48.9	2010	46.0
Togo	4.0	2010	59.6	26.8	8.6	16.5	17.8	14.6	12.8	−3.3	63.8	88.8	85.8	92.1	43.9	2010	30.0
Tunisia	80.0	2005	60.5	161.4	105.6	125.8	4.5	83.5	90.1	1.9	0.0	32.5	0.0	0.0	94.6	2006	5.6
Uganda	2.0	2008	52.2	22.2	6.5	10.3	12.3	17.8	18.6	1.1	60.7	90.7	51.0	72.6	58.0	2011	31.0
Zambia	8.4	2008	73.0	63.7	20.5	28.4	8.5	12.9	11.6	−2.6	10.6	73.3	66.7	81.4	46.5	2007	44.0
Zimbabwe	1.0	2009	...	...	...	...	...	...	...	...	...	...	44.6	69.0	66.2	2011	57.0
Latin America and the Caribbean																	
Antigua and Barbuda	51.1	2007	71.8	537.2	425.3	446.2	1.2	168.6	184.5	2.3	0.0	0.0	0.0	33.1	100.0	2010	...
Argentina	96.8	2008	75.3	671.3	262.3	333.4	6.2	115.7	112.1	−0.8	0.0	0.0	0.0	16.3	99.4	2010	7.7
Aruba	99.2	2003	...	...	...	...	...	...	...	...	...	...	...	...	...	...	...
Bahamas	100.0	1995	71.3	1228.0	775.3	788.5	0.4	512.3	491.5	−1.0	0.0	0.0	0.0	0.0	99.0	2008	4.7
Barbados	100.0	1995	71.0	732.0	549.3	617.8	3.0	249.3	279.6	2.9	0.0	0.0	0.0	0.0	100.0	2008	5.1
Belize	25.0	2009	76.6	200.8	123.2	154.5	5.8	53.2	54.4	0.5	0.0	16.0	0.0	39.1	94.3	2010	5.3
Bolivia (Plurinational State of)	42.7	2009	74.2	87.6	35.4	43.8	5.5	12.0	16.0	7.3	0.0	63.3	0.0	34.1	71.1	2008	19.0
Brazil	100.0	2009	68.7	769.4	181.5	233.2	6.5	147.7	159.7	2.0	0.0	0.0	0.0	0.0	98.9	2010	5.6
Colombia	87.7	2010	83.0	358.5	167.2	187.5	2.9	73.2	42.6	−12.6	0.0	0.0	7.0	47.9	99.2	2011	9.2
Costa Rica	100.0	2009	72.8	686.3	314.1	420.5	7.6	134.3	129.7	−0.9	0.0	0.0	19.9	55.2	95.3	2010	4.0
Cuba	100.0	2011	94.7	573.8	450.9	483.8	1.8	24.5	27.2	2.7	0.0	0.0	0.0	0.0	99.9	2011	7.3

Table B.11 The multiple dimensions of health coverage

Mayor area, region or country	Extent of coverage		Financial resources: Composition. level and trends (2011)		Trends in government expenditure on health (constant US$ per capita)			Trends in out-of-pocket expenditure (constant US$ per capita)					Human resources (and access indicators)		Live births attended by skilled health staff		Maternal mortality rate (2010)
	Estimate of health coverage as a percentage of total population[1,6]	Year	Percentage of health expenditure not financed by out of pocket[2,3,7]	Per capita health expenditure not financed by private households' out-of-pocket payments (US$)[3]	Government expenditure on health in constant US$ per capita (2007)[2]	Government expenditure on health in constant US$ per capita (2011)[2]	Trends in per capita government expenditure on health (constant US$ per capita | 2007–11; (% average annual change)[3]	Out-of- pocket expenditure in constant US$ per capita (2007)[2]	Out-of- pocket expenditure in constant US$ per capita (2011)[2]	Trends in per capita out-of-pocket expenditure on health (constant US$ per capita | 2007–11; % average annual change)[3]	Coverage gap due to financial resources deficit (benchmark: US$60 MDG target for 2015 in low income)[2,9,10]	Coverage gap due to financial resources deficit, % (benchmark: median in low vulnerability group US$239)[3,10]	Coverage gap due to health professional staff deficit (WHO benchmark: 23)[3,8,9]	Coverage gap due to health professional staff deficit: (benchmark relative: 41.1)[3,8,13]	% live births attended by skilled health staff[2,4]	Year	Maternal mortality rate (modelled estimate. per 10.000 live births)[5]
Chile	93.1	2011	62.8	675.2	228.1	313.8	8.3	211.1	248.3	4.1	0.0	0.0	50.6	72.3	99.7	2010	2.5
Dominica	13.4	2009	76.4	319.5	196.1	289.0	10.2	97.9	85.6	-3.3	0.0	0.0	0.0	0.0	100.0	2011	...
Dominican Republic	26.5	2007	60.0	177.5	97.8	129.5	7.3	87.5	104.9	4.6	0.0	25.7	0.0	26.6	95.3	2010	15.0
Ecuador	22.8	2009	50.6	167.9	74.1	93.1	5.9	114.1	125.0	2.3	0.0	29.8	0.0	19.3	89.2	2010	11.0
El Salvador	21.6	2009	67.7	170.0	112.2	128.8	3.5	69.2	65.7	-1.3	0.0	28.9	0.1	44.1	84.6	2008	8.1
Guatemala	30.0	2005	46.6	99.7	54.8	54.0	-0.4	89.4	81.3	-2.3	0.0	58.3	0.0	6.6	51.3	2009	12.0
Grenada																	
Guyana	23.8	2009	82.0	163.9	31.2	62.9	19.1	11.4	14.3	5.7	0.0	31.4	69.4	82.9	87.4	2009	28.0
Haiti	3.1	2001	77.9	44.9	6.1	8.3	8.0	10.2	1.8	-35.6	54.2	81.2	88.1	93.3	26.1	2006	35.0
Honduras	12.0	2006	54.3	...	56.1	63.3	3.1	62.1	63.0	0.4	...	...	42.6	67.9	66.3	2006	10.0
Jamaica	20.1	2007	68.5	...	106.8	111.3	1.0	69.9	68.3	-0.6	...	...	36.7	64.6	98.0	2009	11.0
Mexico	85.6	2010	52.2	...	228.2	253.7	2.7	255.6	238.6	-1.7	...	...	0.0	0.0	95.3	2009	5.0
Nicaragua	12.2	2005	60.4	...	47.2	54.1	3.5	36.2	42.1	3.9	...	...	42.6	67.9	73.7	2007	9.5
Panama	51.8	2008	73.2	514.1	242.6	387.8	12.4	112.3	154.2	8.2	0.0	0.0	0.0	19.4	83.6	2009	9.2
Paraguay	23.6	2009	43.9	154.4	37.8	60.8	12.6	50.5	88.5	15.1	0.0	35.4	0.0	39.6	84.6	2008	9.9
Peru	64.4	2010	61.7	178.1	98.4	110.1	2.9	59.6	72.6	5.1	0.0	25.5	5.8	47.3	85.0	2011	6.7
Saint Kitts and Nevis	28.8	2008	58.2	344.6	248.3	258.4	1.0	208.0	190.1	-2.2	0.0	0.0	0.0	0.0	100.0	2008	...
Saint Lucia	35.5	2003	48.9	246.2	179.9	215.8	4.7	221.8	244.9	2.5	0.0	0.0	6.3	47.5	98.5	2010	3.5
Saint Vincent and the Grenadines	9.4	2008	81.7	253.4	181.0	214.2	4.3	39.3	48.1	5.1	0.0	0.0	0.0	0.0	98.3	2010	4.8

Table B.11 The multiple dimensions of health coverage

Mayor area, region or country	Extent of coverage		Financial resources: Composition. level and trends (2011)										Human resources (and access indicators)		Live births attended by skilled health staff		Maternal mortality rate (2010)
					Trends in government expenditure on health (constant US$ per capita)			Trends in out-of-pocket expenditure (constant US$ per capita)									
	Estimate of health coverage as a percentage of total population[1,6]	Year	Percentage of health expenditure not financed by out of pocket[2,3,7]	Per capita health expenditure not financed by private households' out-of-pocket payments (US$)[3]	Government expenditure on health in constant US$ per capita (2007)[2]	Government expenditure on health in constant US$ per capita (2011)[2]	Trends in per capita government expenditure on health (constant US$ per capita | 2007–11; (% average annual change)[3]	Out-of- pocket expenditure in constant US$ per capita (2007)[2]	Out-of- pocket expenditure in constant US$ per capita (2011)[2]	Trends in per capita out-of-pocket expenditure on health (constant US$ per capita | 2007–11; % average annual change)[3]	Coverage gap due to financial resources deficit (benchmark: US$60 MDG target for 2015 in low income)[2,9,10]	Coverage gap due to financial resources deficit, % (benchmark: median in low vulnerability group US$239)[3,10]	Coverage gap due to health professional staff deficit (WHO benchmark: 23)[3,8,9]	Coverage gap due to health professional staff deficit: (benchmark relative: 41.1)[3,8,13]	% live births attended by skilled health staff[2,4]	Year	Maternal mortality rate (modelled estimate. per 10.000 live births)[5]
Suriname	...	...	89.0	408.4	114.3	131.9	3.6	25.4	27.3	1.9	0.0	0.0	0.0	0.0	86.5	2006	13.0
Trinidad and Tobago	...	...	61.5	587.6	340.6	396.2	3.9	287.2	299.7	1.1	0.0	0.0	0.0	0.0	96.9	2006	4.6
Uruguay	97.2	2010	86.9	960.3	251.5	394.0	11.9	62.7	76.3	5.0	0.0	0.0	0.0	0.0	99.7	2009	2.9
Venezuela, Bolivarian Republic	100.0	2010	43.0	238.7	167.3	117.0	-8.5	185.5	181.8	-0.5	0.0	0.1	0.0	38.3	98.1	2011	9.2
North America																	
Canada	100.0	2011	85.6	4820.0	2550.7	2751.0	1.9	535.5	562.0	1.2	0.0	0.0	0.0	0.0	98.5	2010	1.2
United States	84.0	2010	88.7	7635.6	3183.3	3488.5	2.3	897.4	857.8	-1.1	0.0	0.0	0.0	0.0	99.4	2010	2.1
Asia																	
Afghanistan	...	...	20.6	11.5	2.8	5.1	15.6	21.8	25.8	4.3	89.2	95.2	86.2	92.3	38.6	2011	46.0
Armenia	100.0	2009	42.6	60.3	33.1	31.0	-1.7	43.7	49.6	3.2	0.7	74.8	0.0	0.0	99.5	2010	3.0
Azerbaijan	2.9	2006	29.9	106.7	24.8	33.2	7.6	93.4	108.5	3.8	0.0	55.3	0.0	0.0	88.6	2006	4.3
Bahrain	100.0	2006	83.4	617.2	431.9	346.2	-5.4	117.1	70.7	-11.8	0.0	0.0	0.0	21.9	97.3	2009	2.0
Bangladesh	1.4	2003	38.7	...	5.4	7.5	8.6	9.9	12.6	6.0	...	...	75.7	86.4	31.1	2011	24.0
Bhutan	90.0	2009	84.7	78.8	63.7	58.4	-2.2	11.0	10.7	-0.7	0.0	67.0	50.9	72.6	58.2	2010	18.0
Brunei Darussalam	100.0	2010	85.2	846.5	538.2	519.9	-0.9	97.7	90.4	-1.9	0.0	0.0	0.0	0.0	99.7	2011	2.4
Cambodia	26.1	2009	43.1	22.1	5.5	8.3	11.1	13.4	21.1	12.1	55.3	90.8	55.8	75.2	71.0	2010	25.0
China	96.9	2010	65.2	181.4	44.7	89.1	18.8	41.9	55.4	7.2	0.0	24.1	0.0	29.0	99.6	2010	3.7
Cyprus	65.0	2008	50.6	1074.8	576.1	667.3	3.7	646.3	761.6	4.2	0.0	0.0	0.0	0.0	98.3	2009	1.0
Georgia	25.0	2008	35.1	109.9	25.9	34.6	7.6	103.2	123.9	4.7	0.0	54.0	0.0	0.0	97.4	2010	6.7

Table B.11 The multiple dimensions of health coverage

Mayor area, region or country	Extent of coverage		Financial resources: Composition. level and trends (2011)										Human resources (and access indicators)		Live births attended by skilled health staff		Maternal mortality rate (2010)
					Trends in government expenditure on health (constant US$ per capita)			Trends in out-of-pocket expenditure (constant US$ per capita)									
	Estimate of health coverage as a percentage of total population[1,6]	Year	Percentage of health expenditure not financed by out of pocket[2,3,7]	Per capita health expenditure not financed by private households' out-of-pocket payments (US$)[3]	Government expenditure on health in constant US$ per capita (2007)[2]	Government expenditure on health in constant US$ per capita (2011)[2]	Trends in per capita government expenditure on health (constant US$ per capita | 2007–11; (% average annual change)[3]	Out-of- pocket expenditure in constant US$ per capita (2007)[2]	Out-of- pocket expenditure in constant US$ per capita (2011)[2]	Trends in per capita out-of-pocket expenditure on health (constant US$ per capita | 2007–11; % average annual change)[3]	Coverage gap due to financial resources deficit (benchmark: US$60 MDG target for 2015 in low income)[2,9,10]	Coverage gap due to financial resources deficit, % (benchmark: median in low vulnerability group US$239)[3,10]	Coverage gap due to health professional staff deficit (WHO benchmark: 23)[3,8,9]	Coverage gap due to health professional staff deficit: (benchmark relative: 41.1)[3,8,13]	% live births attended by skilled health staff[2,4]	Year	Maternal mortality rate (modelled estimate. per 10.000 live births)[5]
Hong Kong (China), Special Administrative Region	100.0	2010	...	...	...	...	...	...	...	...	...	...	...	...	...	...	...
India	12.5	2010	40.6	24.0	8.2	12.6	11.3	22.0	24.7	3.0	65.1	90.0	33.1	62.5	57.7	2009	20.0
Indonesia	59.0	2010	50.1	47.6	17.2	15.6	-2.3	21.0	22.5	1.8	20.7	80.1	31.6	61.7	79.8	2010	22.0
Iran, Islamic Republic of	90.0	2005	41.5	143.8	81.1	66.1	-5.0	101.2	97.2	-1.0	0.0	39.8	9.0	49.1	99.0	2007	2.1
Iraq	...	...	80.7	267.5	27.2	61.8	22.8	11.9	13.9	3.8	0.0	0.0	15.7	52.8	88.5	2011	6.3
Israel	100.0	2011	78.6	1907.8	968.7	1060.5	2.3	322.2	368.4	3.4	0.0	0.0	0.0	0.0	...	...	0.7
Japan	100.0	2010	83.6	3552.2	2459.7	3192.7	6.7	493.4	656.7	7.4	0.0	0.0	0.0	0.0	99.8	2011	0.5
Jordan	75.0	2006	75.3	295.3	130.4	160.9	5.4	78.3	58.6	-7.0	0.0	0.0	0.0	0.0	99.1	2007	6.3
Kazakhstan	70.0	2001	58.5	266.1	79.4	117.5	10.3	71.8	84.2	4.0	0.0	0.0	0.0	0.0	99.4	2010	5.1
Korea, Democratic People's Republic	...	...	...	...	4.7	...	...	...	...	...	...	...	0.0	0.0	100.0	2009	8.1
Korea, Republic of	100.0	2010	67.1	1084.7	676.2	920.1	8.0	420.7	527.9	5.8	0.0	0.0	0.0	0.0	99.9	2009	1.6
Kuwait	100.0	2006	83.9	1258.2	631.5	697.3	2.5	155.0	137.0	-3.0	0.0	0.0	0.0	0.0	98.6	2010	1.4
Kyrgyzstan	83.0	2001	65.6	46.8	18.9	22.2	4.1	16.6	12.8	-6.3	45.1	80.4	0.0	0.0	98.3	2010	7.1
Lao People's Democratic Republic	11.6	2009	60.3	22.2	5.6	9.5	14.4	12.6	7.7	-11.7	62.6	90.7	57.3	76.1	37.0	2010	47.0
Lebanon	48.3	2007	43.5	270.8	189.0	122.2	-10.3	213.0	270.6	6.2	0.0	0.0	0.0	0.0	98.0	2004	2.5
Malaysia	100.0	2010	58.3	201.6	114.4	137.4	4.7	76.7	88.2	3.5	0.0	15.6	0.0	0.0	98.6	2010	2.9
Maldives	30.0	2011	50.9	277.3	172.0	182.7	1.5	72.1	201.9	29.4	0.0	0.0	0.0	0.0	94.8	2009	6.0

Table B.11 The multiple dimensions of health coverage

Mayor area, region or country	Extent of coverage		Financial resources: Composition. level and trends (2011)										Human resources (and access indicators)		Live births attended by skilled health staff		Maternal mortality rate (2010)
					Trends in government expenditure on health (constant US$ per capita)			Trends in out-of-pocket expenditure (constant US$ per capita)									
	Estimate of health coverage as a percentage of total population[1,6]	Year	Percentage of health expenditure not financed by out of pocket[2,3,7]	Per capita health expenditure not financed by private households' out-of-pocket payments (US$)[3]	Government expenditure on health in constant US$ per capita (2007)[2]	Government expenditure on health in constant US$ per capita (2011)[2]	Trends in per capita government expenditure on health (constant US$ per capita | 2007–11; (% average annual change)[3]	Out-of- pocket expenditure in constant US$ per capita (2007)[2]	Out-of- pocket expenditure in constant US$ per capita (2011)[2]	Trends in per capita out-of-pocket expenditure on health (constant US$ per capita | 2007–11; % average annual change)[3]	Coverage gap due to financial resources deficit (benchmark: US$60 MDG target for 2015 in low income)[2,9,10]	Coverage gap due to financial resources deficit, % (benchmark: median in low vulnerability group US$239)[3,10]	Coverage gap due to health professional staff deficit (WHO benchmark: 23)[3,8,9]	Coverage gap due to health professional staff deficit: (benchmark relative: 41.1)[3,8,13]	% live births attended by skilled health staff[2,4]	Year	Maternal mortality rate (modelled estimate. per 10.000 live births)[5]
Mongolia	81.9	2009	60.3	96.9	34.0	42.7	5.8	25.0	29.6	4.4	0.0	59.5	0.0	0.0	99.0	2010	6.3
Myanmar	...	...	19.3	4.4	0.6	0.8	6.1	4.4	4.9	3.2	94.7	98.2	41.0	67.0	70.6	2010	20.0
Nepal	0.1	2010	51.7	...	5.7	7.5	7.0	9.2	10.4	3.3	...	...	72.8	84.8	36.0	2011	17.0
Occupied Palestinian Territory	16.2	2004	...	...	...	...	...	...	...	...	...	...	...	...	...	...	...
Oman	97.0	2005	88.6	529.7	268.7	290.5	2.0	40.1	41.2	0.6	0.0	0.0	0.0	0.0	98.6	2008	3.2
Pakistan	26.6	2009	37.0	11.0	6.1	5.3	-3.5	13.9	12.3	-3.0	81.8	95.4	43.0	68.1	45.0	2011	26.0
Philippines	82.0	2009	44.1	42.5	17.8	19.5	2.3	28.0	32.7	4.0	41.1	82.2	0.0	0.0	62.2	2008	9.9
Qatar	100.0	2006	86.4	1533.6	1093.4	942.2	-3.7	207.4	163.6	-5.8	0.0	0.0	0.0	0.0	100.0	2012	0.7
Saudi Arabia	26.0	2010	82.0	621.0	361.4	369.3	0.5	85.9	98.0	3.3	0.0	0.0	0.0	31.0	100.0	2011	2.4
Singapore	100.0	2010	39.6	904.8	306.2	483.2	12.1	799.8	941.3	4.2	0.0	0.0	0.0	0.0	99.7	2011	0.3
Sri Lanka	100.0	2010	54.1	52.2	25.5	26.2	0.7	21.7	27.0	5.6	35.7	78.2	0.0	41.2	98.6	2007	3.5
Syrian Arab Republic	90.0	2008	49.0	49.5	30.1	30.9	0.6	31.3	32.1	0.7	25.6	79.3	0.0	23.6	96.2	2009	7.0
Tajikistan	0.3	2010	39.9	21.6	4.8	8.4	15.1	15.8	17.1	2.0	72.6	91.0	0.0	0.0	88.4	2007	6.5
Thailand	98.0	2007	86.3	174.2	78.5	93.1	4.4	14.9	16.7	2.8	0.0	27.1	24.7	57.9	99.4	2009	4.8
Timor-Leste	...	...	96.0	44.4	40.2	23.4	-12.7	1.1	1.3	3.6	15.8	81.4	26.9	59.1	29.6	2010	30.0
Turkmenistan	82.3	2011	60.8	78.4	60.5	90.2	10.5	31.4	58.2	16.7	0.0	67.2	0.0	0.0	99.5	2006	6.7
United Arab Emirates	100.0	2010	83.8	1374.5	569.9	743.2	6.9	283.3	161.7	-13.1	0.0	0.0	0.0	24.0	100.0	2010	1.2
Uzbekistan	100.0	2010	56.1	49.6	14.6	23.3	12.5	18.8	21.8	3.7	21.7	79.2	0.0	0.0	99.6	2006	2.8
Viet Nam	61.0	2010	44.3	42.0	20.4	24.3	4.5	28.4	34.2	4.7	41.4	82.4	6.6	47.7	91.9	2011	5.9
Yemen	42.0	2003	21.9	19.4	13.9	10.1	-7.7	32.4	37.9	4.0	73.5	91.9	61.0	78.2	35.7	2006	20.0

Table B.11 The multiple dimensions of health coverage

Mayor area, region or country	Extent of coverage		Financial resources: Composition. level and trends (2011)										Human resources (and access indicators)		Live births attended by skilled health staff		Maternal mortality rate (2010)
					Trends in government expenditure on health (constant US$ per capita)			Trends in out-of-pocket expenditure (constant US$ per capita)									
	Estimate of health coverage as a percentage of total population[1,6]	Year	Percentage of health expenditure not financed by out of pocket[2,3,7]	Per capita health expenditure not financed by private households' out-of-pocket payments (US$)[3]	Government expenditure on health in constant US$ per capita (2007)[2]	Government expenditure on health in constant US$ per capita (2011)[2]	Trends in per capita government expenditure on health (constant US$ per capita | 2007–11; (% average annual change)[3]	Out-of- pocket expenditure in constant US$ per capita (2007)[2]	Out-of- pocket expenditure in constant US$ per capita (2011)[2]	Trends in per capita out-of-pocket expenditure on health (constant US$ per capita | 2007–11; % average annual change)[3]	Coverage gap due to financial resources deficit (benchmark: US$60 MDG target for 2015 in low income)[2,9,10]	Coverage gap due to financial resources deficit, % (benchmark: median in low vulnerability group US$239)[3,10]	Coverage gap due to health professional staff deficit (WHO benchmark: 23)[3,8,9]	Coverage gap due to health professional staff deficit: (benchmark relative: 41.1)[3,8,13]	% live births attended by skilled health staff[2,4]	Year	Maternal mortality rate (modelled estimate. per 10.000 live births)[5]
Europe																	
Albania	23.6	2008	45.0	114.6	77.2	97.4	6.0	94.1	121.6	6.6	0.0	52.1	0.0	0.0	99.3	2009	2.7
Andorra	...	...	80.4	2458.3	1781.6	1792.9	0.2	570.3	479.4	−4.2	0.0	0.0	0.0	0.0	...	...	...
Austria	99.3	2010	83.7	4417.3	3073.0	3283.9	1.7	667.5	710.1	1.6	0.0	0.0	0.0	0.0	98.6	2009	0.4
Belarus	100.0	2010	73.3	225.1	165.2	164.6	−0.1	56.3	62.2	2.5	0.0	5.8	0.0	0.0	99.9	2009	0.4
Belgium	99.0	2010	80.9	4013.4	2637.5	2991.5	3.2	752.9	753.4	0.0	0.0	0.0	0.0	0.0	99.4	2009	0.8
Bosnia and Herzegovina	59.2	2004	68.7	338.2	181.0	238.3	7.1	103.0	109.8	1.6	0.0	0.0	0.0	0.0	99.9	2009	0.8
Bulgaria	87.0	2008	57.1	...	169.6	180.9	1.6	118.3	141.4	4.6	...	...	0.0	0.0	99.6	2008	1.1
Croatia	97.0	2009	85.4	...	673.9	658.5	−0.6	96.4	113.8	4.2	...	...	0.0	0.0	99.9	2010	1.7
Czech Republic	100.0	2011	84.9	1279.5	782.7	872.1	2.7	121.1	157.6	6.8	0.0	0.0	0.0	0.0	99.7	2010	0.5
Denmark	100.0	2011	86.8	5772.4	4133.2	4354.2	1.3	683.0	673.2	−0.4	0.0	0.0	0.0	0.0	98.5	2011	1.2
Estonia	92.9	2011	81.4	803.5	479.7	531.5	2.6	133.8	125.2	−1.7	0.0	0.0	0.0	0.0	99.4	2011	0.2
Finland	100.0	2010	80.8	3496.7	2585.4	2733.8	1.4	672.1	700.4	1.0	0.0	0.0	0.0	0.0	98.6	2011	0.5
France	99.9	2011	92.5	4582.5	3066.6	3090.5	0.2	274.9	300.5	2.3	0.0	0.0	0.0	0.0	97.5	2010	0.8
Germany	100.0	2010	87.6	4270.1	2883.1	3126.7	2.0	467.9	511.5	2.3	0.0	0.0	0.0	0.0	98.6	2008	0.7
Greece	100.0	2010	70.2	1626.0	1281.2	1100.9	−3.7	646.6	498.9	−6.3	0.0	0.0	0.0	0.0	...	...	0.3
Hungary	100.0	2010	73.8	800.9	476.6	452.0	−1.3	179.9	182.6	0.4	0.0	0.0	0.0	0.0	99.1	2010	2.1
Iceland	100.0	2010	81.8	3259.4	4014.9	3507.0	−3.3	780.5	795.2	0.5	0.0	0.0	0.0	0.0	...	...	0.5
Ireland	100.0	2011	85.5	3882.0	2773.0	2740.6	−0.3	501.5	565.8	3.1	0.0	0.0	0.0	0.0	99.8	2010	0.6
Italy	100.0	2010	80.1	2751.0	2009.5	2083.2	0.9	527.8	537.4	0.5	0.0	0.0	0.0	0.0	99.8	2009	0.4
Latvia	70.0	2005	62.7	...	313.5	246.0	−5.9	180.2	166.7	−1.9	...	...	0.0	0.0	98.8	2010	3.4

Table B.11 The multiple dimensions of health coverage

Mayor area, region or country	Extent of coverage		Financial resources: Composition. level and trends (2011)										Human resources (and access indicators)		Live births attended by skilled health staff		Maternal mortality rate (2010)
					Trends in government expenditure on health (constant US$ per capita)			Trends in out-of-pocket expenditure (constant US$ per capita)									
	Estimate of health coverage as a percentage of total population[1,6]	Year	Percentage of health expenditure not financed by out of pocket[2,3,7]	Per capita health expenditure not financed by private households' out-of-pocket payments (US$)[3]	Government expenditure on health in constant US$ per capita (2007)[2]	Government expenditure on health in constant US$ per capita (2011)[2]	Trends in per capita government expenditure on health (constant US$ per capita | 2007–11; (% average annual change)[3]	Out-of- pocket expenditure in constant US$ per capita (2007)[2]	Out-of- pocket expenditure in constant US$ per capita (2011)[2]	Trends in per capita out-of-pocket expenditure on health (constant US$ per capita | 2007–11; % average annual change)[3]	Coverage gap due to financial resources deficit (benchmark: US$60 MDG target for 2015 in low income)[2,9,10]	Coverage gap due to financial resources deficit, % (benchmark: median in low vulnerability group US$239)[3,10]	Coverage gap due to health professional staff deficit (WHO benchmark: 23)[3,8,9]	Coverage gap due to health professional staff deficit: (benchmark relative: 41.1)[3,8,13]	% live births attended by skilled health staff[2,4]	Year	Maternal mortality rate (modelled estimate. per 10.000 live births)[5]
Liechtenstein	95.0	2008	...	...	...	...	...	...	...	...	...	...	...	...	...	...	...
Lithuania	95.0	2009	73.6	...	426.4	436.0	0.6	155.2	170.6	2.4	...	...	0.0	0.0	100.0	2006	0.8
Luxembourg	97.6	2010	88.6	7790.5	5260.2	5247.0	−0.1	765.3	712.8	−1.8	0.0	0.0	0.0	0.0	100.0	2003	2.0
Malta	100.0	2009	66.6	...	894.6	910.3	0.4	416.6	482.5	3.7	...	...	0.0	0.0	99.8	2010	0.8
Moldova, Republic of	75.7	2004	55.1	123.1	44.3	61.7	8.6	44.8	60.8	7.9	0.0	48.5	0.0	0.0	99.5	2005	4.1
Monaco	...	...	93.0	6699.8	4257.0	5149.3	4.9	341.1	407.0	4.5	0.0	0.0	0.0	0.0	...	...	...
Montenegro	95.0	2004	70.0	464.3	234.4	285.9	5.1	94.8	128.2	7.8	0.0	0.0	0.0	0.0	99.5	2009	0.8
Netherlands	98.9	2010	94.9	5690.2	3683.2	4091.3	2.7	264.1	242.8	−2.1	0.0	0.0	0.0	0.0	100.0	2007	0.6
Norway	100.0	2011	86.4	7767.2	4676.8	4767.4	0.5	835.5	755.7	−2.5	0.0	0.0	0.0	0.0	99.1	2010	0.7
Poland	97.5	2010	77.1	693.5	394.5	485.7	5.3	137.9	155.9	3.1	0.0	0.0	0.0	0.0	99.8	2010	0.5
Portugal	100.0	2010	72.7	1679.6	1194.6	1147.3	−1.0	456.1	489.1	1.8	0.0	0.0	0.0	0.0	100.0	2001	0.8
Romania	94.3	2009	80.8	...	227.2	252.9	2.7	47.8	61.2	6.4	...	...	0.0	0.0	98.5	2009	2.7
Russian Federation	88.0	2011	64.6	521.2	216.1	240.6	2.7	100.1	142.5	9.2	0.0	0.0	0.0	0.0	99.7	2009	3.4
San Marino	...	...	85.3	...	2900.1	2486.1	−3.8	471.7	432.6	−2.1	...	...	0.0	0.0	100.0	2008	...
Serbia	92.1	2009	63.8	396.9	237.3	253.0	1.6	134.7	147.4	2.3	0.0	0.0	0.0	0.0	99.7	2010	1.2
Slovakia	94.8	2010	74.3	...	491.1	563.9	3.5	191.3	231.5	4.9	...	...	0.0	19.7	99.5	2009	0.6
Slovenia	100.0	2011	...	...	964.9	1079.9	2.9	177.9	192.1	1.9	...	...	0.0	0.0	99.9	2009	1.2
Spain	99.2	2010	...	...	1497.1	1611.0	1.8	424.9	440.4	0.9	...	...	0.0	0.0	...	...	0.6
Sweden	100.0	2011	83.1	4428.5	3284.8	3459.1	1.3	665.8	723.4	2.1	0.0	0.0	0.0	0.0	...	...	0.4
Switzerland	100.0	2010	75.0	6840.3	3527.0	4209.7	4.5	1819.0	1609.0	−3.0	0.0	0.0	0.0	0.0	100.0	2006	0.8
The Former Yugoslav Republic of Macedonia	94.9	2006	61.7	206.1	143.9	144.6	0.1	79.4	90.1	3.2	0.0	13.8	0.0	0.0	99.7	2011	1.0

Table B.11 The multiple dimensions of health coverage

Mayor area, region or country	Extent of coverage		Financial resources: Composition. level and trends (2011)											Human resources (and access indicators)		Live births attended by skilled health staff		Maternal mortality rate (2010)
					Trends in government expenditure on health (constant US$ per capita)			Trends in out-of-pocket expenditure (constant US$ per capita)										
	Estimate of health coverage as a percentage of total population[1,6]	Year	Percentage of health expenditure not financed by out of pocket[2,3,7]	Per capita health expenditure not financed by private households' out-of-pocket payments (US$)[3]	Government expenditure on health in constant US$ per capita (2007)[2]	Government expenditure on health in constant US$ per capita (2011)[2]	Trends in per capita government expenditure on health (constant US$ per capita | 2007–11; (% average annual change)[3]	Out-of- pocket expenditure in constant US$ per capita (2007)[2]	Out-of- pocket expenditure in constant US$ per capita (2011)[2]	Trends in per capita out-of-pocket expenditure on health (constant US$ per capita | 2007–11; % average annual change)[3]	Coverage gap due to financial resources deficit (benchmark: US$60 MDG target for 2015 in low income)[2,9,10]	Coverage gap due to financial resources deficit, % (benchmark: median in low vulnerability group US$239)[3,10]	Coverage gap due to health professional staff deficit (WHO benchmark: 23)[3,8,9]	Coverage gap due to health professional staff deficit: (benchmark relative: 41.1)[3,8,13]	% live births attended by skilled health staff[2,4]	Year	Maternal mortality rate (modelled estimate. per 10.000 live births)[5]
Turkey	86.0	2011	83.9	583.9	117.2	153.7	7.0	37.7	33.1	−3.2	0.0	0.0	0.0	3.4	91.3	2008	2.0
Ukraine	100.0	2011	58.5	155.3	84.7	86.1	0.4	47.5	64.1	7.8	0.0	35.0	0.0	0.0	98.7	2007	3.2
United Kingdom	100.0	2010	90.8	3277.3	2721.1	2902.8	1.6	339.8	322.3	−1.3	0.0	0.0	0.0	0.0	99.0	1998	1.2
Oceania																	
Australia	100.0	2011	80.2	4761.1	2220.9	2305.7	0.9	593.3	665.4	2.9	0.0	0.0	0.0	0.0	99.1	2008	0.7
Cook Islands	...	...	92.5	568.2	358.5	418.6	4.0	30.7	33.9	2.6	0.0	0.0	0.0	0.0	100.0	2009	...
Fiji	100.0	2010	79.0	132.7	101.9	92.4	−2.4	21.0	28.4	7.8	0.0	44.5	0.0	35.2	99.7	2010	2.6
Kiribati	...	...	98.7	174.7	127.6	89.6	−8.4	...	1.5	...	0.0	26.9	0.0	0.0	98.3	2010	...
Marshall Islands	...	...	87.4	458.3	394.5	387.9	−0.4	58.7	58.6	−0.0	0.0	0.0	0.0	26.4	86.2	2007	...
Micronesia	...	...	91.0	348.2	247.2	...	...	17.8	...	...	0.0	0.0	0.0	7.1	100.0	2009	10.0
Nauru	...	...	92.2	630.2	333.0	257.1	−6.3	13.9	23.0	13.5	0.0	0.0	0.0	0.0	97.4	2007	...
New Zealand	100.0	2011	89.5	3280.7	1970.2	2301.6	4.0	273.9	290.4	1.5	0.0	0.0	0.0	0.0	95.7	2007	1.5
Niue	...	...	99.2	2171.1	1348.5	...	...	10.3	...	...	0.0	0.0	0.0	0.0	100.0	2007	...
Palau	...	...	88.4	821.9	667.3	597.2	−2.7	92.6	92.5	−0.0	0.0	0.0	0.0	0.0	100.0	2010	...
Papua New Guinea	...	...	88.3	69.6	27.5	35.9	6.8	4.3	5.3	5.5	31.3	70.9	80.7	89.2	42.7	2011	23.0
Solomon Islands	...	...	97.0	130.0	53.4	88.8	13.6	2.2	2.9	6.8	0.0	45.6	5.2	47.0	70.1	2007	9.3
Tonga	...	...	88.9	194.8	141.9	112.8	−5.6	17.1	15.0	−3.1	0.0	18.5	0.0	0.0	99.0	2010	11.0
Tuvalu	...	...	...	...	415.1	430.4	0.9	0.5	...	...	...	...	0.0	0.0	93.1	2007	...
Vanuatu	100.0	2010	93.1	124.4	83.5	76.3	−2.2	5.8	6.0	0.5	0.0	48.0	28.6	60.1	74.0	2007	11.0
Western Samoa	...	...	92.9	230.8	120.3	147.6	5.3	12.6	12.0	−1.2	0.0	3.4	0.0	43.6	80.8	2009	10.0

Sources

1 *OECD countries:* OECD (Organisation for Economic Co-operation and Development). OECD Health Data 2012 (Health care coverage). Available at: http://www.oecd.org/health/health-systems/oecdhealthdata.htm [6 June 2014]
Non-OECD countries: consult detailed sources available at: http://www.social-protection.org/gimi/gess/RessFileDownload.do?ressourceId=37218;

2 WHO (World Health Organization): National Health Accounts (Global Health Expenditure database). Available at: http://apps.who.int/nha/database [6 June 2014].

3 ILO calculations based on WHO (World Health Organization): National Health Accounts (Global Health Expenditure database) and Global Health Observatory (see below).

4 WHO (World Health Organization): Global Health Observatory. Available at: http://apps.who.int/gho/data/view.main [6 June 2014].

5 World Bank: World Development Indicators. Available at: http://data.worldbank.org/datacatalog/world-development-indicators [6 June 2014].

Notes

n.a: Not applicable.

…: Not available.

6 Estimate of health coverage as a percentage of total population. Coverage includes affiliated members of health insurance or estimation of the population having free access to health care services provided by the State. Consult detailed data and sources available at: http://www.social-protection.org/gimi/gess/RessourceDownload.action?ressource.ressourceId=37218.

7 Out-of-pocket expenditure as a percentage of total health expenditure: see table B.10.

8 Percentage of the population not covered due to professional health staff deficit (based on 1. median value in low vulnerability group of countries or 2. WHO benchmark).
The ILO staff access deficit indicator reflects the supply side of access availability – in this case the availability of human resources at a level that guarantees at least basic, but universal, effective access to everybody. To estimate access to the services of skilled medical professionals (physicians and nursing and midwifery personnel), it uses as a proxy the relative difference between the density of health professionals in a given country and its median value in countries with a low level of vulnerability (population access to services of medical professionals in countries with low vulnerability is thus used as a benchmark for other countries). The relative ILO benchmark corresponds to the median value in the group of countries assessed as 'low vulnerable' (regarding the structure of employment and poverty). Based on 2011 data from WHO (number of physicians, nursing and midwifery personnel per 10,000), the estimated median value is 41.1 per 10,000 poopulation when weighted by total population.
Another way to look at it is to refer to population not covered due to a deficit from the supply side (see second part of example below). Then, the ILO staff access deficit indicator estimates the dimension of the overall performance of health-care delivery as a percentage of the population that has no access to health care if needed. This value is above the minimum set by WHO for primary care delivery, which is 23 per 10,000.
Professional staff includes physicians and nursing and midwifery personnel as defined by WHO. See Indicator definitions and metadata (http://apps.who.int/gho/indicatorregistry/App_Main/view_indicator.aspx?iid=3105, accessed May 2014).

9 WHO benchmark: It has been estimated, in the *World Health Report 2006*, that countries with fewer than 23 physicians, nurses and midwives per 10,000 population generally fail to achieve adequate coverage rates for selected primary health-care interventions as prioritized by the Millennium Development Goals framework (WHO Health Statistics 2012, pp. 82: http://www.who.int/gho/publications/world_health_statistics/WHS2012_IndicatorCompendium.pdf, accessed May 2014).

10 Coverage gap due to financial resources deficit based on median value in low vulnerability group of countries. The ILO financial deficit indicator follows the same principle as the access deficit indicator regarding total health spending (in US$ per capita and per year) except out-of-pocket payments. The relative median value in 2011 in group of countries assessed as 'low vulnerable' is estimated at 239 US$ per capita and per year.

11 According to the World Health Organization, ensuring access to the types of interventions and treatments needed to address MDGs 4, 5 and 6 requires on average "little more than US$ 60 per capita [annually] by 2015": WHO, *The World Health Report: Health systems financing: The path to universal coverage*, World Health Organization (Geneva, 2010).

12 Aggregate measures are weighted by total population (2012) from United Nations Population Division, *UN World Population Prospects*, 2012 Revision.

13 Example of calculation of the ILO Coverage gap due to health professional staff deficit using a relative benchmark.

	Algeria	Burkina Faso
Total of health professional staff [A=B+C]	106776	7671
Number of nursing and midwifery personnel [B]	65919	7129
Number of physicians [C]	40857	542
Total population (in thousands) [D]	38482	10051
Number of health professional per 10000 persons [F=A÷D×10]	27,75	7,63
The ILO staff access deficit indicator [(benchmark-valuecountry X)÷benchmarck×100]	32,5	81,4
If referring to population covered:		
Total population covered if applying benchmark* (thousands) [E=A÷benchmark×10]	25980	1866
Total population not covered due to health professional staff deficit (thousands) [F=D−E]	12502	8185
Percentage of total population not covered due to health professional staff deficit G=F÷D×100	32,5	81,4

* Relative ILO benchmark: 41.1 professional health staff per 10,000 persons.

Table B.12 Public social protection expenditure, 1990 to latest available year (% of GDP)

Major area, region or country	Total public social protection expenditure and health expenditure (% of GDP)																		Public health care (% of GDP)			Public social protection (excluding health care) (% of GDP)		
	1990	Year	1995	Year	2000	Year	2005	Year	2007	Year	2009	Year	2010–11	Year	2012–13	Year	Latest for disaggregation	Year	Latest available year	Year	Source	Latest available year	Year	Source
Regional average (weighted by total population)																								
Africa	2.7		2.8		3.7		4.3		4.8		5.4		5.1											
North Africa	4.2		4.3		5.9		6.4		8.4		9.5		9.0											
Sub-saharan Africa	2.4		2.5		3.2		3.8		3.9		4.4		4.2											
Asia and the Pacific	3.4		2.8		3.5		3.0		4.1		5.3		5.3											
Middle East	4.9		5.2		6.6		7.6		6.5		8.8		8.7											
Western Europe	20.9		23.6		23.3		24.8		24.1		27.2		26.7											
Central and Eastern Europe	12.8		15.5		14.6		16.6		16.2		19.7		17.6											
Latin America and the Caribbean	8.0		9.6		10.2		11.4		12.0		13.6		13.2											
North America	14.0		15.8		14.7		16.1		16.4		19.2		19.4											
World	5.8		6.0		6.5		6.7		7.3		8.8		8.6											
Africa																								
Algeria	7.60	1990	4.50	1995	6.30	1999	7.45	2005	8.04	2007	9.73	2009	8.53	2011	...	...	9.73	2011	3.17	2011	WHO	5.36	2011	ILO
Angola	...	...	...	...	...	...	...	...	...	...	...	...	6.79	2011	...	...	6.79	2011	2.15	2011	WHO	4.64	2011	African Economic Outlook
Benin	1.33	1990	2.59	1995	2.62	2000	3.25	2005	3.31	2007	4.31	2009	4.20	2010	...	...	4.20	2010	2.22	2010	WHO	1.98	2010	World Bank
Botswana	...	...	2.52	1997	4.42	2000	7.67	2005	...	...	7.15	2009	6.59	2010	...	...	6.59	2010	3.49	2010	WHO	3.00	2010	ILO
Burkina Faso	...	...	2.44	1995	3.53	2000	5.19	2005	6.01	2007	5.58	2009	5.07	2011	...	...	5.07	2011	3.27	2011	WHO	1.80	2011	ILO
Burundi	1.71	1990	3.30	1995	3.68	2000	4.23	2005	5.54	2007	4.91	2009	4.94	2010	...	...	4.94	2010	2.89	2011	WHO	2.05	2010	UNICEF
Cabo Verde	...	...	...	...	...	...	...	...	6.98	2008	7.16	2009	6.87	2010	...	...	6.87	2010	2.38	2010	IMF	4.49	2010	IMF
Cameroon	2.20	1990	1.70	1995	1.53	2000	1.92	2005	...	...	2.20	2009	2.33	2010	...	...	2.33	2010	1.52	2010	WHO	0.81	2010	ILO/SSI
Central African Republic	...	...	...	...	0.83	2000	0.74	2005	0.78	2008	0.81	2009	2.45	2011	2.55	2012	2.55	2012	1.93	2012	IMF	0.62	2012	GSW
Chad	...	...	...	...	3.07	2000	2.04	2005	1.18	2007	1.17	2009	1.31	2010	...	...	1.31	2010	1.01	2010	WHO	0.30	2010	ILO*
Congo	2.20	1990	2.88	1995	2.07	2000	2.13	2005	2.55	2007	2.24	2009	2.79	2010	...	...	2.79	2010	1.39	2010	WHO	1.40	2010	ILO/SSI
Congo, Democratic Republic of	...	...	...	...	0.27	2000	1.73	2005	2.73	2007	5.33	2009	3.71	2011	3.48	2012	3.48	2012	2.76	2012	WHO	0.73	2012	GSW

Table B.12 Public social protection expenditure, 1990 to latest available year (% of GDP)

Major area, region or country	Total public social protection expenditure and health expenditure (% of GDP)																		Public health care (% of GDP)			Public social protection (excluding health care) (% of GDP)		
	1990	Year	1995	Year	2000	Year	2005	Year	2007	Year	2009	Year	2010–11	Year	2012–13	Year	Latest for disaggregation	Year	Latest available year	Year	Source	Latest available year	Year	Source
Côte d'Ivoire	1.60	1990	1.70	1995	1.73	2000	1.75	2005	...	...	2.06	2009	1.95	2011	...	...	1.95	2011	0.87	2011	IMF	1.08	2011	National
Djibouti	...	...	...	...	...	...	...	...	7.29	2007	...	...	...	...	...	...	7.29	2007	5.34	2007	WHO	1.95	2007	World Bank
Egypt	4.37	1990	5.30	1995	8.57	2000	8.81	2005	12.91	2007	14.21	2009	13.21	2011	...	...	13.21	2011	1.48	2011	IMF	11.73	2011	IMF
Equatorial Guinea	...	...							1.38	2007	3.90	2009	2.78	2010	...	...	2.78	2010	2.43	2010	WHO	0.35	2010	IMF
Eritrea	...	...			2.16	2000	1.38	2005	1.73	2007	1.68	2009	1.64	2011	...	...	1.64	2011	1.25	2011	WHO	0.39	2011	ILO*
Ethiopia	1.50	1990	2.05	1995	6.02	2001	4.55	2005	2.79	2007	2.94	2009	3.17	2010	...	...	3.17	2010	2.56	2010	WHO	0.61	2010	IMF
Gambia	3.10	1990	3.20	1995	2.54	2000	2.96	2003	2.38	2007	2.95	2009	2.98	2010	...	...	2.98	2010	2.48	2010	WHO	0.50	2010	ILO
Ghana	2.20	1990	3.62	1995	3.11	2000	6.56	2005	5.85	2007	5.01	2009	5.39	2010	...	...	5.39	2010	3.02	2010	WHO	2.37	2010	ILO*
Guinea	0.80	1990	0.80	1995	1.26	2000	1.05	2005	1.43	2007	2.15	2009	2.47	2010	...	...	2.47	2010	2.01	2010	WHO	0.46	2010	ILO
Guinea-Bissau	...	...	...	...	2.52	2000	...	...	3.87	2007	4.63	2009	5.44	2010	...	...	5.44	2010	2.31	2010	WHO	3.13	2010	ILO
Kenya	1.47	1990	1.54	1995	1.51	2000	2.35	2005	3.05	2007	3.31	2009	2.61	2011	3.26	2013	3.26	2013	2.33	2013	IMF	0.93	2013	GSW
Lesotho	7.30	1990	4.90	1995	5.47	2002	4.39	2006	5.21	2007	6.13	2008	8.16	2010	...	...	8.16	2010	7.98	2010	IMF	0.18	2010	IMF
Liberia	8.00	1990	10.00	1995	12.78	2000	11.47	2005	...	...	...	...	...	...	...	...	11.47	2005	1.60	2005	WHO	9.87	2005	IMF
Madagascar	1.36	1990	1.47	1995	2.98	2001	2.62	2005	3.01	2007	2.53	2008	2.39	2010	...	...	2.39	2010	2.08	2010	IMF	0.31	2010	IMF
Malawi	...	...	...	...	...	...	...	...	5.91	2007	...	...	...	...	...	...	5.91	2007	4.51	2007	WHO	1.40	2007	ODI
Mali	...	...	...	...	...	...	...	...	...	...	...	...	4.88	2010	...	...	4.88	2010	2.82	2010	WHO	2.07	2010	World Bank
Mauritania	1.00	1990	3.62	1995	4.27	2000	3.96	2005	3.06	2007	4.07	2009	4.87	2010	...	...	4.87	2010	4.03	2010	WHO	0.84	2010	ILO
Mauritius	4.93	1990	5.76	1995	6.90	2000	7.72	2005	7.19	2007	8.48	2009	9.12	2011	...	...	9.12	2011	2.39	2011	IMF	6.73	2011	IMF
Morocco	2.40	1990	3.54	1995	3.92	1999	4.78	2005	5.98	2007	6.45	2009	6.57	2010	...	...	6.57	2010	2.07	2010	WHO	4.51	2010	ILO
Mozambique	3.50	1990	3.50	1995	4.51	2000	4.71	2005	4.29	2007	4.49	2009	5.32	2010	...	...	5.32	2010	3.29	2010	WHO	2.02	2010	ILO
Namibia	3.90	1990	3.90	1995	3.98	2000	4.20	2005	5.40	2007	6.20	2009	7.40	2011	...	...	7.40	2011	2.80	2011	WHO	4.60	2011	ILO/SSI
Niger	1.90	1990	2.00	1995	1.82	2000	3.48	2005	3.26	2007	3.29	2009	2.91	2010	...	...	2.91	2010	2.38	2010	WHO	0.53	2010	ILO
Nigeria	...	...	...	...	...	...	...	...	...	...	3.70	2009	2.83	2010	...	...	2.83	2010	1.71	2010	ODI	1.12	2010	ODI
Rwanda	1.90	1990	...	...	2.15	2000	4.71	2005	5.66	2007	6.87	2009	7.31	2010	...	...	7.31	2010	5.72	2010	WHO	1.60	2010	National
Sao Tome and Principe	...	...	...	...	...	...	...	...	4.83	2008	6.37	2009	4.93	2010	...	...	4.93	2010	4.19	2010	IMF	0.74	2010	IMF
Senegal	4.30	1990	2.98	1995	3.40	2000	4.79	2005	5.05	2007	...	...	5.34	2010	...	...	5.34	2010	3.28	2010	WHO	2.06	2010	ILO/SSI
Seychelles	11.00	1990	11.60	1995	11.46	2002	9.77	2005	11.77	2007	7.51	2008	7.52	2011	...	...	7.52	2011	3.14	2011	IMF	4.39	2011	IMF

Table B.12 Public social protection expenditure, 1990 to latest available year (% of GDP)

Major area, region or country	Total public social protection expenditure and health expenditure (% of GDP)																Public health care (% of GDP)			Public social protection (excluding health care) (% of GDP)		
	1990	Year	1995	Year	2000	Year	2005	Year	2007	Year	2009	Year	2010–11	Year	2012–13	Year	Latest for disaggregation	Year	Latest available year	Year	Source	Latest available year	Year	Source
Sierra Leone	1.90	1990	2.00	1995	4.26	2000	4.16	2005	3.11	2007	2.07	2009	...	...	...	...	2.07	2009	1.46	2009	WHO	0.61	2009	ILO
South Africa	5.97	1990	6.78	1996	6.88	2000	8.92	2005	8.90	2007	10.17	2009	9.79	2010	...	...	9.79	2010	4.74	2010	IMF	5.05	2010	IMF
Sudan	1.10	1990	1.49	1995	1.36	1996	1.72	2005	2.33	2007	2.46	2008	2.27	2010	...	...	2.27	2010	1.99	2010	WHO	0.29	2010	ILO*
Swaziland	...	...	2.94	1995	3.07	2000	...	...	...	...	7.90	2000	7.32	2010	...	...	7.32	2010	5.54	2010	WHO	1.78	2010	IMF
Tanzania, United Republic of	1.90	1990	2.00	1995	2.05	2000	3.29	2005	5.39	2007	6.08	2009	6.81	2010	...	...	6.81	2010	4.48	2010	ILO	2.33	2010	ILO/SSI
Togo	1.70	1990	2.79	1995	3.71	2000	4.24	2005	4.49	2007	5.49	2009	5.73	2010	...	...	5.73	2010	3.42	2010	WHO	2.31	2010	ILO
Tunisia	7.00	1990	7.52	1995	6.94	2000	8.08	2005	8.22	2007	8.83	2009	10.40	2011	...	...	10.40	2011	1.50	2011	IMF	8.91	2011	IMF
Uganda	...	...	0.90	1998	4.27	2000	4.17	2005	3.15	2007	3.04	2009	3.46	2011	...	...	3.46	2011	2.30	2011	IMF	1.16	2011	IMF
Zambia	2.30	1990	2.50	1995	3.91	2000	5.44	2005	4.75	2007	5.32	2009	5.46	2011	...	...	5.46	2011	3.66	2011	WHO	1.80	2011	ILO
Zimbabwe	3.30	1990	3.50	1995	5.57	2000	3.93	2005	...	...	2.00	2009	5.60	2011	...	...	5.60	2011	4.30	2011	National	1.30	2011	National
Asia and the Middle East																								
Afghanistan	0.80	1990	0.80	1995	0.76	2003	2.23	2006	3.66	2007	4.21	2009	5.60	2011	...	...	5.60	2011	3.61	2011	IMF	1.99	2011	IMF
Armenia	4.30	1990	5.73	1995	3.08	2000	3.35	2005	3.49	2007	9.54	2009	8.46	2011	8.61	2013	8.61	2013	1.65	2013	ADB	6.97	2013	GSW
Azerbaijan	6.78	1990	3.10	1995	8.57	2000	7.08	2005	6.30	2007	8.86	2009	8.27	2011	...	...	8.27	2011	1.01	2011	IMF	7.26	2011	IMF
Bahrain	3.17	1990	3.64	1995	3.26	2000	2.87	2005	3.03	2007	4.73	2009	4.01	2010	...	...	4.01	2010	2.40	2010	IMF	1.61	2010	IMF
Bangladesh	0.71	1990	1.10	1995	1.12	2000	1.17	2005	2.04	2007	2.28	2009	2.69	2011	...	...	2.69	2011	1.11	2011	ADB	1.58	2011	ADB
Bhutan	3.12	1990	4.16	1995	5.69	2000	4.77	2005	5.19	2007	5.01	2009	4.58	2011	5.20	2012	5.20	2012	3.03	2012	ADB	2.17	2012	ADB
Cambodia	1.97	1990	0.76	1995	1.05	2000	1.24	2005	1.35	2007	1.67	2009	1.79	2011	2.23	2013	2.23	2013	1.45	2013	ADB	0.79	2013	GSW
China	5.20	1990	3.19	1995	4.70	2000	2.76	2005	5.01	2007	6.81	2009	6.83	2010	...	...	6.83	2010	1.27	2010	IMF	5.56	2010	IMF
Georgia	5.00	1990	5.69	1997	5.13	2000	7.16	2005	6.39	2007	9.32	2009	8.01	2011	8.22	2012	8.22	2012	1.60	2012	IMF	6.63	2012	ADB
Hong Kong (China)	2.43	1990	4.66	1995	4.52	2000	4.59	2005	4.15	2007	4.75	2009	4.58	2011	5.17	2012	5.17	2012	2.92	2012	ADB	2.25	2012	ADB
India	1.73	1990	1.55	1995	1.61	2000	1.54	2005	1.87	2007	2.59	2009	2.64	2011	2.39	2012	2.39	2012	0.96	2012	WHO	1.42	2012	GSW
Indonesia	...	...	1.61	1995	1.80	1999	2.04	2004	2.75	2007	2.94	2009	2.63	2010	...	...	2.63	2010	1.03	2010	WHO	1.60	2010	ILO/SSI
Iran, Islamic Republic of	4.70	1990	6.10	1995	8.85	2001	9.85	2005	10.36	2007	13.41	2009	12.53	2010	...	...	12.53	2010	1.84	2010	IMF	10.69	2010	IMF
Iraq	...	...	...	...	...	...	...	...	...	...	12.14	2009	11.65	2010	...	...	11.65	2010	6.36	2010	WHO	5.30	2010	ILO*
Israel	14.20	1990	17.37	1995	17.17	2000	16.27	2005	15.46	2007	15.95	2009	16.02	2011	15.81	2013	16.02	2011	4.33	2011	OECD	11.69	2011	OECD

Table B.12 Public social protection expenditure, 1990 to latest available year (% of GDP)

Major area, region or country	Total public social protection expenditure and health expenditure (% of GDP)																		Public health care (% of GDP)			Public social protection (excluding health care) (% of GDP)		
	1990	Year	1995	Year	2000	Year	2005	Year	2007	Year	2009	Year	2010–11	Year	2012–13	Year	Latest for disaggregation	Year	Latest available year	Year	Source	Latest available year	Year	Source
Japan	11.11	1990	14.07	1995	16.28	2000	18.49	2005	18.75	2007	22.40	2009	23.56	2011	...	...	23.56	2011	6.81	2011	OECD	16.75	2011	OECD
Jordan	7.05	1990	7.42	1995	8.44	2000	16.23	2005	13.14	2007	10.63	2009	12.11	2011	...	...	12.11	2011	3.31	2011	IMF	8.80	2011	IMF
Kazakhstan	7.50	1990	8.00	1995	8.67	2000	6.99	2005	6.24	2007	7.11	2009	6.38	2011	...	...	6.38	2011	2.27	2011	IMF	4.11	2011	IMF
Kiribati	...	...	...	...	8.50	2000	11.24	2005	11.58	2007	10.64	2009	10.10	2011	...	...	10.10	2011	8.52	2011	ADB	1.58	2011	ADB
Korea, Republic of	2.82	1990	3.25	1995	4.82	2000	6.51	2005	7.65	2007	9.40	2009	9.14	2011	9.30	2012	9.14	2011	4.00	2011	OECD	5.13	2011	OECD
Kuwait	9.40	1990	11.12	1995	13.49	2000	6.54	2005	5.29	2007	8.00	2009	11.44	2011	...	...	11.44	2011	2.23	2011	IMF	9.21	2011	IMF
Kyrgyzstan	8.65	1990	9.56	1995	3.69	2000	5.10	2005	5.52	2007	5.91	2009	8.30	2011	9.58	2012	9.58	2012	3.83	2012	ADB	5.75	2012	ADB
Lao People's Democratic Republic	1.30	1990	2.98	1995	1.67	2000	1.33	2005	1.39	2008	2.54	2009	1.74	2010	...	...	1.74	2005	1.22	2010	WHO	0.52	2010	ADB
Lebanon	4.50	1990	3.15	1995	2.33	2000	1.29	2005	3.23	2007	1.25	2009	1.12	2011	...	...	1.12	2011	0.77	2011	IMF	0.36	2011	IMF
Libyan Arab Jamahiriya	...	...	...	...	...	...	2.47	2005	...	...	6.60	2009	6.55	2010	...	...	6.55	2010	2.11	2010	WHO	4.44	2010	ILO
Macau	...	...	4.66	1999	4.47	2000	3.25	2005	2.78	2007	5.07	2009	5.12	2011	...	...	5.12	2011	1.35	2011	IMF	3.77	2011	IMF
Malaysia	2.70	1990	2.05	1995	2.40	2000	2.50	2005	2.74	2007	3.20	2009	2.89	2011	2.99	2012	2.99	2012	1.99	2012	ADB	1.00	2012	ADB
Maldives	...	...	4.77	1995	5.12	2000	8.05	2005	5.16	2007	7.32	2009	4.28	2011	6.22	2012	6.22	2012	0.36	2012	IMF	5.86	2012	ADB
Mongolia	13.19	1990	6.04	1995	9.97	2000	8.74	2005	10.56	2007	14.18	2009	...	2011	8.87	2012	8.87	2012	3.13	2012	ADB	5.75	2012	ADB
Myanmar	1.75	1990	0.76	1995	0.49	2000	0.40	2004	0.43	2007	0.44	2009	0.96	2011	...	...	0.94	2010	0.24	2010	IMF	0.70	2010	ILO
Nepal	1.96	1990	1.17	1995	1.73	2000	1.51	2005	1.78	2007	3.07	2010	2.31	2011	2.19	2013	2.19	2013	1.53	2013	IMF	0.66	2013	GSW
Oman	2.50	1990	3.52	1995	3.58	2000	3.88	2005	3.11	2007	3.19	2009	3.80	2011	...	...	3.80	2011	1.49	2011	IMF	2.31	2011	IMF
Pakistan	1.50	1990	0.35	1995	0.27	2000	0.44	2005	0.50	2007	1.66	2009	1.68	2010	...	...	1.68	2010	0.38	2010	National	1.30	2010	ADB
Philippines	1.06	1990	0.80	1995	1.09	2000	0.93	2005	1.00	2007	1.23	2009	1.75	2011	1.55	2012	1.55	2012	0.56	2012	ADB	0.99	2012	ADB
Qatar	...	...	...	...	2.65	2004	2.28	2005	1.50	2007	2.13	2009	1.74	2010	...	...	1.74	2010	1.53	2010	IMF	0.22	2010	IMF
Saudi Arabia	...	...	...	...	...	...	...	...	...	...	3.90	2009	3.64	2011	...	...	3.64	2011	2.54	2011	WHO	1.10	2011	IMF
Singapore	1.35	1990	1.96	1995	1.61	2000	1.16	2005	1.39	2007	3.52	2009	2.83	2011	...	...	2.83	2011	1.20	2011	IMF	1.63	2011	IMF
Sri Lanka	5.34	1990	6.76	1995	4.41	2000	5.62	2005	4.48	2007	3.65	2009	3.14	2011	3.00	2012	3.00	2012	1.31	2012	IMF	1.69	2012	IMF
Syrian Arab Republic	...	...	...	...	3.22	2000	3.08	2005	2.21	2007	1.99	2009	1.91	2010	...	...	1.91	2010	1.57	2010	WHO	0.35	2010	IMF
Taiwan	8.00	1990	9.50	1995	9.94	2000	10.13	2005	9.85	2007	10.54	2009	9.68	2010	...	...	9.68	2010	3.32	2010	National	6.36	2010	National
Tajikistan	...	...	1.45	1995	2.74	2000	4.37	2005	3.91	2007	4.86	2009	5.31	2011	6.75	2012	6.75	2012	1.79	2012	ADB	4.96	2012	ADB

Table B.12 Public social protection expenditure, 1990 to latest available year (% of GDP)

Major area, region or country	Total public social protection expenditure and health expenditure (% of GDP)																		Public health care (% of GDP)			Public social protection (excluding health care) (% of GDP)		
	1990	Year	1995	Year	2000	Year	2005	Year	2007	Year	2009	Year	2010–11	Year	2012–13	Year	Latest for disaggregation	Year	Latest available year	Year	Source	Latest available year	Year	Source
Thailand	1.47	1990	1.83	1995	2.57	2000	3.67	2005	6.18	2007	8.17	2009	7.24	2011	...	...	7.24	2011	2.27	2011	IMF	4.98	2011	IMF
Timor-Leste	...	...	...	...	...	...	...	...	1.08	2007	4.26	2009	3.49	2011	4.24	2013	4.24	2013	1.64	2013	ADB	2.61	2013	GSW
United Arab Emirates	...	...	2.31	1997	2.13	1999	...	...	...	...	...	...	3.76	2011	...	...	3.76	2011	1.59	2011	WHO	2.16	2011	IMF
Uzbekistan	...	...	...	...	...	...	13.14	2005	12.80	2009	12.84	2009	11.16	2010	...	...	11.16	2010	2.73	2010	WHO	8.43	2010	ADB
Viet Nam	2.50	1990	4.99	1995	4.06	2000	4.21	2005	6.04	2008	6.46	2009	6.28	2010	...	...	6.28	2010	2.54	2010	WHO	3.74	2010	ADB
Yemen	...	...	...	...	1.38	2000	1.59	2005	1.47	2007	2.15	2009	5.90	2011	...	...	5.90	2011	1.50	2011	IMF	4.40	2011	IMF
Europe																								
Albania	8.00	1990	10.02	1995	10.77	1998	9.87	2005	10.49	2007	10.82	2009	10.83	2011	...	...	10.83	2011	2.68	2011	IMF	8.15	2011	IMF
Austria	23.79	1990	26.52	1995	26.58	2000	27.14	2005	26.26	2007	29.12	2009	27.89	2011	28.29	2013	27.89	2011	7.51	2011	OECD	20.37	2011	OECD
Belarus	13.29	1990	16.67	1995	16.00	2000	18.48	2005	18.49	2007	18.06	2009	15.80	2011	...	...	15.80	2011	4.00	2011	IMF	11.80	2011	IMF
Belgium	24.85	1990	26.23	1995	25.29	2000	26.53	2005	25.99	2007	29.70	2009	29.73	2011	30.73	2013	29.73	2011	8.64	2011	OECD	21.09	2011	OECD
Bosnia and Herzegovina	...	...	...	...	13.02	2003	14.01	2005	13.80	2007	16.93	2009	17.45	2011	...	...	17.45	2011	6.95	2011	WHO	10.50	2011	IMF
Brunei Darussalam	2.71	1990	3.60	1995	3.29	2000	2.55	2005	...	...	2.95	2009	2.31	2011	...	...	2.31	2011	1.60	2011	ADB	0.71	2011	ADB
Bulgaria	10.90	1990	14.84	1995	17.20	2000	16.78	2005	15.83	2007	17.18	2009	17.20	2011	...	...	17.20	2011	4.31	2011	Eurostat/ IMF	12.88	2011	IMF
Croatia	20.83	1990	17.22	1995	22.83	2000	19.17	2005	18.78	2007	21.06	2009	20.96	2011	...	...	20.96	2011	6.18	2011	IMF	14.78	2011	IMF
Cyprus	8.10	1990	10.30	1995	14.84	2000	18.40	2005	18.20	2007	21.10	2009	22.60	2011	...	...	22.60	2011	3.35	2011	Eurostat	19.47	2011	Eurostat
Czech Republic	15.34	1990	17.38	1995	19.09	2000	18.70	2005	18.14	2007	20.71	2009	20.78	2011	21.77	2013	20.78	2011	6.69	2011	OECD	14.09	2011	OECD
Denmark	25.14	1990	28.92	1995	26.36	2000	27.73	2005	26.45	2007	30.19	2009	30.58	2011	30.79	2013	30.58	2011	7.61	2011	OECD	22.98	2011	OECD
Estonia	...	...	15.30	1999	13.94	2000	13.09	2005	12.75	2007	20.04	2009	18.24	2011	17.74	2013	20.08	2010	5.36	2010	OECD	14.73	2010	OECD
Finland	24.11	1990	30.67	1995	24.23	2000	26.15	2005	24.69	2007	29.44	2009	29.22	2011	30.53	2013	29.22	2011	7.25	2011	OECD	21.97	2011	OECD
France	25.10	1990	29.30	1995	28.61	2000	30.12	2005	29.71	2007	32.07	2009	32.02	2011	33.02	2013	32.02	2011	8.23	2011	OECD	23.78	2011	OECD
Germany	21.73	1990	26.62	1995	26.60	2000	27.29	2005	25.08	2007	27.78	2009	25.89	2011	26.18	2013	25.89	2011	6.84	2011	OECD	19.05	2011	OECD
Greece	16.62	1990	17.50	1995	19.32	2000	21.14	2005	21.57	2007	23.88	2009	24.41	2011	22.00	2013	24.41	2011	5.54	2011	OECD	18.87	2011	OECD
Hungary	...	...	25.10	1995	20.72	2000	22.49	2005	23.02	2007	23.93	2009	21.92	2011	21.56	2013	22.87	2010	5.14	2010	OECD	17.74	2010	OECD
Iceland	13.74	1990	15.21	1995	15.25	2000	16.35	2005	15.26	2007	18.47	2009	18.06	2011	17.22	2013	18.06	2011	7.12	2011	OECD	10.94	2011	OECD
Ireland	17.31	1990	18.06	1995	13.38	2000	16.02	2005	16.75	2007	23.61	2009	23.35	2011	21.59	2013	23.72	2010	6.39	2010	OECD	17.34	2010	OECD

Table B.12 Public social protection expenditure, 1990 to latest available year (% of GDP)

Major area, region or country	Total public social protection expenditure and health expenditure (% of GDP)																Public health care (% of GDP)			Public social protection (excluding health care) (% of GDP)		
	1990	Year	1995	Year	2000	Year	2005	Year	2007	Year	2009	Year	2010–11	Year	2012–13	Year	Latest for disaggregation	Year	Latest available year	Year	Source	Latest available year	Year	Source
Italy	19.87	1990	19.80	1995	23.13	2000	24.90	2005	24.70	2007	27.81	2009	27.50	2011	28.44	2013	27.50	2011	7.27	2011	OECD	20.23	2011	OECD
Kosovo	...	...	...	...	...	...	...	...	...	...	6.10	2009	...	...	...	...	6.10	2009	2.30	2009	World Bank	3.80	2009	World Bank
Latvia	15.20	1990	15.19	1997	15.68	2000	12.28	2005	10.98	2007	16.69	2009	14.91	2011	...	...	14.91	2011	2.63	2011	Eurostat	12.27	2011	Eurostat
Lithuania	13.00	1990	13.02	1996	15.71	2000	12.82	2005	14.00	2007	20.60	2009	16.26	2011	...	...	16.26	2011	4.06	2011	Eurostat	12.20	2011	Eurostat
Luxembourg	19.14	1990	20.76	1995	20.89	2000	22.81	2005	20.29	2007	23.57	2009	22.58	2011	23.38	2013	23.02	2010	6.49	2010	OECD	16.53	2010	OECD
Malta	...	...	16.11	1995	16.59	2000	18.20	2005	17.78	2007	19.71	2009	18.32	2011	...	...	18.32	2011	4.01	2011	Eurostat	14.32	2011	Eurostat
Montenegro	25.00	1990	20.00	1995	20.58	2000	18.70	2005	16.93	2007	21.91	2009	20.05	2011	...	...	20.05	2011	6.24	2011	WHO	13.81	2011	World Bank
Moldova, Republic of	15.00	1990	18.40	1996	15.16	2000	15.52	2005	17.48	2007	21.41	2009	18.61	2011	18.30	2013	18.30	2013	5.20	2013	IMF	13.10	2013	GSW
Netherlands	25.57	1990	23.81	1995	19.76	2000	20.73	2005	21.15	2007	23.18	2009	23.42	2011	24.30	2013	23.42	2011	7.73	2011	OECD	15.69	2011	OECD
Norway	22.31	1990	23.35	1995	21.31	2000	21.59	2005	20.47	2007	23.29	2009	22.37	2011	22.88	2013	22.37	2011	6.53	2011	OECD	15.84	2011	OECD
Poland	14.92	1990	22.61	1995	20.50	2000	21.02	2005	19.69	2007	21.52	2009	20.51	2011	20.94	2013	20.51	2011	4.65	2011	OECD	15.87	2011	OECD
Portugal	12.49	1990	16.46	1995	18.87	2000	23.04	2005	22.73	2007	25.55	2009	25.02	2011	26.38	2013	25.43	2010	6.93	2010	OECD	18.50	2010	OECD
Romania	12.00	1990	12.70	1995	14.17	2000	13.20	2005	13.19	2007	16.88	2009	17.39	2010	...	...	17.39	2010	4.19	2010	Eurostat	13.21	2010	Eurostat
Russian Federation	12.00	1990	11.13	1995	10.06	2000	12.67	2005	12.75	2007	16.93	2009	15.97	2011	...	...	15.97	2011	3.96	2011	IMF	12.01	2011	IMF
San Marino	...	...	...	...	23.25	2002	23.08	2004	21.40	2007	21.40	2009	21.40	2010	...	...	21.40	2010	6.08	2010	IMF	15.32	2010	IMF
Serbia	25.00	1990	21.00	1995	20.90	2000	23.13	2007	23.13	2007	25.86	2009	24.05	2011	...	...	24.05	2011	6.32	2011	IMF	17.73	2011	IMF
Slovakia	19.00	1990	18.75	1995	17.90	2000	16.30	2005	15.72	2007	18.74	2009	18.10	2011	17.95	2013	18.10	2011	6.71	2011	OECD	11.39	2011	OECD
Slovenia	22.00	1990	23.00	1995	21.77	2000	21.10	2005	19.52	2007	22.58	2009	23.74	2011	23.78	2013	23.74	2011	6.32	2011	OECD	17.42	2011	OECD
Spain	19.95	1990	21.41	1995	20.16	2000	21.08	2005	21.34	2007	25.98	2009	26.41	2011	27.43	2013	26.41	2011	7.22	2011	OECD	19.19	2011	OECD
Sweden	30.24	1990	32.03	1995	28.43	2000	29.07	2005	27.34	2007	29.82	2009	27.56	2011	28.64	2013	28.30	2010	7.00	2010	OECD	21.31	2010	OECD
Switzerland	13.45	1990	17.46	1995	17.85	2000	20.18	2005	18.51	2007	20.17	2009	19.53	2011	19.10	2013	20.55	2010	6.74	2010	OECD	13.82	2010	OECD
The Former Yugoslav Republic of Macedonia	23.00	1990	17.99	1995	18.74	2000	17.20	2005	18.41	2007	18.24	2009	17.56	2010	...	...	17.56	2010	4.08	2010	WHO	13.48	2010	ILO*
Turkey	5.68	1990	5.59	1995	9.77	2000	9.87	2005	10.51	2007	12.82	2009	13.11	2011	...	...	13.11	2011	5.90	2011	OECD	7.21	2011	OECD
Ukraine	...	...	19.80	1997	18.07	2000	23.94	2005	22.47	2007	27.19	2009	17.42	2011	...	...	17.42	2011	3.82	2011	IMF	13.60	2011	IMF
United Kingdom	16.75	1990	19.91	1995	18.56	2000	20.54	2005	20.37	2007	24.05	2009	23.56	2011	23.77	2013	23.84	2010	7.49	2010	OECD	16.35	2010	OECD

Table B.12 Public social protection expenditure, 1990 to latest available year (% of GDP)

Major area, region or country	Total public social protection expenditure and health expenditure (% of GDP)																		Public health care (% of GDP)			Public social protection (excluding health care) (% of GDP)		
	1990	Year	1995	Year	2000	Year	2005	Year	2007	Year	2009	Year	2010–11	Year	2012–13	Year	Latest for disaggregation	Year	Latest available year	Year	Source	Latest available year	Year	Source
Latin America and the Caribbean																								
Antigua and Barbuda	...	...	5.24	1995	5.35	2000	5.51	2005	...	...	5.82	2009	7.09	2011	...	...	7.09	2011	4.05	2011	WHO	3.05	2011	ILO
Argentina	15.05	1990	16.91	1995	16.45	2000	15.18	2005	17.38	2007	21.10	2009	18.13	2010	...	...	18.13	2010	5.34	2010	ECLAC	12.79	2010	ECLAC
Aruba	5.50	1990	16.40	1995	14.70	2000	15.30	2005	...	...	17.80	2009	...	...	...	...	17.80	2009	9.60	2009	National	8.20	2009	National
Bahamas	3.40	1990	3.74	1995	3.31	2000	3.57	2005	4.00	2007	4.94	2009	6.29	2011	...	...	6.29	2011	3.50	2011	National	2.79	2011	National
Barbados	8.60	1990	9.91	1995	8.54	2000	9.68	2005	10.06	2007	9.85	2009	11.41	2010	...	...	11.41	2010	4.34	2010	WHO	7.07	2010	ILO
Belize	2.37	1990	4.08	1995	3.39	2000	3.85	2005	5.06	2007	6.33	2009	5.76	2011	...	...	5.76	2011	3.76	2011	WHO	2.00	2011	ILO/SSI
Bolivia	...	...	8.56	1996	10.02	2000	10.40	2005	9.58	2007	11.81	2009	12.12	2010	...	...	12.12	2010	3.62	2010	ECLAC	8.50	2010	ECLAC
Brazil	13.65	1990	15.48	1995	16.26	2000	17.96	2005	19.25	2007	21.18	2009	21.29	2010	...	...	21.29	2010	5.79	2010	ILO	15.50	2010	ILO/SSI
Chile	9.88	1990	11.07	1995	12.81	2000	10.05	2005	9.38	2007	11.32	2009	10.43	2011	10.18	2012	10.43	2011	3.63	2011	OECD	6.80	2011	OECD
Colombia	3.68	1990	8.33	1995	7.32	2000	9.67	2005	9.80	2007	11.38	2009	10.49	2010	...	...	10.49	2010	1.91	2010	ECLAC	8.58	2010	ECLAC
Costa Rica	12.06	1990	11.28	1995	12.47	2000	11.88	2005	12.10	2007	15.42	2009	15.45	2010	...	...	15.45	2010	6.57	2010	ECLAC	8.88	2010	ECLAC
Cuba	16.39	1990	18.86	1995	14.43	2000	19.76	2005	21.05	2007	21.41	2009	22.80	2010	...	...	22.80	2010	9.70	2010	ECLAC	13.10	2010	ECLAC
Dominica	2.20	1990	7.03	1995	6.78	2000	6.34	2005	6.31	2007	6.77	2009	7.99	2010	...	...	7.99	2010	4.19	2010	WHO	3.80	2010	ILO
Dominican Republic	3.42	1990	2.76	1995	3.42	2000	5.03	2005	5.52	2007	5.29	2009	4.82	2010	...	...	4.82	2010	1.75	2010	ECLAC	3.07	2010	ECLAC
Ecuador	1.39	1990	1.66	1995	1.12	2000	2.12	2005	2.89	2007	3.93	2009	4.37	2010	...	...	4.37	2010	2.07	2010	ECLAC	2.30	2010	ECLAC
El Salvador	1.19	1990	3.30	1995	6.25	2000	8.84	2005	8.32	2007	8.64	2009	7.77	2011	...	...	7.77	2011	3.80	2011	IMF	3.97	2011	IMF
Grenada	...	...	4.13	1995	4.72	2000	4.59	2005	4.57	2007	4.95	2009	4.27	2010	...	...	4.27	2010	2.63	2010	WHO	1.64	2010	National*
Guatemala	2.02	1990	2.61	1995	3.82	2000	4.65	2005	4.35	2007	4.60	2009	4.39	2011	...	...	4.39	2011	1.25	2011	ECLAC	3.14	2011	ECLAC*
Guyana	4.62	1990	5.80	1995	8.25	2000	8.16	2003	6.80	2007	9.72	2009	8.18	2010	...	...	8.18	2010	4.48	2010	WHO	3.70	2010	ILO
Haiti	...	...	...	...	...	...	...	...	...	...	...	...	...	...	3.27	2013	3.27	2013	2.21	2013	GSW	1.06	2013	GSW
Honduras	2.88	1990	2.47	1995	3.05	2000	3.29	2005	3.26	2007	4.21	2009	4.39	2010	...	...	4.39	2010	3.45	2010	ECLAC	0.94	2010	ECLAC
Jamaica	4.50	1990	3.82	1995	3.63	2000	4.44	2005	3.98	2007	4.25	2009	4.42	2011	...	...	4.42	2011	2.82	2011	IMF	1.61	2011	IMF
Mexico	3.26	1990	4.33	1995	5.30	2000	6.92	2005	6.90	2007	8.22	2009	7.72	2011	7.41	2012	7.72	2011	2.76	2011	OECD	4.97	2011	OECD
Nicaragua	3.85	1990	4.17	1995	4.76	2000	6.31	2005	6.54	2007	6.95	2009	...	...	...	...	6.95	2009	4.06	2009	ECLAC	2.89	2009	ECLAC
Panama	3.36	1990	4.73	1995	5.05	2000	3.72	2005	5.45	2007	6.57	2009	6.59	2010	...	...	6.59	2010	2.24	2010	ECLAC	4.35	2010	ECLAC

Table B.12 Public social protection expenditure, 1990 to latest available year (% of GDP)

Major area, region or country	Total public social protection expenditure and health expenditure (% of GDP)																Public health care (% of GDP)			Public social protection (excluding health care) (% of GDP)		
	1990	Year	1995	Year	2000	Year	2005	Year	2007	Year	2009	Year	2010–11	Year	2012–13	Year	Latest for disaggregation	Year	Latest available year	Year	Source	Latest available year	Year	Source
Paraguay	1.58	1990	4.44	1995	5.01	2000	4.18	2005	5.21	2007	6.35	2009	6.35	2010	...	...	6.35	2010	2.28	2010	ECLAC	4.07	2010	ECLAC
Peru	2.31	1990	4.20	1995	5.71	2000	6.55	2005	6.06	2007	6.82	2009	6.85	2010	...	...	6.85	2010	1.58	2010	ECLAC	5.27	2010	ECLAC
Saint Kitts and Nevis	5.00	1990	5.27	1995	5.59	2000	4.84	2005	4.48	2008	4.73	2009	5.61	2010	...	...	5.61	2010	2.60	2010	WHO	3.01	2010	National
Saint Lucia	...	...	3.91	1995	4.46	2000	4.69	2005	4.51	2007	6.58	2009	5.97	2010	...	...	5.97	2010	4.25	2010	WHO	1.72	2010	ILO
Saint Vincent and the Grenadines	5.75	1990	6.10	1995	7.18	2000	6.65	2005	6.81	2007	9.20	2009	8.25	2010	...	...	8.25	2010	3.90	2010	IMF	4.35	2010	ILO
Trinidad and Tobago	3.60	1990	3.67	1995	4.60	2000	5.77	2005	4.97	2007	7.02	2008	8.96	2010	...	...	8.96	2010	3.32	2010	ECLAC	5.64	2010	ECLAC
Uruguay	13.84	1990	18.07	1995	17.79	2000	16.35	2005	17.89	2007	18.17	2009	17.90	2010	...	...	17.90	2010	4.85	2010	ECLAC	13.05	2010	ECLAC
Venezuela, Bolivarian Republic of	4.46	1990	4.16	1995	6.05	2000	6.88	2005	7.97	2006	8.33	2009	6.85	2010	...	...	6.85	2010	1.55	2010	ECLAC	5.30	2010	ECLAC
North America																								
Canada	18.11	1990	18.87	1995	16.50	2000	16.95	2005	16.84	2007	19.20	2009	18.14	2011	18.16	2013	18.63	2010	7.97	2010	OECD	10.66	2010	OECD
United States	13.55	1990	15.47	1995	14.54	2000	16.00	2005	16.31	2007	19.16	2009	19.56	2011	20.03	2013	19.92	2010	8.57	2010	OECD	11.34	2010	OECD
Oceania																								
Australia	13.21	1990	16.19	1995	17.32	2000	16.51	2005	16.39	2007	17.84	2009	18.16	2011	19.52	2013	18.16	2011	7.61	2011	OECD	10.55	2011	OECD
Cook islands	...	...	8.17	1995	5.24	2000	7.50	2005	6.34	2007	7.09	2009	6.74	2010	...	...	6.74	2010	3.75	2010	ADB	2.99	2010	ILO
Fiji	1.62	1990	2.09	1995	2.36	2000	2.33	2005	3.39	2008	3.60	2009	3.37	2010	...	...	...	...	1.87	2010	ADB	...	...	...
Marshall Islands	20.00	1990	...	...	28.96	2000	22.93	2005	24.37	2008	25.79	2009	24.01	2010	...	...	24.01	2010	14.37	2010	WHO	9.64	2010	ADB
Nauru	5.00	1990	5.00	1995	6.00	2000	12.52	2005	19.33	2007	9.59	2009	9.49	2010	...	...	9.49	2010	8.33	2010	WHO	1.15	2010	ADB
New Zealand	21.45	1990	18.58	1995	19.04	2000	18.06	2005	18.55	2007	21.24	2009	21.40	2011	22.37	2013	21.20	2010	8.39	2010	OECD	12.81	2010	OECD
Palau	...	...	...	...	...	...	...	...	13.95	2008	14.38	2009	15.79	2010	...	...	15.79	2010	8.79	2010	WHO	7.00	2010	ADB
Papua New Guinea	3.28	1990	3.23	1995	3.79	2000	3.46	2005	3.38	2008	3.16	2009	4.60	2011	4.39	2012	4.39	2012	3.27	2012	GSW	1.12	2012	GSW
Solomon Islands	3.80	1990	4.00	1995	4.00	2000	8.07	2005	6.27	2007	8.43	2009	8.25	2010	...	...	8.25	2010	6.95	2010	WHO	1.30	2010	ADB
Tonga	3.18	1990	3.06	1995	6.36	2000	8.11	2005	...	...	...	...	5.18	ADB	...	...	8.11	2005	7.06	2011	ADB	1.05	2011	ADB
Tuvalu	...	...	...	...	...	...	13.36	2005	...	...	...	...	...	...	...	...	13.36	2005	8.68	2005	WHO	4.68	2005	ILO
Vanuatu	...	...	4.28	1995	5.08	2000	4.20	2005	6.01	2007	5.21	2009	5.43	2010	...	...	5.43	2010	4.68	2010	WHO	0.75	2010	ADB
Western Samoa	...	...	3.87	1995	5.03	2000	4.34	2005	4.60	2007	6.09	2009	5.54	2011	4.95	2012	4.95	2012	3.87	2012	ADB	1.07	2012	ADB

Notes

…: Not available.

* Estimates.

Global estimates weigthed by total population 2012 (UN *World Population Prospects*, 2012 Revision).

[a] Data available for both health and social protection (excluding health) expenditure. Year for which both are available may differ from the latest data available when considering total public social protection expenditure.

Sources

ADB (Asian Development Bank): *Key Indicators for Asia and the Pacific 2013: Part III – Regional trends and tables: Government and governance* (Manila, 2014). Available at: http://www.adb.org/publications/key-indicators-asia-and-pacific-2013?ref=publications/series/key-indicators-for-asia-and-the-pacific [6 June 2014]. Consistent with IMF data for last years for which such data are available.

European Commission, Eurostat, *Living conditions and welfare: Social Protection Database* (ESSPROS) (Luxembourg, 2013). Available at: http://epp.eurostat.ec.europa.eu/portal/page/portal/living_conditions_and_social_protection/data/database [6 June 2014]

GSW (Government Spending Watch). Available at: http://www.governmentspendingwatch.org/spending-data [20 May 2014].

ILO (International Labour Office): ILO Social Security Inquiry; Indicator: E-1f: Public social protection expenditure excluding health benefit in kind as a percentage of GDP (Geneva, 2014). Available at: http://www.ilo.org/dyn/ilossi/ssiindic.viewMultiIndic3?p_lang=en&p_indicator_code=E-1f [6 June 2014].

IMF (International Monetary Fund): Government Finance Statistics, March 2014. *Public social protection (excluding health) expenditure in percentage of GDP* (Washington, DC, 2014).

OECD (Organisation for Economic Co-operation and Development). OECD Social and welfare statistics: Social Expenditure Database (SOCX) (Paris, 2013). Available at: http://stats.oecd.org/Index.aspx?datasetcode=SOCX_AGG [6 June 2014].

ECLAC (United Nations Economic Commission for Latin America and the Caribbean): Statistics and indicators, social public expenditure (Santiago de Chile, 2014). Available at: http://www.cepal.org/default.asp?idioma=IN [6 June 2014].

WHO (World Health Organization): National Health Accounts (Global Health Expenditure database). Available at: http://apps.who.int/nha/database [6 June 2014].

Table B.13 Public social protection expenditure by guarantee, latest available year (percentage of GDP)

Major area, region or country	Public social protection expenditure (total)		Public health care expenditure (% of GDP)			Public social protection expenditure for older persons (% of GDP)			Public social protection expenditure for persons of active age (% of GDP)															Public social protection expenditure for children (% of GDP)		
									Social benefits for persons of active age (excluding general social assistance)			Unemployment			Labour market programme			Sickness. maternity. employment injury, disability			General social assistance (% of GDP)					
	Latest available year (a)	Year	Latest available year (a)	Note	Year	Latest available year (a)	Note	Year	Latest available year (a)	Note	Year	Latest available year (a)	Note	Year	Latest available year (a)	Note	Year	Latest available year (a)	Note	Year	Latest available year (a)	Note	Year	Latest available year (a)	Note	Year
Regional average (weighted by total population)																										
Africa	4.3		2.6			1.3			0.4			...			...			...			0.2			0.2		
North Africa	10.0		3.2			5.0			1.1			...			...			...			0.3			0.4		
Sub-saharan Africa	4.3		2.6			1.1			0.3			...			...			...			0.2			0.1		
Asia and the Pacific	4.6		1.5			2.0			0.4			...			...			...			0.4			0.2		
Western Europe	27.1		7.9			11.1			5.0			...			...			...			0.9			2.2		
Central and Eastern Europe	17.8		4.4			8.3			3.0			...			...			...			1.3			0.8		
Latin America and the Caribbean	13.9		4.0			4.6			2.0			...			...			...			2.6			0.7		
North America	17.0		8.5			6.6			2.8			...			...			...			1.1			0.7		
Middle East	11.0		2.0			3.3			1.5			...			...			...			3.4			0.8		
World	8.8		2.8			3.3			1.5			...			...			...			0.7			0.4		
Africa																										
Algeria	9.73	2009	3.62	4	2009	5.14	2	2009	0.32	2	2009	0.02	2	2009	...		...	0.30	2	2009	0.20	2	2009	0.44	2	2009
Angola	6.79	2011	2.15	4	2011	2.50	2	2011	1.64	2	2011	...		...	...		...	1.64	2	2011	0.50	2	2010	0.00	2	2010
Benin	4.20	2010	2.22	4	2010	1.40	1	2010	0.10	1	2010	n.a.	13	2010	...		...	0.10	1	2010	0.10	1	2010	0.38	1	2010
Botswana	7.15	2009	3.99	4	2009	1.31	5	2009	1.26	1	2009	n.a.	13	2009	...		...	1.26	1	2009	...		...	0.59	1	2009
Burkina Faso	5.58	2009	3.60	4	2009	0.90	1	2009	0.19	1	2009	n.a.	13	2009	...		...	0.17	1	2009	0.71	1	2009	0.18	1	2009
Burundi	5.32	2010	3.27	4	2010	0.70	1	2010	0.16	1	2010	n.a.	13	2010	...		...	0.16	1	2010	1.05	1	2010	0.14	1	2010
Cameroon	2.20	2009	1.27	4	2009	0.50	1	2009	0.37	1	2009	n.a.	13	2009	...		...	0.37	1	2009	...		...	0.05	1	2009
Cabo Verde	7.16	2009	2.48	10	2009	2.50	5	2010	1.94	1	2010	n.a.	13	2010	...		...	1.94	1	2010	...		...	0.24	2	2010

Table B.13 Public social protection expenditure by guarantee, latest available year (percentage of GDP)

Major area, region or country	Public social protection expenditure (total)		Public health care expenditure (% of GDP)			Public social protection expenditure for older persons (% of GDP)			Public social protection expenditure for persons of active age (% of GDP)															Public social protection expenditure for children (% of GDP)		
									Social benefits for persons of active age (excluding general social assistance)			Unemployment			Labour market programme			Sickness. maternity. employment injury, disability			General social assistance (% of GDP)					
	Latest available year (a)	Year	Latest available year (a)	Note	Year	Latest available year (a)	Note	Year	Latest available year (a)	Note	Year	Latest available year (a)	Note	Year	Latest available year (a)	Note	Year	Latest available year (a)	Note	Year	Latest available year (a)	Note	Year	Latest available year (a)	Note	Year
Central African Republic	1.36	2010	0.66	10	2010	0.56	1	2010	0.09	1	2010	n.a.	13	2010	...		...	0.09	1	2010	...		...	0.05	1	2010
Chad	1.31	2010	1.01	4	2010	0.21	1	2010	0.06	1	2010	n.a.	13	2010	...		...	0.06	1	2010	...		...	0.03	1	2010
Congo	2.79	2010	1.39	4	2010	1.00	1	2010	0.25	1	2010	0.00	1	2010	...		...	0.25	1	2010	0.05	1	2010	0.10	1	2010
Congo, Democratic Republic of	2.25	2005	1.77	4	2005	0.40	5	2005	0.07	1	2005	n.a.	13	2005	...		...	0.07	1	2005	...		...	0.05	1	2005
Côte d'Ivoire	1.95	2011	0.87	10	2011	0.60	6	2010	0.22	6	2010	n.a.	13	2010	...		...	0.22	1	2010	...		...	0.26	6	2010
Djibouti	7.29	2007	5.34	4	2007	1.50	5	2007	...		...	n.a.	13	2010	...		...	...		...	...		...	...		...
Egypt	12.57	2010	1.44	10	2010	3.00	5	2010	...		...	...		...	...		...	...		...	...		...	...		...
Equatorial Guinea	3.90	2009	3.41	4	2009	0.30	1	2010	0.17	1	2010	n.a.	13	2009	...		...	0.17	1	2009	...		...	0.02	1	2010
Eritrea	1.64	2011	1.25	4	2011	0.30	5	2001	...		...	n.a.	13	2001	...		...	...		...	...		...	...		...
Gambia	2.96	2005	2.46	4	2005	0.10	5	2003	0.20	1	2003	n.a.	13	2003	...		...	0.20	1	2003	0.20	1	2003	0.00	1	2003
Ghana	5.01	2009	2.81	4	2009	1.30	5	2010	0.65	1	2010	n.a.	13	2009	...		...	0.65	1	2009	...		...	0.25	2	2011
Guinea-Bissau	5.44	2010	2.31	4	2010	2.30	1	2010	0.65	1	2010	n.a.	13	2010	...		...	0.65	1	2010	0.10	1	2010	0.08	1	2010
Kenya	2.84	2011	1.53	10	2010	1.14	1	2010	0.05	2	2010	n.a.	13	2010	...		...	0.05	2	2010	0.10	2	2010	0.02	2	2010
Lesotho	6.13	2009	5.98	10	2008	1.77	7	2008	...		...	n.a.	13	2008	...		...	...		...	...		...	...		...
Liberia	11.47	2005	1.60	4	2005	0.14	5	2010	...		...	n.a.	13	2010	...		...	...		...	...		...	...		...
Libya	6.55	2010	2.11	4	2010	2.00	1	2010	...		...	n.a.	13	2010	...		...	...		...	...		...	...		...
Mali	4.88	2010	2.82	4	2010	1.59	5	2010	0.25	1	2009	n.a.	13	2009	...		...	0.25	1	2009	0.10	2	2010	0.13	2	2010
Mauritania	4.47	2009	3.37	4	2009	0.60	5	2007	...		...	n.a.	13	2009	...		...	...		...	...		...	...		...
Mauritius	9.12	2011	2.39	10	2011	5.02	1	2011	0.88	1	2011	0.01	1	2011	...		...	0.87	1	2011	0.50	2	2011	0.33	1	2011
Morocco	6.57	2010	2.07	4	2010	2.90	5	2011	1.50	1	2010	n.a.	13	2010	...		...	1.50	1	2010	0.05	1	2010	0.06	1	2010
Mozambique	5.32	2010	3.29	6	2010	1.84	5	2010	0.12	1	2010	n.a.	13	2010	...		...	0.12	1	2010	0.06	1	2010	...		...
Namibia	7.40	2011	2.80	4	2011	3.20	1	2011	0.30	1	2011	n.a.	13	2011	...		...	0.30	1	2011	0.80	1	2011	0.30	1	2011

Table B.13 Public social protection expenditure by guarantee, latest available year (percentage of GDP)

Major area, region or country	Public social protection expenditure (total)		Public health care expenditure (% of GDP)			Public social protection expenditure for older persons (% of GDP)			Public social protection expenditure for persons of active age (% of GDP)															Public social protection expenditure for children (% of GDP)		
									Social benefits for persons of active age (excluding general social assistance)			Unemployment			Labour market programme			Sickness. maternity. employment injury, disability			General social assistance (% of GDP)					
	Latest available year (a)	Year	Latest available year (a)	Note	Year	Latest available year (a)	Note	Year	Latest available year (a)	Note	Year	Latest available year (a)	Note	Year	Latest available year (a)	Note	Year	Latest available year (a)	Note	Year	Latest available year (a)	Note	Year	Latest available year (a)	Note	Year
Niger	3.29	2009	2.69	4	2009	0.70	5	2006	...		...	...		...	...		...	...		...	...		...	...		...
Nigeria	3.70	2009	2.30	12	2009	0.91	5	2004	0.29	1	2009	n.a.	13	2004	...		...	0.29	1	2004	0.20	1	2009	0.00	13	2004
Rwanda	6.87	2009	5.37	4	2009	0.75	1	2009	0.50	1	2009	n.a.	13	2009	...		...	...		...	0.10	1	2009	0.15	1	2009
Senegal	5.34	2010	3.28	4	2010	1.78	5	2010	0.15	1	2010	n.a.	13	2010	...		...	0.15	1	2010	0.05	1	2010	0.08	1	2010
Seychelles	7.52	2011	3.14	10	2011	3.00	2	2010	1.39	2	2010	n.a.	13	2010	...		...	1.00	2	2010	...		...	0.00	13	2010
Sierra Leone	2.07	2006	1.46	4	2009	0.47	5	2009	0.14	1	2010	n.a.	13	2010	...		...	0.14	1	2010	...		...	...		...
South Africa	9.79	2010	4.74	10	2010	2.18	5	2010	1.63	1	2010	0.17	1	2010	...		...	1.45	1	2010	...		...	1.24	1	2010
Swaziland	7.32	2010	5.54	4	2010	0.60	7	2010	1.18	1	2010	n.a.	13	2010	...		...	1.18	1	2010	0.00	1	2010	0.00	13	2010
Tanzania, United Republic of	6.81	2010	4.48	1	2010	1.89	1	2010	0.03	1	2010	n.a.	13	2010	...		...	0.03	1	2010	0.40	1	2010	0.00	1	2010
Togo	5.49	2009	3.28	4	2009	2.00	1	2009	0.01	1	2009	n.a.	13	2009	...		...	0.01	2	2009	0.00	2	2009	0.20	2	2009
Tunisia	10.40	2011	1.50	10	2011	4.70	1	2010	3.36	1	2010	...		2010	...		...	2.35	1	2010	0.70	1	2010	0.15	1	2010
Uganda	3.46	2011	2.30	10	2011	0.40	5	2011	0.38	1	2010	n.a.	13	2011	...		...	0.38	1	2011	0.30	1	2011	0.08	1	2011
Zambia	5.46	2011	3.66	4	2011	1.40	5	2008	0.35	1	2008	n.a.	13	2008	...		...	0.35	1	2008	0.05	1	2011	0.00	1	2008
Zimbabwe	5.60	2011	4.30	2	2011	0.95	1	2010	0.05	1	2010	n.a.	13	2010	...		...	0.05	2	2010	0.08	2	2011	0.22	2	2010
Asia																										
Afghanistan	3.70	2010	2.50	10	2010	0.50	5	2010	0.18	3	2010	n.a.	3	2010	0.13	3	2010	0.05	3	2010	0.31	3	2010	0.20	3	2010
Armenia	8.46	2011	1.68	3	2011	3.64	3	2011	1.00	3	2011	0.50	3	2011	0.09	3	2011	0.42	3	2011	0.02	3	2011	2.12	3	2011
Azerbaijan	7.88	2010	1.04	10	2010	4.20	3	2010	0.58	3	2010	0.08	3	2010	0.05	3	2010	0.45	3	2010	1.53	3	2010	0.54	3	2010
Bahrain	4.01	2010	2.40	10	2010	1.00	1	2010	0.51	1	2010	0.01	1	2010	0.00	1	2010	0.50	1	2010	0.11	1	2010	0.00	13	2010
Bangladesh	2.69	2011	1.11	3	2011	0.71	3	2011	0.46	3	2011	n.a.	13	2011	0.45	3	2011	0.02	3	2011	0.32	3	2011	0.09	3	2010
Bhutan	4.77	2010	2.97	3	2010	0.68	3	2010	0.03	3	2011	n.a.	13	2010	...		...	0.03	3	2010	0.00	3	2010	1.09	3	2010
Brunei Darussalam	2.95	2009	2.04	14	2009	...		...	...		...	...		...	...		...	...		...	...		...	...		...
Cambodia	1.79	2011	1.26	3	2011	0.15	3	2011	0.10	3	2011	n.a.	13	2011	0.10	3	2011	0.00	3	2011	0.18	3	2011	0.10	3	2011

Table B.13 Public social protection expenditure by guarantee, latest available year (percentage of GDP)

Major area, region or country	Public social protection expenditure (total)		Public health care expenditure (% of GDP)			Public social protection expenditure for older persons (% of GDP)			Public social protection expenditure for persons of active age (% of GDP)															Public social protection expenditure for children (% of GDP)		
									Social benefits for persons of active age (excluding general social assistance)			Unemployment			Labour market programme			Sickness. maternity. employment injury, disability			General social assistance (% of GDP)					
	Latest available year (a)	Year	Latest available year (a)	Note	Year	Latest available year (a)	Note	Year	Latest available year (a)	Note	Year	Latest available year (a)	Note	Year	Latest available year (a)	Note	Year	Latest available year (a)	Note	Year	Latest available year (a)	Note	Year	Latest available year (a)	Note	Year
China	6.83	2010	1.27	10	2010	2.89	3	2009	1.90	3	2009	0.14	1	2009	0.20	3	2009	1.55	3	2009	0.54	3	2009	0.22	3	2009
Georgia	8.01	2011	1.64	10	2011	3.90	3	2011	0.77	3	2011	n.a.	13	2011	0.00	3	2011	0.77	3	2011	1.40	3	2011	0.31	3	2011
Hong Kong (China), Special Administrative Region	4.58	2011	2.34	3	2011	1.60	5	2011	0.60	1	2011	n.a.	13	2010	...		...	0.60	1	2010	0.03	1	2010	0.07	1	2010
India	2.56	2010	1.06	4	2010	0.75	3	2010	0.60	3	2010	...	3	2009	0.50	3	2010	0.10	3	2010	0.10	3	2010	0.06	3	2010
Indonesia	2.63	2010	1.03	4	2010	0.45	3	2010	0.09	3	2010	n.a.	13	2010	0.07	3	2010	0.03	3	2010	0.38	3	2010	0.68	3	2010
Iran, Islamic Republic of	13.41	2009	1.97	10	2009	3.60	1	2009	1.80	1	2009	0.30	1	2009	...		...	1.50	1	2009	5.04	1	2010	1.00	1	2010
Iraq	12.14	2009	7.07	4	2009	3.90	3	2009	...		...	n.a.	13	2009	...		...	...		...	...		...	...		...
Israel	16.02	2011	4.33	8	2011	5.27	8	2011	3.81	8	2011	0.32	8	2011	0.14	8	2011	3.35	8	2011	0.71	8	2011	1.90	8	2011
Japan	22.40	2009	7.15	8	2009	11.83	8	2009	2.26	8	2009	0.71	8	2009	0.43	8	2009	1.13	8	2009	0.37	8	2009	0.79	8	2009
Jordan	12.11	2011	3.31	10	2011	7.51	1	2010	0.67	1	2010	n.a.	13	2010	0.01	1	2010	0.66	1	2010	0.60	1	2010	0.02	1	2010
Kazakhstan	6.38	2011	2.27	10	2011	2.70	5	2011	1.00	1	2011	...		...	...		...	...		...	0.21	1	2011	0.20	1	2011
Korea, Republic of	9.19	2010	4.12	8	2010	2.36	8	2010	1.24	8	2010	0.31	8	2010	0.38	8	2010	0.54	8	2010	0.68	8	2010	0.78	8	2010
Kuwait	11.44	2011	2.23	10	2011	3.50	1	2011	...		...	n.a.	13	2011	...		...	...		...	...		...	...		...
Kyrgyzstan	8.30	2011	3.31	3	2011	1.54	3	2010	3.11	3	2010	0.01	3	2010	0.01	3	2010	3.08	3	2010	0.02	3	2010	0.33	3	2010
Lao People's Democratic Republic	1.74	2005	1.22	4	2010	0.10	3	2010	0.06	3	2010	n.a.	13	2010	...		...	0.06	3	2010	0.34	3	2010	0.02	3	2010
Malaysia	2.99	2012	1.99	3	2012	0.89	3	2012	0.07	3	2012	n.a.	13	2012	0.00	3	2012	0.07	3	2012	0.03	3	2012	0.02	3	2012
Maldives	5.74	2010	3.63	10	2010	1.66	3	2010	0.23	3	2010	n.a.	13	2010	0.01	3	2010	0.22	3	2010	0.21	3	2010	0.02	3	2010
Mongolia	18.61	2011	2.97	3	2011	7.82	3	2011	1.97	3	2011	0.18	3	2011	0.38	3	2011	1.41	3	2011	5.53	3	2011	0.33	3	2011
Myanmar	0.96	2004	0.26	10	2011	0.60	5	2011	0.06	1	2011	n.a.	13	2011	...		...	0.06	1	2011	0.04	1	2011	0.00	2	2011
Nepal	2.33	2011	1.61	10	2011	0.54	3	2011	0.07	3	2011	n.a.	13	2011	0.01	3	2011	0.06	3	2011	0.02	3	2011	0.09	3	2011
Pakistan	1.68	2010	0.38	2	2010	1.01	3	2010	0.03	3	2010	n.a.	13	2010	0.03	3	2010	0.00	3	2010	0.25	3	2010	0.01	3	2010

Table B.13 Public social protection expenditure by guarantee, latest available year (percentage of GDP)

Major area, region or country	Public social protection expenditure (total)		Public health care expenditure (% of GDP)			Public social protection expenditure for older persons (% of GDP)			Public social protection expenditure for persons of active age (% of GDP)															Public social protection expenditure for children (% of GDP)		
									Social benefits for persons of active age (excluding general social assistance)			Unemployment			Labour market programme			Sickness. maternity. employment injury, disability			General social assistance (% of GDP)					
	Latest available year (a)	Year	Latest available year (a)	Note	Year	Latest available year (a)	Note	Year	Latest available year (a)	Note	Year	Latest available year (a)	Note	Year	Latest available year (a)	Note	Year	Latest available year (a)	Note	Year	Latest available year (a)	Note	Year	Latest available year (a)	Note	Year
Philippines	1.55	2012	0.56	3	2012	0.58	3	2012	0.27	3	2012	n.a.	13	2012	0.02	3	2012	0.25	3	2012	0.01	3	2012	0.14	3	2012
Singapore	2.83	2011	1.20	10	2011	0.70	1	2011	0.91	1	2011	n.a.	13	2011	0.02	1	2011	0.89	1	2011	0.01	1	2011	0.01	1	2011
Sri Lanka	3.14	2011	1.26	10	2011	1.68	3	2011	0.04	3	2011	n.a.	13	2011	0.02	3	2011	0.01	3	2011	0.02	3	2011	0.15	3	2011
Syrian Arab Republic	1.99	2009	1.63	4	2009	1.30	5	2004	...		...	...		...	...		...	...		...	...		...	...		...
Taiwan	10.54	2009	3.75	2	2009	4.74	2	2009	1.09	2	2009	0.29	1	2009	0.19	2	2009	0.61	2	2009	0.53	2	2009	0.43	2	2009
Tajikistan	5.31	2011	1.80	3	2011	0.85	3	2011	1.88	3	2010	0.02	3	2010	0.02	3	2010	1.83	3	2010	0.35	3	2011	0.43	3	2011
Thailand	7.24	2011	2.27	10	2011	4.20	3	2011	0.31	3	2011	0.11	3	2011	0.00	3	2011	0.20	3	2011	0.01	3	2011	0.45	3	2011
Timor-Leste	4.24	2010	0.83	3	2010	1.40	3	2010	0.10	3	2010	n.a.	13	2010	0.10	3	2010	0.00	3	2010	1.22	3	2010	0.69	3	2010
Uzbekistan	11.16	2010	2.73	4	2010	5.75	3	2010	0.69	3	2010	...	3	2010	0.00	3	2010	0.69	3	2010	0.10	3	2010	1.88	3	2010
Viet Nam	6.28	2010	2.54	4	2010	3.13	3	2010	0.51	3	2010	0.02	3	2010	0.16	3	2010	0.33	3	2010	0.09	3	2010	0.02	3	2010
Yemen	1.86	2010	1.13	10	2010	0.50	2	2010	0.17	1	2010	n.a.	13	2010	...		...	0.17	2	2010	0.05	2	2010	0.01	2	2010
Europe																										
Albania	10.83	2011	2.68	10	2011	5.20	5	2011	2.67	2	2010	...		...	...		...	...		...	...		...	0.28	2	2010
Austria	29.10	2009	7.32	8	2009	14.00	8	2009	4.58	8	2009	1.10	8	2009	0.85	8	2009	2.63	8	2009	0.44	8	2009	2.76	8	2009
Belarus	16.35	2011	4.55	10	2010	10.00	5	2009	1.06	1	2010	...		...	...		...	1.06	1	2010	0.34	2	2010	0.40	2	2010
Belgium	29.70	2009	8.11	8	2009	10.20	8	2009	7.76	8	2009	3.68	8	2009	1.40	8	2009	2.68	8	2009	1.02	8	2009	2.62	8	2009
Bosnia and Herzegovina	17.45	2011	6.95	4	2011	9.40	5	2009	0.80	1	2010	0.10	1	2010	...		...	0.70	1	2010	0.10	1	2010	0.20	5	2010
Bulgaria	17.20	2011	4.31	9	2011	8.31	9	2010	2.73	9	2010	0.49	9	2010	...		...	2.24	9	2010	0.40	9	2010	1.45	9	2010
Croatia	21.16	2011	6.38	10	2010	10.60	5	2010	3.09	2	2010	0.40	2	2010	...		...	2.69	2	2010	0.14	1	2010	0.96	2	2010
Cyprus	21.31	2010	3.27	9	2010	9.91	9	2010	3.98	9	2010	1.04	9	2010	...		...	2.95	9	2010	2.75	9	2010	2.20	9	2010
Czech Republic	20.71	2009	6.71	8	2009	8.55	8	2009	4.40	8	2009	1.02	8	2009	0.22	8	2009	3.17	8	2009	0.20	8	2009	0.85	8	2009
Denmark	30.19	2009	7.68	8	2009	8.17	8	2009	9.44	8	2009	2.30	8	2009	1.61	8	2009	5.53	8	2009	1.61	8	2009	3.29	8	2009
Estonia	20.04	2009	5.18	8	2009	8.07	8	2009	5.58	8	2009	1.09	8	2009	0.24	8	2009	4.25	8	2009	0.15	8	2009	1.06	8	2009
Finland	29.44	2009	6.79	8	2009	11.13	8	2009	7.77	8	2009	1.98	8	2009	0.92	8	2009	4.88	8	2009	1.21	8	2009	2.54	8	2009

Table B.13 Public social protection expenditure by guarantee, latest available year (percentage of GDP)

Major area, region or country	Public social protection expenditure (total)		Public health care expenditure (% of GDP)			Public social protection expenditure for older persons (% of GDP)			Public social protection expenditure for persons of active age (% of GDP)															Public social protection expenditure for children (% of GDP)		
									Social benefits for persons of active age (excluding general social assistance)			Unemployment			Labour market programme			Sickness. maternity. employment injury, disability			General social assistance (% of GDP)					
	Latest available year (a)	Year	Latest available year (a)	Note	Year	Latest available year (a)	Note	Year	Latest available year (a)	Note	Year	Latest available year (a)	Note	Year	Latest available year (a)	Note	Year	Latest available year (a)	Note	Year	Latest available year (a)	Note	Year	Latest available year (a)	Note	Year
France	32.07	2009	8.99	8	2009	14.11	8	2009	4.80	8	2009	1.53	8	2009	0.99	8	2009	2.29	8	2009	1.29	8	2009	2.89	8	2009
Germany	27.12	2010	8.52	8	2010	11.00	8	2010	4.97	8	2010	1.53	8	2010	0.94	8	2010	2.50	8	2010	0.81	8	2010	1.82	8	2010
Greece	23.88	2009	6.52	8	2009	13.16	8	2009	2.04	8	2009	0.72	8	2009	0.22	8	2009	1.11	8	2009	0.89	8	2009	1.27	8	2009
Hungary	23.93	2009	5.08	8	2009	10.45	8	2009	4.88	8	2009	0.88	8	2009	0.45	8	2009	3.54	8	2009	0.75	8	2009	2.76	8	2009
Iceland	18.47	2009	6.17	8	2009	2.22	8	2009	5.12	8	2009	1.68	8	2009	0.04	8	2009	3.40	8	2009	1.70	8	2009	3.27	8	2009
Ireland	23.72	2010	6.39	8	2010	5.84	8	2010	6.32	8	2010	2.60	8	2010	0.96	8	2010	2.75	8	2010	1.03	8	2010	4.15	8	2010
Italy	27.81	2009	7.42	8	2009	15.56	8	2009	3.38	8	2009	0.79	8	2009	0.44	8	2009	2.15	8	2009	0.07	8	2009	1.38	8	2009
Latvia	17.60	2010	2.95	9	2010	8.39	9	2010	4.49	9	2010	1.70	9	2010	...		...	2.79	9	2010	0.29	9	2010	1.48	9	2010
Lithuania	18.30	2010	4.29	9	2010	7.89	9	2010	3.66	9	2010	0.78	9	2010	...		...	2.88	9	2010	0.33	9	2010	2.13	9	2010
Luxembourg	23.57	2009	6.65	8	2009	7.67	8	2009	4.86	8	2009	1.17	8	2009	0.50	8	2009	3.19	8	2009	0.82	8	2009	3.58	8	2009
Malta	19.57	2008	4.28	9	2010	10.41	9	2010	3.08	9	2010	0.60	9	2010	...		...	2.49	9	2010	0.56	9	2010	1.24	9	2010
Moldova, Republic of	18.61	2011	5.17	10	2011	7.40	5	2012	...		...	...		...	...		...	...		...	...		...	...		...
Montenegro	20.05	2011	6.24	4	2011	11.00	5	2011	1.54	1	2011	...		...	0.25	5	2011	1.29	5	2011	1.12	5	2011	0.15	5	2011
Netherlands	23.18	2009	7.90	8	2009	6.07	8	2009	5.77	8	2009	1.45	8	2009	1.22	8	2009	3.11	8	2009	1.73	8	2009	1.71	8	2009
Norway	23.29	2009	6.17	8	2009	7.41	8	2009	6.26	8	2009	0.43	8	2009	0.47	8	2009	5.36	8	2009	0.89	8	2009	2.56	8	2009
Poland	21.52	2009	5.17	8	2009	11.84	8	2009	3.56	8	2009	0.28	8	2009	0.63	8	2009	2.65	8	2009	0.21	8	2009	0.75	8	2009
Portugal	25.55	2009	7.20	8	2009	12.47	8	2009	4.39	8	2009	1.21	8	2009	0.77	8	2009	2.41	8	2009	0.31	8	2009	1.19	8	2009
Romania	17.39	2010	4.19	9	2010	8.87	9	2010	2.48	9	2010	0.41	9	2010	...		...	2.07	9	2010	0.23	9	2010	1.63	9	2010
Russian Federation	15.97	2011	3.96	10	2011	6.80	5	2011	2.90	1	2010	0.18	1	2010	...		...	2.72	1	2010	1.77	1	2010	0.55	1	2010
Serbia	24.00	2010	6.51	10	2010	12.84	9	2010	3.25	9	2010	0.75	9	2010	...		...	2.50	9	2010	0.40	9	2010	1.00	9	2010
Slovakia	18.74	2009	6.01	8	2009	7.36	8	2009	3.49	8	2009	0.68	8	2009	0.23	8	2009	2.59	8	2009	0.40	8	2009	1.48	8	2009
Slovenia	22.58	2009	6.80	8	2009	10.96	8	2009	3.71	8	2009	0.48	8	2009	0.33	8	2009	2.90	8	2009	0.52	8	2009	0.59	8	2009
Spain	25.98	2009	7.04	8	2009	9.88	8	2009	7.40	8	2009	3.45	8	2009	0.86	8	2009	3.09	8	2009	0.47	8	2009	1.18	8	2009
Sweden	29.82	2009	7.30	8	2009	10.75	8	2009	7.60	8	2009	0.73	8	2009	1.12	8	2009	5.75	8	2009	1.18	8	2009	2.99	8	2009

Table B.13 Public social protection expenditure by guarantee, latest available year (percentage of GDP)

Major area, region or country	Public social protection expenditure (total)		Public health care expenditure (% of GDP)			Public social protection expenditure for older persons (% of GDP)			Public social protection expenditure for persons of active age (% of GDP)															Public social protection expenditure for children (% of GDP)		
									Social benefits for persons of active age (excluding general social assistance)			Unemployment			Labour market programme			Sickness. maternity. employment injury, disability			General social assistance (% of GDP)					
	Latest available year (a)	Year	Latest available year (a)	Note	Year	Latest available year (a)	Note	Year	Latest available year (a)	Note	Year	Latest available year (a)	Note	Year	Latest available year (a)	Note	Year	Latest available year (a)	Note	Year	Latest available year (a)	Note	Year	Latest available year (a)	Note	Year
Switzerland	18.37	2008	6.02	8	2008	6.56	8	2008	3.79	8	2008	0.53	8	2008	0.33	8	2008	2.94	8	2008	0.73	8	2008	1.27	8	2008
The Former Yugoslav Republic of Macedonia	18.08	2009	4.08	4	2010	8.00	5	2010	...		...	...		...	...		...	...		...	...		...	...		...
Turkey	13.11	2011	5.90	8	2011	6.98	8	2011	0.24	8	2011	0.06	8	2011	0.00	8	2011	0.17	8	2011	0.00	8	2011	0.00	8	2011
Ukraine	17.42	2011	3.82	10	2011	7.90	1	2011	2.41	1	2011	0.17	1	2011	...		...	2.25	1	2011	2.74	1	2011	0.54	1	2011
United Kingdom	24.05	2009	8.08	8	2009	6.76	8	2009	4.07	8	2009	0.46	8	2009	0.33	8	2009	3.28	8	2009	1.67	8	2009	3.47	8	2009
Latin America and the Caribbean																										
Antigua and Barbuda	5.82	2009	2.95	4	2006	2.50	1	2006	0.27	1	2006	0.00	1	2006	0.00	0	0	0.27	1	2006	0.00	1	2006	0.10	1	2006
Argentina	21.10	2009	6.21	12	2009	6.79	2	2009	5.12	2	2009	0.05	2	2009	...		...	5.07	2	2009	2.03	12	2009	0.95	2	2009
Aruba	17.80	2009	9.60	2	2009	4.30	1	2009	1.09	1	2009	0.04	1	2009	...		...	1.05	1	2009	1.81	1	2009	1.00	1	2009
Bahamas	6.29	2011	3.50	2	2011	1.93	2	2011	0.86	2	2011	0.11	2	2011	...		...	0.75	2	2011	0.00	2	2011	0.00	1	2011
Barbados	9.85	2009	3.75	4	2009	4.08	1	2009	1.83	1	2009	0.61	1	2009	...		...	1.22	1	2009	0.18	1	2009	0.00	13	2009
Belize	5.85	2011	3.85	4	2010	0.23	1	2010	0.64	1	2010	n.a.	13	2010	...		...	0.64	1	2009	1.13	1	2010	0.00	12	2010
Bolivia (Plurinational State of)	10.41	2008	3.21	12	2008	2.70	2	2009	2.54	2	2009	n.a.	13	2009	...		...	2.54	2	2009	1.46	1	2008	0.50	1	2009
Brazil	21.29	2010	5.79	1	2010	7.76	1	2010	2.60	1	2010	0.67	1	2010	0.26	1	2010	1.66	1	2010	4.54	1	2010	0.60	1	2010
Chile	10.43	2011	3.63	8	2011	3.30	8	2011	1.28	8	2011	0.04	1	2011	0.25	8	2011	0.99	8	2011	1.30	8	2011	0.93	8	2011
Colombia	10.49	2010	1.91	12	2010	3.50	5	2010	3.94	1	2009	n.a.	13	2009	...		...	3.94	1	2009	0.75	12	2010	0.39	12	2009
Costa Rica	15.45	2010	6.57	12	2010	2.76	5	2009	3.42	1	2010	n.a.	13	2010	...		...	3.42	1	2010	2.31	12	2010	0.39	12	2009
Cuba	22.80	2010	9.70	21	2010	...		...	...		...	...		...	...		...	...		...	2.67	1	2010	...		...
Dominica	7.99	2011	4.19	4	2010	3.15	1	2011	0.50	1	2011	n.a.	13	2011	...		...	0.50	1	2011	0.15	1	2011	0.00	1	2011
Dominican Republic	4.82	2010	1.75	12	2010	0.70	5	2010	1.97	1	2010	n.a.	13	2010	...		...	1.97	1	2010	...		...	0.40	12	2010
Ecuador	4.37	2010	2.07	12	2010	1.80	5	2010	0.15	1	2010	n.a.	13	2010	...		...	0.15	1	2010	0.00	12	2010	0.35	12	2009
El Salvador	7.77	2011	3.80	10	2011	1.70	5	2010	1.25	1	2010	n.a.	13	2010	...		...	1.25	1	2010	0.75	12	2009	0.27	12	2010
Grenada	4.95	2009	3.05	4	2009	2.00	5	2006	...		...	n.a.	13	2006	...		...	...		...	...		...	...		...

Table B.13 Public social protection expenditure by guarantee, latest available year (percentage of GDP)

Major area, region or country	Public social protection expenditure (total)		Public health care expenditure (% of GDP)			Public social protection expenditure for older persons (% of GDP)			Public social protection expenditure for persons of active age (% of GDP)															Public social protection expenditure for children (% of GDP)		
									Social benefits for persons of active age (excluding general social assistance)			Unemployment			Labour market programme			Sickness. maternity. employment injury, disability			General social assistance (% of GDP)					
	Latest available year (a)	Year	Latest available year (a)	Note	Year	Latest available year (a)	Note	Year	Latest available year (a)	Note	Year	Latest available year (a)	Note	Year	Latest available year (a)	Note	Year	Latest available year (a)	Note	Year	Latest available year (a)	Note	Year	Latest available year (a)	Note	Year
Guatemala	4.60	2009	1.40	12	2009	1.20	5	2009	1.68	1	2009	n.a.	13	2009	...		...	1.68	1	2009	0.00	12	2009	0.32	12	2009
Guyana	9.72	2009	5.32	4	2009	0.07	5	2010	...		...	n.a.	13	2010	...		...	...		...	...		...	...		...
Haiti	3.27	2013	2.21	27	2013	...		...	...		...	...		...	...		...	...		...	...		...	...		...
Honduras	4.39	2010	3.45	12	2010	0.21	1	2010	0.20	1	2010	n.a.	13	2010	...		...	0.20	1	2009	0.29	12	2010	0.24	12	2010
Jamaica	4.42	2011	2.82	10	2011	0.12	5	2009	0.39	1	2009	n.a.	13	2009	...		...	0.39	1	2009	0.77	1	2009	0.33	12	2011
Mexico	7.72	2011	2.76	8	2011	1.88	8	2011	0.09	1	2011	n.a.	13	2011	0.03	8	2011	0.06	8	2011	1.92	8	2011	1.08	8	2011
Nicaragua	6.95	2009	4.06	12	2009	1.60	2	2009	0.50	2	2009	n.a.	13	2009	...		...	0.50	2	2009	0.68	1	2009	0.11	12	2009
Paraguay	6.35	2010	2.28	12	2010	1.63	5	2010	1.54	1	2010	n.a.	13	2010	...		...	1.54	1	2010	0.70	1	2010	0.20	1	2010
Peru	6.85	2010	1.58	12	2010	2.47	5	2010	0.78	1	2010	n.a.	13	2010	...		...	0.78	1	2010	1.88	12	2010	0.14	12	2009
Saint Kitts and Nevis	5.61	2010	2.60	4	2010	1.30	1	2009	1.52	1	2009	n.a.	13	2009	...		...	1.52	1	2009	0.19	1	2009	0.00	1	2009
Saint Lucia	6.58	2009	4.68	4	2009	1.20	1	2009	0.50	1	2009	n.a.	13	2009	...		...	0.50	1	2009	0.10	1	2009	0.10	1	2009
Saint Vincent and the Grenadines	6.52	2004	3.22	10	2006	1.50	5	2006	1.20	1	2006	n.a.	13	2009	...		...	1.20	1	2006	0.40	1	2006	0.20	1	2006
Trinidad and Tobago	7.02	2008	3.41	12	2008	2.80	1	2008	0.20	1	2008	n.a.	13	2008	...		...	0.20	1	2008	0.51	1	2008	0.10	1	2008
Uruguay	18.17	2009	4.85	12	2010	8.90	1	2010	0.84	1	2010	0.36	1	2010	...		...	0.48	1	2010	3.08	1	2010	0.50	1	2010
Venezuela, Bolivarian Republic of	7.97	2006	1.80	12	2006	4.98	5	2010	...		...	...		...	...		...	...		...	...		...	...		...
North America																										
Canada	18.63	2010	7.97	8	2010	4.40	8	2010	2.30	8	2010	0.81	8	2010	0.30	8	2010	1.19	8	2010	3.18	8	2010	0.78	8	2010
United States	19.92	2010	8.57	8	2010	6.89	8	2010	2.85	8	2010	1.13	8	2010	0.13	8	2010	1.59	8	2010	0.91	8	2010	0.70	8	2010
Oceania																										
Australia	17.90	2010	6.21	8	2010	5.07	8	2010	3.49	8	2010	0.51	8	2010	0.31	8	2010	2.67	8	2010	0.58	8	2010	2.55	8	2010
Fiji	3.37	2010	1.87	3	2010	0.77	3	2010	0.01	3	2010	n.a.	13	2010	0.01	3	2010	0.00	3	2010	0.16	3	2010	0.57	3	2010
Kiribati	10.37	2010	8.72	14	2010	...		...	...		...	...		...	...		...	...		...	...		...	...		...

Table B.13 Public social protection expenditure by guarantee, latest available year (percentage of GDP)

Major area, region or country	Public social protection expenditure (total)		Public health care expenditure (% of GDP)			Public social protection expenditure for older persons (% of GDP)			Public social protection expenditure for persons of active age (% of GDP)															Public social protection expenditure for children (% of GDP)		
									Social benefits for persons of active age (excluding general social assistance)			Unemployment			Labour market programme			Sickness. maternity. employment injury, disability			General social assistance (% of GDP)					
	Latest available year (a)	Year	Latest available year (a)	Note	Year	Latest available year (a)	Note	Year	Latest available year (a)	Note	Year	Latest available year (a)	Note	Year	Latest available year (a)	Note	Year	Latest available year (a)	Note	Year	Latest available year (a)	Note	Year	Latest available year (a)	Note	Year
Marshall Islands	24.01	2010	14.37	4	2010	7.11	3	2010	0.73	3	2010	n.a.	13	2010	0.11	3	2010	0.62	3	2010	0.00	3	2010	1.81	3	2010
Nauru	9.49	2010	8.33	4	2010	0.88	3	2010	0.28	3	2010	n.a.	13	2010	0.00	3	2010	0.28	3	2010	0.00	3	2010	0.00	3	2010
New Zealand	21.20	2010	8.39	8	2010	4.74	8	2010	3.39	8	2010	0.46	1	2010	0.26	8	2010	2.67	8	2010	1.23	8	2010	3.46	8	2010
Palau	15.79	2010	8.79	4	2010	5.07	3	2010	0.25	3	2010	n.a.	13	2010	0.00	3	2010	0.24	3	2010	0.00	3	2010	1.69	3	2010
Papua New Guinea	4.39	2010	3.27	14	2012	0.10	3	2010	0.20	3	2010	n.a.	13	2010	0.00	3	2010	0.00	3	2010	0.72	3	2010	0.10	3	2010
Solomon Islands	8.25	2010	6.95	4	2010	1.25	3	2010	0.05	3	2010	0.03	1	2010	0.02	3	2010	0.00	3	2010	0.00	3	2010	0.00	3	2010
Tonga	8.11	2005	7.06	3	2005	0.90	3	2005	0.05	3	2005	n.a.	13	2005	0.04	3	2005	0.01	3	2005	0.07	3	2005	0.04	3	2005
Tuvalu	13.36	2005	8.68	4	2005	3.31	1	2005	1.37	2	2005	n.a.	13	2005	0.14	1	2005	1.23	1	2005	0.00	1	2005	0.00	1	2005
Vanuatu	5.43	2010	4.68	4	2010	0.22	3	2010	0.16	3	2010	n.a.	13	2010	0.00	3	2010	0.16	3	2010	0.02	3	2010	0.36	3	2010
Western Samoa	5.54	2011	4.34	3	2011	0.65	3	2011	0.12	3	2011	n.a.	13	2011	0.10	3	2011	0.02	3	2011	0.38	3	2011	0.06	3	2011

Notes

...: Not available.

n.a.: Not applicable.

[a] Differences in global estimates from table B.12 result from differences in reference years and in number of countries considered.

Sources

[1] ILO (International Labour Office): ILO Social Security Inquiry. Available at: http://www.ilo.org/dyn/ilossi/ssimain.home [6 June 2014].

[2] National source: Ministry of Finance.

[3] ADB (Asian Development Bank): ADB Social Protection Index database. Available at: http://spi.adb.org/spidmz/index.jsp [6 June 2014].

[4] WHO (World Health Organization): National Health Accounts (Global Health Expenditure database). Available at: http://apps.who.int/nha/database [6 June 2014].

[5] World Bank pensions data. Available at: http://web.worldbank.org/WBSITE/EXTERNAL/TOPICS/EXTSOCIALPROTECTION/EXTPENSIONS/0,,contentMDK:23231994~menuPK:8874064~pagePK:148956~piPK:216618~theSitePK:396253,00.html [20 Apr. 2014].

[6] UNICEF country report.

[7] HelpAge International: HelpAge's social pensions database. Available at: http://www.pension-watch.net/about-social-pensions/about-social-pensions/social-pensions-database/ [6 June 2014].

[8] OECD (Organisation for Economic Co-operation and Development). OECD Social and welfare statistics: Social Expenditure Database (SOCX) (Paris, 2013). Available at: http://stats.oecd.org/Index.aspx?datasetcode=SOCX_AGG [6 June 2014].

[9] European Commission, Eurostat, Living conditions and welfare: Social Protection Database (ESSPROS) (Luxembourg, 2013). Available at: http://epp.eurostat.ec.europa.eu/portal/page/portal/living_conditions_and_social_protection/data/database [6 June 2014]

[10] IMF (International Monetary Fund): Government Finance Statistics, March 2014 (Washington, DC, 2014).

[11] Overseas Development Institute (ODI).

[12] UN ECLAC (United Nations Economic Commission for Latin America and the Caribbean): Statistics and indicators, social public expenditure (Santiago de Chile, 2014). Available at: http://www.cepal.org/default.asp?idioma=IN [6 June 2014].

[13] SSA (Social Security Administration of the United States); ISSA (International Social Security Association). Social security programs throughout the world (Washington, DC and Geneva): The Americas, 2013; Europe, 2012; Asia and the Pacific, 2012; Africa, 2013. Available at: http://www.ssa.gov/policy/docs/progdesc/ssptw/ [6 June 2014].

[14] GSW (Government Spending Watch). Available at: http://www.governmentspendingwatch.org/spending-data [20 May 2014].

Bibliography

Adato, M.; Bassett, L. 2008. "What is the potential of cash transfers to strengthen families affected by HIV and AIDS? A review of the evidence on impacts and key policy debates", Brief 10 in *HIV, livelihoods, food and nutrition security: Findings from renewal research (2007–2008)* (Washington, DC, International Food Policy Research Institute).

ADB (Asian Development Bank). 2010. *Toward universal social security coverage in the People's Republic of China*, Observations and Suggestions Series (Manila). Available at: http://www.adb.org/publications/toward-universal-social-security-coverage-prc [16 Apr. 2014].

ADB. 2013. *The Social Protection Index: Assessing results for Asia and the Pacific* (Manila). Available at: http://www.adb.org/sites/default/files/pub/2013/social-protection-index.pdf [3 May 2014].

ADB. 2014. *Asian Development Outlook: Fiscal policy for inclusive growth* (Manila). Available at: http://www.adb.org/sites/default/files/pub/2014/ado-2014.pdf [16 Apr. 2014].

Adema, W.; Fron, P.; Ladaique, M. 2011. *Is the European welfare state really more expensive? Indicators on social spending, 1980–2012; and a manual to the OECD Social Expenditure database (SOCX)*, OECD Social, Employment and Migration Working Papers, No. 124 (Paris, OECD). Available at: http://www.oecd-ilibrary.org [16 Apr. 2014].

Adema, W.; Fron, P.; Ladaique, M., 2014. "How much do OECD countries spend on social protection and how redistributive are their tax/benefit systems?", in *International Social Security Review*, Vol. 67, No. 1, pp. 1–25.

Ahluwalia, M. Forthcoming. *Cash transfer programmes, poverty reduction and empowerment of women in India* (Geneva, ILO).

Aiyar, S.; Duval, R.; Puy, D.; Wu, Y.; Zhang, L. 2013. *Growth slowdowns and the middle-income trap*, IMF Working Paper WP 13/71 (Washington, DC, IMF, Asia and Pacific Department). Available at: http://www.imf.org/external/pubs/cat/longres.aspx?sk=40411.0 [16 Apr. 2014].

Alber, J.; Heisig, J.P. 2011. *Do new labour activation policies work? A descriptive analysis of the German Hartz reforms* (Berlin, Social Science Research Center Berlin (WZB)). Available at: http://skylla.wz-berlin.de/pdf/2011/i11-211.pdf [16 Apr. 2014].

Alderman, H.; Yemtsov, R. 2012. *Productive role of safety nets*, Social Protection Discussion Paper 1203 (Washington, DC, World Bank).

Aleksynska, M.; Bonnet, F.; Da Silva Gama Nogueira, A.; Saget, C. 2013. *Addressing employment, labour market and social protection challenges in G20 countries: Key measures since 2010*, background report for the ILO–OECD report for the G20 Task Force on Employment (Geneva, ILO).

Alviar García, H. 2013. "Social policy and the new development state: The case of Colombia", in D.M. Trubek et al. (eds): *Law and the new developmental state: The Brazilian experience in Latin American context* (Cambridge, Cambridge University Press).

Amarante, V.; Arim, R.; Dean, A. 2013. "Unemployment insurance design and its effects: Evidence for Uruguay," in *Revista Desarrollo y Sociedad*, Vol. 71, No. 1, pp. 7–42. Available at: http://www.scielo.org.co/pdf/dys/n71/n71a01.pdf [16 Apr. 2014].

Arpaia, A.; Curci, N.; Meyermans, E.; Peschner, J.; Pierini, F. 2010. *Short time working arrangements as response to cyclical fluctuations*, European Economy Occasional Paper 64 (Brussels, European Commission). Available at: http://ec.europa.eu/social/BlobServlet?docId=6475&langId=en [16 Apr. 2014].

Asante, A.; Martins, N.; Otim, M.; Dewdney, J. 2014. "Retaining doctors in rural Timor-Leste: A critical appraisal of the opportunities and challenges", in *Bulletin of the World Health Organization*, Vol. 92, pp. 277–282.

Aslam, A.; Berkes, E.; Fukač, M. 2013. *Afghanistan: Balancing social and security spending in the context of shrinking resource envelope*, Working Paper No. 13/133 (Washington, DC, IMF).

Attanasio, O.P.; Battistin, E.; Fitzsimons, E.; Mesnard, A.; Vera-Hernández, M. 2005. *How effective are conditional cash transfers? Evidence from Colombia*, Briefing Note No. 54 (London, Institute for Fiscal Studies). Available at: http://www.ifs.org.uk/bns/bn54.pdf [16 Apr. 2014].

Avram, S.; Figari, F.; Leventi, C.; Levy, H.; Navicke, J.; Mataganis, M.; Militaru, E.; Paulus, A.; Rastringina, O.; Sutherland, H. 2013. *The distributional effects of fiscal consolidation in nine countries*, EUROMOD Working Paper (Colchester, Institute for Social and Economic Research, University of Essex). Available at: https://www.iser.essex.ac.uk [16 Apr. 2014].

Babajanian, B.; Hagen-Zanker, J. 2012. *Social protection and social exclusion: An analytical framework to assess the links,* Background Note (London, Overseas Development Institute). Available at: http://www.odi.org.uk/publications/6889-social-protection-social-exclusion-design-analytical-framework [16 Apr. 2014].

Baird, S.; Ferreira, F.H.G.; Özler, B.; Woolcock, M. 2013. *Relative effectiveness of conditional and unconditional cash transfers for schooling outcomes in developing countries: A systematic review* (Oslo, The Campbell Collaboration). Available at: http://www.campbellcollaboration.org/lib/download/2954/> [16 Apr. 2014].

Ball, L.; Leigh, D.; Loungani, P. 2011. "Painful Medicine", in *Finance and Development*, Vol. 48, No. 3, pp. 20–23 (Washington, DC, IMF).

Barham, T. 2010. "A healthier start: The effect of conditional cash transfers on neo-natal and infant mortality", in *Journal of Development Economics*, Vol. 94, No. 1, pp. 74–85.

Barrientos, A. 2007. *Does vulnerability create poverty traps?*, Chronic Poverty Research Centre Working Paper 76 (Brighton, Institute of Development Studies). Available at: http://www.chronicpoverty.org/uploads/publication_files/WP76_Barrientos.pdf [16 Apr. 2014].

Barrientos, A. 2013. *Social assistance in developing countries* (Cambridge, Cambridge University Press).

Barrientos, A.; Byrne, J.; Villa, J.M.; Peña, P. 2013. *Social transfers and child protection*, Office of Research Working Paper (New York, UNICEF). Available at: http://www.unicef-irc.org/publications/691 [16 Apr. 2014].

Barrientos, A; Niño-Zarazúa, M.; Maitrot, M. 2010. *Social Assistance in Developing Countries database (version 5.0)* (Manchester and London, Brooks World Poverty Institute and Overseas Development Institute). Available at: http://www.chronicpoverty.org/publications/details/social-assistance-in-developing-countries-database [16 Apr. 2014].

Basso, G.; Dolls, M.; Eichhorst, W.; Leoni, T.; Peichl, A. 2012. "The effects of the recent economic crisis on social protection and labour market arrangements across socio-economic groups", in *Intereconomics*, Vol. 47, No. 4, pp. 217–223.

Behrendt, C. 2013. "Investing in people: Implementing the extension of social security through national social protection floors", in D. Kucera and I. Islam (eds): *Beyond macroeconomic stability: Structural transformation and inclusive development* (Basingstoke, Palgrave Macmillan), pp. 228–259.

Behrendt, C.; Bonnet, F.; Cichon, M.; Hagemejer, K. 2011. "Social security: Three lessons from the global crisis", in IILS (ed.): *The global crisis: Causes, responses and challenges* (Geneva, ILO), pp. 167–180. Available at: http://www.ilo.org/wcmsp5/groups/public/@dgreports/@dcomm/@publ/documents/publication/wcms_155824.pdf [8 May 2014].

Behrendt, C.; Cichon, M.; Hagemejer, K.; Kidd, S.; Krech, R.; Townsend, P. 2009. "Rethinking the role of social security in development", in P. Townsend (ed.): *Building decent societies: Rethinking the role of social security in state building* (Basingstoke, Palgrave Macmillan), pp. 325–336.

Behrendt, C.; Woodall, J. Forthcoming. "Pensions and other social security income transfer systems", in J. Berg (ed.): *Labour market institutions and inequality: Building just societies in the 21st century* (Cheltenham, Edward Elgar).

Berg, A.G.; Ostry, J.D. 2011. *Inequality and unsustainable growth: Two sides of the same coin?*, IMF Staff Discussion Note (Washington, DC, IMF). Available at: https://www.imf.org/external/pubs/cat/longres.aspx?sk=24686.0 [16 Apr. 2014].

Berg, J.; Salerno, M. 2008. "The origins of unemployment insurance: Lessons for developing countries", in J. Berg and D. Kucera (eds): *In defence of labour market institutions: Cultivating justice in the developing world* (Basingstoke, Palgrave Macmillan), pp. 80–99.

Berg, J.; Tobin, S. 2011. "Income-led growth as a crisis response: Lessons from Brazil", in IILS (ed.): *The global crisis: Causes, responses and challenges* (Geneva, ILO), pp. 181–192. Available at: http://www.ilo.org/wcmsp5/groups/public/---dgreports/---dcomm/---publ/documents/publication/wcms_155824.pdf [16 Apr. 2014].

Bertranou, F.; Cetrángolo, O.; Grushka, C.; Casanova, L. 2012. *Beyond the privatization and re-nationalisation of the Argentine pension system: Coverage, fragmentation, and sustainability*, Social Science Research Network Working Paper, Nov. Available at: http://ssrn.com/abstract=2191202 [16 Apr. 2014].

Bertranou, F.; Maurizio, R. 2012a. "Semi-conditional cash transfers in the form of family allowances for children and adolescents in the informal economy in Argentina," in *International Social Security Review*, Vol. 65, No. 1, pp. 53–72.

Bertranou, F.; Maurizio, R. 2012b. *Monetary transfers for children and adolescents in Argentina: Characteristics and coverage of a "system" with three components*, IPC Research Brief No. 30 (Brasilia, International Policy Centre for Inclusive Growth). Available at: http://www.ipc-undp.org/pub/IPCPolicyResearchBrief30.pdf [16 Apr. 2014].

Birdsall, N. 2010. *The (indispensable) middle class in developing countries; or, The rich and the rest, not the poor and the rest*, Working Paper No. 207 (Washington, DC, IMF).

Blanchard, O. 2008. "IMF spells out need for global fiscal stimulus", in *IMF Survey Magazine*, 29 Dec.

Blanchard, O.; Jaumotte, F.; Loungani, P. 2013. *Labor market policies and IMF advice in advanced economies during the great recession*, IMF Staff Discussion Note SDN 13/02 (Washington, DC, IMF).

Blanchard, O.; Leigh, D. 2013. *Growth forecast errors and fiscal multipliers*, IMF Working Paper No. 13/1 (Washington, DC, IMF).

Bonnet, F.; Saget, C.; Weber, A. 2012. *Social protection and minimum wages responses to the 2008 financial and economic crisis: Findings from the ILO/World Bank Inventory*, Employment Working Paper No. 113 (Geneva, ILO). Available at: http://www.ilo.org/wcmsp5/groups/public/---ed_emp/---emp_elm/documents/publication/wcms_175204.pdf [16 Apr. 2014].

Bonnet, F.; Tessier, L. 2013. *Mapping existing international social protection statistics and indicators that would contribute to the monitoring of social protection extension through social protection floors*, Extension of Social Security ESS Paper No. 38 (Geneva, ILO).

Bontout, O.; Lokajickov, T. 2013. *Social protection budgets in the crisis in the EU*, Working Paper No. 1/2013 (Brussels, European Commission). Available at: http://ec.europa.eu/social/BlobServlet?docId=10224&langId=en [16 Apr. 2014].

Busch, K.; Hermann, C.; Hinrichs, K.; Schulten, K. 2013. *Euro crisis, austerity policy and the European social model: How crisis policies in southern Europe threaten the EU's social dimension* (Berlin, Friedrich Ebert Foundation). Available at: http://library.fes.de/pdf-files/id/ipa/09656.pdf [16 Apr. 2014].

CAGED/IPEADATA. Available at: http://www.ipeadata.gov.br/ [16 Apr. 2014].

Calvo, E.; Bertranou, F.; Bertranou, E. 2010. "Are old-age pension system reforms moving away from individual retirement accounts in Latin America?", in *Journal of Social Policy*, Vol. 39, No. 2, pp. 223–234.

Carter, J.; Bédard, M.; Peyron Bista, C. 2013. *Comparative review of unemployment and employment insurance experiences in Asia and worldwide* (Bangkok, ILO). Available at: http://www.ilo.org/asia/whatwedo/publications/WCMS_229985/lang--en/index.htm [16 Apr. 2014].

Case, A. 2001. *Does money protect health status? Evidence from South African pensions*, NBER Working Paper No. 8495 (Cambridge, MA, National Bureau of Economic Research).

Casey, B.H. 2012. "The implications of the economic crisis for pensions and pension policy in Europe", in *Global Social Policy*, Vol. 12, No. 3, pp. 246–265. Available at: http://gsp.sagepub.com/content/12/3/246.abstract [16 Apr. 2014].

Casey, B.H. 2014. "From pension funds to piggy banks: (Perverse) consequences of the Stability and Growth Pact since the crisis", in *International Social Security Review*, Vol. 67, No. 1, pp. 27–48.

CBPP (Center on Budget and Policy Priorities). 2014. "Today's safety net cuts poverty nearly in half, provides health care to millions, and has long-term benefits for children", in *Chart book: The war on poverty at 50* (Washington, DC).

Cecchini, S.; Madariaga, A. 2011. *Programas de transferencias condicionadas: Balance de la experiencia reciente en América Latina y el Caribe* (Santiago de Chile, United Nations Economic Commission for Latin America and the Caribbean). Available at: http://www.eclac.cl/cgi-bin/getProd.asp?xml=/publicaciones/xml/6/44126/P44126.xml&xsl=/dds/tpl/p9f.xsl [16 Apr. 2014].

CESR (Center for Economic and Social Rights). 2012. *Fiscal fallacies: Eight myths about the age of austerity and human rights responses* (New York).

Chang, H.-J. 2010. "How to 'do' a developmental state: Political, organizational, and human resource requirements for the developmental state", in O. Edigheji (ed.): *Constructing a democratic developmental state in South Africa: Potentials and challenges* (Cape Town, HSRC Press). Available at: http://hajoonchang.net/2010/01/05/constructing-a-democratic-developmental-state-in-south-africa-potentials-and-challenges/ [16 Apr. 2014].

Chile Superintendencia de Pensiones. 2010. *Unemployment insurance in Chile*. Available at: http://www.safp.cl/portal/informes/581/articles-8556_recurso_1.pdf [16 Apr. 2014].

Chronic Poverty Advisory Network. 2014. *The Chronic Poverty Report 2014–2015: The road to zero extreme poverty* (London, Overseas Development Institute). Available at: http://www.odi.org.uk/sites/odi.org.uk/files/odi-assets/publications-opinion-files/8834.pdf [8 May 2014].

Cichon, M. 2013. "The Social Protection Floors Recommendation, 2012 (No. 202): Can a six-page document change the course of social history?", in *International Social Security Review*, Vol. 66, Nos 3–4, pp. 21–43.

Cichon, M.; Hagemejer, K. 2007. "Changing the development policy paradigm: Investing in a social security floor for all", in *International Social Security Review*, Vol. 60, Nos 2–3, pp. 169–196.

Cichon, M.; Hagemejer, K.; Woodall, J. 2006. *Changing the paradigm in social security: From fiscal burden to investing in people* (Geneva, ILO).

Clasen, J.; Clegg, D. 2011. "Unemployment protection and labour market change in Europe: towards 'triple integration'?", in J. Clasen and D. Clegg (eds): *Regulating the risk of unemployment: national adaptations to post-industrial labour markets in Europe* (Oxford, Oxford University Press), pp. 1–12.

Clasen, J.; Goerne, A. 2011. "Exit Bismarck, enter dualism? Assessing contemporary German labour market policy," in *Journal of Social Policy*, Vol. 40, No. 4, pp. 795–810.

Clements, B.; Coady, D.; Eich, F.; Gupta, S.; Kangur, A.; Shang, B.; Soto, M. 2012. *The challenge of public pension reform in advanced and emerging market economies*, IMF Occasional Paper (Washington, DC, IMF).

Coady, D.; Gillingham, R.; Ossowski, R.; Pietrowski, J.; Tareq, S.; Tyson, J. 2010. *Petroleum product subsidies: Costly, inequitable, and rising*, IMF Staff Discussion Note No. SPN/10/05 (Washington, DC, IMF). Available at: http://www.imf.org/external/pubs/ft/spn/2010/spn1005.pdf [8 May 2014].

Cooke, E.F.A.; Hague, S.; Cockburn, J.; El Lahga, A.-R.; Tiberti, L. 2014. *Estimating the impact on poverty of Ghana's fuel subsidy reform and a mitigating response* (Accra, UNICEF and Partnership for Economic Policy). Available at: http://www.unicef.org/ghana/1389903137_PEP_UNICEF_Ghana_WP_201_public.pdf [3 May 2014].

Cornia, G.A.; Stewart, F.; Jolly, R. 1987. *Adjustment with a human face: Protecting the vulnerable and promoting growth* (Oxford, Clarendon).

Cunha, N.; Pellerano, L.; Mueller, J.; Lledo, V.; Xiao, Y.; Gitton, P. 2013. *Towards a Mozambican social protection floor. Consolidating a comprehensive social protection system in Mozambique: Analysis of policy alternatives and costs*, Extension of Social Security ESS Paper No. 41 (Geneva, ILO).

de Brauw, A.; Hoddinott, J. 2008. *Is the conditionality necessary in conditional cash transfer programmes? Evidence from Mexico*, International Poverty Centre One Pager (Brasilia, International Poverty Centre).

De Schutter, O.; Sepúlveda, M. 2012. *Underwriting the poor:* A *global fund for social protection* (New York, United Nations).

Dercon, S. 2003. *Risk and poverty:* A *selective review (or: can social protection reduce poverty?)* (Oxford, Oxford University Department of Economics).

DfID (UK Department for International Development); HelpAge International; Hope & Homes for Children; Institute of Development Studies; ILO; Overseas Development Institute; Save the Children UK; United Nations Development Programme; United Nations Children's Fund; World Bank. 2009. *Joint statement on advancing child-sensitive social protection*. Available at: http://www.unicef.org/aids/files/CSSP_joint_statement_10.16.09.pdf [16 Apr. 2014].

Dornan, P.; Porter, C. 2013. "The implications of conditionality in social assistance programmes", in Rebecca Surender and Robert Walker (eds): *Social policy in a developing world* (Cheltenham, Edward Elgar), pp. 155–171.

DSD (Department of Social Development, South Africa); SASSA (South African Social Security Agency); UNICEF South Africa. 2012. *The South African Child Support Grant impact assessment: Evidence from a survey of children, adolescents and their households* (Pretoria). Available at: http://www.unicef.org/southafrica/SAF_resources_csg2012s.pdf [16 Apr. 2014].

Duflo, E. 2000. *Grandmothers and granddaughters: Old age pension and intra-household allocation in South Africa*, NBER Working Paper No. 8061 (Washington, DC, National Bureau of Economic Research). Available at: http://www.nber.org/papers/w8061.pdf [16 Apr. 2014].

Durán-Valverde, F.; Pacheco, J.F. 2012. *Fiscal space and the extension of social protection: Lessons learnt from developing countries*. Extension of Social Security ESS Paper No. 33 (Geneva, ILO). Available at: http://www.ilo.org/gimi/gess/RessFileDownload.do?ressourceId=34168 [16 Apr. 2014].

Economic Policy Research Institute. 2004. *The social and economic impact of South Africa's social security system* (Cape Town, South Africa Department of Social Development).

Ehmke, E. Forthcoming. *Study on national experiences in building social protection floors: The Indian MGNREGS* (Geneva, ILO).

Eichhorst, W.; Kaufmann, O.; Konle-Seidl, R. 2008. *Bringing the jobless into work? Experiences with activation schemes in Europe and the US* (Berlin, Springer).

EIU (Economist Intelligence Unit). 2014. *Out of office: An overview of workplace absenteeism in Europe* (London).

Epstein, G. 2009. *Rethinking monetary and financial policy: Practical suggestions for monitoring financial stability while generating employment and poverty reduction*, Employment Working Paper No. 37 (Geneva, ILO).

EsSalud; ILO. 2013. *El sisteme de salud del Perú: Situación actual y estrategias para orientar la extensión de la cobertura contributiva* (Lima).

EU Commissioner for Human Rights. 2013. *Safeguarding human rights in times of economic crisis* (Strasbourg, Council of Europe).
EU Social Protection Committee. 2009: *Updates of current and prospective theoretical pension replacement rates 2006–2046*, Report by the Indicator Sub-Group (ISG) of the Social Protection Committee (SPC) (Brussels, European Commission). Available at: http://ec.europa.eu/social/BlobServlet?docId=4307&langId=en, http://ec.europa.eu/social/BlobServlet?docId=4308&langId=en [16 Apr. 2014].
EU Social Protection Committee. 2013: *Social policy reforms for growth and cohesion: Review of recent structural reforms 2013*, Report of the Social Protection Committee (Brussels: European Commission). Available at: http://ec.europa.eu/social/BlobServlet?docId=10976&langId=en [16 Apr. 2014].
Eurofound (European Foundation for the Improvement of Living and Working Conditions). 2013. *Social partners' involvement in pension reform in the EU* (Dublin). Available at: http://www.eurofound.europa.eu/docs/eiro/tn1304032s/tn1304032s.pdf [16 Apr. 2014].
European Commission. 2008. *ESSPROS manual* (Luxembourg, Office for Official Publications of the European Commission).
European Commission. 2011a. *Promoting social protection in EU development cooperation: Public consultation*, Issues Paper No. D.3/NT/AMD (2011) (Brussels). Available at: http://ec.europa.eu/europeaid/news/promoting-social-protection_public-consultation_en.htm [16 Apr. 2014].

European Commission. 2012a. *Social protection in European Union development cooperation: Communication from the Commission to the European Parliament, the Council, the European Economic and Social Committee and the Committee of the Regions*, COM(2012) 446 final (Brussels).
European Commission. 2012b. *European Employment Observatory review: Long-term unemployment 2012* (Luxembourg, Publications Office of the European Union). Available at: http://www.eu-employment-observatory.net [2 Apr. 2014].
European Commission. 2012c. *The 2012 ageing report: Economic and budgetary projections for the 27 EU Member States (2010–2060)* (Brussels). Available at: http://ec.europa.eu/economy_finance/publications/european_economy/2012/2012-ageing-report_en.htm [16 Apr. 2014].
European Commission. 2012d. *Pension adequacy in the European Union 2010–2050* (Brussels). Available at: http://ec.europa.eu/social/BlobServlet?docId=7805&langId=en [16 Apr. 2014].
European Commission. 2013. *Mutual Information System on Social Protection Systems (MISSOC)* (Brussels). Available at: http://ec.europa.eu/social/main.jsp?catId=815&langId=en [2 Apr. 2014].
European Commission. 2014a. *Policy roadmap for the 2014 implementation of the Social Investment Package* (Feb. 2014) (Brussels). Available at: http://ec.europa.eu/social/BlobServlet?docId=11150&langId=en [16 Apr. 2014].
European Commission. 2014b. *Employment and social developments in Europe 2013* (Brussels). Available at: http://ec.europa.eu/social/main.jsp?catId=88&langId=en&eventsId=972&furtherEvents=yes [2 Apr. 2014].
European Parliament. 2014a. "Inquiry: how Parliament evaluated the impact of Troika measures", in *European Parliament News*, 13 Jan. (Strasbourg). Available at: http://www.europarl.europa.eu/news/en/news-room/content/20140110STO32308/html/Inquiry-how-Parliament-evaluated-the-impact-of-Troika-measures [16 Apr. 2014].
European Parliament. 2014b. "Parliamentarians call for more legitimacy in economic policy-making in the EU", in *European Parliament News*, 23 Jan. (Strasbourg). Available at: http://www.europarl.europa.eu/news/en/news-room/content/20140122STO33435/html/Parliamentarians-call-for-more-legitimacy-in-economic-policy-making-in-the-EU [16 Apr. 2014].
Eurostat. 2013. "In 2012, a quarter of the population was at risk of poverty or social exclusion: Corresponding to around 125 million persons", News Release 184/2013 (Luxembourg). Available at: http://epp.eurostat.ec.europa.eu/cache/ITY_PUBLIC/3-05122013-AP/EN/3-05122013-AP-EN.PDF [16 Apr. 2014].

Evans, T.G.; Chowdhury, A.M.R.; Evans, D.B.; Fidler, A.; Lindelow, M.; Mills, A.; Scheil-Adlung, X. 2012. *Thailand's universal coverage scheme: Achievements and challenges – An independent assessment of the first 10 years (2001–2010), Synthesis report* (Bangkok, Health Systems Research Institute). Available at: http://uhcforward.org/sites/uhcforward.org/files/book018.pdf [16 Apr. 2014].

Eyal, K.; Woolard, I. 2013. *School enrolment and the Child Support Grant: Evidence from South Africa*, National Income Dynamics Study, Working Paper Series (Cape Town, Southern Africa Labour and Development Research Unit). Available at: http://opensaldru.uct.ac.za/handle/11090/689 [16 Apr. 2014].

FAO (Food and Agriculture Organization). 2004. *Globalization of food systems in developing countries: Impact on food security and nutrition*, FAO Food and Nutrition Paper No. 83 (Rome). Available at: http://www.fao.org/docrep/007/y5736e/y5736e00.HTM [16 Apr. 2014].

FAO. 2012. *The state of food insecurity in the world 2012: Economic growth is necessary but not sufficient to accelerate reduction of hunger and malnutrition* (Rome). Available at: http://www.fao.org/publications/sofi/2012/en/ [16 Apr. 2014].

FAO. 2014. *From protection to production: The role of cash transfer programmes in fostering broad-based economic development in sub-Saharan Africa* (Rome). Available at: http://www.fao.org/fileadmin/user_upload/p2p/Documents/PtoP_short_description_11feb14.pdf [16 Apr. 2014].

Figari, F.; Matsaganis, M.; Sutherland, H. 2013. "Are European social safety nets tight enough? Coverage and adequacy of minimum income schemes in 14 EU countries", in *International Journal of Social Welfare*, Vol. 22, No. 1, pp. 3–14.

Fiszbein, A.; Schady, N. 2009. *Conditional cash transfers: Reducing present and future poverty* (Washington, DC, World Bank). Available at: https://openknowledge.worldbank.org/handle/10986/2597 [16 Apr. 2014].

Fultz, E.; Francis, J. 2013. *Cash transfer programmes, poverty reduction and empowerment of women:* A *comparative analysis. Experiences from Brazil, Chile, India, Mexico and South Africa* (Geneva, ILO). Available at: http://www.ilo.org/wcmsp5/groups/public/---dgreports/---gender/documents/publication/wcms_233599.pdf [16 Apr. 2014].

G20. 2009. Leaders' statement, G20 Pittsburgh Summit, Pittsburgh, United States, 24–25 Sep. Available at: http://www.g20.utoronto.ca/2009/2009communique0925.html [16 Apr. 2014].

G20. 2011. Final declaration, G20 Summit, Cannes, France, 3–4 Nov. Available at: http://www.g20.utoronto.ca/2011/2011-cannes-declaration-111104-en.html [16 Apr. 2014].

G20. 2012. Leaders' declaration, G20 Summit, Los Cabos (Mexico), 18–19 June. Available at: http://www.g20.utoronto.ca/2012/2012-0619-loscabos.html [16 Apr. 2014].

García, M.; Moore, C.M.T. 2012. *The cash dividend: The rise of cash transfer programs in sub-Saharan Africa* (Washington, DC, World Bank). Available at: https://openknowledge.worldbank.org/handle/10986/2246 [16 Apr. 2014].

Gauthier, A.H. 2010. *The impact of the economic crisis on family policies in the European Union* (Brussels, European Commission). Available at: http://europa.eu/epic/docs/final-revised.pdf [16 Apr. 2014].

Ghellab, Y.; Varela, N.; Woodall, J. 2011. "Social dialogue and social security governance: A topical ILO perspective", in *International Social Security Review*, Vol. 64, No. 4, pp. 39–56.

GIZ (Deutsche Gesellschaft für internationale Zusammenarbeit). 2012. *Social protection and its contribution to social cohesion and state building* (Eschborn). Available at: http://www.odi.org.uk/publications/6720-social-protection-social-cohesion-state-building [16 Apr. 2014].

GIZ; ILO; P4H. 2012. *Actuarial review of the NSSF employment injury branch and assessment of social health insurance for the National Social Security Fund (NSSF) and The National Social Security Fund for Civil Servants (NSSFC)* (Phnom Penh). Available at: http://www.social-protection.org/gimi/gess/ShowRessource.action?ressource.ressourceId=30954 [16 Apr. 2014].

Global Health Workforce Alliance; WHO. 2014. A *universal truth: No health without a workforce* (Geneva). Available at: http://www.who.int/workforcealliance/knowledge/resources/hrhreport2013/en/ [16 Apr. 2014].

Grammenos, S. 2013. *European comparative data on Europe 2020 and housing conditions* (Leeds, Academic Network of European Disability Experts). Available at: http://www.humanconsultancy.com/news?newsid=4 [16 Apr. 2014].

Guajardo, J.; Leigh, D.; Pescatori, A. 2011. *Expansionary austerity: New international evidence*, IMF Working Paper No. 11/158 (Washington, DC, IMF).

Guardiancich, I. (ed.) 2012. *Recovering from the crisis through social dialogue in the new EU Member States: The case of Bulgaria, the Czech Republic, Poland and Slovenia* (Geneva, ILO). Available at: http://www.ilo.org/wcmsp5/groups/public/---europe/---ro-geneva/---sro-budapest/documents/publication/wcms_203443.pdf [8 May 2014].

Hagemejer, K. 2005. "Sustainable, safe and adequate pensions in the ageing society: Policy dilemmas", in *Polityka Społeczna*, Vol. 1, No. 1, pp. 11–17. Available at: http://www.social-protection.org/gimi/gess/RessourceDownload.action?ressource.ressourceId=32290 [16 Apr. 2014].

Hagemejer, K.; McKinnon, R. 2013. "The role of national social protection floors in extending social security to all", in *International Social Security Review*, Vol. 66, No. 3–4, pp. 3–19.

Hagemejer, K.; Scholz, W. 2004. "Nachhaltig, sicher und angemessen? Die Reformstrategie der Weltbank und die Rentenreformen in Polen, Ungarn, Tschechien und anderen osteuroäischen Ländern", in *Deutsche Rentenversicherung*, Nos 11–12, pp. 778–789.

Hagen-Zanker, J.; Morgan, J. 2011. *South Africa's cash social security grants: Progress in increasing coverage*, Development Progress project (London, Overseas Development Institute).

Hall, D. 2010. *Why we need public spending* (London, University of Greenwich). Available at: http://www.psiru.org/reports/why-we-need-public-spending [16 Apr. 2014].

Handa, S.; Park, M.J.; Darko, R.O.; Osei-Akoto, I.; Davis, B.; Diadone, S. 2013. *Livelihood empowerment against poverty impact evaluation* (Carolina Population Center, University of North Carolina).

Hauben, H.; Coucheir, M.; Spooren, J.; McAnaney, D.; Delfosse, C. 2012. *Assessing the impact of European governments' austerity plans on the rights of people with disabilities* (Brussels, European Foundation Centre). Available at: http://www.efc.be/programmes_services/resources/Documents/Austerity%20European%20Report_FINAL.pdf [16 Apr. 2014].

HelpAge International. 2013. *Global AgeWatch Index 2013: Insight report* (London). Available at: http://www.helpage.org/global-agewatch/ [16 Apr. 2014].

HelpAge International. 2014. *Home care for older people: The experience of ASEAN countries* (London). Available at: http://www.eldis.org/go/home&id=66957&type=Document#.Uz8FHq15PSk [16 Apr. 2014].

Hermann, C. 2013. *Crisis, Structural Reform and the Dismantling of the European Social Model(s)*, Working Paper 20/2013 (Berlin, Institute for International Political Economy). Available at: http://www.ipe-berlin.org/fileadmin/downloads/working_paper/ipe_working_paper_26.pdf [15 Apr. 2014].

Hermeto Camilo de Oliveira, A.M.; Caetano, A. Forthcoming. *Cash transfer programmes, poverty reduction and empowerment of women in Brazil* (Geneva, ILO).

Hernandez-Pena, P.; Poulier, J.P. et al. 2013. "Health worker remuneration in WHO member States", in *World Health Organization Bulletin*, Vol. 91, No. 11, pp. 808–815.

Hickey, S. 2010. *The politics of social protection in Africa: What do we get from a "social contract" approach?*, Background Paper to the European Report on Development (Florence, Robert Schumann Centre for Advanced Studies). Available at: http://erd.eui.eu/media/BackgroundPapers/Hickey.pdf [16 Apr. 2014].

Hirose, K. (ed.). 2011. *Pension reform in Central and Eastern Europe in times of crisis, austerity and beyond* (Budapest, ILO Regional Office for Central and Eastern Europe).

Holmes, R.; Jones, N. 2013. *Gender and social protection in the developing world: Beyond mothers and safety nets* (London and New York, Zed Books).

Holzmann, R.; Pouget, Y.; Vodopivec, M.; Weber, M. 2011. *Severance pay programs around the world: History, rationale, status, and reforms*, SP Discussion Paper No. 1111 (Washington, DC, World Bank). Available at: http://go.worldbank.org/ZDUAM7JPI0 [16 Apr. 2014].

Hujo, K. (ed.). 2012. *Mineral rents and the financing of social policy: Opportunities and challenges* (Baasingstoke, UN Research Institute for Social Development and Palgrave Macmillan).

Hujo, K.; McClanahan, S. (eds). 2009. *Financing social policy: Mobilizing resources for social development* (Basingstoke, UN Research Institute for Social Development and Palgrave Macmillan).

IBGE (Instituto Brasileiro de Geografia e Estatística). 2012. *Síntese de indicadores sociais: Uma análise das condições de vida da população brasileira 2012* (Rio de Janeiro).

IILS (International Institute for Labour Studies). 2011a. *Making recovery sustainable: Lessons from country innovations* (Geneva). Available at: http://www.ilo.org/wcmsp5/groups/public/---dgreports/---dcomm/---publ/documents/publication/wcms_153764.pdf [16 Apr. 2014].

IILS. 2011b. *Brazil: An innovative income-led strategy* (Geneva). Available at: http://www.ilo.org/global/publications/books/WCMS_153768/lang--en/index.htm [16 Apr. 2014].

IILS. 2011c. *Germany: A job-centered approach* (Geneva). Available at: http://www.ilo.org/wcmsp5/groups/public/---dgreports/---dcomm/---publ/documents/publication/wcms_153779.pdf [16 Apr. 2014].

IILS. 2012. *World of Work Report 2012: Better jobs for a better economy* (Geneva). Available at: http://www.ilo.org/global/research/global-reports/world-of-work/WCMS_179453/lang--nl/index.htm [16 Apr. 2014].

ILO (International Labour Office). 2000. *World Labour Report: Income security and social protection in a changing world* (Geneva).

ILO. 2008a. *Can low-income countries afford basic social security?,* Social Security Policy Briefings (Geneva). Available at: http://www.ilo.org/gimi/gess/ShowRessource.action?ressource.ressourceId=5951 [16 Apr. 2014].

ILO. 2008b. *Saving lives, protecting jobs: International HIV/AIDS workplace education programme. SHARE: Strategic HIV/AIDS Responses in Enterprises: Second report* (Geneva). Available at: http://www.ilo.org/global/about-the-ilo/newsroom/news/WCMS_092043/lang--en/index.htm [16 Apr. 2014].

ILO. 2009a. *Recovering from the crisis:* A *global jobs pact*, Adopted by the International Labour Conference, 98th Session, Geneva, 2009 (Geneva). Available at: http://www.ilo.org/jobspact/WCMS_115076/lang--en/index.htm [16 Apr. 2014].

ILO. 2009b. *Protecting people, promoting jobs:* A *survey of country employment and social protection policy responses to the global economic crisis in 54 countries*, report to the G20 Leaders' Summit, Pittsburgh, 24–25 Sep. (Geneva).

ILO. 2010a. *World Social Security Report 2010/11: Providing coverage in the time of crisis and beyond* (Geneva). Available at: http://www.ilo.org/global/publications/ilo-bookstore/order-online/books/WCMS_146566/lang--en/index.htm [16 Apr. 2014].

ILO. 2010b. *Extending social security to all:* A *guide through challenges and options* (Geneva). Available at: http://www.ilo.org/global/publications/ilo-bookstore/order-online/books/WCMS_146616/lang--en/index.htm [16 Apr. 2014].

ILO. 2010c. *Accelerating a job-rich recovery in G20 countries: Building on experience*, an ILO report, with substantive contributions from OECD, to the meeting of G20 labour and employment ministers, 20–21 Apr. 2010, Washington, DC (Geneva). Available at: http://www.ilo.org/public/libdoc/jobcrisis/download/g20_report_accelerating.pdf [16 Apr. 2014].

ILO. 2010d. *Maternity at work:* A *review of national legislation. Findings from the ILO Database of Conditions of Work and Employment Laws* (Geneva). Available at: http://www.ilo.org/global/publications/books/WCMS_124442/lang--en/index.htm [16 Apr. 2014].

ILO. 2010e. *ILO contribution to the pension reform in Chile* (Santiago de Chile).

ILO. 2011a. *Social security for social justice and a fair globalization: Recurrent discussion on social protection (social security) under the ILO Declaration on Social Justice for a Fair Globalization, 2011*, Report VI, International Labour Conference, 100th Session, Geneva, 2011 (Geneva). Available at: http://ilo.org/ilc/ILCSessions/100thSession/on-the-agenda/social-protection/lang--en/index.htm [16 Apr. 2014].

ILO. 2011b. *Report of the Director-General: A new era of social justice*, Report I(A), International Labour Conference, 100th Session, Geneva, 2011 (Geneva). Available at: http://www.ilo.org/ilc/ILCSessions/100thSession/reports/reports-submitted/WCMS_155656/lang--en/index.htm [16 Apr. 2014].

ILO. 2011c. *Social security and the rule of law: General survey concerning social security instruments in the light of the 2008 Declaration on Social Justice for a Fair Globalization*, Report III (Part 1B), International Labour Conference, 100th Session, Geneva, 2011 (Geneva). Available at: http://www.ilo.org/wcmsp5/groups/public/---ed_norm/---relconf/documents/meetingdocument/wcms_152602.pdf [3 May 2014].

ILO. 2012a. *The strategy of the International Labour Organization. Social security for all: Building social protection floors and comprehensive social security systems* (Geneva). Available at: http://www.ilo.org/secsoc/information-resources/publications-and-tools/books-and-reports/WCMS_SECSOC_34188/lang--en/index.htm [16 Apr. 2014].

ILO. 2012b. *The youth employment crisis: Time for action*, Report V, International Labour Conference, 101st Session, Geneva, 2012 (Geneva). Available at: http://www.ilo.org/washington/areas/youth-employment/WCMS_175421/lang--en/index.htm [16 Apr. 2014].

ILO. 2012c. *Social protection assessment based national dialogue: Towards a nationally defined social protection floor in Indonesia* (Jakarta). Available at: http://www.ilo.org/jakarta/whatwedo/publications/WCMS_195572/lang--en/index.htm [16 Apr. 2014].

ILO. 2012d. *Global Employment Trends for Women 2012* (Geneva). Available at: http://www.ilo.org/global/research/global-reports/global-employment-trends/WCMS_195447/lang--en/index.htm [16 Apr. 2014].

ILO. 2012e. *World of Work Report 2012: Better jobs for a better economy* (Geneva). Available at: http://www.ilo.org/global/research/global-reports/world-of-work/WCMS_179453/lang--nl/index.htm [16 Apr. 2014].

ILO. 2012f. "China's latest revolution: Basic health care for all", 3 Sep. Available at: http://www.ilo.org/global/about-the-ilo/newsroom/features/WCMS_188582/lang--en/index.htm [16 Apr. 2014].

ILO. 2013a. *World Report on Child Labour: Economic vulnerability, social protection and the fight against child labour* (Geneva). Available at: http://www.ilo.org/ipec/Informationresources/WCMS_178184/lang--en/index.htm [16 Apr. 2014].

ILO. 2013b. *Global Wage Report 2012/13: Wages and equitable growth* (Geneva). Available at: http://www.ilo.org/global/research/global-reports/global-wage-report/2012/WCMS_194843/lang--de/index.htm [16 Apr. 2014].

ILO. 2013c. *Global Employment Trends 2013: Recovering from a second jobs dip* (Geneva). Available at: http://www.ilo.org/global/research/global-reports/global-employment-trends/2013/WCMS_202326/lang--nl/index.htm [16 Apr. 2014].

ILO. 2013d. *Global Employment Trends for Youth 2013: A generation at risk* (Geneva). Available at: http://www.ilo.org/global/research/global-reports/global-employment-trends/youth/2013/WCMS_212423/lang--en/index.htm [16 Apr. 2014].

ILO. 2013e. *Working Conditions Laws Report 2012:* A *global review* (Geneva). Available at: http://www.ilo.org/wcmsp5/groups/public/---ed_protect/---protrav/---travail/documents/publication/wcms_235155.pdf [16 Apr. 2014].

ILO. 2013f. *Tackling the jobs crisis in Portugal*, Report of the ILO Inter-Departmental Task Force on European Crisis Countries for the high-level conference on "Tackling the jobs crisis in Portugal", Lisbon, 4 Nov.

ILO. 2013g. *Transitioning from the informal to the formal economy*, Report V(1), International Labour Conference, 103rd Session, Geneva, 2014 (Geneva). Available at: http://www.ilo.org/wcmsp5/groups/public/---ed_norm/---relconf/documents/meetingdocument/wcms_218128.pdf [3 May 2014].

ILO. 2013h. *The informal economy and decent work: supporting transitions to formality: a resource guide* (Geneva), Available at: http://www.ilo.org/wcmsp5/groups/public/---ed_emp/---emp_policy/documents/publication/wcms_212689.pdf [3 May 2014].

ILO. 2013i. *Employment and social protection in the new demographic context*, Report IV, International Labour Conference, 102nd Session, Geneva, 2013 (Geneva). Available at: http://www.ilo.org/wcmsp5/groups/public/---ed_norm/---relconf/documents/meetingdocument/wcms_209717.pdf [3 May 2014].

ILO. 2014a. *Global Employment Trends 2014: Risk of a jobless recovery?* (Geneva). Available at: http://www.ilo.org/global/research/global-reports/global-employment-trends/2014/WCMS_233953/lang--en/index.htm [16 Apr. 2014].

ILO. 2014b. *Employment policies for sustainable recovery and development: Recurrent discussion under the ILO Declaration on Social Justice for a Fair Globalization*, Report VI, International Labour Conference, 103rd Session, Geneva, 2014 (Geneva). Available at: http://www.ilo.org/wcmsp5/groups/public/---ed_norm/---relconf/documents/meetingdocument/wcms_240032.pdf [16 Apr. 2014].

ILO. 2014c. Forthcoming. *Global Wage Report 2014/15* (Geneva).

ILO. 2014d. *World of Work Report 2014: Developing with jobs* (Geneva).

ILO. 2014e. *Maternity and paternity at work: Law and practice across the world* (Geneva).

ILO; EU (European Union); IILS (International Institute of Labour Studies). 2011. A *review of global fiscal stimulus*, EC–IILS Joint Discussion Paper Series No. 5. Available at: http://www.ilo.org/inst/research/addressing-crisis-challenges/discussion-paper-series/WCMS_194175/lang--en/index.htm [16 Apr. 2014].

ILO; OECD (Organisation for Economic Co-operation and Development). 2013. *Addressing employment, labour market and social protection challenges in G20 countries: Key measures since 2010* (Geneva and Paris). Available at: http://www.ilo.org/wcmsp5/groups/public/---dgreports/---dcomm/---publ/documents/publication/wcms_217544.pdf [16 Apr. 2014].

ILO; UNDP (United Nations Development Programme). 2009. *Work and family: Towards new forms of reconciliation with social co-responsibility* (Santiago de Chile). Available at: http://www.ilo.org/gender/Informationresources/Publications/WCMS_111375/lang--en/index.htm [16 Apr. 2014].

ILO; World Bank. 2012. *Joint synthesis report: Inventory of policy responses to the financial and economic crisis* (Geneva and Washington, DC). Available at: http://ilo.org/empelm/pubs/WCMS_186324/lang--en/index.htm [16 Apr. 2014].

ILO; World Bank; DfID (UK Department for International Development); UNICEF (United Nations Children's Fund); ISSA (International Social Security Association); ODI (Overseas Development Institute); International Policy Center for Inclusive Growth; HelpAge International. 2013. *Joint proposal on international social protection data harmonisation*, input to 3rd meeting of the Social Protection Inter-Agency Cooperation Board (SPIAC-B) (Geneva and Washington, DC). Available at: http://www.ilo.org/newyork/issues-at-work/social-protection/social-protection-inter-agency-cooperation-board/third-meeting/WCMS_227154/lang--en/index.htm [16 Apr. 2014].

IMF (International Monetary Fund). 2003. *Proposed features of a sovereign debt restructuring mechanism* (Washington, DC). Available at: http://www.imf.org/external/np/pdr/sdrm/2003/021203.htm [16 Apr. 2014].

IMF. 2008. *Food and fuel prices: Recent developments, macroeconomic impact, and policy responses – an update* (Washington, DC). Available at: http://www.imf.org/external/np/pp/eng/2008/091908.pdf [8 May 2014].

IMF. 2009. *Creating policy space: Responsive design and streamlined conditionality in recent low-income country programs* (Washington, DC). Available at: http://www.imf.org/external/np/pp/eng/2009/091009a.pdf [16 Apr. 2014].

IMF. 2010a. *Exiting from crisis intervention policies* (Washington, DC). Available at: http://www.imf.org/external/np/pp/eng/2010/020410.pdf [16 Apr. 2014].

IMF. 2010b. *Strategies for fiscal consolidation in the post-crisis world*, Departmental Paper No. 10/4 (Washington, DC). Available at: http://www.imf.org/external/pubs/cat/longres.aspx?sk=23878.0 [16 Apr. 2014].

IMF. 2010c. *Financial sector taxation: The IMF's report to the G-20 and background material* (Washington, DC).

IMF. 2012. *Iceland: 2012 Article IV consultation and first post-program monitoring discussion*, IMF Country Report No. 12/89 (Washington, DC). Available at: http://www.imf.org/external/pubs/ft/scr/2012/cr1289.pdf [16 Apr. 2014].

IMF. 2013a. *World Economic Outlook October 2013: Transitions and tensions* (Washington, DC). Available at: http://www.imf.org/external/pubs/ft/weo/2013/02/ [16 Apr. 2014].

IMF. 2013b. *Energy subsidy reform: Lessons and implications* (Washington, DC). Available at: http://www.imf.org/external/np/fad/subsidies/ [16 Apr. 2014].

IMF. 2013c. *Regional economic outlook Asia and Pacific: Shifting risks, new foundations for growth* (Washington, DC). Available at: http://www.imf.org/external/pubs/ft/reo/2013/apd/eng/areo0413.htm [16 Apr. 2014].

IMF; World Bank. 2006. *Fiscal space policy for growth and development: An interim report*, Background Paper for the Development Committee Meeting, (Washington, DC).

IPEA (Instituto de Pesquisa Econômica Aplicada). 2013. *Duas décadas de desigualdade e pobreza no Brasil medidas pela Pnad/IBGE*, Comunicados do Ipea No. 159. Available at: http://www.ipea.gov.br/portal/index.php?option=com_content&view=article&id=20005 [16 Apr. 2014].

Islam, I.; Chowdhury, A. 2010a. *Fiscal consolidation, growth and employment: What do we know?*, G24 Policy Brief No. 57.

326 Islam, I.; Chowdhury, A. 2010b. *The fallacy of austerity-based fiscal consolidation*, G24 Policy Brief No. 58.

ISSA (International Social Security Association). 2012. *Return-to-work programmes: Supporting health and employability*, Social Policy Highlight No. 22 (Geneva). Available at: http://www.issa.int/details?uuid=c4133419-78dc-49f9-a005-4d74470d11ae [16 Apr. 2014].

ISSA (International Social Security Association). 2013. *Social security coverage extension in the BRICS: A comparative study on the extension of coverage in Brazil, the Russian Federation, India, China and South Africa* (Geneva). Available at: http://www.issa.int/content/download/176183/3493137/file/2-BRICS-report.pdf [3 Apr. 2014].

Jackson, C.; Butters, S.; Byambaa, E.; Davies, M.; Perkins, N. 2011. *Lessons from social protection programme implementation in Kenya, Zambia and Mongolia*, IDS Research Report, Vol. 2011, No. 69 (Brighton, Institute for Development Studies). Available at: http://www.ids.ac.uk/publication/lessons-from-social-protection-programme-implementation-in-kenya-zambia-and-mongolia [16 Apr. 2014].

Jackson, R. 2013. *Attitudes toward the role of the family, the individual, and the State in providing retirement income: Survey evidence from emerging East Asia* (Washington, DC, Center for Strategic and International Studies).

Kar, D.; Curcio, K. 2011. *Illicit financial flows from developing countries: 2000–2009* (Washington, DC, Global Financial Integrity).

Karanikolos, M.; Mladovsky, P.; Cylus, J.; Thomson, S.; Basu, S.; Stuckler, D.; Mackenbach, J.P.; McKee, M. 2013. "Financial crisis, austerity, and health in Europe", in *The Lancet*, Vol. 381, Issue No. 9874, pp. 1323–1331. Available at: http://www.thelancet.com/journals/lancet/article/PIIS0140-6736(13)60102-6/abstract [16 Apr. 2014].

Kentikelenis, A.; Karanikolos, M.; Papanicolas, I.; Basu, S.; McKee, M.; Stuckler, D. 2011. "Health effects of financial crisis: Omens of a Greek tragedy", in *The Lancet*, Vol. 378, Issue No. 9801, pp. 1457–1458. Available at: http://www.thelancet.com/journals/lancet/article/PIIS0140-6736(11)61556-0/fulltext [16 Apr. 2014].

Kentikelenis, A.; Karanikolos, M.; Reeves, A.; McKee, M.; Stuckler, D. 2014. "Greece's health crisis: From austerity to denialism", in *The Lancet*, Vol. 383, Issue No. 9918, pp. 748–753. Available at: http://www.thelancet.com/journals/lancet/article/PIIS0140-6736(13)62291-6/abstract [16 Apr. 2014].

Kruger, A. 2002. *A new approach to sovereign debt restructuring* (Washington, DC, IMF).

Krugman, P. 2012. *End this depression now* (New York, Norton).

Künzel, S. 2012. "The local dimension of active inclusion policy", in *Journal of European Social Policy*, Vol. 22, No. 3, pp. 3–16. Available at: http://esp.sagepub.com/content/22/1/3 [16 Apr. 2014].

Lagarde, C. 2011. "Don't let fiscal brakes stall global recovery", in *Financial Times*, 15 Aug. Available at: http://www.ft.com/cms/s/0/315ed340-c72b-11e0-a9ef-00144feabdc0.html#axzz30yG76vCO [8 May 2014].

Lancet Commission (*The Lancet*–University of Oslo Commission on Global Governance for Health). 2013. "Global health 2035: A world converging within a generation", in *The Lancet*, Vol. 382, Issue 9908, pp. 1898–1955. Available at: http://www.thelancet.com/journals/lancet/article/PIIS0140-6736(13)62105-4/fulltext [16 Apr. 2014].

Lancet Commission (*The Lancet*–University of Oslo Commission on Global Governance for Health). 2014. *The political origins of health inequity: Prospects for change*. Available at: http://www.thelancet.com/journals/lancet/article/PIIS0140-6736(13)62407-1/fulltext [16 Apr. 2014].

Lieuw-Kie-Song, M. 2011. *Integrating public works and cash transfers in Ethiopia: Implications for social protection, employment and decent work*, International Poverty Centre Working Paper No. 84 (Brasilia, International Policy Centre for Inclusive Growth). Available at: http://www.ipc-undp.org/pub/IPCWorkingPaper84.pdf [16 Apr. 2014].

Lieuw-Kie-Song, M.; Philip, K.; Tsukamoto, M.; Van Imschoot, M. 2011. *Towards the right to work: Innovations in Public Employment Programmes (IPEP)*, Employment Working Paper No. 69 (Geneva, ILO). Available at: http://www.ilo.org/employment/Whatwedo/Publications/working-papers/WCMS_158483/lang--en/index.htm [18 Apr. 2014].

Lødemel, I.; Trickey, H. (eds). 2001. *"An offer you can't refuse": Workfare in international perspective* (Bristol, Policy Press).

Lustig, N.; Pessino, C.; Scott, J. 2014. "The impact of taxes and social spending on inequality and poverty in Argentina, Bolivia, Brazil, Mexico, Peru, and Uruguay: Introduction to the special issue", in *Public Finance Review*, Vol. 42, No. 3, pp. 287–303.

Martínez Franzoni, J.; Sanchéz-Ancochea, D. 2014. Forthcoming. "Public social services", in J. Berg (ed.): *Labour market institutions and inequality: Building just societies in the 21st century* (Cheltenham, Edward Elgar).

McCord, A. 2012. *Public works and social protection in sub-Saharan Africa: Do public works work for the poor?* (Tokyo, New York and Paris, United Nations University Press).

Mesa-Lago, C. 2012. "Re-reforms of privatized pension systems in the world: A comparative study of Chile, Argentina, Bolivia and Hungary", in *Zeitschrift für ausländisches und internationales Arbeits- und Sozialrecht*, Vol. 26, No. 3, pp. 189–314.

Minujin, A.; Nandy, S. (eds). 2012. *Global child poverty and well-being: Measurement, concepts, policy and action* (Bristol, Policy Press).

Mladovsky, P.; Drivastava, D.; Cylus, J.; Karanikolos, M.; Evetovits, T.; Thomson, S.; McKee, M. 2012. *Health policy responses to the financial crisis in Europe* (Copenhagen, WHO, Regional Office for Europe). Available at: http://www.euro.who.int/__data/assets/pdf_file/0009/170865/e96643.pdf [8 May 2014].

Mokomane, Z. 2012. *Anti-poverty family-focused policies in developing countries*, Background Paper to the Twentieth Anniversary of the International Year of the Family, 2014 (New York, UNDESA). Available at: http://www.un.org/esa/socdev/family/docs/BP_POVERTY.pdf [18 Apr. 2014].

Molyneux, M. 2007. *Change and continuity in social protection in Latin America: Mothers at the service of the state?* (Geneva, United Nations Research Institute for Social Development). Available at: http://www.unrisd.org/80256B3C005BCCF9/search/BF80E0A84BE41896C12573240033C541 [3 May 2014].

Monchuk, V. 2014. *Reducing poverty and investing in people: The new role of safety nets in Africa* (Washington, DC, World Bank). Available at: https://openknowledge.worldbank.org/handle/10986/16256 [18 Apr. 2014].

Moore, M. 2013. *Obstacles to increasing tax revenues in low income countries*, Working Paper No. 15 (Brighton, International Centre for Tax and Development). Available at: http://www.ids.ac.uk/publication/obstacles-to-increasing-tax-revenues-in-low-income-countries [18 Apr. 2014].

Morduch, J. 1995. "Income smoothing and consumption smoothing", in *Journal of Economic Perspectives*, Vol. 9, No. 3, pp. 103–114.

Nawal, D.; Sekher, T.V.; Goli, S. 2013. "Decomposing the socioeconomic inequality in utilisation of maternal health-care services in selected Asian and sub-Saharan African countries", in *The Lancet*, special issue on "Global health metrics and evaluation", 17 June, p. S97.

OECD (Organisation for Economic Co-operation and Development). 2008. *Growing unequal? Income distribution and poverty in OECD countries* (Paris). Available at: http://www.oecd.org/document/4/0,3343,en_2649_33933_41460917_1_1_1_1,00.html#NEWS [8 May 2014].

OECD. 2009a. *Promoting pro-poor growth: Social protection* (Paris). Available at: http://www.oecd.org/dac/povertyreduction/promotingpro-poorgrowthsocialprotection.htm [18 Apr. 2014].

OECD. 2009b. *Social Expenditure database (SOCX)* (Paris). Available at: http://www.oecd.org/social/expenditure.htm [3 Apr. 2014].

OECD. 2009c. *Doing better for children* (Paris).

OECD. 2010a. *Latin American Economic Outlook 2011: How middle class is Latin America?* (Paris). Available at: http://www.oecd-ilibrary.org/development/latin-american-economic-outlook-2011_leo-2011-en [18 Apr. 2014].

OECD. 2010b. *Sickness, disability and work: Breaking the barriers. A synthesis of findings across OECD countries* (Paris). Available at: http://www.oecd-ilibrary.org/social-issues-migration-health/sickness-disability-and-work-breaking-the-barriers_9789264088856-en [20 Apr. 2014].

OECD. 2010c. *Obesity and the economics of prevention: Fit not fat* (Paris). Available at: http://www.oecd.org/els/health-systems/obesityandtheeconomicsofpreventionfitnotfat.htm [20 Apr. 2014].

OECD. 2010d. *OECD Economic Outlook No. 87* (Paris). Available at: http://www.oecd-ilibrary.org/economics/data/oecd-economic-outlook-statistics-and-projections/oecd-economic-outlook-no-87_data-00492-en;jsessionid=e9ecb59hs92k.delta?isPartOf=/content/datacollection/eo-data-en [20 Apr. 2014].

OECD. 2011a. *Doing better for families* (Paris). Available at: http://www.oecd.org/social/soc/doingbetterforfamilies.htm [20 Apr. 2014].

OECD. 2011b. *Divided we stand: Why inequality keeps rising* (Paris). Available at: http://www.oecd.org/social/soc/dividedwestandwhyinequalitykeepsrising.htm [20 Apr. 2014].

OECD. 2012a. *Pensions Outlook 2012* (Paris). Available at: http://www.oecd.org/finance/private-pensions/oecdpensionsoutlook2012.htm [20 Apr. 2014].

OECD. 2012b. *Social spending after the crisis: Social expenditure SOCX data update 2012* (Paris). Available at: http://www.oecd.org/social/expenditure.htm [3 Apr. 2014].

OECD. 2012c. *Restoring public finances (2012 update)* (Paris). Available at: http://www.oecd.org/gov/budgeting/restoringpublicfinances-reportoutliningthefiscalconsolidationplansof30oecdcountries.htm [20 Apr. 2014].

OECD. 2013a. *Pensions at a Glance 2013: Retirement-income systems in OECD and G20 countries* (Paris). Available at: http://www.oecd.org/pensions/pensionsataglance.htm [20 Apr. 2014].

OECD. 2013b. *Crisis squeezes income and puts pressure on inequality and poverty: New results from the OECD income distribution database* (Paris). Available at: http://www.oecd.org/els/soc/OECD2013-Inequality-and-Poverty-8p.pdf [20 Apr. 2014].

OECD. 2013c. *International Migration Outlook 2013* (Paris). Available at: http://www.oecd.org/els/mig/imo2013.htm [20 Apr. 2014].

OECD. 2013d. *Health at a Glance 2013: OECD indicators* (Paris). Available at: http://www.oecd.org/els/health-systems/health-at-a-glance.htm [20 Apr. 2014].

OECD. 2013e. *Development Co-operation Report 2013: Ending poverty* (Paris). Available at: http://www.oecd.org/dac/dcr2013.htm [20 Apr. 2014].

OECD. 2014a. *Fragile States 2014: Domestic revenue mobilisation* (Paris). Available at: http://www.oecd.org/dac/incaf/resourceflowstofragilestates.htm [20 Apr. 2014].

OECD. 2014b. *OECD Family Database* (Paris). Available at: www.oecd.org/social/family/database [20 Apr. 2014].

OHCHR (Office of the UN High Commissioner for Human Rights). 2012. *Thematic study on the work and employment of persons with disabilities*, Report of the Office of the United Nations High Commissioner for Human Rights, A/HRC/22/25 (Geneva). Available at: http://www.ohchr.org/Documents/Issues/Disability/A-HRC-22-25_en.pdf [18 Apr. 2014].

OHCHR (Office of the High Commissioner for Human Rights). 2013. *Report on austerity measures and economic, social and cultural rights*, presented to ECOSOC, Substantive Session of 2013, Geneva, 1–26 July, E/2013/82 (Geneva). Available at: http://www.ohchr.org/Documents/Issues/Development/RightsCrisis/E-2013-82_en.pdf [18 Apr. 2014].

Ortiz, I.; Burke, S.; Berrada, M.; Cortes, H. 2013. *World protests 2006–2013*, Working Paper, Sep. (New York, Initiative for Policy Dialogue and Friedrich-Ebert-Stiftung).

Ortiz, I; Chai, J.; Sire, X.R. 2010. *Protecting salaries of frontline teachers and health workers*, UNICEF Policy and Practice Working Paper. Available at: http://www.unicef.org/socialpolicy/index_53314.html [20 Apr. 2014].

Ortiz, I.; Cummins, M. 2013. *The age of austerity:* A *review of public expenditures and adjustment measures in 181 countries*, Working Paper (New York and Geneva, Initiative for Policy Dialogue and the South Centre). Available at: http://policydialogue.org/files/publications/Age_of_Austerity_Ortiz_and_Cummins.pdf [20 Apr. 2014].

Ortiz, I.; Cummins, M. (eds). 2012. A *recovery for all: Rethinking socio-economic policies for children and poor households* (New York, UNICEF, Division of Policy and Practice).

Ortiz, I.; Moreira Daniels, L.; Engilbertsdóttir, S. 2012. *Child poverty and inequality: New perspectives* (New York, UNICEF). Available at: http://www.unicef.org/socialpolicy/index_62108.html [20 Apr. 2014].

Ostry, J.D.; Berg, A.G.; Tsangarides, C.G. 2014. *Redistribution, inequality, and growth*, IMF Staff Discussion Note No. 14/02 (Washington, DC, IMF). Available at: http://www.imf.org/external/pubs/ft/sdn/2014/sdn1402.pdf [20 Apr. 2014].

Oxfam. 2013. A *cautionary tale: The true cost of austerity and inequality in Europe*, Briefing Paper (London). Available at: http://policy-practice.oxfam.org.uk/publications/a-cautionary-tale-the-true-cost-of-austerity-and-inequality-in-europe-301384 [20 Apr. 2014].

Padoan, P.C. 2010. *How to correct global imbalances*, OECD Observer No. 279, May. Available at: http://www.oecdobserver.org/news/archivestory.php/aid/3248/How_to_correct_global_imbalances.html [20 Apr. 2014].

Patel, L.; Hochfeld, T.; Moodley, J. 2013. "Gender and child sensitive social protection in South Africa", in *Development Southern Africa*, Vol. 30, No. 1, pp. 69–83.

Patel, L.; Hochfeld, T.; Moodley, J.; Mutwali, R. 2012. *The gender dynamics and impact of the child support grant in Doornkop, Soweto* (Johannesburg, University of Johannesburg, Center for Social Development in America). Available at: http://www.childwatch.uio.no/publications/research-reports/gender%20dynamics%20and%20child%20support.pdf [20 Apr. 2014].

Pollin, R.; Epstein, G.; Heintz, J. 2008. *Pro-growth alternatives for monetary and financial policies in sub-Saharan Africa*, Policy Research Brief No. 6 (Brasilia, UNDP International Poverty Centre).

Rawdanowicz, L.; Wurzel, E.; Christensen, A.K. 2013. *The equity implications of fiscal consolidation*, OECD Economics Department Working Paper No. 1013 (Paris). Available at: http://dx.doi.org/10.1787/5k4dlvx2wjq0-en [8 May 2014].

Ray, R.; Kozameh, S. 2012. *Ecuador's economy since 2007*, Working Paper (Washington, DC, Center for Economic and Policy Research).

Razavi, S.; Arza, C.; Braunstein, E.; Cook, S.; Goulding, K. 2012. *Gendered impacts of globalization: Employment and social protection*, Gender and Development Paper No. 16 (Geneva, United Nations Research Institute for Social Development). Available at: http://www.unrisd.org/80256B3C005BCCF9/search/6E16D1DC33F5D82BC12579D000478859?OpenDocument [20 Apr. 2014].

Republic of Kenya. 2010. *Constitution of Kenya 2010*. Available at: https://www.kenyaembassy.com/pdfs/The%20Constitution%20of%20Kenya.pdf [20 Apr. 2014].

Reynaud, E. (ed.). 2000. *Social dialogue and pension reform* (Geneva, ILO).

Ringen, S.; Ngok, K. 2013. *What kind of welfare state is emerging in China?*, UNRISD Working Paper No. 2013-2 (Geneva, United Nations Research Institute for Social Development). Available at: http://www.unrisd.org/80256B3C005BCCF9/search/28BCE0F59BDD3738C1257BE30053EBAC?OpenDocument [20 Apr. 2014].

Robalino, D.A.; Vodopivec, M.; Bodor, A. 2010. *Savings for unemployment in good or bad times: Options for developing countries*, IZA Discussion Paper No. 4516 (Bonn, Institute for the Study of Labor).

Ryder, G. 2013. *Avoiding the risk of a slow growth trap*, Statement to the International Monetary and Financial Committee and Development Committee (Washington, DC, IMF).

Sanfilippo, M.; de Neubourg, C.; Martorano, B. 2012. *The impact of social protection on children: A review of the literature*, UNICEF Office of Research Working Paper (New York, UNICEF). Available at: http://www.unicef-irc.org/publications/666 [20 Apr. 2014].

Sarfati, H.; Ghellab, Y. 2012. *The political economy of pension reforms in times of global crisis: State unilateralism or social dialogue?*, Working Paper No. 37 (Geneva, ILO). Available at: http://www.ilo.org/ifpdial/information-resources/publications/WCMS_176346/lang--en/index.htm [20 Apr. 2014].

Sarra, J. 2008. *Employee and pension claims during company insolvency: A comparative study of 62 jurisdictions* (Toronto, Carswell).

Save the Children. 2012a. A *chance to grow: How social protection can tackle child malnutrition and promote economic opportunities* (London). Available at: https://www.savethechildren.org.uk/resources/online-library/chance-grow [20 Apr. 2014].

Save the Children. 2012b. *What cash transfer programming can do to protect children from violence, abuse and exploitation: Review and recommendations* (London). Available at: http://www.savethechildren.org.uk/resources/online-library/cash-and-child-protection [20 Apr. 2014].

Scheil-Adlung, X.; Bonan, J. 2012. *Can the European elderly afford the financial burden of health and long-term care? Assessing impacts and policy implications*, Extension of Social Security ESS Paper No. 31 (Geneva, ILO). Available at: http://www.ilo.org/gimi/gess/ShowRessource.action?ressource.ressourceId=30228 [20 Apr. 2014].

Scheil-Adlung, X.; Bonan, J. 2013. "Gaps in social protection for health care and long-term care in Europe: Are the elderly faced with financial ruin?", in *International Social Security Review*, Vol. 66, No. 1, pp. 25–48. Available at: http://dx.doi.org/10.1111/issr.12001 [20 Apr. 2014].

Scheil-Adlung, X.; Bonnet, F. 2011. "Beyond legal coverage: Assessing the performance of social health protection", in *International Social Security Review*, Vol. 64, No. 3, pp. 21–38.

Scheil-Adlung, X.; Kuhl, C. 2012. *Evidence on gender inequities in social health protection: The case of women living in rural areas*, Extension of Social Security ESS Paper No. 29 (Geneva). Available at: http://www.social-protection.org/gimi/gess/ShowRessource.action?ressource.ressourceId=28986 [20 Apr. 2014].

Scheil-Adlung, X.; Sandner, L. 2010. *Paid sick leave: Incidence, patterns and expenditure in times of crises*, Extension of Social Security ESS Paper No. 27 (Geneva, ILO). Available at: http://www.ilo.org/secsoc/information-resources/publications-and-tools/Workingpapers/WCMS_207675/lang--en/index.htm [20 Apr. 2014].

Schmitt, V.; Sakunphanit, T.; Prasitsiriphol, O. 2013. *Social protection assessment based national dialogue: Towards a nationally defined social protection floor in Thailand* (Bangkok, United Nations/Royal Thai Government Joint Team on Social Protection). Available at: http://www.ilo.org/secsoc/information-resources/publications-and-tools/books-and-reports/WCMS_213264/lang--en/index.htm [20 Apr. 2014].

Sehnbruch, K. 2006. "Unemployment insurance or individual savings accounts: Can Chile's new scheme serve as a model for other developing countries?", in *International Social Security Review*, Vol. 59, No. 1, pp. 27–48.

Sekabaraga, C.; Soucat, A.; Diop, F.; Martin, G. 2011. "Innovative financing for health in Rwanda: A report of successful reforms", in P. Chunam-Pole and M. Angwafo (eds): *Yes, Africa can: success stories from a dynamic continent* (Washington, DC, World Bank), pp. 403–416. Available at: http://siteresources.worldbank.org/AFRICAEXT/Resources/258643-1271798012256/Rwanda-health.pdf [20 Apr. 2014].

Sepúlveda, M. 2012. *The human rights based approach to recovery from the global economic and financial crises, with a focus on those living in poverty*, Report of the Independent Expert on the Question of Human Rights and Extreme Poverty, Magdalena Sepúlveda Carmona, Human Rights Council (A/HRC/17/34). Available at: http://www2.ohchr.org/english/bodies/hrcouncil/docs/17session/A-HRC-17-34.pdf [20 Apr. 2014].

Sepúlveda, M. 2014. *From undeserving poor to rights holder: A human rights perspective on social protection systems*, Working Paper (London, Development Pathways). Available at: http://www.developmentpathways.co.uk/downloads/working-papers/from-undeserving-poor-to-rights-holder---magdalena-sepulveda.pdf [20 Apr. 2014].

Sepúlveda, M.; Nyst, C. 2012. *The human rights approach to social protection* (Helsinki, Ministry of Foreign Affairs of Finland). Available at: http://www.ohchr.org/Documents/Issues/EPoverty/HumanRightsApproachToSocialProtection.pdf [20 Apr. 2014].

Skoufias, E.; Parker, S. 2001. *Conditional cash transfers and their impact on child work and schooling: Evidence from PROGRESA program in Mexico,* FCND Discussion Paper No. 123 (Washington, DC, International Food Policy Research Institute). Available at: http://www.ifpri.org/publication/conditional-cash-transfers-and-their-impact-child-work-and-schooling-0?print [20 Apr. 2014].

Soares, S.; Perez Ribas, R.; Veras Soares, F. 2010. *Targeting and coverage of the Bolsa Família Programme: Why knowing what you measure is important in choosing the numbers*, IPC Working Paper No. 71 (Brasilia, International Policy Centre for Inclusive Growth). Available at: http://www.ipc-undp.org/pub/IPCWorkingPaper71.pdf [20 Apr. 2014].

Social Protection Floor Advisory Group. 2011. *Social protection floor for a fair and inclusive globalization* (Geneva, ILO). Available at: http://www.ilo.org/global/publications/books/forthcoming-publications/WCMS_165750/lang--en/index.htm [20 Apr. 2014].

Solt, F. 2009. "Standardizing the world income inequality database", in *Social Science Quarterly*, Vol. 90, No. 2, pp. 231–242. Available at: http://myweb.uiowa.edu/fsolt/swiid/swiid.html [20 Apr. 2014].

Solt, F. 2013. Standardized World Income Inequality Database (SWIID), Version 4.0, Sep. Available at: http://myweb.uiowa.edu/fsolt/swiid/swiid.html [20 Apr. 2014].

SSA (Social Security Administration of the United States); ISSA (International Social Security Association). 2012. *Social security programs throughout the world: Europe, 2012* (Washington, DC and Geneva). Available at: http://www.ssa.gov/policy/docs/progdesc/ssptw/2012-2013/europe/ [20 Apr. 2014].

SSA (Social Security Administration of the United States); ISSA (International Social Security Association). 2013a. *Social security programs throughout the world: Asia and Pacific, 2012* (Washington, DC and Geneva). Available at: http://www.ssa.gov/policy/docs/progdesc/ssptw/2012-2013/asia/ [20 Apr. 2014].

SSA (Social Security Administration of the United States); ISSA (International Social Security Association). 2013b. *Social security programs throughout the World: Africa, 2013* (Washington, DC and Geneva). Available at: http://www.socialsecurity.gov/policy/docs/progdesc/ssptw/2012-2013/africa/ [20 Apr. 2014].

SSA (Social Security Administration of the United States); ISSA (International Social Security Association). 2014. *Social security programs throughout the world: The Americas, 2011* (Washington, DC and Geneva). Available at: http://www.socialsecurity.gov/policy/docs/progdesc/ssptw/2010-2011/americas/ [20 Apr. 2014].

Stiglitz, J. 2009. "The global crisis, social protection and jobs", in *International Labour Review*, Vol. 148, Nos 1–2, pp. 1–13. Available at: http://dx.doi.org/10.1111/j.1564-913X.2009.00046.x [20 Apr. 2014].

Stolz, S.M.; Wedow, M. 2010. *Extraordinary measures in extraordinary times: Public measures in support of the financial sector in the EU and the United States*, Occasional Paper Series No. 117 (Frankfurt, European Central Bank). Available at: http://www.ecb.europa.eu/pub/pdf/scpops/ecbocp117.pdf [15 Apr. 2014].

Stuckler, D.; Basu, S. 2013. *The body economic: Why austerity kills* (New York, Basic Books).

Subbarao, K.; Ninno, C.D.; Andrews, C.; Rodríguez-Alas, C. 2013. *Public works as a safety net: Design, evidence, and implementation* (Washington, DC, World Bank). Available at: http://go.worldbank.org/OPT7HUOS10 [20 Apr. 2014].

Sumner, A. 2010. *Global poverty and the new bottom billion: What if three-quarters of the world's poor live in middle-income countries?*, IDS Working Paper (Brighton, Institute for Development Studies). Available at: http://www.ids.ac.uk/publication/global-poverty-and-the-new-bottom-billion-what-if-three-quarters-of-the-world-s-poor-live-in-middle-income-countries [20 Apr. 2014].

Tangcharoensathien, V.; Prakongsai, P.; Limwattananon, S.; Patcharanarumol, W.; Jongudomsuk, P. 2009. "From targeting to universality: Lessons from the health system in Thailand", in Peter Townsend (ed.), pp. 310–322.

Taylor, J.E.; Kagin, J.; Filipski, M.; Thome, K. 2013. *Evaluating general equilibrium impacts of Kenya's cash transfer programme for orphans and vulnerable children (CT-OVC)* (Rome, Food and Agriculture Organization). Available at: http://www.fao.org/fileadmin/user_upload/p2p/Publications/Kenya_LEWIE_2013.pdf [20 Apr. 2014].

Taylor, J.E.; Thome, K.; Davis, B. 2013. *Evaluating the spillover effects of social cash transfer programs*, The 3rd Annual Transfer Project Workshop, "Evaluating the impact of social cash transfers in sub-Saharan Africa", Lusaka, 23–25 Apr. 2013. Available at: http://www.cpc.unc.edu/projects/transfer/events/third-annual-research-workshop/Paper3LocaleconomyeffectsofCTinSSATaylor.pdf [20 Apr. 2014].

Temin, M. 2010. *HIV-sensitive social protection: What does the evidence say?*, Paper prepared for IDS, UNICEF and UNAIDS meeting on "The evidence for HIV-sensitive social protection", Brighton, UK, 14–15 June 2010.

Thomas, A.; Picos-Sánchez, F. 2012. *Shifting from social security contributions to consumption taxes: The impact on low-income earner work incentives*, OECD Taxation Working Paper No. 11 (Paris, OECD). Available at: http://www.oecd-ilibrary.org/taxation/shifting-from-social-security-contributions-to-consumption-taxes_5k95qw92l521-en [20 Apr. 2014].

Tirivayi, N.; Knowles, M.; Davis, B. 2013. *The interaction between social protection and agriculture:* A *review of evidence* (Rome, Food and Agriculture Organization).

Townsend, P. (ed.). 2009. *Building decent societies: Rethinking the role of social security in state building* (Basingstoke, Palgrave). Available at: http://www.palgrave.com/products/title.aspx?pid=370307 [8 May 2014].

UN (United Nations). 2000. *General comment No. 14: The right to the highest attainable standard of health*. Doc. E/C.12/2000/4 (Geneva, United Nations Economic and Social Council, Committee on Economic, Social and Cultural Rights). Available at: http://tbinternet.ohchr.org/_layouts/treatybodyexternal/Download.aspx?symbolno=E%2fC.12%2f2000%2f4&Lang=en [20 Apr. 2014].

UN. 2008. *General comment No. 19: The right to social security (Art. 9)*. Doc. E/C.12/GC/19 (Geneva, United Nations Economic and Social Council, Committee on Economic, Social and Cultural Rights). Available at: http://tbinternet.ohchr.org/_layouts/treatybodyexternal/Download.aspx?symbolno=E%2fC.12%2fGC%2f19&Lang=en [20 Apr. 2014].

UN. 2009a. *Global financial crisis: UN system joint initiatives* (New York, UN System Chief Executives Board for Coordination (CEB)). Available at: http://www.ilo.org/public/libdoc/igo/2009/433767.pdf [8 May 2014].

UN. 2009b. *Report of the Commission of Experts of the President of the United Nations General Assembly on Reforms of the International Monetary and Financial System* (New York).

UN. 2010a. *Report on the World Social Situation 2010: Rethinking poverty* (New York). Available at: http://www.un.org/esa/socdev/rwss/docs/2010/fullreport.pdf [20 Apr. 2014].

UN. 2010b. *Keeping the promise: United to achieve the Millennium Development Goals*, Resolution adopted by the General Assembly, 22 Sep. 2010, MDG Summit, High Level Plenary Meeting of the General Assembly No. A/RES/65/1 (New York).

UN. 2010c. *Till debt do us part: The urgency of a sovereign debt workout mechanism*, UN-DESA Policy Brief No. 29 (New York, UN Department of Economic and Social Affairs).

UN. 2012a. *The future we want*, Resolution adopted by the General Assembly, Rio de Janeiro, Sep.

UN. 2012b. *Guiding principles on extreme poverty and human rights*, submitted by the Special Rapporteur on Extreme Poverty and Human Rights, Magdalena Sepúlveda Carmona, Human Rights Council, 21st Session, New York, July. Available at: http://www.ohchr.org/EN/Issues/Poverty/Pages/DGPIntroduction.aspx [20 Apr. 2014].

UN. 2012c. *Global health and foreign policy*, Resolution adopted by the UN General Assembly, 67th Session, New York, 12 Dec. Available at: http://www.un.org/ga/search/view_doc.asp?symbol=A/67/L.36 [20 Apr. 2014].

UN. 2013a. *Economic empowerment through inclusive social protection and poverty reduction strategies*, Conference of States Parties to the Convention on the Rights of Persons with Disabilities, 6th Session, New York, 17–19 July. Available at: http://www.un.org/disabilities/documents/COP/crpd_csp_2013_2.doc [20 Apr. 2014].

UN. 2013b. *The Millennium Development Goals Report 2013* (New York). Available at: http://www.un.org/millenniumgoals/pdf/report-2013/mdg-report-2013-english.pdf [20 Apr. 2014].

UN. 2013c. *World Economic Situation and Prospects 2013* (New York).

UN. 2013d. *The report on the world social situation: Inequality matters* (New York, UN Department of Economic and Social Affairs). Available at: http://www.un.org/en/development/desa/publications/world-social-situation-2013.html [20 Apr. 2014].

UN. 2013e. *Economic and social survey of Asia and the Pacific 2013: Forward-looking macroeconomic policies for inclusive and sustainable development* (Bangkok, UN Economic and Social Commission for Asia and the Pacific). Available at: http://www.unescap.org/publications/survey/surveys/survey2013.pdf [20 Apr. 2014].

UNCTAD (United Nations Conference on Trade and Development). 2011. *Development-led globalization: Towards sustainable and inclusive development paths* (Geneva).

UNCTAD. 2012. *Trade and Development Report 2012: Policies for inclusive and balanced growth* (Geneva).

UNCTAD. 2013. *Trade and Development Report 2013: Adjusting to the changing dynamics of the world economy* (Geneva).

UNDP (United Nations Development Programme). 2007. *Fiscal space for what? Analytical issues from a human development perspective*, Paper for G20 Workshop on Fiscal Policy, Istanbul, 30 June–2 July 2007.

UNDP. 2009. *Human Development Report 2009* (New York). Available at: http://hdr.undp.org/en/content/human-development-report-2009 [20 Apr. 2014].

UNDP. 2010. *Social protection in fiscal stimulus packages: Some evidence* (New York, UNDP Office of Development Studies).

UNDP. 2011. *Illicit financial flows from the least developed countries: 1990–2008* (New York).

UNDP. 2013. *Humanity divided: Confronting inequality in developing countries* (New York). Available at: http://www.undp.org/content/dam/undp/library/Poverty%20Reduction/Inclusive%20development/Humanity%20Divided/HumanityDivided_Full-Report.pdf [8 May 2014].

UNDP. 2014. *Humanity divided: Confronting inequality in developing countries* (New York). Available at: http://www.undp.org/content/undp/en/home/librarypage/poverty-reduction/humanity-divided--confronting-inequality-in-developing-countries.html [20 Apr. 2014].

UNDP; RCPAR (Regional Centre for Public Administration Reform). 2011. *Economic crisis responses from a governance perspective in Eastern Europe and Central Asia: Regional report* (New York and Bratislava). Available at: http://www.rcpar.org/contents_en.asp?id=475 [20 Apr. 2014].

UN ECOSOC (United Nations Economic and Social Council). 2009. *Recovering from the crisis: A Global Jobs Pact (Resolution)*, Substantive session of 2009, Geneva, 6–31 July. Available at: http://www.ilo.org/wcmsp5/groups/public/@ed_norm/@relconf/documents/meetingdocument/wcms_108456.pdf [20 Apr. 2014].

UNESCO (United Nations Educational, Scientific and Cultural Organization). 2014. *Teaching and learning: Achieving quality for all. Education for All global monitoring report 2013/14* (Paris). Available at: http://unesdoc.unesco.org/images/0022/002256/225660e.pdf [3 May 2014].

UNFPA (United Nations Population Fund); HelpAge International. 2012. *Ageing in the twenty-first century: A celebration and a challenge* (New York and London). Available at: http://www.helpage.org/resources/ageing-in-the-21st-century-a-celebration-and-a-challenge/ [20 Apr. 2014].

UNICEF (United Nations Children's Fund). 2010. *Protecting salaries of frontline teachers and health workers*, Social and Economic Policy Working Brief (New York). Available at: http://www.unicef.org/socialpolicy/files/Protecting_Salaries_of_Frontline_Teachers_and_Healthcare_Workers_final%281%29.pdf [20 Apr. 2014].

UNICEF. 2012. *Integrated social protection systems: Enhancing equity for children* (New York). Available at: http://www.unicef.org/socialpolicy/files/Presentation_Jennifer_Yablonski_UNICEF__20_Feb_2012.pdf [20 Apr. 2014].

UNICEF. 2013. *The State of the World's Children 2013: Children with disabilities* (New York). Available at: http://www.unicef.org/sowc2013/ [20 Apr. 2014].

UNICEF. 2014. *The State of the World's Children 2014 in Numbers: Every child counts* (New York). Available at: http://www.unicef.org/publications/index_71829.html [20 Apr. 2014].

UNICEF; ILO. 2013. *Supporting workers with family responsibilities: Connecting child development and the decent work agenda* (New York and Geneva). Available at: http://www.ilo.org/travail/areasofwork/work-and-family/WCMS_217181/lang--en/index.htm [20 Apr. 2014].

UNRISD (United Nations Research Institute for Social Development). 2010. *Combating poverty and inequality: Structural change, social policy and politics* (Geneva). Available at: http://www.unrisd.org/publications/cpi [20 Apr. 2014].

Vaughan-Whitehead, D. 2013. *Public sector shock: The impact of policy retrenchment in Europe* (Geneva and Cheltenham, ILO and Edward Elgar).

Vaughan-Whitehead, D. 2014. "Is Europe losing its soul? The European social model in times of crisis. Conference organized by the International Labour Office in collaboration with the European Commission", in D. Vaughan-Whitehead (ed.): *The European social model in times of economic crisis and austerity policies* (Geneva, ILO), pp. 1–52.

Vodopivec, M. 2009. *Introducing unemployment insurance to developing countries*, Social Protection Discussion Paper Series No. 0907 (Washington, DC, and Bonn, World Bank and IZA). Available at: http://www.iza.org/en/webcontent/publications/policypapers/viewAbstract?policypaper_id=6 [20 Apr. 2014].

Whitehouse, E. 2012. *Adequacy (1): Pension entitlements, replacement rates and pension wealth*, World Bank Pension Indicators and Database Briefing No. 3 (Washington, DC, World Bank). Available at: http://www-wds.worldbank.org/external/default/WDSContentServer/WDSP/IB/2012/06/30/000426104_20120630145406/Rendered/PDF/703490BRI0P109070036B00PUBLIC00NC03.pdf [20 Apr. 2014].

WHO (World Health Organization). 2010. *World Health Report 2010. Health systems financing: The path to universal coverage* (Geneva). Available at: http://www.who.int/whr/2010/en/ [20 Apr. 2014].

WHO. 2011a. *Impact of economic crises on mental health* (Geneva).

WHO. 2011b. *Sustainable health financing structures and universal coverage*, Resolution No. WH64.9 adopted by 64th World Health Assembly (Geneva).

WHO. 2012. *Spending on health: A global overview*, Fact sheet No. 319 (Geneva).

WHO; World Bank. 2011. *World report on disability* (Geneva and Washington, DC). Available at: http://www.who.int/disabilities/world_report/2011/en/ [20 Apr. 2014].

Witter, S.; Arhinful, D.; Kusi, A.; Zakariah-Akoto, S. 2007. "The experience of Ghana in implementing a user fee exemption policy to provide free delivery care", in *Reproductive Health Matters*, Vol. 15, No. 30, pp. 61–71.

Woodall, J.; Hagemejer, K. 2009. *How can we maintain pension levels in pay-as-you-go schemes? Maintaining pension levels in PAYG schemes in ageing societies: Rules versus discretion*, International Social Security Association Technical Seminar on Pensions, Paris, 1–2 Oct. 2009. Available at: http://www.ilo.org/secsoc/information-resources/publications-and-tools/articles/WCMS_SECSOC_32289/lang--en/index.htm [20 Apr. 2014].

Woolard, I.; Harttgen, K.; Klasen, S. 2010. *The evolution and impact of social security in South Africa*, Background Paper to the *European Development Report 2010* (Florence, Robert Schumann Centre for Advanced Studies). Available at: http://erd.eui.eu/media/BackgroundPapers/Woolard-Harttgen-Klasen.pdf [8 May 2014].

World Bank. 2003. *The contribution of social protection to the Millennium Development Goals* (Washington, DC).

World Bank. 2012. *Resilience, equity and opportunity: The World Bank's social protection and labor strategy 2012–2022* (Washington, DC). Available at: http://go.worldbank.org/2SVY7NI3Y0 [20 Apr. 2014].

World Bank. 2014. *World Development Report 2014: Risk and opportunity – Managing risk for development* (Washington, DC). Available at: http://go.worldbank.org/OSAT4FHFP0 [20 Apr. 2014].

Xu, K.; Evans, D.; Kawabata, K. 2003. "Household catastrophic health expenditure: A multi-country analysis", in *The Lancet*, Vol. 362, No. 9378, pp. 111–17. Available at: http://www.thelancet.com/journals/lancet/issue/vol362no9386/PIIS0140-6736(00)X3809-3 [20 Apr. 2014].

Yablonski, J.; O'Donnell, M. 2009. *Lasting benefits: The role of cash transfers in tackling child mortality* (London, Save the Children UK).

Zaid, A.; Sherry, H.; El-Badrawi, M.; Haber, J. 2014. *Arab uprisings and social justice: implications of IMF subsidy reform policies* (Washington, DC, New America Foundation). Available at: http://middleeast.newamerica.net/sites/newamerica.net/files/policydocs/Policy_Paper_Arab_Uprisings_and_Social_Justice.pdf [8 May 2014].

International databases referred to in this report

Asian Development Bank: Key Indicators for Asia and the Pacific 2013, Part III – Regional Trends and Tables: Government and governance. Available at: http://www.adb.org/publications/key-indicators-asia-and-pacific-2013?ref=publications/series/key-indicators-for-asia-and-the-pacific [20 Apr. 2014].

Asian Development Bank: Social Protection Index database. Available at: http://spi.adb.org/spidmz/index.jsp [20 Apr. 2014].

Council of Europe: Mutual Information System on Social Protection of the Council of Europe (MISSCEO) (Strasbourg). Available at: http://www.coe.int/t/dg3/socialpolicies/socialsecurity/missceo/missceo_EN.asp [20 Apr. 2014].

Eurofound: European Working Conditions Observatory. Available at: http://www.eurofound.europa.eu/working/.

European Commission: Mutual Information System on Social Protection (MISSOC). Available at: http://www.missoc.org/MISSOC/MISSOCII/MISSOCII/index.htm [20 Apr. 2014].

European Employment Observatory. Available at: http://www.eu-employment-observatory.net/ [3 May 2014].

European Labour Law Network. Available at: http://www.labourlawnetwork.eu/ [3 May 2014].

Eurostat: http://epp.eurostat.ec.europa.eu/portal/page/portal/statistics/ [5 May 2014].

Eurostat: Income and Living Conditions database. Available at: http://epp.eurostat.ec.europa.eu/portal/page/portal/income_social_inclusion_living_conditions/data/database [20 Apr. 2014].

HelpAge International: Global AgeWatch Index. Available at http://www.helpage.org/global-agewatch/ [20 Apr. 2014].

HelpAge International: Pension Watch. Available at http://www.pension-watch.net/ [20 Apr. 2014].

ILO (International Labour Office): ILO Employment protection legislation database (EPLex). Available at http://www.ilo.org/dyn/eplex/termmain.home?p_lang=en [20 Apr. 2014].

ILO (International Labour Office): ILO International labour standards and national legislation database (NORMLEX) (incorporates the former ILOLEX and NATLEX databases). Available at: http://www.ilo.org/dyn/normlex/en/ [20 Apr. 2014].

ILO (International Labour Office): Key Indicators of the Labour Market (KILM), 8th edition. Available at: http://www.ilo.org/empelm/what/WCMS_114240/lang--en/index.htm [20 Apr. 2014].

ILO (International Labour Office): ILO LABORSTA labour statistics database (ILOSTAT). Available at: http://www.ilo.org/ilostat/ [20 Apr. 2014].

ILO (International Labour Office): ILO Social Protection Platform (formerly GESS platform). Available at: http://www.social-protection.org/ [20 Apr. 2014].

ILO (International Labour Office): ILO Social Security Inquiry database. Available at http://www.ilo.org/dyn/ilossi/ssimain.home [20 Apr. 2014].

ILO (International Labour Office): Working Conditions Laws database. Available at: http://www.ilo.org/dyn/travail/travmain.home [20 Apr. 2014].

IMF (International Monetary Fund): World Economic Outlook database. Available at: http://www.imf.org/external/pubs/ft/weo/2013/02/weodata/index.aspx [8 May 2014].

ISSA (International Social Security Association): Social Security Country Profiles (incorporates information from SSA/ISSA Social security programs throughout the world: see below). Available at: http://www.issa.int/country-profiles [20 Apr. 2014].

OECD Family database. Available at: http://www.oecd.org/els/family/ [20 Apr. 2014].

OECD Health Statistics database. Available at: http://stats.oecd.org/index.aspx?DataSetCode=HEALTH_STAT [20 Apr. 2014].

OECD Income Distribution database. Available at: http://www.oecd.org/els/soc/income-distribution-database.htm [20 Apr. 2014].

Solt, Frederick: Standardized World Income Inequality Database (SWIID, Version 4.0). Available at: http://myweb.uiowa.edu/fsolt/swiid/swiid.html [20 Apr. 2014].

SSA (Social Security Administration); ISSA (International Social Security Association): Social security programs throughout the world. Available at: http://www.ssa.gov/policy/docs/progdesc/ssptw/ [20 Apr. 2014].

United Nations: World Population Prospects, 2012 Revision. Available at: http://esa.un.org/wpp/ [20 Apr. 2014].

UN ECLAC (United Nations Economic Commission for Latin America and the Caribbean): Conditional Cash Transfer Programmes database: Non-contributory social protection programmes in Latin America and the Caribbean database. Available at: http://dds.cepal.org/bdptc/en/ [20 Apr. 2014].

WHO (World Health Organization): Global Health Observatory. Available at http://apps.who.int/ghodata/ [20 Apr. 2014].

WHO (World Health Organization): National Health Accounts. Available at: http://www.who.int/health-accounts/en/ [20 Apr. 2014].

World Bank pensions data. Available at: http://web.worldbank.org/WBSITE/EXTERNAL/TOPICS/EXTSOCIALPROTECTION/EXTPENSIONS/0,,contentMDK:23231994~menuPK:8874064~pagePK:148956~piPK:216618~theSitePK:396253,00.html [20 Apr. 2014].

World Bank: World Development Indicators. Available at: http://data.worldbank.org/data-catalog/world-development-indicators [20 Apr. 2014].